African Economic Outlook

2011

AFRICAN DEVELOPMENT BANK

DEVELOPMENT CENTRE OF THE ORGANISATION FOR ECONOMIC CO-OPERATION AND DEVELOPMENT

UNITED NATIONS DEVELOPMENT PROGRAMME

UNITED NATIONS ECONOMIC COMMISSION FOR AFRICA

The opinions expressed and arguments employed in this publication are the sole responsibility of the authors and do not necessarily reflect those of the African Development Bank; the OECD, its Development Centre or the governments of their member countries; the United Nations Development Programme; the UN Economic Commission for Africa; the European Union; or those of the Secretariat of the African Caribbean and Pacific Group of States or its member states.

ISBN 978-92-64-11175-2 (print)
ISBN 978-92-64-11178-3 (PDF)

Foreword

This is the tenth edition of the *African Economic Outlook* (AEO), which over the past decade has become the leading annual review of the state of the African economy. When the first *Outlook* was launched in 2002, as a joint project of the OECD Development Centre and the African Development Bank (AfDB), Africa had just passed through a period of low growth and declining living standards that had caused widespread Afro-Pessimism. There has been a major change since then and we can now look back at a decade of African Renaissance with average growth of almost 6% between 2001 and 2008. Africa has also shown considerable resilience to the deep global economic crisis of 2008/2009.

This *Outlook* portrays a continent sustaining economic expansion. But Africa is marching into serious headwinds, notably caused by high food and fuel prices and political upheavals in a number of countries. As a result, while sub-Saharan Africa will still show strong growth as expected, North Africa will grow more slowly, all leading to a lower average growth for Africa of just below 4% in 2011. Assuming economic normality returns, growth is expected to accelerate to almost 6% in 2012, returning thereafter to levels achieved before the crisis.

Our analysis also shows that Africa has attracted increasing flows of foreign direct investment (FDI). But, so far about three quarters of Africa's FDI inflows are invested in oil-exporting countries, while oil-importing countries are benefitting relatively little. Countries thus need to further improve the business environment for domestic and foreign investors. They must improve infrastructure and power supply and reduce red tape, which continues to restrain the private sector in many countries. Recent social unrest has revealed the need for more accountability and better governance in Africa.

This report highlights the challenges to further boost growth and the need, at the same time, to broaden the sources of growth to more sectors and regions. Reducing income inequality and further improving health and education are crucial to alleviating poverty and making economic growth more inclusive, so that the whole population can reap the benefits.

The *Outlook* theme chapter looks at "Africa and its Emerging Partners". It shows that Africa benefits increasingly from trade, investment and general economic co-operation with emerging economies, such as Brazil, China, India, Korea and Turkey. This is complementary to the links with other advanced economies, which continue to play a key role as partners for the continent. New partnerships between advanced and developing countries and a new paradigm around growth and development will support Africa's prosperity, create opportunities for the people in Africa and build a key pillar in our joint fight against poverty.

Our joint commitment in producing this report is to provide evidence-based policy advice on key development challenges, based on sound and objective analysis, peer learning and good governance.

Donald Kaberuka
President,
African Development
Bank Group, Tunis

Angel Gurría
Secretary-General,
Organisation for
Economic
Co-operation and
Development, Paris

Helen Clark
Administrator,
United Nations
Development
Programme, New York

Abdoulie Janneh
Executive Secretary,
United Nations
Economic Commission
for Africa,
Addis Ababa

Acknowledgements

The *African Economic Outlook* was prepared by a consortium of four teams from the African Development Bank (AfDB), the OECD Development Centre, the United Nations Development Programme (UNDP) and the United Nations Economic Commission for Africa (UNECA). The Outlook thereby benefitted from the overall guidance of Mthuli Ncube (Chief Economist and Vice President, AfDB), Mario Pezzini (Director, OECD Development Centre), Pedro Conceição (Chief Economist and Head of the Strategic Advisory Unit, Regional Bureau for Africa, UNDP) and Emmanuel Nnadozie (Director of the Trade, Finance and Economic Development Division, UNECA). Willi Leibfritz acted as Co-ordinator.

The AfDB task team was led by Charles Lufumpa, Léonce Ndikumana and Désiré Vencatachellum. Key team members included Peter Walkenhorst, Beejaye Kokil, Barfour Osei, Alex Mutebi Mubiru and Ahmed Moummi. The team at the OECD Development Centre was led by Helmut Reisen, Henri-Bernard Solignac-Lecomte and Jean-Philippe Stijns, the team at the UNDP by Janvier Nkurunziza, and the team at UNECA by Adam Elhiraika.

Part I on Africa's performance and Prospects was drafted by Willi Leibfritz, based on the forecast provided by the AfDB Statistics Department (Chapter 1), Jan Rieländer (Chapter 2), Stephen Karingi, Daniel Tanoe, Emmanuel Chinyama and Laura Páez (Chapter 3), Janvier Nkurunziza (Chapter 4) and Jan Rieländer, Bakary Traoré, Said Adejumobi and Kaleb Demeksa (Chapter 5). Part II on Africa's Emerging Partners was co-ordinated by Jean-Philippe Stijns and Alberto Amurgo Pacheco with key input from Vinaye Dey Ancharaz, and very able research assistance of Bakary Traoré, Gregory De Paepe, Myriam Dahman-Saidi and Christina Wolf.

The country notes were drafted by Kossi Robert Eguida (Algeria), Laura Recuero Virto and Sebastian Nieto Parra (Angola), Olivier Manlan (Benin), Wilberforce Mariki and Roger Dhiwayo (Botswana), Tankien Dayo (Burkina Faso), Janvier Nkurunziza (Burundi), Aissatou Gueye (Cameroun), Laura Recuero Virto and Bakary Traoré (Cape Verde), Kalidou Diallo (Central African Republic), Facinet Sylla (Chad), Léonce Yapo (Comores), Ahmed Moummi (Congo, Rep.), Steve Gui-Diby (Congo Dem. Rep.), Wautabouna Ouattara (Côte d´Ivoire), Audrey Vergnes (Djibouti), Alberto Amurgo Pacheco and Andrew Mold (Equatorial Guinea), Alemayehu Geda (Ethiopia), Sylvain Ndo (Gabon), Hee-Sik Kim (Gambia), Barfour Osei (Ghana), Mohamed Ben Abdallah (Guinea), Alberto Amurgo Pacheco and Gregory De Paepe (Guinea-Bissau), Laureline Pla and Désiré Vencatachellum (Kenya), Albert Mafusire (Lesotho), Richard Schiere (Liberia), Emmanuele Santi (Libya), Marco Stampini and Laureline Pla (Madagascar), Adeleke Salami (Malawi), Léandre Bassolé and Mamadou Diagne (Mali), Mohamed Safouane Ben Aïssa (Mauritania), John Anyanwu (Mauritius), Fatima Zohra Allaoui (Morocco), Laura Recuero Virto and Gregory De Paepe (Mozambique), Souleymane Abdallah (Niger), Barfour Osei (Nigeria), Shimeles Abebe (Rwanda), Gregory De Paepe and John Mullally (São Tomé & Príncipe), Peter Ondiege (Seychelles), Zuzana Brixiova and Jamal Zayid (Sierra Leone), Emelly Mutambatsere and Jean-Philippe Stijns (South Africa), Adam Elhiraika (Sudan), Edirissa Nseera (Swaziland), Alex Mutebi Mubiru (Tanzania), Marcellin Ndong-Ntah (Togo), Audrey Verdier-Chouchane (Tunisia), Edward Sennoga (Uganda), Emmanuel Chinyama (Zambia), Barbara Barungi and Kupukile Mlambo (Zimbabwe) and the following research institutes: Centre de Recherches Economiques Appliquées (CREA, Sénégal) and Egyptian Centre for Economic Studies (ECES, Egypt). The work on the country notes greatly benefitted from the valuable contributions of local consultants.

The committee of peer reviewers of the country notes included: Elizabeth Asiedu, Sylvain Eloi Dessy, Anne-Marie Geourjon, Mwangi Kimenyi, Caroline Lambert, Bertrand Laporte and Pierre Pestieau.

The macroeconomic framework and database used to produce the forecast and statistical annex was managed by Beejaye Kokil at the African Development Bank. Valuable statistical inputs for updating the database and running the AEO model were provided by Mohamed Safouane Ben Aïssa, Anouar Chaouch, Ousman Gajigo, Hilaire Kadisha, Koua Louis Kouakou, Fessou Emessan Lawson and Nirina Letsara at the AfDB Statistics Department, as well as Vararat Atisophon and Gregory De Paepe at the OECD Development Centre. Aymen Dhib, Michèle Girard, Aissatou Gueye and Josiane Koné provided very important statistical and organisational assistance.

The project also benefitted from the assistance provided by Rhoda Bangurah, Yvette Chanvoédou and Abiana Nelson.

The country maps were produced by Magali Geney, who also was responsible for the design and layout of the report. The maps and diagrams used in this publication in no way imply recognition of any states or political boundaries by the African Development Bank Group, the Organisation for Economic Co-operation and Development, its Development Centre, the United Nations Development Programme, the United Nations Economic Commission for Africa, the European Union, or the authors.

The report benefited from extremely valuable inputs and comments from a large number of African government representatives, private-sector operators, civil society members, country economists and sector specialists in the AfDB country operations departments and Field Offices, experts in the European Commission delegations in Africa, as well as the Directorate for Development Cooperation, the Directorate for Financial and Enterprise Affairs and the Economics Department of the OECD. Part II on Africa's Emerging Partners drew heavily from the knowledge of international experts gathered in Paris on October 12, 2010, as well as special papers contributed by Vinaye Dey Ancharaz (AfDB), Helmut Asche (University of Leipzig), Xavier Cirera (IDS, Sussex), Ricardo Markwald (FUNCEX, Brazil), Catherine Grant, Memory Dube and Geoffrey Chapman (SAIIA, Johannesburg), Philippe Hugon (Université de Paris Ouest), Raphael Kaplinsky (The Open University, Milton Keynes), Peter Kragelund (Roskilde University), Dorothy McCormick (IDS, Nairobi), Marc Raffinot (Université Paris Dauphine, LEDa-DIAL) and Dieudonné Bleossi Dahoun (Ministry of Finance of Benin), Edouard Turkisch and Christina Wolf (OECD Development Centre).

Adrià Alsina and Vanda Legrandgérard managed the editorial process and supervised the development of the Content Management System. They oversaw the production of the publication in both paper and electronic forms with the assistance of Michèle Girard, Roger Hobby, Ly Na Dollon and Elizabeth Nash, of the OECD Development Centre. The dedication of the editing, translation and proofreading team was essential to the timely production of this report.

This publication has been produced with the assistance of the European Union. The contents of this publication are the sole responsibility of the authors and can in no way be taken to reflect the views of the European Union. The support of the African, Caribbean and Pacific Group of States was essential to initiating and sustaining the project, as was additional support by Belgium, France, Ireland, Portugal and Spain.

African Economic Outlook

Executive Summary

Africa´s economies have weathered the global economic and financial crisis relatively well and have rebounded in 2010. The continent is expected to continue on its path of recovery although serious headwinds weigh on the momentum for expansion in 2011, notably the political events in North Africa and the high fuel and food prices. The dismal situation in Libya and Côte d´Ivoire shows once again how citizens suffer and economies are brought to a halt when political transitions are not pursued in a peaceful way.

Part I of this year's *African Economic Outlook* analyses Africa's macroeconomic and structural developments. It examines how the African continent, its regions and countries, have fared during the global crisis and forecasts economic developments in 2011 and 2012. It describes changes in external financial flows and discusses trade policies and measures to foster regional integration. Furthermore, it discusses why poverty reduction has remained relatively slow in Africa and characterises the status and trends of human development.

Part II explores the relationship between Africa and its emerging partners and casts new light on the impacts for Africa´s development.

Africa's Performance and Prospects

Macroeconomic Prospects

Africa´s economies have rebounded from the slump which had been caused by the global recession. In 2010, *Africa´s average rate of growth* amounted to 4.9%, up from 3.1% in 2009. The political events in North Africa are likely to depress the continent's growth to 3.7% in 2011. However, this forecast is surrounded by considerable uncertainty. Risks are related to the global economy, notably the impact of the earthquake and nuclear crisis in Japan, and to Africa, in particular the development in Libya and Côte d´Ivoire and how this affects neighbouring countries. With the assumption that economic normality returns in these countries, Africa´s average growth is expected to accelerate to 5.8% in 2012.

North Africa is expected to be the only region with lower growth in 2011 compared to the previous year (less than 1% after 4.6% in 2010). Under the assumption of a return to normal economic life, growth of the region is expected to rebound again in 2012. *East Africa* is likely to continue on its growth path of above 6% during the projection period, while growth in West Africa is expected to decelerate to below 6% due to the events in Côte d´Ivoire. In Southern Africa and in Central Africa growth is projected to accelerate, but remain lower than in East and West Africa.

Monetary policies are expected to gradually tighten to respond to inflation concerns related to higher food and energy prices. But, as in most countries, underlying inflationary pressures are expected to remain subdued; there is no need for vigorous tightening. Policies should focus more on core inflation and inflation expectations rather than on the temporary increase of headline inflation.

Africa´s average *fiscal deficit* is expected to increase in 2011 to below 4% of GDP but decline again to slightly above 3% in 2012. But the average masks large differences across countries. However, if disbursements of ODA fall short of expectations as donor countries are facing fiscal problems, and if African governments introduce food and fuel subsidies to protect households from high prices, deficits could be significantly larger. Furthermore, the large number of national elections on the continent this year also bears the risk that office holders will raise spending to get political support from voters, and such "election-cycle politics" would also undermine fiscal consolidation.

After the deterioration in 2009, which had been caused by the fall in commodity prices and export volumes, *external positions* improved as commodity prices and export volumes recovered. But current account positions have generally not regained the levels prior to the global crisis and in some oil-importing countries imbalances are widening.

The current economic recovery in Africa is likely to reduce the cyclical component of unemployment, but structural unemployment remains high in many countries. In North Africa, where economic activity has been disrupted by the political upheavals, unemployment is likely to further increase in 2011. *Youth unemployment* has long been a major problem in North Africa (but also in many other African countries) and contributed to the political unrest which led to the overthrow of governments in Tunisia and Egypt. Labour markets have not been flexible enough to absorb the growing supply of young workers. Given Africa´s rapidly growing population, the demographic pressure on labour markets will continue in many African countries. But in North Africa and Southern Africa the demographic pressure on labour markets will ease as the youth population is projected to remain close to current levels.

A comprehensive approach is needed to address the problem of unemployment in general and of youth unemployment in particular. Improvements are needed both on the supply and the demand side of labour markets. More needs to be done to improve the quality of labour supply so that it better matches the skills required by employers. This also refers to university graduates who are vulnerable to unemployment if their skills do not match job requirements. At the same time labour demand needs to be boosted by further improving framework conditions for economic growth in general and for private sector activity in particular, including through the creation of new firms.

African policy makers must be aware of several sources of global and domestic risks. Economic and social stability needs to be sustained – or where it is disrupted – be quickly restored. Policy requirements are to pursue prudent macro policies and at the same time implement appropriate measures to cope with higher commodity prices. In resource-rich countries, part of the windfall profits could, for example, be put into sovereign wealth funds in order to prepare for the time when prices fall again or resources will be depleted. Given the currently high food prices, governments, which have the necessary resources, might consider protecting vulnerable groups from hunger by providing targeted subsidies, while refraining from costly food and fuel subsidies to the general public. Furthermore, framework conditions for farmers should be further improved so that they are able to increase investment and productivity in response to higher agricultural prices.

External Financial Flows

During the last decade, financial flows to Africa have increased rapidly. Between 2000 and 2010 the sum of Foreign Direct Investment (FDI), portfolio investment and Official Development Assistance (ODA) increased almost five-fold from USD 27 billion to USD 122 billion.

FDI is an especially important source of investment in Africa and over the last decade has amounted to one fifth of Africa´s gross fixed capital formation. FDI to African countries peaked in 2008 at USD 72 billion, five times the value of FDI receipts in 2000. During the global crisis in 2009 Africa´s FDI inflows fell by 20%, to USD 59 billion. Estimates for 2010 point to a further decline to around USD 50-52 billion. Looking forward, the global recovery with high growth in emerging countries, high commodity prices and improvements in economic conditions in many African countries should further stimulate FDI in Africa. However, the recent political events in parts of Africa, notably North Africa with the war in Libya, will likely hold off foreign investors in this region. In recent years, North Africa has been the top destination-region for FDI in Africa, receiving a little more than one-third of all FDI flows to Africa.

Africa´s FDI inflows continue to be unevenly distributed, with a large share going to a limited number of countries. About three-quarters of Africa´s FDI is invested in oil exporting countries. Attracting investment into diversified and higher value-added sectors remains a challenge. Some progress has been made recently in the services sector, led by telecommunication, which is attracting increased investor interest.

OECD countries are the most important source of FDI flows to African countries, accounting for more than 70% of Africa´s FDI inflows between 2000 and 2009. South Africa, Egypt and Nigeria were main beneficiaries of OECD investment in Africa and most of OECD FDI in Africa came from the United Kingdom, France and the United States.

Data on FDI to Africa from non-OECD countries is difficult to obtain. According to its statistical bulletin, China invested USD 5.5 billion in sub-Saharan Africa in 2008, representing almost 10% of its outward FDI. This investment from China was up from USD 70 million in 2003 but declined to USD 1.1 billion in 2009. However, this number understates China´s engagement as activities of state-owned enterprises often involve a range of other financing instruments and are not counted as FDI.

FDI of other emerging economies is also largely in extractive industries but sometimes combines investment in mining with the development of industrial complexes for these sectors and the construction of necessary infrastructure. Moreover, emerging economies also invest in manufacturing at an increasing rate.

Intra-African FDI has equally gained in importance with most of it made in neighbouring countries, focussing on manufacturing and services, thus boosting regional integration and also contributing to diversification. South Africa is the most vital source of intra-African FDI. Libya has invested in many African countries, and Egypt, Morocco and Tunisia have also invested large parts of their outward FDI stocks in Africa. Given this importance of North Africa as a source of intra-African FDI, the recent political turmoil in this region will likely have adverse effects on FDI inflows of African countries in the near term.

ODA to Africa has been rising steadily over the last decade, from USD 15 billion in 2000 to USD 48 billion in 2009. Despite this increase, donors risk failing to meet their Gleneagles commitments made in 2005. In 2009, overall ODA to Africa was almost a quarter short of the target. Net bilateral ODA from DAC donors to Africa totalled USD 28 billion in 2009, of which USD 25 billion went to sub-Saharan Africa. This number represents an increase of 3% in real terms over 2008 for all of Africa and an increase of 5.1% for sub-Saharan Africa --an increase which helped African countries to mitigate the adverse effect of the global economic crisis.

Among non-DAC members, China, India and Saudi Arabia are the most important providers of concessional loans and grants to Africa. Developing country partners tend to combine commercial with developmental interests and financing modalities. For example, export credits do not fall within the ODA definition, but they play an increasingly large role in relations between Africa and its developing country partners.

Trade Policies and Regional Integration

African trade has rebounded in 2010 spurred by the recovery of global trade and in particular demand from emerging markets. A growing services trade has also been consistent with global trends over the past years, signalling Africa's increasing potential and prospects in different services subsectors.

Progress under the Doha Development Round (DDR) and the Economic Partnership Agreements (EPA) negotiations continues to be slow and highly contingent upon compromises between the parties, which aim to balance policy space, developmental goals and deeper market access. Further, the dynamics of other trade relations for Africa, notably under trade preference schemes such as the African Growth and Opportunity Act (AGOA) and South-South co-operation through trade and investment with China have gained increasing importance in the African economic development and diversification agenda over the past years.

African leaders have taken a number of initiatives aimed at advancing the regional integration process in Africa. In particular, the development of Minimum Integration Programmes, the rationalisation of the Regional Economic Communities (RECs), and the recognition of eight RECs as the main building blocks of the African Union, have helped these Communities to continue to play a significant role in achieving Africa's regional integration vision.

Some RECs such as Economic Community of West African States (ECOWAS), Economic Community of Central African States (ECCAS), Common Market of Eastern Southern Africa (COMESA), Southern African Development Community (SADC) and East African Community (EAC) have established Free Trade Areas while others such as Community of Sahel-Saharan States (CEN-SAD) are steadily working towards this objective. Furthermore, EAC and COMESA launched their customs unions in 2005 and 2009, respectively, while, SADC and ECCAS are expected to do so soon and ECOWAS is expected to follow suit in 2015. The Arab-Maghreb Union (UMA), CEN-SAD, and the Intergovernmental Authority Development (IGAD) are to implement their customs union projects in the near future. In addition to these strides, some RECs seek also to harmonise their agendas for establishing Free Trade Areas (FTA) to create larger trading blocs, such as a grand FTA between SADC, COMESA and EAC.

Despite these promising developments, challenges which significantly affect the RECs include: the prevalence of political instability in some parts of the continent, lack of economic diversification, continued multiple and overlapping memberships, inadequate financial resources to buttress the integration processes, and poor implementation of commonly agreed protocols and decisions.

There are also challenges concerning connectivity. *Regional infrastructure development in Africa* is crucial for economic growth and sustainable development. Despite efforts to implement a coherent programme of activities in the areas of energy, transport and communications, Africa remains one of the continents with weak infrastructure networks; this contributes significantly to higher production and transaction costs, and undermines the competitiveness of businesses.

The current status of infrastructure developments in Africa remains mixed. Some sectors have recorded significant progress while others are lagging. The situation in the continent is characterised by insufficient and low quality infrastructure on the one hand, and inefficient and expensive services on the other. For example, only 20% of road networks in Africa are paved and transport services are expensive due to supplier cartels. To overcome these shortcomings, continental efforts in the field of roads development include trans-African highways.

Even less satisfactory is the situation of the railway network, which in comparison to other regions and continents shows a very low density. In addition, the network is generally old and technically outdated, resulting in a low share of rail freight in intra-African trade.

Finally, the global picture of Africa's share in air transport remains modest, relying mostly on three major hubs, namely, Johannesburg, Nairobi and Addis Ababa. South African Airways, Kenya Airways and Ethiopian Airlines remain the three major airlines in Africa. In 2004, Africa's share was 5.2% of passenger traffic and approximately 3.6% of freight.

Human Development

The international community set the goal of eradicating extreme poverty and hunger in the Millennium Declaration adopted in 2000. The community specified two targets in the Millennium Development Goals (MDGs): over the period 1990-2015, halving the proportion of people whose income is less than 1 US dollar a day using 1993 purchasing power parities (PPP), and halving the number of people suffering from hunger. The poverty line was revised to USD 1.25 in 2005 PPPs after estimates for purchasing power parity exchange rates were revised in late 2007. From 54% in 1981, the rate of poverty increased to 59% in 1996 before declining to 51% in 2005, the last year for which comparable data is available. It has been estimated that as a result of slower growth in the wake of the global crisis and the rebound of food prices, poverty might have increased in 2009 and 2010.

While Africa has made progress in reducing poverty between 1996 and 2005, the rate of poverty reduction has been slow relative to other developing regions, due to three main factors: First, Africa experienced relatively high levels of economic growth only since the 2000s, so the growth rates during the 1990s were not high enough to make a substantial impact on poverty. In order to halve poverty by 2015, a cross-country econometric analysis established that African economies would need to grow by 7% per year on average. Despite a clearly improved growth performance in the first decade of the new century with average growth of 5.3%, Africa remained below this mark. Second, growth in Africa has not been high enough in sectors where the poor live or work. Although this situation has improved in many countries since 1996, Africa's growth often originated from sectors with weak linkages to the rest of the economy, such as the mineral and oil sectors, so that the economic expansion has had little impact on job creation and poverty reduction. Third, relatively high inequality in Africa reflects that growth benefited a small part of the population and the benefits to the poor were limited. In this regard, poverty reduction policies will need to combine high economic growth with a reduction in inequality, while ensuring that the sources of economic growth are broad based.

The limitations of income-based measures of progress and wellbeing motivated the creation of the Human Development Index (HDI) by UNDP in 1990. This measure reflects a people-centred understanding of development. It measures human development by integrating indicators of education and health with income. Although by 2010 Africa as a whole had the lowest HDI of any region, the trend between 2000 and 2010 shows that all African countries, except Zimbabwe, improved their human development score. Sub-Saharan Africa made, on average, the most rapid progress of any region. The regional HDI increased by 23%, followed by South Asia, where the increase was 17% over the same period. This improvement was due to rising income per capita in the 2000s in most African countries, and to genuine progress in access to knowledge and better health outcomes.

As expected, an Inequality-Adjusted Human Development Index (IHDI) shows that relatively high levels of income inequality are associated with low human development. In contrast, the Gender Inequality Index (GII) shows a few African countries performing much better than on the other dimensions of human development. The implication is that some dimensions of human development (e.g. gender equality) can be significantly improved even in very poor countries, as they do not necessarily require financial resources, which constitute one of the most binding constraints to development in such countries.

To sustain progress in human development, Africa will need to take simultaneous actions on several fronts rather than focus on only one objective. For example, economic growth will improve human development if it is inclusive and pro-poor. Similarly, investing in social sectors will produce sustainable human development if investment is accompanied by efforts to create more economic opportunities that benefit a large segment of the population. Moreover, some dimensions of human development, for example gender equality, will improve if African governments make the deliberate choice to pursue policies that promote gender equality. In this regard, the quality of economic policy will probably be as important as the resources used to advance the cause of human development in Africa.

Political and Economic Governance

The first quarter of 2011 has been among the most turbulent in Africa's history. Peaceful popular uprisings toppled long-standing authoritarian regimes in Tunisia and Egypt. Neighbouring Libya descended into a civil war in which the international community intervened with military force. The future development in Libya and the repercussions on its neighbours are difficult to predict.

In 2011, the continent will experience a record number of 28 national-level elections in 20 countries. An outstanding electoral event has been Southern Sudan's peaceful January referendum in favour of separation from Northern Sudan. This will come into force in July 2011.

In 2010, 13 countries held largely peaceful elections. The presidential election in Guinea that put an end to the institutional crisis generated by the coup d'état in 2008 and the peaceful constitutional referendum in Kenya were significant milestones after the post-election violence in 2008. The crisis and widespread violence in Côte d'Ivoire after a contested presidential election in November marked the low point.

The report takes stock of Africa´s political and economic governance in 2010 based on the same measures as in last year´s AEO. The main findings of this stocktaking are:

- 2010 was a year of intensifying civil protests, as measured by the number of demonstrations and strikes, pointing to the high level of economic and other grievances felt by many African populations. Yet 2010 was also a year of decreasing violence, which points to a positive trend of more peaceful and democratic expressions of demands that bodes well for Africa's development.
- Violence erupted in several countries, most prominently the post-election violence in Côte d'Ivoire and inter-religious conflicts in Nigeria and Egypt. However, of the 13 legislative and presidential elections held, only the one in Côte d'Ivoire was followed by large-scale violence. Violence around other elections was significant but of minor scale.
- Despite an increase in public protests, government responses in the form of violence and restricting political measures (bans of press, demonstrations, etc.) continued their downward trend. Our indicator of political hardening, which combines various means of government oppression into a single variable, indicates that 2010 was the year with the most relaxed stance of governments since the beginning of the series in 1996.

- The Political Freedom Index (PFI) from Freedom House, which measures political rights and civil liberties, classifies nine African countries as "free", 24 as "partly free" and 20 as "not free" in 2010. All countries that experienced revolts in 2011 had very low values for civil liberties and political rights and were classified as "not free". Concerning freedom of the press, progress was mixed with 21 countries improving their rating while in 22 countries the situation for the press worsened.
- Despite significant efforts to fight piracy around the Horn of Africa, it increased significantly over the last years. The pirates' radius now reaches from the coasts of Oman to Tanzania and almost reaches the Maldives and causes significant economic costs to international traders and the countries in the region.
- Corruption remains a serious problem in Africa with 27 out of 47 African countries classified as having "rampant corruption". Additionally, in 17 countries corruption is perceived as a "serious challenge" by country experts and business people. As in 2009, only in Botswana, Mauritius and Cape Verde is corruption perceived as a lesser challenge.
- A number of African countries registered remarkable economic improvements with respect to *economic governance.* According to *Doing Business 2011*, among the top thirty most improved economies, a third of them are in sub-Saharan Africa. In the top ten are three sub-Saharan African countries: Rwanda, Cape Verde and Zambia. The improved conditions are generally attributed to better regulations and continued ease of doing business in many African countries. Measures focused on facilitating the process to start a business, improving access to bank credits, and better enforcing contracts. However, much remains to be done in Africa to upgrade conditions for doing business to international standards.

Africa and its Emerging Partners

The 2011 edition of this *Outlook*'s thematic chapter investigates the rise of Africa's emerging partners. It analyses policy options for African policy-makers to make the best out of Africa's rapid integration into the global economy. The decade that began at the onset of the new century saw emerging partners swiftly rise from a relatively marginal position to one of fully fledged partners. Africa's trade volumes with its emerging partners have doubled in nominal value over the decade and now amount to 37% of Africa's total trade. While China represents Africa's leading emerging partner, having surpassed the United States in volume, the continent's trade with its other emerging partners, taken together, is even larger than its trade with China alone. China represents more than a third of Africa's trade with emerging partners.

The EU and the US remain the most important sources of Foreign Direct Investment (FDI) for African countries. When it comes to Official Development Assistance (ODA), traditional partners also dominate, although the share of emerging partners is growing fast. However, those are only the tip of the iceberg: emerging partners provide Africa with a range of alternative finance modalities that defy FDI and ODA definitions. They tend to adopt a more holistic approach to promoting their exports, supporting direct investment, and offering development assistance.

Africa's business relations with emerging partners are often complementary to those with traditional partners. Because of their diversity, emerging partners offer African countries new opportunities to exchange goods, technology and development models. They make mass consumption goods affordable to the nascent African middle-class and supply production goods adapted to the productive conditions of developing countries. These goods have the potential to help African firms increase their productivity and move up global value chains.

The co-operation activities of emerging partners are also typically complementary to those of traditional partners. The latter have focused their assistance, mostly through ODA, on poverty reduction, health, education and governance. Emerging partners, not only China, are more focused on removing infrastructural bottlenecks.

African manufactured exports have roughly doubled over the last 10 years, mostly driven by the demand of emerging partners. Fears that the intensifying co-operation with emerging partners is boosting Africa's indebtedness are not supported by available evidence. However, a risk of re-indebtment persists, particularly for the weakest African states. Similarly, existing aggregate governance indicators show no sign of a worsening of corruption. Policy autonomy is affected differently for different groups of African countries: the resource-abundant ones stand to widen their policy space more than others.

However, these general benign trends do not guarantee economic diversification and, thus, policy has a role to play. African countries have to frame their engagement with their emerging partners within a home-grown strategy of national development, particularly with respect to longer-term industrial and agricultural policy. Where absorption capacity is low, large infrastructure investments need to be accompanied by proper budgeting of maintenance costs and consistency with the country's development strategy.

Most African countries still need to enhance their bargaining position vis-à-vis traditional *and* emerging partners to ensure that these partnerships are actually mutually beneficial and African countries get their fair share of the benefits. Policy options include leveraging the rise in commodity prices to negotiate the supply of infrastructure for diversification, industrialisation and economic development, and holding traditional partners to account on their aid promises.

Faster progress in regional integration is imperative, so that African countries do not engage in "incentive wars", trying to outbid each other for FDI and aid. Better co-ordination means more bargaining power. Besides, from a financing perspective, regional, larger-scale projects would attract more consideration from emerging partners, especially those using Sovereign Wealth Funds (SWFs).

To promote regional integration, African countries can leverage complementarities between partners: traditional partners have the mechanisms to support the Regional Economic Communities (RECs) secretariats, while emerging partners can give additional impetus to build cross-border infrastructure. They would thereby help to boost intra-regional trade, in turn contributing to a virtuous circle of deeper economic integration that would bring closer together the visions of regional actors.

10th Edition of the *African Economic Outlook*

An unprecedented change in Africa's economic performance, and with it a shift in the way the world sees the continent, has occurred since independence and accelerated markedly over the last ten years. The *African Economic Outlook (AEO)*, celebrating its tenth edition this year, has been monitoring in great detail the economic pulse of Africa and has accompanied Africa's growth by stimulating policy dialogue, identifying best practice and encouraging policy reform.

The AEO provides comprehensive comparative data and analysis of African countries, comprising economic, social and political trends, highlighting African countries' distinctive histories, resources, and political systems in order to understand the drivers of the countries' performance and short-term outlook. Between 2001 and 2011, the AEO's coverage has increased from 22 countries to 51 countries.

In the 2000s, the slight recovery experienced in the 1990s accelerated further, and for some countries it turned into an outright boom. Prior to the 2009 global economic crisis, Africa enjoyed over 5% annual growth for nearly a decade.

Africa's performance from 1961 to 2012: growth of real GDP (percentage)

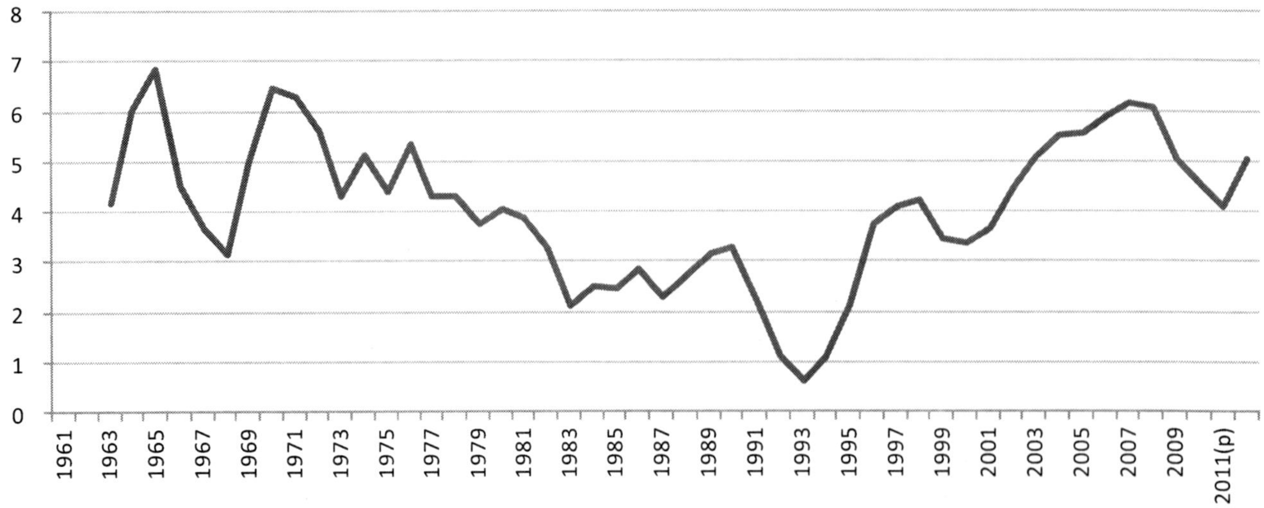

Notes: Three-year moving average of GDP growth; 2010 estimated; 2011-12 predicted.
Source: Calculations based on African Economic Outlook and World Bank data.

At first sight, when looking at the strong performance of the continent over the last decade, oil and other natural resource producers seem to have had the lion's share of economic success. But the turnaround of Africa is not simply the result of favourable commodity prices. Some deeper factors were at work over the past ten years: *i)* During the last decade, many countries have implemented much stronger economic policies, as shown by their control of inflation, improved public finances and building-up of foreign reserves. *ii)* There is evidence of slow but steady improvements in governance, including a deepening of democracy and strengthening of civil society. *iii)* Relations with donors improved substantially. The Heavily Indebted Poor Country (HIPC) initiative and the Multilateral Debt Relief Initiative (MDRI) have brought an end to Africa's debt crisis. The 2005 Paris Declaration and the 2008 Accra High Level Forum reinforced the commitments made by donors on improving aid effectiveness and managing for development results. *iv)* New technology provides opportunities for growth and poverty reduction: Africa is the fastest growing mobile phone market in the world; and *v)* a new class of political leaders and entrepreneurs contributed to the continent's progress of the past decade.

How can African countries capitalise on the progress achieved in the past decade to achieve sustainable growth and poverty reduction? What can policy makers and the international community do to help set Africa on a firm footing of growth?

In 2010, these important questions led to the adoption in Seoul of a G20 Consensus for Shared Growth and a Multi-Year Action Plan to promote growth in developing countries. The plan includes actions on domestic resource mobilisation, financial inclusion, private investment and job creation, infrastructure, human resources and development, food security, growth resilience, and knowledge sharing. All of these topics have been thoroughly analysed by the *African Economic Outlook*, making it a particularly timely and relevant tool.

The future of Africa's development rests on knowledge, entrepreneurship and governance. By stimulating dialogue on what works in Africa, promoting peer learning and sharing knowledge on key solutions to development challenges, the AEO helps broker an informed dialogue on Africa economies and build a critical mass of informed citizens, the actors of change in today's Africa.

The power of social medias in bringing hundreds of thousands of people into the streets in North Africa clearly shows that modern communication technology has vastly lowered the costs of knowledge and also enhanced the ability of citizens, once informed, to organise themselves collectively into pressure groups. Spreading knowledge is thus crucial to build informed citizenships and societies and to drive change.

With this in mind the *African Economic Outlook* has grown into an online platform, accessible free-of-charge at www.africaneconomicoutlook.org. Its goal is to distil and share the lessons learned, highlight best practices and provide a platform for African and non-African entrepreneurs, policy makers and activists. This goal is as important today as it was ten years ago when this project was launched.

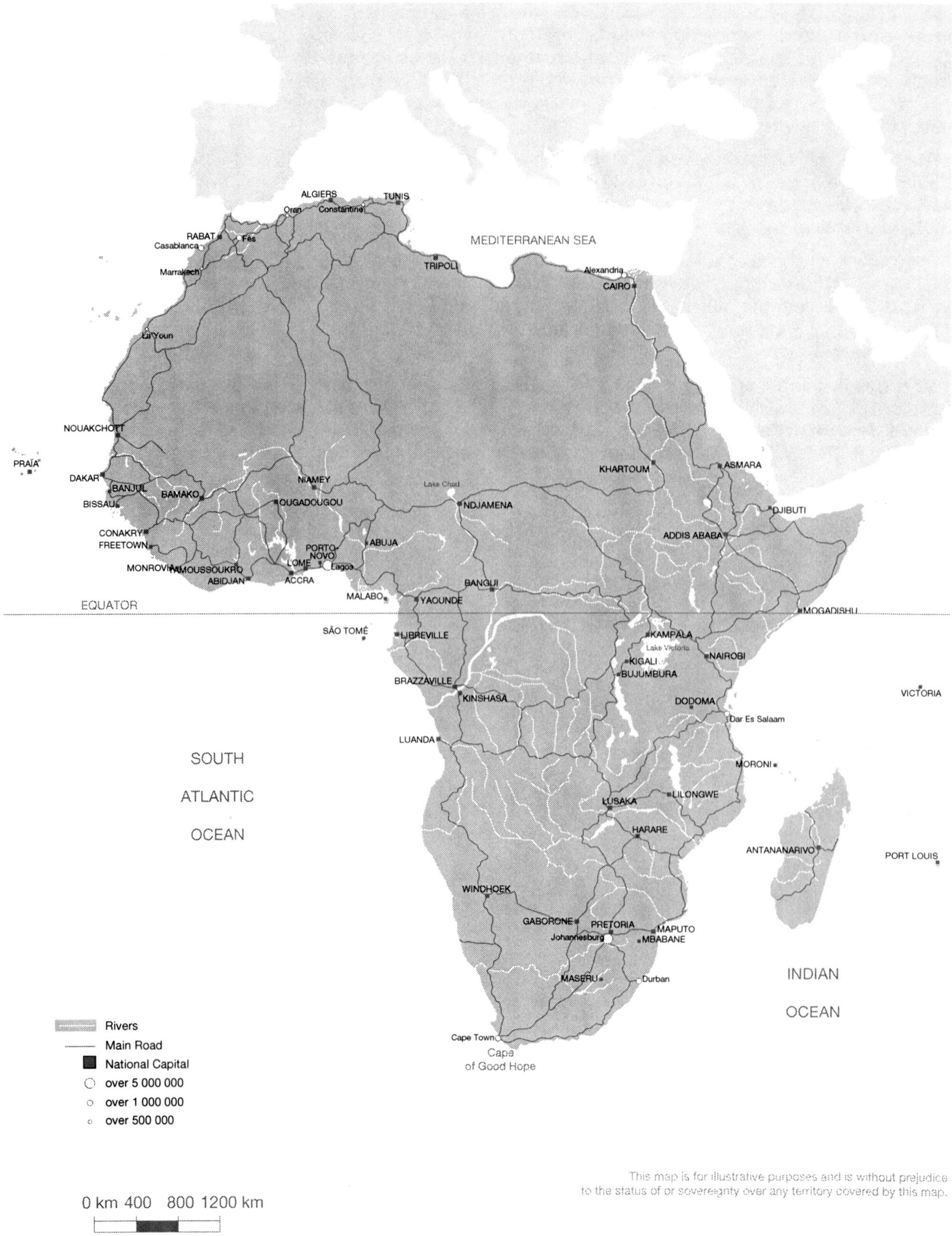

This map is for illustrative purposes and is without prejudice to the status of or sovereignty over any territory covered by this map.

Part One

Africa's Performance and Prospects

Chapter 1: Macroeconomic Prospects

This chapter explores the economic performance and prospects of the African continent and its regions and countries. It also examines the main driving forces of this development and discusses the chances and risks of a sustained recovery. The main finding is that Africa´s growth accelerated in 2010 and the recovery will continue, albeit at a moderate pace. The continent benefits from further growth of world trade and high commodity prices and from a broadening of the recovery. At the same time, high food and oil prices are restraining the income of African consumers. In several countries, notably in north Africa and Côte d´Ivoire, the recent political upheavals and related uncertainty are weighing on the growth prospects for 2011.

Africa is growing but there are risks

Africa´s economies are recovering, mainly driven by higher commodity prices and export volumes. The global financial and economic crisis of 2008/2009 had interrupted the period of high growth, with Africa´s GDP growth halving from an average annual rate of around 6% in the years prior to the crisis to 3.1% in 2009. Since then Africa´s economic climate has, in general, improved significantly, and expectations have overall been favourable. In 2010 Africa´s average rate of growth amounted to 4.9%, but due to the political events in North Africa the continent's growth will be depressed to 3.7% in 2011. At the time of writing there was, however, still considerable uncertainty about developments in several countries, notably in Libya and Côte d'Ivoire, and thus also about the overall effect of these events on Africa´s growth. With the assumption that economic normality returns, Africa´s average growth is expected to accelerate to 5.8% in 2012 (see Figures 1.1 and 1.2 and Box 1.1). (The detailed macroeconomic forecast for Africa and its regional groupings is presented in Table A.1 at the end of this chapter).

Figure 1.1: Africa´s economic growth

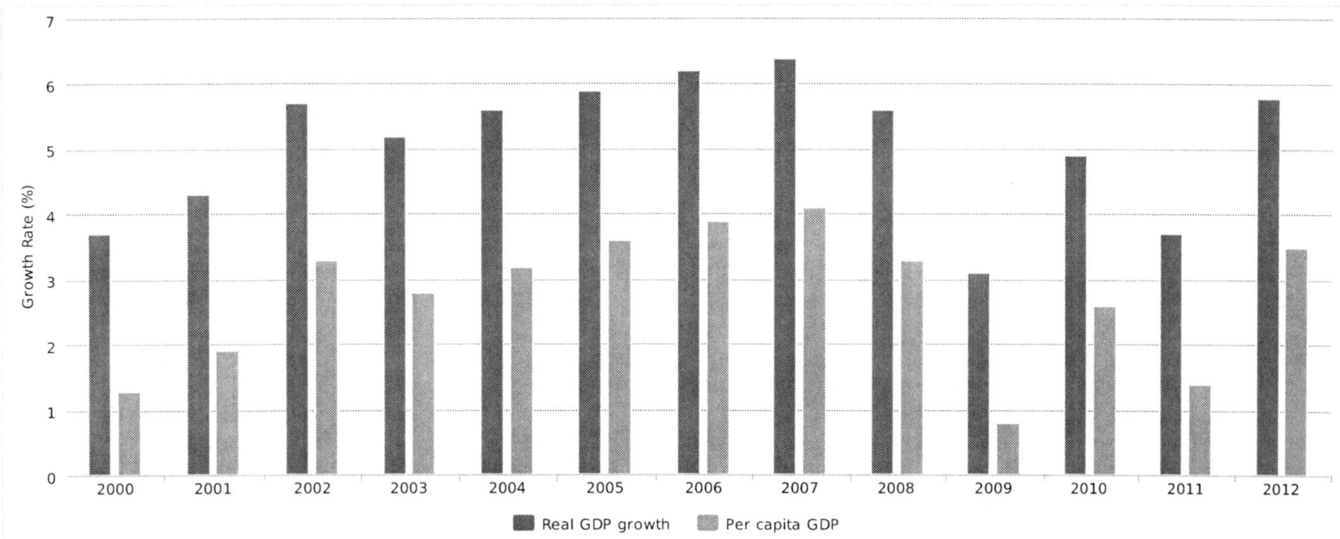

Source: African Development Bank.

StatLink http://dx.doi.org/10.1787/888932403116

Figure 1.2: Africa´s current economic situation and expectations for the next six months

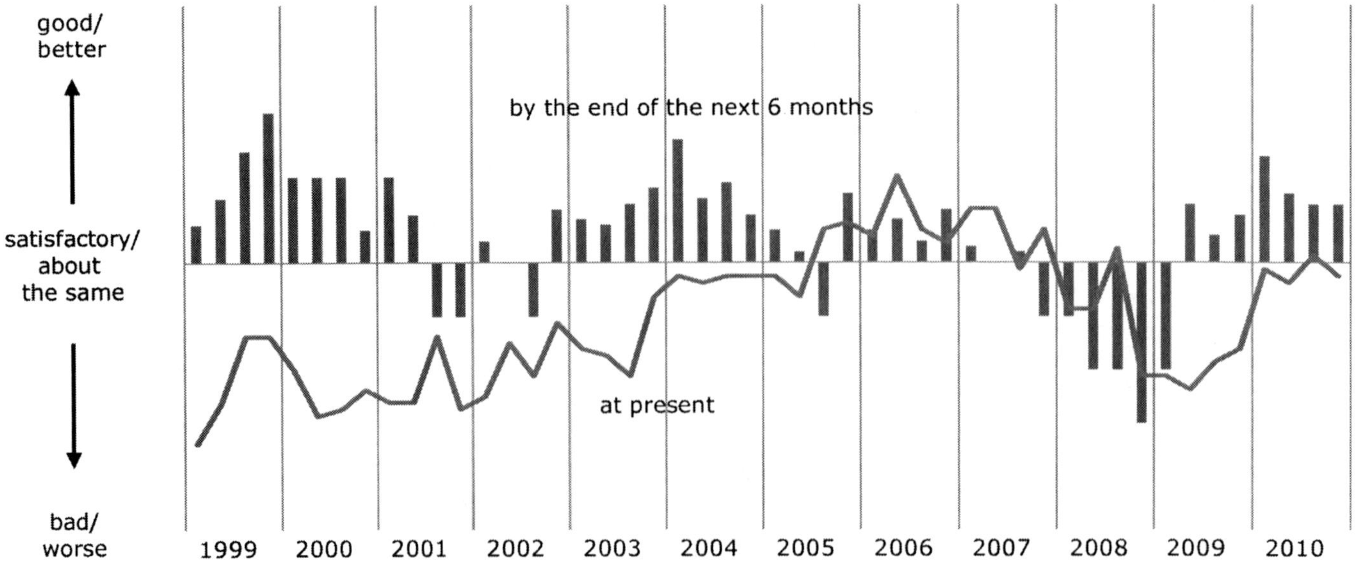

Source: Ifo Institute for Economic Research, African Development Bank.

The two indicators displayed in this graph represent the judgement of poll participants about the present economic situation and the expected economic situation by the end of the next six months. According to these indicators, the current economic activity is judged close to a satisfactory level and further improvements are expected for the next six months.

StatLink http://dx.doi.org/10.1787/888932403135

This forecast for Africa is based on the assumption that the world economy will continue to expand, but at a more moderate pace than in 2010 (see Box 1.2)

Box 1.1. Economic climate indicator for Africa

The economic climate indicators as shown in Figure 1.2 for Africa are from the Ifo World Economic Survey (WES). This survey is conducted by the German Ifo Institute for Economic Research Munich in co-operation with the International Chamber of Commerce (ICC) in Paris and, for Africa, in co-operation with the African Development Bank. Every three months it assesses global economic trends by polling economic experts world wide about current economic developments in their respective countries. This allows for a rapid, up-to-date assessment of the economic situation prevailing around the world. The survey questionnaire focuses on qualitative information: on assessment of a country's general economic situation and expectations regarding important economic indicators. It has proved to be a useful tool because it reveals economic changes earlier than do traditional economic statistics. Africa´s coverage in the survey has recently been extended, and it now includes 34 countries, although in some countries with only a few participants. The WES plans to further improve the country coverage in Africa and also the number of participants in Arican countries.

Given Africa´s population growth of above 2%, GDP per capita is expected to increase on average by 1.4% in 2011 and 3.5% in 2012, after less than 1% in 2009. While the acceleration of per capita growth is commendable, in 2011 it will not be sufficient to significantly reduce poverty. Income per capita growth will be too low in many countries, notably in countries that suffer from terms of trade losses due to higher import prices for food and energy. This is currently the case in resource-poor countries, while resource-rich countries benefit from terms of trade gains, so that real income of resource-rich countries increases faster than real output (see Figures 1.3 and 1.4).[1] Furthermore, in many countries, notably resource-rich countries, income and wealth are unequally shared, and stronger average income growth does not necessarily reduce poverty.

Figure 1.3: Terms of trade in selected resource-rich countries

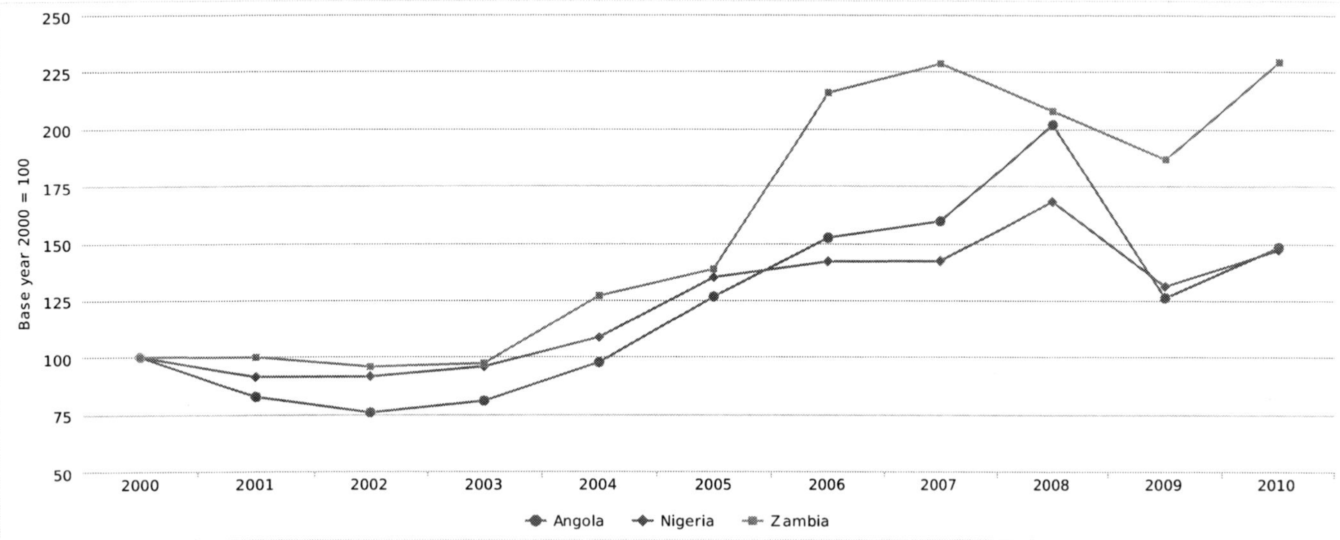

Source: African Development Bank based on IMF data.

StatLink http://dx.doi.org/10.1787/888932403154

Figure 1.4: Terms of trade in selected resource-poor countries

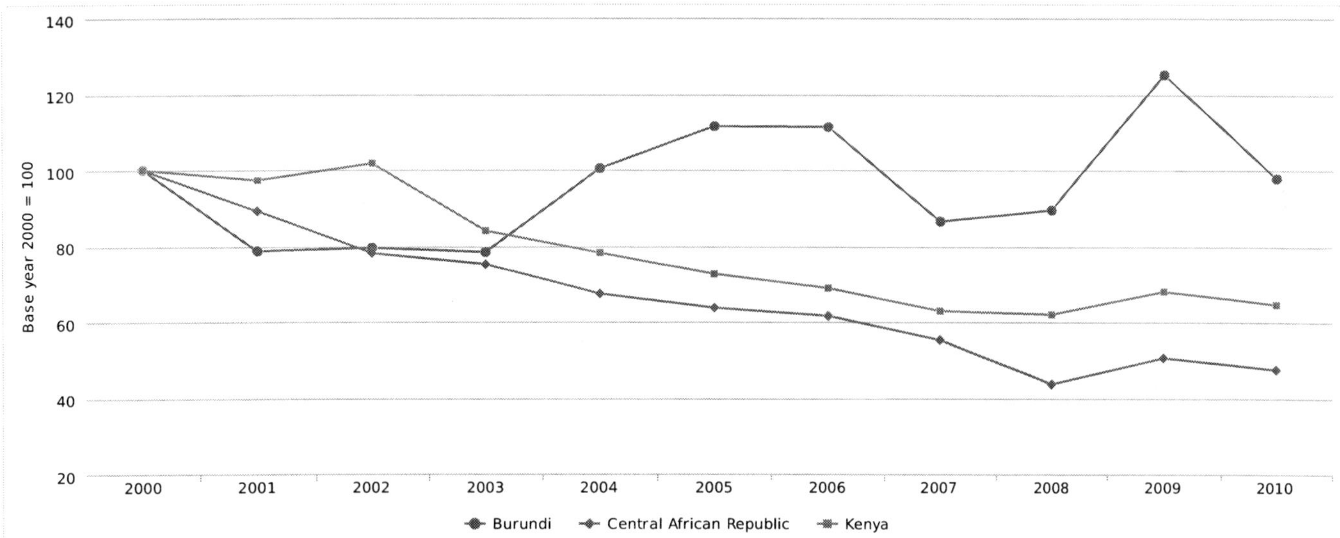

Source: African Development Bank based on IMF data.

StatLink http://dx.doi.org/10.1787/888932403173

The export-led recovery is broadening

Africa´s recovery in 2010 and into 2011 has been largely driven by export volumes and commodity prices. In 2010 real exports increased by 3.1% after a decline of 2.5% in 2009. Exports are likely to remain an important engine of growth, but domestic demand is also strengthening in many countries. Several resource-rich countries, such as Botswana, Algeria, Chad, Gabon and Nigeria, use the additional government revenues from natural resources to finance government spending on infrastructure investment and public consumption. Countries also sometimes use the additional revenues to support private households, thus boosting domestic demand. In several countries, such as Cameroon, Kenya, South Africa, Senegal and Tanzania, domestic demand is expected to drive growth to a large extent. However, the high food and fuel prices are constraining real private consumption in many countries. Furthermore, remittances to Africa are expected not to increase in 2011 as the recent political events in Libya and Côte d'Ivoire are seriously affecting workers' remittances to neighbouring countries.[2] (see Figure 1.5).

Figure 1.5: Migrant remittances to Africa

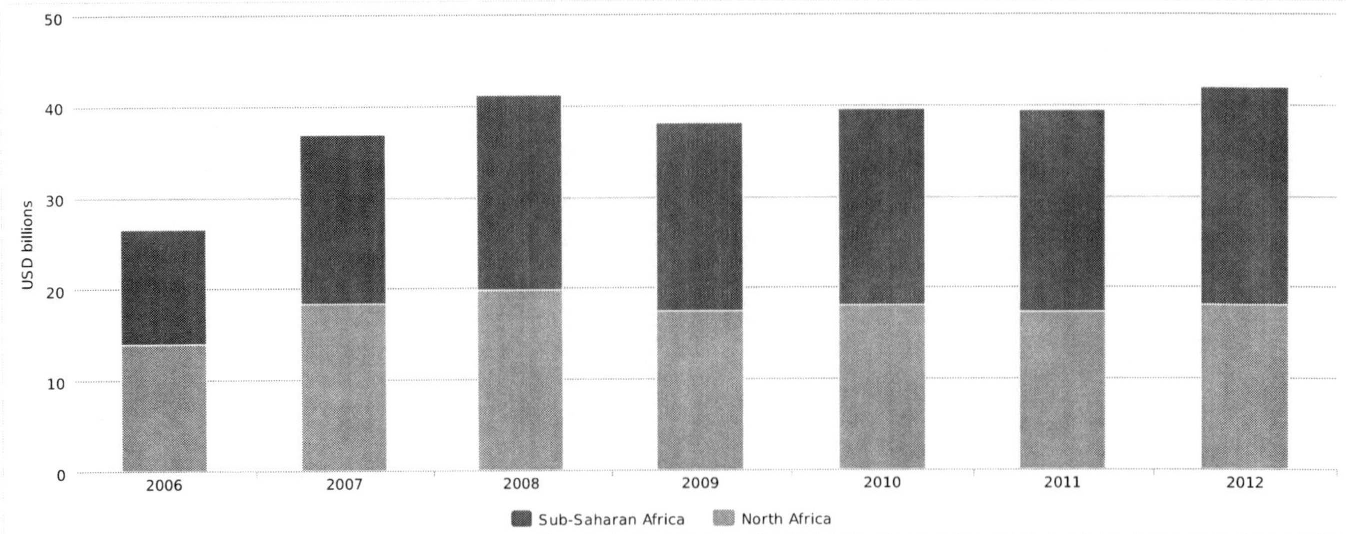

Source: African Development Bank.

Estimates for 2010 and forecasts for 2011 and 2012.

StatLink http://dx.doi.org/10.1787/888932403192

On the supply side, Africa's economic expansion is boosted by a few sectors, which vary, however, due to the different characteristics of the countries. In resource-rich countries, the mining sector has again become the main driver of growth, and in some countries new oil fields are coming on stream. In countries using higher export earnings to finance infrastructure investment, the construction sector is growing quickly.

In many African countries, the agricultural sector dominates economic activity. This sector's share in GDP is 40% or above in Burundi, Central African Republic, Republic of Congo, Ethiopia, Guinea Bissau, Niger, Liberia, Sierra Leone and Togo, and between 20% and 40% in Benin, Burkina Faso, Cameroon, Chad, Côte d'Ivoire, Guinea, Ghana, Kenya, Madagascar, Malawi, Mozambique, Nigeria, Tanzania, Sudan, Uganda and Zambia. In most of Africa, the agricultural sector has performed relatively well in 2010 due to favourable weather conditions. This also helped to mitigate the adverse effect from higher global food prices. But in several countries, agricultural production suffered, notably in Tunisia due to drought, and in Benin and Uganda due to floods. With the assumption of normal weather conditions, Africa's agricultural production is expected to further expand and contribute to GDP growth. However, agriculture remains highly vulnerable to the vagaries of nature.

The service sector is also an important contributor to African growth. In several countries, such as in South Africa (related to the soccer world cup), Botswana, Mauritius, Morocco, Seychelles, Tanzania, Egypt and Tunisia, tourism regained momentum in 2010. In Egypt and Tunisia, tourism will, however, decline in 2011 due to the recent political events and related security concerns.

Other services, such as trade, transport, financial services and real estate, are also supporting growth. Furthermore, the diffusion of new technologies, such as mobile phones and computers, continues to boost the quantity and quality of services. While in most African countries access to information and communications technologies (ICT) services is very low, many countries are now promoting the diffusion of ICT, which helps to raise Africa's growth potential (AEO, 2009).

When compared to developing countries in Asia, Africa's manufacturing sectors continue to lag behind. In many African countries, the share of manufacturing in GDP amounts to only around 10% or less. Manufacturing sectors are larger (with GDP shares between 15% and 20%), such as in Cameroon, Côte d'Ivoire, Egypt, Lesotho, Madagascar, Mauritius, Morocco, Namibia, South Africa, Tunisia and Zimbabwe. There are a number of reasons for the relatively weak industrial activity in Africa. Infrastructure bottlenecks, unreliable power supply and red tape continue to be major constraints in many countries. Africa's manufacturing firms are also facing fierce import competition, notably from emerging countries such as China. Furthermore, in resource-rich countries, the competitiveness of non-mining sectors is weakened if commodity exports drive up the real exchange rate relative to that of their competitors (an effect known as Dutch-disease).

Resource-rich countries are trying to prevent excessive appreciation by intervening in foreign exchange markets and accumulating foreign reserves, a policy that has also been criticised. The accumulation of foreign exchange reserves - beyond levels needed to cover imports and to insure the country against speculative currency attacks and a slump in resource prices – cannot be an end in itself. But such „excess reserves" may be the result of currency intervention to avoid excessive currency appreciation that could cause Dutch disease effects and harm non-resource exports. Rapid use of these reserves for financing social spending and consumption could lead to higher inflation and a real currency appreciation that the central bank intervention aimed at avoiding in the first place. However, the holding of high foreign reserves also entails costs as their real rate of return may be low. Excessive foreign reserves could instead be used to finance imports of capital goods and other spending, which helps to raise growth potential. Such use of foreign reserves would contain inflation and Dutch disease effects and foster economic development. There are currently fiftteen Sovereign Wealth Funds (SWFs) in Africa, but these are generally small and and their main objective is to stabilize the economy. They could potentially play a bigger role for Africa´s development but this also requires that their fiscal transparency and corporate governance structure is further improved (Triki T. and I. Faye, 2011).

Several resource-rich countries are attempting to diversify their economies by stimulating non-mining sectors. Zambia, for example, is establishing economic zones, and Botswana is implementing an Economic Diversification Drive (EDD), which favours public procurement from local manufacturers and service providers.

In South Africa, manufacturing production was hit in 2009 by the global recession. Manufacturing production recovered in 2010, although it has not yet attained its pre-crisis level. South Africa´s industrial production continues to be hampered by structural constraints, such as infrastructure bottlenecks, a relatively weak growth of export markets in Europe and the strong rand exchange rate. Egypt's manufacturing sector, which had also declined during the global recession, rebounded in 2010, driven by exports. Lesotho's manufacturing sector, which textiles and clothing dominate, also declined in 2009 and recovered gradually in 2010. Since the peak in 2004, the textile and clothing sector has suffered significant job losses and continues to face fierce competition from Asian firms. In Namibia the main driver of growth in manufacturing is processing of fish and other food. This activity remained resilient during the global crisis and continued in 2010. In 2011 African manufacturing sectors are likely to further expand, driven by higher exports. However, structural impediments and foreign competition continue to constrain growth.

Box 1.2. Prospects for the international economy

The world economy has shown a remarkable recovery from the deep slump of 2009 (Figure 1.6). Expansionary policies in all major regions of the world helped this recovery. After declining by 0.5% in 2009, world output increased by 5% in 2010. The recovery of the global economy is likely to be sustained in 2011 and 2012, but at a more moderate pace. While higher food and fuel prices are likely to affect global consumption, the earthquake and tsunami in Japan will temporarily reduce global output. At the time of writing, the developments in Japan and their impact on the global economy are, however, still highly uncertain. With the assumption that the impact on the global economy will remain moderate, world output growth is expected to amount to around 4.5% in both 2011 and 2012. World trade (volume) is projected to increase by around 7% in 2011 and 2012, down from 12.4% in 2010.

European economies achieved average growth of 1.8% in 2010. In response to the sovereign debt crisis, which erupted in Greece (in the first months of 2010), in Ireland (in November) and in Portugal (in April 2011), international bailout packages were put together for these countries (EUR 110 billion, EUR 85 billion and EUR 80 billion respectively). Furthermore, a European Stability Mechanism (ESM) was launched as a permanent system to deal with debt crisis and to become effective after 2013.

In 2011, the ECB is expected to only moderately increase interest rates. As a first step it has lifted on the 7th of April ist main interest rate from 1% to 1.25%. European governments are withdrawing fiscal stimulus measures, cutting spending and – sometimes – raising taxes to reduce their historically high budget deficits. This exit from expansionary policies all over Europe is likely to restrain short-term demand. It is expected that the 27 countries of the European Union growth will amount to around 2% in 2011 and 2012, after 1.8% in 2010 and -4.1% in 2009. Growth remains uneven across Europe. In several European countries, notably Greece, Ireland, Portugal and Spain, economic conditions will remain fragile.

The ***US economy*** also recovered in 2010, with growth of 2.8%, compensating the GDP decline in 2009 (-2.6%). While output recovered, unemployment remained at a historically high level. Core consumer prices rose by less than 1%, keeping deflationary risks alive. The Federal Reserve responded by again buying government bonds and mortgage-backed securities (quantitative easing or QE 2). At the same time, the expansionary fiscal policy stance was extended. In 2011 the effects of the replenishment of stocks, which boosted demand in 2010, are subsiding. Additionally, capacity in real estate markets continues to depress the construction sector. High unemployment, households deleveraging debt levels and high oil prices weigh on consumer spending, but the strong performance of equity markets provides some support through wealth effects. The recovery of GDP from the deep 2009 recession continues to remain more subdued than the recoveries from earlier recessions with growth remaining close to 3% in both 2011 and 2012.

Japan´s economy also recovered from the deep recession with real GDP increasing by almost 4% in 2010, which was not enough to compensate for the decline of more than 6% in 2009. Growth was mainly driven by private consumption, which had been boosted by fiscal stimulus measures and by the revival of exports. Investment activity remained subdued. Japan was hit in March 2011 by a huge earthquake and tsunami, which caused many casualties, seriously damaged nuclear power plants and disrupted the whole economy. This event could also affect the economies of neighbouring countries and possibly the world economy. Prior to this catastrophe, growth in Japan was expected to amount to 1%-2% in 2011 and 2012. As production has been disrupted by the earthquake, GDP will probably decline in the first half of 2011 but later recover due to reconstruction activities, although the timing of this recovery and the overall effect on 2011 remains uncertain.

China´s economy weathered the global crisis very well, helped by large-scale fiscal expansion. In 2009 growth amounted to above 9% and accelerated in 2010 to above 10%. At the same time, inflationary pressures increased due to higher food prices, driven by supply bottlenecks both in China and abroad. Strong economic growth and high bank liquidity also fuelled inflationary pressures, notably in the real estate sector. The People´s Bank of China responded by raising reserve requirements and lifting interest rates. These measures and the more subdued external demand are expected to reduce growth to around 9.5% in both 2011 and 2012. In March 2011, China published its twelfth five-year plan (2011-2015), which aims at a more moderate growth of 7%. This plan also stresses a broader development objective, including environmental goals, more equal income distribution, and shifting the growth pattern from exports and investment growth more towards private consumption and from manufacturing more towards services. If successful, this strategy will have important implications not only for China, but also for its trading partners, including Africa.

India´s economy has also continued its impressive performance, with growth of above 10%% in 2010 (after 6.8% in 2009). Growth was mainly driven by domestic demand, notably private consumption and investment. Exports of services (mainly in software) also remained strong, while other exports contributed relatively little. As inflationary pressures were mounting, the Central Bank raised interest rates. The appreciating exchange rate has also helped to mitigate inflation. It is expected that growth will gradually slow down to around 8% in 2011 and 2012. But India is also facing bottlenecks that weigh on medium-term growth, such as in infrastructure (notably roads, electricity), shortage of skills and rigid labour markets.

Latin America´s economies recovered from their 2009 recession as countries benefited from the rebound of primary commodity prices. Brazil's recovery was also driven by public consumption in the run-up to presidential elections. When inflationary pressures mounted, some countries responded by increasing interest rates. But this, together with generally favourable economic prospects, attracted capital imports, drove up exchange rates and reduced international competitiveness. Some countries responded by intervening in foreign exchange markets and restraining capital imports, for example by levying taxes, as in Brazil. Growth in Latin America is expected to weaken due to subdued import demand of industrial countries. In Brazil growth is expected to amount to 4.5% in 2011 and around 4% in 2012 after 7.5% in 2010 and -0.6% in 2009.

Figure 1.6: World economic growth

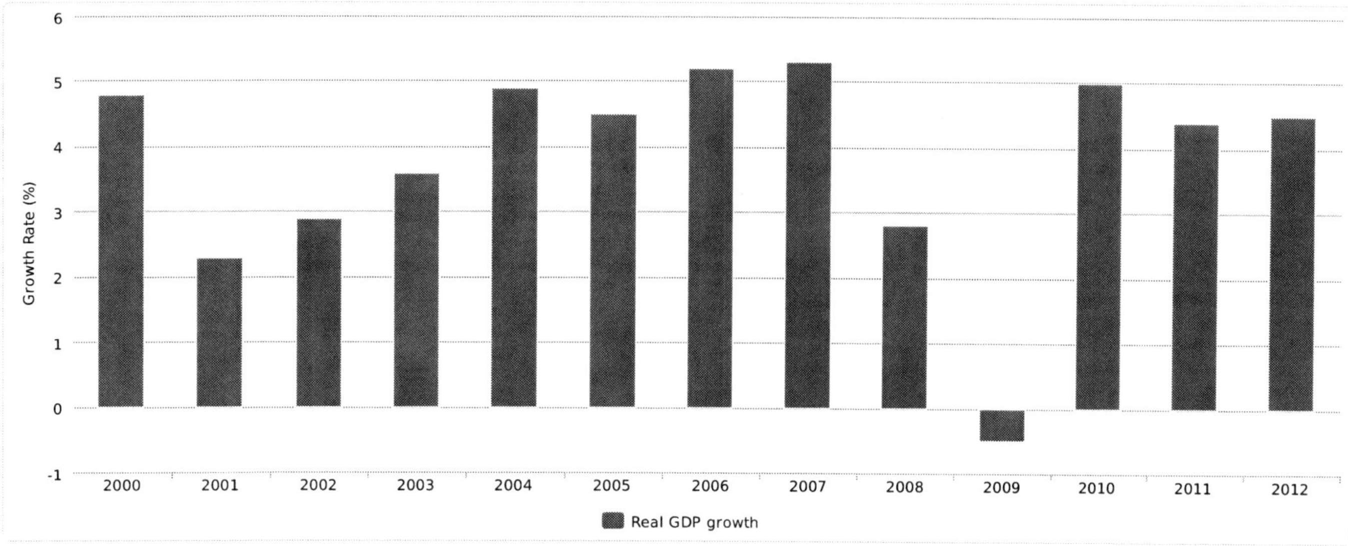

Source: African Development Bank, International Monetary Fund.

StatLink http://dx.doi.org/10.1787/888932403211

Political upheaval causes near stagnation in North Africa

In 2010 the economic expansion was above average in resource-rich countries that benefit from the revival in commodity demand, oil and non-oil commodity prices, and trade. In 2011 growth is expected to accelerate in most African countries, with some important exceptions. Several African countries have to cope not only with higher food and oil bills, but also with political instability and social unrest. The political upheavals and related uncertainty in northern Africa in the first half of 2011 disrupted economic activity. In ***Tunisia*** and ***Egypt***, large-scale strikes and demonstrations led to production losses in the first months of the year, and the security situation discouraged tourism, which is a major earner of export revenues in both Tunisia and Egypt. In ***Libya*** the recent political upheaval is causing a double-digit fall in oil production and aggregate output. Due to these events, growth in ***North Africa*** is expected to slow to below 1% in 2011, down from 4.7% in 2010. Under the assumption of a return to normal economic life, growth of the region is expected to accelerate to around 5% in 2012. These projections are subject to a large margin of error. Given north Africa´s weight of around a third of the continent´s GDP, the events in this region are depressing Africa´s growth in 2011 by more than one percentage point.

East Africa is expected to continue on its growth path of above 6% during the projection period, while growth in West Africa is expected to decelerate to below 6% due tot he events in Côte d´Ivoire. ***Southern Africa,*** the only African region with negative growth in 2009, recovered in 2010 and is expected to further strengthen, with growth reaching 4.5% in 2011 and 5.5% in 2012. In ***Central Africa,*** growth is projected to accelerate to 5.3% in 2011 and to 5.7% in 2012 (Table 1.1 and Figure 1.7).

Table 1.1: Growth by regions (real GDP growth in percentage)

	2009	2010	2011	2012
Africa	3.1	4.9	3.7	5.8
Central Africa	2.6	4.7	5.3	5.7
Eastern Africa	5.7	6.2	6.7	6.7
Northern Africa	3.5	4.6	0.7	5.1
Southern Africa	-0.5	3.3	4.5	5.5
Western Africa	5.6	6.7	6	6.8

Source: African Development Bank.

StatLink http://dx.doi.org/10.1787/888932405700

Figure 1.7: Contributions of regions to Africa's growth

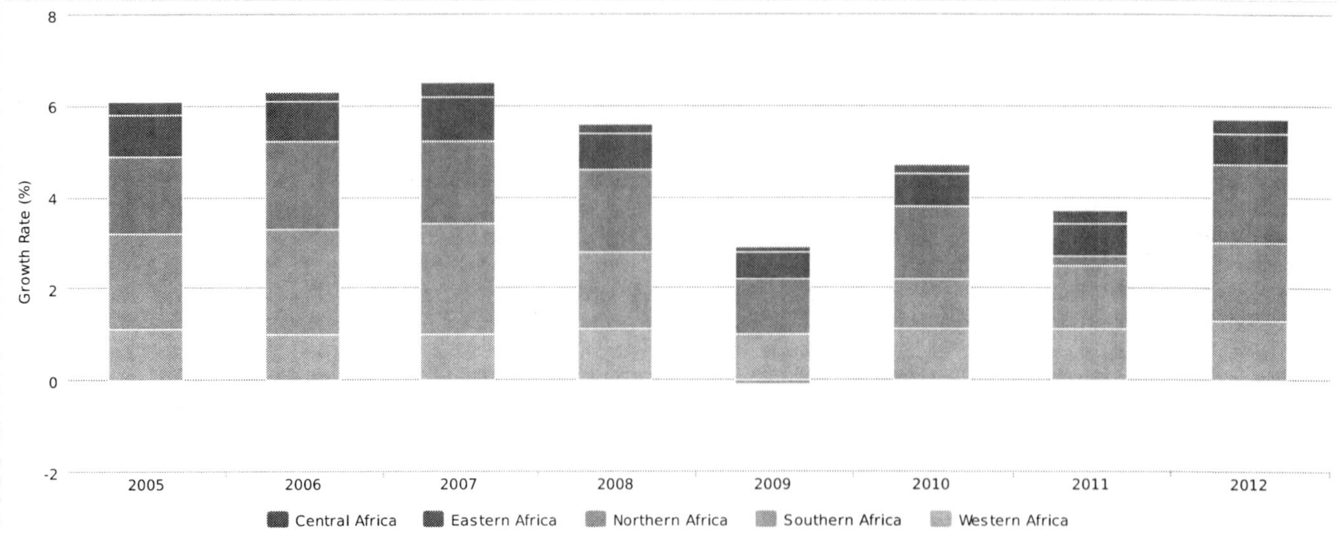

Source: African Development Bank.

StatLink http://dx.doi.org/10.1787/888932403230

The high oil price and increasing oil production continue to boost growth of African ***oil-exporting countries***. But the events in Libya affect average GDP growth of this group of countries, which is expected to decelerate to below 3 % in 2011 before accelerating again to around 6% in 2012 (under the assumption that normal economic activity in Libya resumes). In ***oil-importing countries***, average growth accelerated in 2010 to 4.2 % (up from less than 2% in 2009) and is expected to further strengthen to 4.9% in 2011 and to 5.4 % in 2012 (see Annex Table 1.A).

Among individual countries, Ghana and Ethiopia are projected to lead the African growth league in 2011. In contrast, political conflicts are causing output to fall in Libya and Côte d´Ivoire. The events in Egypt and Tunisia and the political uncertainty in Madagascar are also weighing on these countries´ growth (see Figures 1.8 and 1.9).

Figure 1.8: Growth of GDP (%)

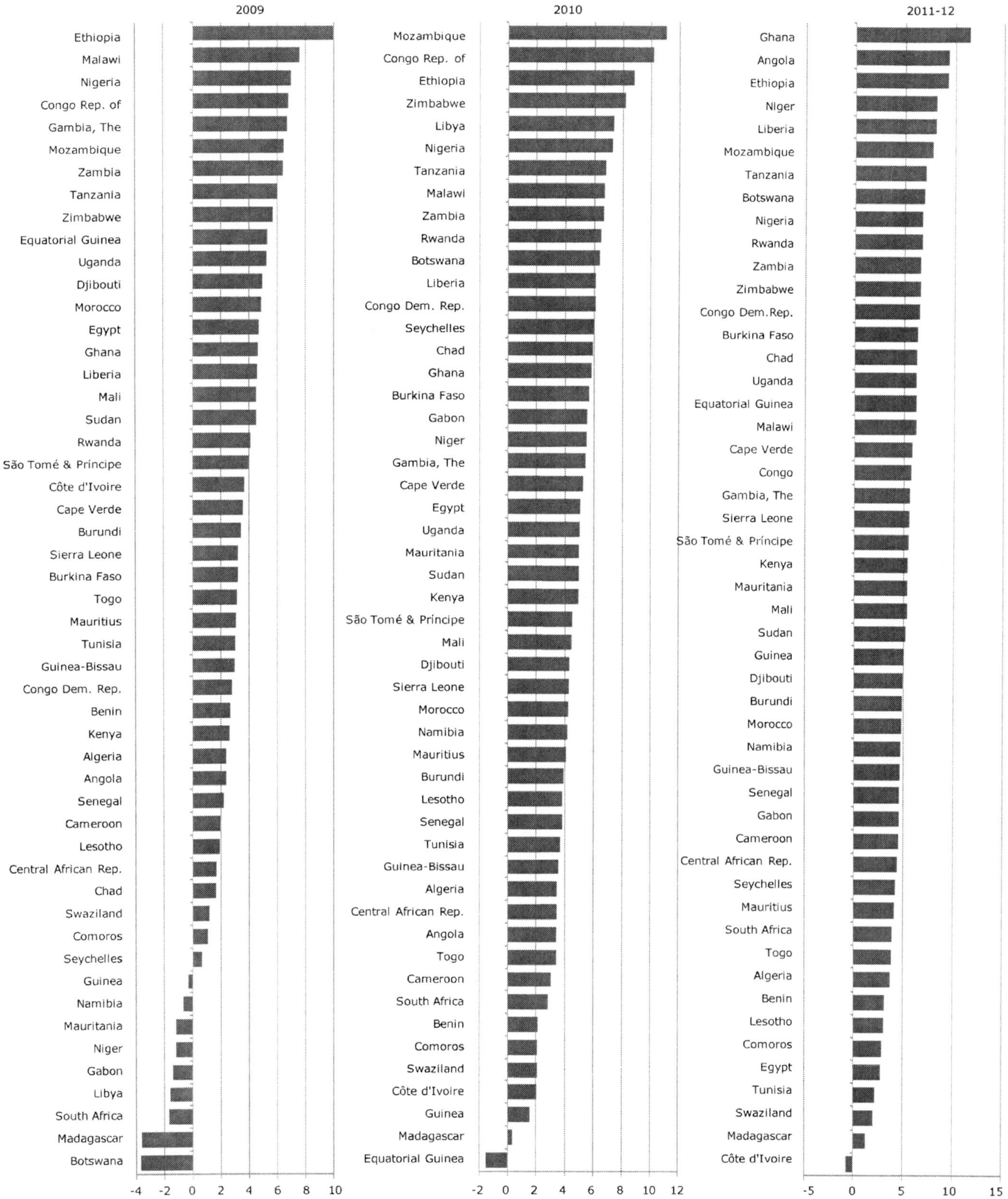

Source: African Development Bank.

StatLink http://dx.doi.org/10.1787/888932403249

Figure 1.9: Growth of per capita GDP (%)

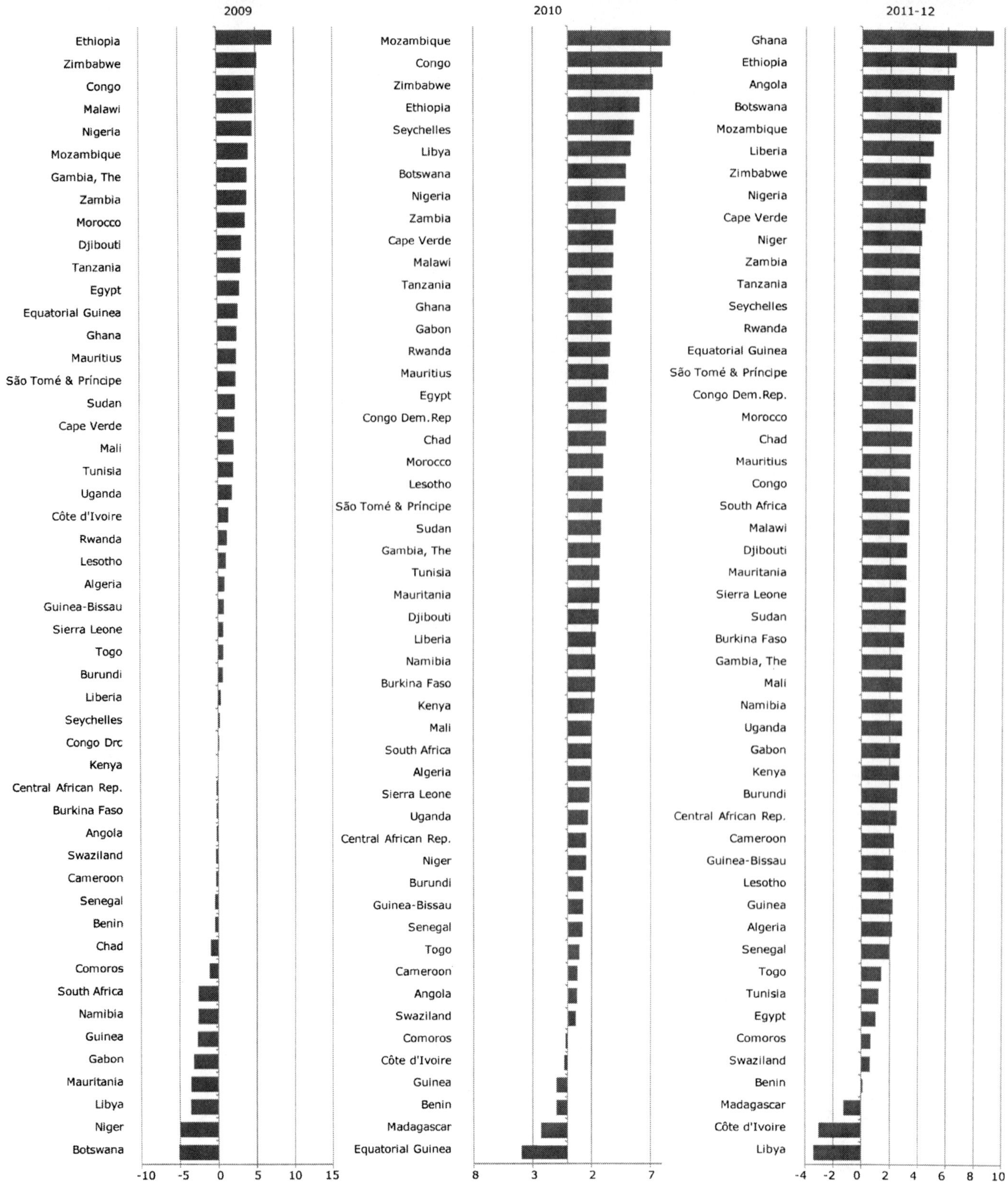

Source: African Development Bank.

StatLink http://dx.doi.org/10.1787/888932403268

High prices are boosting growth of commodity exporters

Driven by the expansion of global demand, commodity prices continued to increase in 2010, and in first months of 2011 some prices reached a new historical peak (see Figures 1.10 - 1.13). The ***oil price*** (crude Brent) has sharply increased from its trough of USD 30 per barrel in December 2008 and was at the time of writing fluctuating around USD 110, around three-fourths of its all-time high of USD 145 in July 2008. The latest oil price spike of between USD 110 and USD 120 was caused by the events in Libya. Changes in the price of oil depend, however, on further political developments in oil producing countries, notably Libya, and also on the supply response to the recent hike in oil prices. Some OPEC member countries, such as Saudi Arabia, have increased production in response to the price hike, but others have not followed. The technical assumption used in this report is that during the projection period 2011/12, the oil price will decline again to around USD 90 per barrel. Oil price uncertainty will continue to be a major risk factor for economic growth in the near term. African oil exporters, notably Nigeria, Algeria Angola and Sudan, are benefiting from the oil price boom. Not so Libya, which has the continent's largest oil reserves, as the political upheaval has caused a sharp decline in oil production and aggregate output. While oil exporters benefit from windfall gains on output, net exports and government revenue, oil importing countries are suffering from losses in output and a worsening of current accounts. This is a particular problem for Highly Indebted Poor Countries (HIPCs). The impact of higher oil prices on the economies also depends on how countries respond to the oil price shock. If governments contain the impact of the shock by controlling petroleum prices and/or providing subsidies output declines less in the short-term, but budget deficits increase, which could cause output losses in the longer term.

The ***price of gold*** has continued its steep rise during 2010 and into 2011, driven by global demand that aimed at hedging against financial market and exchange rate risks. The escalation of violence in Libya has further boosted the price of gold. The soaring gold price benefits countries such as South Africa, Ghana, Zimbabwe, Tanzania, Guinea and Mali, Africa´s main producers of gold. Africa accounts for around 30% of global gold production.

Other metal prices have recovered from their trough in early 2009, driven by global demand. The price of ***copper*** has reached a new historical peak, providing windfall gains to copper producing countries. Zambia is Africa's biggest copper producer, followed by the Democratic Republic of Congo and South Africa. The price of ***aluminum*** has recovered at a more moderate pace. South Africa and Mozambique are Africa´s largest aluminium producers, followed by Egypt, Ghana, Nigeria and Cameroon.

Export prices for agricultural products have further increased in the course of 2010 and into 2011. ***Cotton*** has recorded the sharpest price increase, caused by higher global demand (notably from China) and supply shortages due to poor crops in Pakistan and export restrictions in India. In Africa, Burkina Faso, Chad, Mali and Benin are main producers of cotton. The ***cocoa*** price has experienced sharp swings at high levels, affected by the events in Côte d´Ivoire, the world´s largest producer. The price tumbled after the news about good harvests in Côte d´Ivoire, but it jumped again after the export ban on cocoa by EU. This ban was intended to cut the funding of the incumbent president, Mr. Gbagbo and to support Mr. Ouattara, the internationally recognised winner of the presidential elections, but it also hurt farmers. After Mr. Gbagbo has been caught, the export ban has been lifted. Prices of ***coffee*** are also rising fast due to poor harvests in major producing countries, such as Colombia and Brazil. The high prices are benefiting African producers, such Ethiopia and Kenya, and help to absorb the impact of lower production due to bad weather conditions in some coffee-growing regions.

Import prices of basic foodstuffs have increased sharply in the course of 2010, with prices of wheat and maize rising much faster than the price of rice. African farmers benefit from higher agricultural prices, but consumers, notably in urban areas, are suffering. In several countries the hardship falling on populations has contributed to large-scale political unrest, although other problems, notably high youth unemployment and insufficient political freedom, have also played roles.

The causes for the recent hike of food prices are diverse. Increasing global demand as well as supply constraints played roles. Financial market speculation has also been criticised as a booster, although the size of this effect is controversial (see Box 1.3).

Figure 1.10: Oil price and gold price (base January 2000 = 100)

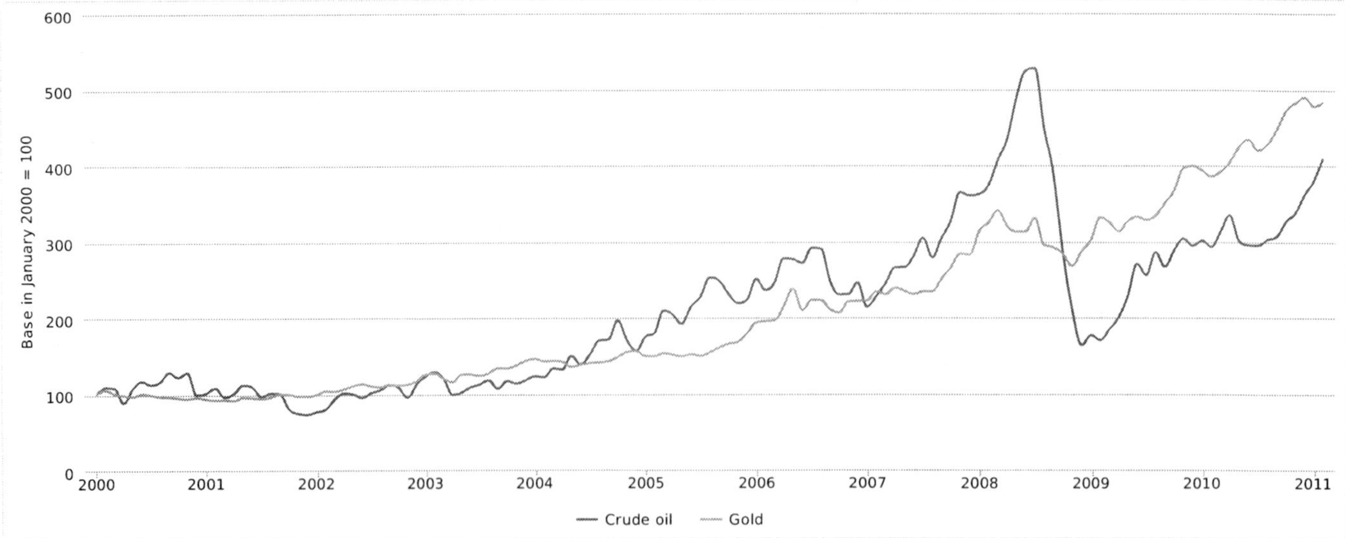

Source: African Development Bank, World Bank.

StatLink http://dx.doi.org/10.1787/888932403287

Figure 1.11: Copper and aluminium prices (base January 2000 = 100)

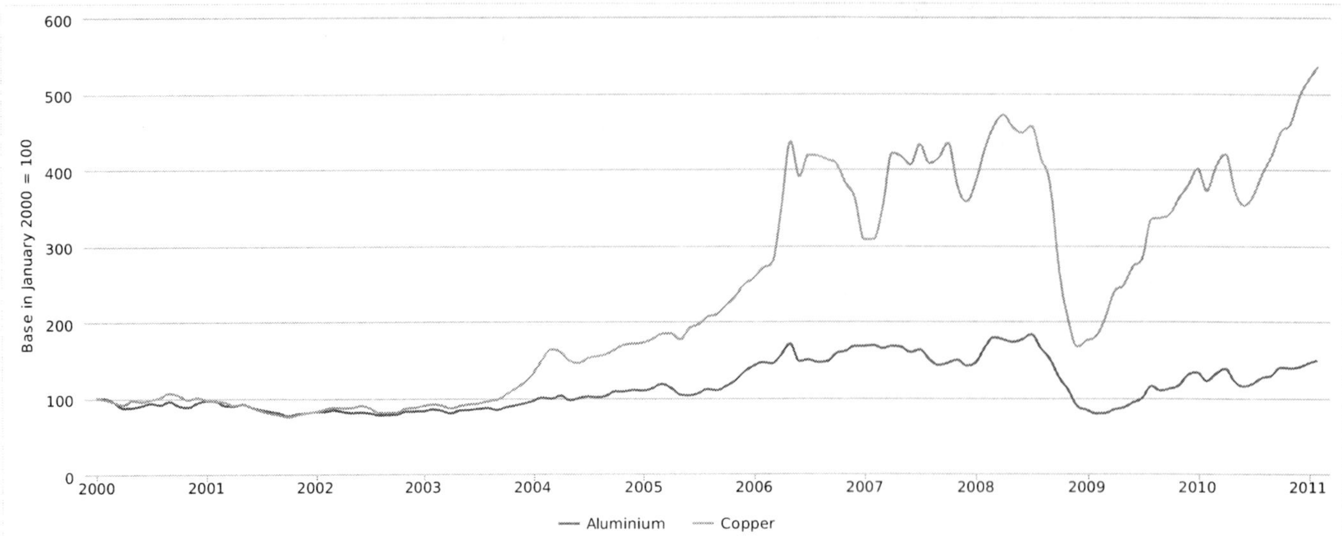

Source: African Development Bank, World Bank.

StatLink http://dx.doi.org/10.1787/888932403306

As the African continent is a net food importer, the sharp increase in food prices will increase the import bill. This is putting pressure on the balance of payments and raising inflation. Where governments increase food subsidies to protect their population, the burden is shifted to government budgets, causing deficits to rise and/or other spending to be cut. The countries within the group of Low-Income-Food-Deficit Countries (LIFDC) are particularly vulnerable to higher food prices (AfDB, 2011; Salami *et al.*, 2011). According to the 2010 classification of the Food and Agriculture Organization (FAO), of the 77 countries of this worldwide group, 43 are in Africa, around 80% of all African countries. To prevent (or respond to) social unrest, countries are taking measures to tackle the effects of higher food prices. For example, in Egypt, which is a large importer of food – it imports 40% of its total foodstuffs and 60% of its wheat – the number of ration-card beneficiaries has increased.

Figure 1.12: Export prices of agricultural products (base January 2000 = 100)

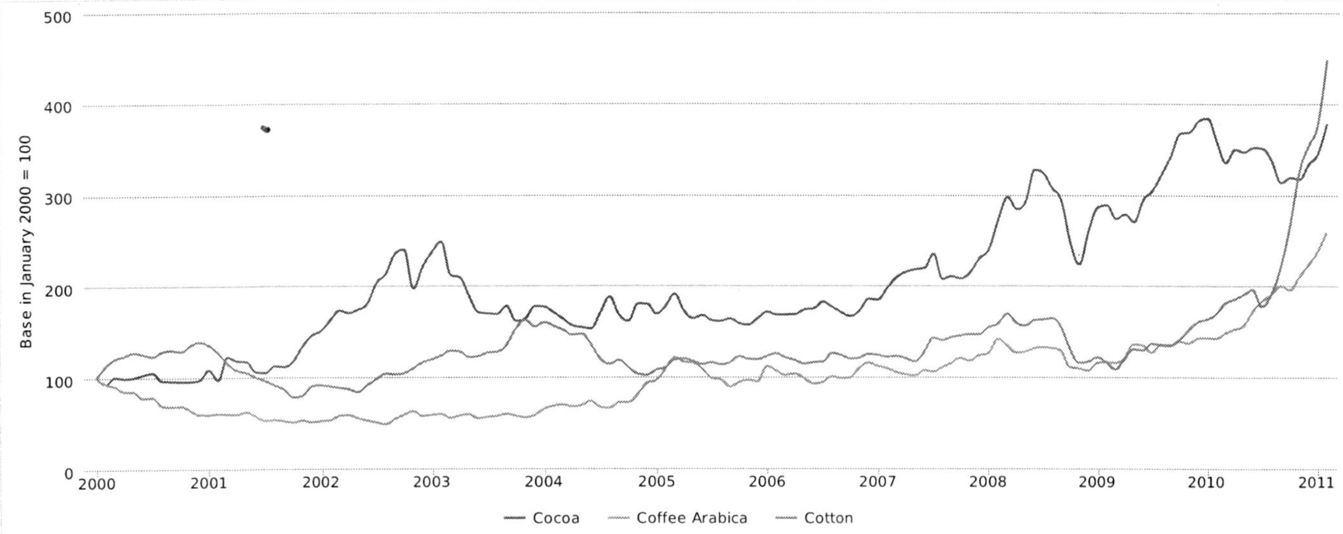

Source: African Development Bank, World Bank.

StatLink http://dx.doi.org/10.1787/888932403325

Figure 1.13: Import prices of basic foodstuffs (base January 2000 = 100)

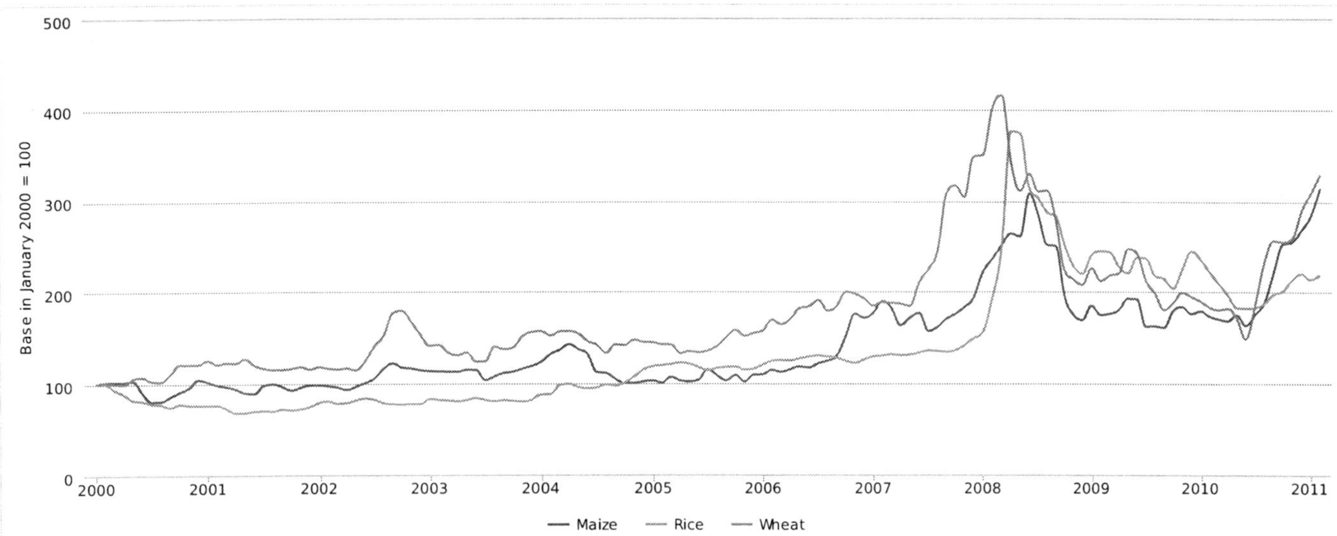

Source: African Development Bank, World Bank.

StatLink http://dx.doi.org/10.1787/888932403344

Box 1.3: What is causing food price inflation?

After the sharp decline from their peak in the second half of 2008, international food prices soared again in 2009 and 2010. Prices for cereals, cooking oils and sugar increased most, while the increase of meat prices was more moderate. Global supply and demand imbalances in agricultural commodity markets appear to have been a main driving factor for this recent increase.

On the supply side, unfavourable weather conditions in important producing countries affected sugar and wheat prices. Among the sugar-producing countries, Brazil (the most important producer) suffered from dry weather, and India's output in the biggest sugar growing region (Uttar Pradesh) was reduced by heavy rainfalls, infestations and crop diseases. Among producers of wheat, Australia's crops were damaged by heavy rainfall, and several other wheat-producing countries also suffered from unfavourable weather conditions. Following the lower production due to drought, the Russian Federation banned its wheat exports, which reduced supply to international markets. Additionally, unfavourable weather conditions negatively affected agricultural production in several countries in Africa, such as Benin, Madagascar, Morocco, Mozambique, Tunisia and Zimbabwe. But in most other African countries, favourable weather conditions boosted harvests, thus mitigating the effect of high global food prices. Nonetheless, food security remains critical for vulnerable groups.

On the demand side, the growing world population is often mentioned as a main driver of food prices. While this is true for the medium and longer term, it cannot explain the recent price hike. Thus, together with the supply disruptions, other demand-side factors appear to have been more important, notably that countries increased their stocks to protect their populations from higher prices. Other factors driving food prices (both on the supply and demand sides) are higher energy prices and the expansion of biofuel production. The sharp increase of petroleum prices is increasing not only costs for production (including prices of fertilizers) and transport of agricultural products, but it also makes it more profitable to transform agricultural products into biofuels. Regulations (as in the European Union) and subsidies for ethanol (as in the United States) favour the use of biofuels. The additional demand for agricultural products, which can be used for biofuel production, increases their prices. As consumers shift their demand to cheaper products, those prices also rise. At the same time, farmers find it more profitable to use their land for the production of biofuel inputs, which reduces the supply of food production and further increases food prices.

Factors outside agricultural markets, such as the relatively weak exchange rate of the US dollar, are also blamed for driving commodity prices. As commodity prices are denominated in US dollars, a weaker dollar encourages replenishing stocks, thus increasing demand while producers of commodities are demanding a higher price (in US dollars), thereby driving up prices. However, it is difficult to isolate exchange rate effects from other factors that changed at the same time, notably the recovery of the global economy. Financial market speculation is also blamed as a culprit for the volatility and recent increase of commodity prices. It is true that in recent years more money is flowing into commodity markets, also fuelled by excess liquidity in financial markets due to expansionary monetary policies. However, there are different views regarding to what extent this affects prices as the causal relationship between spot prices and futures prices is not very clear.

Inflation is increasing again due to higher food and fuel prices

Africa´s average inflation rate, which had declined to 7.7% in 2010 (from 10.1% in 2009), is expected to increase marginally to 8.4% in 2011 before sliding back again to 7.4% in 2012. The median inflation, which is not affected by countries with extremely high inflation, amounted to 4.7% in 2010 (down from 7.1% in 2009) and is projected to accelerate to 5.9% in 2011 before declining to and 5.3% in 2012. The main reason for the uptick of inflation rates in 2011 is the increase in energy and food prices. Among the 51 countries covered in this report, the majority will record inflation rates between 2 % and 5.5 % in 2011 and 2012. This is not excessive for developing countries in particular, as part of this price increase stems from higher import prices for food and energy so that core inflation is lower. But in some countries (such as Ethiopia, Sudan, Egypt and Angola) inflation is expected to remain above 10%.

Monetary policy: moving towards moderate tightening

Given moderate inflationary pressures during 2010, central banks in Africa often saw room to further ease monetary policies. Nonetheless, in many countries bank-lending rates remained relatively high, and bank credits to the private sector relatively low. This provides further evidence of a relatively weak transmission of monetary policy measures to private sector activity (Kasekende and Brownbridge, 2010). In 2011 monetary policies have to cope with the challenge to control inflation in the light of imported inflation from higher oil and food prices, while at the same time accommodating the economic recovery.

Monetary policies in Africa are expected to gradually tighten to respond to inflation concerns. As in most countries where underlying inflationary pressures are expected to remain subdued, there is no need for vigorous tightening. Policies should focus more on core inflation and inflation expectations rather than on the temporary increase of headline inflation, caused by spikes in food and energy prices. The conditions for monetary authorities are, however, quite different across the individual countries and country groups.

Monetary policies of African countries are implemented within three different frameworks: *a)* fixed exchange rate regimes, such as the West African Economic and Monetary Union (WAEMU),[3] the Economic and Monetary

Union of Central Africa (CEMAC)[4] and the Common Monetary Area (CMA)[5] in southern Africa; *b)* targeting of monetary aggregates, such as broad money as intermediate target and reserve money as operational target, and *c)* inflation targeting. But there are also hybrid systems, with countries (such as Kenya) using elements of the different systems (Kasekende and Brownbridge, 2010).

Inflation continued to decline in 2009 and 2010 in most African countries, independent of their monetary policy frameworks. In fixed exchange rate regimes, the peg with the euro is clearly helping to control inflation. Indeed, countries with exchange rates linked to the euro tend to have lower inflation than countries without such pegging. However, the "one-size-fits-all" monetary policy also entails costs, as the monetary conditions (*i.e.,* the interest rate-exchange rate mix) may be too tight for some countries and too loose for others. For example, in Senegal the inflation rate was below WAEMU average (around -1% in 2009 and around 1% in 2010), suggesting that monetary conditions were, perhaps, too tight for this country. In contrast, in Equatorial Guinea, where inflation tends to be above the CEMAC average, the real exchange rate tends to appreciate, which reduces competitiveness of the non-oil sector.

Countries that are targeting monetary aggregates (such as Ethiopia, Tanzania, Uganda and Mozambique) have been more flexible. These countries have used both monetary policies and exchange rate policies to control inflation and at the same time try to sustain competitiveness. While inflationary pressures generally declined, the level of inflation remained mostly higher than in countries with fixed exchange rate regimes. In Ethiopia, Tanzania, Uganda and Mozambique, nominal exchange rates depreciated in 2010, which supported exports but increased import prices. In these countries, inflation amounted to between 9% and 11% in 2010. While in the first three countries inflation was lower than a year earlier, in Mozambique it was significantly higher.

South Africa is pursuing its monetary policy in an inflation-targeting framework. When the rate of inflation approached the lower band of the target range of 3%-6%, helped by the appreciation of the rand, the central bank cut interest rates. In Ghana, another country with inflation targeting, inflation declined significantly, from around 19% in 2009 to 8% in 2010, but it remained above the target of 5%. The appreciation of the (trade-weighted) exchange rate following the earlier sharp depreciation helped ease inflationary pressures.

Over the past five years CEMAC and WAEMU countries had higher inflation than members of the East African Community (EAC) and the South African Customs Union (SACU). At the same time, EAC achieved on average the highest growth among these regions. It is clear that very high inflation is detrimental growth, but at lower levels the interrelationship between inflation and growth is less clear. There could be a trade-off between growth and keeping inflation at a very low level (*e.g.* through pegging the exchange rate to a low-inflation country or country group like the euro zone) as monetary conditions may become too tight. However, allowing higher inflation is no panacea for attaining higher growth, as other conditions must also be fulfilled. For example, SACU members had on average higher inflation than CEMAC and WAEMU members but not higher growth (see Figure 1.11). This was, however, partly due to the recession, which hit the SACU region particularly hard and led to negative growth in 2009. In the four years prior to this crisis (2005-2008), the SACU region achieved higher growth (4.9%) than WAEMU (3.8%) and CEMAC (4.6%) but still lower growth than EAC (6.9%).

Figure 1.14: Growth and inflation in African regions

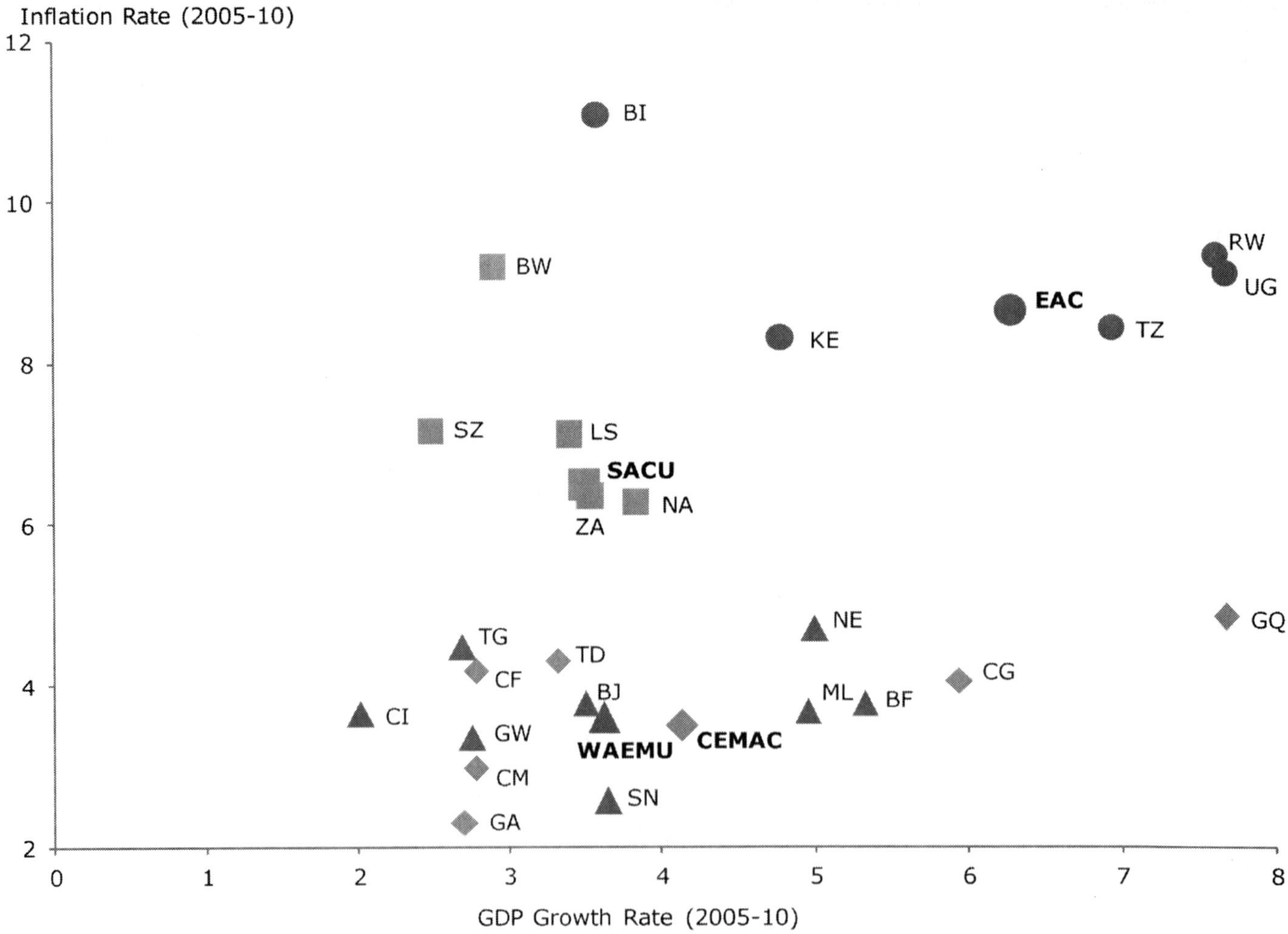

Source: African Development Bank.

CEMAC member countries: Cameroon (CM), Central African Republic (CF), Congo Rep. (CG), Gabon (GA), Equatorial Guinea (GQ), Chad (TD). EAG member countries: Burundi (BI), Kenya (KE), Rwanda (RW), Tanzania (TZ), Uganda (UG).SACU member countries: Botswana (BW), Lesotho (LS), Namibia (NA), South Africa (ZA), Swaziland (SZ).WAEMU member countries: Benin (BJ), Burkina Faso (BF), Côte d´Ivoire (CI), Guinea Bissau (GW), Mali (ML), Niger (NE), Senegal (SN), Togo (TG).

StatLink http://dx.doi.org/10.1787/888932403363

Fiscal and external positions are affected by commodity prices

Developments in global commodity markets heavily influence the development of fiscal balances and current accounts in African countries. But the impact on individual countries is quite different across countries and depends on their natural resource wealth. In ***oil-exporting countries***, both current accounts and fiscal balances generally improved in 2010, driven by higher oil prices and oil revenues. This is a reversal of the development in 2009, when declining oil prices caused a deterioration of both the current account and the fiscal balance. But fiscal and current account positions have generally not yet regained the levels prior to the global crisis. Both are projected to deteriorate slightly in 2011, but to improve again in 2012 (see Figure 1.15). The slight deterioration in 2011 is due to the disruption of oil production in Libya as without this event oil exporters´ fiscal and current account positions would have continued to improve.

In ***oil-importing countries***, current accounts have on average sligtly improved in 2010 but are expected to deteriorate again in 2011 and 2012 (see Figure 1.16). Higher import bills for oil and food are taking their toll, and higher exports generally do not offset these. The external positions of these countries are sometimes also affected by fiscal policies. For example, where an increase in public spending is not accompanied by higher public revenue or by private net savings, both the fiscal and the external positions deteriorate, causing a twin-deficit. But high domestic cost and price pressures or large capital inflows, which lead to an uncompetitive real exchange rate, can also cause external imbalances. Where current account deficits are to a large extent financed through foreign direct investment (FDI) equity inflows, they are sustainable, as this kind of financing does not increase external debt. In contrast, financing deficits by short-term capital inflows increases foreign debt and makes countries vulnerable to swings in market perceptions. Thus, following prudent fiscal policies, sustaining competitive real exchange rates and improving conditions for domestic and foreign investors help to prevent unsustainable external positions.

The continent´s average fiscal deficit amounted to 5.2% of GDP in 2009. It declined to 3.3% in 2010 as revenues recovered, but it is expected to increase again to almost 4% in 2011. This increase is caused by the deterioration of fiscal balances in North Africa in the wake of political upheavals. In 2012 Africa´s average fiscal deficit is projected to decline again to slightly above 3% of GDP. However, fiscal consolidation will be uneven across the continent. While some countries (such as Angola and Republic of Congo) will record high surpluses, other countries (such as Cape Verde, Chad, Egypt, Guinea Lesotho and Swaziland) will continue to run relatively high fiscal deficits. Several countries (such as Burundi, Republic of Congo, Central African Republic, Nigeria and South Africa) have implemented or are planning additional fiscal reforms (notably, improving tax collection). These reforms aim at creating fiscal space for higher spending and/or reducing the dependence on donor support.

Budget projections as described in this report are subject to considerable uncertainty. Disbursements of Official Development Assistance (ODA) may fall short of expectations as donor countries are facing fiscal problems. Furthermore, African governments may introduce food and fuel subsidies to protect households from high import prices. Finally, the large number of national elections on the continent this year brings the risk that in many countries office holders will raise spending to get political support from voters, and such "pork-barrel politics" could undermine fiscal consolidation.

Figure 1.15: Current account and fiscal balance in oil-exporting countries

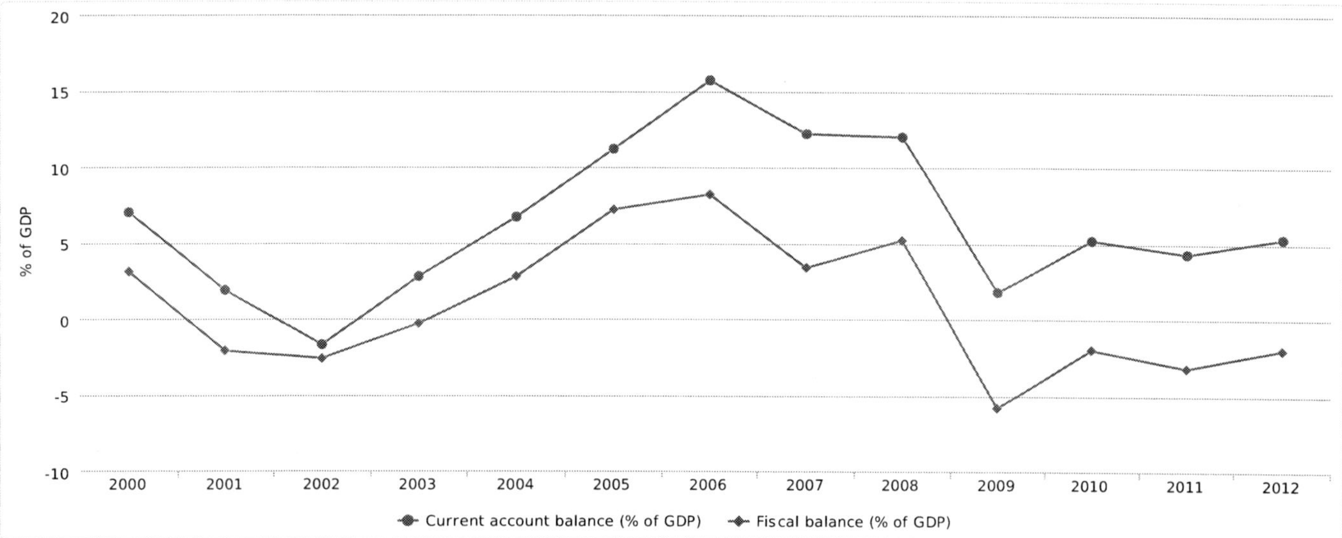

Source: African Development Bank.

StatLink http://dx.doi.org/10.1787/888932403382

Figure 1.16: Current account and fiscal balance in oil-importing countries

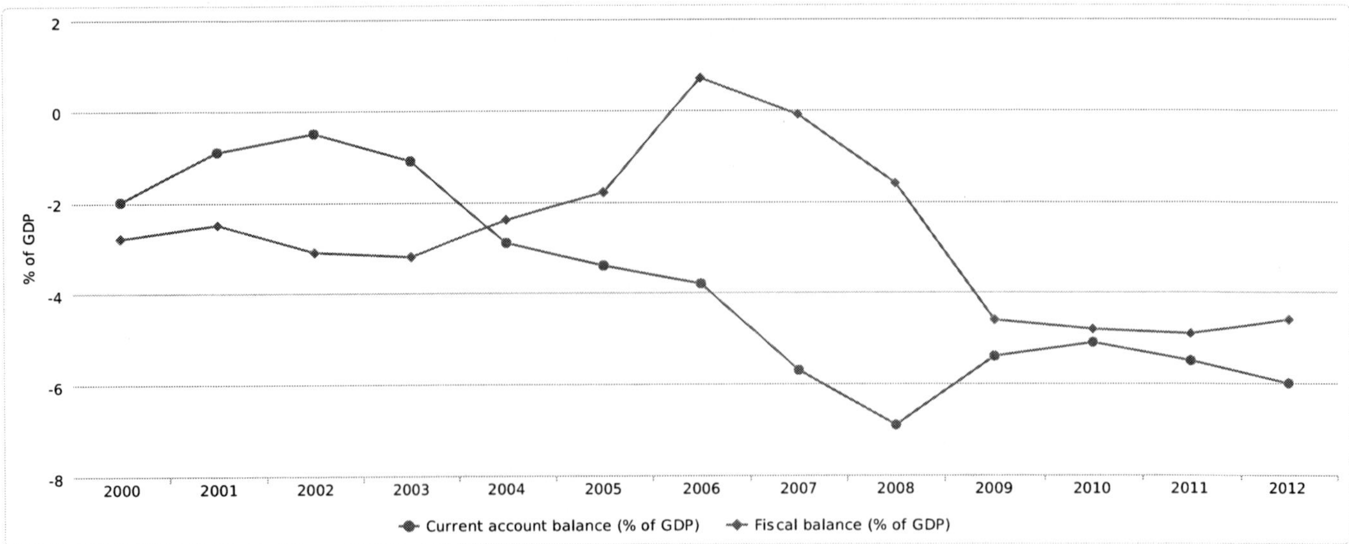

Source: African Development Bank.

StatLink http://dx.doi.org/10.1787/888932403401

The challenge of reducing youth unemployment

While the current economic recovery is likely to reduce the cyclical component of unemployment in Africa, structural unemployment nevertheless remains high in many countries. In north Africa, where economic activity has been disrupted by the political upheavals, unemployment is likely to further increase in 2011. Youth unemployment has become a major problem in north Africa and contributed to political unrest, which led to the overthrow of governments in Tunisia and Egypt. According to a recent study by the International Labour Office (ILO), the youth unemployment rate in north Africa amounted to 23.7% in 2009 (down from 26.5% in 1998), and it is estimated to have remained at around the same level in 2010 (ILO, 2010). This is twice as high as in sub-Saharan Africa, where the youth unemployment rate was 11.9% in 2009, down from 13.5% in 1998 (ILO, 2010).

The relatively low unemployment rate of the youth in sub-Saharan Africa as recorded in this ILO study is somewhat surprising. As it is very difficult to get reliable labour market data, part of the relatively low rate may be due to statistical problems. However, given high poverty levels and lack of better alternatives in the labour market and education in many of these countries, the relatively low unemployment rate also reflects people's need to survive by accepting any kind of work, including indecent jobs (ILO, 2010). Another reason for the relatively low unemployment rate is that people have given up seeking employment due to lack of opportunities and are not counted as unemployed as they are not actively looking for a job.

In parts of Africa, and notably in the north, labour markets have not been flexible enough to absorb the growing supply of young workers. Given Africa´s rapidly growing population, the pressure on labour markets continues to increase. Over the past decade, Africa´s population increased by over 217 million to more than one billion. One-fifth of the population are at age 15-25 and thus at the age of entering the labour market and looking for a job. Both total population and youth population increased by 2 %, or 2.3% per year from 2000 to 2010. During the current decade, Africa´s population is projected to further increase by more than 23% (2. % per year), and the youth population by almost 20% (1.8% per year). While in eastern, central, and western Africa demographic pressures on labour markets continue, in north Africa and southern Africa, where population growth is more moderate, the youth population will stop rising and remain close to current levels (see Table 1.2).

A comprehensive approach is needed to address the problem of unemployment in general and of youth unemployment in particular. Improvements are needed both on the supply and the demand side of labour, with policies depending on country specifics. In many countries, more needs to be done to improve the quality of labour supply so that it better matches the skills required by firms. This also refers to university graduates, who are vulnerable to unemployment if their skills do not match job requirements. At the same time, labour demand needs to be boosted by further improving conditions for economic growth in general and for private sector activity in particular, including through the creation of new firms.

Table 1.2: Demographic trends in Africa (million persons)

	2000	2010	2020	2000/2010 (change in %)	2010/2020 (change in %)
Africa	-	-	-	-	-
Population	819.5	1033.1	1276.4	25.8	23.6
Of which age group 15-24	166	208.9	250.3	26.1	19.8
Northern Africa	-	-	-	-	-
Population	179.5	212.9	247.6	18.6	16.3
Of which age group 15-24	37.9	42.6	42.4	12.4	-0.5
Eastern Africa	-	-	-	-	-
Population	252.7	327.2	420.2	29.5	28.4
Of which age group 15-24	50.7	67.1	85.5	32.3	27.4
Western Africa	-	-	-	-	-
Population	237.8	306.1	383.2	28.7	25.2
Of which age group 15-24	47.8	61.1	76.9	27.8	28.8
Middle Africa	-	-	-	-	-
Population	98.1	128.9	164.3	31.4	27.5
Of which age group 15-24	19	26.3	33.9	38.4	28.9
Southern Africa	-	-	-	-	-
Population	51.4	58	61.1	12.8	5.3
Of which age group 15-24	10.6	11.8	11.6	11.3	-1.7

Source: World Population Prospects: the 2008 Revision; UN population database, medium variant.

StatLink http://dx.doi.org/10.1787/888932405719

Risks and policy challenges for African economies

This forecast for Africa for 2011 and 2012 rests on several assumptions, which may turn out to be too optimistic or too pessimistic. It has been assumed that the recovery of the world economy and world trade will be sustained and that prices of oil and non-oil commodities will remain high, although at somewhat lower levels than during the first quarter of 2011.

However, there are both upside and downside risks to this forecast. On the upside, the global recovery may be stronger than expected as confidence recovers in many parts of the world. A stronger growth of global demand would also boost Africa´s growth. With the recent events in the global economy following the earthquake and nuclear crisis in Japan, however, the upside risk may be small.

On the downside, the global recovery could be weaker than assumed here. If oil prices persist at high levels of USD 110 to USD 120, global growth would be restrained. The hike in oil prices is shifting wealth from oil-importing countries to oil-exporting countries, raising global savings in the oil-exporting countries (as oil exporters have generally a higher savings rate than oil importers), increasing headline inflation and reducing real demand. If monetary policies of oil-importing countries are tightened in response to higher headline inflation, global growth would be further reduced.

Besides these external risks, upside and downside risks also exist within Africa. Most importantly is how countries will cope with social discontent and political tensions, which have flared up in several countries. It is currently unclear how fast peace will be restored in Libya.

Furthermore, in countries with relatively large agricultural sectors, aggregate output also depends on agricultural production and thus also on weather conditions. The technical assumption of normal weather may turn out to be too optimistic or too pessimistic.

Finally, given the high food and energy prices and also the large number of forthcoming national elections, further social and political unrest could emerge in several African countries.

African policy makers must be aware of these global and domestic risks. Economic and social stability need to be sustained, or, where they are disrupted, be quickly restored. Policy requirements are to pursue prudent macro policies and at the same time implement appropriate measures to cope with higher commodity prices.

In resource-rich countries, part of windfall profits should be put into sovereign wealth funds in order to be prepared when prices fall again or resources will be depleted. Given the high food prices, governments, which have the necessary resources, should protect vulnerable groups from hunger by providing targeted and cost-effective support, while refraining from costly food and fuel subsidies to the general public. Furthermore, business conditions for farmers should be further improved so that they are able to increase investment and productivity in response to higher agricultural prices.

Table 1.a: Macroeconomic developments in Africa

	2009	2010	2011	2012
Real GDP Growth (%)				
Central Africa	2.6	4.7	5.3	5.7
Eastern Africa	5.7	6.2	6.7	6.7
Northern Africa	3.5	4.6	0.7	5.1
Southern Africa	-0.5	3.3	4.5	5.5
Western Africa	5.6	6.7	6.0	6.8
Africa	3.1	4.9	3.7	5.8
Memorandum items				
North Africa (including Sudan)	3.6	4.6	1.1	5.1
Sub-Saharan Africa	2.7	5.0	5.5	6.2
Oil-exporting countries	4.1	5.4	2.7	6.1
Oil importing countries	1.9	4.2	4.9	5.4
Consumer Prices (Inflation in %)				
Central Africa	10.0	5.5	4.8	4.4
Eastern Africa	16.7	9.3	11.3	9.3
Northern Africa	9.1	7.1	8.8	7.7
Southern Africa	8.0	6.4	6.6	6.7
Western Africa	10.3	10.4	9.2	7.3
Africa	10.0	7.7	8.4	7.4
Memorandum items				
North Africa (including Sudan)	9.3	7.7	9.3	7.9
Sub-Saharan Africa	10.5	7.8	7.8	7.1
Oil-exporting countries	11.5	10.0	10.4	8.7
Oil importing countries	8.3	5.0	6.1	5.8
Overall Fiscal Balance, including grants (% GDP)				
Central Africa	-2.3	0.5	-0.2	0.2
Eastern Africa	-2.6	-3.3	-3.5	-4.2
Northern Africa	-4.0	-2.4	-6.9	-5.3
Southern Africa	-6.5	-3.3	-2.8	-2.2
Western Africa	-8.0	-6.1	-2.0	-1.2
Africa	-5.2	-3.3	-3.9	-3.2
Memorandum items				
North Africa (including Sudan)	-3.8	-2.3	-6.1	-4.9

Sub-Saharan Africa	-6.1	-3.9	-2.6	-2.1
Oil-exporting countries	-5.8	-2.0	-3.2	-2.0
Oil importing countries	-4.6	-4.8	-4.9	-4.6
External Current Account, including grants (% GDP)				
Central Africa	-6.0	-3.1	-2.3	-2.4
Eastern Africa	-7.4	-8.3	-7.7	-9.2
Northern Africa	0.1	3.2	0.1	1.3
Southern Africa	-5.7	-2.8	-4.0	-3.2
Western Africa	6.4	7.0	10.0	9.7
Africa	-1.6	0.4	-0.2	0.2
Memorandum items				
North Africa (including Sudan)	-0.8	2.0	-0.6	0.3
Sub-Saharan Africa	-2.1	-0.5	0.0	0.2
Oil-exporting countries	1.8	5.2	4.3	5.3
Oil importing countries	-5.4	-4.9	-5.5	-6.0

Source: African Development Bank.

StatLink http://dx.doi.org/10.1787/888932405738

Notes

1. As real GDP is a measure of output, it deviates from real income if terms of trade change. If import prices increase more than export prices, the terms of trade deteriorate and per real capita income increases less than per capita GDP. In contrast, if export prices increase more than import prices, the terms of trade improve and real income increases more than output.
2. For a general discussion on the economic effects of remittances, see Ratha *et al.* (2011).
3. The WAEMU members are Benin, Burkina Faso, Côte d´Ivoire, Guinea Bissau, Mali, Niger, Senegal and Togo.
4. The CEMAC members are Cameroon, Central African Republic, Chad, Republic of Congo, Equatorial Guinea and Gabon.
5. In the CMA the currencies of Lesotho and Swaziland are pegged to the South African rand.

References

AfDB and OECD (2009), African Economic Outlook, OECD, Paris.

African Development Bank (2011), "Towards Food Security in Africa: Challenges, Policies and the Role of the Bank", Brief for the C-10 Meeting in Addis Ababa, March.

ILO (2010), *Global Employment Trends for Youth*, International Labour Office, Geneva.

IMF (2011), *World Economic Outlook*, International Monetary Fund, April.

Kasekende, L. and M. Brownbridge (2010), "Post Crisis Monetary Frameworks in Sub-Saharan Africa", paper presented at the African Economic Conference, Tunis, October.

Ratha, D., S. Mohapatra, C. Özden, S.Plaza, W, Shaw and A. Shimeles (2011), "Leveraging Migration for Africa, Remittances, Skills, and Investments", report prepared by the Migration and Remittances Unit of the World Bank and the Development Research Department of the African Development Bank, Washington, DC.

Salami, A., Z. Brixiova, H. Kandil and A. Mafusire (2011), "Towards Food Security in Africa: Challenges, Policies and the Role of the African Development Bank, *Africa Economic Brief*, Volume 2, No. 2, April.

Triki, T. and I. Faye (2011), "Africa's Quest for Development: Can Sovereign Wealth Funds Help?", *International Financial Review*, No.12.

WES (2011), Ifo *World Economic Survey*, www.cesifo-group.de/portal/page/portal/ifoHome/b-publ/b2journal/50publwes.

World Population Prospects (2008 Revision), United Nations Population Database, esa.un.org/unpp/

Chapter 2: External Financial Flows

The last decade has been one of impressive changes in the volume and composition of financial flows to Africa. Between 2000 and 2010 the sum of foreign direct investment (FDI), portfolio investment and official development assistance (ODA) increased almost fivefold, from USD 27 billion in 2000 to an estimated USD 126 billion in 2010 (OECD/DAC, 2010; UNCTAD, 2010a; IMF, 2010a). It is the changing composition of these flows, however, that best represents Africa's new economic dynamism: since 2005 Africa has attracted more FDI than ODA flows. Moreover, Africa's share of global FDI flows has risen over the last decade, from 0.7% in 2000 to 4.5% in 2010. These figures offer an impressive testimony to Africa's changing role in the world and its increasing ability to harness the opportunities from globalisation. Nevertheless, some challenges remain.

Foreign Direct Investment in Africa continues to be concentrated in a few countries and sectors, with 15 oil-exporting countries receiving 75% of FDI flows, pointing to a further need for diversification. Many governments are tackling this challenge and show commitment to improving institutional frameworks. The outlook for FDI flows to Africa in 2011 is basically good given the strong recovery in many parts of the world and rising resource prices. The current uncertainty in north Africa renders predictions difficult, however, as the region has been Africa's top FDI destination for the last five years.

Official Development Aid globally reached USD 120 billion in 2009, a 0.7% increase in real terms against 2008. ODA increased despite the financial crisis and its severe impact on government budgets in donor countries. Net bilateral ODA from donors that are members of the OECD Development Assistance Committee (DAC) to Africa totalled USD 28 billion in 2009, of which USD 25 billion went to sub-Saharan Africa. This represents an increase of 3% in real terms over 2008 for all of Africa and an increase of 5.1% for sub-Saharan Africa.

Direct investment flows

FDI is an especially important source of investment in Africa. Over the last decade, FDI's share of gross fixed capital formation in Africa has, at 20%, been twice the global average and 8% above that of other developing countries (UNCTAD, 2010b). Although it is of growing importance for the whole continent, FDI continues to be unevenly distributed. A large share of FDI goes to extractive industries in a limited group of countries. Attracting investment into diversified and higher value-added sectors remains a challenge for Africa. Many governments are tackling this challenge and show commitment to improving institutional frameworks.

Figure 2.1 shows that FDI to African countries peaked in 2008 at USD 72 billion (UNCTAD 2010a), five times the value of FDI receipts in 2000. The rise in FDI up to 2008 was supported by the surge in prices for raw materials, particularly oil, which triggered a boom in commodity-related investment. The global financial crisis had a twofold negative impact. First, investors suffered and reduced their investment volume. At the same time, the crisis lowered demand for Africa's commodities. This lowered demand has reduced capital investment in those sectors and countries where most foreign investment has historically been concentrated in Africa. Consequently, FDI inflows to African countries fell by 20%, to USD 59 billion in 2009. For 2010 the United Nations Conference on Trade and Development (UNCTAD) estimates a further decline to USD 50 billion, while the International Monetary Fund (IMF) estimates FDI to African countries at USD 52 billion in 2010.

Figure 2.1: FDI and ODA flows to Africa 2000-11 (billion USD, current)

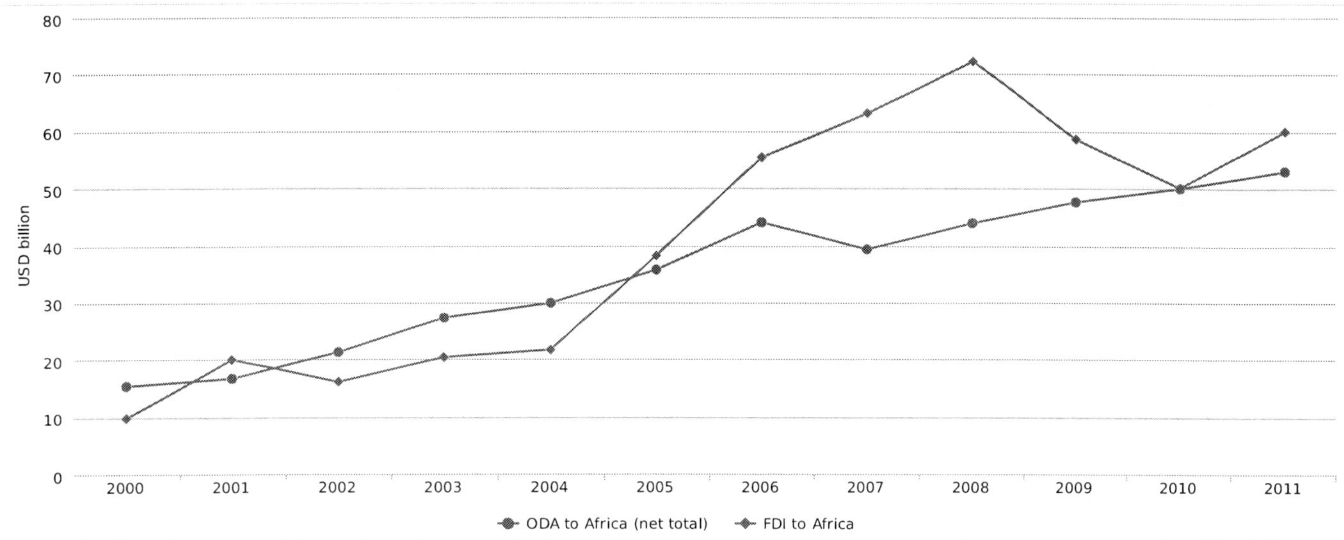

Source: OECD/DAC for ODA, UNCTAD for FDI 2000-2010.

Projections for 2011: FDI: IMF; ODA: Simple forecast (author's calculation)

StatLink http://dx.doi.org/10.1787/888932403420

Measured in shares of global FDI, inflows to African countries have been rising steadily over the last decade, from 0.7% in 2000 to 5.3% in 2009. However, Africa's shares of global FDI dipped slightly in 2010, to 4.5%. This drop in Africa's share is largely due to a quicker recovery of FDI flows from the financial crisis elsewhere in the world.

In terms of sectors, the services sector, led by the telecommunications industry, became the dominant FDI recipient in 2009 and attracted the largest share of cross-border mergers and acquisitions (M&As) in Africa (UNCTAD, 2010b). The primary sector, in turn, experienced pressure from low commodity prices and lack of credit. Nevertheless, FDI in Africa continues to be concentrated in a few countries and sectors, pointing to a further need for diversification. As Figure 2.2 shows, between 2000 and 2009, about 75% of FDI to Africa flowed to oil-exporting countries. For FDI from OECD member countries, this percentage is even higher: 85%.

Figure 2.2: FDI flows to countries exporting oil vs countries without oil 2000-09 (billion USD, current)

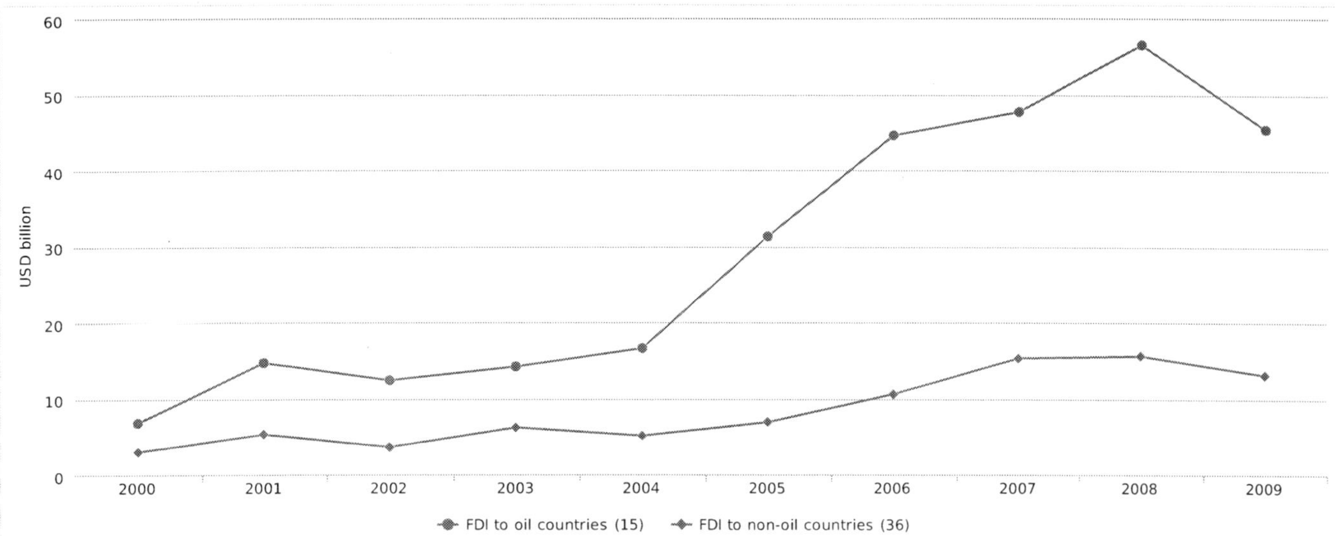

Source: UNCTAD FDI data, own calculation

StatLink http://dx.doi.org/10.1787/888932403439

From 2008 to 2009, net cross-border mergers and acquisitions (M&As) fell much more sharply than overall FDI, by 75% from an all-time high of USD 21 billion in 2008 to USD 5 billion in 2009. However, these cross-border M&As rebounded by 50% in 2010 to USD 8 billion, compared with a global rebound of only 37% (UNCTAD, 2010b). The biggest M&A deal related to Africa was Indian telecom Bharti Airtel's USD 10.7 billion acquisition of the African assets of Kuwait's Zain. This deal is not included in the preceding numbers, however, as it does not involve any financial flows to Africa but only a change of ownership of African assets between foreigners. In contrast, Japan's Nippon Telegraph and Telephone's USD 3 billion purchase of the South African IT firm Dimension Data Holdings brought significant financial flows to Africa. Major equity market deals included miner African Barrick Gold's nearly USD 900 million London IPO, while the top debt market issuance was nearly USD 2 billion South African sovereign bonds (ThomsonReuters, 2010).

A number of factors influence the possibilities for FDI to Africa in 2011. On the positive side, the global economy continues to recover from the financial crisis, especially the emerging economies that play an increasingly important role in Africa. In combination with rising commodity prices, this economic recovery makes for a favourable scenario for resource-exporting countries that can expect increasing FDI flows. As investors, especially from emerging partners, become more comfortable with the overall African business environment, the global upswing will also likely increase investment in other sectors.

However, negative factors also influence the 2011 possibilities for FDI to Africa. Specifically, the political developments in North Africa and the Middle East since the beginning of 2011 will likely have a negative effect on FDI and portfolio flows to Africa in the near future through two channels. North Africa has been important as both a destination of FDI inflows from outside of Africa and as a source of intra-African FDI. Owing to the current political uncertainty, foreign investors will likely hold off on the region, and North African investors will be much less active in the rest of Africa. To a lesser extent, a similar assessment holds true for the Middle East, which has been a key source of investment in Africa. A larger negative effect of North Africa on FDI to Africa is conceivable if investors interpret recent events in North Africa as a sign of increasing political instability across the continent.

FDI destinations in Africa

In 2009[1] Angola received the largest amount of FDI, at USD 13.1 billion. Angola was followed by Egypt, with USD 6.7 billion, and South Africa and Nigeria with USD 5.7 billion each[2]. In 2010 Angola is estimated to have received USD 7.9 billion, equivalent to 15% of all FDI to Africa in that year. Egypt, with USD 6.8 billion, and Nigeria, with USD 4.5 billion, follow. Libya, Morocco, the Republic of Congo and Sudan each received between USD 3 billion and USD 4 billion in FDI in 2010, while South Africa ranked eighth with USD 2 billion in FDI.

In terms of regional aggregates, **Northern Africa** has been the top destination for FDI in Africa between 2004 and 2008 and again in 2010, receiving a little more than one-third of all FDI flows to Africa. North Africa thus benefited enormously from the strong growth of FDI to the continent. In addition to attractive oil resources in Algeria, Libya, Egypt, Sudan and Tunisia, this surge is due to efforts by a number of governments in the region to open their economies to more foreign investment. In 2010 North Africa received USD 20 billion, up from USD 18.3 billion in 2009 but still significantly lower than its peak of USD 24 billion in 2008. Although Egypt receives by far the greatest amount of FDI in North Africa, its regional share has dropped from almost 40% in 2008 to 34% in 2010. Together with Egypt, Algeria saw a drop in FDI from USD 2.5 billion in 2009 to USD 1.5 billion in 2010. FDI to Libya is estimated to have increased USD 2.7 billion in 2009 to USD 3.8 billion in 2010.

Middle Africa has been the second FDI destination over the last years. The region was the first destination in 2009 with USD 18.7 billion, one third of FDI to African countries, but it fell back to USD 14 billion in 2010. The bulk of this investment is linked to the oil industry. Angola is by far the biggest FDI recipient in the region and accounts for about two-thirds of investments. The Republic of Congo comes second, with USD 2 billion in 2009 and USD 3.2 billion in 2010, followed by Equatorial Guinea with USD 1.7 billion in 2009 and USD 1.4 billion in 2010.

Table 2.1: FDI flows to African regions 2005-10 (billion USD, current)

	2005	2006	2007	2008	2009	2010
Africa	38.2	55.4	63.1	72.2	58.6	52.3
Northern Africa	12.2	23.1	24.8	24.1	18.3	19.7
Middle Africa	9.4	12.1	15.7	20.9	18.7	14.4
Western Africa	7.1	16.0	9.5	11.1	10.0	9.1
Southern Africa	7.3	0.6	7.1	10.4	6.6	3.1
Eastern Africa	2.1	3.6	6.0	5.7	5.0	6.0

Source: 2005-09 UNCTAD; 2010 IMF estimates from October 2010.

StatLink http://dx.doi.org/10.1787/888932405757

Western Africa has received about 20% of FDI to Africa over the last five years, attracting USD 10 billion in 2009 and USD 9 billion in 2010. Nigeria's oil industry is the main destination in the region. Nigeria received almost USD 6 billion in 2009 and USD 4.5 billion in 2010, accounting for 50% of FDI to the region. Ghana is the second largest recipient of FDI in the region, with USD 1.5 billion in 2010. FDI to Ghana has increased tenfold over the last five years, linked to Ghana's recent oil discoveries (production will start this year). This dynamism is only topped by Niger, which received USD 900 million in 2010, up from USD 30 million in 2005, and Liberia, which increased its FDI from practically nothing in 2005 to USD 350 million in 2010.

Over the last five years, about 11% of FDI to African countries has gone to **Southern Africa**, reaching USD 6.6 billion in 2009, down from USD 10 billion in 2008. In 2010 southern Africa experienced a further drop to USD 3 billion. South Africa is the main FDI destination in the region, accounting for 85% during 2007-09. Unlike in most other African countries, much foreign investment in South Africa goes to the manufacturing sector. Especially in the automotive industry, South Africa has successfully applied investment incentives to develop an export-manufacturing industry (International Strategic Analysis, 2011a). Elsewhere in the region, foreign investment will be targeted at the large mining and tourism industries in countries such as Namibia and Botswana (International Strategic Analysis, 2011ab.

Eastern Africa's share of FDI to African countries is the smallest, amounting to 8% over the last five years. For 2010 FDI to eastern Africa is estimated at USD 6 billion, up from USD 5 billion in 2009. Zambia has been the region's top recipient, with about USD 1 billion annually over the last three years, mainly directed at its mining industry. With almost 900%, Mozambique had the highest east African growth rate over the last five years, reaching USD 900 million in 2010. This surge consists mainly of megaprojects in resource extracting industries, notably in coal and aluminium. These megaprojects reward Mozambique's efforts in setting up special economic zones (SEZs) and providing attractive legal and fiscal conditions for investors. Except for Uganda, where oil reserves have recently been discovered, the other countries in the region have no significant natural resources, attracting lower amounts of FDI. Although low in value, east Africa's share of investment in terms of numbers of projects is significant. During the first quarter of 2010, 25% of African greenfield investment projects were in the region, reflecting the focus on market seeking investment in the productive and service sectors, which are much smaller in value than extractive industry projects.

Sources of FDI

Developed countries are the most important source of FDI flows to African countries, accounting for 72% between 2000 and 2008 (UNCTAD, 2010c). Hit hard by the global economic crisis, OECD countries substantially reduced their foreign investment activities. According to FDI outflow data compiled by the OECD (n.d.), member countries reduced their global FDI outflows by 43% from USD 1.8 trillion in 2008 to USD 1 trillion in 2009. OECD FDI flows to Africa also took a hit, but to a much lesser extent: from USD 34 billion in 2008 to USD 29 billion in 2009. As a result Africa's share of OECD FDI outflows grew from 2% in 2008 to 3% in 2009, up from less than 1% in 2000. Despite this positive development, FDI from the OECD is concentrated in a few countries and sectors and does not reach the whole continent equitably. During 2007-09 60% of OECD investment in Africa was made in three countries (South Africa, Egypt and Nigeria). The largest OECD investors in Africa are companies from the United Kingdom, France and the United States, having historically mainly invested in extractive industries.

Data on FDI to Africa from non-OECD countries are difficult to obtain. In a sample of ten African countries, whose central banks provided the AEO with their own data on FDI inflows,[3] OECD countries accounted for 83% of FDI inflows between 2005 and 2010. The Middle East constituted the second most important region of investors, followed by African countries (intra-African investments). China and India make up roughly 3% of FDI to these ten African countries, with India's share being larger than China's. According to China's statistical bulletin, in 2008 China invested USD 5.5 billion in sub-Saharan Africa, representing 9.82% of its outward FDI. This investment from China was up from USD 70 million in 2003 but declined to USD 1.1 billion in 2009 (IMF, 2011). South Africa, where the Chinese Industrial and Commercial Bank acquired a 20% stake in the Standard Bank, recorded most of the 2008 growth.

These numbers might seem low. However, data on FDI flows from emerging economies to Africa should be seen in the context of a broad variety of financing mechanisms that these countries provide to Africa. Export credits, for example, play a much more significant role in the Africa portfolios of emerging economies than in OECD countries. Generally, investments from private entities from emerging economies in Africa are most likely to be registered as FDI, whereas deals involving state-owned enterprises often involve a range of financing instruments and are not accounted for as FDI.

Although still largely focused on extractive industries, growing investments by emerging economies in Africa have the potential to become key drivers of economic development. Several deals by emerging partners in Africa combine the development of resource extractions with the development of industrial complexes and the construction of necessary infrastructure. Moreover, emerging economies invest increasingly in other sectors, starting to build local manufacturing capacity.

African investors are an equally critical source of more diversified FDI. Most African investment in Africa is made in neighbouring countries, focusing on manufacturing and services rather than primary commodities. Intra-African investment therefore benefits and helps to drive regional integration and structurally balanced economic development in Africa. The increasing volume of intra-African FDI is thus very positive.

South Africa is the most vital source of intra-African FDI and the second most important developing country investor in Africa after China. The share of African host economies in South Africa's outward FDI stock reached almost USD 11 billion in 2008, representing 22%, compared with 5% in 2000. In 2009 South Africa invested USD 1.6 billion (FDI outflows) in other African countries, a reversal from its disinvestment activities during 2008 and a return to an active foreign investment strategy in Africa.

Northern Africa ranks second as a source of intra-African FDI. Libya's sovereign wealth fund, the Libyan Africa Portfolio Fund for Investment (LAP), has over USD 5 billion in capital and invests, both directly and through its subsidiaries, in a wide range of sectors in many African countries. Egypt's Orascom also has a broad portfolio of investments throughout Africa, notably in telecommunications and construction. Morocco holds 55% of its stocks of outward FDI in North Africa, and Tunisia 84% (IMF, 2010 a). Given this importance of North Africa as a source of intra-African FDI, the recent political turmoil in this region will likely negatively affect these flows in the near future.

African outward FDI

Although intra-African investment is growing in importance, it does not yet make up the majority of foreign investment flows originating in Africa. Between 2000 and 2009, 63% of all African FDI outflows were invested in OECD countries. In 2009 this ratio was 56% of a total of USD 5 billion outward FDI (Combining data from UNCTAD, 2010a and OECD,n.d.) On the one hand, this investment can play a critical role in bringing expertise to the continent through acquisitions in more advanced economies. On the other hand, this large share of African investment going to OECD countries instead of other African countries presents an untapped potential.

Portfolio investment

Figure 2.3 shows that, compared with FDI in Africa, portfolio investment is still small, but of growing importance. At only USD 2 billion, or 13% of FDI in 2000, portfolio investment started to play a significant role in Africa around 2004, with a volume of USD 8 billion, 23% of FDI. Portfolio investment flows to Africa peaked in 2006 at USD 24 billion and took a deep hit during the following years, bottoming at USD -22 billion in 2008. Since then an equally steep and impressive recovery has followed: in 2010 portfolio flows to Africa amounted to USD 22 billion, just USD 2 billion shy of the peak of 2006, and equivalent to 30% of FDI.

Figure 2.3: Foreign direct investment and portfolio investment in Africa (billion USD, current)

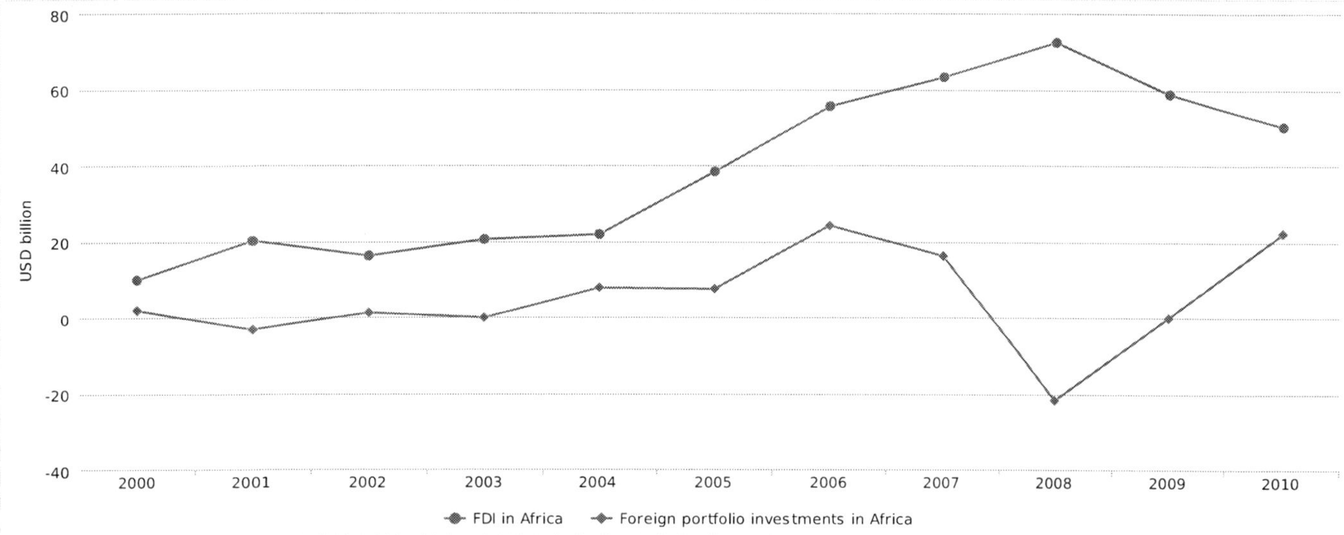

Source: UNCTAD for FDI; IMF for Portfolio.

StatLink http://dx.doi.org/10.1787/888932403458

South Africa is by far the most important destination for portfolio investment in Africa. Over the period 2000-10, portfolio flows going to South Africa amounted to 128% of all flows to Africa (mainly because Libya had negative portfolio flows of USD 28 billion during this period). In 2010 South Africa received USD 17.5 billion in portfolio flows, 80% of the continent's total. Another USD 8 billion, or 36% of the total, went to Egypt, whereas Libya had a net outflow of USD 4 billion, or -18% of the total African portfolio volume. Libya's high net outflows reflect the activities of its sovereign wealth fund, which has become a central player in African investment.

The IMF's Coordinated Portfolio Investment Survey (CPIS) collects information on the stock of cross-border holdings of equities and debt securities from 75 investor countries and territories (IMF 2010b).[4] In 2009 the portfolio investment stock of these 75 countries in Africa was USD 150 billion, consisting of 72% equity securities and 28% debt securities. This was also the ratio for the rest of the decade. The United States held a portfolio investment stock of USD 66 billion in Africa in 2009, or 44% of the total investment stock of all countries responding to the survey, followed by Luxembourg with USD 19 billion and Mauritius and the United Kingdom with USD 8 billion each. These figures reflect Mauritius's critical role as an investment gateway to Africa.

Aside from Mauritius, which is by far the most important source of intra-Africa portfolio investment, the intra-African dynamics of portfolio investment are similar to those of FDI, with South Africa and the northern African countries as the main sources of investment. The only continental respondents to the CPIS, Egypt held 0.2% and South Africa 0.8% of all portfolio stock in Africa.

Box 2.1: A glimpse at African investment policy developments

Global trends in Foreign Direct Investment (FDI) are often tied to developments in investment policy. Certainly, FDI inflows to Africa have increased substantially over the last decades, and so has liberalisation of investment policies - especially in sub-Saharan Africa. Policy reforms are essential to create an enabling environment for boosting domestic as well as foreign investment as a means for African governments to reach their development objectives.

In recent years, Africa has made more progress than any other region in economic freedom rankings, with countries such as Rwanda joining the ranks of top global reformers (Heritage Foundation Index of Economic Freedom, 2011; World Bank *Ease of Doing Business Index*, 2011). However, many African countries continue to manifest some regulatory shortcomings, such as in property registration and land titles, in attracting more and better investment.

African governments have undertaken a number of policy initiatives towards investment promotion and further liberalisation of their investment frameworks. These initiatives include:

Further Promotion and Facilitation of Investment:

The Zambia Development Agency facilitated joint ventures between local and foreign investors by providing a match-making facility and streamlining the business licences process;

Mozambique launched reforms to improve investor protection and strengthen the legislative framework for Public Private Partnerships (PPPs), concessions and megaprojects;

Rwanda, Mozambique and Uganda strengthened their legislative environments through launching company laws or improving existing laws aimed at easing business start-up procedures;

Burkina Faso created the Autorité de Régulation des Marchés Publics, a regulatory body aimed at enhancing transparency of public procurement procedures;

Namibia enacted measures authorising foreign banking institutions to open local branches;

Burundi removed nominal screening procedures for foreign investors.

Tax Policy Reforms:

South Africa launched a tax incentive programme for investors in the manufacturing sector;

Namibia reduced the corporate tax rate for non-mining companies by 1% (2010 Income Tax Bill);

Burundi embarked on tax exemptions for real estate purchases related to new investments and for goods purchased to establish new businesses;

Cameroon eliminated the corporate registration tax through the 2010 Revenue Bill.

International Investment Rule Making:[5]

Mozambique and Spain signed a bilateral investment treaty (BIT);

Mauritius and Australia signed an income tax treaty.

Recent Focus on Investment in Agriculture: With 60% of the world's remaining uncultivated farmland (McKinsey Global Institute, 2010), Africa has started to attract large-scale foreign investments for agricultural production. Recent policies at country level to attract more and better investment in the sector include:

Burkina Faso adopted a rural land management law that ensures equitable access to rural lands and effective management of land disputes to promote agricultural productivity. In addition, the country has streamlined property registration by allowing transfer taxes to be paid at the land registry.

Kenya set up an insurance system for pastoralists in the north of the country.

Despite these initiatives, attracting more and better agricultural investment remains a challenge for African policy makers. In this regard, international initiatives – such as Principles for Responsible Agricultural Investment that respect Rights, Livelihoods and Resources by the World Bank, the Food and Agriculture Organisation (FAO), UNCTAD and the International Fund for Agricultural Development (IFAD); or the Voluntary Guidelines on responsible governance of tenure of land and other natural resources by the FAO – can support governments in designing sound policy frameworks for responsible agricultural investment. Other instruments, such as the OECD Policy Framework for Investment in Agriculture (PFIA), can also help African governments enhance policy coherence for agricultural investment. These efforts complement the advances made by the New Partnership for Africa's Development (NEPAD) to boost investment for Africa's agricultural development through the Comprehensive Africa Agriculture Development Programme (CAADP).

Overall, African countries have continued to strengthen their investment frameworks. This has been one of the factors, alongside improved macroeconomic management, that have contributed to Africa's resilience to the recent global financial crisis. Moreover, FDI continues to serve as a vital source of growth and development for African people and economies, particularly through spurring employment creation, technology and knowledge transfer, and export diversification.

Source: Provided by the NEPAD-OECD Africa Investment Initiative.

Growth of aid to Africa

Global ODA

Given the financial crisis and its severe impact on government budgets in donor countries, global ODA volumes decreased slightly, from USD 121.5 billion in 2008 to USD 120 billion in 2009. Despite this drop, 2009 ODA represents a higher share of DAC members' combined gross national income owing to the economic contraction in DAC-member economies: ODA was 0.31% in 2009 compared to 0.30% in 2008.[6] These numbers, however, understate the important increase in core development funding. If debt relief[7] and humanitarian aid are excluded, bilateral aid for development programmes and projects rose by 8.5% in real terms. This continues a strong trend over recent years.

At the Gleneagles G8 and Millennium +5 summits in 2005, donors made specific commitments to increase their aid. When quantified by the OECD Secretariat, the pledges implied lifting aid from around USD 80 billion in 2004 to nearly USD 130 billion in 2010. At constant 2004 prices, these pledges represent 0.36% of estimated gross national income (GNI) in 2010. The OECD now estimates that the recent economic contraction has, by cutting nominal GNI, reduced the value of the commitments made for 2010 to around USD 126 billion (in constant 2004 USD), or USD 46 billion over the 2004 level. Donors are estimated[8] to have delivered USD 108 billion in 2010, falling short of the Gleneagles target by USD 18 billion (in 2004 USD).

Nevertheless, the increase in aid since 2004 is significant: USD 28 billion (2004 USD) over the 2004 baseline, with the ODA/GNI ratio rising over the same period from 0.26% to an estimated 0.32%. This is the largest volume increase ever in ODA over such a period and does not depend on the large increase in debt relief that boosted the aid numbers in 2005-07. The continued growth in ODA has shown that aid pledges are effective when backed up with adequate resources, political will and firm multi-year spending plans. ODA will continue to rise in 2010, unlike other financial flows to developing countries, which have fallen sharply since the onset of the global financial crisis.

As for other categories of international financial flows, new players are entering into development assistance, offering additional financial resources and new ways of engaging with Africa. Development assistance funding from the 23 members of the OECD's DAC account for about 90% of global aid flows, roughly based on the DAC method of accounting. The total gross development assistance flows from countries beyond the DAC has been estimated at USD 12 billion in 2009. China's development assistance is estimated at USD 2 billion to USD 3 billion, Russia's at USD 800 million, India's at USD 500 million, Brazil's at USD 360 million, and South Africa's at USD 100 million (Smith and Zimmermann, forthcoming).

Africa

ODA to Africa has been rising steadily over the last decade, from USD 15 billion in 2000 to USD 30 billion in 2004 and to USD 48 billion in 2009. Despite this increase, donors risk failing to meet their Gleneagles commitments made in 2005. In real terms (2004 USD, the basis for the Gleneagles commitments), overall ODA to Africa in 2009 was USD 38 billion, and an estimated USD 42 billion in 2010,[9] USD 13 billion (or 24%) short of the target.

Net bilateral ODA from DAC donors to Africa totalled USD 28 billion in 2009, of which USD 25 billion went to sub-Saharan Africa. This number represents an increase of 3% in real terms over 2008 for all of Africa and an increase of 5.1% for sub-Saharan Africa.

DAC data indicate that humanitarian aid decreased slightly, from USD 5.5 billion in 2008 to USD 5.2 billion in 2009. Bilateral debt relief doubled, from USD 2 billion in 2008 to USD 4 billion in 2009. The other ODA flows increased and reached USD 38 billion in 2009 from USD 36 billion in 2008. All are shown in Figure 2.4.

Figure 2.4: Net ODA disbursements to Africa 2000-09 (billion USD, current)

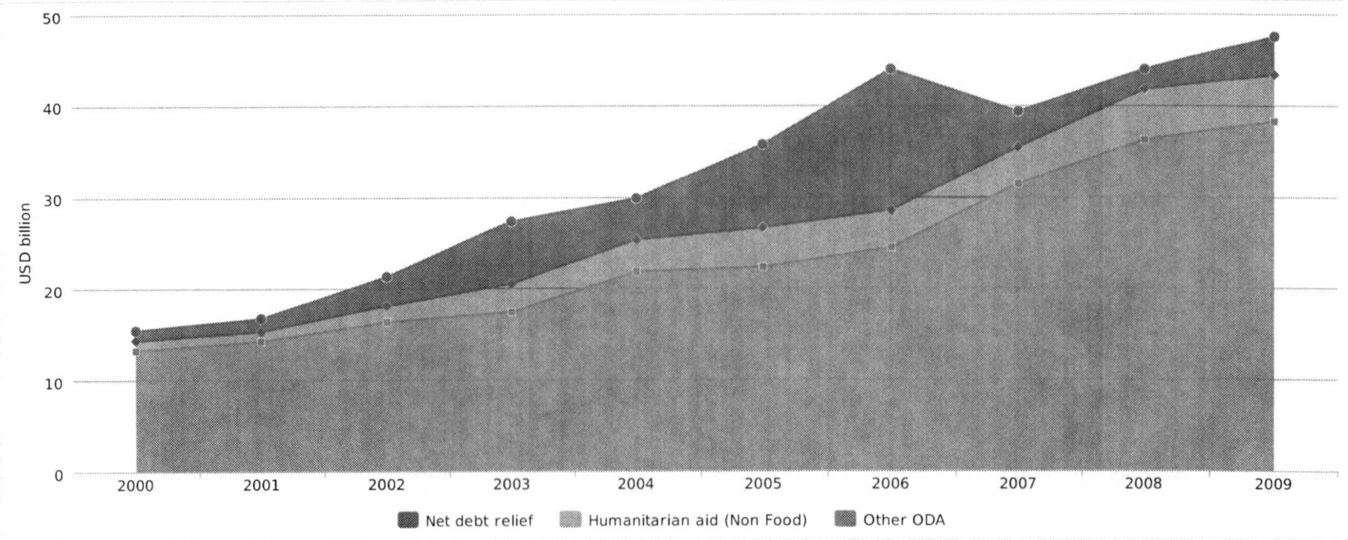

Source: OECD/DAC.

StatLink http://dx.doi.org/10.1787/888932403477

One country offering additional financial resources is China, whose co-operation with Africa has grown rapidly. At the fourth Forums for China-Africa Co-operation (FOCAC), held in November 2009, China pledged to provide USD 10 billion in concessional loans to African countries. China also pledged USD 1 billion in special loans for small and medium-sized African enterprises. India also promised help to Africa, pledging, at the First India-Africa Forum Summit in 2008, to provide USD 5.4 billion in loans and USD 500 million in grants to the continent over the five to six following years. Major initiatives include the Pan-African e-Network Project, the Techno-Economic Approach for Africa-India Movement (TEAM 9) and the Special Commonwealth African Assistance Programme (SCAAP).

In addition to aid from China and India, South Africa's development co-operation amounted to USD 108.7 million in the 2009/10 fiscal year. Almost all of South Africa's development co-operation is directed at the African continent, with a strong focus on member countries of the Southern African Development Community (SADC). The biggest among the Arab donors, Saudi Arabia provided Africa with USD 5.5 billion in gross ODA in 2008. The Saudi Fund for Development finances investment projects through concessional loans, targeted at transportation and energy infrastructure (60%), agriculture (18%) and social sectors (13%). Of these loans, 28% are directed at countries in sub-Saharan Africa.

Focusing on pure development assistance in line with DAC's ODA definition[10] misses the full picture of financial flows directed at development between Africa and other developing countries. The development finance that emerging economies supply to Africa comes largely in modalities different from those which traditional partners provide. Under the framework of aid effectiveness, DAC donors have spent the last decade putting in practice a number of strict rules separating development assistance from other forms of economic co-operation such as trade and investment. "Tied" aid, development assistance funds that were linked to products and services from the donating country, has been largely phased out, aiming to promote fair competition for aid contracts and ensure value for money (2001 OECD/DAC Recommendation on Untying Official Development Assistance and 2008 Accra Agenda for Action). Developing country partners, on the other hand, pursue a different strategy, one that combines commercial with developmental interests and financing modalities.

For example, export credits do not fall within the ODA definition, but they play an increasingly large role in relations between Africa and its developing country partners. The sum of all export credits from China in 2006 reached close to USD 1.2 billion. In the case of India, export credits went up from USD 50 million in 2004 to USD 89 million in 2010 (Chanana, 2009). Emerging partners also use what is called "mixed credits", *i.e.* a financing package that combines concessional rate and market rate loans (Brautigam, 2010a). For China, Brautigam (2010b) estimates an annual average of USD 7.1 billion of such financing over the period 2007-09. This estimate is much higher than the DAC's USD 1.9 billion estimate for 2009, which accounts only for concessional finance. Part II of this report provides an in-depth discussion of Africa's emerging partners and their expanding interactions with Africa, including both FDI and development assistance from emerging partners.

Notes

1. All data up to 2009 from UNCTAD (2010a); 2010 estimates from IMF (2010a).
2. For Angola the IMF reports USD 4.2 billion in 2009. For the other countries the reported data are the same.
3. Morocco, Republic of Congo, Djibouti, Gabon, Tanzania, Mauritius, Malawi, Nigeria, Rwanda and Uganda..
4. Respondents: Argentina, Aruba, Australia, Austria, The Bahamas, Bahrain, Barbados, Belgium, Bermuda, Brazil, Bulgaria, Canada, Cayman Islands, Chile, Colombia, Costa Rica, Cyprus, Czech Republic, Denmark, Egypt, Estonia, Finland, France, Germany, Gibraltar, Greece, Guernsey, Hong Kong SAR of China, Hungary, Iceland, India, Indonesia, Ireland, Isle of Man, Israel, Italy, Japan, Jersey, Kazakhstan, Republic of Korea, Kuwait, Latvia, Lebanon, Luxembourg, Macao SAR of China, Malaysia, Malta, Mauritius, Mexico, Netherlands, Netherlands Antilles, New Zealand, Norway, Pakistan, Panama, Philippines, Poland, Portugal, Romania, Russian Federation, Singapore, Slovak Republic, Slovenia, South Africa, Spain, Sweden, Switzerland, Thailand, Turkey, Ukraine, United Kingdom, United States, Uruguay, Vanuatu and Venezuela.
5. These measures were signed in 2010 and have not yet been ratified.
6. Specific data are available at stats.oecd.org/qwids
7. Debt relief had been especially high owing to exceptional Paris Club packages for Iraq and Nigeria in 2005 and 2006, but fell sharply thereafter.
8. ODA figures for 2010 will be available in April 2011.
9. See footnote 8.
10. The DAC defines ODA as "those flows to countries and territories on the DAC List of ODA Recipients and to multilateral development institutions which are: i) ***provided by official agencies***, including state and local governments, or by their executive agencies; and ii) each transaction of which: a) is administered with the promotion of the ***economic development and welfare of developing countries*** as its main objective; and b) is ***concessional in character*** and conveys a grant element of at least 25% (calculated at a rate of discount of 10%)." See www.oecd.org/dac/stats/methodology.

References

2008 Accra Agenda for Action, www.oecd.org/dataoecd/30/63/43911948.pdf

Brautigam, D. (2010a), "China, Africa and the international aid architecture", Working Paper No. 107. African Development Bank Group, Tunis.

Brautigam, D. (2010b), "Chinese Finance of Overseas Infrastructure". prepared for the OECD-IPRCC China-DAC Study Group, OECD, Paris.

Chanana, D. (2009), India's Transition to a Global Donor – Limitations and Prospects, Area: International Cooperation and Development ARI, 123/2010, Elcano Royal Institute of International and Strategic Studies, Madrid.

Heritage Foundation (2011), 2011 Index of Economic Freedom, http://www.heritage.org/index/.

IMF (International Monetary Fund) (2010a), World Economic Outlook Database, 6 October 2010.

IMF (2010b), Coordinated Portfolio Investment Survey Database, www.imf.org/external/np/sta/pi/datarsl.htm, updated November 2010.

IMF (2011), "New Growth Drivers for Low-Income Countries: The Role of BRICs, prepared by the Strategy", Policy and Review Department, Washington, D.C.

International Strategic Analysis (2011a), Regional Report Sub-Saharan Africa, March 2011, Cleveland.

International Strategic Analysis (2011b), South Africa Country Report, March 2011, Cleveland.

McKinsey Global Institute (2010), Lions on the Move: The Progress and Potential of African Economies, http://bit.ly/9DF7Dk.

OECD (n.d.), International Direct Investment Database, accessible through OECD.StatExtracts, stats.oecd.org, accessed 25 March 2011.

OECD/DAC (Development Assistance Committee) (2001), DAC Recommendation on Untying Official Development Assistance to the Least Developed Countries, OECD Document: DCD/DAC(2001)12/FINAL, http://www.oecd.org/dataoecd/14/56/1885476.pdf.

OECD/DAC (2010), Development Aid Rose in 2009 and Most Donors Will Meet 2010 Aid Targets, 14 April 2010, http://www.oecd.org/document/11/0,3746,en_2649_37413_44981579_1_1_1_37413,00.html.

Smith, K. and Zimmermann, F. (forthcoming), "More Actors, More Money, More Ideas for International Development Co-Operation", *Journal of International Development*.

ThomsonReuters (2010), Africa M&A Surges to Record $44 bln in 2010, af.reuters.com/article/investingNews/idAFJOE70I0IZ20110119, accessed 18 March 2011.

UNCTAD (United Nations Conference for Trade and Development) (2010 a), Foreign Direct Investment Data Series, accessible via UNCTADStats, unctadstat.unctad.org, updated 17 September 2010,

UNCTAD (2010b), World Investment Report, United Nations Publication, Geneva.

UNCTAD (2010c), Economic Development in Africa Report 2010 – South-South Co-operation: Africa and the New Forms of Development Partnership, United Nations Publication, Geneva.

World Bank (2011), *Ease of Doing Business Index*, http://www.doingbusiness.org/.

Chapter 3: Trade Policies and Regional Integration

Following the global economic crisis, African trade recovered, mainly spurred by growing demand from emerging markets. Services trade also increased, underscoring Africa's increasing potential and prospects in different services subsectors.

The Doha Development Round (DDR) and the Economic Partnership Agreements (EPAs) negotiations again saw little progress in 2010. A positive outcome will depend on the compromises parties are willing to make, which balance policy space, developmental goals and deeper market access concerns. Given the stalemate in these negotiations, trade preference agreements such as the African Growth and Opportunity Act (AGOA) and South-South Co-operation with partners such as China have gained attention in the African development and diversification agenda.

The regional integration process on the continent has advanced thanks to important initiatives, such as the development of Minimum Integration Programmes (MIPs) and the rationalisation of the Regional Economic Communities (RECs). Some RECs have already launched their free trade areas, while others are steadily working towards this objective.

Despite these positive developments, most RECs continue to face challenges. These include political instability, poor economic diversification, multiple and overlapping memberships, insufficient financial resources to support their integration processes, and poor implementation of commonly agreed protocols and decisions.

Africa's economic growth and sustainable development greatly depend on regional infrastructure development. Nonetheless, implementing a coherent programme of activities covering energy, transport and communications remains one of the continent's main shortcomings and undermines Africa's competitiveness. To overcome these shortcomings and buttress regional competitiveness, continental infrastructure development must target low-quality, outdated and insufficient infrastructure. Greater regional efforts should address Africa's infrastructure deficit, particularly in the transport sector.

Developments in international trade negotiations during 2010

As in previous years, Africa noted poor progress in the DDR negotiations in the World Trade Organization (WTO) during 2010. Though the closure of the DDR was expected to be achieved by December 2005, discussions have advanced slowly since 2008. Negotiations in 2010 barely progressed beyond informal meetings, with the result of cross-sectoral negotiations being postponed. Nevertheless, 2010 saw some highlights, such as the "banana deal" (AfDB *et al.*, 2010) and progress on cotton trade and non-tariff barriers negotiations, with notable engagement of the African Group in the latter (UNECA and AUC, 2011).

Despite renewed commitments at the highest level during the January 2011 World Economic Forum in Davos to seek closure to the DDR, it has become clear that no "early harvest" will be possible for least developed countries (LDCs),[1] given the virtual halt of negotiations. This situation raises questions on the development gains that a large majority of African nations are foregoing, and it calls for a reassessment of how the DDR is dealing with development concerns in the current negotiations. Further, if policy space is not adequately afforded in the single undertaking through elements such as appropriate flexibilities, special and differential treatment, and deep market access commitments of relevance to Africa, the ability of African countries to work on economic transformation and industrialisation objectives through their trade agenda may be compromised severely in the future.

The stalemate in negotiations since 2005 has also shifted attention to other types of trade relations in Africa. Trade preference arrangements – such as the AGOA (see Box 3.1) and South-South Co-operation with other developing economies such as China, India and Brazil – represent important mechanisms in the furtherance of Africa's economic development and diversification agenda.

Box 3.1: Revisiting existing trade partnerships: A decade of trade preferences under the African Growth and Opportunity Act (AGOA)

The African Growth and Opportunity Act (AGOA) has ruled over US-Africa trade relations since 2000 with some measurable success. African exports to the United States increased from USD 23 billion in 2000 to USD 81 billion in 2008, despite exclusion of key African exports such as sugar, peanuts, dairy and tobacco. During that period, foreign direct investment (FDI) and employment also increased, with over 300 000 new jobs created in Africa.

Despite these highlights, it is often argued that AGOA has not been able to contribute to greater trade diversification, growth and development. The benefits of AGOA have been unevenly distributed across countries and sectors. Roughly half of the sub-Saharan eligible countries are currently benefiting, and only in a handful of sectors. Africa's inability to diversify trade in agricultural products, which account for less than 1% of AGOA exports, is partly due to quotas on sugar, tobacco, dairy and peanuts. Further, although AGOA has been extended to 2015, the uncertainty of AGOA's future has kept required investment levels at bay, leaving little time for Africa to raise its productive capacity and consolidate the gains of this preferential act.

An extension of AGOA beyond 2015 would afford investors sufficient time to recoup returns on investments and thereby take full advantage of AGOA. However, other challenges faced by AGOA beneficiaries also need to be addressed. For example, competition has increased since the elimination in 2005 of the Multi-Fibre Arrangement (MFA), which opened up the apparel sector to Asian countries. This led to a preference erosion, disinvestment, and unemployment in countries where AGOA had originally promoted some industrialisation in the textile sector. Further, AGOA fails to consider the impact a removal of an African country from the AGOA beneficiary list may have on other regional trading partners, destroying existing regional value chain creation. Finally, AGOA also lacks mechanisms for promoting innovative ideas for public-private partnerships for infrastructure investment, improving operating efficiency and locking in logistics services market reforms, especially pertaining to transport regulation in Africa.

Although AGOA may have had a positive impact in the past, it needs to be improved to accommodate these challenges. A revision of AGOA should focus on ensuring more inclusiveness, accessibility and permanence. Doing so will extend benefits to all of sub-Saharan Africa and promote a wider range of export products. A revised AGOA should also reorientate FDI away from oil, textiles and apparel and towards agriculture. It can do this by assisting beneficiaries in complying with standards and sanitary and phytosanitary (SPS) measures and by tackling supply-side constraints. Finally, targeted export diversification and sectoral carve-outs to avoid trade preference erosion in the future also need to be included.

Source: See ERA (2011) and Páez, *et al.* (2010).

As with the DDR negotiations, EPA negotiations saw little progress during 2010. Discussions appear to revolve around the same contentious issues of previous years. These issues include the development dimension of the EPAs, definitions of "substantially all trade" (SAT) and "most favoured nation" (MFN), export taxes, regional integration, quantitative restrictions, special agricultural safeguards, a rendezvous clause and rules of origin, among others (African Union, 2010a).

As with multilateral trade negotiations, how a final agreement deals with these contentious issues will condition the strategic use of trade policies to address development and industrialisation concerns in Africa. For example, a prohibition on export taxes in the EPAs will mean that some African countries may not have sufficient policy space to confront revenue and value additional concerns lying at the heart of their fiscal and industrial policy objectives. These countries may thus need to broaden their tax base to account for revenue loss. Equally, a narrowly based definition of substantially all trade and the most favoured nation may sever opportunities of future trade agreements with third parties. Thus, these narrowly based definitions may hinder lock in economic transformation policies targeting export-led growth. Finally, rules of origin that do not allow for cumulation across African LDCs, regardless of membership to a particular EPA, will impinge on regional value chain creation. These rules will also lessen the impact of regional integration policies that target landlockness through trade facilitation, among other measures.

Considering the challenges, agreeing on comprehensive EPAs in the near future seems unlikely. African countries have indicated through an EPA position paper (African Union, 2010b) their willingness to consider the viability of an EPA deal in relation to other alternatives. Such alternatives include: *i)* deferring and sequencing EPAs to regional integration processes; *ii)* postponing EPA negotiations until after WTO negotiations on the

General Agreement on Tariffs and Trade (GATT) Article XXIV conclude; *iii)* instead of EPAs, extending the "Everything but Arms" (EBA) initiative to all African countries; *iv)* improving the European Union's generalised scheme of tariff preferences (GSP) regime, or *v)* discontinuing EPAs and focusing on regional integration and South-South Co-operation instead. In particular, the last option once again indicates the rising interest in trade and investment partnerships with Asian economies, such as China (see Box 3.2).

Box 3.2: South-South co-operation: The rising importance of Africa-China partnerships

Africa-China co-operation partnerships are mainly taking place through trade, investment and aid. Often these three modalities appear to be inter-related, reflecting complementary and/or competitiveness relationships between both parties. For example, Chinese resource-seeking FDI (*e.g.* minerals and oil to be exported to China) has an aid component through infrastructure development, which has been the case in countries such as Sudan and Angola. Though needed, infrastructure development should not come at the expense of resource depletion and environmental degradation. Policies targeting sustainable development and linking industrial activities with the local economy will help strike a balance between resource exploitation and industrialisation in Africa.

Chinese FDI in retail trade is another example of complementary/competitive relations through local presence and commercialisation of Chinese products in Africa. In some African countries, such as Nigeria and Ghana, this has translated into a preference for Chinese (manufactured and food) products. This preference, in turn, has led to a crowding out of local and regional products, even in cases where the former may be of lower quality than the latter, owing to price considerations. The trade balance has thus skewed in favour of China. Clear rules promoting regional diversification, value chain creation and safeguarding against preference erosion could help maximise the benefits from China-Africa trade relations without undermining regional integration and consumer protection considerations.

Learning-seeking and market-seeking FDI is exemplary in the field of services, which is also becoming an important target of Chinese FDI in Africa. For example, South Africa is benefiting from complementarities because Chinese financial firms have large markets and capital but lack the world-class skills in financial markets that South Africa possesses. South African financial firms gain in their capital base from Chinese investment, enabling them to expand into Africa and also globally into other developing country financial markets.

South-South co-operation between China and Africa faces several major challenges. First, there is the need to ensure that as Chinese trade and FDI increase, they also build (backward) linkages into the economy through local capacity building and partnerships. Concerning aid, Africa needs to formulate concrete aid needs based on sustainable development impacts rather than simply target the volume of aid flowing to the continent. Finally, Africa's economic space could replicate Chinese market conditions, if the continent is taken as a common market. Win-win opportunities for goods, services and capital exchanges between these two markets could be identified, especially if African leaders emphasise development in their dialogue with Chinese counterparts.

Source: AERC (2010) and see Part II of this report.

Developments in regional integration in Africa

Regional integration remains an important vehicle for enhancing Africa's development and growth prospects, including boosting trade both within and outside the continent. Consequently, African leaders have taken a number of initiatives, through various African Union decisions, aimed at advancing the regional integration process. These initiatives include the transformation of the Organization of African Unity (OAU) into the African Union (AU), the implementation of the New Partnership for Africa's Development (NEPAD), the rationalisation of the RECs through the moratorium on the creation of new RECs, and the recognition of only eight RECs as the main building blocks of the African Union. The African Union Commission (AUC) is in the process of implementing the Minimum Integration Programmes to ensure that all the RECs are putting into practice the stages of the Abuja Treaty within the same timeframe.

The RECs continue to play a significant role in achieving Africa's regional integration vision by pursuing and implementing various programmes. In the area of trade and market integration, some RECs, such as the Economic Community of West African States (ECOWAS), Economic Community of Central African States (ECCAS), Common Market for Eastern and Southern Africa (COMESA), South African Development Community (SADC) and East African Community (EAC), have launched their free trade areas. Other RECs, such as the Community of Sahel-Saharan States (CEN-SAD), are steadily working towards this objective. Furthermore, EAC has been a full customs union since 2005, while COMESA launched its customs union more recently in 2009. ECOWAS is expected to launch its customs union by 2015. The customs union agenda of SADC and ECCAS, which was envisaged to materialise in 2010, is now expected to be launched during 2011. Arab Maghreb Union (UMA), CEN-SAD, and Intergovernmental Authority on Development (IGAD) have yet to implement their customs union. In addition to these strides, momentum exists among some RECs to harmonise their Free Trade Agendas (FTA) to create larger trading blocs. The ongoing initiative on the grand FTA (SADC, COMESA and EAC) is a good example of this new trend towards unifying the sub-regional markets.

Despite these positive developments, a number of RECs continue to face enormous challenges that significantly affect their progress to higher phases of the integration agenda. These challenges also hinder the attainment of the continental vision of a common market in the not too distant future. Major challenges include prevalence of political instability in some parts of the continent, lack of economic diversification, continued multiple and overlapping memberships, inadequate financial resources to buttress the integration processes, lack of integration between national and regional or continental development policies and poor implementation of commonly agreed protocols and decisions at regional and continental levels.

The conflict situation in Africa has exacerbated poverty across the continent and made it even more difficult to accelerate economic growth and Africa's development agenda. Conflicts have resulted in loss of human life, displacement of people, high numbers of refugees, child soldiers, high incidence of vulnerability and social exclusion, destruction of socio-economic infrastructure and erosion of institutional capacity.

Inadequate financial resources and lack of absorption capacity also continue to impede the implementation of regional integration activities and programmes by RECs and other pan-African institutions. Assessed contributions from OECD member countries are not adequate to finance the execution of activities and programmes. To a large extent, RECs depend on external assistance to carry out their activities and programmes. Further, duplication of functions and programmes and overlapping memberships by pan-African institutions and sub-regional organisations also exert pressure on the limited resources from OECD member countries, contributing to poor delivery of results.

Implementation of Minimum Integration Programmes (MIP)

The African Union Commission, in close collaboration with the RECs, has developed the Minimum Integration Programme (MIP). The MIP comprises a set of activities, projects and programmes to be implemented by the RECs in order to accelerate the regional and continental integration process. The MIP has identified the following key areas of the integration agenda to focus on trade, infrastructure development, free movement of people, and peace and security. The Conference of African Ministers In Charge of Regional Integration endorsed the MIP, which the AU Assembly subsequently approved.

The African Union Commission has developed an Implementation Action Plan to deliver on the MIP. The action plan currently faces a number of challenges, including lack of funding. Efforts, however, are being made by implementing agencies (RECs, member countries, the African Union Commission) to mobilise resources. Paramount to these efforts is a proposal by the African Union to establish an integration fund dedicated to supporting the activities and programmes of the MIP. The AU Assembly has approved this initiative, and the AU Commission will soon undertake a pre-feasibility study on the establishment of the fund. Furthermore, the RECs are in the process of mainstreaming the action plan into their programmes and sensitising their member countries about it.

All pan-African institutions, including the RECs, are making efforts to accelerate the implementation of regional integration activities and programmes in Africa. Most notable efforts include the ongoing Tripartite Free Trade Area among the member countries of EAC, COMESA and SADC. Box 3.3 describes some of the recent developments in this area.

Box 3.3: Africa's proposed Free Trade Areas (FTAs)

In an effort to fast-track the attainment of the African Economic Community, as outlined in the Abuja Treaty, RECs are implementing a number of activities and programmes. These include the recent Decision by Heads of State and Government of the COMESA, SADC and EAC member countries to establish a single FTA. The inter-Regional Economic Communities FTA is expected to help enlarge African markets, unlock productive potential, and increase intra-Africa trade. It would also help facilitate free movement of business people across the RECs by opening up the borders. At the same time, it would make the enlarged market and economic bloc more attractive to foreign direct investments, in particular those motivated by economies of scale.

To help accelerate the achievement of inter-FTAs in Africa, the United Nations Economic Commission for Africa (UNECA) is in the process of carrying out a study. Among other things, the study will analyse the impact of inter-FTAs on African economies, assess the benefits and costs to countries, and examine the impact on RECs' efficiency and effectiveness. The study will also consider the impact of inter-RECs' free trade areas on the EPAs that the African countries are currently negotiating with the European Union. The study will assist countries in making informed decisions on their participation in the inter-REC FTAs.

Regional infrastructure developments

Regional infrastructure development, particularly in the areas of transport, communications and energy infrastructure and services, is crucial for economic growth and sustainable development. Despite efforts to put in place a coherent programme of activities in these areas, Africa remains one of the continents with weak infrastructure networks. These weak networks contribute significantly to higher production and transaction costs, and they undermine business competitiveness.

Recent diagnostic studies in Africa show that infrastructure is responsible for more than half of Africa's recent improved growth performance and has the potential to contribute even more in the future. Africa's infrastructure networks increasingly lag behind those of other developing countries and are characterised by missing regional links and stagnant household access (World Bank, 2010). These same findings for Africa indicate that the infrastructure needs are around USD 93 billion per year for the coming ten years. After capturing efficiency gains and considering domestic and external spending projections, a financing gap of around USD 31 billion per year, mostly in the power sector, would still prevail.

With the delivery of the much-needed infrastructure and its services alone, economic growth will not happen. Therefore, investing in infrastructure and services would have to be accompanied with support to sector governance and regulatory reforms, trade facilitation measures etc. so that reduced costs and time savings can be transmitted to the end-users.

Continental infrastructure development initiatives

The importance of accessible and efficient infrastructure as a tool for achieving regional integration for sustained economic development has been on the minds of African leaders since the 1970s. The years 1978 to 2000 were devoted to the programme of the United Nations Transport and Communications Decade in Africa (UNTACDA), supplemented by the sub-Saharan Africa Transport Policy Programme (SSATP), for the development of these sectors. These programmes were added to by other recent initiatives, including the NEPAD Medium to Long Term Strategic Framework (MLTSF) and the Programme for Infrastructure Development in Africa (PIDA).

In an effort to accelerate the continent's infrastructure development, the African Union, the African Development Bank, the New Partnership for Africa's Development (NEPAD is a programme), as well as the Regional Economic Communities, are currently in the process of formulating PIDA. The objectives of PIDA are to promote socio-economic development and poverty reduction in Africa through improved access to integrated regional and continental infrastructure networks and services.

The current status of infrastructure developments in Africa remains mixed. Some sectors have recorded significant progress compared to others. The current situation is by and large unsatisfactory, characterised by insufficient and low-quality infrastructure on the one hand, and inefficient and expensive services on the other. For example, the total length of classified road networks in Africa is estimated to be about 2.3 million kilometres, of which 20% is paved. In contrast, the required or desired level of social and economic development is estimated at an average of 7.6 kilometres per 100 square kilometres. Other road infrastructure developments include Trans-African Highway 1 (TAH1); Trans-African Highway 5 (TAH5), and Trans-African Highway 7 (TAH7).

Compared with that of roads, the picture in the railway network is not very satisfactory. Africa's railway network consists of about 89 000 kilometres for an area of about 29.6 million square kilometres, representing a density of about 2.5 kilometres per 1 000 square kilometres. This is much lower compared with 40 kilometres per 1 000 square kilometres for Europe. Fourteen of the mainland countries in Africa do not have railway lines or sections of international lines. In addition, the railway network in Africa is generally old and technically outdated. The poor railway network has resulted in a low share of rail freight in intra-African trade. More investments need to be made to improve the situation.

Africa's global share of air transport remains modest. However, this modest share relies on only three major hubs, namely, Johannesburg, Nairobi and Addis Ababa. South African Airways, Kenya Airways and Ethiopian Airlines remain the three major airlines in Africa. In 2004 Africa's share of world passenger traffic stood at about 5.2% and its share of world freight traffic at approximately 3.6%. During the same year, the sector generated 470 000 jobs on the continent, resulting in an income estimated at USD 11.3 billion (1.7% share in the African gross domestic product). In addition to job opportunities, air freight plays a growing role in the competitiveness of goods in world markets for high-value, time-sensitive cargo (such as horticultural and floricultural products), particularly to landlocked countries.

Notes

1. WTO trade ministerial negotiations follow the principle of a single undertaking, meaning that once negotiations on all the aspects have been concluded, countries are able to adopt them. Therefore, though some negotiation issues may have been successfully concluded, these cannot be implemented until agreement is reached on the remaining issues. The "Early Harvest" was proposed as a means to enable LDCs to benefit from the early consensus on some issues, recognising that the single undertaking could take longer than expected. See ICTSD (2010).

References

AERC (African Economic Research Consortium) (2010), Proceedings from the Conference on Africa-China Relations, Hilton Hotel, Addis Ababa, 28-30 September.

AfDB, OECD and UNECA (2010), *African Economic Outlook 2010*, OECD, Paris.

AfDB, OECD and UNECA (2011), *African Economic Outlook 2011*, OECD, Paris.

African Union (2010a), "EPA Negotiations Co-ordination Meeting Report", AU Conference of Ministers of Trade, 6th Ordinary Session, Kigali, 29 October – 2 November.

African Union (2010b), "African Union Commission-Regional Economic Communities Common Position Paper on EPAs", AU Conference of Ministers of Trade, 6th Ordinary Session, Kigali, 29 October – 2 November 2010.

AUC (2004), *The Mission, Vision and Strategic Framework of the African Union Commission (2004-2007)*, African Union Commission, Addis Ababa.

AUC (2006), *The Review of Millennium Development Goals and the Millennium Declaration: An African Common Position*, African Union Commission, Addis Ababa.

ICTSD (2010), "No Early Harvest for LDCs' Top WTO Priorities", *Bridges*, Vol. 14, No. 1, International Centre for Trade and Sustainable Development, Geneva, p. 6.

Mkwezalamba, M. and E. Chinyama (2007), "Implementation of Africa's Integration and Development Agenda: Challenges and Prospects", *African Integration Review*, Vol. 1.

OAU (2000), Constitutive Act of the African Union, Organisation of African Unity, Addis Ababa.

OAU (1991), Treaty Establishing the African Economic Community, Organisation of African Unity, Addis Ababa.

Páez, L., S. Karingi, M. Kimenyi and M. Paulos (2010), "A Decade (2000-2010) of African-US Trade Under the African Growth and Opportunity Act (AGOA): Challenges, Opportunities and a Framework for Post AGOA Engagement", paper presented at the African Economic Conference 2010, Tunis, 27-29 October, www.uneca.org/aec/2010/papers.htm

UNECA, AfDB and AUC (2010), *Assessing Regional Integration in Africa IV: Enhancing Intra-African Trade*, Economic Commission for Africa, Addis Ababa.

UNECA and AUC (2011), *Economic Report on Africa 2011: Governing Development in Africa. The Role of the State in Economic Transformation*, Economic Commission for Africa, Addis Ababa.

World Bank (2010), "Africa's Infrastructure: A Time for Transformation", World Bank, Washington DC.

Chapter 4: Human Development

This chapter discusses the rate of poverty reduction in Africa compared to other developing regions and characterises the status and trends of human development in Africa on the basis of the United Nations Development Programme's Human Development Index (HDI).

Concerning the issue of poverty reduction, the international community set the goal of eradicating extreme poverty and hunger in the Millennium Declaration adopted in 2000. The community specified two targets in the Millennium Development Goals (MDGs): over the period 1990-2015, halving the proportion of people whose income is less than US dollars (USD) 1 a day, and halving the number of people suffering from hunger. While Africa made progress in reducing poverty, the region has recorded a slow rate of poverty reduction relative to other developing regions. This has been due to three main factors. First, Africa experienced relatively high levels of economic growth only since the 2000s, so the average growth rates since 1990 were not high enough to make a substantial impact on poverty. Second, growth in Africa has not been high enough in sectors where the poor live or work. Although this situation has improved in many countries since 1996, Africa's growth often originated from sectors with weak linkages to the rest of the economy, having little impact on job creation and poverty reduction. Third, relatively high inequality in Africa reflects that growth benefited a small part of the population and the benefits to the poor were limited. In this regard, poverty reduction policies will need to combine high economic growth with a reduction in inequality while ensuring that the sources of economic growth are broad-based.

Concerning the status of human development, the limitations of national income as a measure of progress motivated the creation of the Human Development Index (HDI) by the United Nations Development Programme (UNDP) in 1990. This measure reflected a people-centred understanding of development. Although by 2010 Africa as a whole had the lowest HDI of any region, the trend between 2000 and 2010 shows that all African countries but Zimbabwe improved their human development. Sub-Saharan Africa made, on average, the most rapid progress of any region. The regional HDI increased by 23%, followed by South Asia, where the increase was 17% over the same period. This improvement was due to rising income per capita in the 2000s in most African countries, and to genuine progress in access to knowledge and better health outcomes. Also, to some degree, improvement in human development in 2010 relative to 2000 was due to the relatively low initial level of HDI in 2000 following a decline in HDI between 1990 and 2000.

To sustain progress in human development, Africa will need to take simultaneous actions on several fronts rather than focus on only one objective. For example, economic growth will improve human development if it is inclusive and pro-poor. Similarly, investing in social sectors will produce sustainable human development if investment is accompanied by efforts to create more economic opportunities that benefit a large segment of the population. Moreover, some dimensions of human development, for example gender equality, will improve if African governments make the deliberate choice to pursue policies that promote gender equality. In this regard, the quality of economic policy will probably be as important as the resources used to advance the cause of human development in Africa.

Economic growth, inequality and poverty: why has poverty reduction been slow in Africa?

At the Millennium Summit in September 2000, where the Millennium Development Goals (MDGs) were adopted, the international community set the goal of eradicating extreme poverty and hunger, with two specific targets. First, over the period 1990-2015, halve the proportion of people whose income is less than USD 1 a day. Second, halve the number of people suffering from hunger. Measuring poverty is not only important for establishing the progress that has been achieved in terms of reaching the set targets, but also for knowing the extent to which economic growth and socio-economic policies affect the process of poverty reduction.

When the MDG targets were set, the indicator chosen to determine progress in poverty reduction was the incidence of extreme poverty, measured by calculating the proportion of people living on less than USD 1 per day using 1993 purchasing power parities (PPPs). After revisions of the estimates for purchasing power parities exchange rates were introduced in late 2007, the extreme poverty line was revised upwards to USD 1.25 in 2005 PPPs. This measure of poverty is called headcount ratio.

The complexity of the concept of poverty and its measurement has generated passionate debates about the methodologies used to measure poverty, the poverty lines that should be used to compare poverty incidence across countries, and the different results that different poverty lines and different methodologies have produced. Some have also argued that relying on household data to measure poverty makes the analysis of poverty dynamics in Africa difficult given the time separating household surveys. Attempts to rectify this problem by using other methods and different data sources remain contested.[1]

Using the poverty line of USD 1.25 a day in 2005 PPPs, the proportion of sub-Saharan Africa's population living in extreme poverty increased from 54% in 1981 to 59% in 1996. By 2005, the most recent year for which comparable data are available, the proportion had declined to 51% (Chen and Ravallion, 2008). Hence, from 1996 to 2005, the proportion of poor people in Africa had been reduced by 8%. However, as a result of the crisis that has been affecting world economies since 2007, it has been estimated that the number of poor people in Africa might have increased by 50 million in 2009 and by another 39 million in 2010 (Ravallion, 2009a) relative to a baseline scenario with the absence of the crisis. This may have slowed the progress that the continent had been making until the onset of the crisis.

The poverty dynamic appears to mirror the evolution of economic growth rates. In the 1980s, the average per capita income of the African countries in the sample was USD 1 955 in 2005 PPP exchange rates. In 1996 the average income per capita had declined to USD 1 887, and it was USD 2 163 in 2005. As a result of the economic crisis, African rates of economic growth declined. From an average growth rate of 6% a year in 2006-08, the rate of growth declined to 2.5% in 2009. The *African Economic Outlook 2010* projected that growth in 2010 would be around 4.5% and in 2011 around 5.2% (AfDB *et al.*, 2010). Taking into account the average rate of population growth of about 2.5% per year, these rates of economic growth indicate that relative to the period from 1996 to 2008, income per capita in the period 2009-10 was much lower. In fact, the rate of economic growth in 2009 suggests that there was no increase in income per capita that year.

These statistics suggest that growth of income per capita reduces poverty.[2] As high economic growth increases per capita income, more people are pulled out of poverty, other things being equal. This reduces the proportion of poor people in the population. But to what extent will growth contribute to poverty reduction in Africa, and why has poverty reduction in Africa been slower than in other regions?

Owing to the paucity of reliable cross-country data on poverty incidence and its determinants in Africa, very few studies have attempted to deal with these questions at the regional level. Quantitative evidence shows that three key factors explain the weak response of poverty to economic growth in Africa. The first is that despite the rise in growth rates over the period 1996-2008, Africa's average growth rates have not been high enough to have as strong an impact on poverty reduction as in other regions. The second factor is that the growth process in Africa has been more weakly linked with poverty reduction than in other regions. The third factor is that relatively high rates of inequality, as well as high levels of poverty, have hampered poverty reduction in Africa.

In an early attempt to analyse poverty at the continental level using cross-country quantitative analysis, the Economic Commission for Africa (ECA) (1999) found that sub-Saharan Africa would need to grow by 7% per year to meet the first MDG of halving poverty by 2015.[3] This finding suggests that if African countries are reducing poverty more slowly than other regions, the reason could be that the growth rates in Africa have not been high enough. Indeed, over the period 2001-09, the continent's average rate of economic growth was 5.3% per year. Only 9 out of 53 countries – Angola, Chad, Equatorial Guinea, Ethiopia, Mozambique, Nigeria, Sierra Leone, Sudan and Uganda – recorded average GDP growth rates that were higher or equal to 7% per year (AfDB *et al.*, 2010). The implication is that to have a more substantial effect on poverty reduction, economic growth in more African countries will need to be higher than it has been so far.

A deeper analysis of the relationship between economic growth and poverty reduction in Africa shows that in the majority of the fastest growing countries, defined as the countries with growth rates higher than the African average of 5.3% of GDP over the period 2001-09, economic growth had the weakest effect on poverty reduction.[4] Out of 44 countries for which there is information on growth elasticities of poverty, 14 recorded high economic growth rates as defined here.[5] These countries are Angola, Burkina Faso, Cape Verde, Chad, Ethiopia, Ghana, Mali, Mozambique, Nigeria, Rwanda, Sierra Leone, Tanzania, Uganda and Zambia. However, only three countries (Cape Verde, Ethiopia and Ghana), or about one-fifth of the fastest growing countries, have high growth elasticities of poverty, defined as elasticities higher than the African average of -1.717 (see Table 4.1). Among the fastest growing countries, no oil or mineral exporter has a high growth elasticity of poverty. On the other hand, oil producers (although some are small oil producers) with high growth elasticities of poverty have low growth rates.

Table 4.1: Growth and inequality elasticities of poverty (USD 1.25 in 2005 PPP)

	Elasticities		Comparative ratio
	Growth (1)	Inequality (2)	Absolute (1)/(2)
East Asia and Pacific	-2.5	3.4	0.7
Eastern Europe and Central Asia	-4.0	6.4	0.6
Latin America and Caribbean	-3.1	5.1	0.6
Middle East and North Africa	-3.2	4.9	0.7
South Asia	-2.0	2.5	0.8
Sub-Saharan Africa	-1.5	1.7	0.9
Africa	-1.7	2.0	0.9

Source: Based on Fosu (2011).

The fourth column shows the absolute value of the ratio of growth elasticity over inequality elasticity of poverty. It is just a way of showing the relative importance of these two. A value less than one means that the effect of inequality dominates the growth effect.

StatLink http://dx.doi.org/10.1787/888932405776

The weak growth elasticity of poverty suggests that Africa has been unable to reduce poverty as needed, even in some countries where the growth rate was relatively high. This illustrates that growth alone is not a sufficient condition for poverty to decline, raising the question of why growth in Africa is weakly related to poverty reduction relative to other regions. As Table 4.1 shows, sub-Saharan Africa has the lowest average growth elasticity of poverty.[6] It is half of the elasticity in Latin America and the Caribbean and only two-fifths of the elasticity in eastern Europe and Central Asia.

The weak response of poverty reduction to economic growth may be due to the growth process not being inclusive enough, partially because it was not strongly linked to activities and economic sectors where the poor are. This could have been because growth did not take place in the sectors where the poor work (*e.g.* in agriculture), or in areas where the poor live (in rural areas), or simply if growth did not involve the poor by using their labour. It is known that high fuel and mineral commodity prices have strongly influenced the growth process in many of the fastest growing African economies in the period from 1996 to 2008, given that fuels and minerals account for the largest share of Africa's exports (AfDB *et al.*, 2010).[7] These commodities, particularly fuel, are produced in "enclave" industries using highly capital-intensive technologies that tend to exclude the poor. Therefore, even rapid growth can have limited impact on poverty reduction when growth is generated from sectors weakly linked to the rest of the economy, particularly the sectors where large numbers of poor people are active. The limited impact of economic growth in reducing poverty creates a vicious cycle. Higher poverty diminishes even further the capacity of economic growth to reduce poverty (Ravallion, 2009b).

Countries with high levels of poverty can enhance the poverty impact of growth if their growth strategies focus investments on sectors where the poor are more active. Growth needs to be associated with employment creation, especially in rural areas where most of the poor live, because employment is the main channel through which economic growth affects poverty (Nkurunziza, 2007). This has not been the case in most African countries in the past, even though the situation may have changed to some extent in some countries. In this regard, the recent trend to refocus economic development in Africa on agriculture and rural sector development is expected to have a stronger impact on poverty reduction, as it will make agriculture and the rural economy important sources of economic growth.

Economic inequality is the third factor that inhibits the responsiveness of poverty to economic growth. The growth effect is stronger in more equal societies where different segments of the population more equally share the benefits of growth. In less equal societies, additional income created by economic growth is appropriated by a small group that accounts for a disproportionately large share of a country's income. In a particular country, the extent to which economic growth reduces poverty depends on the level of inequality because economic growth and inequality have an opposite effect on poverty. Even though at the aggregate level Africa has the lowest inequality elasticity of poverty, on average, relative to other regions, the last column of Table 4.1 shows that the negative effect of inequality on poverty outweighs the positive effect of economic growth. Elasticity estimates show that 61% of countries in Africa have inequality elasticities higher than growth elasticities of poverty, four out of five of the highest inequality elasticities of poverty being for North African countries (Fosu, 2011).

On the basis of these factors, poverty reduction policies solely focusing on economic growth would have a more limited impact on poverty in cases where initial levels of inequality are high and persistent. In fact, if additional income arising from economic growth were equally distributed, reducing the negative effect of inequality on poverty reduction, poverty rates would fall faster than at the current rate (Bigsten and Shimeles, 2003). Therefore, as inequality in sub-Saharan Africa over the period from 1981 to 2005 has tended to be persistent, the slow pace of the decline in inequality helps to explain why the impact of growth on poverty has been so unrelentingly low. To accelerate the rate of poverty reduction, the progress made in terms of increasing economic growth will need to be scaled-up, while, at the same time, finding ways to reduce inequality.

The status of human development in Africa as measured by the Human Development Index

It is clear that focusing on economic growth alone as a strategy to combat poverty is ineffective. Income inequality and other forms of inequality are also important determinants of poverty and wellbeing. The tendency to centre the development discourse on increasing national income misses several dimensions of human development, such as having good health and accessing quality education and equitable justice. The limitations of national income as a measure of progress motivated the creation of the Human Development Index (HDI) by UNDP in 1990. This measure was developed to reflect a more people-centred understanding of development. The capabilities approach introduced by Amartya Sen, one of the architects of the HDI, provided the underlying theory of the human development paradigm behind the HDI.[8] This composite index combines several dimensions of well-being to measure progress. These dimensions are access to knowledge, healthy life and standard of living. Other composite indicators produced by the *Human Development Reports* (HDRs) have explored gender-based inequities and multidimensional poverty. In the 2010 edition of the HDR, UNDP introduced innovations in the measurement of the HDI and new ways of adjusting the HDI to account for income and gender inequality. Box 4.1 provides the details on the construction of these indices, and Table 4.2 reports the values of HDI and other indices discussed in Box 4.1.

Box 4.1: Constructing the HDI and other indices

The HDI is a composite measure summarising achievements in three different dimensions of human development: health, knowledge and standard of living. Until the 2010 edition of the *Human Development Report*, life expectancy at birth was used to capture the progress in health; adult literacy rate - with a two-third weight - was used together with a combination of primary, secondary and tertiary gross enrolment ratios - with one-third weight - to measure knowledge; and gross domestic product (GDP) per capita in USD purchasing power parity terms was introduced as a proxy for the standard of living. These indicators were then re-scaled to take values between 0 and 1. The Human Development Index (HDI) was calculated as the simple average of the three indices.[9]

The 2010 edition of the *Human Development Report* (*HDR 2010*) introduced innovations in the computation of the HDI. First, indicators of knowledge were changed from literacy rates and enrolment ratios to mean years of schooling and expected years of schooling.

These two indicators were aggregated using a geometric mean. Second, following criticism that the linear aggregation formulae used to compute the HDI allowed for perfect substitutability across the different dimensions, the new HDI used a geometric mean to generate the average of the three sub-indices. With a geometric mean, there is imperfect substitutability across the different indicators of human development.[10] Generally, the new method generated lower indices relative to those produced before *HDR 2010*. However, changes in HDI country ranks due to the new methodology are moderate; most countries keep their ranking.

The *HDR 2010* introduced an inequality-adjusted human development index (IHDI). It is computed as the geometric mean of geometric means of each dimension of human development included in the traditional HDI. Inequalities in each sub-index are accounted for by "discounting" each dimension's average according to its level of inequality across the population. This means that in cases of perfect equality, HDI=IHDI. Where inequality is high, IHDI is lower than HDI. Therefore, HDI can be interpreted as the index of potential human development in the absence of inequality, while IHDI is the actual level of human development. The difference between the two indices shows the position of a country relative to its potential under perfect equality (see Table 4.2).[11]

The Gender Inequality Index (GII) has also been modified. Building on the past Gender-related Development Index (GDI), which was derived on the basis of the same indicators used to compute the HDI but by decomposing it into its male and female components, the new index uses different indicators to assess women's disadvantages in three dimensions: reproductive health using maternal mortality ratio and adolescent fertility rate; empowerment using parliamentary representation and attainment of secondary and higher education; and participation in the labour market using the labour market participation rate. The index is calculated by first aggregating the indicators by each gender using geometric means, following the procedure described for the other indices; then the geometric means are aggregated across genders using a harmonic mean.[12]

Table 4.2 reports African countries' indices of human development: Human Development Index (HDI), Inequality-Adjusted Human Development Index (IHDI) and Gender Inequality Index (GII). Information in Table 4.2 also makes it possible to analyse the trends in HDI to assess progress in human development in Africa over time.

Table 4.2: Indices of human development

	HDI 1990	HDI 2000	HDI 2010	GII 2008
Algeria	0.5	0.6	0.7	0.6
Angola	-	-	0.4	-
Benin	0.3	0.4	0.4	0.8
Botswana	0.6	0.6	0.6	0.7
Burkina Faso	-	-	0.3	-
Burundi	0.2	0.2	0.3	0.6
Cameroon	0.4	0.4	0.5	0.8
Cape Verde	-	0.5	0.5	-
Central African Republic	0.3	0.3	0.3	0.8
Chad	-	0.3	0.3	-
Comoros	-	-	0.4	-
Congo	0.5	0.5	0.5	0.7
Congo, The Democratic Republic of the	0.3	0.2	0.2	0.8
Côte d'Ivoire	0.4	0.4	0.4	0.8
Djibouti	-	-	0.4	-
Egypt	0.5	0.6	0.6	0.7
Equatorial Guinea	-	0.5	0.5	-
Ethiopia	-	0.2	0.3	-
Gabon	0.6	0.6	0.6	0.7
Gambia	0.3	0.3	0.4	0.7
Ghana	0.4	0.4	0.5	0.7
Guinea	-	0.3	0.3	-
Guinea-Bissau	-	0.3	0.3	-
Kenya	0.4	0.4	0.5	0.7
Lesotho	0.5	0.4	0.4	0.7
Liberia	-	0.3	0.3	0.8
Libya	-	0.7	0.8	0.5
Madagascar	-	0.4	0.4	-
Malawi	0.3	0.3	0.4	0.8
Mali	0.2	0.2	0.3	0.8
Mauritania	0.3	0.4	0.4	0.7
Mauritius	0.6	0.7	0.7	0.5
Morocco	0.4	0.5	0.6	0.7

Mozambique	0.2	0.2	0.3	0.7
Namibia	0.6	0.6	0.6	0.6
Niger	0.2	0.2	0.3	0.8
Nigeria	-	0.4	0.4	-
Rwanda	0.2	0.3	0.4	0.6
Sao Tome and Principe	-	0.5	0.5	-
Senegal	0.3	0.4	0.4	0.7
Sierra Leone	0.2	0.2	0.3	0.8
South Africa	0.6	0.6	0.6	0.6
Sudan	0.3	0.3	0.4	0.7
Swaziland	0.5	0.5	0.5	0.7
Tanzania, United Republic of	0.3	0.3	0.4	-
Togo	0.4	0.4	0.4	0.7
Tunisia	0.5	0.6	0.6	0.5
Uganda	0.3	0.3	0.4	0.7
Zambia	0.4	0.3	0.4	0.8
Zimbabwe	0.3	0.2	0.1	0.7
Sub-Saharan Africa	0.4	0.3	0.4	0.7
Africa	0.4	0.4	0.4	0.7
East Asia and Pacific	0.5	0.6	0.6	0.5
South Asia	0.4	0.4	0.5	0.7
Latin America and the Caribbean	0.6	0.7	0.7	0.6
OECD	0.8	0.9	0.9	0.3

Source: Based on UNDP (2010).

StatLink http://dx.doi.org/10.1787/888932405795

The trends of the HDI show that all African countries but Zimbabwe experienced an improvement in their human development between 2000 and 2010. Although African countries are still ranked as having the lowest level of human development relative to other regions, sub-Saharan Africa made, on average, the most important progress over the period 2000-10. The regional HDI increased by 23%, followed by South Asia, where the increase was 17% over the same period.

The improvement in Africa from 2000 to 2010 was due to three main factors. First, most African countries experienced higher economic growth in the 2000s relative to the decade before. Given that the level of income is a component of HDI, higher GDP translated into better human development, to some degree. Second, there was genuine progress in the other two dimensions of human development.

Access to knowledge and better health care improved as most countries in Africa increased their investment in social sectors over the last decade. Thus, almost all the countries had higher HDIs in 2010 than in 2000. They were led by Rwanda, Sierra Leone, Ethiopia, Mozambique, Burundi, Mali, Niger and Uganda, which each increased their HDI by more than 20% between 2000 and 2010.

Third, to some degree, the strong improvement in human development in Africa from 2000 to 2010 reflects a rebound from the social and economic reversals of the 1990s. Africa is the only region where human development worsened between 1990 and 2000, from an average HDI of 0.354 to 0.319. Between 1990 and 2000, out of 35 countries for which data are available, 11 experienced a decline in their HDI. Political instability and the resulting decline in income, health and education are the most likely factors that explain the decline in human development in some countries. In southern Africa, the decline in human development in the 1990s could be the result of the scourge of HIV/AIDS, which ravaged the region more than anywhere else in Africa before its spread was more or less stabilised in the 2000s. In the Democratic Republic of Congo, Republic of Congo, Lesotho, South Africa, and Zambia, HDIs in 2010 had increased from their values in 2000 but still were lower than in 1990.

As expected, introducing inequality into the calculation of the HDI systematically reduces the values of the traditional index of human development, although the rankings between the two indices are not significantly affected. The difference between HDI and IHDI appears to be more pronounced in countries with large inequalities. Although on average Africa has the lowest indices of both HDI and IHDI, across regions the difference is more pronounced with IHDI, indicating more widespread inequalities in Africa than elsewhere. For example, whereas Africa's average HDI index is half of the OECD's, Africa's IHDI is one-third of OECD's IHDI. This is also the case when Africa is compared with other developing regions. Africa's HDI is two-thirds of the value for East Asia and the Pacific region. These results confirm findings that inequality has a strong negative effect on human development. A positive interpretation of these findings is that Africa could substantially improve its human development if it addressed inequalities.

The Gender Inequality Index (GII) shows that some African countries perform much better here than on the other dimensions of human development. Out of 169 countries ranked for both HDI and GII, Burundi, one of the poorest countries in the world, moves up 87 places relative to HDI, from 166th to 79th. The country's performance is primarily due to its low adolescent fertility rate and its relatively high proportion of seats held by female members in parliament. Other countries with remarkable progress in gender equality relative to the overall situation of human development include Rwanda, Mauritius and Mozambique. The message from these findings is that important improvements of some dimensions of human development are possible even in very poor countries, as they do not necessarily require financial resources that these countries lack.

Overall, the trends in human development show that Africa is making progress but that it will have to do much more to attain the level of human development enjoyed in other regions. The implication is that human development in Africa will need to improve much faster than in other regions if the continent is to close the current gap. As the cases of improvement of the GII in Burundi, Rwanda, Mauritius and Mozambique show, Africa has the capacity to quickly improve human development to some degree by at least focusing on some dimensions that do not require out-of-reach resources. For example, increasing women's representation in public structures could be easily done in a relatively short period of time, as the examples of Burundi and Rwanda have demonstrated. It is up to the African countries' leadership to make this policy choice. It is also expected that the efforts undertaken in several African countries over the last ten years to improve their social sectors by heavily investing in education and health will bear fruit over time. If these efforts are sustained, Africa will increase its chances of closing the gap in human development with other developing regions. Realistically, progress will be relatively slow in some areas. For example, it will take some countries several years to increase their income per capita to levels that will substantially reduce poverty. Reducing inequalities will also take time, considering that this will require balancing out competing interests in African societies.

It is important to note that not just one response to the issues discussed in this chapter will be enough to substantially improve the status of human development in Africa. To be successful, Africa will need to take simultaneous actions on several fronts. For example, economic growth will improve human development if it is inclusive and pro-poor, which means that growth policies will have to encourage a broad-based growth process that benefits as many people as possible. Similarly, investing in social sectors will not produce sustainable human development if these investments are not accompanied by efforts to create more economic opportunities that benefit a large segment of the population. Moreover, some dimensions of human development, for example gender equality, will not improve even if there is high economic growth and declining income inequality unless African governments deliberately choose to promote gender equality. In this regard, in addition to the resources devoted to the improvement of human development, the quality of economic policy will determine the progress African countries will be able to achieve.

Notes

1. See, for example, the study by Pinkovskiy and Sala-i-Martin (2010) and some criticism and counter-criticism at http://blogs.worldbank.org/africacan/is-african-poverty-falling and http://www.salaimartin.com/academics-and-books/65-altres/552-response-to-martin-ravallion-and-the-world-bank.html.
2. On the positive effect of economic growth on poverty reduction, see also Dollar and Kraay (2002).
3. As an illustration of the limited data even the most influential studies were based on ECA (1999) and Ali and Thorbecke (2000) as well as Fosu (2008 and 2010) used a sample of only 16 African countries, with one data point each for urban and rural poverty.
4. The results in Table 4.1 are based on a model of poverty specified as follows: growth in the poverty rate is modelled as a negative function of growth in income and a positive function of the growth in inequality, initial inequality, measured by the Gini coefficient, as well as the ratio of the poverty line to income. The reduction in poverty is specified as depending on the interaction between income growth and the initial level of inequality, income growth and the ratio of the poverty line to income, growth in inequality and the initial level of inequality, and growth in inequality and the ratio of the poverty line to income (Fosu, 2011).The extent to which these factors are important is empirically determined and represented by the income and inequality elasticities of poverty (Table 4.1). These elasticities are defined as the ratio of the percentage change in poverty measured as P0 to the percentage change in income per capita expressed in 2005 PPPs, and as the ratio of the percentage change in poverty to the percentage change in inequality measured by the Gini coefficient. The data are from the World Bank (2010a).
5. These elasticities were estimated using a limited number of household surveys at country level, so they should be treated as only indicative of the strength of the relationship between economic growth, inequality and poverty reduction. Also, given that the timeframe for which there are data on poverty differs from country to country, comparisons of these elasticities across countries should be made with caution.
6. See also World Bank (2010b).
7. Growth of non-mineral commodity exporting countries has also been strong but volatile.
8. For a detailed discussion of the origins of the HDI and the theory underlying it, see Fukuda-Parr and Kumar (2003).
9. Dimensional indicators were rescaled into indices using the following formulae: (actual value-minimum value)/(maximum value-minimum value), where maximum and minimum values were goalposts chosen for each indicator. For example, the maximum goalpost for adult literacy rate was 100, with a minimum goalpost of zero. Minimum values were considered to be "subsistence" values or "natural" zeros. In *HDR 2010*, minimum values for life expectancy are 20 years; zero years for both education variables and USD 163 for per capita gross national income (UNDP, 2010).
10. These methodological changes have raised a passionate debate in the literature (see, for example, aidwatchers.com/2010/12/page/2/ and http://hdr.undp.org/en/humandev/lets-talk-hd/2010-12a/
11. The derivation of the IHDI is based on the Atkinson (1970) family of inequality measures. For more technical details, see Technical Note 2 in UNDP (2010).
12. Maternal mortality ratio and adolescent fertility rate are coded as "na" (not applicable) for the male gender. See Technical Note 3 in UNDP (2010) for details on the averaging of the sub-indices.

References

AfDB, OECD and UNECA (2010), *African Economic Outlook 2010*, OECD, Paris.

Ali, A.A. and E. Thorbecke (2000),"The State and Path of Poverty in Sub-Saharan Africa: Some Preliminary Results", *Journal of African Economies*, Vol. 9, Supplement 1, Oxford University Press, Oxford, pp. 9-40.

Atkinson, A. (1970), "On the Measurement of Inequality", *Journal of Economic Theory*, Vol. 2, No. 3, pp. 244-263.

Bigsten, A. and A. Shimeles (2003), "Prospect for Pro-Poor Growth Strategies in Africa", *WIDER Research Paper*, No. 42/2004, Helsinki.

Chen, S. and M. Ravallion (2008), "The Developing World is Poorer than We Thought, but No Less Successful in the Fight against Poverty", *Policy Research Working Paper*, No. 4703, World Bank, Washington, DC.

Dollar, D. and A. Kraay (2002), "Growth is Good for the Poor", *Journal of Economic Growth*, Vol. 7, No. 3, pp. 195–225.

ECA (1999), *Economic Report on Africa*, Economic Commission for Africa, Addis Ababa.

Fosu, A. (2008), "Inequality and the Growth-Poverty Nexus: Specification Empirics Using African Data", *Applied Economics Letters*, Vol. 15, No. 7, pp. 563-566.

Fosu, A. (2010), "Income Distribution and Growth's Ability to Reduce Poverty", The American Journal of Economics and Sociology, Vol. 69, No. 3, pp. 1034-1053.

Fosu, A. (2011), "Growth, Inequality and Poverty Reduction in Developing Countries: Recent Global Evidence", Working Paper, No. 2011/01, UNU-WIDER, Helsinki.

Fukuda-Parr, S. and A.K.S. Kumar (eds.) (2003), *Readings in Human Development*, Oxford University Press, Oxford.

Nkurunziza, J.D. (2007), "Generating Rural Employment in Africa to Fight Poverty", in J.A. Ocampo and K.S. Jomo (eds.), *Towards Full and Decent Employment*, Orient Longman Publisher, pp. 158-190.

Pinkovskiy, M. and X. Sala-i-Martin (2010), "African Poverty is Falling... Much Faster than You Think!", *NBER Working Paper*, No. 15775, NBER, Cambridge, MA.

Ravallion, M. (2009a), "The Crisis and the World's Poorest", Special Report pp. 16-18, World Bank, Washington, DC.

Ravallion, M. (2009b), "Why Don't We See Poverty Convergence?", *Policy Research Working Paper*, No. WPS4974, World Bank, Washington, DC.

UNDP (2010), "The Real Wealth of Nations: Pathways to Human Development", *Human Development Report 2010*, United Nationsl Development Programme, New York.

World Bank (2010a), POVCAL Online 2010, On-line tool for poverty measurement developed by the Development Research Group of the World Bank. World Bank, Washington, DC. iresearch.worldbank.org/PovcalNet/povcalSvy.html

World Bank (2010b), *Global Monitoring Report 2010: The MDGs after the Crisis*, World Bank, Washington, DC.

Young, A. (2009), "The African Growth Miracle", Working Paper, Department of Economics, LSE, London.

Chapter 5: Political Governance

2010 was a year of intensifying civil protests, pointing to the high level of economic and other grievances felt by many African populations. Yet, despite an increase in public protests, government responses in the form of violence and restrictive political measures (bans of press, demonstrations etc.) continued their downward trend from 2009 and were much less aggressive than in 2008. However, Freedom House continues to classify 20 African countries as "not free".

In 2010, 13 countries held largely peaceful elections. The presidential election in Guinea that put an end to the institutional crisis generated by the *coup d'état* in 2008 and the peaceful constitutional referendum in Kenya were significant milestones after the post-election violence in 2008. The crisis and widespread violence in Côte d'Ivoire after a contested presidential election in November marked the low point.

The first quarter of 2011 has been among the most turbulent in Africa's history. Peaceful popular uprisings toppled long-standing authoritarian regimes in Tunisia and Egypt. Neighbouring Libya descended into a civil war in which the international community intervened with military force. The future development in Libya and the repercussions on its neighbours are difficult to predict.

In 2011, the continent will experience a record number of 28 national-level elections in 20 countries. An outstanding electoral event has been Southern Sudan's peaceful January referendum in favour of separation from Northern Sudan. This will come into force in July 2011.

This chapter takes the events of early 2011 as a lens for describing the political landscape of Africa in 2010. The analysis is based on a 15-year dataset covering civil tension (in the form of strikes, demonstrations and victims of violence by non-government actors) and government responses (in the form of violence, arrests, bans, curfews and states of emergencies as measures of suppression, as well as lifting of bans, releases of political prisoners and others as measures of a softening stance) in 25 African countries[1] (see the methodology section of the statistical annex for further details). The analysis is also based on measures of freedom and democracy from Freedom House and Reporters Without Borders.

Public protests, violence and conflicts

Some of the events of late 2010 and early 2011 can be interpreted as the results of longer processes at work over previous years. Intensifying civil protests characterised 2010, pointing to the high level of economic and other grievances felt by many African populations. In September 2010, large protests against the high cost of living paralysed Mozambique's capital, Maputo, for more than a week. Given the steep increase in food and fuel prices (and their large share in average African consumption baskets) that began in the second half of 2010 and has not come to a halt so far, the potential for further public protest in 2011 is high.

In 2010 the measure of demonstrations as used in this report reached its highest level since 2006 and its second highest since the start of the time series in 1996 (see Figure 5.1). Strikes in the sample were driven more strongly by larger events than in previous years. There were significantly more strikes with more than 5 000 participants than in previous years,[2] pointing to increased social pressures and civil societies' capacity to mobilise. These large protests, and especially the recent revolutions in North Africa, also bear witness to the important role of easily accessible new media and communication technology as tools of social organisation.

Yet 2010 was also a year of decreasing violence. The measure of violence by non-government actors was much lower in 2010 than in 2009 (for the 25-country sample). The combination of decreasing violence and increasing public protests points to a positive trend of more peaceful and democratic expressions of demands that bodes well for Africa's development. The expression of public dissent through strikes and demonstrations in order to claim improved public services, better living conditions or social change can be an important driver of development.

Violence between communities can erupt for a host of reasons. Nigeria suffered from severe confrontations over access to land and inter-religious conflicts (Christian and Muslim) in the region of Jos in early 2010, costing between 1 000 and 1 500 lives. In April 2011, violence erupted in the north of the country after the presidential elections, which were won by the incumbent president M. Jonathan, a Christian from southern Nigeria against M. Buhari, a Muslim from the northern part of the country. In Egypt a January 2010 attack on Copts left seven dead and was followed by large protests and in December, similar protests erupted after a bomb killed 21 in a Coptic church. One would note, however, that Muslims and Copts were united in the peaceful uprising against the authoritarian regime of Mubarak.

To obtain a full picture, these observations of post-election violence and strife between communities must be put in the wider electoral context. Of the 13 legislative and presidential elections held in 2010, only the one in Côte d'Ivoire was followed by large-scale violence. Violence around other elections was of minor scale and there are many positive examples of the electoral process on the continent (see below).

Figure 5.1: Public protests, public violence and food price indices (base year 1996 = 100)

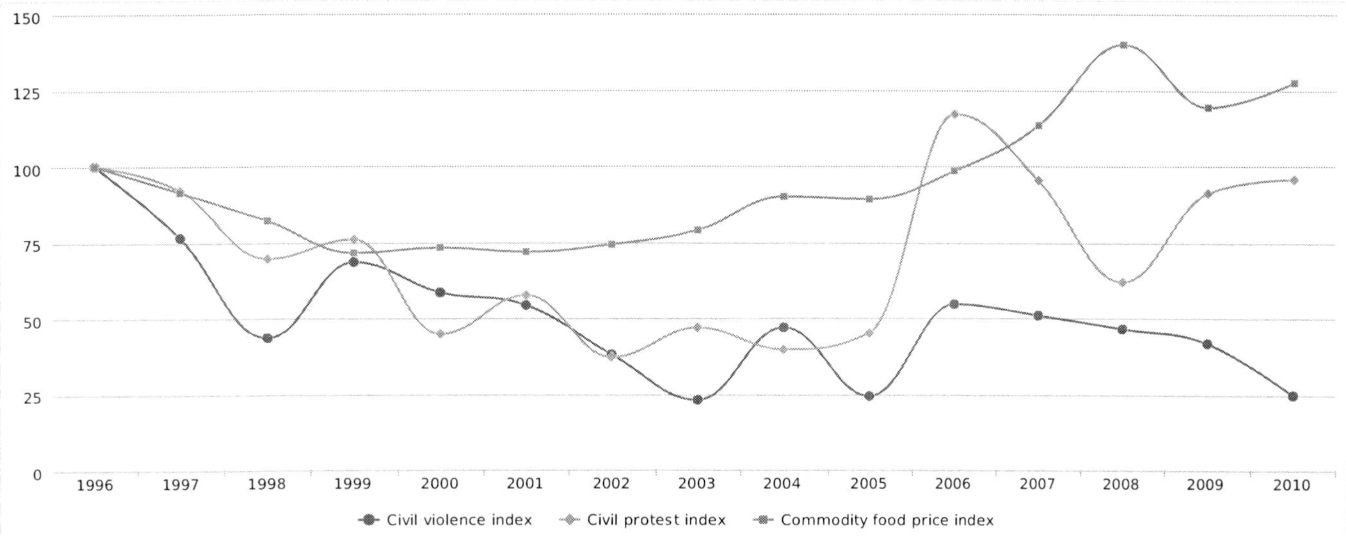

Source: Public Protests and Violence: Authors' calculations based on AFP information; Commodity Price Index: IMF.

StatLink http://dx.doi.org/10.1787/888932403496

Government responses and political freedom

Despite an increase in public protests, government responses in the form of violence and restrictive political measures (bans of press, demonstrations, etc.) continued their downward trend from 2009 and were much less aggressive than in 2008. The measure of violence exerted by government forces was 30% lower in 2010 than in 2009. Arrests of protesters, journalists and members of civil society and the opposition, on the other hand, were up by 20% from 2009. Although still far below (65%) their peak in 2008, the higher number of arrests in 2010 suggests that governments turned to arrests as a means of reaction to increasing public protests. As Figure 5.2 shows, in terms of the indicator of political hardening, which combines various means of government oppression into a single variable, 2010 was the year with the most relaxed stance of governments since the beginning of the series in 1996.

Figure 5.2: Political hardening index 1996-2010 (base year 1996 = 100)

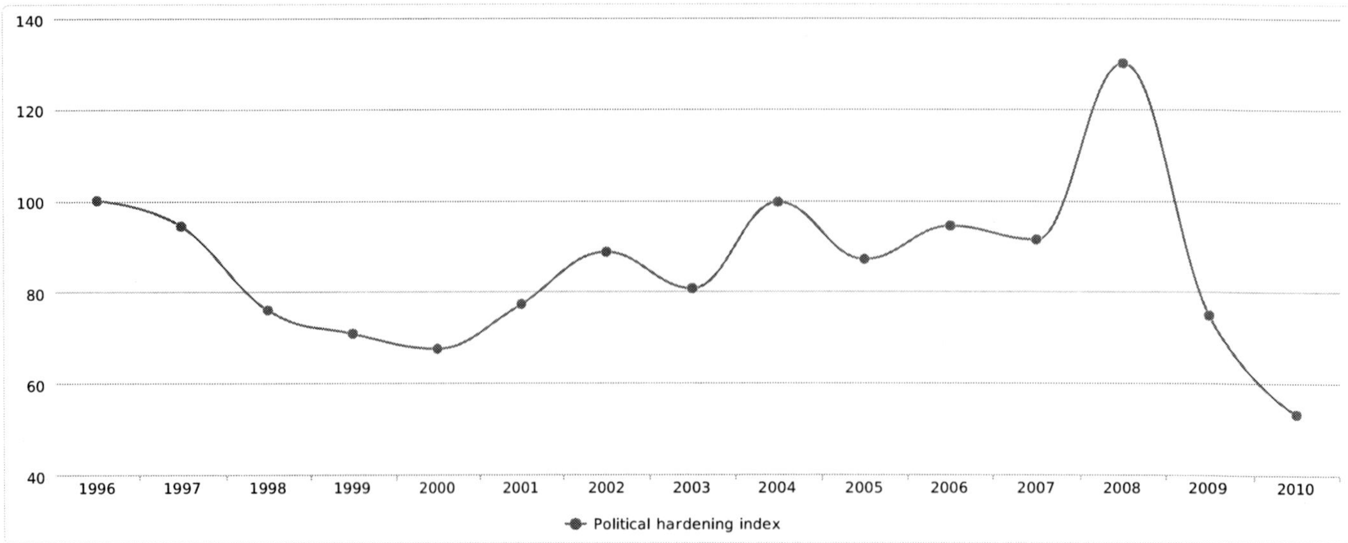

Source: Authors' calculations based on AFP information.

StatLink http://dx.doi.org/10.1787/888932403515

The observation of a softer government stance in 2010 has to be put in the wider context of political and civil liberties in Africa, however. As Table 5.1 shows, the Political Freedom Index (PFI) from Freedom House, which measures political rights and civil liberties in 2010,[3] classifies 9 African countries as "free", 24 as "partly free" and 21 as "not free". Due to its transition from military rule to a democratically elected government, Guinea achieved a change in classification to "partly free" from "not free" in previous years. Across categories the PFI counts improvements but also setbacks. In addition to Guinea, the countries of Kenya, Nigeria and Tanzania saw an improvement of either political or civil rights, while another four countries (Burundi, Côte d'Ivoire, Djibouti, Ethiopia) experienced a worsening. As Table 5.1 shows, Tunisia, Egypt, Libya and Côte d´Ivoire, all of which experienced revolts in the first months of 2011 had very low values for civil liberties and political rights in 2010 and were classified as "not free".

Reporters Without Borders (2010) annually compiles a Press Freedom Index, reflecting "the degree of freedom that journalists and news organisations enjoy in each country, and the efforts made by the authorities to respect and ensure respect for this freedom." In Africa 21 countries improved their rating during 2010, compared to 22 where the situation for the press worsened. With Namibia, Cape Verde, Ghana, Mali, South Africa and Tanzania, six African countries achieved a rating in the "satisfactory" category, as did many OECD member countries such as, for example, France, the United Kingdom and the United States. At the other end of the scale, 7 African countries (Eritrea, Sudan, Rwanda, Equatorial Guinea, Tunisia, Somalia, Libya) fall among the 20 countries at the bottom of the ranking. Tunisia and Libya, two of these seven low-ranked countries, are at the centre of the public revolts that have unfolded in North Africa.

Looking back, the political hardening index shows that 2008 was the year with the "hardest" stance of government repression since the beginning of the series in 1996. Comparison of Figures 5.1 and 5.2 for 2008 shows a spike in government oppression on the one hand and a drop in civil protests on the other against the backdrop of a spike in food prices.[4] Assuming that such a sharp rise in food prices would cause significant grievances[5] and pressures leading to public protests, the figures' revealing of the opposite, namely, lower levels of public protests than in adjacent years, potentially indicates a tough and preventive stance by governments. In 2008, nine governments out of the sample of 25 countries banned strikes and demonstrations in 26 instances, compared to five countries and 12 instances in 2007 and only three countries and 3 instances of bans in 2009. Thus, given that food prices may remain high, Africa might experience similar bouts of strong and preventive government responses to expected protests in the coming years.

Table 5.1: Freedom in Africa in 2010

Country	Freedom Status	Political Rights	Civil Liberties
Algeria	Not Free	6	5
Angola	Not Free	6	5
Benin*	Free	2	2
Botswana*	Free	3	2
Burkina Faso	Partly Free	5	3
Burundi	Partly Free	5 (up)	5
Cameroon	Not Free	6	6
Cape Verde*	Free	1	1
Central African Republic	Partly Free	5	5
Chad	Not Free	7	6
Comoros*	Partly Free	3	4
Congo (Brazzaville)	Not Free	6	5
Congo (Kinshasa)	Not Free	6	6
Côte d'Ivoire	Not Free	7 (down)	6 (down)
Djibouti	Not Free (down)	6 (down)	5 (down)
Egypt	Not Free	6	5
Equatorial Guinea	Not Free	7	7
Eritrea	Not Free	7	7
Ethiopia	Not Free (down)	6 (down)	6 (down)
Gabon	Not Free	6	5
Gambia	Partly Free	5	5
Ghana*	Free	1	2
Guinea	Partly Free (up)	5 (up)	5 (up)
Guinea-Bissau	Partly Free	4	4
Kenya	Partly Free	4	3 (up)
Lesotho*	Partly Free	3	3
Liberia*	Partly Free	3	4
Libya	Not Free	7	7
Madagascar	Partly Free	6	4
Malawi*	Partly Free	3	4
Maldives*	Partly Free	3	4
Mali*	Free	2	3
Mauritania	Not Free	6	5

Mauritius*	Free	1	2
Morocco	Partly Free	5	4
Mozambique	Partly Free	4	3
Namibia*	Free	2	2
Niger	Partly Free	5	4
Nigeria	Partly Free	4 (up)	4
Rwanda	Not Free	6	5
São Tomé and Príncipe*	Free	2	2
Senegal*	Partly Free	3	3
Seychelles*	Partly Free	3	3
Sierra Leone*	Partly Free	3	3
Somalia	Not Free	7	7
South Africa*	Free	2	2
Sudan	Not Free	7	7
Swaziland	Not Free	7	5
Tanzania*	Partly Free	3 (up)	3
Togo	Partly Free	5	4
Tunisia	Not Free	7	5
Uganda	Partly Free	5	4
Zambia*	Partly Free	3	4
Zimbabwe	Not Free	6	6

Source: Freedom in the World 2011, Political Freedom Index, Freedom House. The ratings reflect events from January 1, 2010, through December 31, 2010; 1 represents the most free and 7 the least free rating; * indicates a country's status as an electoral democracy; (up) or (down) indicates an improvement or decline in ratings or status since the last survey.

Electoral processes

In 2010, presidential elections took place in nine countries: Burkina Faso, Burundi, Comoros, Côte d'Ivoire, Guinea, Rwanda, Sudan, Tanzania and Togo. In addition, parliamentary elections occurred in seven countries: Burundi, Egypt, Ethiopia, Mauritius, São Tomé and Principe, Sudan and Tanzania. Two referenda also took place, in Kenya and Madagascar. In turn, 2011 has already witnessed five presidential elections (Benin, Central African Republic, Niger, Nigeria and Uganda) and five parliamentary elections (Cape Verde, Central African Republic, Chad, Nigeria and Uganda) and will be Africa's record election year, with a total of 28 elections at the national level. On top of this, two key referenda have already taken place in the first quarter of 2011 (see Table 5.2). In January the referendum in Southern Sudan confirmed the separation of Southern Sudan from the North. In March the Egyptian population voted in the first constitutional referendum after the January and February revolution against the Mubarak regime.

The largely peaceful presidential election in Guinea was the first democratic election in Guinea since independence in 1958 and put an end to the institutional crisis generated by the 2008 *coup d'état* which had followed the death of President Lansana Conté. After Moussa Dadis Camara, leader of the military junta, left the country after being injured in an assassination attempt in late 2009, then vice president Sékouba Konaté took over the government and focused on the organisation of presidential elections. Konaté himself did not run in the elections. After several postponements of the second round of elections, Alpha Condé won against Cellou Dalein Diallo with 52.52% of the vote. Although the elections were largely successful, violence linked to the two rounds of elections resulted in several hundred injured and between five and ten killed protesters.

The other African presidential election that brought about a leadership change took place in Comoros in November and December 2010. With its electoral law passed in 2005 and first democratic elections in 2006, Comoros successfully embraced democracy after a legacy of military dictatorship. As a federation of the three islands Anjouan, Mohéli and Grande Comore, the federal presidency rotates between these islands every four years. In 2010 it was Mohéli's turn to provide a president. In the first round, people in Mohéli voted in a primary election. In the second round, voters from all three islands elected Ikililou Dhoinine as president from among the top three candidates of the first round. The elected president Dhoinine will take office on 26 May 2011, the final day of the official period of transition.

In Africa, opposition parties often face difficulties in accessing public space for campaign and debate in preparation for elections, which results in biased democratic competition. For example, Ethiopia was downgraded from "partly free" to "not free" by Freedom House because of "massive repression that accompanied national elections" (Freedom House, 2011). The ruling party and its allies won 99% of the official vote, confirming this assessment. Rwanda and Burundi also posed concerns "due to heightened repression in the run-up to national elections" (ibid.). In both countries the incumbent presidents were confirmed in office with results of over 90%. Moreover, both countries experienced incidences of violence around election time. In Burkina Faso, Blaise Compaoré has been ruling since a bloody *coup* in 1987. Among claims of widespread fraud, Compaoré was re-elected with 80.2% of the vote in 2010, almost exactly the same result as five years earlier. In early 2011 the capital Ouagadougou has been the site of large, at times violent protests by civilians and military. Egypt's parliamentary elections, which resulted in a 95% vote for Mubarak's ruling party, were, in hindsight, a clear measure of the repressiveness of the government against which the people revolted in 2011.

In Côte d'Ivoire, after six postponements since 2005, two rounds of presidential elections took place on 21 October and 28 November. For the first time, the country's three principal political opponents (the incumbent president Laurent Gbagbo, and Alassane Ouattara and Henri Konan Bédié who were prime minister and president before the *coup d'état* in 2002) faced each other in the elections. In the second round, Ouattara won against Gbagbo with 54.1% of the votes, according to the Independent Electoral Commission. In response the Constitutional Council declared the results invalid. Subsequently, each candidate declared himself winner and rightful president. The international community, including the United Nations, AU, ECOWAS, the European Union and the United States have affirmed their support for Ouattara and called on Gbagbo to step down, which he refused to do. After the failure of several mediation attempts by ECOWAS and the AU, in March heavy fights broke out between the supporters of Ouattara and Gbagbo. Rebel troops took control of the capital and arrested Gbagbo on April 11. Ouattara has since assumed the presidency. UN and French troops had intervened in the fights by shelling positions of Gbagbo's troops to prevent the use of heavy weaponry against civilians.

In terms of referenda, Kenya's peaceful constitutional referendum on 4 August 2010 and the citizens' affirmative vote for a new constitution that had been supported by the two main opposition parties mark great progress after the 2008 post-election violence. Kenya's post-election violence also spawned significant progress for the role of the International Criminal Court (ICC, founded in 1998) in prosecuting election-related violence. In a case without international precedents, in December 2010 the ICC named six individuals against whom it will start prosecution, including two cabinet ministers and the head of Kenya's civil service. Although the Kenyan parliament responded with an overwhelming vote for a recommendation to leave the ICC, so far the country co-operates. The six suspects followed a summons to The Hague on 7 April 2011. Given continued incidences of election-related violence in Africa, the ICC's role in the Kenyan case will be of great importance for the whole continent.

2011 will be a record election year in Africa with a total of 28 elections at the national level. In the first four months there have been already five presidential elections (Benin, Central African Republic, Niger, Nigeria and Uganda) and five parliamentary elections (Cape Verde, Central African Republic, Chad, Nigeria and Uganda). Most of these elections were relatively peaceful with the exception of Nigeria where, as mentioned above, violence erupted after the presidential election.

In addition to the elections, two key referenda have already taken place in the first quarter of 2011. In January the referendum in Southern Sudan decided the separation of Southern Sudan from the North. Despite widespread fears of violence, this historic vote proceeded smoothly between 9 and 15 January, and international observers commended it as free and fair. Of Southern Sudanese voters, 98.83% voted for independence from Northern Sudan, which will come into effect on 9 July 2011. The referendum had been among the outcomes of the 2005 peace agreement ending the civil war between Northern and Southern Sudan.

After the revolution against the Mubarak regime in January and February, in March the Egyptian population voted in the first constitutional referendum. In this first referendum in North Africa brought about by a popular uprising, 77.27% of voters approved constitutional reforms, including a limitation on the presidency to at most two four-year terms, judicial supervision of elections, a commission to draft a new constitution following the parliamentary election, and easier access to presidential elections by candidates. The referendum will be followed by new parliamentary elections during the second half of 2011. Presidential elections had been planned for 2011, but following the revolution they will most likely be postponed to 2012.

In Tunisia, following the revolution and departure of former President Ben Ali after 23 years in power, the interim government announced elections of a council of representatives on 24 July 2011 to rewrite the constitution. Once elected, the constitutional council could either appoint a new government or ask the current executive to carry on until presidential or parliamentary elections are held (BBC, March 2011).

In Niger, the presidential election ended peacefully after the second round on 12 March 2011 with the victory of Mahamadou Issoufou, who had won 58% of the vote. The successful election ended the constitutional crisis that been continuing since 2009 when then president Mamadou Tandja continued to stay in office despite the end of his official term. In February 2010, a military junta under the label "Supreme Council for the Restoration of Democracy" had taken power through a *coup d'état* and the capture of President Tandja.

Benin's presidential elections of 13 March 2011 went about peacefully and were considered "free and fair" by the AU's observer mission.[6] Incumbent Boni Yayi won a second term with 53% of the vote. The national electoral commission confirmed this result after a short period of heated protest of fraud by runner-up Houngbedji.

Both the Central African Republic and Uganda witnessed smooth general elections that confirmed incumbents as was generally expected. Yoweri Museveni has ruled Uganda for 25 years and was re-elected with 68% of the vote. In his second electoral victory, François Bozizé has been reaffirmed as president of the Central African Republic with 64% of the vote after having acceded to power as leader of a rebel army in 2003.

Table 5.2: National elections in Africa in 2010 and 2011		
	2010	**2011**
Algeria		
Angola		
Benin		Presidential (13 March), National Assembly (17 April)
Botswana		
Burkina Faso	Presidential (21 Nov)	
Burundi	Parliamentary and Presidential (Jun and Jul)	
Cameroon		Presidential (October)
Cape Verde		Parliamentary (6 Feb), Presidential (July)
Central African Rep.		Parliamentary (Jan and March) and Presidential (23 Jan)
Chad		Presidential (May) and Parliamentary (13 Feb)
Comoros	Presidential (7 Nov and 26 Dec)	
Congo		
Congo, Dem. Rep.		Presidential and Parliamentary (1st round November 27)
Côte d'Ivoire	Presidential (31 Oct and 28 Nov)	
Djibouti		Presidential (8 April)
Egypt	Parliamentary (November)	Referendum (March 19) (Presidential elections originally planned for 2011, but will likely be postponed until 2012)
Ethiopia	Parliamentary (23 May)	
Equatorial Guinea		
Gabon		Legislative elections (December)
Gambia		
Ghana		
Guinea	Presidential (27 Jun and 7 Nov)	
Guinea-Bissau		
Kenya	Referendum (4 Aug)	
Lesotho		
Liberia		Presidential, Parliamentary (October)
Madagascar	Referendum (17 Nov)	Presidential (scheduled for May, but will likely be postponed to September), Parliamentary (September)
Malawi		

Mali		
Mauritania		Parliamentary (November)
Mauritius	Parliamentary (Jul)	
Morocco		
Mozambique		
Namibia		
Niger	Referendum (31 Oct)	Presidential (8 Jan and 12 March)
Nigeria		Parliamentary (2 April), Presidential (9 April)
Rwanda	Presidential (9 Aug)	
São Tomé and Principe	Parliamentary (1 Aug)	Presidential (July 2011)
Senegal		
Seychelles		Presidential (1stround May 21)
Sierra Leone		
South Africa		
Sudan (Southern)	"Parliamentary and Presidential (11 Apr)	
Referendum (Jul)"	Referendum (9 Jan)	
Swaziland		
Tanzania	Parliamentary and Presidential (31 Oct)	
Togo	Presidential (4 Mar)	
Tunisia		Constitutional Assembly (24 July)
Uganda		Presidential and Parliamentary (Feb 18)
Zambia		Presidential, Parliamentary (October)
Zimbabwe		Potentially presidential elections, but pressure to postpone is strong

Peace and security

The year 2010 witnessed four *coups d'état*, one of which was successful. In Niger military forces led by Colonel Salou Djibo toppled President Mamadou Tandja on 18 February. In reaction to the illegitimate overthrowing of the government in Niger, the AU suspended the country's membership the day after the *coup*. Madagascar experienced two attempted *coups* against President Andry Rajoelina, who himself had taken power in a military-backed *coup* in March 2009. Guinea Bissau witnessed the fourth *coup* attempt in three years

Two areas of interrelated, highly violent and often border-transcending conflicts continue to characterise sub-Saharan Africa (Heidelberg Institute for International Conflict Research, 2010). In the first area, encompassing the states of Nigeria[7], Chad, Sudan, Ethiopia and Somalia, most conflicts remained on a highly violent level. The second area of highly violent conflicts include the states of the Great Lakes region: Burundi, Rwanda, Uganda, the Central African Republic, and the Democratic Republic of Congo. In this region, the tendency of conflicts to transcend borders increased, as a Burundian rebel group resumed activities in the eastern Democratic Republic of Congo, while the Ugandan Lord's Resistance Army remained highly active in Sudan, as well as in the Democratic Republic of Congo and the Central African Republic.

As in previous years, sub-Saharan Africa was the region with the most (six) UN peacekeeping missions administered by the Department of Peace Keeping Operations (DPKO). The UN peacekeeping mission in the Democratic Republic of Congo (MONUC) used to be the UN's largest peacekeeping mission until 2010, when it was renamed the UN Organization Stabilization Mission in the DRC (MONUSCO) and 2 000 troops were withdrawn. The other ongoing peacekeeping missions in Africa are the UN Operation in Côte d'Ivoire (UNOCI), in progress since 2004; the UN Mission in the Central African Republic and Chad (MINURCAT), in progress since 2007; the UN/AU Mission in Darfur (UNAMID), in progress since 2007; the UN Mission in Sudan (UNMIS), in progress since 2005; and the UN Mission in Liberia (UNMIL), in progress since 2003.

In addition to peacekeeping missions, in 2010 the international community also applied sanctions with the intent to sustain or restore peace and security. In 2010 the UN maintained six sanction committees concerning sub-Saharan Africa (Côte d'Ivoire, Democratic Republic of Congo, Liberia, Rwanda, Somalia, Sudan), one less than in previous years. The committee concerning Sierra Leone was closed down. A new arms embargo and travel bans were imposed on Eritrea, however, sanctioning its support for antigovernment militants in Somalia.

In 2010 the African Union was engaged in two active missions: AMISOM in Somalia as well as the hybrid UN-AU mission in Darfur (UNAMID), which the North Atlantic Treaty Organization (NATO) also supports. The ongoing AMISOM mission brought the conflict in Somalia for the first time to Uganda, one of the major contributors of troops to the mission. The Somali Al-Shabaab claimed responsibility for two simultaneous bomb attacks in the Ugandan capital, Kampala, on 11 July, killing more than 80 people.

In addition to its support to UNAMID, NATO runs the counter-piracy operation around the Horn of Africa. Despite NATO's significant efforts, however, according to the National Geospatial Intelligence Agency's Maritime Safety Portal, piracy in the region has increased significantly over the last years, from 146 attacks by pirates against maritime vessels in 2008 to 376 such attacks in 2010. The pirates' radius now stretches from the coasts of Oman to Tanzania and almost reaches the Maldives. The average ransom has increased from US dollars (USD) 150 000 in 2004 to USD 5.4 million in 2010. In 2009 approximately USD 177 million was paid in ransom to Somali pirates. This sum rose to an estimated USD 238 million in 2010 (Bowden, 2010). Bowden (2010) estimates the global annual cost of piracy to be between USD 7 billion and USD 12 billion, including USD 2 billion for international military operations around the Horn of Africa. Although these costs represent less than 0.1% of world trade (Chalk, 2008), some African countries have to bear high costs. Egypt, for example, has been affected by reduced traffic primarily caused by piracy. Revenue from the Suez Canal is expected to fall from USD 5.1 billion in FY08 to USD 3.6 billion in FY10, a 30% decrease in two years (Wasser, 2009). Bowden (2010) estimates the annual cost of Somali piracy to Egypt at USD 642 million and to Kenya at USD 414 million.

Beyond such instances of direct costs of conflicts, many African countries will likely be confronted with the costly consequences of the escalating conflicts in Libya and Côte d'Ivoire. The Libyan civil war has caused an additional increase in oil prices, negatively affecting those countries that have to import oil. Côte d'Ivoire's conflicts since 2002 have had a negative impact on its landlocked neighbours, such as Mali and Burkina Faso, which have historically depended on the port of Abidjan for their trade. Both countries have been suffering from a significant rise in the prices of imported goods since the recent outbreak of renewed violence in Côte d'Ivoire.

Corruption

Despite both the efforts recorded in some countries and rising domestic and international attention, corruption remains a serious problem in Africa. According to Transparency International's Corruption Perception Index,[8] which ranks countries according to perception of corruption in the public sector, in 2010, 34 out of 47 African countries scored less than 3 (out of 10), indicating that corruption is rampant. Additionally, 16 countries scored between 3 and 5, where corruption is perceived as a serious challenge by country experts and businesspeople. As in 2009, only Botswana, Mauritius and Cape Verde scored more than 5. The situation in South Africa continues to deteriorate: while in 2007 South Africa numbered among the best performers on the continent, in 2010 its score declined to 4.5, from 4.7 in 2009 and 4.9 in 2008.

Overall, 2010 registered more improvements than setbacks, with 26 countries ranking higher in 2010 than in 2009, against 17 ranking lower. Countries that score 3.0 or above and are perceived as relatively less corrupt still face enormous challenges in the fight against corruption, exacerbated by poor enforcement of anti-corruption laws. In these countries, high-profile anti-corruption cases and scandals continue to be frequently reported and risk undermining political stability as well as the governments' capacity to provide effective basic services. Unfortunately, Senegal and Madagascar continued their downward trend from 2009 and dropped below 3; that is, from corruption being a "serious challenge" to it being "rampant". But in several countries, such as Rwanda, Ghana and Lesotho, the situation improved despite remaining a serious challenge.

As in the past, the CPI results clearly indicate that corruption is particularly challenging in fragile states, exacerbating political instability. Somalia, once again, features at the bottom of the ranking with a score of 1.1. Continued conflict and corruption traps Somalia in political and economic collapse, preventing structural reforms. Burundi, only recently emerged from civil war, does only a little better with a score of 1.8. Other countries scoring at the bottom of the ranking, with 2.0 or less, include Angola, the Democratic Republic of Congo, Guinea, Equatorial Guinea, Chad and Sudan.

Table 5.3: Corruption perception index

	Global rank 2009	CPI 2009	Global rank 2010	CPI 2010
Botswana	37	5.6	33	5.8
Mauritius	42	5.4	39	5.4
Cape Verde	46	5.1	45	5.1
Seychelles	54	4.8	49	4.8
South Africa	55	4.7	54	4.5
Namibia	56	4.5	56	4.4
Tunisia	65	4.2	59	4.3
Ghana	69	3.9	62	4.1
Rwanda	89	3.3	66	4
Lesotho	89	3.3	78	3.5
Malawi	89	3.3	85	3.4
Morocco	89	3.3	85	3.4
Liberia	97	3.1	87	3.3
Djibouti	111	2.8	91	3.2
Gambia	106	2.9	91	3.2
Swaziland	79	3.6	91	3.2
Burkina Faso	79	3.6	98	3.1
Egypt	111	2.8	98	3.1
Sao Tome and Principe	111	2.8	101	3
Zambia	99	3	101	3
Algeria	111	2.8	105	2.9
Senegal	99	3	105	2.9
Benin	106	2.9	110	2.8
Gabon	106	2.9	110	2.8
Ethiopia	120	2.7	116	2.7
Mali	111	2.8	116	2.7
Mozambique	130	2.5	116	2.7
Tanzania, United Republic of	126	2.6	116	2.7
Eritrea	126	2.6	123	2.6
Madagascar	99	3	123	2.6
Niger	106	2.9	123	2.6
Uganda	130	2.5	127	2.5
Nigeria	130	2.5	134	2.4

Sierra Leone	146	2.2	134	2.4
Togo	111	2.8	134	2.4
Zimbabwe	146	2.2	134	2.4
Mauritania	130	2.5	143	2.3
Cameroon	146	2.2	146	2.2
Côte d'Ivoire	154	2.1	146	2.2
Libya	130	2.5	146	2.2
Central African Republic	158	2	154	2.1
Comoros	143	2.3	154	2.1
Congo	162	1.9	154	2.1
Guinea-Bissau	162	1.9	154	2.1
Kenya	146	2.2	154	2.1
Congo, The Democratic Republic of the	162	1.9	164	2
Guinea	168	1.8	164	2
Angola	162	1.9	168	1.9
Equatorial Guinea	168	1.8	168	1.9
Burundi	168	1.8	170	1.8
Chad	175	1.6	171	1.7
Sudan	176	1.5	172	1.6

Source: Transparency International.

The Corruption Perception Index ranks countries according to perception of corruption in the public sector on a scale from 10 (very clean) to 0 (highly corrupt).

StatLink http://dx.doi.org/10.1787/888932405852

Economic Governance

A number of African countries registered remarkable economic improvements in recent years. According to *Doing Business 2011*, among the top thirty most improved economies, a third are from sub-Saharan Africa. In the top ten are three sub-Saharan African countries: Rwanda, CapeVerde and Zambia. The improved economies are generally attributed to better regulations and continued ease of doing business in many African countries. The report *Doing Business 2011* has also identified several areas of improvements in the economic governance of many African countries.

In the area of paying taxes, significant improvements have taken place in many parts of the continent. Zimbabwe reduced the corporate income tax rate from 30% to 25%; it also lowered the capital gains tax from 20% to 5% and simplified the payment of corporate income tax by allowing quarterly payments through commercial banks. Burundi also introduced laws that would simplify paying taxes by replacing the transactions tax with a value added tax. Similarly, the Republic of Congo reduced its corporate income tax rate from 38% to 36% in 2010. Cape Verde eliminated the stamp duties on sales and checks. Madagascar continued to reduce corporate tax rates, while Sierra Leone replaced sales and service taxes with a goods and service tax. On the other hand, Chad increased taxes on business through changes to its social security contribution rates. Kenya also increased the administrative burden of paying taxes by making it mandatory to quarterly file payroll taxes.

The starting a business indicator also registered positive changes in many countries. Zambia eased business start-up by getting rid of the minimum capital requirement. Cameroon also made starting a business easier by establishing a new one-stop shop and eliminating rules that required verifying business premises and associated fees. Zimbabwe eased business start-up by lowering registration fees and speeding up the process. Kenya eased business start-up by reducing the time it takes to get the memorandum and articles of association stamped, merging the tax and value added tax registration procedures and digitizing records at the registrar. Mozambique also took steps to ease business start-up by introducing a simplified licensing process.

An important measurement of good economic governance in a given country is the country's ability to enforce contractual agreements. In this regard, several African countries have taken important steps designed to improve contract enforcements. For example, Zambia improved contract enforcement by introducing an electronic case management system in the courts; the system provides electronic referencing of cases and a database of laws. Guinea-Bissau established a new commercial court, which has helped to speed up the enforcement of contracts. Malawi simplified contract enforcement by amending the law that raised the ceiling for commercial claims that can be brought to the magistrate's courts. Other countries have also have taken measures to improve the efficiency of their court systems, greatly reducing the time to file and serve claims.

Obtaining credit continues to be a major problem for individual businesses as well as corporations. Nonetheless, some countries have managed to tackle the problem. For example, Ghana enhanced access to credit by creating a centralized collateral registry and by granting an operating license to a private credit bureau that began operations in April 2010. Rwanda also enhanced access to credit by allowing potential borrowers the right to inspect their own credit report and requiring that loans, regardless of their size, be reported to the central bank's public credit registry. Uganda enhanced access to credit by establishing a new private credit bureau.

However, in spite of the positive changes, sub-Saharan Africa remains at the bottom in seven of the ten components of economic freedom measured in the 2010 "Index of Economic Freedom," published annually by The Wall Street Journal and The Heritage Foundation. While there is no doubt that sub-Saharan Africa has a long way to go in improving its economic governance environment, many analysts and experts believe that the current positive trend will continue. These experts expect that many countries will introduce new laws and regulations that will create better and more conducive environments for businesses to be effective development partners.

Table 5.4: African index of economic freedom, 2003-11

	World Rank	Score								
	2011	**2003**	**2004**	**2005**	**2006**	**2007**	**2008**	**2009**	**2010**	**2011**
Algeria	132	57.7	58.1	53.2	55.7	55.4	56.2	56.6	56.9	52.4
Angola	161	-	-	-	43.5	44.7	46.9	47	48.4	46.2
Benin	117	54.9	54.6	52.3	54	55.1	55.2	55.4	55.4	56
Botswana	40	68.6	69.9	69.3	68.8	68.1	68.2	69.7	70.3	68.8
Burkina Faso	85	58.9	58	56.5	55.8	55.1	55.7	59.5	59.4	60.6
Burundi	148	-	-	-	48.7	46.9	46.2	48.8	47.5	49.6
Cameroon	136	52.7	52.3	53	54.6	55.6	54.3	53	52.3	51.8
Cape Verde	65	56.1	58.1	57.8	58.6	56.5	57.9	61.3	61.8	64.6
Central African Republic	152	60	57.5	56.5	54.2	50.6	48.6	48.3	48.4	49.3
Chad	165	52.6	53.1	52.1	50	50.1	47.8	47.5	47.5	45.3
Comoros	167	-	-	-	-	-	-	-	-	43.8
Congo	168	47.7	45.9	46.2	43.8	44.4	45.4	45.4	43.2	43.6
Congo, The Democratic Republic of the	172	-	-	-	-	-	-	-	-	40.7
Côte d'Ivoire	122	56.7	57.8	56.6	56.2	54.9	53.9	55	54.1	55.4
Djibouti	125	55.7	55.6	55.2	53.2	52.4	51.2	51.4	51	54.5
Egypt	96	55.3	55.5	55.8	53.2	54.4	58.5	58	59	59.1
Equatorial Guinea	157	53.1	53.3	53.3	51.5	53.2	51.6	51.3	48.6	47.5
Eritrea	176	-	-	-	-	-	-	-	-	36.7
Ethiopia	144	48.8	54.5	51.1	50.9	53.6	52.5	53	51.2	50.5
Gabon	110	58.7	57.1	54.8	56.1	54.8	54.2	55	55.4	56.7
Gambia	105	56.3	55.3	56.5	57.3	57.7	56.9	55.8	55.1	57.4
Ghana	95	58.2	59.1	56.5	55.6	57.6	57	58	60.2	59.4
Guinea	137	54.6	56.1	57.4	52.8	54.5	52.8	51	51.8	51.7
Guinea-Bissau	159	43.1	42.6	46	46.5	46.1	44.4	45.4	43.6	46.5
Kenya	106	58.6	57.7	57.9	59.7	59.6	-	58.7	57.5	57.4
Lesotho	156	52	50.3	53.9	54.7	53.2	52.2	49.7	48.1	47.5
Liberia	160	-	-	-	-	-	-	-	-	46.5
Libya	173	34.6	31.5	32.8	33.2	37	38.7	43.5	40.2	38.6
Madagascar	81	62.8	60.9	63.1	61	61.1	62.4	62.2	63.2	61.2
Malawi	119	53.2	53.6	53.6	55.4	52.9	52.7	53.7	54.1	55.8
Mali	114	58.6	56.6	57.3	54.1	54.7	55.6	55.6	55.6	56.3

Mauritania	134	59	61.8	59.4	55.7	53.6	55.2	53.9	52	52.1
Mauritius	12	64.4	64.3	67.2	67.4	69.4	72.6	74.3	76.3	76.2
Morocco	93	57.8	56.7	52.2	51.5	56.4	55.6	57.7	59.2	59.6
Mozambique	109	58.6	57.2	54.6	51.9	54.7	55.4	55.7	56	56.8
Namibia	73	67.3	62.4	61.4	60.7	63.5	61.4	62.4	62.2	62.7
Niger	126	54.2	54.6	54.1	52.5	53.2	52.9	53.8	52.9	54.3
Nigeria	111	49.5	49.2	48.4	48.7	55.6	55.1	55.1	56.8	56.7
Rwanda	75	47.8	53.3	51.7	52.8	52.4	54.2	54.2	59.1	62.7
Sao Tome and Principe	150	-	-	-	-	-	-	-	-	49.5
Senegal	121	58.1	58.9	57.9	56.2	58.1	58.3	56.3	54.6	55.7
Seychelles	142	-	-	-	-	-	-	47.8	47.9	51.2
Sierra Leone	149	42.2	43.6	44.8	45.2	47	48.3	47.8	47.9	49.6
South Africa	74	67.1	66.3	62.9	63.7	63.5	63.4	63.8	62.8	62.7
Swaziland	97	59.6	58.6	59.4	61.4	60.1	58.4	59.1	57.4	59.1
Tanzania, United Republic of	108	56.9	60.1	56.3	58.5	56.8	56.5	58.3	58.3	57
Togo	153	46.8	47	48.2	47.3	49.7	48.9	48.7	47.1	49.1
Tunisia	100	58.1	58.4	55.4	57.5	60.3	60.1	58	58.9	58.5
Uganda	80	60.1	64.1	62.9	63.9	63.1	63.8	63.6	62.2	61.7
Zambia	91	55.3	54.9	55	56.8	56.2	56.2	56.6	58	59.7
Zimbabwe	178	36.7	34.4	35.2	33.5	32	29.4	22.7	21.4	22.1

Notes

1. The following countries are included in this sample: Algeria, Chad, Côte d'Ivoire, Tunisia, Nigeria, Mali, Botswana, Burkina Faso, Cameroon, Egypt, Equatorial Guinea, Ethiopia, Gabon, Ghana, Kenya, Mauritius, Morocco, Mozambique, Namibia, Senegal, South Africa, Tanzania, Uganda, Zambia, Zimbabwe.
2. Across Africa strikes for improved salaries and working conditions at the production sites of large multinational corporations have multiplied. In April 2010, workers at the Guinean Fria aluminium factory (part of Russia's Rusal) obtained a significant salary increase, as did 7 000 striking workers at an ArcelorMittal plant in Algeria in January 2010. In Cameroon strikers at the independent port of Douala operated by French multinational Bolloré obtained similar results in April 2010 (*Jeune Afrique*, 2010).
3. The PFI is based on measures of several components of political freedom. These measures include free and fair elections; honest tabulation of ballots; the extent to which citizens are free to organise in different political parties or groupings; whether there is a significant vote for the opposition and a realistic possibility of coming to power through elections; self-determination and freedom from any kind of domination; reasonable self-determination for cultural, ethnic, religious and other minority groups; and the extent to which political power is decentralised.
4. The decline in violence by non-government actors since 2006 was largely due to the declining intensity of the conflicts in the Darfur region and Côte d'Ivoire.
5. Ivanic and Martin (2008), for example, find that the large increases in food prices in 2007 and 2008 "appear likely to raise overall poverty in low-income countries substantially."
6. http://news.xinhuanet.com/english2010/world/2011-03/15/c_13780370.htm
7. Between 2006 and 2009, Nigeria's oil production dropped from 2.6 to about 1.7 million barrels per day. This drop was due to attacks against production sites and kidnappings of international staff by MEND, an armed rebel group.
8. "Transparency International defines corruption as the abuse of entrusted power for private gain. [...] The 2010 CPI draws on different assessments and business opinion surveys carried out by independent and reputable institutions. [...] Broadly speaking, the surveys and assessments used to compile the index include questions relating to bribery of public officials, kickbacks in public procurement, embezzlement of public funds, and questions that probe the strength and effectiveness of public sector anti-corruption efforts" (Transparency International, 2010).

References

Bowden, A. (2010), "The Economic Cost of Maritime Piracy", *One Earth Future Working Paper*, oneearthfuture.org/images/imagefiles/The%20Economic%20Cost%20of%20Piracy%20Full%20Report.pdf, accessed March 2011.

British Broadcasting Corporation (BBC), 3 March 2011,

www.bbc.co.uk./news/world-middle-east-12642942, accessed April 2011.

Chalk, P. (2008), *The Maritime Dimensions of International Security: Terrorism, Piracy and Challenges for the United States*, RAND Corporation, Santa Monica.

Freedom House (2011), Freedom in the World 2011 – The Authoritarian Challenge to Democracy, www.freedomhouse.org/template.cfm, accessed March 2011.

Heidelberg Institute of International Conflict Research (2010), Conflict Barometer 2010, Department of Political Science, Universidade de Heidelberg, www.hiik.de/en/konfliktbarometer.

Ivanic, M. and W. Martin (2008), "Implications of Higher Global Food Prices for Poverty in Low-Income Countries", *Agricultural Economics*, Vol. 39, supplement, pp. 405–416.

Jeune Afrique (2010), No. 2583, 11 July 2010.

National Geospatial Intelligence Agency (n.d.), Maritime Safety Information Portal, msi.nga.mil/NGAPortal/MSI.portal, accessed March 2011.

Reporters without Borders (2010), Press Freedom Index 2010, en.rsf.org/press-freedom-index-2010,1034.html, accessed March 2011.

Transparency International (2010), Corruption Perceptions Index 2010, Berlin, www.transparency.org/policy_research/surveys_indices/cpi/2010/.

Wasser, L. (2009), "Somali Piracy Costs Suez Canal Business", San Francisco Chronicle, 29 April 2009.

Part Two

Africa and its Emerging Partners

Chapter 6: Africa and its Emerging Partners

- Global transformation brings historic opportunities
- Africa must unite to bargain with "old" and "new" powers

Africa has gone through a remarkable decade of economic transformation. The continent is abuzz with talk of new investment, new cities, new airports, new refineries: The new African Lions.

Before, the talk was how many billions of dollars Africa needs. Now, leaders speak equally of Chinese yuan, Indian rupees, Brazilian reals, Korean won and Turkish lira – the currencies of the emerging economic powers drawn to Africa whose sustained growth played a key role helping the continent weather the global economic crisis of 2008-09.

The dramatic decade opened a new era of opportunity for the continent. Trade between Africa and its new partners is now worth USD 673.4 billion a year. And this year's *African Economic Outlook* describes and analyses Africa's surge in relations with their "emerging partners", who are now on the top table of economic decision making alongside the "traditional partners" from Europe and North America. The study also looks at what can be expected in the future.

Drawing on milestone studies on Africa and South-South relations,[1] this report provides a new insight into Africa's expanding partnerships after the 2008-09 crisis dramatically shifted the centre of the world's economic gravity away from OECD members towards the east and south. Africa is benefiting from investment, trade and aid, but also from the macroeconomic, political and strategic advantages that the rise of emerging countries has produced.

The *African Economic Outlook*'s traditional theme chapter casts new light on the diversity of Africa's changing relations. China takes centre stage, but other emerging partners together make up a larger share of many of the dealings. Africa's top five emerging partners are China, India and Brazil -- along with Korea and Turkey.

Europe and North America's trade share has quickly eroded, but they still account for more than half of Africa's trade and foreign investment stock, and their economic health remains key to Africa's growth performance. Nevertheless, Africa's rebalancing act turns the page on 50 years of over-reliance on the West, a period sometimes dubbed the post-colonial era. Links with the traditional partners face profound changes.

Outlook experts give a cautiously positive verdict on concerns about the impact of the emerging partners on Africa's development. Prospects are good for the transfer of technology and access to finance. There is no evidence to suggest that the new players are hindering Africa's industrialisation, debt sustainability or governance, but Africa needs a clear engagement strategy and all sides must show greater transparency.

To maximise development benefits from the new partnerships, African nations can draw lessons from their dealings with traditional partners and the successful experience of the rising economic powers. Vision and ownership turn global opportunities into sustained and shared growth. The economic independence that African economies are gaining from globalisation can be sustained if countries draw up their own development policies and co-ordinate them at regional and continental level to better negotiate with their traditional and emerging partners.

Box 6.1. Defining Africa's "emerging partners"

A strong case has been made against calling economies such as India or China "new partners", as they have had long-lasting relations with Africa (Kragelund, forthcoming).

The notion of "emerging partners" used here tries to capture two characteristics:

1. they are considered "emerging" economies in the global context;
2. their economic relations with Africa have been marginal until the last decade but are rising fast and are expected to grow further.

For this study, "emerging partners" are economic partners of African countries which did not belong to the club of traditional "donors", the OECD Development Assistance Committee (DAC), at the outset of the millennium. Korea is the only country to have joined the committee since then, in 2010, thereby aligning its development policy and practices with DAC norms and manifesting its intention to comply with its principles and guidelines. (*)

Of course, this category brings together partners at markedly different stages of engagement with African countries. One of the contributions of this report is to document, analyse and draw policy conclusions from this heterogeneity.

It also shows that any typology of Africa's global economic relations is doomed to be short-lived, given the pace at which they change in nature and magnitude.

(*) As of March 2011, the 24 members of the DAC are Australia, Austria, Belgium, Canada, Denmark, Finland, France, Germany, Greece, Ireland, Italy, Japan, Korea, Luxembourg, Netherlands, New Zealand, Norway, Portugal, Spain, Sweden, Switzerland, United Kingdom, the United States and the European Commission. Eleven OECD countries are not DAC members: Chile, Czech Republic, Estonia, Hungary, Iceland, Israel, Mexico, Poland, Slovak Republic, Slovenia and Turkey. See www.oecd.org/dac.

Africa pushes aside post-colonialism

Africa's shifting role in globalisation

The world can no longer simply be divided between North and South, developed and developing countries. To understand the complexity of the shift, this report takes and develops James Wolfensohn's concept of a "four-speed" world of *Affluent*, *Converging*, *Struggling* and *Poor* countries according to their income and growth rate relative to the industrialised powers (Wolfensohn, 2007). This reveals a new global growth map: some developing countries are beginning to catch up with the living standards of the affluent, others are struggling to break through a middle-income "glass ceiling", while some just cannot shrug off the weight of extreme poverty.

Two distinct time periods emerge. For most developing economies, the 1990s were another "lost decade", hampered by financial crises and instability (Figure 6.1). Some African countries continued to stagnate. Northern and southern Africa struggled, as Latin America did, with growth responding only weakly to reform.

Figure 6.1. The four-speed world in the 1990s

Source: OECD (2010) based on World Bank (2009). This map is for illustrative purposes and is without prejudice to the status of or sovereignty over any territory covered by this map.

In the 2000s, before the economic crisis, much of the developing world enjoyed its first strong growth in many years (Figure 6.2). The new millennium saw Africa's per capita incomes rise faster than high-income countries for the first time since the 1970s. The number of converging countries – those doubling the average per capita growth of high-income OECD nations – rose from 12 to 65. The number of poor countries fell from 55 to 25. China and India grew at three to four times the OECD average during the 2000s.

In Africa, while a group of poor countries – mostly in western and central Africa -- continued to underperform, it is striking that 19 countries made it to the converging category in the 2000s, compared with only two in the 1990s. Most countries which made the leap are still struggling to contain poverty and inequality. However the map below still illustrates a dramatic change in Africa's average growth performance compared with the rest of the world.

Figure 6.2. The four-speed world in the 2000s (before the global economic crisis)

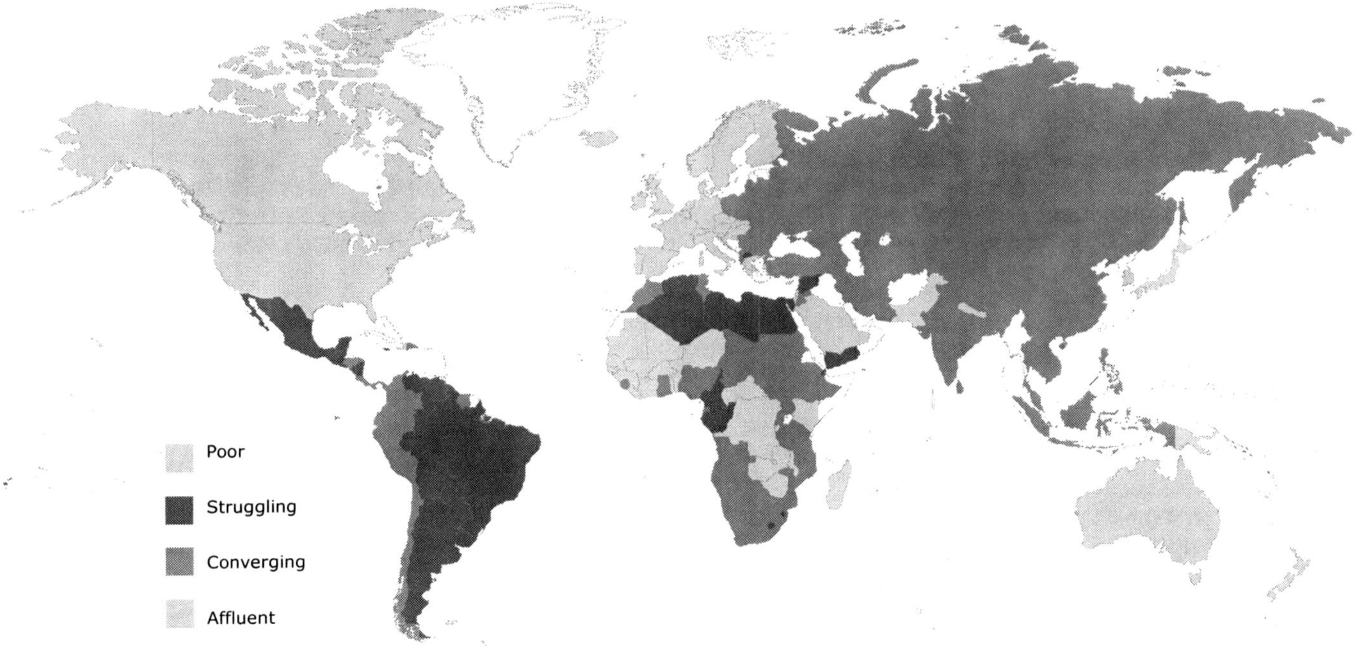

Source: OECD (2010) based on World Bank (2009). This map is for illustrative purposes and is without prejudice to the status of or sovereignty over any territory covered by this map.

Looking at the years when OECD countries fell into recession produces an even more striking picture: about half of Africa's economies graduated to the converging group (Table 6.1). This change should be treated with caution as the size of the gap in economic performance between affluent and other economies in 2009 arguably distorts the medium-term picture. The data reveal, however, that the crisis significantly accelerated the global wealth change and Africa captured much of the benefit. Whether this becomes a durable shift, or whether new growth in the OECD sends some nations back toward divergence, remains to be seen.

The story of Africa and its emerging partners is a key part of the recalibration of the world economy over the past decade. Building on improved policies, the continent has benefited from extra investment, trade and aid, as well as from macroeconomic, political and strategic advantages from the rise of the large emerging countries.

The rapid integration of emerging partners into the world economy started in the 1980s and accelerated with China becoming a member of the World Trade Organization in 2001. China, India and others have enjoyed high growth, rising economic clout and seen a massive reduction in the number of poor people.

Table 6.1: Number of African countries by category in the four-speed world

	1990s	2000s before crisis (2000-07)	2000s including crisis (2000-09)
Affluent	0	0	1
Converging	2	19	28
Struggling	11	10	6
Poor	34	21	14
Total	49	50	49

Source: Updated from OECD (2010). Data unavailable for Libya (columns 1 and 3), Sáo Tome & Principe, Somalia and Zimbabwe (columns 1, 2 and 3).

StatLink http://dx.doi.org/10.1787/888932405871

There has been a global and bilateral impact on growth and poverty in other poor countries, including Africa. The global dimension includes the impact on wages, interest rates, manufactured goods and raw material prices, on global imbalances and net investment. This global dimension is rarely addressed in the context of poverty reduction. Most analysis concentrates on the links between China and Africa: raw materials, trade, investment, export credits, aid and migration.

Indeed, emerging partners do not benefit all African countries. While oil- and mineral-rich countries have benefited disproportionately, others – especially those that do not have diplomatic links with China – have hardly benefited at all.

The "growth engine effect" was documented and analysed by Garroway *et al.* (2010). While in the 1990s the Group of Seven nations led growth by developing countries, in the 2000s the impact of China's growth on low- and middle-income countries has risen significantly. Over the period, a 1% change in China's growth rates will result in a change of about 0.3% in low-income countries and 0.4% for middle-income countries. The impact of OECD countries decreased over the same period. Whether that growth, spurred by China's currency peg to the US dollar, is right for poor countries' development is an ongoing debate. Rodrik (2010) argues that it heightens the reliance of poor countries on exports of unprocessed raw materials, and – through the undervalued Chinese currency – undercuts their industrialisation. Conversely, Garroway *et al.* (*ibid.*) argue that the growth engine effect, by sustaining world demand for goods that poor countries export, has benefited oil and non-oil producing countries alike.

A steady rise in world demand has triggered a "super cycle" in raw material prices (Standard Chartered Bank, 2010). Speeding urbanisation and a rapid growth in the middle classes in emerging countries have a big impact on commodity demand. Urbanisation is particularly commodity-intensive and commodity consumption increases rapidly as incomes approach a level deemed "middle class".[2] On top of this rise in demand, global imbalances have helped push commodity prices higher. Until 2006, the investment of rising foreign exchange reserves in US treasury bonds by the new players depressed global interest rates, boosting commodity prices. Africa has benefited disproportionately as it produces the commodities whose prices are likely to rise most and it holds the highest share of unexploited resources (Collier, 2010).

The boom, if sustained, should generate more benefits for Africa. As emerging countries become advanced economies – notwithstanding any radical change in their growth – as they become richer and demographically more mature, their success will improve export opportunities for Africa. Once the poor share the new wealth, over 2 billion more people will live in countries that import labour-intensive goods and fewer in countries that export them, opening up further opportunities for African goods. The sustained growth of the emerging giants may thus have negative short-term effects on African productive sectors, but it could improve long-term prospects (Chamon and Kremer, 2006). Provided barriers to business and trade are further reduced, African economies stand to gain from the relocation of production away from today's emerging economies.

The International Monetary Fund (2011) believes that changing production patterns in large emerging economies such as China can help low income countries diversify into new products. The experience of Malaysia, Indonesia and Chile, it argues, shows that poor countries with rich natural resources can diversify exports as they grow, provided resource revenues are used to build up productive capacity, including infrastructure and human capital. In addition, Africa needs to promote private sector development, as successive editions of the *African Economic Outlook* have argued. Relations between Africa and its emerging partners thus need to be understood in the context of the global shift in wealth.

Emerging partners go from the balcony to orchestra in a decade

It is easy to underestimate the importance that the new economic forces have taken on for Africa. People know China, India and the rest are a feature of Africa's economic landscape, but do they realise the magnitude of this importance, particularly as trading partners?

Table 6.2 shows the evolution of Africa's exports, imports and total trade with emerging partners over the last decade. Among the clear trends, it shows that Africa's total trade has more than doubled in nominal terms from less than USD 247 billion to USD 629 billion.

Table 6.2: Shares of traditional and emerging partners in Africa's imports, exports and total trade, 2000 and 2009 (in percentage)

	2009			2000		
	Trade	**Exports**	**Imports**	**Trade**	**Exports**	**Imports**
Total traditional partners	63.5	67.6	59	77	78.3	75.4
EU25	44.3	43	45.6	53.5	51.3	56.4
Other TPs	6.1	6.1	6.1	7.5	6.6	8.8
United States	13.1	18.4	7.3	16.1	20.4	10.1
Total emerging partners	36.5	32.4	41	23	21.7	24.6
China	13.9	13.1	14.7	4.7	4.6	4.9
India	5.1	6	4	2.3	2.4	2.1
Korea	2.6	1.3	4	2.6	2.2	3.1
Brazil	2.5	2.4	2.7	1.7	2	1.3
Turkey	2.4	1.6	3.1	1.6	1.9	1.3
Thailand	1.1	0.4	2	0.8	0.6	1.2
Russian Federation	1	0.5	1.6	0.6	0.3	1
Chinese Taipei	0.9	1.1	0.7	1.9	2.3	1.3
United Arab Emirates	0.9	1.3	0.5	0.2	0.2	0.1
Singapore	0.8	0.2	1.4	1	0.5	1.7
Malaysia	0.7	0.5	1	0.5	0.3	0.7
Indonesia	0.7	0.6	0.8	0.8	0.6	1
Argentina	0.5	0.1	0.9	0.6	0.3	1
Saudi Arabia	0.4	0.7	0	0.4	0.6	0
Other countries (58)	3	2.6	3.5	3.3	2.9	3.8
Total	100	100	100	100	100	100
Total value (billion USD)	673.4	350.8	322.5	246.4	142.4	104

Source: OECD Development Centre calculations based on ComTrade data.

StatLink http://dx.doi.org/10.1787/888932405890

Several other trends emerge. First, the share of trade volume conducted with the emerging forces has grown from approximately 23% to 39%. Over the same period, the share for traditional partners shrank from around 77% to 62% (Figure 6.3).

Figure 6.3: Shares of emerging and traditional partners in Africa's trade from 1992 to 2009 (in percentage)

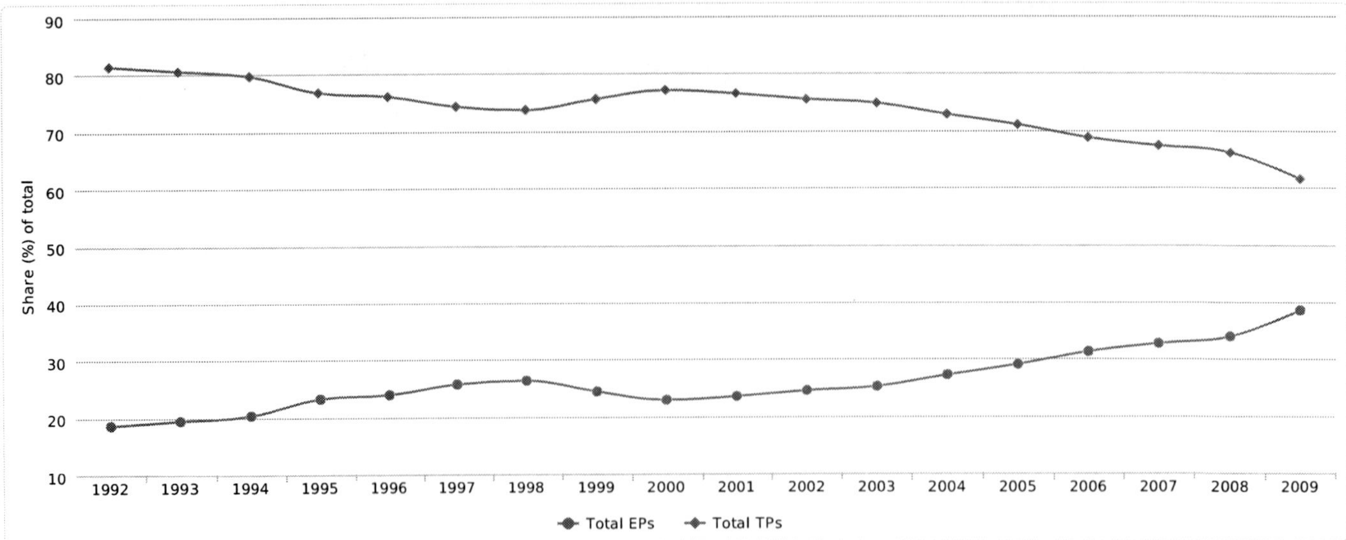

Source: OECD Development Centre calculations based on ComTrade data.

StatLink http://dx.doi.org/10.1787/888932403572

Second, Africa's trade volumes with emerging partners grew remarkably between 2000 and 2009. China represented less than 5% of Africa's trade at the start of the decade. This, however, tripled to nearly 16% by the end. The US share of Africa's trade was more than three times China's in 2000 but was surpassed by China in 2009. All the emerging partners together accounted for less than half of the European Union volume with Africa in 2000. By 2009 their share was almost equal, and on current trends they will soon overtake the EU. However, one should bear in mind that data in Table 6.2 and Figure 6.3 refer to merchandise trade. As much of Africa's services trade is with traditional partners, their total share of trade is higher than that reflected by merchandise trade figures.

Figure 6.4: Africa's total volume of trade and with traditional partners (1992-2009, in billion USD)

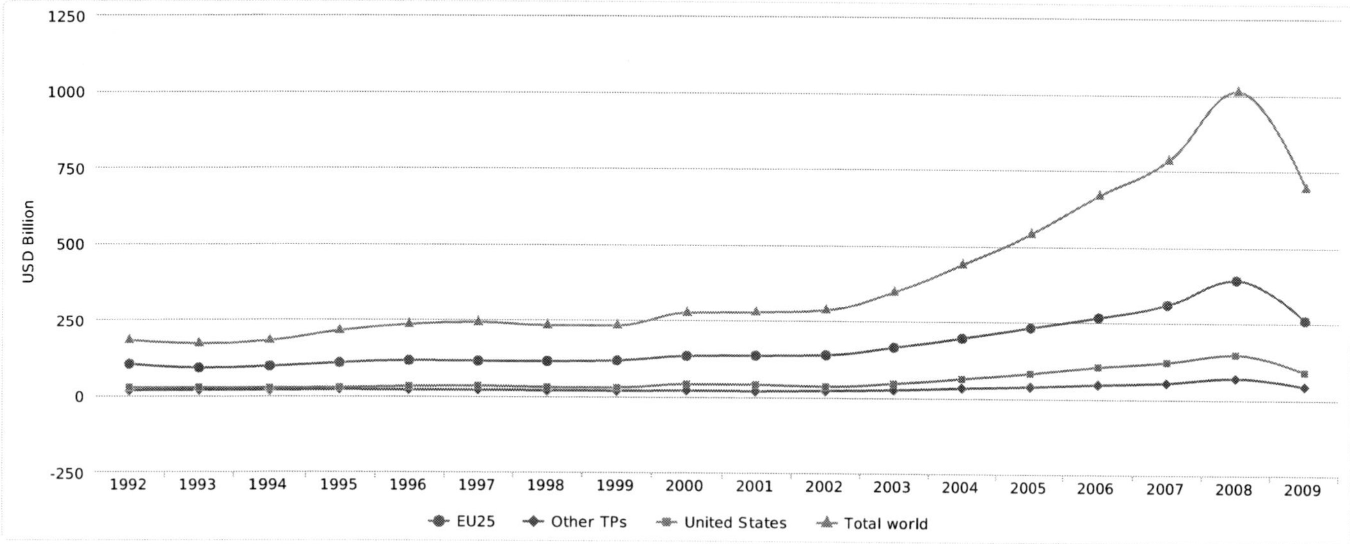

Source: OECD Development Centre calculations based on ComTrade data.

StatLink http://dx.doi.org/10.1787/888932403591

Traditional partners remain key and keep growing

Over the last decade, Africa's trade volume with traditional partners doubled in nominal value, as shown in Figure 6.4. Africa's overall trade volume has more than doubled however which explains why the share of traditional partners decreased. Africa's trade with traditional partners remains crucial, however, at close to 62% according to Figure 6.4. The European Union still represents more than 40% of Africa's trade – the equivalent of USD 256 billion – and almost three times that of China. As African countries strive to make the most of growing relations with the new economic forces, they need to be aware that their older partners remain a very solid and growing base. The downward trend of curves in Figure 6.4 in the year 2009 should not be misunderstood. Africa's trade is not structurally declining – on the contrary: the dip in 2009 reflects the onslaught of the financial crisis. Preliminary data for 2010 suggest that Africa's trade has picked up for the old and new economic forces. Trade for the traditional partners is only decreasing in importance in relative terms and because of Africa's very fast growth of trade with emerging partners.

In terms of foreign direct investment (FDI), the continued dominance of traditional partners is striking. As Figure 6.5. illustrates, OECD countries – including traditional partners – still account for about 80% of FDI flows to Africa. However, the share of non-OECD countries – including Brazil, India and China – has risen from an average of 18% in 1995-99 to 21% for 2000-08. Europe and the United States still dominate FDI to African countries.

One must be careful, however, when comparing investment data between traditional and emerging nations. Assembling reliable data on African FDI is difficult, particularly for the emerging powers. There are large gaps in reported data and large discrepancies between different sources that are hard to explain as it is difficult to access the complete methodology used.

Figure 6.5: African FDI inflows 1995-2008

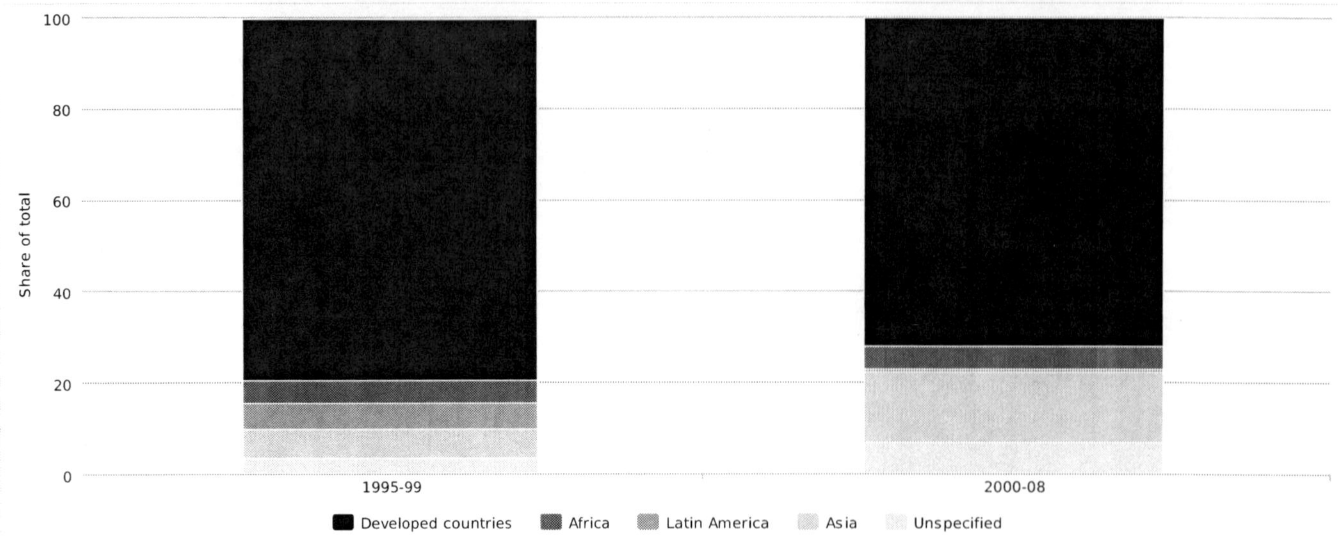

Source: UNCTAD, OECD.

StatLink http://dx.doi.org/10.1787/888932403610

Meanwhile, available evidence points to the relative concentration of current FDI flows from emerging partners into a limited number of countries, typically resource-rich countries. An analysis of Chinese Ministry of Commerce (MOFCOM) data reveals that, by 2009, 76% of Chinese outward FDI in Africa was in countries defined by the IMF (2007) as hydrocarbon- or mineral-rich, namely: Algeria, Angola, Botswana, Cameroon, Congo DR, Congo Republic, Equatorial Guinea, Gabon, Ghana, Guinea, Liberia, Libya, Mauritania, Namibia, Nigeria, Sierra Leone, South Africa, Sudan and Zambia. In general, FDI in Africa is still concentrated in a few countries and sectors. North Africa has been the main recipient of FDI each year since 2004, receiving between 30% and 50% of all FDI to Africa (UNCTAD, 2010b). Between 2000 and 2010, about 75% of FDI to Africa went to oil-exporting countries. For FDI from OECD member-countries this ratio is even higher, at 85%. By implication, FDI from emerging partners is actually less concentrated in oil-exporting countries than that of traditional partners.

A special survey by the AEO team of country authors was conducted for 40 African countries and we collected data from African central banks. We are able to illustrate 11 countries in a comparable fashion in Table 6.3. and to obtain a breakdown by country of origin not available from other sources. The analysis of the AEO data set confirms that the EU and US remain the most important FDI sources of the African countries. In our sample group traditional partners delivered close to 85% of all FDI flows during 2000-04 and 83% for the period 2005-10. The EU is the single largest FDI partner for the ten countries accounting for 55% of total FDI inflows in 2000-04, shrinking to a still dominating 44% in 2005-10. The United States has grown from a quarter of FDI flows to our ten countries in the first half of the decade to close to 37% in the second half. Emerging partners as a whole, on the other hand, still represented only around one tenth of FDI inflows in our sample countries. However, this share has approximately doubled between the first and the second half of the decade. The rise of the emerging economies as investment partners for Africa may thus be underway, with investment flows lagging trade in terms of magnitude. Indeed, emerging partners have already become significant investment partners if one accounts for other types of investment flows besides FDI.

Table 6.3: FDI flows to selected African countries over the last decade, by country of origin (in percentage)

	2000-04	2005-10
Traditional partners	84.8	83.3
EU25	55.5	43.7
United States	25.7	37.4
All other traditional partners	3.5	2.3
Emerging partners	5.6	10.2
China	0.6	0.9
India	0.4	1.7
Latin America	0.3	0.2
Middle East	3.2	6.1
All other emerging partners	1.1	1.3
Intra-African	5	5.6
Unspecified	4.7	0.8

Source: Central Banks from African countries.

The table was constructed using data from all countries where data was available in both periods, namely: Morocco, Republic of Congo (Brazzaville), Djibouti, Gabon, Tanzania, Mauritius, Malawi, Nigeria, Rwanda and Uganda.

StatLink http://dx.doi.org/10.1787/888932405909

Better data for FDI and investment in general are necessary to form policy on engagement with emerging partners. Though incomplete, the data in Table 6.3 likely represent the best available from African governments on FDI broken down by partner, emerging partners included. However, the limited number of countries covered, the lack of a joint country-sectoral breakdown, reliability issues and the tentative nature of the conclusions that have to be derived from it are indications of the importance for African countries to strengthen their statistical capacity. African countries could encourage traditional partners to help their capacity in this area.

Table 6.4 combines the Committee's measures of ODA flows for a few DAC members, the United States, Germany, Britain, France and Japan, with estimates of ODA-equivalent flows for China, Brazil, India, Kuwait, Saudi Arabia, United Arab Emirates and Turkey. The traditional economic powers dominate in official development assistance (ODA), but aid from emerging partners is growing fast. ODA is co-operation as defined and practised by the OECD Development Assistance Committee (DAC). Basically, it is those flows to developing countries and to multilateral institutions which are provided by governments to promote economic development and are primarily concessional in character (OECD, 2008).

Table 6.4a: ODA gross disbursements (OECD DAC definition) from traditional partners, 2009 (in million USD)

	United States	France	Germany	United Kingdom	Japan
Total ODA flows 2009	29659.2	15538.8	13342.3	11698.3	16452.1
Total ODA to Africa	7997.8	6445.5	2297.4	2932.0	1932.9
% Africa of total ODA	27	41	17	25	12

Source: OECD/DAC statistics (except where specified), last accessed 1 April 2011.

StatLink http://dx.doi.org/10.1787/888932405928

Table 6.4b: ODA gross disbursements (OECD DAC definition) from emerging partners (in million USD)

Emerging Donors	China	India	Brazil	Turkey	UAE	Saudi Arabia	Kuwait
Total ODA flows 2009	1947.7*	488*	362*	707.2	1038.24	3245.8*	527.7*
Total ODA to Africa	n.a.	25.93	n.a.	46.96	147.19	n.a.	n.a.
% Africa of total ODA	25%[1]	5-10%[3]	12%[2]	7%	14%		

Source: OECD/DAC statistics (except where specified).

*DAC equivalent estimations of concessional finance by Zimmermann and Smith (forthcoming) (1) According to Chin and Frolic (2007) estimation. (2) In 2009, 68% of USD 362 Million went to international organisations (IPEA, 2010). Of the remainder (humanitarian assistance, scholarships and technical co-operation) around 12% went to Africa (based on own calculation of figures provided in IPEA 2010). (3) Zimmermann and Smith (forthcoming) calculations. Agrawal (2007) estimates Indian ODA to Africa at between 5-10% of Indian total ODA between 2004 and 2007.

The broad range of emerging partnerships

The China trade is important to Africa but all the other emerging players together outweigh China in importance. Figure 6.6 below shows the shares of Africa's total trade, exports and imports, with different emerging partners. China only accounts for 38% of trade volume.

Figure 6.6: Distribution of Africa's total trade with emerging partners (2009, in percentage)

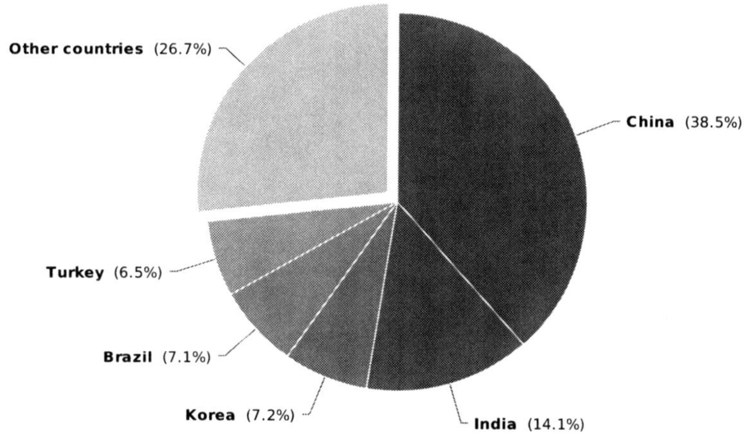

Source: OECD Development Centre calculations based on ComTrade data.

StatLink http://dx.doi.org/10.1787/888932403629

In foreign direct investment, the ranking of emerging economies differs markedly from the trade ranking. Referring to Table 6.3, w ithin the emerging powers, China accounted for about 10% of FDI into the selected countries and this share even showed a slight decline. In contrast, India grew from about 7% to nearly 17% across the two periods. The Sudan country note in this report observes that India is the most important emerging partner after China and is helping to end key infrastructure bottlenecks.[4] But it is FDI from the Middle East that is most striking, about 58% and growing. Direct investment is not, however, the favoured form of investment in Africa for emerging partners, particularly China. So focusing on FDI risks missing a hidden part of the African investment iceberg.

Overall, on top of its quantitative importance as a trading partner and the number of countries it engages with, China is unquestionably leading the way for emerging powers in Africa. Not only because it is at the heart of the shift in global wealth (OECD, 2010) but also because its behaviour and discourse in Africa have helped to change perceptions of the continent. China and most other emerging powers do not see Africa as the "hopeless" continent described by *The Economist* magazine in 2000, but as a continent of opportunities and an investment destination. This attitude is even having an effect on the traditional powers who are reviving their interest with vivid accounts of the "African economic lion" now ready to take its place beside the Chinese dragon and the Indian tiger, according to statements by the World Bank (Okonjo-Iweala, 2010) and a report by the McKinsey Global Institute entitled *Lions on the Move* (Roxburgh *et al.*, 2010). Even *The Economist* revised its view with a feature in 2010 on "Uncaging the Lions".

The number of African countries with which emerging partners conduct trade varies greatly. Table 6.5 tallies the number of African countries with which the emerging powers have total trade above 10 million constant USD.[5] China, India, Korea, Brazil, Thailand, Turkey and Indonesia stand out as having the broadest scope of Africa trade. The smaller emerging nations have a much more limited number of trade links.

Table 6.5: Number of African countries in which emerging partners have significant trade (at least 10 million USD a year)

	Rank	Exports by Africa		Imports by Africa	
	2009	2000	2009	2000	2009
China	1	22	34	30	41
India	6	19	31	28	38
Korea	10	13	15	22	29
Brazil	12	11	10	12	28
Turkey	13	13	13	9	24
Thailand	16	15	14	19	25
Russian Federation	17	6	13	12	15
Chinese Taipei	19	14	10	14	12
United Arab Emirates	20	4	20	4	17
Singapore	22	7	9	14	18
Malaysia	23	6	15	10	22
Indonesia	24	10	9	19	22
Argentina	27	8	3	10	17
Saudi Arabia	29	8	9	0	0
58 others (average)	-	1	1.4	1	2.4

Source: OECD Development Centre calculations based on ComTrade data.

Ranked by total trade volume with Africa in 2009.

StatLink http://dx.doi.org/10.1787/888932405947

Similarly, the number of sectors in which emerging partners conduct trade varies widely. Table 6.6 tallies the number of sectors in Africa in which emerging partners have total trade above 53 million constant USD.[6] Again, China, India, Korea, Brazil, Thailand, Turkey and Indonesia stand out as having the broadest scope of trade across the sectors of trade activity. The smaller emerging players tend to trade in a limited number of sectors.

Table 6.6: Number of sectors in which emerging partners have significant trade with Africa (at least 53 million USD a year)

	Rank	Number of African export sectors		Number of African import sectors	
	2009	2000	2009	2000	2009
China	1	8	9	6	7
India	6	7	7	5	8
Korea	10	6	4	4	6
Brazil	12	4	6	6	9
Turkey	13	6	7	5	7
Thailand	16	4	4	5	6
Russian Federation	17	2	4	4	8
Chinese Taipei	19	4	3	4	4
United Arab Emirates	20	1	6	0	6
Singapore	22	4	4	5	7
Malaysia	23	2	4	4	7
Indonesia	24	4	3	5	6
Argentina	27	1	0	3	4
Saudi Arabia	29	4	4	-	-
58 others (average)	-	0.2	0.4	0.3	0.6

Source: OECD Development Centre calculations based on ComTrade data.

Ranked by total trade volume with Africa in 2009.

StatLink http://dx.doi.org/10.1787/888932405966

As McCormick (forthcoming) emphasises, most attention on the economic changes in Africa is put on China, India and Brazil. But observers are increasingly recognising the contribution to Africa and the global economy of other emerging partners.

If there is consensus on the importance of the major nations there is little agreement on the next tier of emerging partners, maybe because only global giants have a very wide impact. Beyond them, most other partners are important in a limited number of countries and sectors. Scott *et al.* (2010) look for the emerging middle powers that also have significant links in Africa. Applying these criteria to the countries in Table 6.5., Korea and Turkey stand out as obvious candidates for the second tier of Africa's emerging partners, which tend to concentrate on more specialist sectors in a few countries.

This diversity of partners is a tremendous opportunity for Africa. Each wave of countries engaging with Africa brings with it a new array of products, capital goods, technology, know-how and development experience. Each brings new opportunities to trade goods, knowledge and models.

China has a perceived comparative advantage in infrastructure development (Foster *et al.*, 2008), India in learning, skill-intensive areas and services (Sidiropoulos, 2011; Kragelund, 2008), and Brazil in agriculture and agro-processing (White, 2010; Ejigu, 2008). Africa's needs are perhaps most crying in infrastructure, so policy makers and analysts have focused on China. However, Africa's development needs go further. As the 2009 *African Economic Outlook* (AfDB, OECD and UNECA, 2009) highlighted, Africa can use information technology to circumvent some infrastructure bottlenecks. Africa's needs and potential in agriculture – especially in terms of food security and employment (Dorward *et al.*, 2004; Diao *et al.*, 2006; FAO, 2008) – mean new partners such as Brazil are well placed to help the continent move forward.

New and old partners help Africa in complementary ways

The rise of Africa's emerging partners has been widely analysed in terms of a scramble for African resources. The overall picture is more complex and more positive however. New trade routes opened up by the new economies create new opportunities for technology transfer, and the greater range of finance and co-operation possibilities is a boost to African policy makers.

Emerging partners compete for access to Africa's resources, but closer inspection of trade and investment flows in other sectors reveals more complementarity than competition. That is explicitly shown in the case of development co-operation. The 2008 Accra Agenda for Action welcomed co-operation partnerships between African countries and emerging partners and praised South-South co-operation as a "valuable complement to North-South Co-operation" (Zimmermann and Smith, forthcoming). The emerging partners are not a homogenous group however. The opportunities they offer differ in sectors, types of goods traded, underlying technologies and innovation, geographical focus and financing. There are various complementarities between the old and new partners.

Complementarities in products traded ...

African countries buy different goods from the emerging partners compared to those they get from Europe and North America. Imports of affordable consumer goods from Asia help African consumers increase their purchasing power and improve living standards. More affordable and more adapted production goods help African firms increase productivity and move up the global value chain. Typically, flows from the traditional powers are in services, telecommunications and tourism. Consistent with Vernon's global product cycle, the emerging partners are more active in manufacturing and in agriculture.

Table 6.7a illustrates the types of goods in which each country's exports to Africa are concentrated and reveals complementarity between emerging and traditional partners. For instance, the share of commodities, fuels and less sophisticated products among exports from the traditional powers are typically below average while these are above average for several emerging partners. However, China stands out among the new powers in terms of its wide array of products exported to Africa, which compares favourably with the range from Europe and North America. Other emerging partners have a narrower range of exports and in sectors that complement their rivals.

In terms of imports (Table 6.7b), there is clearly competition between the emerging and traditional powers for minerals, oil, precious stones and . The concentration in trade with the old and new partners tend to follow more similar patterns, illustrating the "scramble for resources". The United States, together with the larger emerging partners Brazil, Indonesia, India and China, stand out as the most "commodity-hungry" importers – those for whom oil and minerals account for a disproportionate share of total imports. This benefits resource-rich African countries and offers greater scope for policy making. Beyond this, the emerging powers also contribute to the exploration and exploitation of reserves through their investment and help build up infrastructure and transport. They are enlarging Africa's pool of exploitable resources beyond what the traditional powers alone could handle. The note on Sudan in this report says that although the bulk of investment from emerging partners is resource seeking, it comes with the prospect of leveraging resource-backed loans for crucial infrastructure projects in education, energy and public utilities.

Table 6.7a. Distribution of Africa and its main economic partners by sector (2009): Exports to Africa

Partners	**Foods**			**Raw Mat.**	**Fuels**	**Chem**	**Manufactured goods**				
Sector code[9]	**0**	**1**	**4**	**2**	**3**	**5**	**9**	**8**	**6**	**7**	**Total**
EU25	7.4	**1.3**	0.3	2.3	8.4	**11.4**	2.8	7.3	16.5	**42.1**	100
Other TPs	**14**	0.2	0.1	**3.1**	1.8	**10.8**	1.9	4.2	9.7	**54.3**	100
USA	**12.6**	0.3	**1.7**	**4.9**	8.3	8.7	**11.5**	6.1	6.4	**39.6**	100
China	2.9	0.1	0	0.4	0.6	5.6	0	**18.4**	**30.7**	**41.2**	100
India	5.1	1	0.1	1.3	**19.6**	**17.9**	0.3	5.9	**22.4**	26.6	100
Korea	0.3	0.1	0	0.9	1.3	9.3	0	1.6	9.3	**77.2**	100
Brazil	**46.9**	**2.3**	**2**	**7.6**	3.6	4.4	0.1	2.7	9.5	20.8	100
Turkey	6.1	0.6	0.1	0.5	5.5	5.3	**6.8**	7.4	**46.5**	21.1	100
Thailand	**46.5**	0.4	0.1	0.9	1.5	5.3	0	4	**18.4**	23	100
Russia	**29.2**	0.1	**2.3**	**8.3**	**21.6**	8.1	**4.3**	1.6	17.5	7	100
Chinese Taipei	1.2	0.1	0	0.9	3.1	**12.6**	0.6	6.7	**26.3**	**48.5**	100
United Arab Emirates	**13**	**1.1**	0.6	**3.9**	7.7	**20.2**	**3.6**	**7.7**	16.4	25.9	100
Singapore	1.4	0.1	**2.5**	0.4	**18.9**	4	**43.4**	2.3	4.7	22.4	100
Malaysia	7	0.2	**41.8**	**3**	0.5	8	0.5	7.3	13.3	18.3	100
Indonesia	9.8	0.6	**27.1**	2.5	0.4	**13.5**	-	7.6	**25.9**	12.6	100
Argentina	**63.9**	0.3	**18**	**4.9**	2.4	1.2	-	0.4	7.2	1.6	100
Other Countries	**23.8**	0.7	**3.4**	**4.9**	**9.8**	**12**	1.8	3.3	**25.2**	15.2	100
Intra-African	12	2.7	1	4.4	36.4	8.7	1.1	6.1	14.2	13.4	100
World	**10.4**	**1**	**1.3**	**2.6**	**9.8**	**9.7**	**3**	**7.6**	**18**	**36.5**	100

Source: OECD Development Centre calculations based on ComTrade data. Note: The STIC codification of ComTrade has ten sectors : (0) food & live animals ; (1) beverages and tobacco; (2) crude mater (excluding food and fuels); (3) mineral fuel and lubricants; (4) animal and vegetable oil, fat, and wax; (5) chemicals products; (6) manufactured goods; (7) machinery and transport equipment; (8) miscellaneous manufactured articles; (9)other refined commodities. Columns have been ranked by average degree of industrial sophistication.

StatLink http://dx.doi.org/10.1787/888932403648

Table 6.7b. Distribution of trade between Africa and its main economic partners by sector (2009): Imports from Africa

Partners	**Foods**			**Raw Mat.**	**Fuels**	**Chem**	**Manufufactured goods**				
Sector code	**0**	**1**	**4**	**2**	**3**	**5**	**9**	**8**	**6**	**7**	**Total**
EU25	**11.5**	**0.8**	0.3	4.5	57.1	2.3	1.5	**7.4**	7.7	**6.9**	100
Other TPs	**8.3**	**1**	0.3	**10**	46.1	2.6	1.1	2.1	**23.6**	5.1	100
USA	2.3	0.2	0.2	2.1	**82**	1.2	0.6	3.4	5.1	3.1	100
China	0.9	0.4	0.1	**17.9**	**60.8**	1.3	2.3	0.3	**15**	1.1	100
India	3.6	0	0	**7.3**	**66**	**7**	**12.1**	0.2	3.2	0.6	100
Korea	1.7	**0.9**	0	**12**	57.2	1	0	0.8	**23.7**	2.6	100
Brazil	1.5	0.1	0	1.3	**87.4**	**6**	-	0.1	2.1	1.4	100
Turkey	4.7	**0.9**	0	**7.6**	25.9	**11**	**35.9**	1.8	7.8	4.4	100
Thailand	5.5	0.1	0	**21.5**	37.4	**9.3**	3.3	1.1	**17.3**	4.5	100
Russia	**59.6**	**11.5**	0.2	**11.3**	0	1.4	0.1	**8.1**	4.9	2.9	100
Chinese Taipei	0.5	0.2	0	4.9	**75.6**	1.5	0.2	0.4	**15.4**	1.2	100
United Arab Emirates	**9.8**	0.3	0.2	2.6	2.4	2.3	**62.4**	2.1	**13.6**	4.3	100
Singapore	**17**	0.5	0	3.2	22.7	**8.7**	2.9	3.2	**16.4**	**25.4**	100
Malaysia	**13.6**	0.7	**0.5**	**25.1**	31.6	2.5	0.2	0.5	**19**	**6.2**	100
Indonesia	6.4	0.4	0	**15.2**	**67.7**	**4.6**	-	0.8	3.7	1.3	100
Argentina	2.2	**2.4**	0	**11.9**	33.2	**30.9**	-	1.1	**11.7**	**6.6**	100
Saudi Arabia	**30.3**	**1**	0.3	3.3		1.3	**32.6**	1.4	**24.1**	**5.7**	100
Other Countries	**16.1**	**2.8**	**0.5**	**10.9**	39.7	**10.3**	2.3	3.2	8.7	5.5	100
Intra-African	11.5	1.7	1.2	4.2	32	10.3	0.4	4.6	16.1	18	100
World	**7.9**	**0.8**	**0.3**	**6.6**	**58**	**3.4**	**3.3**	**4.2**	**9.9**	**5.6**	100

Source: OECD Development Centre calculations based on ComTrade data. Note: The STIC codification of ComTrade has ten sectors : (0) food & live animals ; (1) beverages and tobacco; (2) crude mater (excluding food and fuels); (3) mineral fuel and lubricants; (4) animal and vegetable oil, fat, and wax; (5) chemicals products; (6) manufactured goods; (7) machinery and transport equipment; (8) miscellaneous manufactured articles; (9)other refined commodities. Columns have been ranked by average degree of industrial sophistication.

StatLink http://dx.doi.org/10.1787/888932403648

Complementarity is observed in development co-operation as well. In recent decades, traditional partners have focused co-operation efforts on poverty reduction, social sectors and governance. In 1990, 82% of ODA was allocated to agriculture, industry, economic infrastructure and the financial sector. Agriculture and industry saw their share halved by 2004, while the shares for health, education and governance more than doubled over the same period to about 51% of all aid flows in 2004 (Harrigan, 2007). The country notes in this report emphasise that the co-operation programmes of emerging partners complement this sectoral focus by traditional partners. Emerging partners, not just China, seem to focus more on infrastructure and other structural bottlenecks. The Cape Verde note shows that traditional partners focus on governance and institutional capacity building while emerging partners tend to support public infrastructure and human capital formation through university exchange programmes, etc. In Mauritius, emerging partners' engagement targets government priority sectors such as manufacturing, construction, hospitality and the real estate sectors where traditional partners are not present. In Mozambique or Chad, traditional partners tend to intervene in social sectors while emerging partners tend to focus on agriculture and infrastructure or productive projects. The *African Economic Outlook* stakeholder survey confirms that emerging partners are perceived as more effective partners for a number of development objectives (Figure 6.7).[10] This impression is also found in studies: Kragelund (2010) identifies infrastructure and agriculture as key target sectors for Brazil, China and India.

… in technology and innovation …

African countries stand to benefit from Bottom-of-the-Pyramid (BOP)[11] technologies through FDI and other investment and finance from the emerging powers. First, technology embodied in imports from new partners is more likely to contribute to upgrading than those from traditional partners. Despite significantly lower wages, production of high value-added products is rarely transferred to poor countries because of the difficulty of reaching a given level of quality at competitive prices. The most important missing ingredient in technology acquisition is production knowledge, or "the routines of production that cannot be learnt through manuals but have to be acquired through actual practice", which lie at the heart of most innovations (Khan, 2009). When the technology has been designed in a developing country, it makes it easier to adopt, acquire and imitate in African countries (OECD, 2010). Obviously, this does not imply that African countries can readily absorb these technologies. The above argument focuses on the supply side, while on the demand side some African countries are more technology-ready than others.

Figure 6.7: Perceived competitive advantage of various types of development partners in Africa

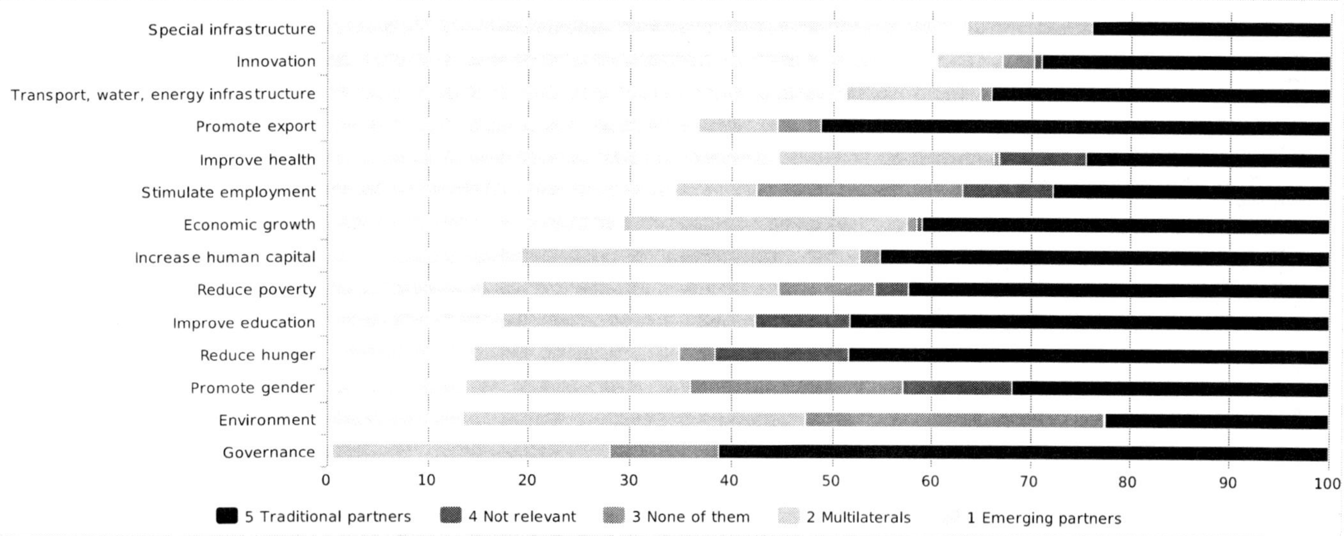

Source: AEO 2011 stakeholder survey.

Figure plots answers to the following question: Who among the following partners are typically most effective at meeting the development objectives of the country?

Second, with the emerging powers increasingly the source of innovation, research and development is no longer the exclusive domain of traditional powers (Hollanders & Soete, 2010). A wave of south-bred innovation will sweep African countries via trade, investment and migratory flows from the emerging economies. African consumers will increasingly buy products incorporating cheaper core technology that meets the needs of poor people (Kaplinsky, forthcoming). In addition, Pal (2008) finds a trend of emerging partners widening their range of investment in Africa as they find an increasingly skilled yet affordable labour force.

… and in geographical focus

Complementarity between emerging partners and traditional partners also exists from a geographical perspective. Table 6.8a shows where Africa's exports went in 2009, and the allocation of this share across African regions. Traditional partners are more present in northern and western Africa while the new powers are more visible in central, eastern and southern Africa. For African imports (Table 6.8b), the traditional powers have a marked presence in northern and southern Africa while the new powers have their footprint in western and eastern Africa. Geography alone does not dictate trade routes, however: southern Africa lies farther away from Europe than any of Africa's regions, but sources about 40% of its imports from Europe, more than western

Africa, geographically closer to Europe. Other systemic, historical and cultural factors are at play.

China and other emerging powers are known to engage countries to which the traditional partners have paid less attention, because it is easier to penetrate their markets. Based on OECD data, the ten top African recipients of OECD investment are South Africa, Egypt, Nigeria, Morocco, Algeria, Congo, Libya, Mauritius, Tunisia and Ghana. China's top recipients are also South Africa, Egypt, Algeria, Mauritius and Nigeria but its list also includes Zambia, Sudan, Democratic Republic of Congo, Ethiopia, Tanzania, Madagascar and Guinea, according to China's Ministry of Commerce (2010). Interestingly, while Egypt is the second FDI destination of OECD countries in Africa, Chinese FDI stock in 2009 in Egypt (USD 285 billion) is roughly the same as in Ethiopia (USD 283.4 billion).

Table 6.8a: Distribution of Africa's exports by type of partners (2009, in percentage)

	Exports (distribution by partners)							
	Eastern Africa	**Middle Africa**	**Northern Africa**	**Southern Africa**	**Western Africa**	**Total Africa**	**Non oil group**	**Oil group**
Total traditional partners	45.9	52.1	73.6	50	65.6	62	57	62.8
EU25	36.8	19.9	57.5	29.6	33.1	39.5	45.9	38.4
Other traditional partners	3.6	3.9	4.9	11.5	3.2	5.6	4.7	5.8
United States	5.5	28.3	11.2	8.9	29.3	16.9	6.4	18.6
Total emerging partners	34.7	44.2	22.5	31.8	27	29.8	29.7	29.8
China	11.5	29	7.2	14.1	3.3	12	9.4	12.4
India	3.4	6.3	2.9	6.6	9.4	5.5	4.6	5.7
Korea	2.2	1.8	0.9	1.6	0.5	1.2	1.3	1.1
Brazil	0.1	0.6	1.9	0.6	6.8	2.2	0.7	2.5
Turkey	0.9	0.1	2.5	1.4	1.1	1.5	1	1.6
Other emerging partners	16.7	6.4	7.1	7.5	5.9	7.3	12.6	6.5
Intra-African	19.4	3.7	3.9	18.2	7.4	8.2	13.3	7.4
Total	100	100	100	100	100	100	100	100
Total value (billion USD)	20.4	68.7	144.7	76.9	71.7	382.2	52.7	329.8

Source: OECD Development Centre calculations based on ComTrade data.

StatLink http://dx.doi.org/10.1787/888932406004

Table 6.8b: Distribution of Africa's imports by types of partners (2009, in percentage)

	Imports (distribution by partners)							
	Eastern Africa	Middle Africa	Northern Africa	Southern Africa	Western Africa	Total Africa	Non oil group	Oil group
Total traditional partners	31.6	51.2	61.6	56.3	45.4	53.1	44.3	56.8
EU25	20.0	41.3	50.6	39.7	33.3	41.1	33.5	44.1
Other traditional partners	6.4	2.5	5.0	8.8	5.1	5.5	5.6	5.5
United States	5.2	7.4	6.1	7.8	7.1	6.5	5.2	7.2
Total emerging partners	41.2	28.6	34.3	34.9	45.5	36.9	40.4	35.6
China	1.3	4.9	2.1	2.3	2.7	2.4	1.8	2.7
India	14.1	12.5	10.5	13.6	18.0	13.2	14.9	12.5
Korea	10.5	2.7	2.2	3.6	3.7	3.6	5.2	3.0
Brazil	1.5	1.3	3.0	2.0	7.9	3.6	5.7	2.7
Turkey	12.6	6.3	11.3	11.9	12.2	11.2	11.3	11.3
Other emerging partners	1.3	0.9	5.1	1.5	1.0	2.8	1.4	3.4
Intra-African	27.2	20.2	4.2	8.8	9.0	9.9	15.3	7.7
Total	100.0	100.0	100	100.0	100.0	100.0	100.0	100.0
Total value (billion USD)	39.7	33.3	150.2	57.8	77.8	358.9	109.6	249.3

Source: OECD Development Centre calculations based on ComTrade data.

StatLink http://dx.doi.org/10.1787/888932406023

A wider range of finance and co-operation modalities

The emerging powers provide development finance for Africa in a different way from traditional partners. Tracking and comparing the two is a challenge. A look at the investment and aid flows in this section shows that the surge in relations with countries that are not members of the OECD Development Assistance Committee (DAC) has led to a broadening of finance possibilities.

Emerging partners, as defined in this report, are not members of the DAC. The exception is Korea which changed status when it joined the DAC in 2010. This chapter looks at the whole of the last decade however, which is why Korea is nonetheless analysed and included as an emerging partner. Korea's graduation from emerging to established development partner is symptomatic of the rapid pace of change in the landscape of Africa's partners.

The Development Assistance Committee has strict principles for conducting and accounting for Official Development Assistance (ODA). The committee has been negotiating "best practice" guiding principles in several areas. One is the relaxation of restrictions preventing aid recipients from buying the goods and services they need from wherever they can get the best quality at the lowest price – i.e. to untie development assistance from trade. Thus, credit granted by governments that are committee members to promote the country's exports is not accounted as official development assistance. Budget support, although not universally practised, is considered superior to finance on a project basis.

Emerging partners tend to adopt a more holistic approach to promoting exports, supporting direct investment and offering development assistance. In partnerships with other southern countries, in Africa and elsewhere, the new economic powers tend to bundle the negotiation and implementation of activities together. South-South co-operation is based on the notion of a win-win relationship where trade and investment are conceived as legitimate, effective ways to further economic development for both sides. For many emerging partners, development co-operation is only one element of a broader engagement aimed at boosting bilateral trade and gaining access to new markets. International co-operation efforts are often conducted jointly with the private sector. For instance, export credit subsidies are used by a government to reduce the risk of market entry for companies, or to reduce operational costs by creating necessary infrastructure (Potter, 2008; Chanana, 2009; Kiala, 2010).

Europe and North America therefore tend to rely on FDI[12] and ODA in their engagement with Africa. The emerging powers are not yet major players in FDI, but they outplay traditional partners in alternative finance, the growth of which has been such that in 2011 the OECD development committee has started to work more actively on these "other official flows" (OOF, see Zimmermann and Smith, forthcoming). China in particular uses the following:

- **Export credits.**[13] It supports national exporters competing for overseas sales. The sum of all export credits by DAC members between 2004 and 2008 averaged USD 4.2 billion, of which less than USD 500 million annually was disbursed to Africa. By contrast, in 2009 China disbursed USD 29.6 billion in export credit globally.[14] India has a high share of classical FDI activity and low levels of export credit relative to China (Athukorala, 2009) but Chanana (2009) reckons that India's Exim Bank extended credit lines of INR 2 266 million (50 million USD) and INR 4 300 million (89 million USD) in 2004 and in 2010, respectively, of which over 60% were targeted to Africa.

- **Natural resource-backed lines of credit**. China's Exim Bank also uses natural resource exports or preferential access to natural resources as collateral for infrastructure projects and as means to repay a loan. The most famous example of such deals concerns the USD 6 billion joint venture negotiated by China with Democratic Republic of Congo in 2007 which is discussed in Box 6.8. Other well-known examples of such credit lines were for USD 2 billion in 2004 and USD 2.5 billion in 2007 issued by Exim Bank for the construction in Angola of 1 300 km of railways, 300 km of roads, hospitals, schools, social housing, telecommunications network and agriculture investment. These credit lines were secured by crude oil exports (Brautigam 2010a). This mode of financing, previously used by Japan in China, became known as the "Angola model" or "resource for infrastructure" (R4I) deals.

- **"Mixed credits". Emerging partners also use financing packages in which concessional and market rate loans are combined** (Brautigam, 2010a). China is the most active emerging partner using hybrid financing mechanisms including mixes of FDI and export credits, the latter sometimes with concessional elements. Brautigam (2010b) estimates that purely concessional loans, zero-interest loans and grant commitments from China to Africa (excluding debt relief) reached USD 1 billion in 2007, USD 1.4 billion in 2008, and USD 2.1 billion in 2009. She also estimates that preferential export credit commitments amounted to USD 2 billion between 2007 and 2009 while non-concessional finance approximated USD 5 billion per year. Taken together, all these alternative financial flows add up to an annual average commitment of USD 7.1 billion over 2007-09, much higher than the Smith and Zimmermann DAC-equivalent global estimate of USD 1.9 billion for 2009, which accounts only for concessional finance (Table 6.4a and 6.4b).

Emerging partners seem to offer a twin benefit: a longer time horizon that allows for a period of loss-financing, combined with the efficiency of the profit-oriented private sector. This method offers African countries a greater potential to move up the value chain, as resources would be extracted and new value-adding processing industries, such as refineries or petro-chemical complexes, are built. Projects that private actors would otherwise be reluctant to finance are undertaken. China's notable examples include the 2007 credit line of more than USD 6 billion that China gave to Democratic Republic of Congo for projects such as 6 000 km of roads linking Kinshasa to the east of the country, 3 000 km of railways, hospitals, schools and social housing (Marysse and Geenen, 2009). In 2010, China made a USD 23 billion deal with Nigeria to construct three oil refineries and a petro-chemical complex. Moreover, some of the new modalities such as resource-for-infrastructure deals are compelling resource rich African countries to re-invest at least part of their resource revenues into wider national development.

Emerging partners other than China are increasingly emulating China's model of mixing aid and investment, albeit on a smaller scale. For instance, in 2007 Senegal struck a USD 2.2 billion agreement with the Indian government and Arcelor Mittal to launch an iron ore extraction project accompanied by plans to construct and renovate railway lines, and to build a steel industry complex and a port. This year's AEO note on Sao Tomé and Principe reports that India has issued a credit line of USD 5 million and a grant of USD 1 million to set up a "technology incubation centre" for the development of small and medium enterprises (SMEs) and for technical co-operation in agriculture, infrastructure and the hydrocarbon sector. In 2010, the Gabonese government announced a EUR 3.5 billion investment by Indian and Singapore multinationals for 1 000 km of roads, 5 000 social housing units and the creation of a special economic zone to process palm oil. By contrast, Brazil follows a more traditional approach, more clearly separating aid and investment. Arab countries' co-operation practices are typically closer to the Western model although their most preferred aid sectors, *e.g.* telecommunications and tourism, reflect the donor's comparative advantage rather than the recipient's development priorities. A case in point is the USD 540 million investment in Democratic Republic of Congo by Rakeen of the United Arab Emirates to build a hotel complex and several commercial centres.

The impact of those changing practices and broadening of actors on the global governance of development assistance are explored in Box 6.2.

Box 6.2. The global governance of development co-operation: changing patterns

Emerging partners' more integrated approach to development partnerships is not as foreign to traditional partners as one may think. For a start, they used to practise tied aid themselves. Traditional partners chose to give up this practice with the "Helsinki-Package" of 1991 under the principle that tied aid distorted trade often to the detriment of the recipient (Morrisey, 1993). Besides, there has always been some degree of diversity in philosophy and practice amongst OECD members. Japan and Korea have traditionally shown more sympathy to combining trade, finance and co-operation than their Western counterparts. This is partly a reflection of their own experience pursuing economic development and making the best of their own development partnerships. Perhaps influenced by the new powers, some traditional partners are seeking fresh synergies between aid and other official flows, including export credits, to promote developing countries' access to long-term finance. Some of these adjustments can be traced back to the rise of emerging partners' engagement. Like some bilaterals, the World Bank lays renewed emphasis in the region's private sector, job creation and competitiveness. Agriculture and rural development as well as infrastructure are featuring more prominently in traditional donors' portfolios than in the last decade.

Conversely, the emerging nations are changing fast and taking on some of the practices and standards of the OECD committee. As their development co-operation matures, they are hitting some of the challenges that Europe and North America have struggled with: coherence between co-operation programmes and national strategic objectives, controlling a large variety of actors, protecting a country's public image as a development partner. These challenges are more acute for large nations with a lot of government layers involved with a large number of development partners. Some non-OECD countries have therefore started using its standards, for example to report their development assistance. United Arab Emirates started reporting assistance in 2010. Others, like Brazil, are opting to report development assistance according to principles that are close to, or inspired by the OECD principles. An increasing number of emerging partners are establishing institutions like the development assistance committee's bodies to inform and direct their development assistance framework.

A more diverse landscape of international co-operation is thus emerging. First, emerging partners are offering alternative ways for African countries to co-operate with them. Second, traditional partners, while remaining committed to their principles of aid effectiveness, policy coherence for development and aid untying, are welcoming these development partnerships (OECD, 2011) and have set out to promote mutual learning with emerging partners (Bogota Statement, March 2010). A notable example of such institutionalised experience-sharing is the China-DAC study group.[15]

However, a single paradigm for international co-operation is unlikely to emerge in the foreseeable future. This need not be bad news, though. From the perspective of African countries, it is doubtful that such a single paradigm would be desirable anyway. Key voices in Africa actually see reason in emerging partners' rise and successes for traditional partners to accelerate their delivering on the Paris Declaration on Aid Effectiveness. Meanwhile, some emerging partners are adopting some principles and practices akin to those of traditional partners. A negative outcome for African countries would be that emerging partners' "unorthodoxy" is used as a reason for traditional partners to slow down on implementing the Paris Declaration. In this context, DAC donors have repeated their commitment to the Paris Declaration. The 2008 Accra Agenda for Action invited providers of South-South Co-operation to help shape the aid effectiveness agenda. The Busan High Level Forum (HLF-4, 2011) is also conceived as a key step in developing a common understanding of "development effectiveness".

Source: OECD Development Centre

Emerging partners, especially China, are viewed as delivering "turn-key projects" and faster than traditional partners. For instance, this report's note on Benin highlights the fact that, in general, emerging partners are perceived as less bureaucratic than traditional partners. Another important difference between emerging and traditional partners concerns the use of policy conditions, an important feature of multilateral and bilateral aid programmes by traditional partners since the 1980s (Nissanke, 2010). However, the reluctance of emerging partners to set conditions does not imply a lack of control on projects. Evidence suggests that Chinese officials are very demanding when it comes to the use and implementation of credit lines (Aguilar and Goldstein, 2009). Further, emerging partners generally offer project-aid rather than programme-aid like traditional partners. Consequently, funds are channelled directly to the contracted emerging partners' firms, providing a strong incentive to complete projects successfully and reducing the risk of fund misappropriation. For instance, the two Chinese deals signed by Exim Bank in Angola specify that 70% of the civil engineering contracts have to be awarded to Chinese firms and at least 50% of the inputs have to be procured by China, a share even higher in practice (Tan-Mullins *et al.*, 2010). There is no evidence, however, that emerging partners' co-operation is systematically more effective. The AEO notes on Angola and Equatorial Guinea point to concerns expressed over the quality of some Chinese projects.[16]

Can triangular co-operation maximise complementarities between emerging and traditional partners? The AEO note on Cape Verde points to a technological centre project involving several emerging and traditional partners. The traditional powers brought finance and the emerging partners know-how that is more adapted to the African context. The Mozambique note reports that Brazil engages in triangular co-operation on research projects to boost agricultural productivity, notably with Japan and South Africa. Box 6.3 explores the potential for triangular co-operation further.

Box 6.3. Triangular co-operation: making the most of the complementarity between Africa's traditional and emerging partners

Broadly, trilateral co-operation is understood as international co-operation with the explicit goal of advancing development, involving three partners, at times explicitly referring to traditional partners, emerging partners and beneficiary countries (see Altenburg and Weikert, 2007).

Core benefits of trilateral co-operation are sought in capacity development and mutual learning processes: "South-South and trilateral co-operation are new modalities of aid that may have a strong potential for capacity development" (Key messages to the Accra High Level Forum Ministerial Meeting, also compare for example Altenburg and Weikert, 2007). The developed country may act as the mere financier for what could essentially be seen as South-South co-operation, or may be fully involved, contributing its expertise and technical advice to the project.

Trilateral cooperation can also aspire to make use of any specific expertise emerging donors are bringing to the table (UNDP, 2004; Yamashiro Fordelone, 2009). In this context, ECOSOC argues that emerging donors, who are still in the process of developing themselves, "are felt to be better placed and have the relevant experience to respond to the needs and problems of programme countries"[17] (ECOSOC, 2008; for a debate of the advantages of intermediate technologies see CUTS-CITEE, 2005). Emerging partners that have been receiving aid in the past (or still continue to do so) are assumed to bring experience and know-how to the table when it comes to advising developing countries: they often share economic, social and political characteristics and language, enabling them to tailor their assistance to local conditions at low transaction cost.

Examples of high-level political co-operation on development in the framework of trilateral co-operation are still scarce and at present exist rather in the form of small-scale co-operation programmes, mostly in training and capacity building. However, it is manifest that various countries are actively seeking trilateral co-operation, with an increasing trend. Among them are Brazil, South Africa and Mexico. Others, such as China, appear to be more cautious in their approach towards trilateral co-operation. This might well be the case as their success in Africa is based upon the dissociation from "traditional donors", with a narrative of never having colonised Africa and also being a developing country. Closely co-operating with Western states would challenge this alternative position. An explicit worry exists in African states about trilateral co-operation, as it might reduce the bargaining power for African governments by lining up the partners in one grouping.

Source: Sven Grimm and Sanne van der Lugt, Centre for Chinese Studies, Stellenbosch University.

Industrialisation, debt and governance: more fear than harm

While a greater diversity of partnerships can benefit Africa's development, there are concerns that the intense activity with new partners could heighten Africa's over-specialisation on unprocessed raw materials, undo the patient work by traditional partners of reducing Africa's debt burden and compromising the quality of governance. The jury is still out on all three counts. While there is no solid evidence for the fears, the risks exist and call for African policy makers collectively to develop enhanced co-ordination amongst themselves and greater transparency by all partners.

New opportunities for African manufacturing

Available data give rise to careful optimism. African manufactured output roughly doubled over the last ten years. And those goods are going more to the emerging economies than to the traditional powers. Yet economic diversification remains a challenge. As Africa integrates into the world economy and positions itself in global value chains (GVC),[18] painful adjustments in some sub-sectors and for segments of the labour market are inevitable.

The rise in African imports from China, and even more so other emerging partners, can be interpreted as trade creation instead of trade diversion (Berthélemy, 2009), the concepts that have been developed to analyze Free Trade Areas. Chinese development and financial assistance act as a subsidy on China's exports to Africa, *i.e.* a distortion from free trade. Through trade creation, more expensive domestic production is replaced by imports from a more efficient partner country, *i.e.* the country starts importing within a trading bloc where it formerly did not import at all. In the case of trade diversion, a distortion from free trade leads to the replacement of initially cheaper imports from third parties by comparatively more expensive products within a trading bloc (Viner, 1950).

South-based manufacturing enhances the welfare of African consumers via prices and functionality. This report's note on Malawi highlights that the presence of emerging partners allows Malawians to access a broader variety of goods and services. For instance, generic Indian pharmaceuticals are cheaper than brands from traditional partners. Generally, China has become over the last decade the largest single supplier of manufactured products to Africa, representing almost a fifth of all African imports in the sector, as shown in Table 6.9a.

Table 6.9a: Africa's imports of manufactured products, by origin (2000-09, in percentage)

	2000	2005	2008	2009
Total traditional partners	75.5	67.1	60.5	58.8
EU25	57.4	51.9	46.6	46
United States	9.5	7.5	6.8	6.8
Other traditional partners	8.6	7.7	7.1	6
Total emerging partners	24.5	32.9	39.5	41.2
China	5.8	11.9	18.4	19.5
Other emerging partners	18.7	21	21.1	21.7
Total	100	100	100	100
Total value (billion USD)	72.7	140.4	249.5	219.6

Source: OECD Development Centre calculations based on ComTrade data.

StatLink http://dx.doi.org/10.1787/888932406042

Fast rising oil exports during the 2000s, driven by prices that rose from USD 35 a barrel on average in 2000 to USD 100 on average in 2009, make it the dominant feature of Africa's trade over that period. Nevertheless, this feature tends to obscure the fact that African manufactured exports – including machinery, transport equipment and processed commodities but excluding processed foodstuff (SITC 6 – 9) – approximately doubled in nominal value between 2000 and 2009, when trade between African countries and emerging powers equalled that between Africa and its traditional partners (Figure 6.8).

Most of the increase in manufactured exports was absorbed by the emerging partners, the smaller ones in particular. This reflects the broad view this report adopts on emerging partners, *i.e.* a definition inclusive of all Southern partners, not just China or a few "giants". Emerging partners engaging on a smaller scale than China, India, Brazil, Korea and Turkey collectively play an important role in helping Africa diversify its production. Table 6.9b below compares the relative shares of emerging partners and traditional partners as markets for African manufactured exports (as opposed to absolute volumes in Figure 6.8). In 2000, Africa exported 3.4% of such products to China and 14.8% to other emerging partners. By 2009, these shares had risen to 11.3% and 22.7% respectively, largely at the expense of the EU and, to a lesser extent, the US.

Table 6.9b: Africa's exports of manufactured products, by destination (2000-09, in percentage)

	2000	2005	2008	2009
Total traditional partners	81.8	76.7	69.2	66
EU25	58.4	54.3	47.3	46.6
United States	14.3	11.8	12	10.3
Other traditional partners	9.1	10.6	9.9	9.1
Total emerging partners	18.2	23.4	30.8	34
China	3.4	5.3	7	11.3
Other emerging partners	14.8	18.1	23.8	22.7
Total	100	100	100	100
Total value (billion USD)	39.3	68.9	104.1	75.8

Source: OECD Development Centre calculations based on ComTrade data.

StatLink http://dx.doi.org/10.1787/888932406061

An increasing share of Africa's manufactured exports goes to developing countries. Emerging partners other than China take more diversified imports from African countries than traditional partners, and increasingly so. By contrast, the share of miscellaneous manufactured goods in Africa's exports to the European Union's original 25 members, the United States and China has actually decreased since 2000.

Some progress can be observed in Africa's manufacturing export performance, but it remains concentrated in a few countries even though the upward trend in African manufactured exports is at play across the continent. African nations need to attract a wide range of emerging partners and engage with other Southern countries. As Figure 6.9 illustrates, a significant take-off in manufacturing exports is observed in the top African industrial exporters, *i.e.* South Africa, Tunisia, Morocco, Egypt, Mauritius and Algeria; a similar pattern is discernible for the rest of Africa taken together. While most countries start from a very low base, the pace of growth has been actually of the same order of magnitude since 2000. Data for 2009, the latest available, have to be interpreted with caution because of the impact of the global crisis.

Figure 6.9: Africa's exports of manufactured goods (1995-2009, in billion USD)

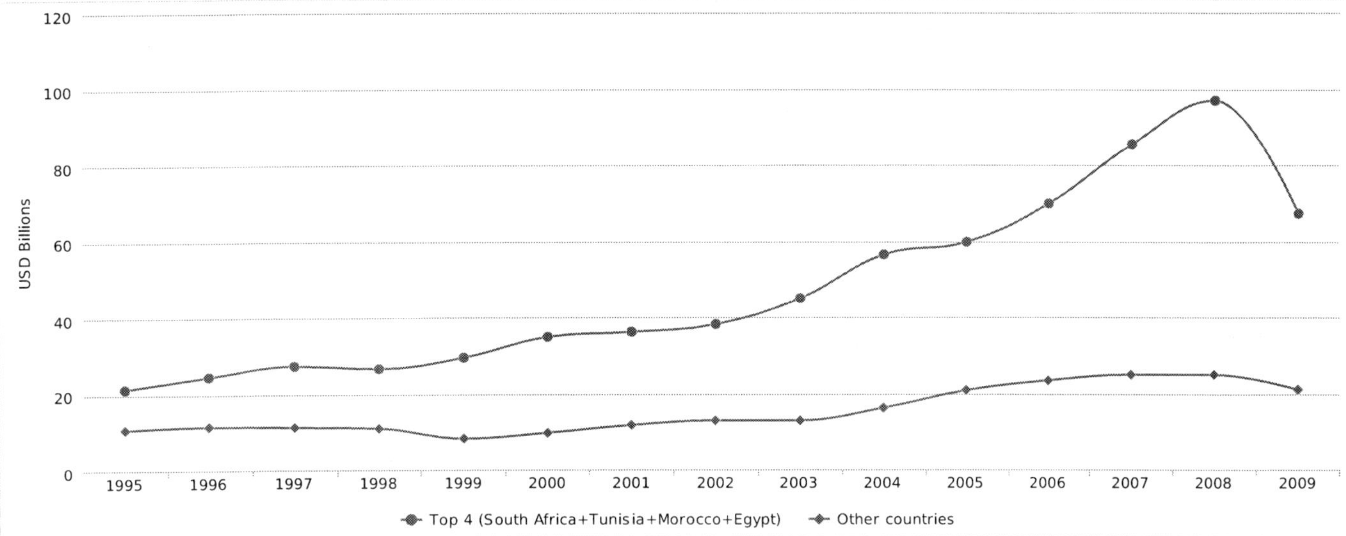

Source: OECD Development Centre calculations based on ComTrade data.

StatLink http://dx.doi.org/10.1787/888932403686

New opportunities for diversification arise from the rebalancing of Africa's economic relations with emerging partners:

1. High commodity prices allow for the accumulation of foreign exchange to finance imports of capital goods necessary for upgrading;
2. Emerging partners are becoming major sources of innovation for Africa. The share of global research and development conducted in developing countries has grown substantially, spreading technology better suited to meeting the growing demand of the "bottom-of-the-pyramid" consumers. Four decades ago, just 2% of global research and development occurred in the developing world, and even then much of it was devoted to meeting the needs of high-income consumers (Singer *et al.*,1970). In 2010, that share had risen to more than one-fifth (Hollanders and Soete, 2010). One driver has been the fast growth in demand by poor consumers, particularly in China and India. Cirera and Markwald (forthcoming) also argue that growing intra-African trade provides additional "South-South" opportunities for diversification and technology upgrading. One example of adapted technology is the use of solar-powered mobile phone chargers linked to new LED light technologies in East Africa. For less than one US dollar a China-sourced system will charge three phones and provide electric light for a family with no connection to the power grid. These consumer benefits are not just in consumption goods, since mobile phones are also important capital goods in agriculture, and lighting helps children to learn at home and in school. Several AEO country notes confirm that emerging partners contribute to technology transfer and diversification: for example, employment creation, higher export earnings, diversification of productive capacity, and technology transfer in Uganda; technology and innovation, employment, and economic diversification in Namibia.
3. Diaspora originating from the new economic powers are an important source of technology transfer through their tacit, specialist knowledge. New techniques introduced by Chinese small investors in farming are a good example.
4. African countries want special economic zones[20] and to copy China's development model by attracting FDI and enhancing the transfer of technology, knowledge and skills (Brautigam and Tang, 2011). The special zones can combine top class infrastructure, expedited customs and administrative procedures with fiscal incentives to overcome barriers to African development (Brautigam, *et al.*, 2010). Job creation is another key goal for African countries, as in the case of the Lekki project in Nigeria (World Bank, 2011). Finally, the special zones build links with the local economy through logistics, forwarding, and insurance and financial services and also when foreign companies contract out transportation, health, catering and housing services to local firms. The AEO country notes observe that Zambia's minerals and Egypt's marble are processed in special economic zones.

Several obstacles must be overcome and adjustments made to seize these opportunities. Productivity differentials between African countries and the emerging economic powers may hold up the diversification of tradeable goods. While African consumers benefit from cheap imports of consumer goods and clothing from the new partners, the further integration of African economies in global value chains may contribute, some fear, to African firms remaining confined at the lower end of production processes (Asche, forthcoming). The most sophisticated product South Africa sends in sizeable amounts to China is steel. The new triangular textile trade provides another illustration (Figure 6.10). Mainly West African countries export raw cotton to China, an important cotton producer which has turned into a long-term net importer (flow 1 in the figure below). Yarn and cloth are sent back mainly to southern Africa (flow 2) as an input into low-tech apparel making at Chinese-run factories for the US market (flow 3). A fourth flow consists in imports of cheap clothing to the whole of Africa.

Box 6.4. Channels of technology and knowledge spillovers

- Labour turnover: workers employed or trained by a foreign firm transfer new skills to local firms by changing jobs or contribute to technology diffusion by setting up enterprises of their own;
- Demonstration effects: local firms adopt foreign investors' superior technologies through imitation and reverse engineering;
- Vertical linkages: foreign firms may transfer technology to local suppliers of inputs or buyers of their finished product. In particular, investment flows by SMEs from emerging partners, seem to carry the best prospects and especially if properly supported in this by public policy.

Source: Saggi (2002).

Figure 6.10. The new Chinese triangular trade in textiles

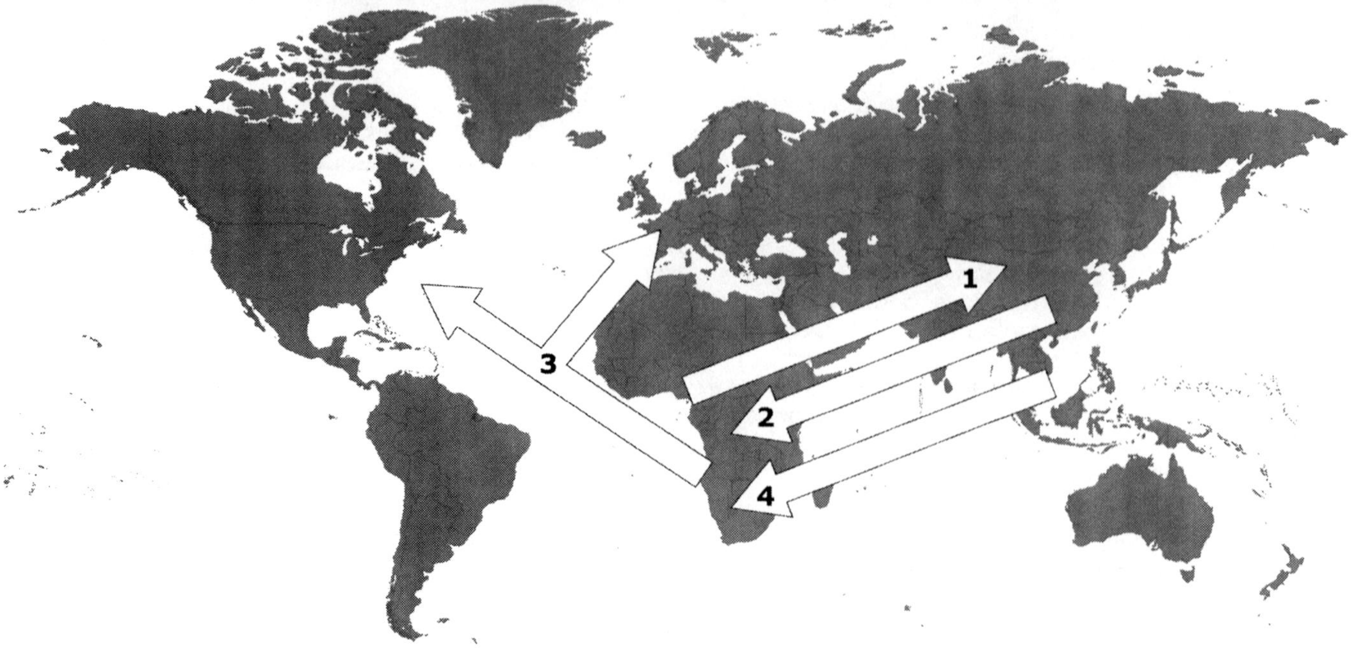

1- Cotton imports from (West) Africa

2- Yarn and fabric exports to Africa (raw material for 3)

3- Clothing exports by Chinese firms in Africa to the USA (AGOA) and EU

4- Clothing exports to Africa (final consumption)

Source: Asche (forthcoming). This map is for illustrative purposes and is without prejudice to the status of or sovereignty over any territory covered by this map.

McCormick (forthcoming) argues that there is no definitive answer to the question of whether Africa's dealings with emerging economies help or hinder industrialisation. The trade, foreign direct investment and development assistance may have different and even contradictory effects. The impact depends on factors such as the form of collaboration; whether projects and programmes fit the capacities of both sides; whether appropriate institutional arrangements are in place; and on general adherence to the principles of mutual understanding, respect, and transparency. Countries should build on existing strengths as they industrialise. African manufacturing tends to be labour-intensive production of fairly simple products, such as processed food, textiles, footwear, furniture, and basic metal products. Comparative advantage in these products may derive from availability of raw materials, innovative capabilities, or traditional skills that can be adapted to new products. Box 6.5 contrasts two examples to illustrate that the strategy sometimes works, but can be derailed by competition from emerging economies.

Box 6.5. The impact of emerging partners on African manufacturing: two contrasting examples

Garment industry: losing to China. Some countries have tried to use the benefits of AGOA to build or revive a labour-intensive export clothing industry. The strategy allowed countries such as Mauritius, Madagascar, Kenya, Lesotho and Swaziland steadily to increase their clothing exports. Since the end of the Multi-fibre Agreement at the beginning of 2005, however, China has massively increased exports of clothing to the United States and Europe. Analysis of COMTRADE data indicates that between 2005 and 2009, Chinese exports to the United States have risen by 457%, from USD 2.1 billion to USD 11.9 billion. At the same time, African countries trying to access the US market saw their market share drop from 2.6% to 1.3%. Clothing is one area in which the indirect competitive effect of Chinese trade has hindered Africa's export development.

Shoe production for the Ethiopia market: small countries with good skills can sometimes win. Like many African countries, Ethiopia saw a flood of Chinese shoe imports in the early 2000s (Gebre-Egziabher 2007; Sonabe *et al.* 2009). In contrast with its neighbours, however, Ethiopia regained control of the domestic market and established itself as a credible exporter of leather shoes to Europe and North America. Ethiopia has a well developed leather sector, which can draw on a huge livestock population (Bini 2004). By the early 2000s the leather sector had begun to upgrade. The shoe industry's subsequent growth was driven by growth of existing shoe firms and new entrants (Sonabe *et al.*, 2009). Many of the new entrants were second generation shoe producers who knew the industry and were more educated than their parents' generation. The new entrants appeared ready to introduce new ideas on product design, production methods, labour management, marketing and procurement to combat the competition from imports and from micro enterprises. The emerging shoe cluster in Addis Ababa seems to have benefited from the availability of raw materials, entrepreneurs' experience and skills in shoemaking, and their ability and willingness to innovate, especially to improve quality (see also UNIDO, 2009).

Source: McCormick (forthcoming).

The risk of high commodity prices exacerbating the over-specialisation on natural resources may be overblown. The 2003-08 commodity price boom was largely driven by increasing demand from China and India (Farooki, 2010). This so-called commodity-price "supercycle" increases the risk of Dutch Disease for African countries – over-specialisation in natural resource exports increases financial windfalls that harm the competitiveness of the non-resource sector through currency appreciation and wage pressures (Corden and Neary, 1982). In practice, however, Dutch-Disease effects caused by the emerging powers are normally limited. First, wage pressures are likely to be small since China takes a lot of Chinese labour for its resource projects, for instance in resource for infrastructure deals (Christensen, 2010). Second, since non-resource trading activities are underdeveloped in Africa, the major issue is to enhance productivity in the non-resource sector rather than avoid external shocks from currency appreciations (Goldstein *et al.*, 2006). Third, Chinese investment in resources has actually financed much-needed infrastructure, removing constraints on growth. Although the Angolan economy remains highly dependent on resources, in 2010 the non-oil sector grew at a faster pace than the oil sector for the third straight year (see the country note for Angola). Fourth, there is no evidence that emerging partners are responsible for some kind of political "resource-curse" as there is no evidence that governance in any African country is worsening because of the new economies.

Special economic zones in Africa have yet to show their potential for technology transfer, value addition and job creation. By 2010, six special zones were under construction in Africa with China's help (Table 6.10). However, not all of them can be expected to succeed, for the same reasons as export processing zones have not always successfully promoted diversification. Whether the economic benefits from special zones will pay back the costs incurred for roads, utilities and telecommunication networks remains an open question, as Ancharaz (forthcoming) shows. The number of special zones in Africa is too small to spark a continent-wide industrial push. Opportunities for technology spillovers are more limited in cases where local firms are barred from the zones – as in Mauritius – or if participation is restricted as some other zones do (Ancharaz, ibid.). Moreover, many countries in need of an industrial zone have been receiving attention from the Chinese developers while those hosting the SEZs are arguably not prepared to benefit fully from the effort.

The fiscal costs of special zones needs to be reviewed as well as the burden they impose on existing infrastructure. The 2010 *African Economic Outlook* emphasised the risks associated with treating local and foreign owners of capital differently in terms of public resource mobilisation. Governments will certainly lose tax revenue from special zones because of the many fiscal concessions granted to operators from emerging economies. Moreover, they may face heavier debt service charges as a result of borrowing to finance infrastructure and services.

Benefiting from knowledge and skill transfers through special economic zones depends on how they are set up (Brautigam and Tang, 2011). African governments must strategically engage zone developers by inviting local investors into the zones, building links to research and development institutes, planning the long-term transfer of shareholder relations, as China did with the special zones it created, sometimes with Singapore partners. In addition, special zones must be a part of a larger regional development plan. The Lekki Free Trade Zone in Nigeria is presented as part of the development for a new city on the Lekki peninsula. The objective is to build a free trade zone and international city to develop trade, tourism and industry. To make the zones benefit Africa, policy makers need to give strong incentives to emerging economies, so they can apply the same stick-and-carrot strategy that was so successful in the emerging nations to foster private business. The Chinese-developed Jin Fei Zone in Mauritius is part of a government effort to attract foreign investment and take advantage of the country's position as a gateway between Asia and Africa. The zone agreement specifies that if the developer cannot meet performance indicators, including attracting about USD 700 million of FDI within eight years, it will have to return the land to the government (World Bank, 2010).

Table 6.10. Overview of China's official African trade and economic co operation zones

Country/ zone	Total investment	Start of planning	Current status	Developers	Industry focus
Zambia, Chambishi	USD 410 million	2003	In operation/ under construction	China Non-ferrous Metal Mining Group	Copper and copper mining-related industries
Zambia, Lusaka	Subzone	Not available	Under construction	China Nonferrous Metals Corporation	Garments, food appliances, tobacco, electronics
Nigeria, Lekki	USD 369 million	2003	Under construction	China Civil Engineering Construction, Jiangning Development Corporation, Nanjing Beyond, China Railway	Transport equipment, textile and light industries, home appliances, telecommunications
Nigeria, Ogun	USD 500 million for the first phase	Early 2004	Under construction	Guangdong Xinguang, South China Developing Group	Construction materials and ceramics, ironware, furniture, wood processing, medicine, computers, lighting
Mauritius, Jin Fei (originally Tianli)	USD 940 million	2006-07	Under construction	Shanxi-Tianli Group, Shanxi Coking Coal Group, Taiyuan Iron and Steel Company	Property development, services (tourism, education, finance), manufacturing (textile and apparel, machinery, high-tech industries)
Ethiopia, Oriental (Eastern)	USD 101 million	2006-07	Under construction	Yonggang (withdrew), Qiyuan Group, Jianglian International Trade, Yangyang Asset Management, Zhangjiagang Free Trade Zone (not a shareholder)	Electric machinery, steel and metallurgy, construction materials

Transparency needed to end debt sustainability fears

Over the past decade, OECD DAC members and multilateral banks eliminated a major part of the debt owed by sub-Saharan African nations as part of the Heavily Indebted Poor Countries (HIPC) initiative – launched by the International Monetary Fund (IMF) and World Bank in 1996 and reinforced in 1999 – and the Multilateral Debt Relief Initiative (MDRI) of the Group of Eight (G8) nations in 2005.

Several studies have highlighted, however, that even with these initiatives the causes of critical debt remain (Berthélemy, 2001; Easterly, 2002).

There have been fears that the emerging economic partners would again plunge borrower nations into a new debt vortex (World Bank & IMF, 2009). No general increase has been seen yet, but the risk remains, especially for the most fragile states.

It is very difficult to assess whether the African countries which have benefited from debt relief are falling into debt again. The action on debt was in most cases too recent and information coherent with data from the past is not yet available. Furthermore, the HIPC initiative is only partially reflected in the statistics. Debt reductions only show up when repayments are made by developed countries for debtor nations. The MDRI, on the other hand, is calculated as a debt reduction.

Many of the Chinese contracts in Africa lay down that repayments be made in natural resources, with complex institutional contracts that make repayments unpredictable in financial terms.[21]

The link between the expansion in the number of Africa's economic partnerships and the continent's debt is also complex. Reisen (2007 and 2008) argues that the emerging powers have had an impact on Africa's debt sustainability in several ways:

Financing can increase debt, but grants, which probably represent a substantial part of the total (see above), tend to lighten the burden by making repayments in currency easier.

Loans, including those made at non-concessional terms, can have a positive impact if they finance productive projects that offer a return higher than the interest rate. This is the case in China's loans to Africa, especially those by Exim Bank, and export credits. They are targeted at improving infrastructure and can strengthen long term growth prospects if properly maintained. Classical debt analysis often does not take into account the relationship between loans and future growth.

The emerging countries also have an impact on resources making possible the repayment of external loans: increases in exports, higher prices for raw materials, lower costs of imported products and public works, grants etc.

Figure 6.11: Africa's post-HIPC debt (external debt in percentage of GDP, 1995-2009)

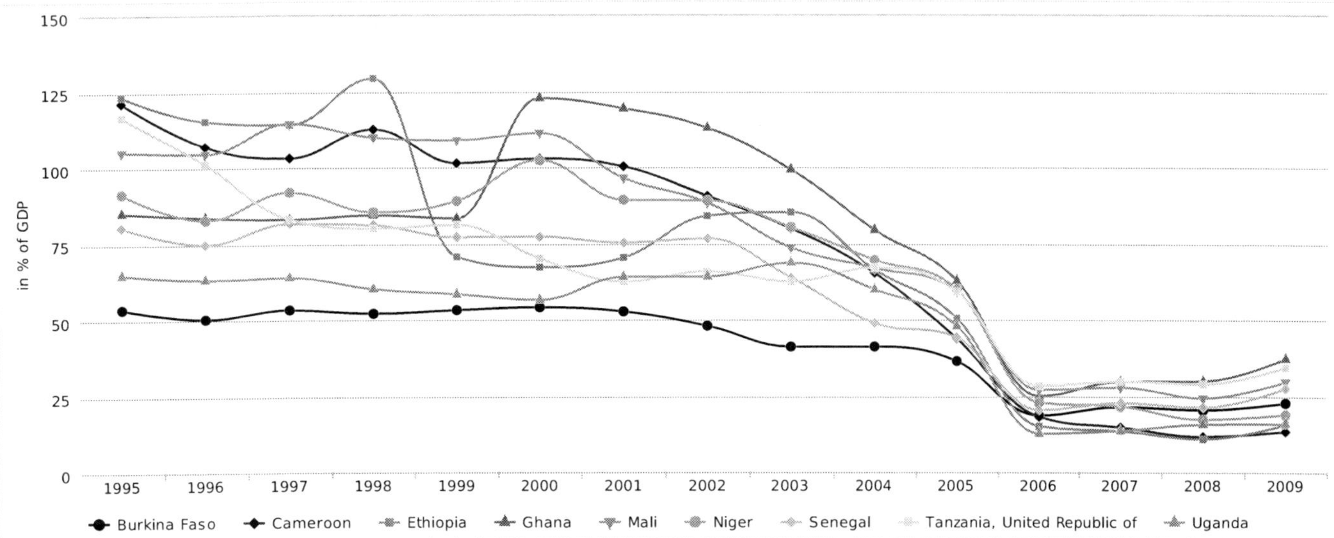

Source: Raffinot and Dahoun (forthcoming), information from the French Development Agency.

StatLink http://dx.doi.org/10.1787/888932403724

With this in mind Figure 6.11 does not indicate any rapid increase in new debt since the reductions accorded by traditional partners in recent years. On the contrary, debt is continuing to fall for countries which have reached the HIPC completion point because they can then get relief under the MDRI. The biggest debt reduction comes after reaching the completion point.[22] Combined with favourable economic circumstances, especially rising raw material prices before and after the 2008 financial and economic crisis, debt reductions have created an unprecedented situation for the financing of African countries. Reisen (*ibid.*) says that overall China barely contributes to Africa's new debts inasmuch as the main beneficiaries of co-operation with China, such as Sudan and Angola, have rich natural resources and have not benefited from debt reductions.

Nevertheless it seems that some African countries that received large debt reductions still face significant risks. Chaponnière (2007) highlights how China's co-operation has spread to low-revenue countries such as Ethiopia, Mali and Tanzania and claims that even if the loans are smaller for countries which do not have raw materials, they can be large in relation to their resources, and also in debt terms if the concessional rates are inadequate.

Raffinot and Dahoun (forthcoming) use the example of Ethiopia to highlight how the emerging economies contribute to the running up of new debts by countries that have benefitted from major debt reduction. According to the published data reproduced in Figure 6.11, Ethiopia's new debt does not seem significant. Nevertheless the most recent figures from the IMF and Ministry of Finance still show that new debt increased quickly after it reached the HIPC completion point at which point Ethoipia also benefitted from the multilateral relief.

Table 6.11: Ethiopia, public debt in % of GDP

	2002/03	2003/04	2004/05	2005/06	2006/07	2007/08	2008/09	2009/10
Public debt	-	-	-	70.5	40.0	39.8	36	40.6
Internal	-	-	-	30.9	28.4	28.1	22	21.5
External (IMF etc)	78.7	73.3	48.9	39.6	11.6	11.7	14.1	19.0
Multilateral	49.6	46.4	39.7	32.2	5.8	-	-	-
Bilateral public	28.6	24.3	6.4	5.1	4.2	-	-	-
Commercial	0.5	2.5	2.9	2.3	1.5	-	-	-

Source: IMF - reports cr08264, cr08260 and cr10175.

Figures on external debt before 2004/05 differ according to the reports.

StatLink http://dx.doi.org/10.1787/888932406099

Ethiopia's public sector debt has practically returned to pre-MDRI levels – it was USD 5.6 billion in 2009/10 against USD 6 billion in 2005/06. While most of the new debt was owed to international financial bodies and the sustainability level does not appear to be under threat, loans from countries that were not members of the Paris Club contributed to the phenomenon.[23] They accounted for 17.5% of total public debt in 2009/10. China's Exim Bank made loans of USD 349 million in November 2009 and USD 25 million[24] in January 2010. China became Ethiopia's third biggest lender in 2009/10 with 11% of its new loans, behind the World Bank's IDA (34.3%) and the IMF on 11.5%. It was also the main bilateral lender ahead of India (4.8%).

The growth in financing from the emerging partners has been accompanied by a change in attitude, especially on the part of China, taking them closer to the lending policies of Africa's traditional partners. China's financing conditions now correspond to the concessionality norms of the traditional powers (Brautigam, 2010a). The two 20-year Chinese loans to Ethiopia had an interest rate of 2% with a grace period of seven and eight years respectively. According to available information, these conditions are in line with OECD DAC terms, say Raffinot and Dahoun (forthcoming). The concessionality rates, calculated with a standard discount rate of 10%, are approximately 58% and 59% respectively. This is part of a general trend to move closer to the practices of the traditional partners.

China has also granted large debt reductions and its increasingly assumes the role of a conventional lender. The emerging economies are seeking a bigger voice in international financial governance not only through their membership of the Group of 20 nations but also their strengthened representation on international bodies. The increase in IMF quota shares given to emerging countries will only heighten the trend.[25] This can be seen in their treatment of indebted African countries where China has announced several debt cancellation initiatives:

More than USD 1 billion owed by Africa's poorest countries was cancelled at the first China-Africa Forum in October 2000. According to Wang & Bio-Tchané (2008), this effectively wiped out almost 10.5 billion Chinese yuan renminbi (CNY), or USD 1.3 billion, between 2000 and 2002.

CNY 10 billion of debt owed by 33 HIPC and Least Developed Countries (LDC) in Africa that had diplomatic relations with China were written off in 2006. China cancelled outstanding debt for the same 33 on interest-bearing loans that became payable in 2009 as part of a three year plan unveiled at the Fourth China-Africa Forum in Sharm El-Sheikh, Egypt, in 2009.

Finally, at the 2010 Millennium Development Goals summit, Prime Minister Wen Jiabao announced the latest figures on China's accumulated debt cancellation so far: CNY 25.6 billion, about USD 3.8 billion, of debt owed by heavily indebted and least developed countries.

China's position is increasingly like that of a traditional lender to Africa. For example, before 2000 Mali's debt to China was "dormant": it was recognised as being owed but in practice no repayment was ever asked for. This posed a technical problem in analysing Mali's debt sustainability as the nominal sum increased while there was no real impact on Mali's repayments. China later adopted a policy more in line with that of traditional creditors, cancelling part of the sum but asking for effective payment of the rest of the amount due.

So, rather paradoxically, the effective weight of debt owed by African countries to China has grown. Even if the terms and conditions for China's loans are different from traditional creditors' (Foster *et al.*, 2008), their philosophies seem to be getting closer.

For all that, China has not openly adopted the standards set by Paris Club creditor nations, nor those of the HIPC initiatives and MDRI (Wang and Bio-Tchané, 2008). In particular it has granted debt reductions to countries, such as Zimbabwe, which are not considered eligible by the Bretton Woods institutions. Neither has China become a member of the Paris Club though it has taken part in meetings that the body has held with non-member creditors and the private sector.

In this context, the Bretton Woods institutions seek to keep Africa's new debts in check by supervising concessionality levels of loans to countries which receive financing from the international bodies. They also use the Debt Sustainability Framework (DSF), which seeks to stop lenders from lending more money to countries that have exceeded their debt ceilings (Box 6.6). This framework is not aimed at emerging partners' financing and but it has also constrained traditional lenders' activities and can potentially act as a brake on lending by emerging partners as well.

To work well, the DSF needs close co-ordination between all creditors. This is hard enough to do between public and private lenders from the traditional partners, but is even more difficult with the new lenders (Djoufelkit-Cottenet, 2006). Their commercial and diplomatic interests could encourage the emerging nations to get around the measures, in particular by hiding information (Reisen and Ndoye, 2008), the more so since the new emerging partners were not involved in drawing up the framework. They could seek clandestine means to be repaid – including through access to raw materials – by countries that would otherwise be in payment default.

Box 6.6. How international finance institutions regulate financing for low revenue countries

As part of their structural adjustment programmes, the IMF and World Bank have introduced conditionalities for external loans, aiming to make sure that countries in adjustment programmes which receive concessional loans do not become victims of new debt which might prevent them from making repayments. Governments have to undertake not to take on debt on non-concessional terms, or at least remain under a fixed low level. This is to prevent a country that receives concessional loans, or grants, taking on debt with "hard" conditions. This would imply a kind of debt transfer – concessional creditors partly financing repayments to other creditors – compromising the notion of equality between creditors.

This practice remains in force in recent programmes such as the IMF's Poverty Reduction and Growth Facility (PRGF) and Extended Credit Facility (ECF). Ethiopia committed itself in its new IMF programme not to take on more than USD 500 million a year of non-concessional loans during the programme. The concessionality rate, which is generally 35%, can rise to 50% in cases like Burundi and 100% for Liberia. This is required for any sovereign financing for a low-revenue country and for some medium-revenue countries, even if the IMF programme does not contain financing.

The World Bank's campaign against non-concessional loans aims to strengthen co-ordination between creditors around the Debt Sustainability Framework (DSF, 2005). It discourages non-concessional loans with dissuasive measures against borrower countries, reducing their International Development Aid (IDA) financing limit or toughening conditions for countries which do not respect minimum concessionality terms. The debt framework aims to stop countries from increasing their debt if they go past certain levels. The levels depend on the quality of their governance as measured by the World Bank's *Country Policy and Institutional Assessment*. The DSF has come under criticism because the forecasts which underpin its analyses do not take into account the relationship between financing received and future resources growth, and it was revised in 2009 to make it less restrictive (IMF, 2009; World Bank and IMF, 2009). It now takes greater account of the impact of growth and excludes from public debt financing taken on by companies without a state guarantee, as long as the operations bear only a limited risk for public finances. See www.imf.org/concessionality.

The risk exists, then, that the fiscal space created by large-scale debt reductions granted by traditional partners will be used to repay new debts, especially on non-concessional terms, to the emerging partners. Ghana is a case in point. Following its MDRI, in 2007 Ghana managed to borrow on the international financial market at rates more than ten times higher than those of bodies such as the World Bank and African Development Bank. Another risk, just as big though less visible, concerns the development of internal public debt. This tends to grow, not only in the emerging countries, but also those with low revenues – such as the case of Ethiopia already highlighted – as internal financial systems strengthen. For most African nations, the Bretton Woods institutions and traditional lenders have little pressure to apply as nations which have reached the HIPC completion point and the end of the MDRI get unconditional debt reductions. Pressure can only be put on the very small number of countries which have not entered the HIPC system.

Tensions have surfaced when debt is reduced after a nation reaches the HIPC completion point. Conditions are applied according to each case. But the example of the Democratic Republic of Congo is among the best documented (Box 6.7).

Box 6.7. Tensions between traditional and emerging lenders – the Democratic Republic of Congo case

The Democratic Republic of Congo entered the debt reduction process late because of its internal troubles. From 2007 contracts were negotiated with China for infrastructure work in return for a mining concession to be operated by a joint venture. At the start the conditions were not very transparent. The deal was said to be worth USD 9 billion, about 80% of the country's GDP. Cappelaere (2011) noted:

"A showdown began with the IMF which opposed easing DR Congo's debt if the state guarantee for the mining part of the Chinese contracts was not removed ... In the end the IMF won. The guarantee was lifted and the contracts scaled back to USD 6 billion, two conditions for letting Congo continue its move toward the 'completion point' so hoped for."

The World Bank, however, maintained its opposition for some time, mainly for reasons of governance in the mining industries (Cappelaere, 2011). Because of its strategic interests, China pressed on with Congolese authorities and ultimately concluded an agreement that allowed it to maintain its presence in DR Congo's mining industry.

To summarise, the impact of financing from the emerging partners is limited so far. In the short term it does not seem to be a threat to the debt sustainability of low-revenue African nations. In any event, China, the biggest creditor among the emerging partners, is adopting an attitude ever closer to that of the traditional creditors. There is still a risk, however, especially for the most fragile nations. Increased transparency in financial transactions between African economies and their partners would reassure Paris Club creditors and strengthen the credibility of the emerging partners as part of the international financial governance structure. Demands for transparency would have a greater chance of success if the African institutions showed greater transparency themselves.

The impact on governance

Contrary to widely held beliefs, there is no evidence that the emerging partners have worsened corruption in Africa (Box 6.8). In fact, there are signs that it may improve national control over the development agenda in some instances.

Kragelund (forthcoming) discusses the impact of the changes of recent years on African ownership over development policies. Ownership is taken to mean using resources to fund a country's own priorities rather than those of donors (UNCTAD, 2007).[26] A first step in the process is forming national strategies that specify clear targets, key policy instruments and effective monitoring mechanisms. Ownership is also linked to the notion of "policy space", which essentially refers to the ability of a state to define its own tailor-made development goals that reflect specific challenges and the availability of resources to attain these goals (UNCTAD, 2007). The new modes of finance and co-operation offered by the emerging partners and the growth-engine effect resulting from eastward and southward shifts in the global economy's centre of gravity both have a positive impact on control over the national agenda.

Box 6.8. Governance indicators: no evidence of worsening as China steps up its engagement

A widespread concern, especially among traditional partners, is that emerging partners - especially China - might harm good governance in resource-rich African countries, and by extension their ability to turn the resource curse into a boon. There is no such evidence when looking at how two of the best known indicators have evolved over the last decade.

When comparing the 2002 and 2009 scores of the **Kaufmann, Kraay and Mastruzzi's** Governance Indicators on *i)* corruption and *ii)* regulatory quality for all 16 sub-Saharan African countries defined by the IMF (2007) as hydrocarbon or mineral rich, she finds:

> Mauritania is the only country that scored significant negative changes on both indicators - but China has not been very involved in the country's resource industry.
>
> In Nigeria, where resources have attracted substantial Chinese engagement, the change in regulatory quality is positive.
>
> In all other countries, neither a positive nor negative change has been seen.

The **Mo Ibrahim Index** measures the delivery of public goods and services to citizens. It lists Angola and the DR Congo among the six countries with the biggest positive change in their score between 2001/02 and 2008/09. The largest increase is reported for Angola and Liberia (+ 15.9 points), Sierra Leone (+ 8.9 points), Burundi (+ 8.1 points), Congo-Brazzaville (+ 6.7 points) and DR Congo, and Zambia (+ 5.5 points). The strong increase for Angola and DR Congo are particularly noticeable, as both countries concluded huge resource-for-infrastructure deals with China.

Source: Wolf (forthcoming)

Co-operation with emerging partners is sometimes described as having "no strings attached" and perceived to increase the policy space of African governments through the funds and increased competition among donors. Some subtle form of conditionality exists in Chinese aid, nonetheless. Chinese aid for infrastructure is often tied to the use of Chinese contractors, inputs and labour. But while economically tied, development co-operation by emerging partners is not explicitly bound to policy conditionality. Even though no simple picture of the relationship between emerging partners and policy space can be drawn, on the whole emerging partners contribute more to the opening of policy space for resource rich, creditworthy African countries (Kragelund, forthcoming).

Positive impacts from the emerging partners' investment flows include making domestic resource mobilisation easier for resource-rich African economies through the commodity boom (OECD and AfDB, 2010). This can help important public investment by reducing the cost of finance, paving the way for greater policy autonomy. Besides, emerging partners' own development experiences point to a multiplicity of potential routes thereby enlarging the pool of paradigms and options that African governments can choose from.

Co-operation with emerging partners is popular among African nations as the infrastructure, government buildings and stadiums are more visible, are built faster and are perceived to be more cost-effective, and less bureaucratic than aid from traditional donors. This report's country note for Benin shows emerging partners targeting the needs identified by the country itself, with faster turnaround than other partners. Similarly, the country note for Burundi reports fast aid disbursement from China. Following a Chinese pledge in November 2006 to build 30 hospitals in Africa, Burundi submitted a request. Work on a first hospital started in May 2009 and was completed in 18 months. In Guinea-Bissau, the AEO reports that China supplied ready-made projects and delivers faster than traditional partners. Authorities consider bilateral co-operation with emerging partners to be less administratively burdensome than with traditional partners, a statement with which the country note for Malawi concurs.

The availability of additional funds is used by African governments to increase policy space, rather than switch between donors, barring a few exceptions such as Zimbabwe. The Burundi country note in this report indicates that new partners such as China have given the government more flexibility in its dealings with donors. For instance, while most partners stopped their co-operation and repatriated their representatives during the 1993-2005 civil war, China stayed on, giving Burundi breathing space during this difficult period. China and Angola have intensified relations, highlighted by several oil-backed loans and credit from China Exim Bank and China Development Bank after 2002. But China has not monopolised Angola's foreign policy. Angola uses its growing economic power to negotiate with other actors (Tan-Mullins *et al.*, 2010). In a similar vein, the Democratic Republic of Congo government has sought to renegotiate its agreement with international actors based on an accord with China Exim Bank to finance infrastructure (Henderson, 2008; UN OSAA, 2010). According to Gabas (2009), the power of African negotiators to renegotiate the Cotonou Agreement with the European Union has been boosted by the presence in Africa of countries such as China.

Emerging partners tend to give priority --and with it, ownership over development policies-- to the president's office rather than dealings with line ministries (Figure 6.12; see also this report's notes on Burkina Faso and Morocco). By contrast, traditional partners have generally dealt with ministers and high-level officials. While the Poverty Reduction Strategy Paper era started a process of decentralising ownership within African countries, the emerging partners may have initiated a reverse process towards centralisation. In Lesotho, the AEO reports that the civil society organisations view China's approach to aid with suspicion, especially noting a lack of transparency. In Chad, complaints were heard about the opacity of the deals.

Figure 6.12: To what extent is each local stakeholder involved in the partnership with emerging partners? (average score)

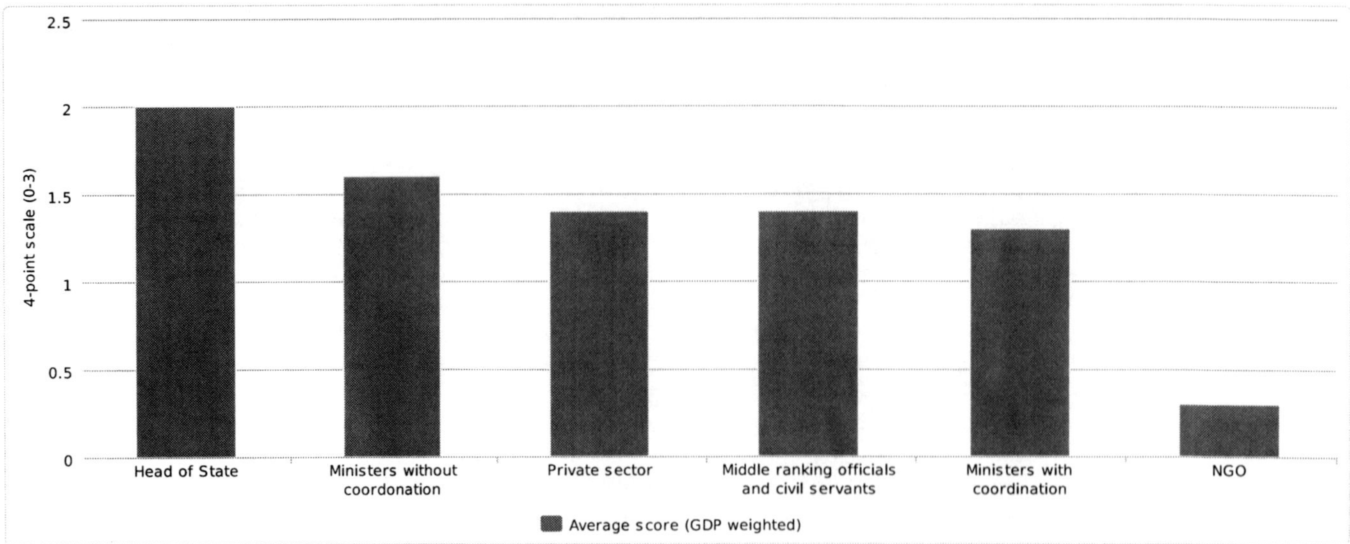

Source: AEO 2011 stakeholder survey. The graph plots the answers to the following question: To what extent does each stakeholder listed below take part in the partnership with emerging partners? "Not at all" = 0, "A little" = 1, "Much" = 2, and "Very much" = 3. Average score GDP-weighted.

StatLink http://dx.doi.org/10.1787/888932403743

The positive effect of emerging partners on African policy autonomy is greatest for resource-rich countries, which benefit from significant investment flows and the ability to renegotiate existing deals with traditional partners (Kragelund, forthcoming). Since emerging partners' dependence on African imports is increasing rapidly – faster than that of traditional partners (UN OSAA, 2010) – primary commodity-exporting African countries may gain further policy space, which could increase their negotiating power *vis-à-vis* traditional partners. But rising commodity prices are not all good news. First, although the demand-led commodity price boom – the so-called "super-cycle" – may continue for a long time (UN OSAA, 2010), commodity prices still tend to fluctuate which reduces policy autonomy (Akyüz, 2008). Second, the commodity boom may postpone necessary reforms. Third, while the availability of cheap loans with relatively long grace periods may finance crucial investments, these loans still have to be repaid.

Seizing new policy opportunities

Africa is becoming more integrated in the world economy and its partnerships are diversifying, revealing unprecedented economic opportunities. But African citizens and investors worry that increased competition in local and export markets will play against them. Governments are struggling to find ways to maximise benefits, minimise risks and provide Africans with the economic and social opportunities that match the needs of a growing population. This requires a leap forward in the quality of policy making and governance, which can be achieved through active engagement with traditional and emerging partners in pursuit of development objectives. Regional co-ordination is also required.

The fast-growing new economic powers have a growing voice in global governance on bodies such as the Group of 20 nations. African countries are also moving on from "post-colonial" North-South relations towards richer, more diverse, more business-centric and more mature partnerships. The changes of the past decade are less of a revolution than a mainstream acceptance of a healthy degree of diversity, complementary approaches and the need for all partners to learn from each other in the pursuit of strong, sustained growth in African countries.

A wider spectrum of co-operation tools is good news for Africa but some longstanding challenges remain, such as the importance of maximising local ownership of the development agenda.[28] This requires a home-grown strategy about how partnerships are to be used as part of long term policies for industry, agriculture and other sectors. As this AEO 2011 report shows, several countries have begun formulating such strategy: Namibia's engagement strategy is formalised and the assistance provided by emerging partners is integrated into the national development plan; similarly, Cameroon's engagement strategy with emerging partners is framed within the country's development vision for 2035. In Morocco, Chinese operators are actively encouraged to invest in the country to counterweigh Chinese imports and ease the commercial deficit; in Cape Verde, the government plays on the full range of partners to modernise productive capacity and infrastructure; in Equatorial Guinea, officials negotiate in Chinese with their Chinese counterparts.

Some old challenges have resurfaced: increased finance can harm the quality of projects funded. For example, large infrastructure investment needs to be accompanied by proper budgeting for maintenance costs and prioritised consistently with a country's development strategy. As Box 6.9 recalls, the continent saw similar challenges during the commodity booms of previous decades and lessons have to be learnt to avoid repeating past mistakes.

Box 6.9. Cautionary lessons from history: Infrastructure spending and African development in the 1960s and 1970s.

The large-scale infrastructure projects seen in Africa in the last decade recall memories of the last major economic boom in the region in the 1960s and 1970s. That boom ended in bust, as economies contracted sharply under unsustainable debt and harsh structural adjustment programmes. The failure of many of the projects of the time became emblematic of an inappropriate development strategy. The building of dams that silted up, useless four-lane highways, huge investments in steel works that never became operational – these are the stories which caused widespread pessimism about development prospects for the region. Too often, the projects were unviable, insufficiently maintained, and inappropriate for the local economic conditions.

Yet it is important to remember the context. At the time, Africa was just getting used to independence, there was much optimism about prospects for economic growth and development. The orthodoxy of the time called for the accumulation of fixed capital machinery, ports and roads. The logic seemed implacable: poor countries have large numbers of underemployed people so labour scarcity could hardly be the problem. It was argued that capital scarcity was the principal bottleneck.

The industrialisation of the Soviet Union in the 1950s, achieved by forced saving for factories, machines and massive infrastructure projects, encouraged the belief that economic growth was determined by investment (Mallaby, 2004). Many post-independence African leaders, from Nasser in Egypt to Nkrumah in Ghana, were impressed with the Soviet model, and inspired to initiate large infrastructure projects in the hope that it would accelerate development. They were also encouraged by the West (*e.g.* Rostow, 1960).

The first warning signs of fundamental flaws came in Ghana. With his plans to turn Ghana into a modern industrial society, President Nkrumah initially made considerable progress (Meredith, 2002). Drawing on plans that had originally been drawn up by the British (Nugent, 2004), schools, hospitals and roads were built at an unprecedented rate, and the major hydroelectric scheme on the Volta river was completed. The Second Five Year Plan (1959-64) allocated even more of a priority to expenditure on infrastructure and social services – 80% of the entire budget. The sustainability of the infrastructure schemes was put into question by changing external conditions, with the precipitous drop in the world price of cocoa in 1961 forcing the government to introduce new and severe taxes, leading to civil unrest. Many of the projects subsequently remained incomplete or abandoned.

In the DR Congo (formerly Zaire), the second phase of the Inga hydroelectric project began in 1973 and was completed in 1977 at the cost of USD 260 million. Work on the 1 100 mile power line to Katanga also began in 1973 and was completed in 1982 at a final cost of close to USD 1 billion, four times the initial estimate. By then, the copper industry was in severe difficulty and expansion plans on which Inga II was predicated were abandoned. Only 18% of Inga II's hydroelectric capacity and 20% of the power-lines capacity were ever used (Meredith, 2005).

In Nigeria oil was first discovered in 1959 and oil revenues began to flow from the mid-1970s. This gave rise to major prestige investments, including the construction of a new capital at Abuja. The government reportedly spent a total of USD 8-10 billion trying to build a steel industry at Ajaokuta steel plant and elsewhere. Ajaokuta was commissioned to start in September 1979, yet 30 years later it had still not produced any steel at all.

What went wrong with projects?

1. The external financing situation sharply changed from the boom of the 1960s and early 1970s and spending had to be sharply curtailed, particularly after the 1982 debt crisis, which pushed borrowing costs prohibitively high and undermined the viability of many projects.
2. Many projects had little or no prospect of economic viability in the first place – some, because of the political nature of the projects themselves (football stadia and presidential palaces), some because of inadequate planning and management. They failed because of inadequate provision for maintenance costs, unrealistic pricings, the prevalence of gross mismanagement (Nissanke, 2010).
3. The human capital did not exist to maintain infrastructures. Hospitals had no doctors and nurses. There was a general lack of engineers and technicians. It was not surprising given skills shortages at the time of independence. Few new African states had more than 200 students undergoing university training. In the former French colonies there were still no universities. According to Meredith (2005), more than three-quarters of high-level manpower in government and private business were foreigners.
4. Foreign expertise did not seem to ease the problems. Foreign experts often failed adequately to identify the right kinds of projects – many of the most resounding failures were financed by bilateral and multilateral donors, such as the Inga hydroelectric project. In a World Bank report (Wapenhans Report, 1992), it was acknowledged that "a culture of loan approval" deeply embedded in senior World Bank management had caused a relentless decline in performance and quality of bank operations. Geographically, the African region had the most problems with some countries having success rates as low as 17.2%. That is to say, four out of five projects in Africa were deemed as failures according to the bank's own criteria (Rich, 2002).

What lessons can be drawn?

History makes it clear that investment decisions concerning infrastructure projects currently conducted by emerging partners need to be properly budgeted for and framed consistently with a sustainable, realistic, home-grown development strategy. Projects that are approved need to clear the hurdle of high and wide relevance for the country's development and chosen to be sustainable not only within the country's current economic conditions but also in times of economic trouble domestically or worldwide.

Source: adapted from Mold (2011).

New challenges are also emerging. A key past issue for Africa has been to cope with the variety of official development assistance programmes of the traditional partners. Yet this fragmentation allowed recipient countries to exploit a degree of competition among donors. The large emerging powers operate on a more co-ordinated scale, posing the opposite difficulty for African governments. Individual countries find it difficult to negotiate with India or China, whose populations exceed that of the whole African continent, and so cannot play off the competition. Most African countries need to enhance their bargaining position to ensure that partnerships are mutually beneficial.

The UN Office of the Special Adviser (UN-OSSA) on Africa in 2010 suggested a framework to guide African governments in their engagement with emerging partners. It stresses the need to monitor trade, aid and foreign direct investment dealings, analyse the strategic objectives of the emerging economies along with the opportunities and threats, and develop a strategic focus to maximise benefits and to gain influence. They must also work with other governments, the African Union, African Development Bank (AfDB) and regional groups to maximise bargaining power and avoid incentive wars.

Kimenyi and Lewis (2011) propose more concrete policy steps: *i)* Achieve national consensus – with civil society and other stakeholders – on national priorities and development needs, and insist that emerging partners channel FDI and co-operation into those areas; *ii)* use the commodities boom to negotiate the supply of infrastructure for diversification, industrialisation and economic development; *iii)* use the "new scramble for Africa" to hold traditional partners to account for their promises on aid, especially in areas where they compete with emerging partners; iv) make provisions for the maintenance of large infrastructure projects financed or constructed by emerging partners.

Kragelund (forthcoming) gives a similar message: African countries should minimise reliance on volatile financial flows from external partners and make sure they use external finance for productive developmental purposes. Resource-rich African countries should leverage their bargaining power with emerging partners to kick off a structural transformation of the economy. They must also build an analytical capacity to monitor financial flows and set priorities and develop an engagement strategy with emerging partners. African countries should acknowledge the great heterogeneity among their emerging partners and seek to balance their interests between them.

The South Africa-China Comprehensive Strategic Partnership made in August 2010 is a blueprint for dealings between Africa and the emerging economies. Both countries undertook to work towards a more balanced trade profile and to encourage trade in manufactured value-added products. China will, according to the document, "increase investment in South Africa's manufacturing industry and promote the creation of value-adding activities in close proximity to the source of raw materials".[29]

Investment frameworks often fail to provide adequate incentives for investors from emerging and traditional partner countries. African governments must make extra efforts to tackle policy and human resource weaknesses that have impeded the work of investment promotion agencies and set up the regulatory framework needed to host, and benefit from, investments, including those flowing into Chinese-developed special economic zones.

Regional co-ordination needed to embrace new giants

With the rapid broadening of Africa's partnerships, regional integration has become crucial. To make the most of the competition amongst partners and acquire a critical mass for negotiations, African governments must co-ordinate policies more effectively and share some of their sovereignty at supra-national level. Existing initiatives under the African Union, including the African Peer-Review Mechanism (APRM) and the New Partnerships for Africa's Development (NEPAD), need to be reinforced and carried out.

Regional integration needs a new impetus. Africa has a clear agenda for economic integration which dates back to the 1960s (Grant *et al.*, forthcoming). However, even though a timetable was set out, progress has been slow and deadlines have not been met. Regional economic communities continue to face the challenges of political instability, poor economic diversification, multiple and overlapping memberships, insufficient financial resources, and poor implementation of commonly agreed protocols and decisions, among others (see Chapter 3).

Traditional partners can support regional economic integration, through their own stated objectives to assist Africa's economic development and the provision of funding, for example to regional groups. Under its African Growth and Opportunities Act (AGOA) the United States put in place regional trade competitiveness hubs to help African sub-regions to take advantage of market access preferences granted under the act. The European Union is negotiating Economic Partnership Agreements with sub-regional groups and is a major provider of development assistance at regional level, with the specific objective of strengthening regional integration.

Emerging partners give help to the financing and building of transport infrastructure, thus helping tackle one major hurdle to regional integration. But more broadly, while the African agenda for regional economic integration has received explicit support from emerging partners, to date most of the engagement has been on a bilateral level (Box 6.10).

Box 6.10. China, India, Brazil and Africa's regional integration agenda

The Forum for Co-operation between Africa and China (FOCAC), which set out China's Africa Policy in 2006 and remains the main framework for the relationship, includes a reference to the African Union and regional groups but is not specific on China's support to these institutions. Some support has been provided for African-led peace and security initiatives, such as the Intergovernmental Authority on Development (IGAD) and the NEPAD. China has offered support for some African Union activities, and recently officials have shown a growing inclination to engage with Africa at a more multilateral level and support regional integration. Yet, China's engagement remains predominantly bilateral, with a strong focus on infrastructure development.

At the India-Africa Summit in April 2008, the Delhi Declaration made it clear that India is seeking to strengthen its partnership with the AU and regional groups. It is not yet clear how this will manifest itself as to date Indian co-operation has largely come in the form of technical training and private sector investment.

When in office Brazil's President Luiz Inacio Lula da Silva was one of the most vocal supporters of Africa's advancement on the international stage, undertaking numerous visits to the continent with private sector representatives. Brazil has however been pursuing co operation largely through bilateral relations. In July 2010, however, ECOWAS and Brazil held a special Summit of Heads of State in Sal (Cape Verde).

Beyond their stated intentions, there are concerns that the new and old economic players and their African counterparts are harming regional integration by striking bilateral trade deals. Asche (forthcoming) argues that this applies to relations with all three major powers: the European Union, United States and China. Bilateral arrangements for investment topics may be fine as long as investment policies are not harmonised in African groups and investment promotion agencies pursue national interests. In trade, however, as African regional groups strive to become customs unions with common external tariffs, agreements on the African side should be concluded regionally rather than bilaterally. Yet, this did not apply to the EU-South Africa Trade, Development and Co-operation Agreement (TDCA), for instance. Trade negotiations over the past decade between the EU and other sub-Saharan countries were meant to have been conducted with regional groups to foster integration, but have become dominated by bilateral negotiations. Africa's regional economic communities are made up of two types of countries. Those classified as Least Developed Countries need not sign proposed arrangements with the EU to continue benefiting from European trade preferences. Those classified as Middle Income Countries stand to lose in EU trade from not signing an economic partnership agreement and becoming subject to appreciable tariffs again, like Cameroon, Côte d'Ivoire or Ghana. In the absence of consensus between least developed and middle income countries on the regional groups, the middle income nations decided to sign individually, in violation of regional treaties, or in small subgroups such as Botswana and others in southern Africa. The EC agreed to separate negotiations with single countries when "complex dynamics in the group" hamper regional agreements, although only on a provisional basis (European Commission, 2010).[30]

On paper, the Chinese attitude is more friendly to regional integration, but in substance it operates in the same way as the bilateral treaties require tariff concessions. Despite the ambitious aspirations of the East African Community (EAC), which declared a common market on 1 July 2010, and a proposed huge free-trade area comprising the EAC, the Common Market for Eastern and Southern Africa (COMESA) and Southern African Development Community (SADC), African regional economic communities will weaken unless African leaders come up with tough backing to put them at the frontline of key trade talks, including with China.

Ultimately, the impact of emerging partners on Africa's regional integration is for African countries to manage and take advantage of international development co-operation, FDI and other development finance on offer. At the end of the day, emerging economic powers cannot map out regional integration for Africa. Their interest is not based on developing country solidarity and Africa's economic health, but on their own economic and political needs (Kimenyi and Lewis, 2011). As le Pere and Sheldon (2007) point out, there are prospects for economic growth from engagement with the emerging powers but the key also lies in the ability of African countries to articulate pro-growth policies; democratisation and inclusive systems of government; improved political and corporate governance; conflict resolution and more competitive labour practices.

At the sub-regional level, governments should consult each other on national and regional priorities, shun "incentives wars" where countries try to outbid each other for investment and aid. Better co-ordination will ensure African countries have more bargaining power (UN-OSAA, 2010). In the same vein, the Paris Declaration on Aid Effectiveness and the Accra Agenda for Action should be put into effect for Africa's regional programmes. As no one country can negotiate with the emerging powers on regional integration, countries need to come together and define a clear and common strategy for engaging with emerging partners. They must identify regional priorities for donor funding and investment. From a financing perspective, many projects in Africa are too small for emerging powers to consider. Only larger regional projects will be attractive for these partners (Box 6.11).

Box 6.11. Sovereign wealth funds: an untapped source for Africa?

Sovereign wealth funds from the new economic powers are increasingly interested in the developing world, and are recycling surpluses towards developing countries.

This represents a major opportunity, as these investments have long-term and stable perspectives, the type of funding needed in developing countries. However, Turkisch (forthcoming) studies historical databases on the funds' transactions and shows that Africa remains underinvested by the operators, despite the major opportunities. African infrastructure investment foreseen by the UN's Millennium Development Goals (MDGs) are only half-funded and Africa will therefore remain highly dependent on external funding. Just 1% of the assets of sovereign wealth funds could fill the gap. The funds have been diversifying beyond natural resources and are particularly noticeable in northern and southern Africa where telecoms and media are popular. Outside of these regions, land has been bought.

However, despite the high returns there are specific barriers to sovereign wealth funds in Africa, which have to be addressed. Some are structural and require long-term policy responses, such as the lack of key technologies. Further, weak sovereign ratings and weak regulatory framework contribute to perceptions of volatility in the returns. Other barriers to investment in Africa are short term. There should be more deliberate and co-ordinated policies to attract and cooperate with sovereign wealth funds. The international community and major financial institutions could also help push the funds toward Africa by creating more vehicles to attract investment and reduce uncertainty through the collection and sharing of relevant information. In particular, the lack of large and liquid investment targets seems to hold back significant investment from the sovereign wealth funds. There is therefore a need for regional co-ordination to offer cross-country infrastructure investment opportunities of scale with the right benefits linked to access to multiple markets.

Source: Turkisch (forthcoming).

The way ahead

A continental level framework for engagement with emerging and traditional economic powers should be developed, probably at African Union level, in consultation with the private sector and civil society. It should aim to outline African objectives and a clear strategy for achieving these goals. The African Union, the African Development Bank, NEPAD and regional economic communities should provide the necessary support for governments to identify national development priorities and monitor trade, aid and investment dealings with emerging partners (UN OSAA, 2010). The UN report (ibid.) argues that the institutions should also "co-ordinate strategic analysis where action is appropriate at the continental or regional level". A race to attract the largest amounts of investment or aid from emerging partners should be avoided. Africa-wide attempts should be made to co-ordinate trade preference regimes with the traditional and emerging partners. This would enable Africa to conduct streamlined trade with the rest of the world at a lower cost. Finally, the same institutions could be used when co-ordinated bargaining is required – and they could serve to protect the interests of non-commodity exporting countries, who have received less attention from emerging partners. Strong and effective regional organisations need well prepared, well structured members that feed valuable policy input into the regional decision-making process and efficiently implement policies and decisions adopted at regional level.

The domestic agenda is equally challenging and calls for sustaining reform. For Africa to reap the full benefits from engagement with the emerging powers, African countries need stable, home-grown, development policies. Opening new space for private sector development is paramount. If Africa fails to form solid strategies and to negotiate proactively, there is a risk that the new global players will push Africa to further specialise in raw material exports. Time is still on Africa's side and it can leverage the new relationships and ensure they contribute to Africa's diversification into manufacturing, services and agriculture. The necessary ownership needs to be established at supra-national level.

Africa does not need more dialogue platforms, but more tangible progress towards regional integration. The emerging partners can help through their infrastructure development. The continent can take pride in its improved macroeconomic management. To preserve this achievement, large infrastructure investments need to be accompanied by proper budgeting of maintenance costs and prioritised consistently with the country's development strategy. Regional co-ordination improves the bargaining power of African countries and helps to raise the scale of investment projects to the level where emerging partners can a make a significant contribution to the development of the private sector, resulting in a virtuous circle of enhanced economic integration at the regional level and beyond.

The shift in global wealth has ended post-colonialism and the broadening of Africa's partnerships reflects the normalisation of its international relations. The challenge is to ensure that this shift results in strong, sustained and shared growth for the continent. To succeed, African countries should unite to take advantage of the competition between those partners and let their models compete and prove their effectiveness.

Pessimists say the emerging economic giants are plundering Africa. Optimists see Africa already belonging to the emerging powers club. This *Outlook*'s conclusion is that there are distinct opportunities but that African policymakers need to ensure that relations with all partners, old and new, are framed to achieve their country's development vision, not their partners'. Spreading the gains throughout African society is the key to the stability and sustained vigour of these emerging partnerships.

Notes

1. See in particular Goldstein et al. (2006), UNCTAD (2010a), UN-OSAA (2010) and AfDB (forthcoming).
2. See Kharas (2010) for an analysis of the rise of the middle class in developing countries.
3. The striking discrepancies in FDI data reported by different sources give a sense of the difficulties related to the analysis of FDI flows: MOFCOM reports USD 390.3 million in 2007 Chinese OFDI flows to Nigeria; the Nigerian Investment Promotion Council reports for the same year inflows from China of USD 43.4 million. Even data coming from different Chinese are contradictory: Deborah Brautigam points out that Chinese official OFDI stock in Nigeria as reported by MOFCOM amounts to USD 795.91 million in 2008 although the Chinese Economic Counsellor speaks of USD 7.24 billion. (Brautigam Blog China in Africa: The Real Story: www.chinaafricarealstory.com/2010/02/chinese-investment-in-africa-whats-real.html)
4. For instance, the Indian Railways — Rites (Rail India Technical and Economic Services) and Ircon — signed an agreement with Sudan Railways for total development of the Sudanese railway system. In 2004 Bharat Heavy Electricity Ltd (BHEL) signed a contract to build a 500 MW thermal power project in Sudan costing USD 457 million. The ICSA (India) Ltd. has signed an agreement with Sudan's National Electricity Corporation for the execution of a turnkey project of USD 139.95 million (2006).
5. This (USD 10 million) threshold has been chosen empirically to illustrate the spread of the corresponding distribution. USD 10 million is equivalent to USD 1 million / sector if country flows are equally distributed across sectors.
6. We use separate deflators for Africa's exports and imports calculated by the IMF. The deflators used have 2000 as base year (2000 = 100).
7. This (USD 53 million) threshold was chosen empirically to illustrate the spread of the corresponding distribution. USD 53 million is equivalent to 1 million / sector times 53 African countries (if the sectoral flows are equally distributed across countries)
8. We use separate deflators for Africa's exports and imports calculated by the IMF. The deflators used have 2000 as base year (2000 = 100).
9. ComTrade has ten sectors : (0) food & live animals; (1) beverages and tobacco; (2) raw materials (excluding food and fuels); (3) mineral fuel and lubricants; (4) animal and vegetable oil, fat and wax; (5) chemical products; (6) manufactured goods; (7) machinery and transport equipment; (8) miscellaneous manufactured articles; (9) other refined commodities. Columns have been ranked by average degree of industrial sophistication.
10. Stakeholder survey methodology: AEO country note authors on fact-finding missions for the economic assessment and macroeconomic forecast gather data from the National Statistical Office and conduct interviews with a range of government officials and representatives of private sector, civil society and international organisations. This year, a special survey was designed to capture and compare the results of interviews of African stakeholders on emerging partners' activities. Responses were collected for 40 countries, representing 83% of the African population and 92% of the continent's GDP. The survey uses qualitative measures on a 5-point scale aiming at providing subjective indicators. Where applicable, answers were weighted according to GDP and/or population.
11. As defined by Prahalad (2005): "those 4 billion people who live on less than $2 a day".
12. FDI reflects the objective of obtaining a lasting interest by a resident entity in one economy in an entity resident in an economy other than that of the investor (OECD benchmark definition). The lasting interest implies the existence of a long-term relationship between the direct investor and the enterprise and a significant degree of influence on the management of the enterprise. For further details, refer to International Direct Investment Statistics, OECD.
13. Governments provide official export credits through Export Credit Agencies (ECAs) in support of national exporters competing for overseas sales. ECAs provide credits to foreign buyers either directly or via private financial institutions benefiting from their insurance or guarantee cover. ECAs can be government institutions or private companies operating on behalf of the government (http://www.oecd.org/about/0,3347,en_2649_34169_1_1_1_1_1,00.html).
14. Conversion from RMB to USD based on the official exchange rate provided by the World Bank's WDI database.
15. www.oecd.org/document/36/0,3746,en_2649_34621_44173540_1_1_1_1,00.html and www.iprcc.org/front/article/article-list.action

16. An USD 8 million general hospital built four years ago by the China Overseas Engineering Group Company in Luanda had to evacuate 150 of their patients after cracks were found in the building.

17. Capacity development on the basis of trilateral co-operation should not be limited to developing countries: as developed countries often pursue policies guided from a developed countries' perspective that might hamper the development of developing countries, "there are requirements for sensitisation and capacity building in developed countries to give the developing country perspective to the stakeholders there" (CUTS-CITEE 2005).

18. Global value chains: "The full range of activities required to bring a product or service from conception through the intermediate phases of production to delivery to consumers and final disposal after use" (Kaplinsky and Morris, 2000); alternatively, "The process of ever-finer specialisation and geographic fragmentation of production, with the more labour intensive parts of production being transferred to developing countries" (Cattaneo, et al. 2010).

19. The manufacturing here is defined as the aggregation of the following ComTrade sectors: (6) manufactured goods; (7) machinery and transport equipment; (8) miscellaneous manufactured articles; (9) other refined commodities. Columns have been ranked by average degree of industrial sophistication.

20. SEZs are generally defined as geographically delimited areas administered by a single body, offering certain incentives (generally duty-free importing and streamlined customs procedures, for instance) to businesses which physically locate within the zone (Farole, 2008).

21. The IMF has applied pressure for greater transparency in contracts, by converting repayments into monetary terms in such examples as the Nouakchott airport in Mauritania.

22. The two initiatives signal a change in logic on debt. The HIPC initiative aimed to reduce debt to a bearable level, while the MDRI sought to end outstanding multilateral debt at 2003 or 2004, depending on the institution (Raffinot, 2008). For countries which benefited at a later stage from the HIPC initiative, the MDRI came into effect at once at the completion point. For details on the progress of African countries in the two debt reduction projects, see Raffinot and Dahoun (forthcoming) and www.africaneconomicoutlook.org .

23. See IMF (2010a and b).

24. According to the Ethiopian finance ministry's statistics bulletin: Federal Republic of Ethiopia (2010). These figures do not appear to include debt owed to the Chinese firm, ZTE, of more than USD 1 billion. Two other loans at market rates were made by China in 2010 for almost USD 700 million. The financial conditions of these loans, which were part of packages, are not known.

25. Following reforms agreed in November 2010, which should take effect in 2012, China will become the IMF's third biggest shareholder (6.39% of the quotas). Brazil (2.31%), India (2.75%) and Russia (2.70%) join the top ten shareholders. Despite the reform, China, which is now the second biggest economy in the world ahead of Japan, still has fewer quotas than Japan, which has 6.46%. http://www.imf.org/external/np/sec/pr/2011/pdfs/quota_tbl.pdf.

26. The focus is thus on control. In that sense, it takes after the definition suggested by Whitfield (2008: 4) that sees ownership as the '*degree of control recipient governments are able to secure over implemented policy outcomes*'.

27. Figure plots answers to the following question: To what extent is each local stakeholder below involved in the partnership with emerging partners?

28. See Zimmermann and McDonnell (2008).

29. "China, South Africa upgrade relations to 'comprehensive strategic partnership'", Xinhua News, 24 August 2010, news.xinhuanet.com/english2010/china/2010-08/24/c_13460144.html

30. Interim Economic Partnership Agreements with Middle-Income Countries have been concluded as "stepping stones" towards full EPAs, under the pressure of the expiration of a World Trade Organization waiver on the previous unilateral trade preferences, in December 2007.

References

Special AEO 2011 papers

Ancharaz, V. D. (forthcoming), "Can Chinese SEZs Spur Industrial Development in Africa?", OECD Development Centre.

Asche, H. (forthcoming), "Domestic Policy Implications of Chinese Economic Engagement in Africa", OECD Development Centre.

Cirera, X. and R. MARKWALD (forthcoming), "The Level of Sophistication and Technological Content of African Exports. Does Africa Benefit from South-South trade?", OECD Development Centre.

Grant, C., M.DUBE and G. CHAPMAN (forthcoming), "How can African Countries Harness Emerging Partners to Foster Regional and Sub-Regional Integration?", OECD Development Centre.

Hugon, P. (forthcoming), « L'Afrique se trouve-t-elle aujourd'hui là où l'Asie se trouvait il y a quelques décennies ? », OECD Development Centre.

Kaplinsky, R. (forthcoming), "Technology Transfer: What Can Africa Expect from China And India?" OECD Development Centre.

Kragelund, P. (forthcoming), "Emerging Partners and Governance: Does the Rise of Emerging Partnerships Increase Ownership of Development Policies and Widen the Policy Space for African Governments?", OECD Development Centre.

McCormick, D. (forthcoming), "Africa and its Emerging Development Partners: Helping or Hindering Industrialisation?", OECD Development Centre.

Raffinot, M. and D.B. Dahoun (forthcoming), « Partenaires émergents: Quels enjeux pour la soutenabilité de la dette africaine », OECD Development Centre.

Turkisch, E. (forthcoming), "Sovereign Wealth Funds as Investors in Africa: Opportunities and Barriers", OECD Development Centre.

Wolf, C. (forthcoming), "Natural Resource Rent Management in Africa in the Presence of New Partners at the Example of China", OECD Development Centre.

Bibliography

AFDB, OECD and UNECA, (2010), African Economic Outlook – Public ressource mobilisation and Aid, Organisation for Economic Cooperation and Development, Development Centre and African Development Bank, Paris.

AFDB, OECD and UNECA, (2009), African Economic Outlook – Innovation and ITC in Africa, Organisation for Economic Cooperation and Development, Development Centre and African Development Bank, Paris.

African Development Bank, (forthcoming), China as an Emerging Development Partner for Africa: Myth or Reality? African Development Bank Group, Tunis.

Agrawal, S., (2007), Emerging donors in International Development Assistance – the India Case. International Development Research Centre, Canada.

Aguilar, R. and A. Goldstein, (2009), "The Chinisation of Africa: The Case of Angola", The World Economy, 32(11).

Akyüz, Y., (2008), Global Rules and Markets: Constraints over Policy Autonomy in Developing Countries, Working Paper No. 87, Policy Integration and Statistics Department, International Labour Office, Geneva.

Altenburg, T. and J. Weikert, (2007), Trilateral Development Cooperation with 'New Donors', Briefing Paper 5/2007, German Development Institute, Bonn.

Athukorala, P.C., (2009), "Outward Foreign Direct Investment from India", Asian Development Review, 26(2).

Bell, R.M., (2007), Technological learning and the development of productive and innovative capacities in the industry and infrastructure sectors of the Least Developed Countries: What roles for ODA? Paper prepared for UNCTAD Division for Africa, Least Developed Countries, Science Policy Research Unit, University of Sussex, Brighton.

Berthélemy, J.C., (2009), Impact of China's Engagement on the Sectoral Allocation of Resources and Aid Effectiveness in Africa. Paper presented at the African Economic Conference 11 - 13 November, Addis Ababa.

Berthélémy, J.C., (2001), HIPC Debt Relief and Policy Reform Incentives, communication à la WIDER Conference on Debt Relief 17-18 août, Helsinki.

Bini, A., (2004), "Upgrading In the Leather Value Chain: The Learning Experience of Ethiopian Tanneries", D. McCormick and C. Rogerson, eds, *Clothing and Footwear in African Industrialisation*, African Institute of South Africa, Pretoria.

Brautigam, D., (2010a), China, Africa and the international aid architecture, Working Paper No. 107, African Development Bank Group, Tunis.

Brautigam, D., (2010b), Chinese Finance of Overseas Infrastructure, prepared for the OECD-IPRCC China-DAC Study Group, Organisation for Economic Cooperation and Development, Paris.

Brautigam, D., T. Farole and X. Tang, (2010), China's Investment in African Special Economic Zones: Prospects, Challenges, and Opportunities, Economic Premise No. 5 March, World Bank, Washington, D.C.

Brautigam, D. and X. Tang, (2011), "African Shenzhen:China's special economic zones in Africa", Journal of Modern African Studies, 49(1).

Cappelaere, P., (2011), Congo (RDC) puissance et fragilité, L'Harmattan, Paris.

Cattaneo, O., G. Gereffi and C. Staritz, (2010), Global Value Chains in a Postcrisis World - A Development Perspective, World Bank, Washington, D.C.

Chamon, M. and M. Kremer, (2006), Economic Transformation, Population Growth And The Long-Run World Income Distribution, Working Paper No. 12038, National Bureau of Economic Research, Cambridge, MA.

Chanana, D., (2009), India's Transition to a Global Donor – Limitations and Prospects, ARI 123/2010, Real Instituto Elcano, Madrid.

Chaponnière, J.R., (2007), "La Chine : une aide difficile à mesurer", La Lettre des économistes de l'AFD, 15.

Chin, G. and R.M. Frolic, (2007), Emerging donors in International Development Assistance– the China Case, International Development Research Centre, Canada.

Christensen, B.V., (2010), China in Africa A Macroeconomic Perspective, Working Paper 230 November 2010, Center for Global Development, Washington, D.C.

Collier, P., (2010), The Plundered Planet: Why We Must - and How We Can - Manage Nature for Global Prosperity, Oxford University Press, Oxford.

Corden, M.W. and P.J. Neary, (1982), "Booming Sector and De-Industrialisation in a Small Open Economy", Economic Journal, 92(368).

CUTS-CITEE, (2005), Trilateral Development Cooperation: An Emerging Trend, CUTS Briefing Paper No. 1/2005, CUTS - Centre for International Trade, Economics & Environment, Jaipur.

Diao, X., P. Hazell, D. Resnick and J. Thurlow, (2006), The Role of Agriculture in Development: Implications for Sub-Saharan Africa, Discussion Paper No. 29, Development Strategy and Governance Division, International Food Policy Research Institute, Washington D.C.

Djoufelkit-Cottenet, H., (2006), "Bilan des annulations PPTE et IADM et perspectives de réendettement", Lettre des économistes, Agence française de développement, 14.

Dorward, A., J. Kydd, J. Morrison and I. Urey, (2004), "A Policy Agenda for Pro-Poor Agricultural Growth", World Development, 32(1).

Easterly, W., (2002), "How Did Heavily Indebted Poor Countries Become Heavily Indebted? Reviewing Two

Decades of Debt Relief", World Development, 30(10).

ECOSOC, (2008), Trends in South- South and Triangular Development Cooperation, Background study for the Development Cooperation Forum, United Nations Economic and Social Council, New York.

Ejigu, M., (2008), "Toward energy and livelihoods security in Africa: Smallholder production and processing of bioenergy as a strategy", Natural Resources Forum, 32.

European Commission, (2010), Trade, Growth and World Affairs. Trade Policy as a Core Component of the EU's 2020 Strategy. 612/4, EU Communication, Brussels.

FAO, (2008), Brazil and African Countries Cooperation - Opportunities for enhancing Smallholder Farming productivity through small scale irrigation and Rainwater Harvesting, Food and Agriculture Organisation, Rome.

Farole, T., (2008), Special Economic Zones in Africa: Comparing Performances and Learning from Global Experience, World Bank, Washington, D.C.

Farooki, M., (2010), China's Commodities Demand, The Financial Crisis And Economic Recovery: What Now For Resource Rich African Economies? Development Policy and Practice Unit The Open University (UK), United Kingdom.

Foster, V., W. Butterfield, C. Chen and N. Pushak, (2008), Building Bridges: China's Growing Role as Infrastructure Financier for Sub-Saharan Africa, Trends and Policy Options No.5, World Bank – PPIAF, Washington, D.C.

Gabas, J.J., (2009), "Emerging Countries and International Cooperation", C. Jaffrelot, ed, The Emerging States. The Wellspring of a New World Order, Columbia University Press, New York.

Garroway, C., B. Hacibedel, H. Reisen and E. Turkisch, (2010), The Renminbi and Poor-Country Growth, Working Paper No. 292, Organisation for Economic Cooperation and Development, Development Centre, Paris.

Gebre-Egziabher, T., (2007), "Impacts of Chinese Imports and Coping Strategies of Local Producers : The Case of Small-scale Footwear Enterprises in Ethiopia", Journal of Modern African Studies, 45(4).

Goldstein, A., N. Pinaud, H. Reisen and X. Chen, (2006), The Rise of China and India - what's in it for Africa? OECD Development Centre Studies, Organisation for Economic Cooperation and Development, Development Centre, Paris.

Harrigan, J., (2007), "The Doubling of Aid to Sub-Saharan Africa: Promises and Problems", Journal of Contemporary African Studies, 25(3).

Henderson, J., (2008), "China and global development: towards a Global-Asian Era? ", Contemporary Politics, 14(4).

Hollanders, H. and L. Soete, (2010), "The growing role of knowledge in the global economy", A World of Science, 8(4).

IMF, (2011), New Growth Drivers for Low-Income Countries: The Role of BRICs, International Monetary Fund, Washington, D.C.

IMF, (2010a), Ethiopia: 2010 Article IV Consultation and First Review of the Arrangement under the Exogenous Shocks Facility—Staff Repor, Country Report No. 10/175, International Monetary Fund, Washington, D.C.

IMF, (2010b), The Federal Democratic Republic of Ethiopia: Second Review of the Arrangement under the Exogenous Shocks Facility—Staff Report, Country Report No. 10/339, International Monetary Fund, Washington, D.C.

IMF, (2009), *Debt Limits in Fund Supported Programs: Proposed New Guidelines*, International Monetary Fund, Washington, D.C.

IMF, (2007), Guide on Resource Revenue Transparency, International Monetary Fund, Washington, D.C.

IPEA, (2010), Cooperação Brasileira para o Desenvolvimento Internacional: primeiro levantamento de recursos investidos pelo governo federal, Boletim de Economia e Política Internacional No. 3, Instituto de Pesquisa Economica Aplicada, Brazil.

Jerve, A.M. and H. Selbervik, (2009), Self Interest and Global Responsibility: Aid Policies of South Korea and India in the Making, CMI Report No. 9, Chr. Michelsen Institute, Bergen.

Kaplinsky, R. and M. Morris, (2000), A Handbook for Value Chain Research, Institute of Development Studies, University of Sussex, Brighton.

Khan, M.H., (2009), Learning, Technology Acquisition and Governance Challenges in Developing Countries, Project Report, Department for International Development, London.

Kharas, H., (2010), The Emerging Middle Class in Developing Countries, Working Paper No. 285, Organisation for Economic Cooperation and Development - Development Centre, Paris.

Kiala, C., (2010), The Impact of China Africa Aid Relations – the Case of Angola, Policy Brief No. 1, African Economic Research Consortium, Nairobi.

Kimenyi, M.S. and Z. Lewis, (2011), "The BRICs and the New Scramble for Africa", E. Aryeetey, E. Asmah, M.S. Kimeny, Z. Lewis, J.M. Mbaku, N. Moyo, J. Mutenyo, J. Page, E.S. Suruma and O. Taiwo, eds, Foresight Africa: The Continent's Greatest Challenges And Opportunities For 2011, Brookings Institution, Africa Growth Initiative, Washington, D.C.

Kragelund, P., (2010), The potential role of non-traditional donors' aid in Africa, Issue Paper No. 11, International Centre for Trade and Sustainable Development, .

Kragelund, P., (2008), "The Return of Non-DAC Donors to Africa: New Prospects for African Development?", Development Policy Review, 26(5).

Le Pere, G. and G. Sheldon, (2007), China, Africa and South Africa: South – South Cooperation in a Global Era, Institute for Global Dialogue, Midrand South Africa.

Mallaby, S., (2006), The World's Banker – A Story of Failed States, Financial Crises, and the Wealth and Poverty of Nations, Penguin Books, New York.

Marysse, S. and S. Geenen, (2009), "Win-win or unequal exchange ? The case of the Sino-Congolese cooperation agreements", Journal of Modern African Studies, 47(3).

Meredith, M., (2005), The State of Africa – A History of Fifty Years of Independence, The Free Press, London.

MOFCOM, (2010), 2009 Statistical Bulletin of China's Outward Foreign Direct Investment, Ministry of Commerce People's Republic of China, Beijing.

Mohan, G. and M. Tan-Mullins, (2009), "Chinese migrants in Africa as new agents of development? An analytical framework", European Journal of Development Research, 21(4).

Mold, A., (2011), Will history repeat itself?: infrastructure spending and African Development, mimeo, Organisation for Economic Cooperation and Development, Development Centre, Paris.

Morrissey, O., (1993), "The Mixing of Aid and Trade Policies", World Economy, 16(1).

Nissanke, M., (2010), "Reconstructing the Aid Effectiveness Debate", G. Mavrotas, ed, Foreign Aid for Development: Issues, Challenges, and the New Agenda, Oxford University Press, Oxford.

Nissanke, M. and A.M. Jerve, (2008), Aid Effectiveness to Infrastructure: A Comparative Study of East Asia and Sub-Saharan Africa. JBICI Research Paper No. 36-1, Japan Bank for International Cooperation, Tokyo.

Nugent, P., (2004), Africa Since Independence, Palgrave MacMillan, Basingstoke.

OECD, (2011), Draft DAC Statement on "Welcoming New Partnerships In International Development Co-Operation", DCD/DAC/A(2011)5, Organisation for Economic Cooperation and Development, Development Cooperation Directorate, Paris.

OECD, (2010), Perspectives on Global Development 2010 - Shifting Wealth, Organisation for Economic Cooperation and Development, Develoment Centre, Paris.

OECD, (2008), Is it ODA? Factsheet November 2008, Organisation for Economic Cooperation and Development, Paris.

Okonjo-Iweala, N., (2010), What's the Big Idea? To reposition Africa as the Fifth BRIC-A Destination for Investment, not just Aid, How has a decade of change shaped development thinking? Harvard Kennedy School, May 14 2010, World Bank.

Pal, P., (2008), Surge in Indian Outbound FDI to Africa: An Emerging Pattern in Globalization, paper presented at the Global Studies Conference May 16-18, University of Illinois, Chicago.

Potter, D.M., (2008), Modes of Asian Development Assistance, Nanzan University, Nagoya.

Prahalad, C.K., (2005), The Fortune at the Bottom of the Pyramid: Eradicating Poverty through Profits, Pearson Education/ Wharton School Publishing, New Jersey.

Raffinot, M., (2008), *La dette des tiers mondes*, La Découverte, Paris.

Reisen, H., (2008), Des donateurs traditionnels aux prêteurs émergents en Afrique, Repères No. 57, Organisation for Economic Cooperation and Development, Development Centre, Paris.

Reisen, H., (2007), Is China Actually Helping Improve Debt Sustainability in Africa? Preliminary draft, International Conference "Emerging Powers in Global Governance" 6-7 July 2007, Organisation for Economic Cooperation and Development, Paris.

Reisen, H. and S. Ndoye, (2008), Prudent versus Imprudent Lending to Africa: From Debt Relief to Emerging Lenders, Working Paper No. 268, Organisation for Economic Cooperation and Development, Development Centre, Paris.

Rich, B., (2002), "The World Bank under James Wolfensohn", P. Jonathan R. and W. Jeffrey A., eds, Reinventing the World Bank, Cornell University Press, London.

Rodrik, D., (2010), Is Chinese Mercantilism Good or Bad for Poor Countries? Project Syndicate.

Rostow, W., (1960), The Stages of Economic Growth: A non-communist manifesto, Cambridge University Press, Cambridge.

Roxburgh, C., N. Dörr, A. Leke, A. Tazi-Riffi, A. van Wamelen, S. Lund, M. Chironga, T. Alatovik, C. Atkins, N. Terfous and T. Zeino-Mahmalat, (2010), Lions on the Move: The Progress and Potential of African Economies, McKinsey Global Institute, New York.

Saggi, K., (2002), "Trade, FDI and International Technology Transfer: A Survey", World Bank Economic Observer, 17(2).

Scott, J., M. vom Hau and D. Hulme, (2010), Beyond the BICs: Identifying the 'Emerging Middle Powers' and understanding their Role in Global Poverty Reduction, BWPI Working Paper No. 137, The University of Manchester, Manchester.

Sidiropoulos, E., (2011), India and South Africa as Partners for Development in Africa? Briefing Paper ASP/AFP BP 2011/01, Chatham House, London.

Singer, H., C. Cooper, R.C. Desai, C. Freeman, O. Gish, S. Hall and G. Oldham, (1970), The Sussex Manifesto: Science and Technology for Developing Countries during the Second Development Decade, Institute of Development Studies, Brighton.

Sonobe, T., J.E. Akoten and K. Otsuka, (2009), "An Exploration into the Successful Development of the Leather-Shoe Industry in Ethiopia", Review of Development Economics, 13(4).

Standard Chartered Bank, (2010), The Super-Cycle Report, Global Research, Standard Chartered Bank, London.

Tan-Mullins, M., G. Mohan and M. Power, (2010), "Redefining 'Aid' in the China–Africa Context", Development and Change, 41(5).

The Economist, (2010), "Uncaging the Lions: Business is Transforming Africa for the Better", The Economist, June 12.

UN OSAA, (2010), Africa's Cooperation with New and Emerging Development Partners: Options for Africa's Development, United Nations Office of the Special Adviser on Africa, New York.

UNCTAD, (2010a), South South Cooperation - Africa and the New Forms of Development Partnership, Economic Development in Africa Report 2010, United Nations Conference on Trade and Development, Geneva.

UNCTAD, (2010b), World Investment Report 2010, United Nations Conference on Trade and Development, Geneva.

UNCTAD, (2007), Reclaiming Policy Space - Domestic Resource Mobilization and Developmental States,

Economic Development in Africa No. UNCTAD/ALDC/AFRICA/2007/1, United Nations Conference on Trade and Development, Geneva.

UNDP, (2004), UNDP /Japan Partnership supporting South-South cooperation: Innovative triangular cooperation towards the Millennium Development Goals (1999-2004), United Nations Development Programme, New York.

UNIDO, (2009), Industrial Development Report. Breaking In and Moving Up: New Industrial Challenges for the Bottom Billion and the Middle-Income Countries, United Nations Industrial Development Organization, Vienna.

Viner, J., (1950), The Customs Union Issue, Carnegie Endowment for International Peace, New York.

Wang, J.Y. and A. Bio-Tchané, (2008), "Africa's Burgeoning Ties with China: Maximizing the Benefits of China's Increasing Economic Engagement with Africa.", Finance and Development, 45(1).

White, L., (2010), "Understanding Brazil's new drive for Africa", South African Journal of International Affairs, 17(2).

Whitfield, L., (2008), "Introduction: Aid and Sovereignty", The Politics of Aid. African Strategies for Dealing with Donors, Oxford University Press, Oxford.

Wolfensohn, J., (2007), "The Four Circles of a Changing World", International Herald Tribune, .

World Bank, (2011), Africa's Future and the World Bank's Support to It, World Bank, Washington, D.C.

World Bank, (2010), Chinese Investments in Special Economic Zones in Africa: Progress, Challenges and Lessons Learned, draft version 2010-11-04, World Bank, Washington, D.C.

World Bank, (2009), IDA Countries and Non-Concessional Debt: Dealing with the Free-Rider Problem in IDA14 Grant-Recipient and Post-MDRI countries, World Bank, Washington, D.C.

World Bank, (1992), Effective Implementation: Key to Development Impact: Report of the World Bank's Portfolio Task Force, (The Wapenhans Report), Working paper M, World Bank, Washington, D.C.

World Bank and IMF, (2009), A Review of Some Aspects of the Low-Income Country Debt Sustainability Framework, World Bank and International Monetary Fund, Washington, D.C.

World Bank (2009), World Development Indicators, CD-ROM Version.

Yamashiro Fordelone, T., (2009), Triangular Cooperation and Aid Effectiveness, Paper presented at the OECD/ DAC Policy Dialogue on Development Cooperation Mexico City, 28–29 September 2009, Organisation of Economic Cooperation and Development.

Zimmermann, F. and I. Mcdonnell, (2008), "Broader Ownership for Development", Development Centre Studies, ed, Financing Development 2008 Whose Ownership? OECD, Paris.

Zimmermann, F. and K. Smith, (forthcoming), More Money, More Actors, More Ideas: For International Development Co-operation, Organisation for Economic Cooperation and Development, Development Cooperation Directorate, Paris.

Part Three

Country Notes

Algeria

Growth in actual gross domestic product (GDP), estimated at 3.5% in 2010, was driven principally by: the oil and gas sector where prices generated a rise in fiscal revenue from exports; the continuation of major public sector infrastructure projects; and a rise in consumer consumption. Medium-term growth prospects are favourable.

Algeria is consolidating its economic performances of the past decade, which have been characterised by a stable macroeconomic framework and tangible progress at the social level. The country must intensify reforms aimed at improving the business climate and competitiveness and encourage private investment. This is essential to encourage diversification in the economy and to create jobs, in particular for young people.

In recent years Algeria has stepped up its economic, cultural and diplomatic ties with emerging countries such as China, Brazil, Russia and Turkey, thereby diversifying trade and developing new forms of co-operation to encourage investment. In 2009 procurement from China represented 12% of total imports; sales to China represented about 1.9% of total exports. The volume of trade between Algeria and Turkey climbed to USD 3.8 billion, placing Turkey in sixth place on Algeria's list of clients and seventh on its list of suppliers.

The oil and gas sector represents the principal source of growth, even though GDP in the non-hydrocarbon sector has also done well in the past several years. Besides oil and gas, it has been the completion and acceleration of major public investment projects and household consumption that drove growth in 2010. However, a growth rate of 3.5% in 2010 remains modest considering the potential of the Algerian economy and is insufficient to bring down unemployment and ease the housing crisis. Growth excluding hydrocarbons reached 5.5% in 2010, below that of the two preceding years (9.3% in 2009 and 6.1% in 2008). Medium-term growth prospects are encouraging, but are subject to variations in the price of oil and gas. Growth should be sustained in the short term by the effects on the oil and gas sectors of increased growth in the world economy resulting in an increase in oil prices favourable to Algeria; major public spending; and an acceleration of the programme of public investment under the 2010-14 plan. Inflation in 2010 stood lower than the relatively high levels experienced the two previous years (4.8% in 2008 and 5.7% in 2009). The rise in prices, in particular in the second quarter, was due mainly to soaring world prices of the principal consumer food products.

At sector level, growth came on the back of good performances in construction, services, agriculture and energy. In 2010 agricultural production grew by almost 11% compared to 9.2% in 2009. Successive investment programmes ongoing since 2004 continue to energise the construction sector, which is posting annual growth rates of 9% to 10%. The added value of the oil and gas sector was reduced slightly in 2010 (because of a drop in production volume) with the prospect of a recovery in 2011 thanks to a projected increase in world demand, to the price effect of oil and gas exports and to investment projects that should help improve productivity in the sector. Industry was stable in 2010 and could even slip to 5% growth from 5.5% in 2009. Production levels in manufacturing industries, a strategic element in overall industrial development, under-performed, especially in the textiles and leather sub-sectors. By contrast the services sector continued to show strong year-on-year growth. With 26% total added value in 2009, the market services sector remains the second biggest contributor to the creation of national wealth and the biggest in terms of production outside the oil and gas sector.

Budgetary policy is still expansionary but remains viable thanks to the significant resources in the Revenue-Regulation Fund (FFR), which is one of the main sources of deficit financing. Heavy demands are made on the state budget to fund major public investment projects, in particular those included in the five-year development plans covering the periods 2005-09 and 2010-14. Government revenue remains dependent on tax revenue from the oil sector, which in the past five years has accounted for over 70% on average of total budget revenue. This dependence makes the economy vulnerable to external shocks. The drop in oil and gas revenue in the past two years, combined with a relatively high level of public spending has led to a deterioration in the public finances illustrated, for the second year running, by budget deficits of about 6.9% of GDP in 2009 and 4.4% in 2010. Monetary policy is focused on control of the money supply, the exchange rate and inflation. The external position was healthy in 2010 in spite of a decline in the current account surplus (5.5% of GDP in 2010, 19.8% in 2008). In 2010 the country registered a trade surplus of USD 16.4 billion compared to USD 5.9 billion in 2009. Foreign exchange reserves were estimated at USD 155 billion at the end of December 2010, equivalent to three years of imports of goods and services. The level of foreign debt remains quite low at 2.7% of GDP (2009).

As far as structural reforms are concerned, in spite of a marked improvement in the regulatory framework that governs them, the business climate overall remains constrained by delays resulting from the need to carry out administrative formalities, as well as the continuing presence of an informal sector. As regards human development, the social indicators are satisfactory. The country is on course to reach the Millennium Development Goals (MDGs). Despite the progress made, Algeria still faces the challenge of unemployment (10% in 2010), especially among young people (about 21.5% unemployment in the 16-24 age bracket), and a lack of housing.

Table 1: Macroeconomic indicators

	2009	2010	2011	2012
Real GDP growth	2.4	3.5	3.9	3.6
CPI inflation	5.7	4.1	4.5	4.1
Budget balance % GDP	-6.9	-4.4	-5.3	-5.7
Current account % GDP	0.3	5.5	5	4.7

Source: National authorities' data; estimates and predictions based on authors' calculations.

Figures for 2010 are estimates; for 2011 and later are projections.

StatLink http://dx.doi.org/10.1787/888932406118

Figure 1: Real GDP growth (N)

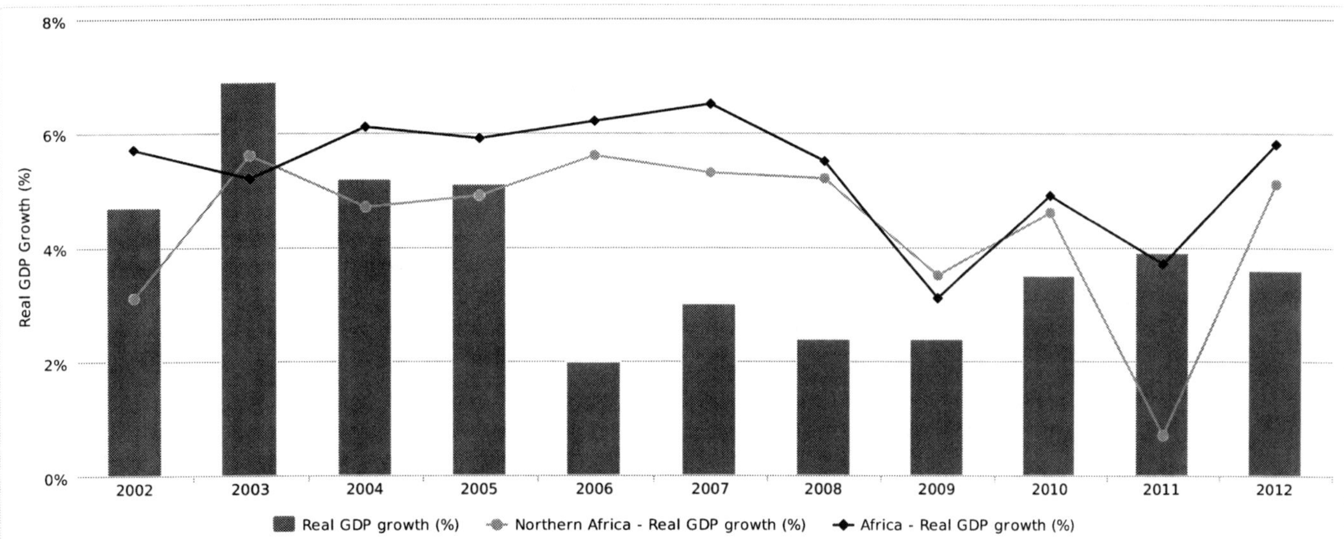

Source: IMF and local authorities' data; estimates and projections based on authors' calculations.

Figures for 2010 are estimates; for 2011 and later are projections.

StatLink http://dx.doi.org/10.1787/888932403762

Angola

Angola's economy remained stagnant in the first half of 2010 as a result of government's accumulated domestic arrears, but it began to recover at the end of the year and the outlook for 2011 and 2012 is positive with the recovery in oil prices.

Economic growth has yet to make a significant impact on poverty, inequality and youth unemployment, which remain critical issues in the country given the high population increase.

In the last ten years Angola's economy has considerably diversified its partners, and the role of emerging economies (outside the African continent) on Angola has dramatically increased.

Angola's economy is largely dependent on the oil sector and it was hard hit by the collapse in oil prices and demand in 2009. For years one of the fastest growing economies in the world, Angola's real gross domestic product (GDP) growth was just 3.4% in 2010, stalled from 2.4% in 2009 (and down from 13.3% in 2008). Despite the recovery in oil prices, growth was hampered by government arrears in construction and infrastructure payments. The outlook is good however and growth is expected to reach 7.5% in 2011 buoyed by high oil prices and by the resumption of the government's Public Investment Programme (PIP).

Inflation remains a challenge for Angola. After years of sustained decreases, inflation rose by 6% in 2008 to reach 13.7% and climbed one percentage point again in 2010. It is expected to decrease in 2011 to 11.7%. Both a deteriorating exchange rate and sharp increases in petrol and diesel prices following the removal of subsidies underlie this increase. Inflation is expected to remain in double digits in 2010 and 2011 due to structural constraints in public transportation and agricultural distribution.

Efforts to bolster the exchange rate in 2009 led to a sharp decrease in monetary reserves. This prompted an overhaul of monetary policy set out in a new constitution that was approved in February 2010. The *Banco Nacional de Angola* (BNA) now shares responsibility for interest and exchange rate policies with the Ministries of Planning and Finance. With budgetary and current account balances beginning to recover in 2010 on the back of rising oil prices, monetary policies are expected to loosen in 2011 to foster private sector activity.

While the non-oil sector has expanded by an average of 14% over the past four years, economic diversification remains shallow. The construction and infrastructure sectors are heavily dependent on the PIP, while growth in agriculture more adequately reflects a catch up after the country's 27-year war that ended in 2002. Mining is still concentrated on oil and diamonds although the resumption of pre-war exploitations of iron ore, gold and copper is underway. Commerce, which developed informally during the war, was severely disrupted in 2010 by the government's displacement of the Roque Santeiro market, previously the largest market in sub-Saharan Africa. Manufacturing is largely concentrated in oil- and gas-related activities.

While public sector capacity to crowd out private investment in a number of sectors remains a concern, the government has managed great social and economic challenges since 2002 without any major outbreak of violence. There is a widespread lack of qualified human resources that acts as a major constraint to growth in the medium term. With an ambitious infrastructure development plan boosted by the country's first credit risk rating and by massive inflows of credit, the government hopes to improve access to basic services in the short term.

Angola's economy remains largely driven by public investment, which is blighted by political patronage and corruption. National planning programmes continue to highlight the need for better co-ordination of public policies, and there is a clear need for a national infrastructure development policy. Efforts are currently being taken to boost the private sector and decrease reliance on public investment.

The adoption of a new constitution in February 2010 further cemented President José Eduardo dos Santos's 30-year grip on power. Presidential elections have been abolished (the president instead being nominated as head of the ruling party) and the post of prime minister has been replaced by that of a vice president directly under the president's authority. Although a limit of two five-year presidential terms has been set, this does not take into account Mr dos Santos' previous decades in power, enabling him to remain president until 2022. The next presidential elections are not scheduled before 2012.

According to the United Nations High Commissioner for Refugees (UNHCR), there are close to 70 000 Angolan refugees in Democratic Republic of Congo, 25 000 in Zambia, 6 000 in Namibia and 2 000 in Congo. These will lose their war refugee status at the end of 2011. The appropriate re-integration of these refugees poses a fresh challenge for the Angolan government added to the key tasks of managing the country's non-renewable national wealth more efficiently, and creating jobs. Better management will require the strengthening of institutions and a relaxing of the leadership's tight hold on power, both political and economic.

Table 1: Macroeconomic indicators

	2009	2010	2011	2012
Real GDP growth	2.4	3.4	7.5	11.1
CPI inflation	13.7	14.7	11.7	12.1
Budget balance % GDP	-8.6	7.3	6.7	8.1
Current account % GDP	-10	1	-3.8	3.5

Source: National authorities' data; estimates and predictions based on authors' calculations.

Figures for 2010 are estimates; for 2011 and later are projections.

StatLink http://dx.doi.org/10.1787/888932406137

Figure 1: Real GDP growth (S)

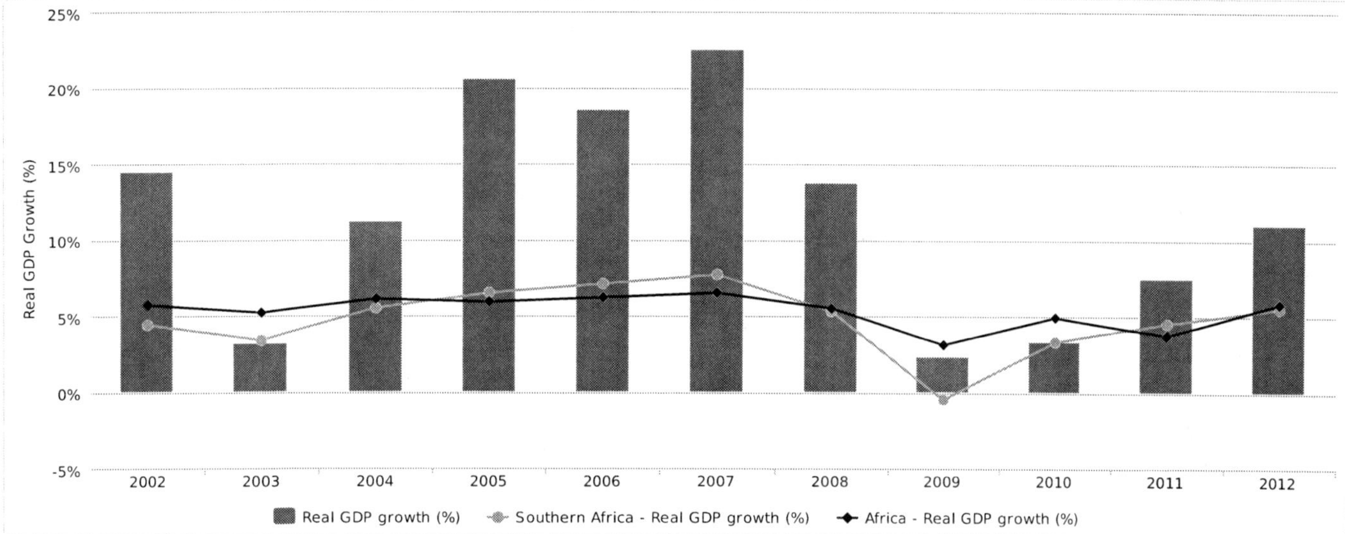

Source: IMF and local authorities' data; estimates and projections based on authors' calculations.

Figures for 2010 are estimates; for 2011 and later are projections.

StatLink http://dx.doi.org/10.1787/888932403781

Benin

After weak growth in 2010, Benin has no choice but to intensify economic, structural and institutional reforms so as to improve its growth projections for 2011 and for 2012 and to increase its chances of achieving the Millennium Development Goals (MDGs).

Human development is still poor in Benin; poverty is a major concern and inequalities within the population are marked.

In addition to its traditional partners, five emerging countries are operating in Benin, mainly in the area of economic and social infrastructure.

Benin's economy is characterised by a labour market dominated by the informal sector which involves about 95% of the working population and plays a major role in income generation. In 2010, activity was slowed down by low agricultural and cotton production, reduced public investment and floods. The cost of these unanticipated factors is evaluated at 0.8 economic growth points. An estimated 8% of the Beninese population, nearly one-third of which lives off agricultural activities, was directly affected. Growth in gross domestic product (GDP) in 2010, which was initially expected to be around 3%, is now estimated at 2.1% in a context of control over inflation, compared to 2.7% in 2009. Projections for 2011 are banking on 2.5% growth, driven by trade with Nigeria, agricultural production and the pursuance of major public projects in the form of road infrastructure, general construction work and agricultural development.

Macroeconomic policy is implemented on the basis of agreements related to the Extended Credit Facility concluded with the International Monetary Fund (IMF) in June 2010, which is backed by other development partners in the form of financial and technical support for budget execution. Fiscal policy has been characterised since 2006 by a significant increase in public expenditure. The lethargy observed in the implementation of reforms, however, has prevented tax revenues from following the same upward trend. In the 2007-10 period, tax revenues increased on average by 12%, whereas expenditure increased by nearly 20%, with a peak between 2007 and 2008 due to rises in wages and investment expenditure.

In 2010, the balance of the State's financial operations showed a deficit down from 4.2% in 2009 to 2.6%. Budget execution has been projected to produce an overall deficit of 2.5% in 2011. External accounts currently show a deficit (estimated at 7% of GDP in 2010), explained in particular by a low level of grants. The country's current-account balance is projected to worsen in 2011 to 8%, mainly as a result of a deteriorating trade balance and declining net services and public and private transfers, which will continue to suffer from the impact of the international economic crisis.

These past few years, Benin has established new partnerships with emerging countries such as India, Saudi Arabia, Abu Dhabi, Kuwait and China. The partnership with China is by far the biggest in terms of volume of trade and number of sectors of activity.

In the political arena, preparation of the presidential and legislative elections scheduled for March and April 2011, coupled with claims from professional interest groups, disrupted the functioning of the administration and certain institutions in 2010.

Benin's human development otherwise remains poor, with an overall Human Development Index (HDI) of 0.435 in 2010, which ranks it 134th out of 169 countries. Benin's HDI has, however, risen since 1975 when it stood at 0.312, thanks to efforts in education and health. Notwithstanding, poverty is still a major concern, with highly marked inequalities within the population. In 2009, monetary poverty affected 35.2% of the population versus 33.3% in 2007. The proportion affected by non-monetary poverty, on the other hand, declined from 39.7% in 2007 to 30.9% in 2009. This means that, while intensifying reforms and pursuing efforts to reduce non-monetary poverty further, focus needs to be placed on structural reforms and income-generating activities. The government needs to accelerate and intensify economic, structural and institutional reforms in order to improve on the current 2.5% and 3.5% growth projections for 2011 and 2012 respectively.

Table 1: Macroeconomic indicators

	2009	2010	2011	2012
Real GDP growth	2.7	2.1	2.5	3.7
CPI inflation	2.2	2.1	2.2	2.9
Budget balance % GDP	-4.2	-2.6	-2.5	-1.6
Current account % GDP	-7.7	-7.1	-8.2	-7.6

Source: National authorities' data; estimates and predictions based on authors' calculations.

Figures for 2010 are estimates; for 2011 and later are projections.

StatLink http://dx.doi.org/10.1787/888932406156

Figure 1: Real GDP growth (W)

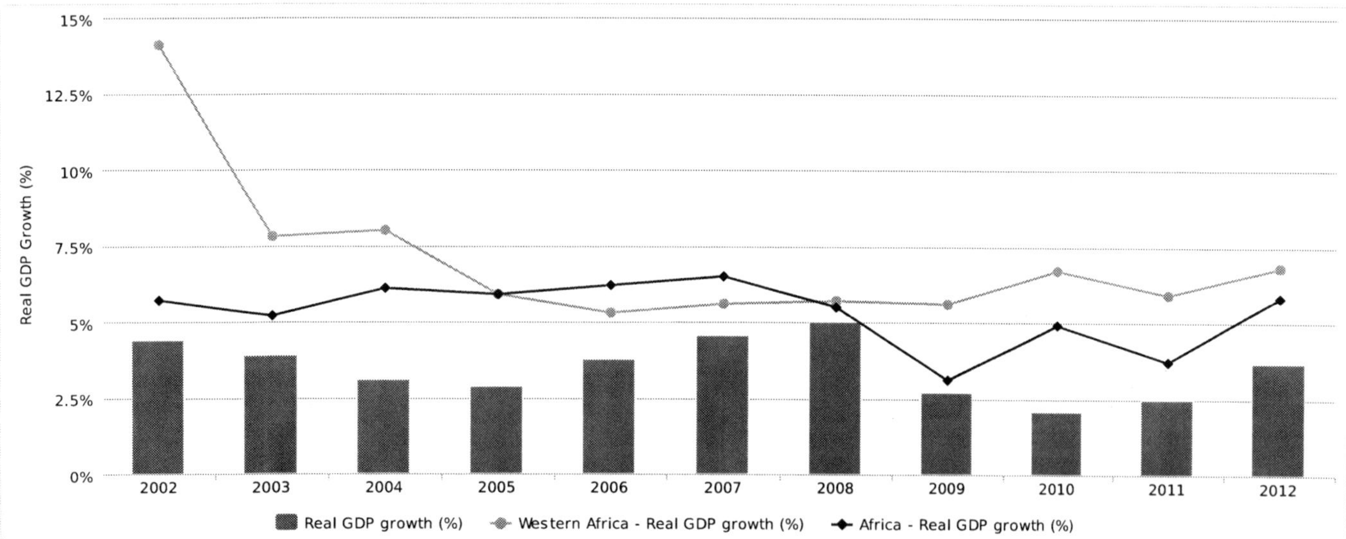

Source: IMF and local authorities' data; estimates and projections based on authors' calculations.

Figures for 2010 are estimates; for 2011 and later are projections.

StatLink http://dx.doi.org/10.1787/888932403800

Botswana

Botswana grew 6.4% in 2010, rebounding strongly from 2009 when the global economic crisis saw the diamond-dependent economy shrink 3.7%.

Botswana is on track to meet most of the Millennium Development Goals (MDGs) by 2015 but HIV/AIDS remains a major challenge.

China continues to be a key donor in many areas while traditional aid partners no longer play such a role as Botswana has become wealthier.

Botswana has developed from Least Developed Country (LDC) status at the time of independence in 1966 to Middle Income Country (MIC) status within three decades, largely due to the effective use of revenues from mineral resources following the discovery of large diamond reserves. Gross domestic product (GDP) per capita more than doubled, at current prices, from 3 180 US dollars (USD) in 2000 to USD 6 760 in 2008 but slipped to USD 6 215 in 2009, reflecting the impact of the global slump on demand for diamonds and other minerals. Despite the impressive progress in per capita income, rates of poverty and inequality are still high.

Botswana's reliance on diamond exports is a challenge for sustainable economic growth. The global economic and financial crisis of 2008 saw the economy shrink 3.7% in 2009, primarily due to substantial fall in diamond demand, but it bounced back to growth of 6.4% in 2010. The economy should grow 6.9% in 2011 and 7.0% in 2012. The current account deteriorated sharply in 2009 and 2010 but should improve and return to surplus in 2011 and 2012. The budget came under pressure too, chalking up large deficits that will take longer to bring under control. Foreign exchange reserves have stabilised at around 17 months of imports.

Inflation fell to 7.0% in 2010 from 8.2% in 2009 but continued well above the central bank's medium-term target of 3.0-6.0%. Inflation should ease into the target range by second quarter 2011 as a hike in VAT and higher controlled prices fall out of the comparison. Lower inflation in South Africa, Botswana's major trade partner, should also help.

The government is promoting the diversification of the economy away from diamonds and Botswana's private sector should provide a solid foundation. Botswana has robust macroeconomic policies, an efficient financial sector, good governance and fairly well developed infrastructure after sustained investment. The result is that the country ranks favourably with its peers. The World Bank's 2011 *Ease of Doing Business* survey ranked Botswana 52 out of 183 countries. On the Corruption Perception Index compiled by Transparency International, Botswana was ranked 33 out of 178 countries in 2010, ahead of all its sub-Saharan African peers.

Botswana is progressing well with the implementation of reforms required to meet the MDGs by 2015. Significant progress has been made in education and in health although HIV/AIDS remains a significant challenge despite proactive measures by the government. Botswana has one of the best Prevention of Mother to Child Transmission (PMCT) programmes in Africa where 96% of babies born under the programme are HIV negative.

Table 1: Macroeconomic indicators

	2009	2010	2011	2012
Real GDP growth	-3.7	6.4	6.9	7
CPI inflation	8.2	7	6.1	5.3
Budget balance % GDP	-5.2	-11.1	-6.9	-6
Current account % GDP	-5.7	1.5	1.9	2.7

Source: National authorities' data; estimates and predictions based on authors' calculations.

Figures for budget balance refer to fiscal year April (n)/ March (n+1).

Figures for 2010 are estimates; for 2011 and later are projections.

StatLink http://dx.doi.org/10.1787/888932406175

Figure 1: Real GDP growth (S)

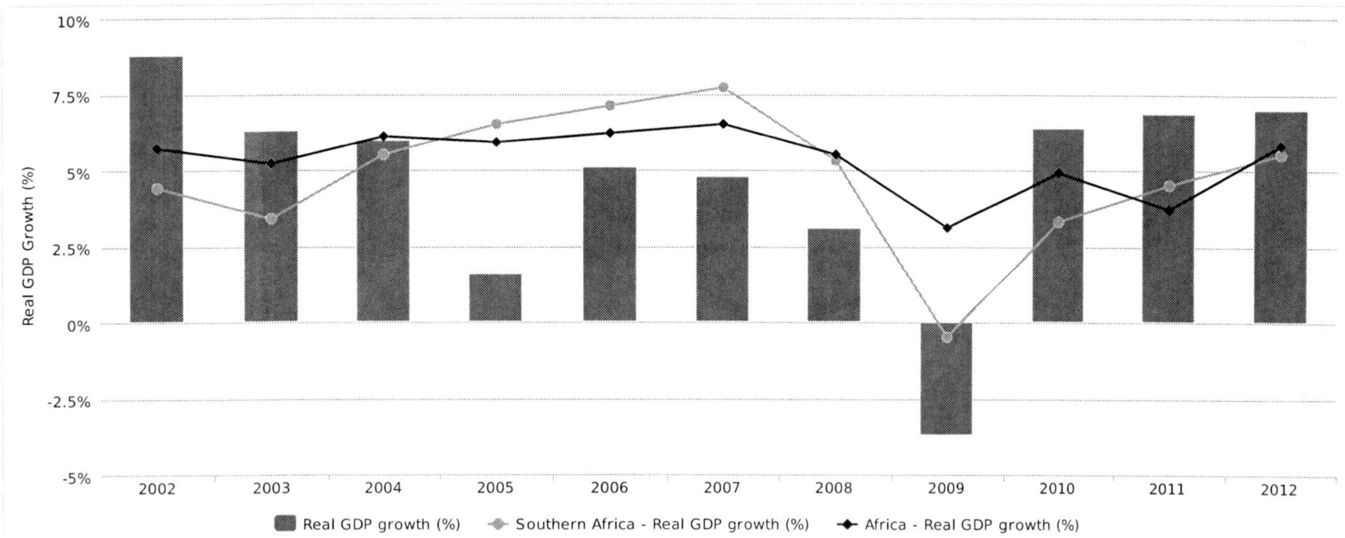

Source: IMF and local authorities' data; estimates and projections based on authors' calculations.

Figures for 2010 are estimates; for 2011 and later are projections.

StatLink http://dx.doi.org/10.1787/888932403819

Burkina Faso

Rising international prices for cotton and gold should consolidate the country's external position and maintain a sustained economic growth dynamic in 2011 and 2012. However, the strong dependence of the export sector on these two products and the dominance of oil products in imports makes external trade highly vulnerable. This is particularly so in the case of shocks associated with adverse fluctuations in world cotton, gold and oil prices and poor climatic conditions.

In terms of economic policy, the authorities should focus on promoting public and private investment in order to strengthen infrastructure and improve economic competitiveness. The political situation is relatively stable in Burkina Faso.

The largest emerging partners are China, India, Chinese Taipei, Thailand and Brazil. The primary focus of interest with these partners are trade (exports and imports), foreign direct investment (FDI) and diplomatic relations.

In 2010, economic growth accelerated over 2009, with real gross domestic product (GDP) growth increasing from 3.2% to 5.7%. The outlook for the economy in 2011 and 2012 is for higher growth, with respective rates of 6.5% and 6.2%.

The macroeconomic policy pursued by the authorities in 2010 was more expansionist than in 2009 and the budget deficit came in at 4.5% of GDP in 2010, against 3.5% in 2009. It was mainly covered by external aid, despite the high risk of over-indebtedness in the medium to long term. This expansionist policy aims at supporting domestic demand, reinforcing the social security net and responding to humanitarian needs for housing and reconstruction caused by the 2009 and 2010 floods. Growth in 2010 was thus led more by consumption than investment. This led to an increase in imports, particularly petroleum products, the effect of which was largely offset by a strong rise in exports, particularly gold. The current account deficit was thus partially absorbed in 2010 to around 2.7% of GDP.

On the social front, indicators have improved but poverty remains a concern. Further, the ongoing crisis in Côte d'Ivoire poses a threat to regional stability.

Table 1: Macroeconomic indicators

	2009	2010	2011	2012
Real GDP growth	3.2	5.7	6.5	6.2
CPI inflation	2.6	0.9	2.5	2.6
Budget balance % GDP	-3.5	-4.5	-4.4	-5.1
Current account % GDP	-4.6	-2.7	-1.3	-0.4

Source: National authorities' data; estimates and predictions based on authors' calculations.

Figures for 2010 are estimates; for 2011 and later are projections.

StatLink http://dx.doi.org/10.1787/888932406194

Figure 1: Real GDP growth (W)

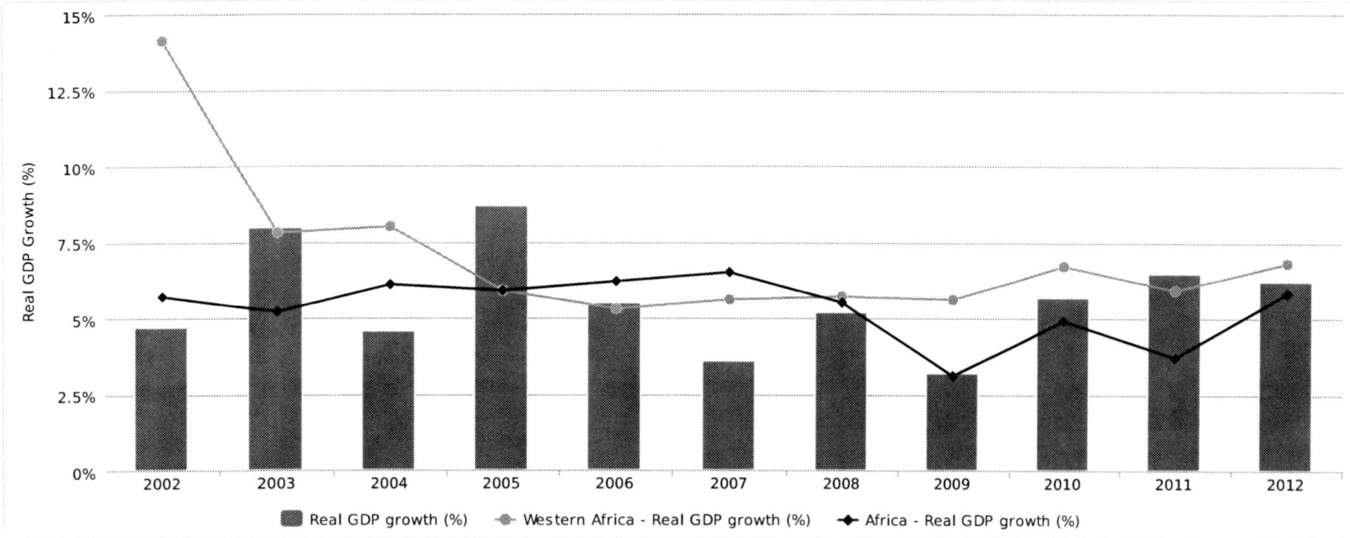

Source: IMF and local authorities' data; estimates and projections based on authors' calculations.

Figures for 2010 are estimates; for 2011 and later are projections.

StatLink http://dx.doi.org/10.1787/888932403838

Burundi

The 2010 growth rate of 3.9% fell short of the government's target, due to political uncertainty and inclement weather.

Burundi's economic growth is held back by political instability and constraints on private sector development.

Co-operation with China, Burundi's main emerging partner, dates from the early 1960s but has intensified in recent years.

Burundi's economy grew by 3.9% in 2010. As in previous years, this rate was below the government's target of 4.5%, mainly as a result of political uncertainty stemming from a series of elections in a politically fractionalised environment, as well as inclement weather. In 2011 and 2012, growth is expected to reach 4.5% and 5.2% respectively. This improvement will be conditional on better weather conditions and a more predictable political environment.

Fiscal policy was neutral, with levels of revenue and expenditure in 2010 similar to those in 2009. Public investment increased by 10%, mostly as a result of the expansion of social sector infrastructure. The rise in public spending combined with a small decline in grants increased the overall deficit from 2% of GDP in 2009 to 3.2% in 2010. Large increases in credit to the government drove money supply upwards. The resulting pressure on domestic prices was counterbalanced by higher food production and lower food price inflation. Overall domestic inflation stood at 7.1%, down from 10.7% in 2009. Over the years, the country's chronic trade deficit has been partly absorbed by current transfers, mostly in the form of aid. Owing to the high level of transfers in 2010, the current account balance declined despite a substantial increase in the trade deficit.

Aid transfers to Burundi might decline over the next two years as a result of the economic crisis affecting its traditional partners as well as poor governance in Burundi. Such a decline would impair the government's ability to deliver basic services. Burundi's long-term financial stability requires that the country find new sources of finance, preferably domestic, and increase efficiency in resource allocation and use.

It is inconceivable that Burundi will reach high and sustained levels of growth unless it can stabilise its political environment, strengthen its embryonic private sector and develop its human resources. The insecurity that followed the 2010 elections will have to be addressed in order to achieve the higher levels of investment and aid flows that are needed to raise growth rates. To strengthen the private sector, the second vice-president is leading a drive to improve the business environment. However, the private sector will not thrive unless more is done to modernise the decaying agriculture sector, which sustains the livelihoods of the large majority of Burundians. Efforts to develop human resources by expanding education and health infrastructure and ensuring its efficiency will help to overcome the shortage of skilled labour.

The development of economic relations with new partners has opened up new opportunities that will help Burundi to diversify its markets and sources of assistance. China stands out as the country's key emerging partner. While China benefits from Burundi's diplomatic backing, there is no indication that this co-operation is driven by China's commercial interests in the country. Burundi is still dependent on its traditional partners, which fund a large share of the country's budget, so there does not seem to be competition between Burundi's partners. The country's needs are so immense that more partnerships should be welcome.

Table 1: Macroeconomic indicators

	2009	2010	2011	2012
Real GDP growth	3.4	3.9	4.5	5.2
CPI inflation	10.7	7.1	8.3	6.9
Budget balance % GDP	-2	-3.2	-4.5	-3.9
Current account % GDP	-15.5	-9.4	-7.9	-11.7

Source: National authorities' data; estimates and predictions based on authors' calculations.

Figures for 2010 are estimates; for 2011 and later are projections.

StatLink http://dx.doi.org/10.1787/888932406213

Figure 1: Real GDP growth (E)

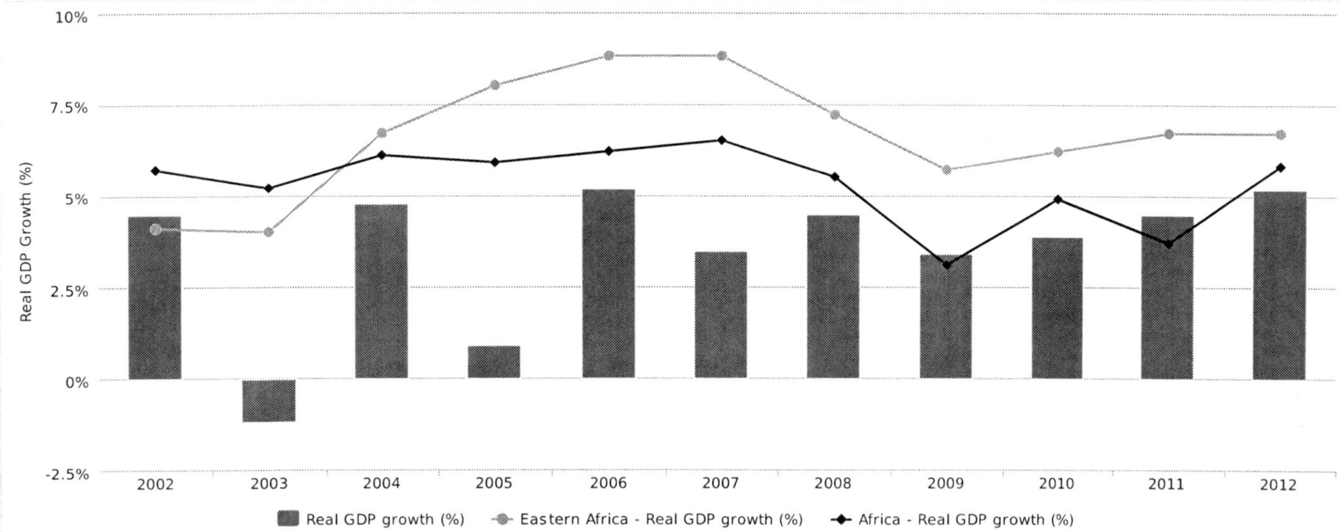

Source: IMF and local authorities' data; estimates and projections based on authors' calculations.

Figures for 2010 are estimates; for 2011 and later are projections.

StatLink http://dx.doi.org/10.1787/888932403857

Cameroon

Recent economic growth is positive but remains weak (3%), well below its potential and the level necessary to meet the Millennium Development Goal (MDG) of reducing poverty by half by 2015. It is driven essentially by the good performance of the main raw material export markets.

The Growth and Employment Strategy Paper (GESP) aims to reduce the country's dependence on raw materials and to create the conditions for the development of a dynamic private sector.

Implementing the GESP requires significant financial resources. Emerging countries that create a financial surplus can, under different conditions from traditional funders, contribute to financing Cameroon's development.

The rate of growth recorded two successive falls between 2007 and 2009. It fell from 3.3% in 2007 to 2.9% in 2008 and to 2% in 2009, before rising more than one percentage point in 2010 to stabilise at 3%. The projections for 2011 and 2012 are 3.8% and 5.3% respectively, based mainly on the strength of internal demand, notably domestic consumption. This has been driven by the benefits of financial arrangements related to the completion of infrastructure projects. Private investment in the non-oil sector should support growth by an average of 0.4 percentage points a year. At the same time, the oil sector should continue to play an important role in growth with the exploitation of reserves in the Bakassi area.

In public finance matters, the authorities have continued efforts aimed at increasing non-oil tax revenues by: *i)* simplifying tax legislation and strengthening governance; *ii)* enlarging the tax base for all economic actors; *iii)* strengthening research into budgetary policies to improve the effectiveness of policy development.

The monetary policy objective set and managed by the Bank of Central African States (BEAC) is price stability. The financial instruments the Bank uses are: the bank base rate, free market policy and compulsory reserves.

In 2010 the inflation rate fell below the community threshold of 3% to settle at 1.4% due to the relative stability of food prices and the freeze on the pump prices of petroleum products.

Cameroon ended 2010 with a current account deficit of 3.6% of gross domestic product (GDP), marginally higher than in 2009 (3.3%). A further deterioration is expected in 2011, with a deficit of 3.8%.

Public sector reform continued in 2010, with completion of the privatisation of certain public sector companies and the creation of a single office as part of an improvement in the business climate.

On the political front, the fight against corruption also continued in 2010. Elections Cameroon (Elecam) continued to establish its representatives throughout the country in preparation for presidential elections planned in 2011. The head of state has met the main opposition leader, Ni John Fru Ndi, for the first time since 1990.

The authorities have continued their policy of improving education and health opportunities, building a new university in Bamenda and new hospitals, and providing better care for people suffering from chronic illness with the creation and outfitting of specialist centres.

Table 1: Macroeconomic indicators

	2009	2010	2011	2012
Real GDP growth	2	3	3.8	5.3
CPI inflation	3	1.4	2.9	3
Budget balance % GDP	-0.4	-0.9	-1.3	-0.4
Current account % GDP	-3.3	-3.6	-3.8	-2.6

Source: National authorities' data; estimates and predictions based on authors' calculations.

Figures for 2010 are estimates; for 2011 and later are projections.

StatLink http://dx.doi.org/10.1787/888932406232

Figure 1: Real GDP growth (C)

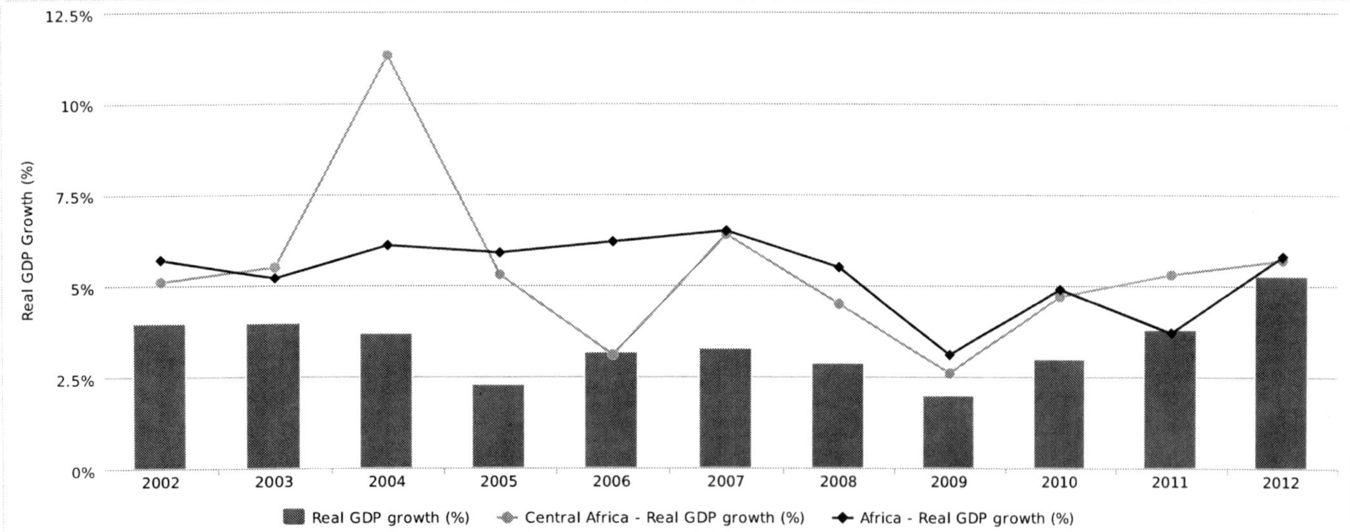

Source: IMF and local authorities' data; estimates and projections based on authors' calculations.

Figures for 2010 are estimates; for 2011 and later are projections.

StatLink http://dx.doi.org/10.1787/888932403876

Cape Verde

Cape Verde's economy has suffered from a steep drop in foreign investment after the global crisis, but has been sustained by a large public infrastructure investment programme. Gross domestic product (GDP) growth has risen 5.3% in 2010, up from 3.6% in 2009.

The country faces a double challenge over the coming years: the need to continue pushing ahead with diversification of the economic structure and a looming increase in social spending following the phasing out of foreign assistance.

The archipelago has a very proactive approach to its many economic partners, concentrating on finding the maximum complementarity in investment projects as well as in development cooperation.

Cape Verde's economy showed signs of recovery from the impact of the global financial crisis with 2010 gross domestic product (GDP) growth estimated to reach 5.3% compared to 3.6% in 2009. In 2010 there were signs of recovery in tourism and air transport and strong support from the Public Investment Programme (PIP). However, in 2010 foreign direct investment (FDI) and associated construction inflows continued to shrink. The outlook remains uncertain for 2011 as investment largely originates from the European Union (EU), which is growing only slowly. Remittances remained fairly constant in 2010 after a slight decrease of 2.2% in 2009.

The inflation rate was 2.1% in 2010, down from 6.7% in 2008, mainly as a result of the euro peg and the large import component of goods and labour of the PIP. Inflation is expected to rise slightly in 2011 because of increases in commodity and fuel prices and the weak resumption in private economic activity.

The government has put in place an ambitious strategy that addresses, on the one hand, the large PIP in infrastructure and, on the other, an improvement of the business environment through the creation of marketing and certification strategies. The extent to which these strategies generate direct benefits for the population and foster high value-added tourism will affect the resilience of the economy in the face of external shocks in the medium term, the trend in poverty rates and ultimately, the success of the government's PIP. In addition, the resumption in FDI flows will be key once the PIP is over as the country depends on external financing for large investment programmes.

To counter the impact of the crisis and to restructure the economy in view of Cape Verde's graduation to Middle Income Country (MIC) status, the government reinforced the 2010-12 PIP to address binding constraints: transport (particularly ports and roads), energy and water. In line with the PIP, the fiscal balance deteriorated considerably from -6.3% in 2009 to -13.7% in 2010 and is expected to remain large in 2011. International reserves are expected to remain at prudential levels in 2010-12, since the deficit is financed by external borrowing. Donor budget support increased considerably in 2010 to counter the crisis.

To reduce its strong dependence on fuel imports, Cape Verde has a 300 million US dollar (USD) plan to cover 25% of its needs with renewable energy by 2011 and 50% by 2020. The country is developing 28 megawatt (MW) onshore wind farms expected to come into operation in June 2011 in Sal, Boavista, São Tiago and São Vicente islands. This is the first large-scale wind project in Africa and the first renewable energy Private Public Parnership (PPP) in sub-Saharan Africa.

Cape Verde is one of the few African countries that may meet the Millennium Development Goals (MDGs) by 2015. Four of the eight goals - achieving universal primary education, promoting gender equality, reducing child mortality and improving maternal health - were attained by the end of 2010. The sustainability of these outcomes largely depends on donor support. Some donors, however, phased out aid in 2010 from certain social sectors. With its graduation to the MIC category, Cape Verde faces reduced access to concessional loans and has requested an extension from 2012 to 2015 in order to access the Low Income Country (LIC) instruments under the assumption that this will prove sufficient to address key structural bottlenecks.

The PIP aims at crowding in private investment in 2011-12 by fostering growth clusters in line with the 2003 Economic Transformation Strategy (ETS): tourism, fisheries (export and processing), creating a transport hub, financial services and information technology. In spite of attempts to use its geopolitical situation and economic stability to find new partners, the country's trade and investment partners remain largely European. Diversification has been slower than expected under government plans.

Cape Verde has asked the EU to extend its LIC status until 2011 while negotiating new commercial agreements including services, favourable rules of origin and quotas for fish exports. Cooperation with Brazil is primarily in the fields of education and capacity building. Exchanges with China are linked to the construction of infrastructure. Cape Verde is reinforcing its relationship with the Economic Community of West African States (ECOWAS). Since 2010 it has been hosting the West African Institute (WEA) and the ECOWAS Centre for Renewable Energy and Energy Efficiency (ECREEE).

On the political front, 2011 is the year of the fourth democratic legislative and presidential elections in Cape Verde. Parliamentary elections took place on 6 February. After a tight race, the ruling African Party for the Independence of Cape Verde (PAICV) won 37 out of 72 parliamentary seats. The main opposition party Movement for Democracy (MPD) picked up 33 seats. Presidential elections will take place six months later.

Table 1: Macroeconomic indicators

	2009	2010	2011	2012
Real GDP growth	3.6	5.3	5.6	6.1
CPI inflation	1.2	2.1	3	2.1
Budget balance % GDP	-6.3	-13.7	-11.3	-8.9
Current account % GDP	-9.9	-18.4	-15.5	-13.2

Source: National authorities' data; estimates and predictions based on authors' calculations.

Figures for 2010 are estimates; for 2011 and later are projections.

StatLink http://dx.doi.org/10.1787/888932406251

Figure 1: Real GDP growth (W)

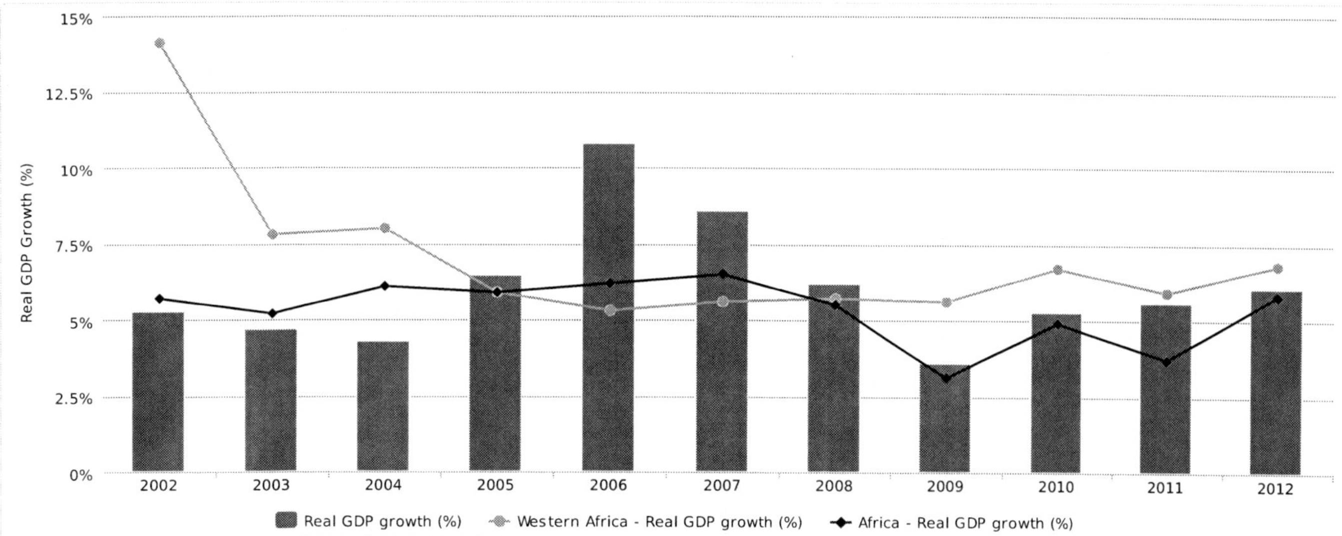

Source: IMF and local authorities' data; estimates and projections based on authors' calculations.

Figures for 2010 are estimates; for 2011 and later are projections.

StatLink http://dx.doi.org/10.1787/888932403895

Central African Republic

After suffering the full effects of the global economic crisis in 2009, the economy is recovering, and this recovery should be consolidated in 2011 and 2012. The Central African Republic remains a fragile, post-conflict country faced with serious structural constraints resulting in particular from poor infrastructure (transport, energy and telecommunications). Its people are among the poorest in Africa.

Despite the reforms being made, the priorities remain to improve governance and strengthen human skills.

The Central African Republic has few partner countries, either traditional or emerging.

The economic recovery in the Central African Republic (CAR) was confirmed in 2010, with real gross domestic product (GDP) growth estimated at 3.4%. This positive growth came a year after the economy had suffered the full effects of the global economic and financial crisis that broke out in 2008. In 2010, the CAR also achieved the objectives set out in the 2008-10 poverty reduction strategy document (PRSP) and the year saw its economic and financial programme negotiated with the International Monetary Fund (IMF), supported through the Extended Fund Facility (EFF) agreed upon with the IMF in December 2006. The sixth and final review of the EFF was approved by the IMF board on 25 August 2010, thus rewarding the efforts made in terms of economic and financial reform. The CAR reached the completion point of the Heavily Indebted Poor Countries (HIPC) Initiative and the Multilateral Debt Relief Initiative (MDRI).

The recurring social, political and military crises of the past two decades have made the CAR a "fragile", "post-conflict" state. These crises have damaged the economic fabric and destroyed the basic socio-economic infrastructure. Since 2005, the CAR has been experiencing an economic recovery and political transition that culminated in the presidential and parliamentary elections on 23 January 2011. Blessed with abundant natural resources, the country is seeing an increase in economic stability and the implementation of financial and structural reforms, as well as the rehabilitation of basic social services.

Whether these economic and social improvements will be consolidated will depend largely on the country's capacity to complete the political stabilisation process and respect the peace agreements, notably through the Disarmament, Demobilisation and Reintegration (DDR) programme adopted during the "Inclusive Political Dialogue" (DPI) conference held in December 2008. The DPI conference brought together the presidential majority, the opposition, politico-military movements, civil society and public bodies. The success of the transition from a period of prolonged instability towards growth and development will also depend on the country's capacity to mobilise more resources than is currently the case. This concern has led the government, in agreement with its main development partners, to organise a roundtable meeting for donors, which is due to take place in 2011.

Table 1: Macroeconomic indicators

	2009	2010	2011	2012
Real GDP growth	1.7	3.4	4.3	4.5
CPI inflation	3.5	1.8	2.5	1.8
Budget balance % GDP	0.7	-0.3	-0.3	-0.5
Current account % GDP	-9.2	-9.9	-12.3	-12.7

Source: National authorities' data; estimates and predictions based on authors' calculations.

Figures for 2010 are estimates; for 2011 and later are projections.

StatLink http://dx.doi.org/10.1787/888932406270

Figure 1: Real GDP growth (C)

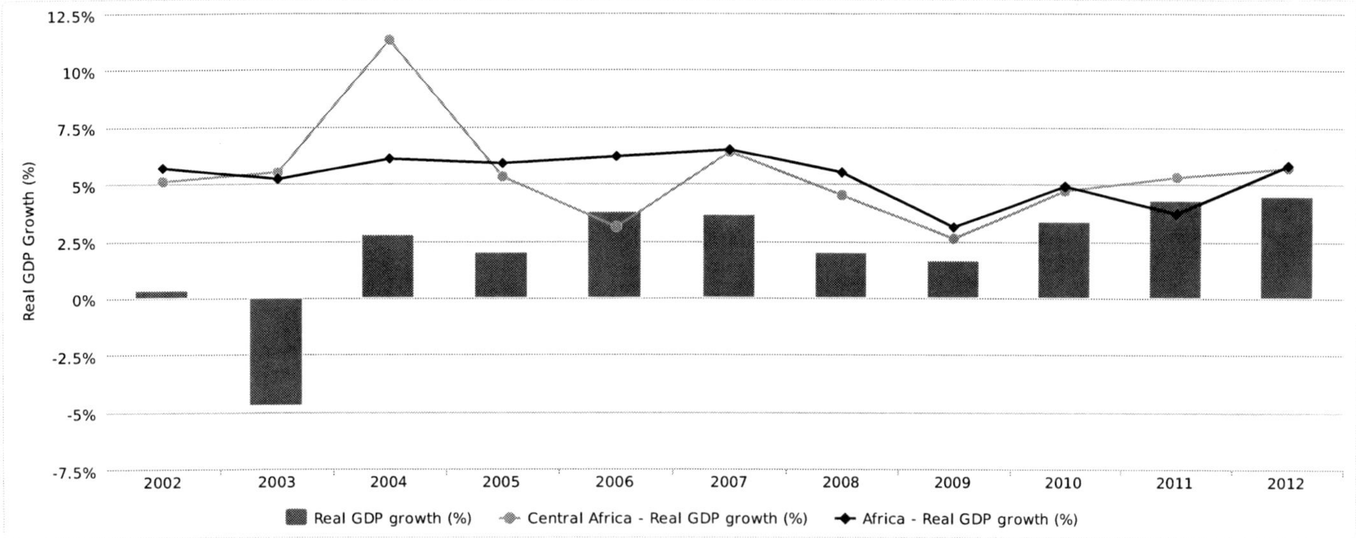

Source: IMF and local authorities' data; estimates and projections based on authors' calculations.

Figures for 2010 are estimates; for 2011 and later are projections.

StatLink http://dx.doi.org/10.1787/888932403914

Chad

An improved security situation and higher oil prices produced better growth (5.9%) in 2010 than 2009 (1.7%). This should hold up in 2011 and 2012, though budget management continues to be a serious problem.

With civil peace being consolidated, the challenges now are the advancing desert and drying-up of Lake Chad, which could harm the economy, the society and peace between farmers and the nomadic population.

Partnership with emerging countries, which focuses on areas of the economy neglected by traditional partners, is dominated by China, which wants to marginalise the presence of Chinese Taipei in Africa, and India, which has a continental strategy and seeks markets.

The economy did fairly well in 2010, growing an estimated 5.9% (up from 1.7% in 2009), with the better security situation a key. Growth was also driven by external factors such as higher world oil prices. The oil sector advanced by only 0.3% however, while the non-oil sector expanded strongly (6.4%, against 3.3% in 2009). As world demand picks up and construction and oil sector investment continues, overall growth is expected to be 5.7% in 2011 and 6.9% in 2012. Inflation fell sharply to 0.6%, from 10.1% in 2009. Public finance management was problematic due to poorly planned investment spending (based on domestic funding) which widely overshot budget limits and increased the primary non-oil deficit to 28.4% (up from 25.1% in 2009). Healthy oil prices substantially improved the external position and strong growth of goods exports (+33.8%) and foreign direct investment (FDI) in the oil sector (+36.8%) reduced the current account deficit to 12.8% of GDP (from 16.9% in 2009).

After decades of fighting, Chad has been fairly peaceful for the past two years due to concerted dialogue inside and outside the country. Presidential, parliamentary and local elections are due in early 2011. The government is also normalising ties with Sudan through a peace agreement and creation of a joint force to patrol the shared border. With civil peace being consolidated, the biggest challenge now is environmental, from the advancing desert and the drying-up of Lake Chad, which could harm the nation's health, damage agriculture, increase poverty and threaten the peaceful cohabitation of farmers and the nomadic population.

Despite progress in 2010, social indicators are still far below those elsewhere in sub-Saharan Africa. The second national household consumption and informal sector survey ECOSIT 2 (*Enquête sur la Consommation des Ménages et le Secteur Informel au Tchad*) showed 55% of people were poor, 87% of them in the countryside. The government aims to reduce the national rate to 41.3% in 2011 – 20.4% in urban areas (from 24.6% in 2003) and 44% in rural areas (58.6% in 2003).

Partnership with emerging countries is mostly with China and India and focuses on areas of the economy neglected by traditional partners. Though Chad produces oil, neither country seems to be interested in its raw materials, and the partnerships are based on FDI, diplomacy, investment in production facilities and to a lesser extent on Chad importing their goods. The tie-up with China is also part of Beijing's efforts to marginalise Chinese Taipei's presence in Africa, while India has a long-term continental strategy and seeks markets.

Table 1: Macroeconomic indicators

	2009	2010	2011	2012
Real GDP growth	1.7	5.9	5.7	6.9
CPI inflation	10.1	0.6	3.1	3.2
Budget balance % GDP	-9.8	-12.5	-9.1	-8.5
Current account % GDP	-16.9	-11.3	-9.5	-9.4

Source: National authorities' data; estimates and predictions based on authors' calculations.

Figures for 2010 are estimates; for 2011 and later are projections.

StatLink http://dx.doi.org/10.1787/888932406289

Figure 1: Real GDP growth (C)

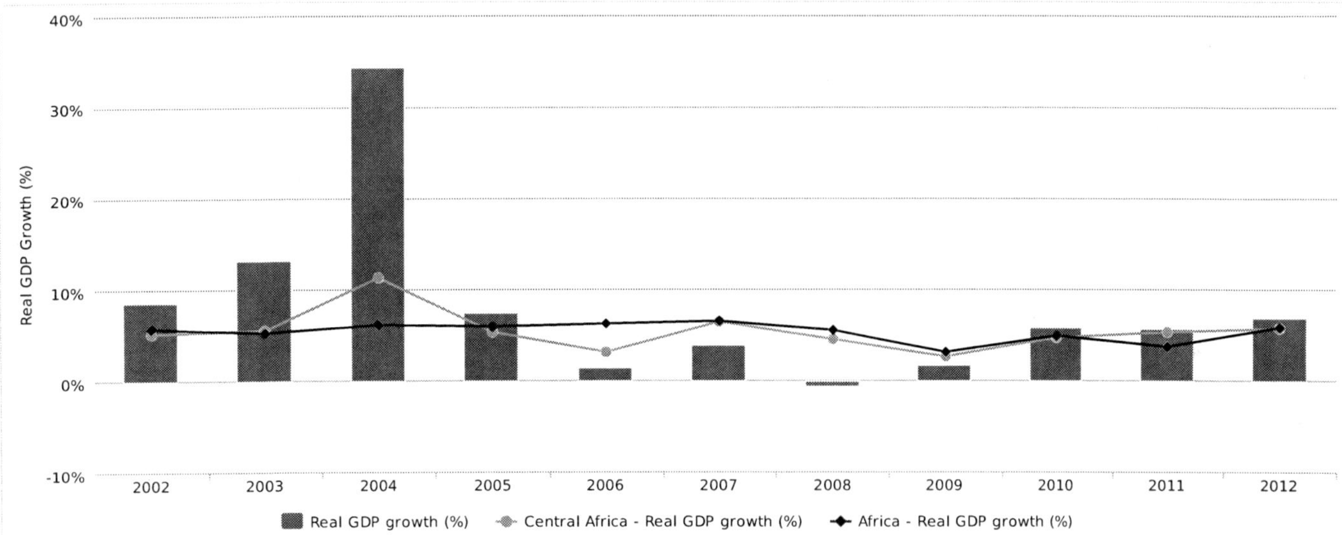

Source: IMF and local authorities' data; estimates and projections based on authors' calculations.

Figures for 2010 are estimates; for 2011 and later are projections.

StatLink http://dx.doi.org/10.1787/888932403933

Comoros

After a period of political instability, the Comorian economy continues to recover slowly, buoyed by investment and emigrants' remittances. The accuracy of the economic forecasts for 2011-12 will depend on a smooth transfer of power to the new president elected in December 2010.

Higher growth will require further structural reforms and fiscal consolidation, increased tax collection and better governance.

The 2010 conference in Qatar on development and investment in Comoros gave a new dimension to partnership with emerging countries. If Comoros is to profit from this external support, an effective mechanism to follow up on the pledges given at the conference is needed.

The Union of the Comoros is an archipelago of three islands (Grande Comore, Anjouan and Moheli), with an undiversified economy and few natural resources. The country has suffered from chronic political instability for a number of years, with repeated coups and secessionist leanings among the islands, and this troubled political climate has hampered its economic and social development.

The Comorian economy has not yet recovered from the consequences of this period of instability, nor from the global recession of the last few years. In 2010, the real gross domestic product (GDP) growth rate was 2.1%, up from 1.1% in 2009. Growth was driven by public investment, the strengthening of the financial sector and the buoyancy of construction, financed by remittances from the Comorian Diaspora.

New measures to increase fiscal resource mobilisation raised tax revenue slightly from 10.4% of GDP in 2009 to an estimated 10.6% in 2010. Total expenditure amounted to 22.7% of GDP, as against 22.1% in 2009. The executed budget exhibited a primary surplus of 4.6% of GDP in 2010 (0.6% in 2009), as a result of the rise in tax revenue and grants.

The country's external position remained poor in 2010, as the current account deficit widened to an estimated 10.2% of GDP despite substantial transfers from expatriates. This trend can be attributed to the increased deficit in the services account, a slight dip in exports and a sharp increase in imports of consumer and capital goods. The current account deficit should average 12% of GDP in 2011-12.

In 2010, the government of Qatar hosted a conference on development and investment in Comoros that elicited pledges estimated at more than 500 million US dollars (USD), notably from the Gulf countries. Qatar provided 20 million euros (EUR) of budget support that enabled Comoros to pay off wage and pension arrears.

Remittances from expatriates, which are a key source of finance and support for the Comorian economy, remained dynamic in 2010 despite the unfavourable international climate. These transfers were facilitated by the opening of branch offices of the Comorian post office in France.

As a result of the reform programme supported by an Extended Credit Facility (ECF) from the International Monetary Fund (IMF) in July 2010, the Comoros reached the decision point of the Heavily Indebted Poor Countries (HIPC) Initiative. The interim debt reduction granted by creditors eased the pressure on Comoros' public finances.

The business climate remained much the same in 2010 as in 2009 – Comoros is still ranked 159th out of 183 countries in the World Bank's *Doing Business* report – but the stabilisation of the political situation and initiatives to clean up the business environment are expected to bring some improvement. Domestic lending rose moderately. This cautious monetary policy is conducted under the terms of the monetary co-operation agreement with France. In 2010, the mandatory reserve requirement of the Central Bank of Comoros (BCC) was increased from 25% to 30% to offset the increase in money supply. This decision was taken to avert the possibility of an inflationary surge following the substantial grants provided to clear the government's wage arrears.

Constitutional reforms and the improvement of the political climate made it possible to carry the 2010 electoral process through to completion. The election brought Vice-President Ikililou Dhoinine to the presidency. The transfer of powers by President Ahmed Sambi should take place by 26 May 2011 at the latest. The economic situation in 2011 will depend on whether the political transition goes smoothly, as well as on structural reforms and public and foreign investment.

Table 1: Macroeconomic indicators

	2009	2010	2011	2012
Real GDP growth	1.1	2.1	2.5	3.2
CPI inflation	4.8	2.9	3	2.8
Budget balance % GDP	0.6	4.1	-3.1	-3.6
Current account % GDP	-7.6	-10.2	-11.7	-12.2

Source: National authorities' data; estimates and predictions based on authors' calculations.

Figures for 2010 are estimates; for 2011 and later are projections.

StatLink http://dx.doi.org/10.1787/888932406308

Figure 1: Real GDP growth (E)

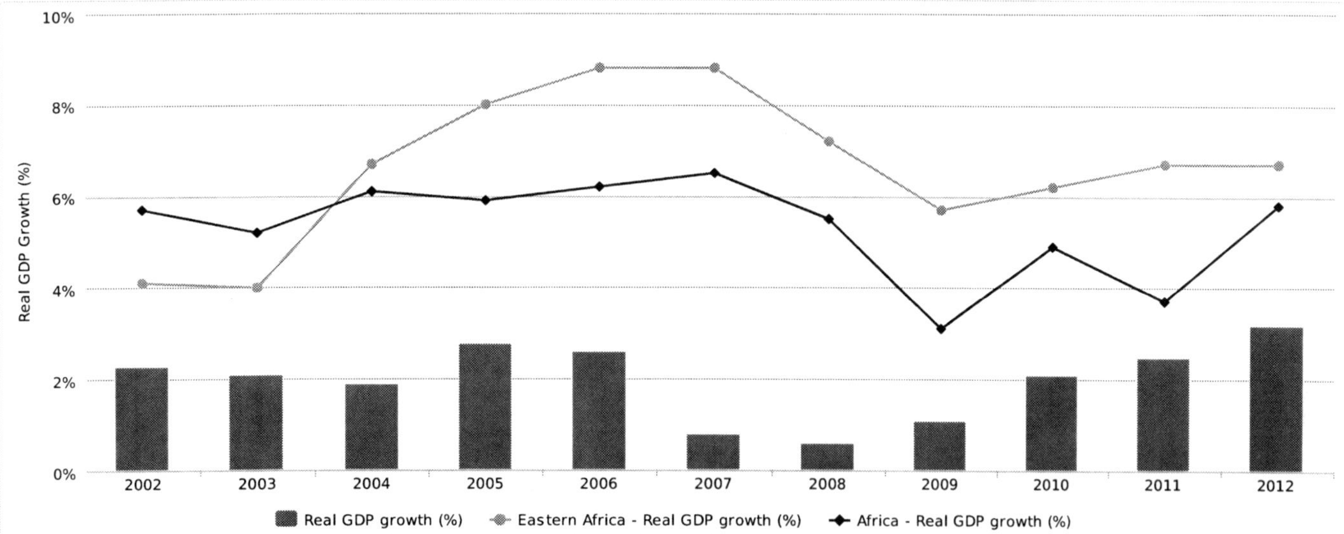

Source: IMF and local authorities' data; estimates and projections based on authors' calculations.

Figures for 2010 are estimates; for 2011 and later are projections.

StatLink http://dx.doi.org/10.1787/888932403952

Congo, Democratic Republic

After slow growth in 2009, the Democratic Republic of Congo (DRC)'s 2010 real gross domestic product (GDP) growth rate, boosted mainly by higher world prices for raw materials, has been estimated at 6.1%, and this pace is projected to continue over the next two years.

Achievement of the HIPC Initiative completion point in June 2010 should lead to social improvements and the application of reforms should benefit the country.

Partnerships with emerging countries (mainly China and India) are allowing the DRC, as a post-conflict country, to broaden its sources of funding for reconstruction.

The economy began to recover in 2010, with estimations showing real GDP growth increasing to 6.1% from 2.8% in 2009 and largely driven by mining, which was buoyed by higher world prices. This in turn stimulated the services sector and infrastructure rehabilitation. Contributors to overall growth were mining (11.8%), construction (10.1%) and wholesale and retail trade (6.3%). The economy is expected to grow at around 6.5% over the next two years.

The budget deficit, which had worsened in 2009 as a result of the world economic crisis, improved in 2010 thanks to higher government revenue, but is expected to worsen again in 2011.

Better co-ordination of monetary and budgetary policies cut inflation to 23.2% in 2010 from 46.2% in 2009, and it is expected to fall sharply to around 10% in 2011. The central bank (BCC) reduced its key interest rate five times during the year and it reached 22% in November 2010.

The revival of the world economy and the country's achievement of completion point under the Heavily Indebted Poor Countries (HIPC) Initiative should greatly improve the DRC's external position. The current-account deficit increased to almost 16% of GDP in 2010, from 10.1% in 2009. It is expected to remain high in 2011 and 2012. Reaching completion point in June 2010 has opened the way to total debt relief of USD 12.3 billion: 11.1 billion under the HIPC Initiative and 1.2 billion under the Multilateral Debt Relief Initiative (MDRI).

The DRC ranks 175th in the World Bank's *Doing Business* report, an improvement of four places mainly due to reforms in setting up businesses, granting building permits and transferring property.

The central bank surveyed commercial-bank loan quality and whether to recapitalise or restructure some banks. Dollarisation is still substantial, with foreign currency making up 85.7% of all bank deposits. Actionable debts were estimated at 4.8% of total debts to the private sector at the end of November 2010, up from 3.6% at the end of December 2009.

Ongoing decentralisation and privatisation are having serious problems, but public-finance management has improved thanks to effective use of resources.

The country's vast road network is still in very poor condition despite efforts to improve it, and electricity supply remains far below the country's needs, but an aid agreement with China and resumption of ties with foreign donors have re-energised these sub-sectors.

The first report by the Extractive Industries Transparency Initiative (EITI) was approved by a multiparty group in January 2010, and several mining contracts have been amended.

Politicians are waiting for general elections due in 2011. Efforts to improve governance have not, however, changed the country's very low ranking in worldwide indexes.

Progress has been made in health and education but most Millennium Development Goals (MDGs) are unlikely to be achieved.

Partnerships with emerging countries include ties with China, India, Korea and Brazil, which are very involved in mining, construction, information and communication technology (ICT), agriculture, technology transfer and social development, with India supplying credit lines, and China grants and soft loans. Chinese enterprises dominate public-works projects and have increased their activity in mining.

Table 1: Macroeconomic indicators

	2009	2010	2011	2012
Real GDP growth	2.8	6.1	6.7	6.4
CPI inflation	46.2	23.2	10.2	9.8
Budget balance % GDP	-4.1	-0.5	-8.3	-6.6
Current account % GDP	-10.1	-15.7	-16.7	-14.3

Source: National authorities' data; estimates and predictions based on authors' calculations.

Figures for 2010 are estimates; for 2011 and later are projections.

StatLink http://dx.doi.org/10.1787/888932406327

Figure 1: Real GDP growth (C)

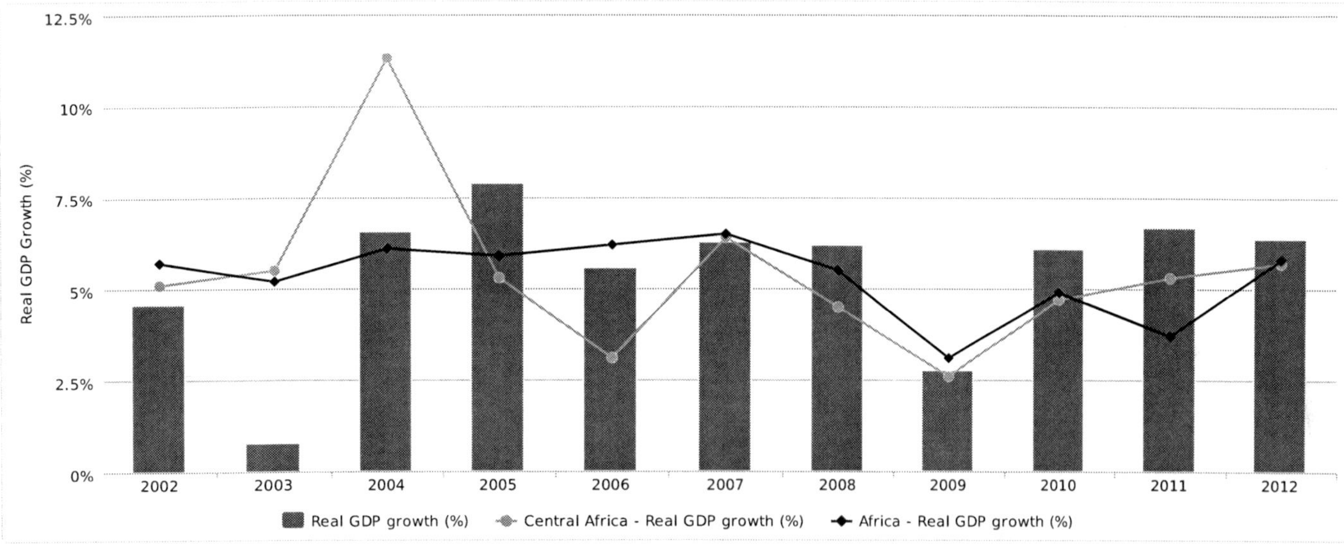

Source: IMF and local authorities' data; estimates and projections based on authors' calculations.

Figures for 2010 are estimates; for 2011 and later are projections.

StatLink http://dx.doi.org/10.1787/888932403971

Congo Republic

Congo registered 10.2% growth in 2010 thanks to an increase in oil production and debt relief obtained under the Heavily Indebted Poor Countries (HIPC) Initiative.

Congo maintains strong and diversified relations with numerous emerging partners in Asia (China and India), the Middle East and South America.

Only two Millennium Development Goals (MDGs) will be achieved in 2015: education for all and gender equality.

Congo's economic performance in 2010 owes a great deal to the increase in its oil production. The latter reached a record level, estimated at 115 million barrels compared to 99 million in 2009. Fiscal reform and debt relief obtained under the HIPC Initiative also consolidated fundamental indicators and improved the budgetary balance. The result was a strong 10.2% growth rate in 2010, with 8.4% expected in 2011. These growth rates nevertheless remain fragile. They depend too heavily on the international oil market and maintenance of a high level of oil production. Medium-term forecasts show that oil production will gradually diminish unless new reserves are discovered. Diversification of the economy remains a crucial issue. Construction, public works and telecommunications continue to thrive. The forestry sector seems to be recovering after having been penalised by the global crisis. Increased demand from Asian countries, particularly China, which is the leading buyer of Congolese timber, is ensuring the industry's survival.

The budgetary balance improved markedly in 2010 to reach 13.9% of gross domestic product (GDP) and is forecast to reach 16.5% in 2011. This is the result of a budgetary policy based on improving the quality of expenditure and implementation of the public contracts code and the public investment management system in line with the Medium-Term Expenditure Framework (MTEF). Revenue should increase 12% in 2011, with oil revenue up 74.3% and fiscal revenue up 17.8%. The Republic of Congo should benefit from XAF 50 billion in 2011 in HIPC resources. Grants should reach XAF 45 billion and state borrowing XAF 115 billion.

Congo's external position progressed in 2010 thanks to good oil price levels, improved productivity from certain reserves and a recovery in timber exports. The current account deficit fell to 2.6% of GDP in 2010 thanks to the increase in exports.

The inflation rate stood at 4.8% in 2010 under the impact of strong domestic demand and an increase in international prices for food products.

Table 1: Macroeconomic indicators

	2009	2010	2011	2012
Real GDP growth	6.8	10.2	8.4	3.1
CPI inflation	3.8	4.8	5.2	3.3
Budget balance % GDP	5.4	13.9	16.5	15.6
Current account % GDP	-20.8	-2.6	0.3	-8.4

Source: National authorities' data; estimates and predictions based on authors' calculations.

Figures for 2010 are estimates; for 2011 and later are projections.

StatLink http://dx.doi.org/10.1787/888932406346

Relations with emerging countries, notably India and China, go back to Congo's independence in 1960. More recently, relations have been forged with other Asian countries, such as Malaysia and Korea, Middle Eastern countries, such as Saudi Arabia and the United Arab Emirates, and Latin American countries, such as Brazil and Argentina.

Asia is Congo's biggest client. It accounted for 56% of total exports in 2009, ahead of Latin America, where Mexico, Brazil and Argentina absorb 20% of Congolese exports. China is the country's leading Asian partner, accounting for 40% of Congo's export sales, principally in the form of oil and timber, compared with 10% for Chinese Taipei. Imports from Asia nevertheless remain at a low level. They take the form mainly of food products and capital equipment but represent less than 8% of the country's total foreign purchases.

Congo is lagging way behind on the Millennium Development Goals (MDGs). It will probably attain only two objectives by 2015 – universal education and sexual equality. Poverty has only slightly diminished, according to the latest study, carried out in 2009. The health situation remains worrying with high levels of infant and maternal mortality and still limited access to drinking water and sanitation. Unemployment remains high, especially among the young, and the average monthly salary level in the public sector does not exceed EUR 100.

Figure 1: Real GDP growth (C)

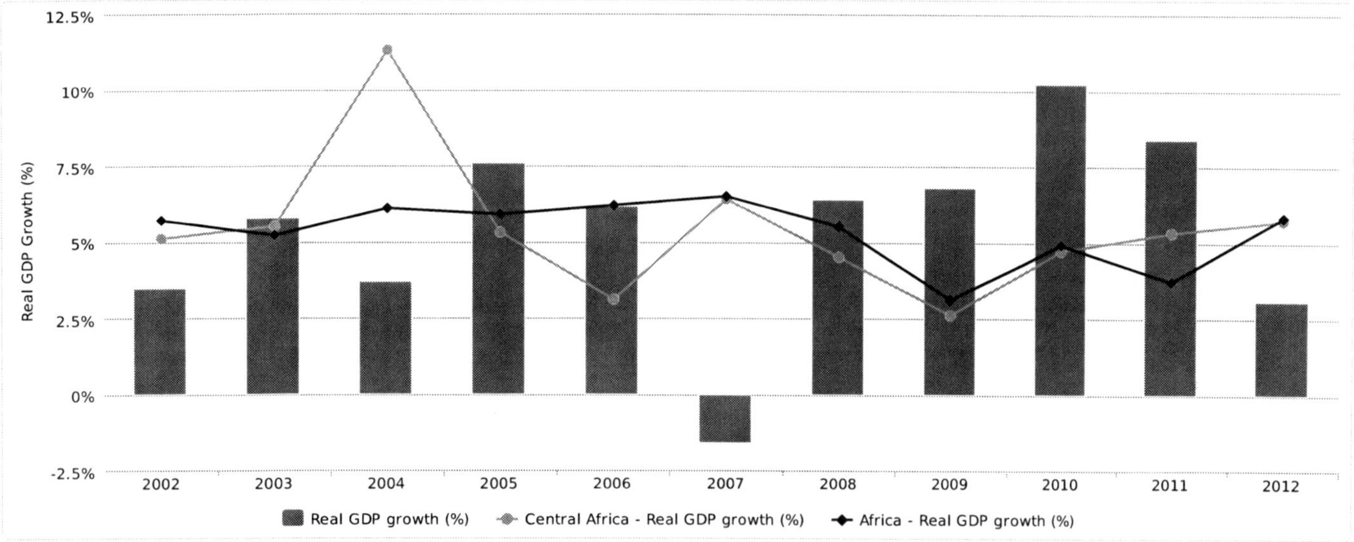

Source: IMF and local authorities' data; estimates and projections based on authors' calculations.

Figures for 2010 are estimates; for 2011 and later are projections.

StatLink http://dx.doi.org/10.1787/888932403990

Côte d'Ivoire

Since the presidential election of 28 November 2010, Côte d'Ivoire has been faced with a grave post-electoral political crisis which has significantly weakened and disrupted economic activity.

Its performance has been affected but it has the necessary resources to turn the economy around once a climate of peace has been established.

Despite its current difficulties, Côte d'Ivoire remains a key country in the West African Economic and Monetary Union (WAEMU) and continues to open its borders to new Asian trading partners.

The political impasse in Côte d'Ivoire following the second round of the presidential elections on 28 November 2010 turned into an armed conflict between the defence and security forces led by the outgoing president Laurent Gbagbo and the republican forces loyal to Alassane Ouattara, the elected president recognised by the international community. After several days of heavy fighting, the pro-Ouattara forces arrested Gbagbo and several of his aides while they were in the bunker of the presidential palace. The escalation of the violence and the use of heavy weaponry have increased the civilian death toll to more than 900 according to the UN, with thousands more injured and massive numbers of Ivorian refugees, especially in neighbouring Liberia and Ghana.

This post-electoral crisis and the sanctions imposed by the international community have had a strong impact on the economy, leaving the country cash-strapped. Nearly all the financial institutions and private firms have had to cease operations due to the insecurity and the suspension of the clearing system by the Central Bank of West African States (BCEAO).

With this economic paralysis, the forecast for 2011 is for a strong fall of 7.3% in real GDP growth, as is made evident in the table below. Nevertheless, a gradual recovery is expected in 2012 (+5.9%) based on the hypothesis of the security situation returning to normal in the second half of 2011, the sanctions being lifted and international co-operation being resumed. Also, the commitment of development partners to support the Ivorian authorities in their efforts for reconciliation and reconstruction will enable trust to be restored, thus fostering private-sector development.

The political crisis has made the already-precarious humanitarian situation worse. By March 2011, around a million Ivorians had been forced out of their homes, while more than 79 000 more had fled mainly to the Ghanaian border, but also to the Liberian border. The lack of drinking water and sanitation in some urban areas, especially in Abidjan, could increase the spread of water-borne diseases. There are enormous risks in terms of Côte d'Ivoire's progress in achieving the Millennium Development Goals (MDGs) by 2015. It is feared that many of the population will fall into poverty, with the level of poverty standing at 48.9% of the population in 2008.

Côte d'Ivoire's medium-term economic and social outlook largely depends upon peace being restored and emergency reconstruction programmes being implemented. Despite the socio-political crisis of the last ten years, Côte d'Ivoire's economic partnerships with emerging countries have markedly increased, particularly those with Asian countries, including, notably, China, Korea, India, Singapore, Thailand, Brunei Darrusalam, Indonesia and Malaysia. Asia is Côte d'Ivoire's third largest trading partner (12.5%), after Europe (44.0%) and Africa (29.0%). China, which is the country's leading Asian partner, still represents a modest share (3.2%) of the economy compared to its wider performance in Africa.

Table 1: Macroeconomic indicators

	2009	2010	2011	2012
Real GDP growth	3.7	2	-7.3	5.9
CPI inflation	4.7	2.7	6.3	3.3
Budget balance % GDP	-1.6	-2.5	-1.9	-3.4
Current account % GDP	7.2	5.9	5.2	4.2

Source: National authorities' data; estimates and predictions based on authors' calculations.

Figures for 2010 are estimates; for 2011 and later are projections.

StatLink http://dx.doi.org/10.1787/888932406365

Figure 1: Real GDP growth (W)

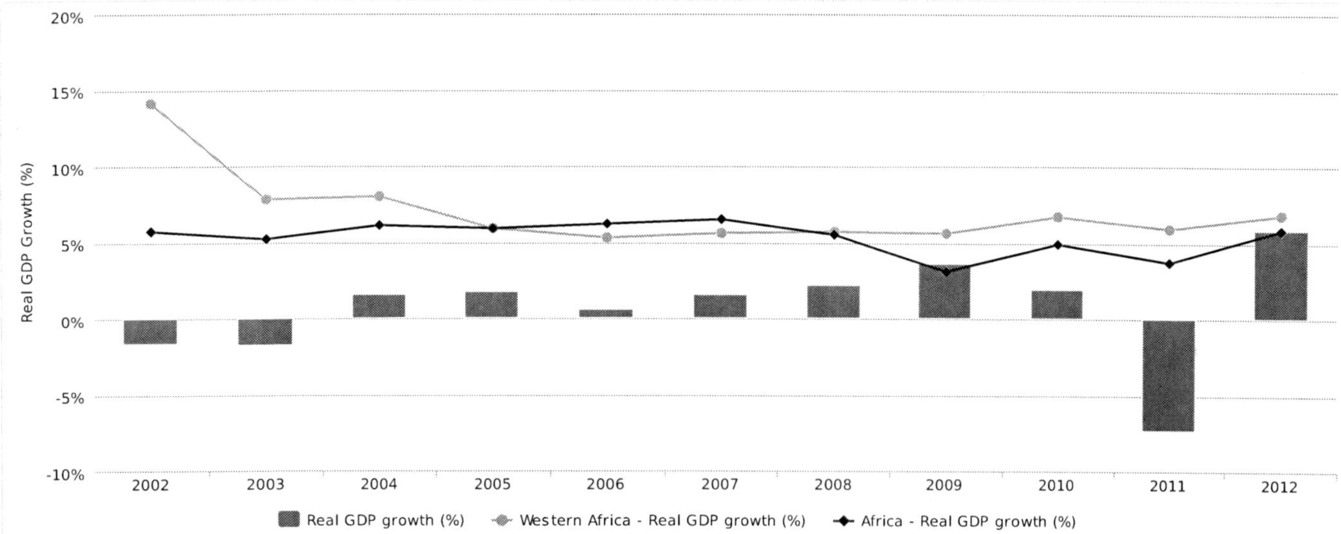

Source: IMF and local authorities' data; estimates and projections based on authors' calculations.

Figures for 2010 are estimates; for 2011 and later are projections.

StatLink http://dx.doi.org/10.1787/888932404009

Djibouti

In spite of a small contraction, Djibouti's economic growth remained steady in 2010. This growth did not, however, lead to a significant reduction in the endemic poverty in the country, which is still faced with significant shortages of energy and water. Djibouti also faces the problem of food insecurity.

Driven by the recovery in port operations and foreign direct investment (FDI), growth should accelerate in 2011 and 2012.

Investment from the Gulf states has been one of the main engines of growth over the past few years.

In 2010 Djibouti saw steady economic growth, at an estimated 4.4%, albeit slightly below the 2009 level of 5%. The less vigorous performance of the economy in 2010 was due to a reduction in port operations, upon which the country's economy is heavily dependent, and the postponement of planned foreign direct investment (FDI). Nevertheless, domestic private investment accelerated.

In 2011 and 2012 the economy is forecast to grow by 4.6% and 5.1% respectively, boosted by a recovery in port operations and FDI.

Following the fiscal slippage in 2009, the authorities tackled the issue of restoring balance to the public finances in 2010 in line with the requirements of the International Monetary Fund (IMF). A three-year IMF programme is in place through an Extended Fund Facility (EFF) agreed upon in 2008. The public deficit of 5.1% of gross domestic product (GDP) in 2009 was cut to 2.7% in 2010.

Inflation, meanwhile, surged from 1.7% in 2009 to 4.2% in 2010. This was mainly caused by dearer food products from the second quarter on and, to a lesser extent, more expensive transport and price rises in the housing, water, electricity, gas and other fuels sub-sector. It should be recalled that the annualised rise in prices reached 12% in 2008.

With the aim of strengthening Djibouti's position as a hub for trade, logistics and related services, as well as a provider of financial services, several road corridors were opened or renovated in 2010.

Furthermore, the authorities have continued to develop the financial sector, passing new laws governing banking, such as stronger legislation regulating banks, and relating to financial cooperatives and Islamic finance. Two new banks came into being, bringing the total number of financial institutions in Djibouti to 11. Other structural reforms have been carried out, including an overhaul of the investment code, legislation on companies and bankruptcies, and the overhaul of the labour code.

Nevertheless, the economy remains little diversified and highly dependent on port operations in the tertiary sector. This accounts for 76% of GDP, while the primary sector contributes a mere 3.9%. The country depends almost entirely on imports for its food supply. Domestic agricultural production covers only 10% of the country's food needs. The country still faces the problem of structural food insecurity, which has been made worse by recurring droughts. Its energy supply is limited and expensive, putting a brake on the country's development. To solve this problem in 2010 the authorities began to construct an electricity interconnection with Ethiopia so they can import power.

Finally, although economic growth is steady it does not yet benefit everyone. Unemployment remains high and poverty affects 70% of the population.

Table 1: Macroeconomic indicators

	2009	2010	2011	2012
Real GDP growth	5	4.4	4.6	5.1
CPI inflation	1.7	4.2	4	3
Budget balance % GDP	-5.1	-2.7	-2.5	-1.3
Current account % GDP	-17.5	-9.1	-14.3	-13.6

Source: National authorities' data; estimates and predictions based on authors' calculations.

Figures for 2010 are estimates; for 2011 and later are projections.

StatLink http://dx.doi.org/10.1787/888932406384

Figure 1: Real GDP growth (E)

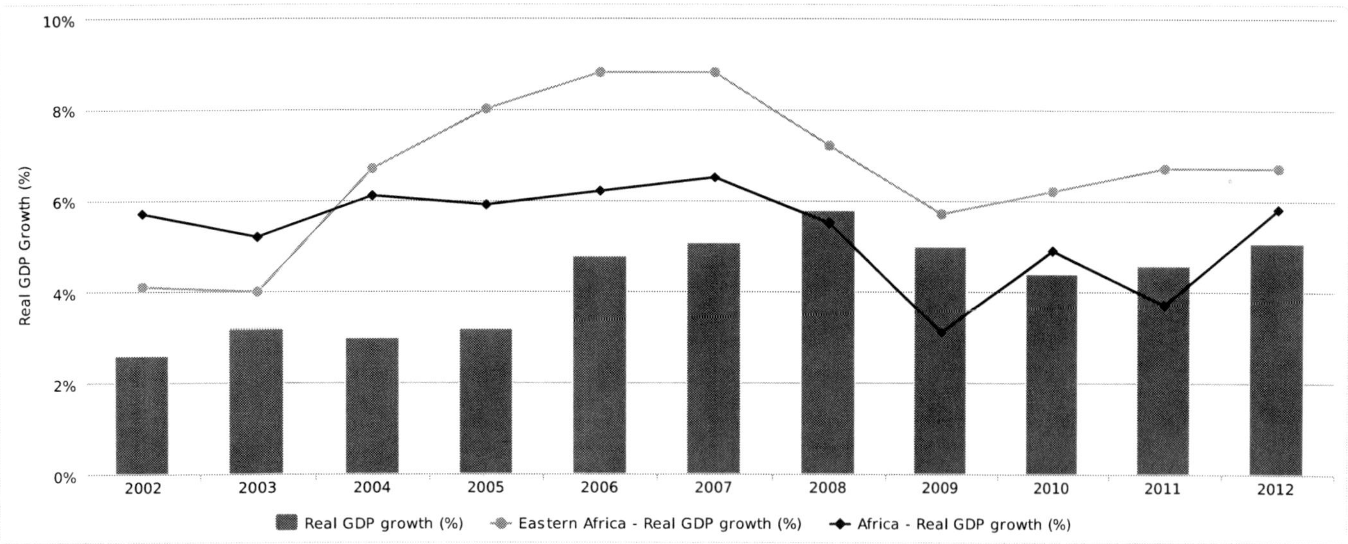

Source: IMF and local authorities' data; estimates and projections based on authors' calculations.

Figures for 2010 are estimates; for 2011 and later are projections.

StatLink http://dx.doi.org/10.1787/888932404028

Egypt

The Egyptian economy grew at an estimated 5.1% in the fiscal year to June 2010 as the country started to recover from the impact of the global financial crisis. Political unrest, which led to the ouster of President Hosni Mubarak in early 2011, will likely dampen growth but the prospect of substantial economic and political reform offers hope for the future.

Egypt suffers from severe social handicaps – poor educational attainment, high unemployment and wide income disparities. Economic growth has not delivered the benefits it should have due to corruption and lack of political reform.

Egypt continues to rely mainly on its traditional partners – the United States of America and the European Union – but emerging country partners are taking on a larger role. Arab countries constitute an important source of foreign direct investment (FDI) and are also a primary destination for young Egyptian migrants.

Egypt has been on the brink of social and political turmoil for the past few years, with evident signs of mounting frustration among citizens, mainly due to the severe socio-economic conditions, constraints on liberties and an uncertain political outlook. Inspired by the Tunisian revolution, Egyptians started a large-scale uprising on 25 January 2011 and after 18 days of protests, Mr. Hosni Mubarak stepped down, bringing to an end his 30-year rule as Egypt's President. Power was handed to the Supreme Council of the Armed Forces which became responsible for conducting the affairs of the State and leading the transitional period according to a constitutional declaration issued on 30 March, until the parliamentary and presidential elections are held towards the end of 2011.

While the Egyptian popular uprising has come with the promise of major political reform, it has led to the temporary disruption of economic activity, below-capacity production and a 55-day shutdown of the stock market. The adverse economic implications thereof will most likely be sustained throughout 2010/11, as the high uncertainty in Egypt will weaken FDI inflows as well as tourism and Suez Canal receipts. Thus, real GDP growth rate is expected to be only 1.6% in 2010/11; down from 5.1% in 2009/10.

The interim government has tried to absorb the anger of protesters by stepping up food subsidies, freezing the plan to phase out energy subsidies and upgrading the status of temporary government workers who have been in their posts for more than three years to permanent workers. While the interim government should indeed be addressing such crucial social priorities, it should also take into account their medium- and long-term implications on fiscal balances.

The budget deficit is expected to rise from 8.1% in 2009/10 to close to 10% in 2010/11, as the interim government boosts spending to offset the impact of the political unrest. The temporary supply shortages that followed the upheaval coupled with rising international prices of food and fuel have been adding to the pressure on the domestic price level since early 2011. Thus the inflation rate is expected to increase from 11.7% in 2009/10 to 13.4% in 2010/11. Similarly, the current account deficit is expected to widen from 2.0% of GDP in 2009/10 to 3.2% in 2010/11 and then fall marginally to 2.9% in 2011/12 as FDI inflows, remittances and the services balance remain vulnerable.

Egypt's partnerships with emerging economies, mainly in non-Arab Asia and the Arab world are still marginal compared to those with the European Union and the United States of America. Although economic relations with emerging partners have been on an upward trend, the political unrest in Egypt and the wider region will hinder trade, particularly with Arab countries as well as FDI inflows and remittances originating from Arab countries. The Egyptian government already allocated 100 million Egyptian pounds (EGP), targeted at addressing employment issues of returning labour from Arab countries, especially Libya.

The restoration of political stability and effective reform are essential if the Egyptian economy is to return to solid growth that benefits the population as a whole. In order to alleviate poverty and improve living standards, the priority has to be a high and sustainable growth rate while addressing social concerns such as unemployment, income distribution and the poor level and quality of education and health services. Fiscal consolidation is key to the realisation of Egypt's economic and social objectives as reform efforts have historically been diluted by poorly targeted government expenditure and a large public debt.

Table 1: Macroeconomic indicators

	2009	2010	2011	2012
Real GDP growth	4.7	5.1	1.6	4
CPI inflation	16.2	11.7	13.4	12.2
Budget balance % GDP	-6.6	-8.1	-9.8	-9.4
Current account % GDP	-2.3	-2	-3.2	-2.9

Source: National authorities' data; estimates and predictions based on authors' calculations.

Fiscal year July (n-1)/ June (n).

Figures for 2010 are estimates; for 2011 and later are projections.

StatLink http://dx.doi.org/10.1787/888932406403

Figure 1: Real GDP growth (N)

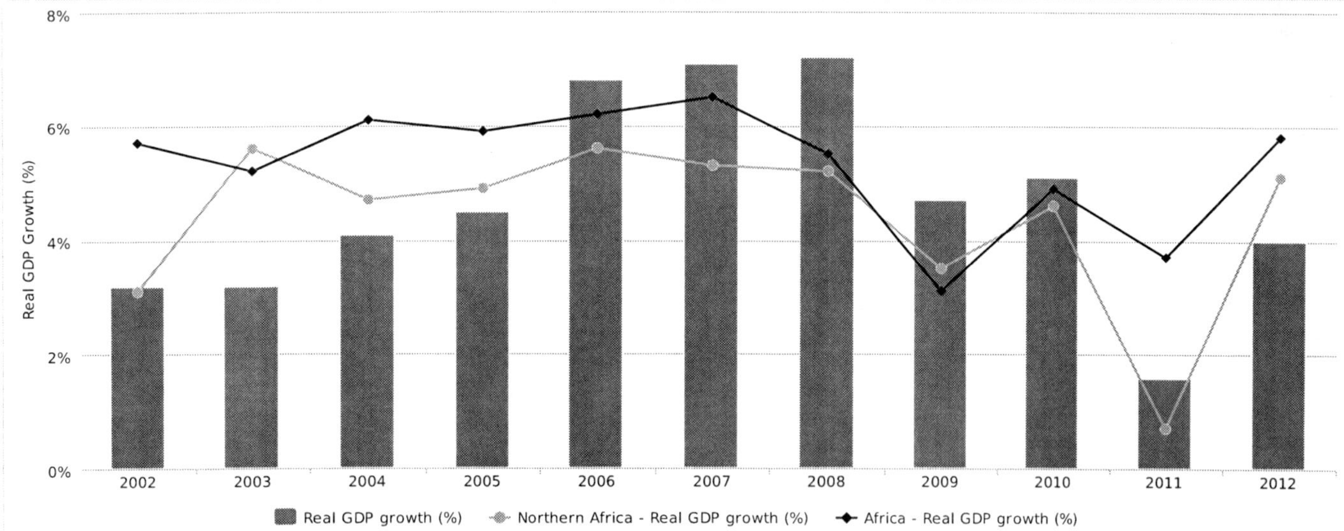

Source: IMF and local authorities' data; estimates and projections based on authors' calculations.

Figures for 2010 are estimates; for 2011 and later are projections.

StatLink http://dx.doi.org/10.1787/888932404047

Equatorial Guinea

During 2010, the economy grew by 1.2% of gross domestic product (GDP). One of the lowest growth rates since oil exploitation began in the mid-1990s.

Over 70% of the population in Equatorial Guinea still falls below the poverty line. A major challenge is to develop the policies to allow the majority of the population to benefit from the country's vast oil wealth.

Oil wealth has attracted the attention of emerging economies in recent years. The main emerging partner is China, followed by a small presence of Chinese Taipei, Cuba, Argentina, Brazil and Russia. Equatorial Guinea lacks the administrative capacity to engage strategically with the emerging partners.

Equatorial Guinea's economy experienced growth of 1.2% of GDP in 2010 as a result of the fall of oil output and the main oil-producing fields reaching their maturity. The economy has been on a downward trend since 2004, when real GDP growth peaked at 38%. 2010 experienced one of the lowest growth rates since oil exploitation of hydrocarbons began in the mid-1990s. It is expected to recover and return to high growth rates of 5.0% and 7.5% in 2011 and 2012. Despite lower outputs from the oil industry, growth will be sustained by the international demand for hydrocarbons and the construction of major infrastructure projects, including those for the hydrocarbon industry.

The recovery of oil prices has had a positive effect on the government budget with the deficit reaching 2.6% of GDP in 2010, up from a deficit of 9.6% of GDP in 2009. Driven by falling imports, the current account rose to a surplus of 2.7% of GDP in 2010, compared to a 7.6% deficit in 2009; it is projected to remain in surplus of 2.9% in 2011 and further 3.8% in 2012. The inflation rate for 2010 was 4.7%. As a result of continued high levels of capital expenditure, inflation is expected to remain in the region of 6.3% in 2011. Equatorial Guinea faces no debt problems due to a budget surplus and external reserves. External debt at the end 2010 was close to 5% of GDP, or XAF 307 billion (CFA Franc BEAC).

Equatorial Guinea lost its Extractive Industries Transparency Initiative (EITI) candidate status in 2010. The government stated its intention to improve the management of the oil sector and reapply for admission. Furthermore, the environment for private-sector activity remains difficult. Equatorial Guinea still ranks among the bottom countries in the World Bank's *Doing Business Index*. It slipped three places in the ranking in 2011 to 164 from 161 in 2010. Key constraints include construction permits, import licences, the perceived high level of corruption, elaborate procedures and an unpredictable judicial environment.

Over 70% of the population in Equatorial Guinea falls below the poverty line, raising questions about the extent to which the country's oil wealth has benefitted the majority of the population. Maternal and infant mortality rates are still very high. Measuring progress towards the Millennium Development Goals (MDGs) with precision is an extremely difficult task because of data deficits and an ongoing controversy about the population census. The country is on track to achieve the MDGs of universal primary education, reducing child mortality, improving maternal health, and combating HIV/AIDS, malaria and other diseases. However, it is not on track to achieve the MDGs of ensuring environmental sustainability and promoting gender equality and empowering women.

On the political front, 2010 has been the first year in office of the new cabinet under the same government, which has been in power since 1979. There have been few signs of political opening or change. Tensions have, nevertheless, remitted since the attack on the presidential palace in early 2009. In 2010, a group of four top military and government officials were sentenced to death for their role in these events. The government is trying to pursue an open-door policy to the rest of the world during 2010 with important investments in major events, including hosting the 2011 summit of the African Union and the 2012 Africa Cup of Nations. The plans for a UNESCO-Obiang Nguema Mbasogo award for scientific achievement were put on hold after intense criticism by the international community. The president´s eldest son, Teodoro Nguema Obiang Mangue, and current Minister of Agriculture, has continued his ascension to power after being promoted to the rank of Lieutenant Colonel in the army and vice-president of the ruling party.

Oil wealth has attracted the attention of emerging economies in recent years. However, the country remains relatively closed. Equatorial Guinea's main emerging partner is China. There is a small presence of Chinese Taipei, Cuba, Argentina, Brazil and Russia. The country's hydrocarbons industry is still dominated by US companies but Chinese companies are increasingly active providing significant credit lines. Equatorial Guinea lacks the administrative capacity to engage strategically with the emerging partners.

Table 1: Macroeconomic indicators

	2009	2010	2011	2012
Real GDP growth	5.3	1.2	5	7.5
CPI inflation	7.2	4.7	6.3	5.6
Budget balance % GDP	-9.6	-2.6	-2.8	-2.7
Current account % GDP	-7.6	2.7	2.9	3.8

Source: National authorities' data; estimates and predictions based on authors' calculations.

Figures for 2010 are estimates; for 2011 and later are projections.

StatLink http://dx.doi.org/10.1787/888932406422

Figure 1: Real GDP growth (C)

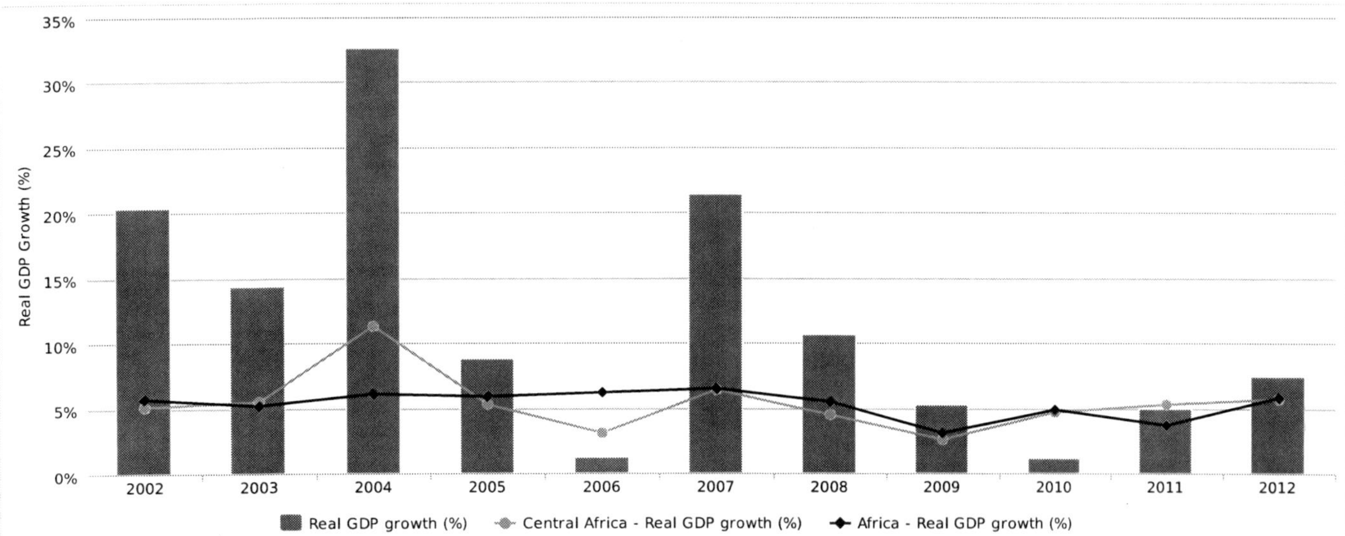

Source: IMF and local authorities' data; estimates and projections based on authors' calculations.

Figures for 2010 are estimates; for 2011 and later are projections.

StatLink http://dx.doi.org/10.1787/888932404066

Ethiopia

Ethiopia is expected to continue on its fast growth track. It recorded average growth of above 10% over the past five years. In 2011, growth is expected to again reach 10% before decelerating slightly to just below 9% in 2012.

Impressive economic growth has put the country on track to reach most of the Millennium Development Goals (MDGs) by 2015. The poverty rate has fallen from almost 39% in 2005 to around 32% in 2010.

Ethiopia is pursuing opportunities for growth and development with new partners such as China, India and Turkey, but needs to exercise caution while adopting a strategy to maximise the benefits.

In 2010, Ethiopia continued to register the fast growth as it has for the last five years. Gross domestic product (GDP) growth in 2010 (2009/10) remained strong at 8.8%. Growth is driven by the service sector (14.5%), followed by the industrial (10.2%) and agricultural (6%) sectors. Except for a rebound in fishing, the rest of the agricultural sub-sectors remained fundamentally unchanged from their levels in 2009. The service sector's leading role is due to hotels and restaurants, financial intermediation, public services and real estate. The country continues to struggle with the macroeconomic challenges of high inflation and very low international reserves. The government's five-year Growth and Transformation Plan was launched in 2010/11. If it is successful, the prospects for 2011 and 2012 are likely to be as positive as in 2010. The plan calls for the agriculture sector to become the major source of economic growth. Industrial growth will also be given particular attention. The government intends to promote industrialisation through increased exports and import substitution. The economy is projected to grow at an average annual rate of 10% in 2011. The agriculture sector is expected to grow by 8.1% while industry and services are expected to show an average annual growth of 20 and 11% respectively during the planned five-year period of the government.

In 2010, although growth remained strong, macroeconomic management was problematic because of the rising level of inflation and a sharp depreciation of the national currency. The government managed to contain inflation through a combination of monetary instruments, i.e. the contraction of credit and money supply growth. The government devalued the national currency by 20% in 2010 with the aim of boosting exports and raising the level of external reserves. The government intends to use monetary policy to keep inflation below 10% starting in 2011 and through the duration of its five-year plan.

Following a drop in merchandise exports in 2009 due mainly to the global economic crisis hitting demand for key traditional export commodities, exports began to bounce back slowly in 2010. Imports remained strong in 2010 at 27.2% of GDP. The government projects this figure will grow to between 30 and 35% of GDP per annum by 2015. The result is a large trade and balance-of-payment deficit. The current account balance is expected to worsen from about minus 6.4% of GDP in 2010/11 to minus 11.9% in 2011/12.

The private sector is confronted with a number of challenges including: *i)* a poor business environment; *ii)* a poorly performing judicial system that fails to address property rights and weak corporate governance; *iii)* a relatively undeveloped financial system; and *iv)* a challenging macroeconomic environment. The government has attempted to address some of these issues by passing a competition law, setting up a public-private partnership forum and attempting to control inflation in 2010. However, the large devaluation in 2010 and the introduction of price controls on 18 goods designated as "basic" at the beginning of 2011 have led to confusion in the market.

The election held in May 2010 was generally peaceful. The ruling EPRDF claimed to win all but two seats in Parliament – thus controlling 99% of the Parliament. Many in the opposition have complained about the lack of political space and intimidation of their supporters by the government. Political tensions in the region remain high because of insecurity in Somalia and the uncertainty associated with the future relations of North and South Sudan following the secession of South Sudan, with which Ethiopia enjoys friendly relations so far. The Ethiopian-Eritrea border dispute remained unresolved in 2010.

Despite limited success in institutionalising democratic governance, the Ethiopian government demonstrated impressive achievements in social and human development as government spending on education, health, agriculture and roads grew at an exemplary rate. In 2010/11, Ethiopia has made significant progress towards achieving the Millennium Development Goals (MDGs). In 2004/05, 38.7% of Ethiopians (about 30 million people) were poor. The figure has gone down to about 32.3% in 2009/10 and is expected to fall further to 31.0% in 2010/11. The decline in rural poverty since 1995/96 is substantial. Ethiopia is also on the right track in relation to education. Given the trend in the 1990s and the recent performance, conservative estimates show that this particular goal is achievable by 2015. However, this success may have come at the expense of quality in education. Ethiopia also appears to be on track to achieve gender parity in primary school enrolment by 2015. The country is also on track with regard to the health related MDGs such as maternal and child mortality, as well as HIV-AIDS and Malaria prevention and treatment.

Table 1: Macroeconomic indicators

	2009	2010	2011	2012
Real GDP growth	9.9	8.8	10	8.6
CPI inflation	36	11.2	17.6	14.3
Budget balance % GDP	-0.9	-2.3	-3.5	-4.1
Current account % GDP	-5	-6.6	-6.4	-11.9

Source: National authorities' data; estimates and predictions based on authors' calculations.

Fiscal year July (n-1)/ June (n)

Figures for 2010 are estimates; for 2011 and later are projections.

StatLink http://dx.doi.org/10.1787/888932406441

Figure 1: Real GDP growth (E)

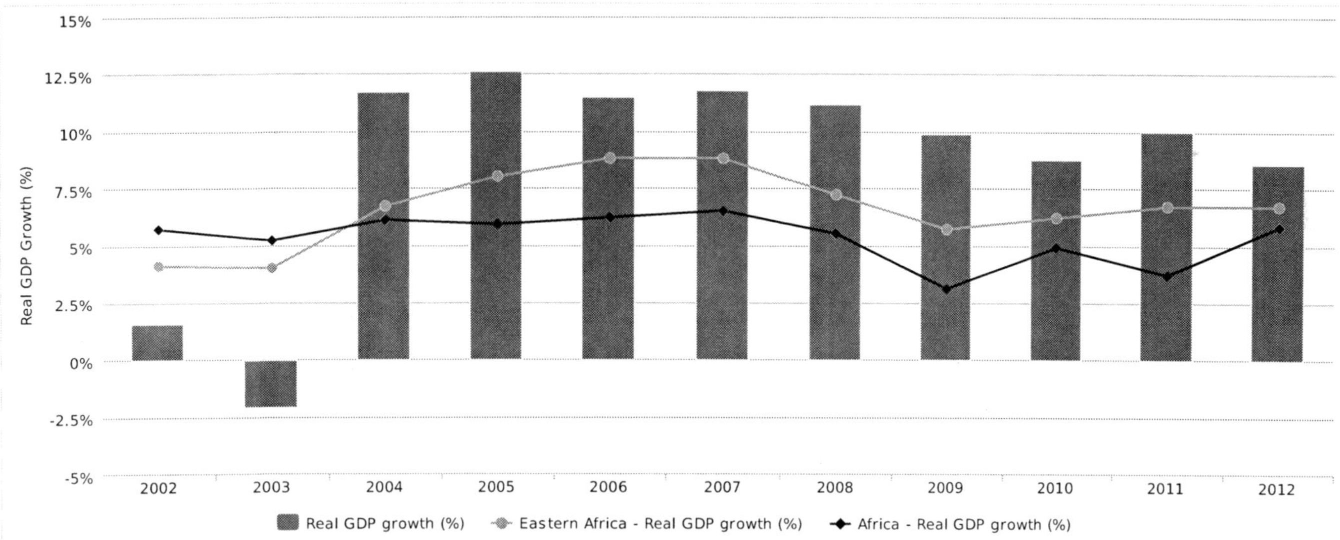

Source: IMF and local authorities' data; estimates and projections based on authors' calculations.

Figures for 2010 are estimates; for 2011 and later are projections.

StatLink http://dx.doi.org/10.1787/888932404085

Gabon

Macroeconomic indicators are improving in a slightly better business climate.

There has been a fresh upsurge in political tension since an opposition leader declared himself president.

Strategic partnerships are expected to generate about 50 000 jobs.

The country's main economic and social indicators improved in 2010, with restored overall growth (5.5%) and a healthier budget situation. The current account surplus grew despite inflation above the target level.

These advances were due to higher investments for the construction of facilities for the Africa Cup of Nations football tournament (CAN 2012) and infrastructure projects for the 50th anniversary of independence celebrations, and to improved international circumstances bringing about better prices for Gabon's raw material exports.

Table 1: Macroeconomic indicators

	2009	2010	2011	2012
Real GDP growth	-1.4	5.5	4.2	4.9
CPI inflation	1.9	3.2	2.7	2.7
Budget balance % GDP	0.2	3.7	4.4	4.6
Current account % GDP	13.6	14.3	16.4	16.6

Source: National authorities' data; estimates and predictions based on authors' calculations.

Figures for 2010 are estimates; for 2011 and later are projections.

StatLink http://dx.doi.org/10.1787/888932406460

Despite a projected slowing of growth in 2011, budget and current balances should improve in 2011 and 2012 after the start, in the second semester of 2010, of projects to upgrade main roads, process timber locally and build low-cost housing.

These projects should meet the serious concerns of the population by providing material benefits, jobs, housing and welfare.

Figure 1: Real GDP growth (C)

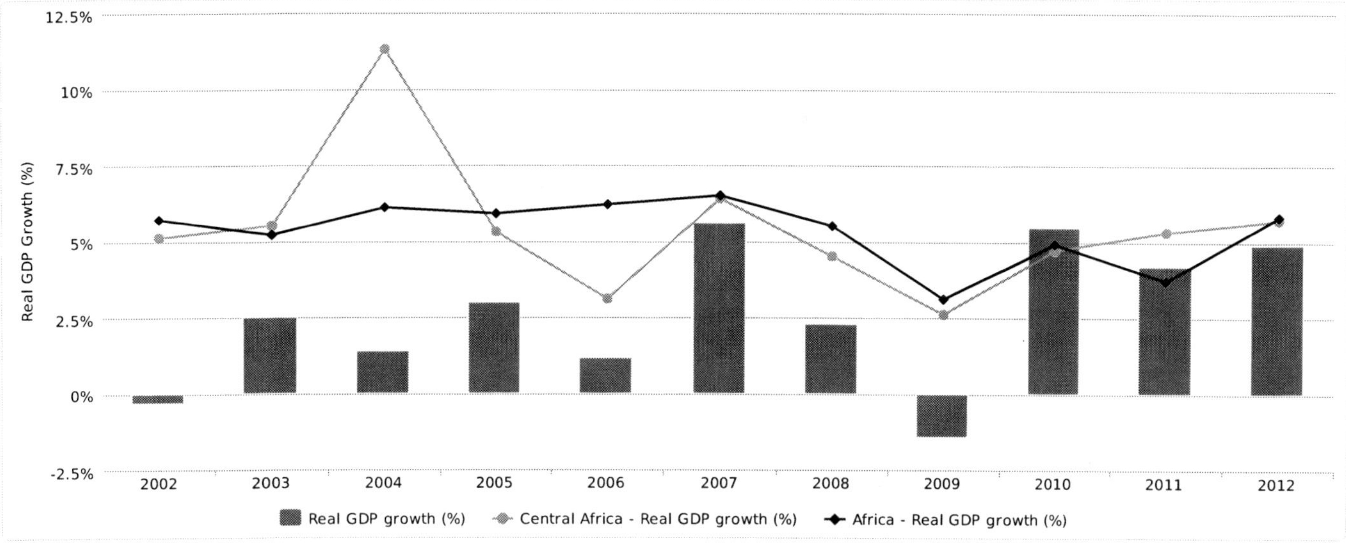

Source: IMF and local authorities' data; estimates and projections based on authors' calculations.

Figures for 2010 are estimates; for 2011 and later are projections.

StatLink http://dx.doi.org/10.1787/888932404104

Gambia

The Gambian economy slowed in 2010, posting growth of 5.4% after 6.7% in 2009, but held up relatively well against the continued negative impact of the global economic slump on trade, tourism and remittances. Growth should pick up to 5.6% in 2011 and 2012.

Gambia's business environment remains challenging although there has been some progress in the banking and communications sector. The government is pursuing initiatives to boost agriculture on which most people depend for their livelihood.

Emerging country partners are important for Gambia, among them Kuwait, Chinese Taipei and Venezuela.

Gambia is a low-income country with a structural food deficit but it has managed to post relatively strong growth rates over the past three years. In 2010, growth slowed to 5.4% from 6.7% in 2009 as the global slump continued to be felt on re-exports, tourism and remittances. Growth should pick up to 5.6% this year and next. Good harvests -- especially of rice -- and gains in the construction and banking sectors drove economic growth. The newly-launched National Agricultural Investment Plan aims to improve agricultural sector productivity.

The government managed to maintain macroeconomic stability in the face of external shocks such as a reduction in grant aid and trade revenues, as well as rising oil and food prices. Debt, both domestic and external, remains a problem and the burden is expected to increase further in the near future. Inflation picked up in the second half of 2010, partly reflecting the Central Bank of the Gambia's financing of the budget deficit. The central bank accordingly hiked interest rates to 15% and succeeded in keeping inflation below its 6% target. Inflation in 2011, driven by higher oil and food prices, is expected to accelerate in the first quarter.

The banking sector is developing, driven by foreign direct investment (FDI). Increased competition and capacity in the industry has increased deposits and credit supply. However, a large share of bank credit has been absorbed by the government and private sector demand for credit is limited.

With the support of development partners, the government launched initiatives to promote the private sector, such as the Growth and Competitiveness Project (GCP) to support foreign trade and investment, and the Gambia National Agricultural Investment Plan (GNAIP) to improve agricultural productivity. GNAIP could be the first step toward broad-based agricultural development, provided that it is complemented by land reform and infrastructure provision. It could also encourage development partners to participate more actively in agricultural development.

The role of emerging country partners in the Gambia has remained relatively limited. Traditional development partners, including the World Bank, the International Monetary Fund (IMF) and the African Development Bank (AfDB), retain crucial roles. Among emerging country partners, Chinese Taipei remains the most important, followed by Cuba and Venezuela while Kuwait exerts a growing influence. The political situation in the Gambia was calm during 2010. There seems to be little interest in institutional reform.

Table 1: Macroeconomic indicators

	2009	2010	2011	2012
Real GDP growth	6.7	5.4	5.6	5.6
CPI inflation	4.6	5.8	5.9	6.3
Budget balance % GDP	-3	-2.7	-2.4	-1.5
Current account % GDP	-10.1	-12.2	-11.9	-11

Source: National authorities' data; estimates and predictions based on authors' calculations.

Figures for 2010 are estimates; for 2011 and later are projections.

StatLink http://dx.doi.org/10.1787/888932406479

Figure 1: Real GDP growth (W)

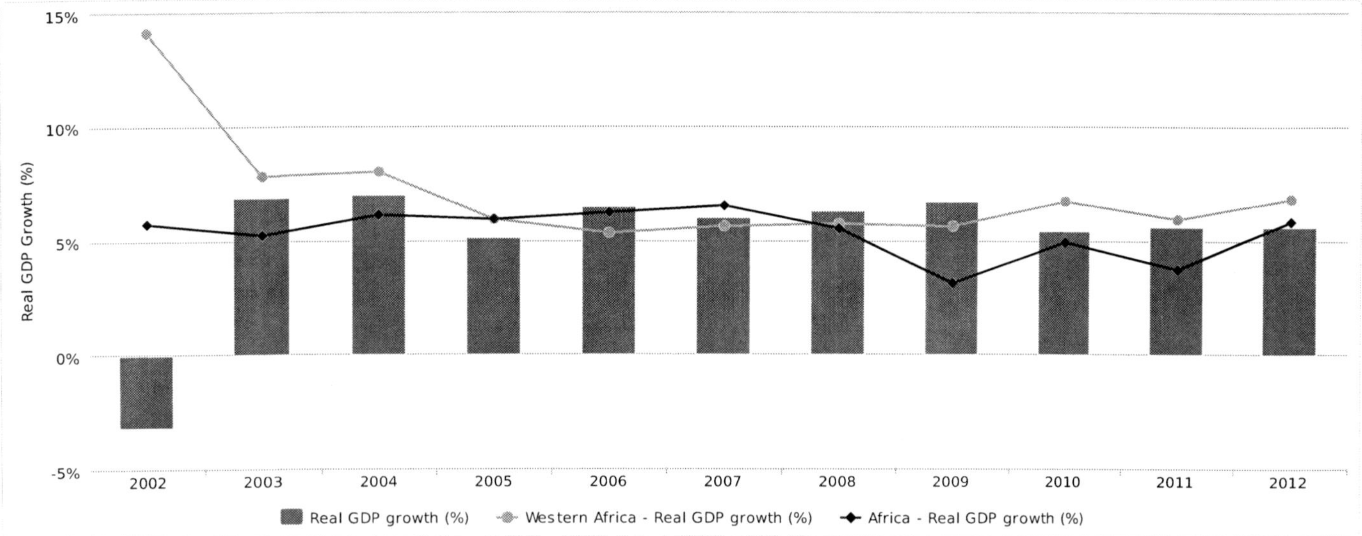

Source: IMF and local authorities' data; estimates and projections based on authors' calculations.

Figures for 2010 are estimates; for 2011 and later are projections.

StatLink http://dx.doi.org/10.1787/888932404123

Ghana

The economy continues to show strong real gross domestic product (GDP) growth which is expected to reach double digits in 2011 and 2012, provided oil revenues are prudently managed.

The macroeconomic environment is stable but fiscal consolidation will be enhanced by reforms to increase domestic resource mobilisation.

The export of oil opens up additional opportunities for co-operation with emerging economies.

Ghana has rebased its national accounts, changing the base year from 1993 to 2006. According to the national authorities, following the rebasing, the size of the economy in real GDP terms has been raised threefold and placed Ghana among the lower middle income group of countries. The rebasing has also suggested greater fiscal space for Ghana with a reduced revenue-to-GDP ratio. While questions on the international acceptability of the new numbers remain, one point is clear: they confirm what most observers have often suggested, namely that the size of the Ghanaian economy has hitherto been grossly under-estimated.

Economic growth has remained strong with real GDP growth reaching an estimated 5.9% in 2010 compared to 4.7% in 2009. Growth prospects are even brighter as real GDP growth of 12.0% and about 11.0% are projected for 2011 and 2012 respectively, largely on account of the start of oil production in commercial quantities in December 2010. In addition, the country's increasingly democratic settlement and social stability have served to boost the confidence of investors, leading to rising investment.

The country's strong growth has been achieved within a sound macroeconomic environment. Prudence in fiscal and monetary management has contributed to the easing of inflationary pressures with declining interest rates. The private sector has responded positively to the government's development programmes and the improved business environment. The rise in bank lending and capital inflows suggests increasing investor confidence. New partnerships between Ghana and emerging economies such as China and South Korea are providing additional sources of financing and expertise for development.

Nevertheless, challenges remain, such as a very weak fiscal stance and fragile external balances. Growing fiscal challenges include large domestic payment arrears. Also, the government's new public sector pay policy – the Single Spine Salary (SSP) policy – requires a huge budgetary outlay, which could threaten macroeconomic stability unless renewed efforts are made to enhance domestic resource mobilisation. Ghana should also adopt a sustainable debt management strategy to avoid post-HIPC (Highly Indebted Poor Countries) debt overhang. In addition, strong and sustainable growth over the next decade will require continued high levels of investment; this will be conditional on prudence in the management of the oil revenues. Besides, unemployment and underemployment are key challenges that require the government to enhance the job-relevant skills of the workforce, especially in the large informal sector of the economy.

Table 1: Macroeconomic indicators

	2009	2010	2011	2012
Real GDP growth	4.7	5.9	12	11
CPI inflation	19.3	8	8.5	6.9
Budget balance % GDP	-7.6	-7.9	-7.7	-5
Current account % GDP	-8.1	-7.6	-6.4	-2.5

Source: National authorities' data; estimates and predictions based on authors' calculations.

Figures for 2010 are estimates; for 2011 and later are projections.

StatLink http://dx.doi.org/10.1787/888932406498

Figure 1: Real GDP growth (W)

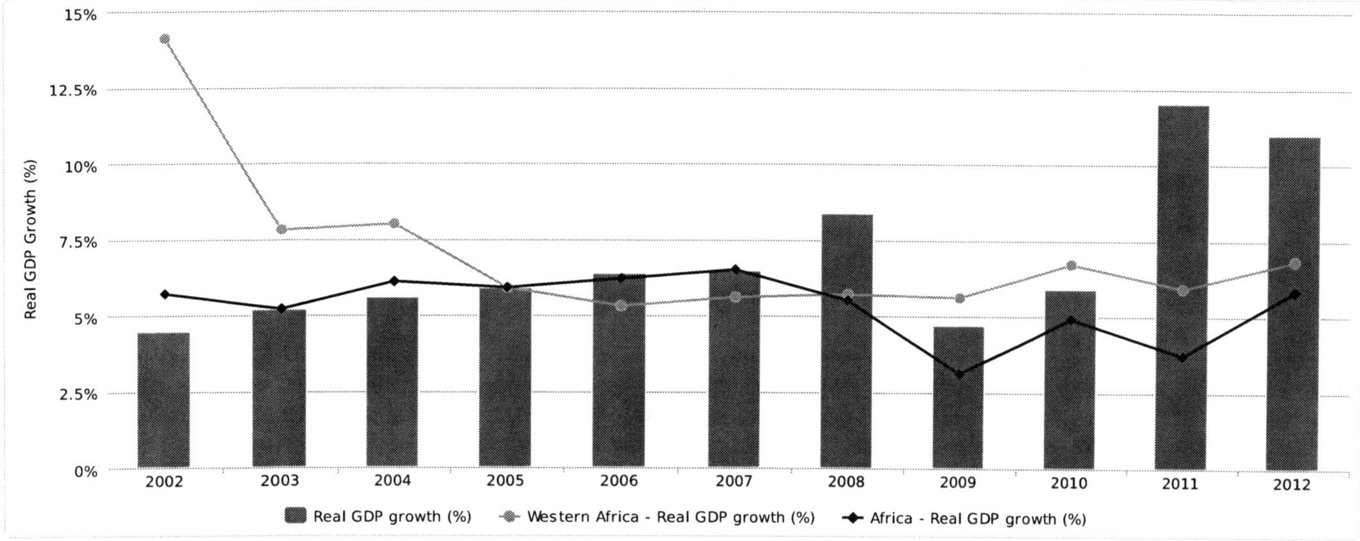

Source: National authorities' data; estimates and predictions based on authors' calculations.

Figures for 2010 are estimates; for 2011 and later are projections.

StatLink http://dx.doi.org/10.1787/888932404142

Guinea

Economic activity in 2010 was affected by a wait-and-see attitude resulting from delays in the presidential election process; growth should pick up in 2011.

Guinea suffers from persistent structural and institutional weaknesses and a business environment that does not encourage private sector development.

Partnership with new emerging countries remains weak, but fairly significant progress is being made.

Guinea is a poor, fragile country, despite considerable unexploited economic potential. It has the world's largest reserves of bauxite (two-thirds of global reserves), as well as large deposits of iron ore, gold and diamonds. It also has the potential to develop other metals, oil and gas. Persistent structural and institutional weaknesses have prevented Guinea from developing a strategic vision and implementing the type of policies needed to reap the full benefit of its mineral wealth.

From 1985 to 2002, Guinea engaged in a process of economic liberalisation and transformation that drove real gross domestic product (GDP) growth to an average of 4% per year over the period (equal to a 0.8% increase in per capita income), while stabilising prices and the exchange rate. Problems in the implementation of reforms between 2003 and 2006 resulted in a 0.6% fall in per capita income, and the economic slump subsequently worsened in 2007 as a result of the global crisis. In response to these difficulties, since 2007 Guinea has been conducting reforms under its second poverty reduction strategy (PRSP2), which is supported by the International Monetary Fund's (IMF) Poverty Reduction and Growth Facility (PRGF) and by other technical and financial partners. The reforms bore fruit in 2008, despite the difficult international context, as growth accelerated from 1.8% in 2007 to 4.9% in 2008. From 2009, however, the economic situation was marked by the combined effects of the economic and financial crisis and the socio-political crisis, resulting in a 0.3% fall in GDP.

The economic situation remains difficult, as reflected in the 2010 indicators. The rate of economic growth is 1.6%, too low to reduce poverty. The high rate of inflation (15.8%) continues to undermine the population's purchasing power. The poverty rate, which stood at 49% in 2002, reached 55% in 2010. Foreign exchange reserves have dwindled to only 1.9 months of imports. Domestic and foreign arrears have rocketed, making it difficult to improve the macroeconomic situation. Added to all this is a substantial reduction in official development assistance (ODA), both bilateral and multilateral, and increased prices for the main imported products, such as food and oil. If these trends are not reversed soon, it will be difficult for Guinea to reach the completion point of the Heavily Indebted Poor Countries (HIPC) Initiative, even though it had nearly attained this important milestone at the end of 2008.

Over the last decade, Guinea has experienced recurring socio-political instability marked by state violence against the civilian population. This socio-political environment is not conducive to private sector development.

The first free elections in Guinea's history were held on 27 June 2010. These elections should lead to a new constitutional order, the return of the army and security forces to barracks and their transformation into a national force for peace, democracy and development.

The stabilisation of the socio-political situation, following the presidential elections in 2010, and the global economic recovery should lead to a pick-up in growth beginning in 2011.

Table 1: Macroeconomic indicators

	2009	2010	2011	2012
Real GDP growth	-0.3	1.6	4.6	5.5
CPI inflation	4.7	15.8	13.5	8.2
Budget balance % GDP	-8.4	-12	-10.8	-9.3
Current account % GDP	-9.2	-8.3	-5.6	-3.6

Source: National authorities' data; estimates and predictions based on authors' calculations.

Figures for 2010 are estimates; for 2011 and later are projections.

StatLink http://dx.doi.org/10.1787/888932406517

Figure 1: Real GDP growth (W)

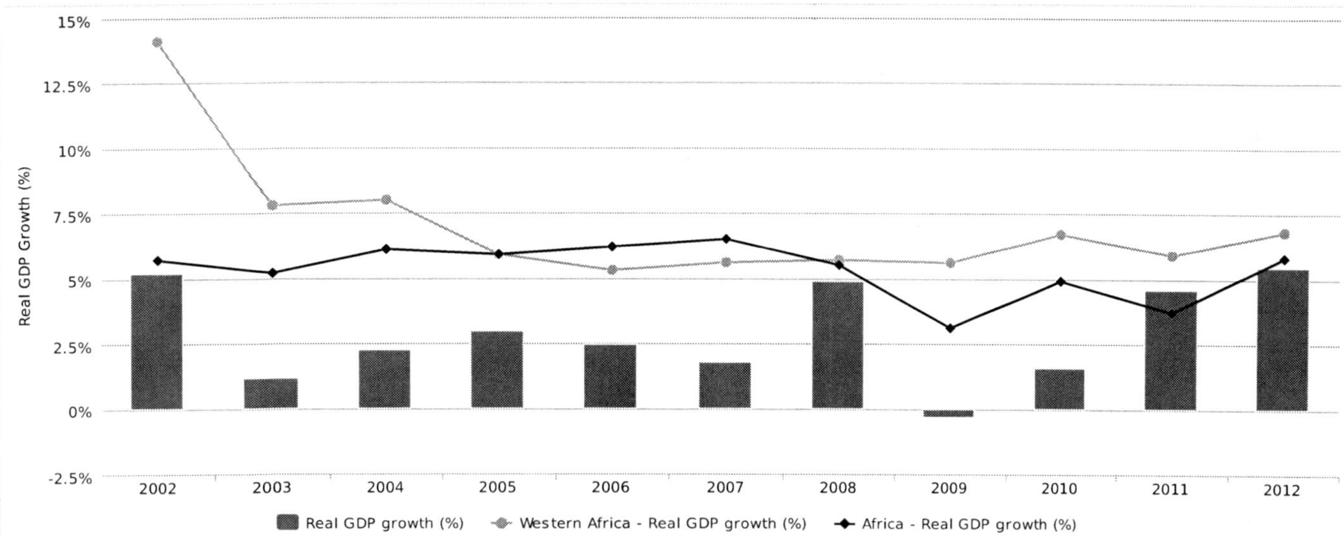

Source: National authorities' data; estimates and predictions based on authors' calculations.

Figures for 2010 are estimates; for 2011 and later are projections.

StatLink http://dx.doi.org/10.1787/888932404161

Guinea-Bissau

Economic growth in Guinea-Bissau reached 3.6% in 2010 thanks to higher cashew nut prices, sustained construction of private housing and investment in major infrastructure projects.

The new government's main political challenges in 2011 will be to bring stability, implement reforms in the defence sector and fight the narcotics trade.

Guinea-Bissau's main emerging partners are China, Brazil and India. China is present primarily through bilateral co-operation and large infrastructure projects, while India has strong trade ties in the cashew nut sector. Brazil has long been involved in capacity-building projects in the education sector.

Economic growth in Guinea-Bissau picked up slightly to 3.6% in 2010 from 3.0% in 2009 thanks to higher cashew nut prices, sustained construction of private housing and major infrastructure projects. The indirect impact of the global economic crisis, felt mainly through lower government export revenues and remittances, has been mitigated by a strong increase in the world demand for cashew nuts. Heightened political instability, however, resulted in the withdrawal of budget support from the European Union (EU), one of the country's main development partners. Economic growth is expected to increase to 4.5% and 4.8% in 2011 and 2012, sustained by increased agricultural production, cashew nut exports and foreign direct investment (FDI) in mining projects and infrastructure. The major downside risk is persistent political instability, which could result in a further decrease in donor funding, hampering the execution of the public investment programme in the coming years. In the medium term, inflation is expected to remain within the Central Bank of West African States' (BCEAO) target of 3%, maintaining the good performance of 2010.

The normalisation of relations with the International Monetary Fund (IMF) in January 2008 continued to yield benefits in 2010. In May, Guinea-Bissau obtained a three-year Extended Credit Facility (ECF) worth Special Drawing Rights 22.4 million (SDR), on top of the Emergency Post Conflict Assistance (EPCA) facility to support the government's 2008 and 2009 economic programmes.

A weather-related drop in cashew nut export volume compared to last year's exceptional performance was offset by higher prices, boosting overall export value and reducing the trade deficit. This improvement in the terms of trade, however, did not compensate for the withdrawal of EU budget support in 2010, and the result was a gradual widening of the current account deficit.

Guinea-Bissau remains highly dependent on subsistence agriculture, the export of cashew nuts and foreign assistance. In order to diversify its economy and foster growth, Guinea-Bissau needs major reforms in public administration (in particular security and defence), as well as investment in agriculture, basic transport and energy infrastructure. The exploitation of its large minerals potential, likely to start soon, could generate substantial resources to finance these investments.

In December 2010, Guinea-Bissau reached completion point under the Heavily Indebted Poor Countries (HIPC) debt relief initiative, which should result in a debt reduction of 1.2 billion US dollars (USD) and qualifies the country for further debt relief under the Multilateral Debt Relief Initiative (MDRI).

Guinea-Bissau's main emerging partners are China, Brazil and India. China has been involved in the country mainly through bilateral co-operation and large infrastructure projects, while India has traditionally had strong trade ties in the cashew nut sector and has only recently started to intensify its bilateral co-operation. Brazil has long been a supporter of capacity-building projects in the education sector and is becoming a significant trade partner.

The attempted coup led by the army vice chief of staff, General Antonio Indjai, and his subsequent controversial appointment as head of the army dominated the political scene in 2010. Political developments resulted in the suspension of budget support from the EU, which had been funding defence and Security Sector Reform (SSR) and paying for the salaries of teachers and civil servants. Donors' financial support in the medium term will depend to a large extent on the return of long-term political stability.

Creating political stability, implementing reforms in the defence sector and fighting the narcotics trade will be the new government's main political challenges in 2011. Economic performance will depend on the government's success in tackling these issues.

Table 1: Macroeconomic indicators

	2009	2010	2011	2012
Real GDP growth	3	3.6	4.5	4.8
CPI inflation	-1.6	2.6	2.7	2.6
Budget balance % GDP	2.8	-0.2	-2	-1.2
Current account % GDP	-4.1	-5.6	-6.2	-6.1

Source: National authorities' data; estimates and predictions based on authors' calculations.

Figures for 2010 are estimates; for 2011 and later are projections.

StatLink http://dx.doi.org/10.1787/888932406536

Figure 1: Real GDP growth (W)

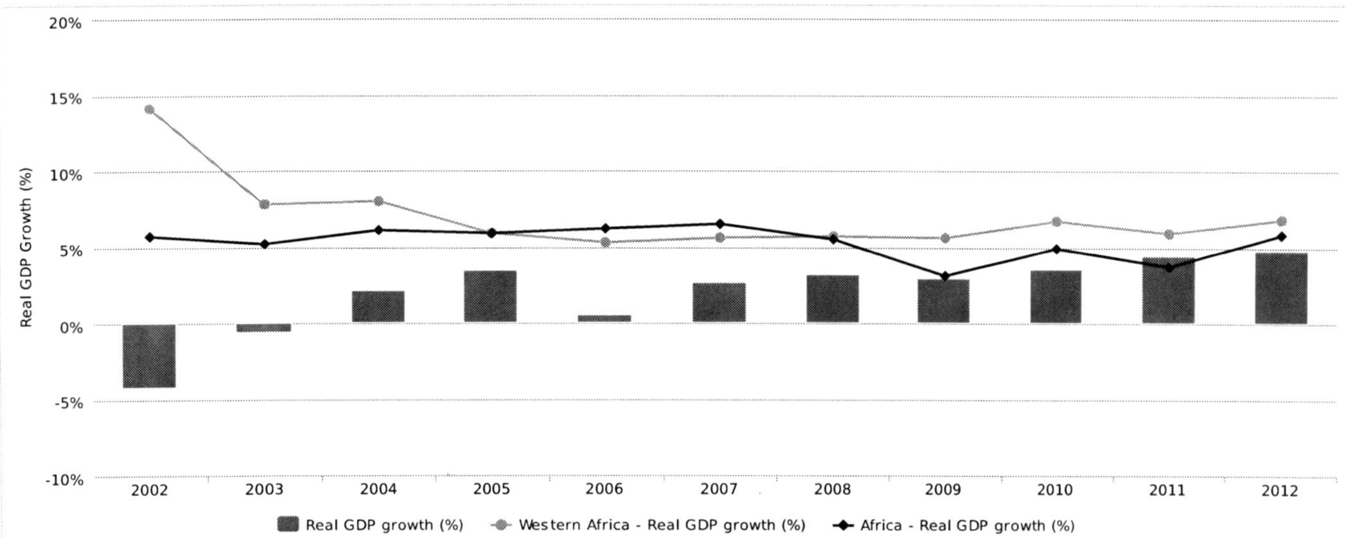

Source: IMF and local authorities' data; estimates and projections based on authors' calculations.

Figures for 2010 are estimates; for 2011 and later are projections.

StatLink http://dx.doi.org/10.1787/888932404180

Kenya

The Kenyan economy grew by 5.0% in 2010, *i.e.* almost twice the 2009 rate. The positive outlook for 2011 is mitigated by Kenya's vulnerability to climate hazards and the need to diversify the economy. Moreover, another political shock could roll back the recent economic and social gains.

The government's Economic Stimulus Progamme played an important part in boosting infrastructure projects and creating credit for SMEs. The stronger performance of the Kenyan economy and the gradual recovery of the global economy in 2010 contributed to the rebound in trading activities at the Nairobi Stock Exchange (NSE).

Since the early 2000s, Kenya has been building new economic partnerships with Middle Eastern and Far Eastern countries, particularly with China.

The macroeconomic performance of the Kenyan economy improved significantly in 2010 compared to 2009. While the economy grew by 2.6% in 2009, it is estimated that the growth rate of GDP nearly doubled to reach 5.0% in 2010. The increase in growth can be attributed to the good rainfall during 2010 and higher prices for Kenyan exports on world markets. The abundance of agricultural output, coupled with increased competition in some key services, helped contain inflation in 2010. However, the Kenyan economy faces two challenges: diversification and the reduction of its dependence on the vagaries of nature.

The outlook for 2011 is promising and a combination of trends could contribute to ensure positive prospects on the short to medium term. The approval of the constitution, continued investment in infrastructure, and government policies targeting development in the private sector should all enhance Kenya's business environment and reinforce a dynamic private sector. Secondly, deepening regional integration and the launch of the East African Community common market are creating a single trading and investment environment in which Kenyan firms to have access to a larger market. Lastly, prudent monetary and fiscal policy is expected to reduce inflation and keep interest rates low, creating a credible and stable macroeconomic environment. Given these prospects, the Kenyan economy is forecast to grow by 5.3% in 2011 and 5.5% in 2012.

This positive outlook may however be mitigated by two main challenges. First, Kenya will need to reduce its high reliance on agricultural outputs to limit its vulnerability to climate hazards by diversifying the economy. Second, Kenya may be vulnerable to another political shock as it faces 2012 elections. Contributing further to the uncertainty weighing on the political environment is the indictment of six high-level Kenyan officials – including the current finance minister and deputy prime minister – by the International Criminal Court for alleged crimes connected to the 2007 post-election violence.

Table 1: Macroeconomic indicators

	2009	2010	2011	2012
Real GDP growth	2.6	5	5.3	5.5
CPI inflation	10.5	4.1	9.8	7.6
Budget balance % GDP	-5.4	-5.8	-6.8	-7.1
Current account % GDP	-5.3	-7.8	-8.5	-9.1

Source: National authorities' data; estimates and predictions based on authors' calculations.

Figures for budget balance refer to fiscal year July (n-1)/ June (n).

Figures for 2010 are estimates; for 2011 and later are projections.

StatLink http://dx.doi.org/10.1787/888932406555

Figure 1: Real GDP growth (E)

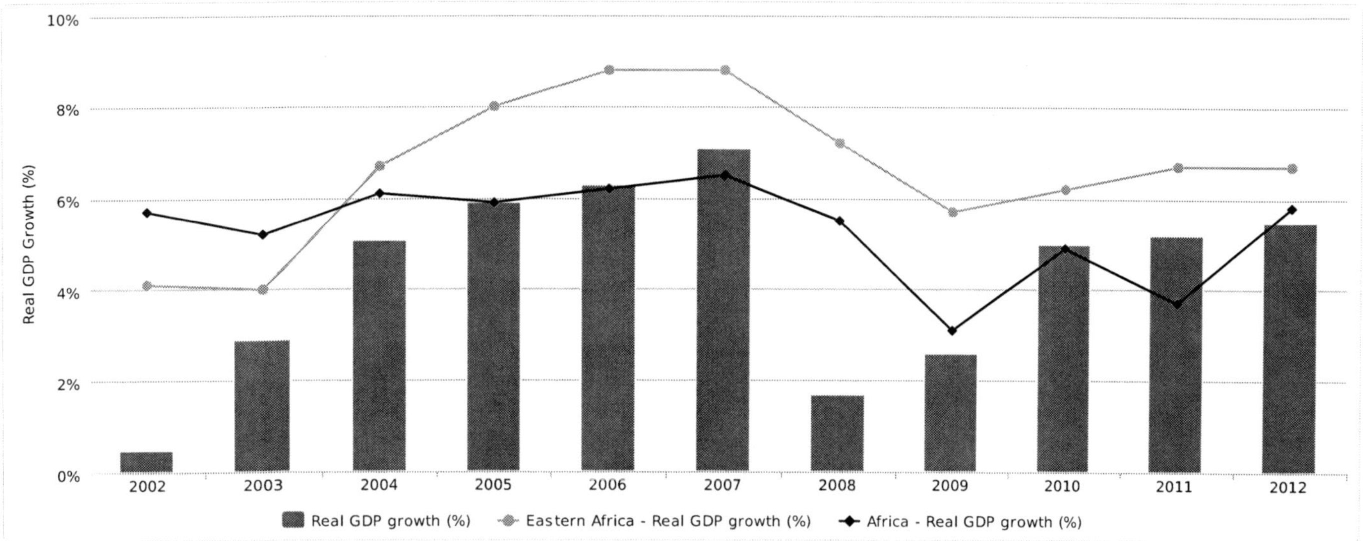

Source: IMF and local authorities' data; estimates and projections based on authors' calculations.

Figures for 2010 are estimates; for 2011 and later are projections.

StatLink http://dx.doi.org/10.1787/888932404199

Lesotho

Rising commodity prices have led to improved viability in mining activities resulting in the reopening of some of the mines that had shut down at the peak of the financial crisis.

While agricultural development remains important for ensuring broad-based growth in Lesotho, the manufacturing and services sectors hold greater promise for diversifying production and job creation.

Increasing diplomatic and economic co-operation between China and Lesotho has opened new opportunities, including duty-free market access for Lesotho's exports to China since 2008.

There are signs of Lesotho's economic recovery from the effects of the global financial crisis, but the damage caused to this small and open economy may last for a while. Lesotho's high export concentration left it vulnerable to the global economic downturn. This was exacerbated by Lesotho's dependency on South Africa, a country that was also affected by the collapse in commodity prices. Lesotho's economic growth declined by about 4.4% in 2008 to 1.9% in 2009. As the global economy began to recover, however, Lesotho's gross domestic product (GDP) in 2010 grew by an estimated 3.8%. This recovery in economic growth can be attributed to both firming commodity prices and high government capital expenditures. The mining and construction sub-sectors, in particular, experienced some buoyancy. In addition, rising commodity prices led to the improved viability of mining activities, resulting in the reopening of some of the mines that had shut down at the peak of the crisis. Furthermore, the government's focus on infrastructure development is driving activity in the construction sector.

Recent efforts by the government of Lesotho to diversify the economy are gaining traction. Thanks to the development of manufacturing, services and the export of water resources, the economy is relying less on subsistence agriculture and remittances. The textiles sector is now the largest employer in the manufacturing sector. Its competitiveness, however, has been negatively affected by the appreciating rand and increased competition from Asian suppliers, and both investment inflows and employment in the sector have declined. Net foreign private capital also fell in 2010, a trend likely to continue in 2011.

The country's growth is expected to be lower in 2011 than in 2010 as no major investments are expected, while recovery in the global economy remains weak. In addition, growth in 2011 is likely to be dampened due to a projected high current-account deficit resulting from higher imports to meet requirements for projects in the construction sector, compounded by continued low Southern Africa Customs Union (SACU) revenues. Slower growth in government expenditure is also a factor in the lower projected economic growth. The government has taken measures, amongst others, to reduce its current expenditure, which includes a freeze on government jobs, and has also committed not to fund new projects during the current fiscal year, 2010/11.

Although the government of Lesotho is making efforts to reduce its budget deficit, it has maintained infrastructure development as a priority. This infrastructure is intended to link remote areas to markets and to enable new investments that would provide opportunities for value addition, especially in the agriculture sector. The country's business environment has remained poor, impacting negatively on inward investments and trade competitiveness. To a large extent, the poor business environment has curtailed the expansion of private-sector activities, and government still accounts for nearly 50% of Lesotho's GDP. Current efforts to improve the business environment are likely to increase private-sector activities. The fundamental elements of this process, however, are either in the very early stages of implementation or have yet to be fully developed and implemented. The passing of the Land Act (2010) and the establishment of the land register, with the pilot phase completed in 2010, will go a long way to address the challenges of financing small- and medium-scale enterprises (SMSEs) and improve the country's attractiveness for foreign investment. The government has also made substantial progress in drafting and completing its industrial and competition policies.

Table 1: Macroeconomic indicators

	2009	2010	2011	2012
Real GDP growth	1.9	3.8	2.9	3.3
CPI inflation	7.3	7.3	7.8	6.8
Budget balance % GDP	-4.9	-9.8	-11.3	-3.4
Current account % GDP	-0.2	-14.9	-14.5	-5.4

Source: National authorities' data; estimates and predictions based on authors' calculations.

Figures for budget balance refer to fiscal year April (n)/ March (n+1).

Figures for 2010 are estimates; for 2011 and later are projections.

StatLink http://dx.doi.org/10.1787/888932414421

Figure 1: Real GDP growth (S)

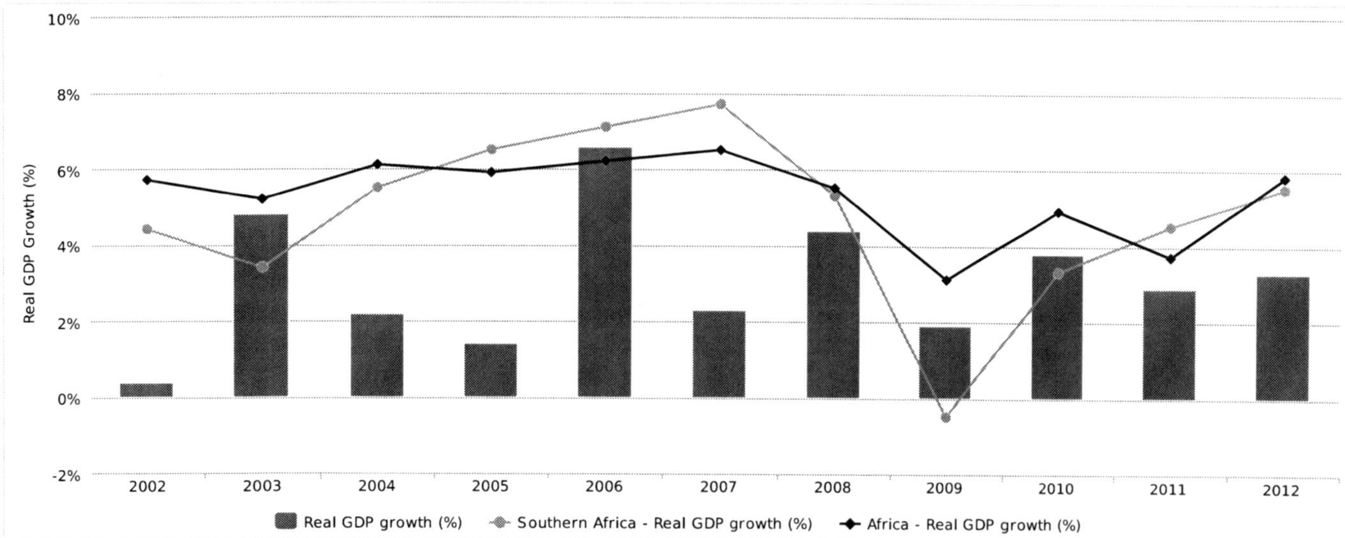

Source: IMF and local authorities' data; estimates and projections based on authors' calculations.

Figures for 2010 are estimates; for 2011 and later are projections.

StatLink http://dx.doi.org/10.1787/888932412065

Liberia

Liberia reached the Heavily Indebted Poor Countries (HIPC) Completion Point in October 2010. This has not only led to the writing off of 4.6 billion US dollars (USD) by Multilateral Development Banks, Paris Club members and commercial creditors, but has also created a positive reform dynamic in the country.

The challenge for Liberia is to make the transition from post-conflict reconstruction to sustainable development. This can only be achieved through further regional integration and regional infrastructure projects, as Liberia is a small country with limited purchasing power.

Companies from emerging partners are mainly active in the extractive industries and palm oil sectors. Of these, China is the largest provider of development assistance and its aid efforts are coordinated with other traditional donors.

Liberia's economy is recovering from the global economic downturn. Growth in 2010 was estimated at 6.1%, up from 4.6% in 2009, driven by an increase in exports and foreign direct investment (FDI). Growth is projected to reach 7.3% in 2011 and 8.9% in 2012. The rise in exports was thanks to an increase in commodity prices, particularly rubber, palm oil and minerals. In 2010, the government also began receiving royalty payments (of USD 1.57 million) from the extractive industries sector and these are projected to grow to USD 30 million by 2015.

The rise in international commodity prices has led to the resumption of investments in the Bong Mines and Yekepa iron ore operations, which were delayed by the 2008 financial crisis. In 2010, large-scale extraction commenced and should generate royalties for the country. There are also expectations that offshore oil will be found in the near future.

Liberia made significant progress by reaching the Completion Point under the Enhanced HIPC Initiative in June 2010 resulting in debt relief of USD 4.6 billion. Reforms required to reach the Completion Point also had the ancillary effect of creating a positive reform dynamic in many sectors including public financial management, implementation of the Extractive Industries Transparency Initiative, health services and harmonisation of the education payroll. In 2010, the government also reached an out-of-court settlement with two 'vulture funds' – Hamsah Investment and Wall Capital – agreeing to repay just over 3% of the USD 43 million it owed on a 1970s debt.

The security situation is generally stable, though fragile, and a sizeable United Nations Mission in Liberia (UNMIL) peacekeeping force remains in the country. Regional instability caused by the political stalemate in neighbouring Côte d'Ivoire has made the situation in Liberia increasingly precarious as the UN has reported that former fighters from Liberia are being recruited in Côte d'Ivoire. Over 10 000 refugees from Côte d'Ivoire are in Liberia and the presidential and legislative elections scheduled for October 2011 provide a further source of insecurity. Finally, there is some concern that Liberia could become a transit point for drugs to Western Europe and the United States.

The overall challenge for Liberia is to make the transition from a period of post-conflict reconstruction to sustainable development. This would require not only a long-term vision as articulated in the Liberia Rising 2030 development plan, but also strong emphasis on regional integration. As Liberia is a small country with limited purchasing power, a strong export policy to regional markets and shared regional infrastructure projects would boost development. Such a policy could be integrated into the next cycle of the country's poverty reduction strategy.

Non-African and African emerging partners are active in Liberia. Non-African countries are mainly active in the private sector and extractive industries, including iron ore and palm oil plantations. Clearly, recent high commodity prices provide an additional incentive to invest in Liberia's relatively risky business environment. Of the non-African emerging partners group, China is the largest public donor giving an estimated USD 20 million annually to Liberia, mainly in the form of tied aid. This aid – which is primarily bilateral – is being used to build infrastructure, and to improve healthcare and education. China is also an observer on various donor co-ordination frameworks and is a member of the country's Economic Management Team, the highest body that reviews development projects managed by the Ministry of Planning and Economic Affairs. The comparatively good coordination between China and Liberia's other development partners has been attributed by traditional donors to the absence of competition or strategic interests in Liberia compared with other resource rich African countries.

In terms of African emerging partners, Nigeria leads the group and Nigerian banks are planning on introducing mobile phone banking to Liberia on the back of the innovation's success in East Africa. Libya is also present with investments in the hotel sector. A rubber processing plant is also planned that will produce tyre-grade rubber for export as well a project to improve food security.

Table 1: Macroeconomic indicators

	2009	2010	2011	2012
Real GDP growth	4.6	6.1	7.3	8.9
CPI inflation	7.6	7.7	4.4	4.8
Budget balance % GDP	-1.6	1.3	-1.9	-2.2
Current account % GDP	-33.2	-40.9	-38.1	-40.6

Source: National authorities' data; estimates and predictions based on authors' calculations.

Figures for budget balance refer to fiscal year July (n-1)/ June (n).

Figures for 2010 are estimates; for 2011 and later are projections.

StatLink http://dx.doi.org/10.1787/888932406593

Figure 1: Real GDP growth (W)

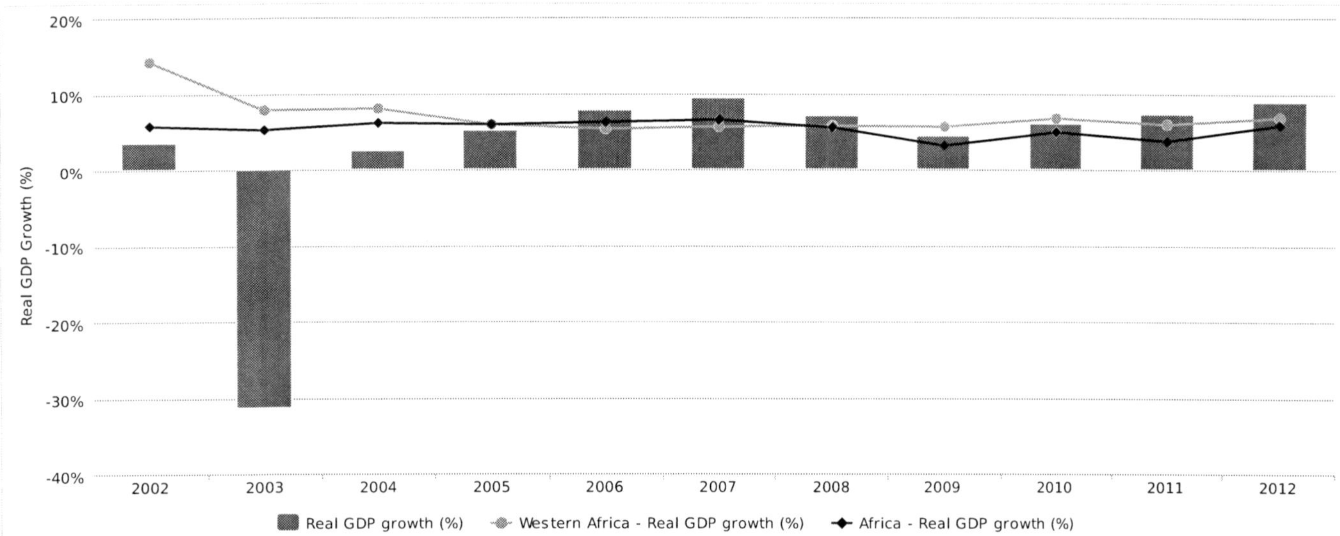

Source: IMF and local authorities' data; estimates and projections based on authors' calculations.

Figures for 2010 are estimates; for 2011 and later are projections.

StatLink http://dx.doi.org/10.1787/888932404237

Libya

Since February 2011 Libya has experienced an escalation of violence which has led the country into an armed conflict, which essentially split its territory into government-controlled and rebel-held areas. The recent political upheaval is likely to cause Gross Domestic Product (GDP) to face a double digit recession after a decade of high growth culminating in an increase of 7.4% in 2010.

While uncertainties persist regarding the duration of the conflict, the country's oil endowement and international attention to the country are likely to secure a relatively fast recovery once the conflict is over. Before the conflict, the country had made major strides towards improving the business environment but private sector activity and investor confidence have been disrupted by the political unrest.

Prior to the conflict, emerging economies were playing an increasingly important role in the Libyan economy with Turkey and China as the most important partners among this group of countries.

Further to the anti-government protests of 17th February, the so called "Day of Rage", Libya has experienced an escalation of violence which has led the country into an armed conflict which persists at the time of writing this report and which has seen the country effectively split between government- controlled areas in the West and anti-government controlled ones in the East. The latter is backed by an international coalition which is enforcing a no-fly zone to protect it from pro-Gaddafi forces.

The country is likely to pay a high price for the conflict, which has effectively paralysed the economy and led to a near halt of Libya's oil production. With considerable oil revenues, a relatively small population and redistributive policies including an extensive social welfare system and subsidies for basic goods, Libya was enjoying the third highest Gross National Income (GNI) per capita and the highest human development index (HDI) in Africa. In 2010, the country was also enjoying robust growth of around 7.4% and was on a similar high-growth trajectory until the conflict erupted. The government had announced plans to increase oil production capacity to 2.5 million barrels per day (bpd) by 2015, but oil production and sales have been brought almost to a halt by the political unrest. The scenario as presented in the table below assumes that oil production and GDP will drop sharply in 2011 but that the political situation will stabilise and the economy recover again in 2012. Given the high uncertainty about how the conflict will evolve, this is just one among other possible scenarios.

The Libyan crisis has also already transcended its boundaries and severly affected some other African countries, namely through humanitarian crises on the borders of neighbouring countries, the loss of remittances from millions of African migrants working in Libya and through the freezing of Libyan assets worldwide. While the global market loss of Libyan oil production has been offset by the increase in supply by other oil producers, risk premia and associated high prices are likely to persist.

On the security and political front, there is no clear indication of either the timing nor the outcome of the crisis. At the time of writing, the Libyan National Council, the self-proclaimed authority in the rebel-area in the eastern part of the country was increasingly recognised as the legitimate authority for the country, while defections in government ranks and diplomatic representations have significantly weakened Gaddafi. The crisis came at a time when Libya was pursuing economic liberalisation which was often accompanied by a gradual opening up of the political system. However, progress in this direction was mixed and many sections of society grew increasingly dissatisfied. Events unfolding in Tunisia and Egypt in the wake of their respective revolutions gave people confidence that a regime change was possible, unleashing a wave of protests and political upheaval.

On human development, the population is likely to suffer a lot from the impact of the conflict. Before the unrest, Libya was expected to achieve all the Millennium Development Goals (MDGs) within the 2015 timeframe. Although the state provided free universal health care and education to its citizens, the main challenge was to improve the quality of both and government attention is now directed towards that aim. Pressing social challenges already included the need to tackle high youth unemployment, to strengthen efforts to conserve Libya's delicate environment and limited natural resources, to encourage women's economic and social participation, and to manage irregular migration. Such challenges are likely to be even further exarcebated by the conflict.

The European Union (EU) remains Libya's largest trade partner. However, economic relations between Libya and the emerging economies, notably China and Turkey, were expanding rapidly. These economic partners were particularly prominent in the rapidly expanding construction sector as foreign construction firms have been contracted to implement the country's large public infrastructure projects. Foreign Direct Investment

(FDI) is still limited, with a few exceptions in the oil sector. Libya was increasingly positioning itself as a "gateway to Africa", an image that appeals to the wishes of Turkey and China to strengthen their economic foothold on the continent. It was also keen on using its partnership with emerging economies to strengthen its negotiating power vis-à-vis its traditional partners. Future relationships may be further adjusted depending on the outcome of the conflict and the respective role played by countries in support to either party, with the highest dividend possibly being assigned to (or taken away from) France and the UK who have been the frontrunners in supporting the no-fly zone and the rebels. In contrast, China and Russia have played a much more cautious role and often criticised the military intervention.

Table 1: Macroeconomic indicators

	2009	2010	2011	2012
Real GDP growth	-1.6	7.4	-19	16
CPI inflation	2.4	4.7	12.1	5.1
Budget balance % GDP	7.1	20.9	-7.1	6.8
Current account % GDP	18.5	28.4	13.7	22.7

Source: National authorities' data; estimates and predictions based on authors' calculations.

Figures for 2010 are estimates; for 2011 and later are projections.

StatLink http://dx.doi.org/10.1787/888932406612

Figure 1: Real GDP growth (N)

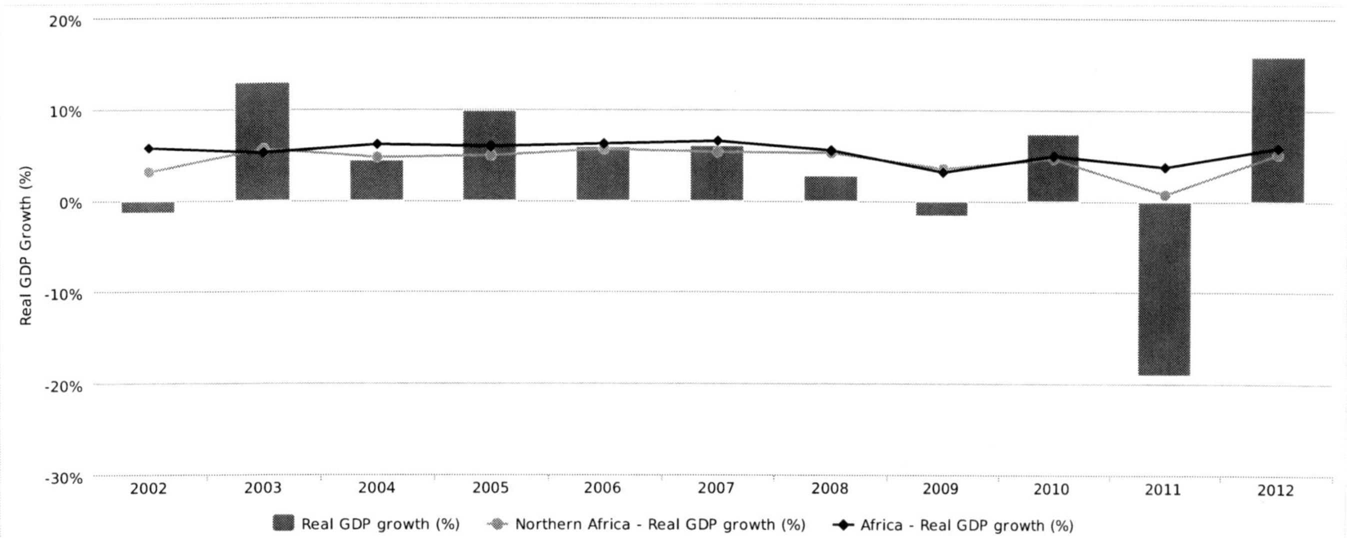

Source: IMF and local authorities' data; estimates and projections based on authors' calculations.

Figures for 2010 are estimates; for 2011 and later are projections.

StatLink http://dx.doi.org/10.1787/888932404256

Madagascar

Madagascar still suffers from the political crisis sparked by the coup of 2009 and the economy grew by only 0.3% in 2010. The international community's refusal to recognise the current government has led to the suspension of most donor aid, hitting growth prospects.

The political and economic uncertainty weighing on Madagascar has produced a 'wait-and-see' attitude among most private investors.

China has become Madagascar's most important emerging country partner. Others such as India, Kuwait, United Arab Emirates, South Korea and Turkey are all significantly less important than China in terms of aid, trade and foreign direct investment (FDI).

Madagascar inched back to growth in 2010, with the country still suffering in the political fallout from the 2009 coup that ousted president Marc Ravalomanana and compounded the impact of the 2008-09 global slump. The economy expanded 0.3% last year after shrinking 3.7% in 2009. This was achieved despite donor countries cutting the development aid that has traditionally funded public investment in infrastructure. The international community does not recognise the political normalisation programme of the current government and so development aid is not expected to return to pre-crisis levels in the short term, with growth expected to be slower as a result.

Growth in 2010 was driven by the extractive industries, with production scaling up at large foreign-owned mines, and by a recovery in tourism. Agricultural output expanded slowly despite good weather while construction and the textile industry continued to contract.

The government has adopted a tight fiscal policy. As revenues fell due to the slowdown in economic activity and aid flows, most ministries suffered cuts that helped contain the budget deficit at a remarkably low 1.6% of gross domestic product (GDP). However, this was achieved at the expense of infrastructure development and maintenance, and threatens to compromise growth prospects in the medium term. At the same time, the Central Bank of Madagascar adopted a prudent monetary policy stance, holding inflation at 9.6% despite a 14% rise in food prices and keeping its key interest rate unchanged in spite of the sluggish economy. In coming years, the main challenge will be to ease constraints on economic growth without generating unsustainable fiscal deficits and excessive inflation.

Economic activity in the private sector remains constrained by the lack of clarity on future political developments. Foreign investment suffers from concerns over the ultimate legal standing of contracts and concessions signed by the current government and from the revision of contracts signed by the previous government. In addition, with political efforts concentrated on establishing the Fourth Republic, very little is being done to reform the business environment.

The informal sector of the economy has grown as the government cut public spending, private investment remained low and companies in export processing zones closed. Although updated estimates on progress towards the Millennium Development Goals (MDGs) are not available, it is most likely that the incidence of poverty has increased since the coup of 2009.

The November 2010 referendum amending the constitution makes it possible that Andry Rajoelina, who seized power in 2009, will be elected president in 2011, although his candidacy is yet to be confirmed. The political environment remains uncertain as both the opposition and most of the international community have not recognised the validity of the referendum while efforts to broker a settlement appear to be making no progress.

In this context, emerging economy partners represent an opportunity for Madagascar. Although China has not recognised the current government, some Chinese companies have continued to sign contracts with it. In 2010, the Chinese group Wuhan Iron and Steel Co (WISCO) made an advance payment of 100 million US dollars (USD) for an iron ore concession. If the iron ore reserves prove to be as large as hoped, the resulting investment may amount to USD 8 billion, by far the largest single foreign direct investment ever made in the country. Given widespread corruption, the challenge is to transform this investment opportunity into development, ensuring the payment of fair royalties and the creation of linkages with the local economy.

Table 1: Macroeconomic indicators

	2009	2010	2011	2012
Real GDP growth	-3.7	0.3	0.6	2
CPI inflation	8.5	9.6	10.1	9.8
Budget balance % GDP	-2.5	-1.6	-1.3	-1.2
Current account % GDP	-20.9	-17	-15.9	-15.3

Source: National authorities' data; estimates and predictions based on authors' calculations.

Figures for 2010 are estimates; for 2011 and later are projections.

StatLink http://dx.doi.org/10.1787/888932406631

Figure 1: Real GDP growth (S)

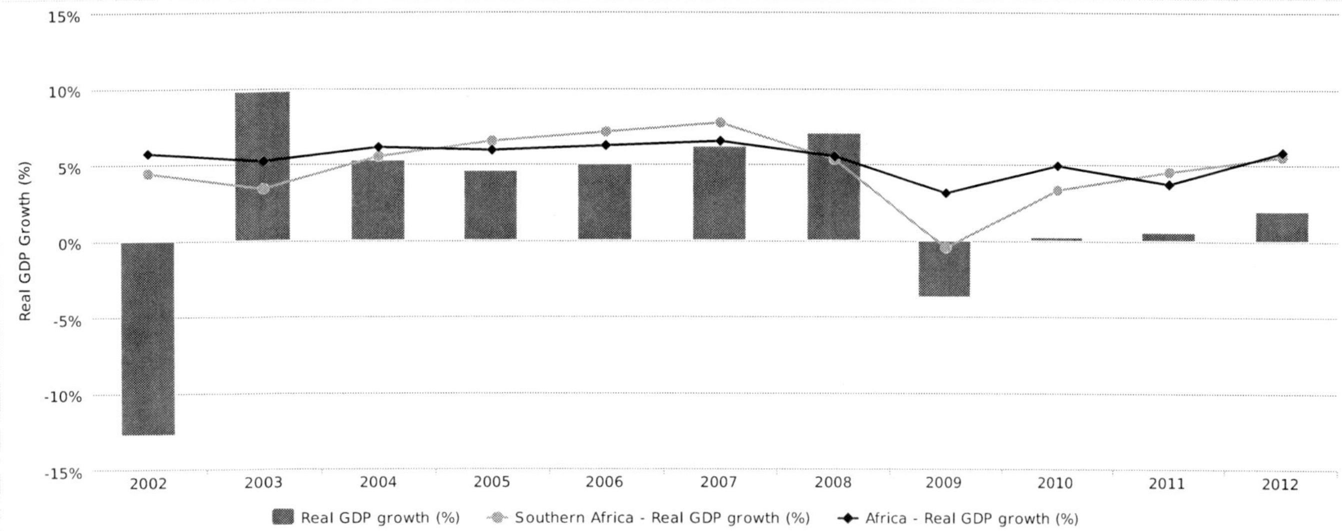

Source: IMF and local authorities' data; estimates and projections based on authors' calculations.

Figures for 2010 are estimates; for 2011 and later are projections.

StatLink http://dx.doi.org/10.1787/888932404275

Malawi

Malawi's real gross domestic product (GDP) is estimated to fall to 6.7% in 2010 from 7.6% in 2009 due to reduced agriculture output for maize and tobacco as a result of the drought experienced in some parts of the country at the beginning of the 2009/10 growing season. The main driving force for economic growth in 2010 has been strong performance in mining and quarrying, construction, financial and insurance services and information and technology.

Private sector growth in Malawi is largely constrained by a poor regulatory environment and inadequate infrastructure in transportation, telecommunications, power and water supply. The authorities have since introduced a number of reforms aimed at improving the business climate. In spite of these reforms, Malawi performed poorly in the 2011 *Doing Business Survey* ranking 133 out of 183 economies, one place lower than in the 2010 survey.

China and India are the most important Emerging Partners (EPs) for Malawi. Other EPs with diplomatic, trade and co-operation agreements albeit at different degrees are Brazil and Cuba. The EPs' interventions have concentrated on infrastructural development, agriculture, education and health. The EPs' investments have increased employment and economic activities in Malawi. Additionally, Chinese and Indian goods are found to be cheaper than Western alternatives on the market.

The political and macroeconomic environment remained stable in Malawi through 2010. Malawi's real gross domestic product (GDP) is estimated to fall to 6.7% in 2010 from 7.6% in 2009. The slight reduction in real GDP growth is largely attributed to reduced agriculture output for maize and tobacco due to the drought experienced in some parts of the country at the beginning of the 2009/10 growing season. The main driving force for economic growth in 2010 has been strong performance in mining and quarrying, construction, financial and insurance services and information and technology. Real GDP growth is forecast at 6.4% in 2011 and 6.0% in 2012 reflecting stability in uranium output and levelling off of productivity gains in the agriculture sector as the agricultural growth rate has peaked.

The recent global financial crisis had a limited impact on Malawi's economy. However, the key sector affected was the export sector, which faced fluctuating international prices (tea, coffee, tobacco) resulting in worsened terms of trade. Official development assistance (ODA), foreign direct investment (FDI) and remittances to Malawi also declined following the global credit crisis. In order to mitigate the impact of the global recession on the Malawi economy, the Reserve Bank of Malawi, among other initiatives, maintained the bank rate at 15.0% and issued Repurchase Agreements (REPO) instruments to combat inflationary pressures.

Malawi has made considerable progress on most Millennium Development Goals (MDGs) targets. According to Malawi's MDG report 2010, the country is on track to attain five of the eight MDG targets by 2015. The five MDG targets that are likely to be achieved are the eradication of extreme poverty, reduction of infant mortality, combating HIV/AIDS, malaria and other diseases, ensuring environmental sustainability, and developing global partnership for development. The three MDG targets in doubt are achieving universal primary education, reducing gender inequality and maternal mortality.

In 2010, the Government of Malawi (GoM) continued with the execution of the Farm Inputs Subsidy Programme (FISP). The FISP in its sixth year of implementation was designed to achieve food security and raise smallholder's income through increased maize and legume production. In the 2010/11 agricultural season, the Government FISP package include subsidies of 160 000 metric tonnes of fertiliser for maize; 8 000 metric tonnes of improved maize seeds and 1 600 metric tonnes of legume seeds. The FISP has been a very successful programme since introduction, leading to record surpluses in maize production including 1.3 million metric tonnes in 2008/09. Although Malawi experienced a prolonged period of abnormal dry weather in some areas in 2010, the country still recorded a surplus of about 900 000 metric tonnes of maize above annual food requirement.

Malawi's Emerging Partners (EPs) have concentrated on infrastructural development, agriculture, education and health. The EPs' investment has generated employment especially for Malawi's youth and their goods are found to be cheaper than western alternatives on the market. The overall advantage is that they are complementing traditional partners and not substituting them. The increasing importance of EPs notwithstanding, the share of traditional partners such as the UK, the USA and the EU in trade, ODA and FDI flows to Malawi is still significant. However, the increasing presence of China and India in Malawi comes with a number of challenges including flooding the market with cheaper Chinese and Indian goods which make local industries uncompetitive.

Table 1: Macroeconomic indicators

	2009	2010	2011	2012
Real GDP growth	7.6	6.7	6.4	6
CPI inflation	8.4	7.7	7.6	6.2
Budget balance % GDP	-3.6	-1.1	-6.3	-7.4
Current account % GDP	-2.1	1.1	-1.6	-3.3

Source: National authorities' data; estimates and predictions based on authors' calculations.

Figures for budget balance refer to fiscal year July (n-1)/ June (n).

Figures for 2010 are estimates; for 2011 and later are projections.

StatLink http://dx.doi.org/10.1787/888932406650

Figure 1: Real GDP growth (S)

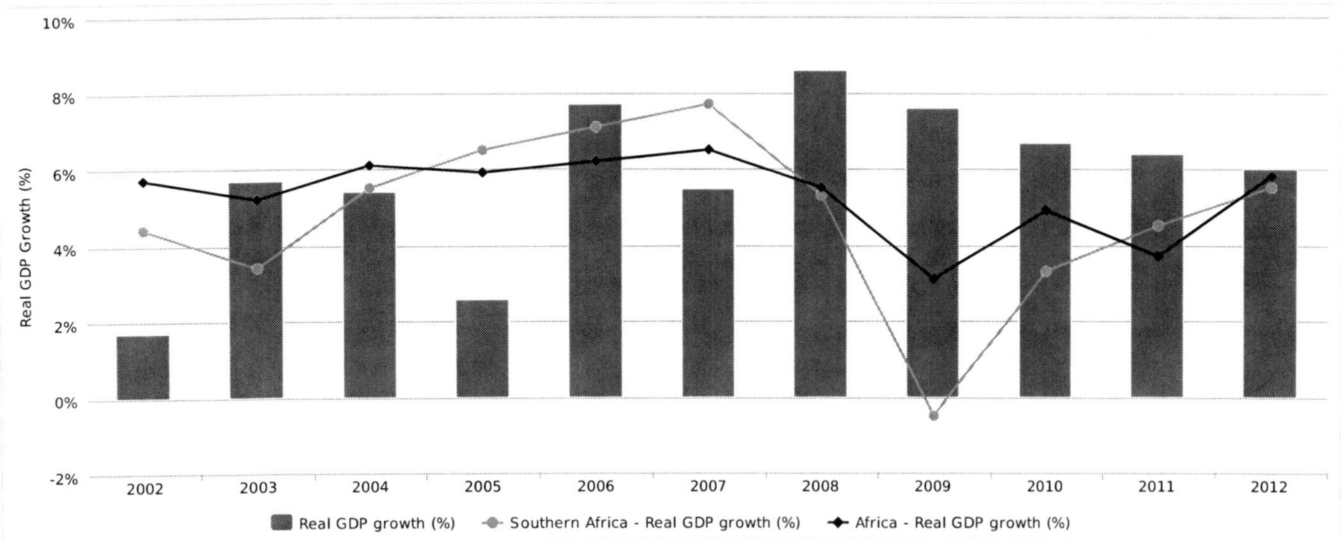

Source: IMF and local authorities' data; estimates and projections based on authors' calculations.

Figures for 2010 are estimates; for 2011 and later are projections.

StatLink http://dx.doi.org/10.1787/888932404294

Mali

The economy grew at the same rate as in 2009, with modest inflation and a contraction in mining. Growth could be impaired if the Côte d'Ivoire political crisis continues.

The government is focusing development policy on agriculture in a bid to make Mali a sub-regional agro-pastoral centre. The Millennium Development Goals are unlikely to be reached by 2015, except for those concerning education and access to safe water. The political scene is starting to reorganise in the run-up to elections in 2012 for president (in April) and parliament (in July).

Mali has strengthened ties with emerging partners, especially China. These partners operate in less formal ways than traditional donors but are not always in tune with the country's growth and poverty reduction plan or its debt policy.

The structure of the economy, dominated by the primary and tertiary sectors (36% and 35.6%of GDP), did not change much in 2010 and should stay largely the same in 2011, with a small decline in the primary and tertiary sectors in favour of the secondary. Real GDP growth in 2010 (4.5%) was the same as in 2009, though lower than expected.

Growth was driven by subsistence farming, transport and telecommunications, which together contributed a third of real GDP growth, and by livestock and commerce. Export crops, including cotton, expanded strongly (up 11.4%) but still made only a marginal contribution to overall growth because of their small share of GDP (2.6%). Mining, especially gold, slumped 16.2% and subtracted 1.1 percentage points from overall GDP growth.

Final consumption (85.1% of GDP) contributed 3.5 percentage points to GDP growth and gross investment (22% of GDP) 1.3 points, while external demand subtracted 0.3 points.

The post-election crisis in Côte d'Ivoire that began in December 2010 slowed Mali's economy, stoked inflation and will undermine prospects until 2012 if it continues. Taking this into account, 2011 growth is forecast as 5.4% if the harvest is good and gold output revives, along with world prices for gold and cotton.

The country strengthened its links with emerging partners, especially China, which was involved in nearly all aspects of economic, social and cultural life. India, Russia, Brazil, Venezuela, Malaysia and Libya also increased their economic and trade ties with Mali, especially in agro-industry, chemicals and construction. Emerging-partner countries' interests are the same as those of traditional partners: they seek access to local and West African regional markets and to natural resources. They are barely active for the moment in the mining sector. The government finds them faster and less formal than traditional partners in carrying out projects, but they are not always in tune with the country's debt policy or anti-poverty programme, the Strategic Framework for Growth and Poverty Reduction (SFGPR).

Table 1: Macroeconomic indicators

	2009	2010	2011	2012
Real GDP growth	4.5	4.5	5.4	5.3
CPI inflation	2.2	1.4	4.1	2.5
Budget balance % GDP	-4.2	-4.1	-4.1	-3.9
Current account % GDP	-7.5	-8.8	-9.6	-10.9

Source: National authorities' data; estimates and predictions based on authors' calculations.

Figures for 2010 are estimates; for 2011 and later are projections.

StatLink http://dx.doi.org/10.1787/888932406669

Figure 1: Real GDP growth (W)

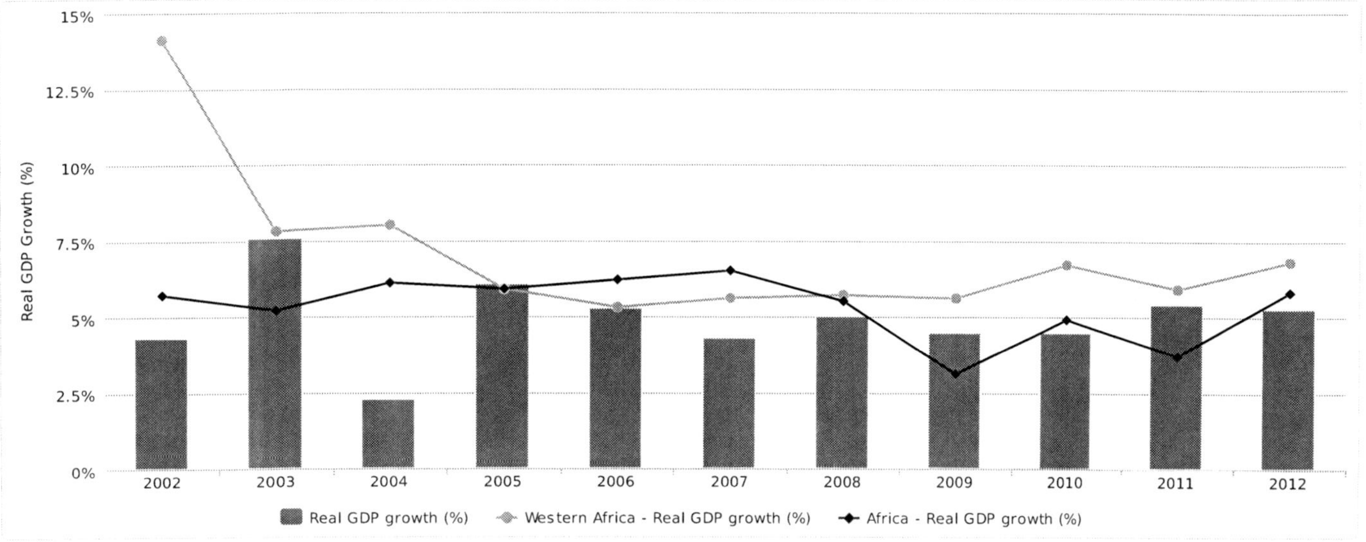

Source: IMF and local authorities' data; estimates and projections based on authors' calculations.

Figures for 2010 are estimates; for 2011 and later are projections.

StatLink http://dx.doi.org/10.1787/888932404313

Mauritania

Growth in the Mauritanian economy recovered in 2010, in the context of significant increases in international mineral prices and the implementation of a public finance reform programme.

Metallic mineral extraction continues to hold a strategic position in the government's development policies, the objective of which is to optimise the management of natural resources. The achievement of the Millennium Development Goals (MDGs) is unlikely by 2015.

Mauritania strengthened its relations with its emerging partners (EPs), particularly with Russia, Brazil, Turkey and China, which rank behind the European Union, the country's historic partner in terms of trade and foreign direct investment (FDI).

The structure of the Mauritanian economy, characterised by the predominance of the secondary and tertiary sectors (with 34.7% of gross domestic product [GDP] and 44.8% of GDP respectively) remained almost entirely unchanged between 2009 and 2010. After a fall in GDP of 1.2% in 2009, the economy should rebound in 2010, with GDP expanding by an estimated 5%. This is expected to become stronger in the coming years with a slight decline in the tertiary sector to the advantage of the primary and secondary sectors. This performance is the outcome of the combined effects of the implementation of the public finances reform programme agreed with the International Monetary Fund (IMF) and the substantial rise in international minerals prices.

Mauritania should build on these results by achieving growth of 5.3% in 2011 and 5.5% in 2012. The authorities are relying on the maintenance of prices of mineral products, notably of iron, copper and gold. They are equally counting on the rationalisation of public expenditure, on an increase in private investment in the mining sector and on the ongoing support of donors. This optimism is reinforced by the close monitoring of the IMF which is aimed at seeing the policy of fiscal consolidation through to a successful conclusion in the framework of a coherent macroeconomic policy. This policy should enable Mauritania to further unblock domestic resources and maintain its debt at a sustainable level.

On the supply side, growth was sustained particularly by the metallic minerals mining sub-sector, which accounted for a quarter of real GDP growth, as well as by the trade and livestock sub-sectors, with contributions of 11.2% and 10.7% respectively. Mining activity grew slightly in 2010 (0.8%), whereas prices on international markets rose significantly. Thus, the prices of iron, copper and gold rose by 60.4%, 46.3% and 25.9% respectively, between 2009 and 2010. Agriculture benefited from a very good season and registered growth of 11.7%. It continued, however, to make a marginal contribution to growth, with a low GDP share of 4.6%. On the demand side, final consumption (estimated at 90.5% of GDP) contributed 6.3 percentage points to growth in 2010. Gross investment expanded by 9.3% in 2010, to around 26.4% of GDP. The volume of exports remained unchanged in 2010 leaving imports (primarily hydrocarbons) to rise by an uncompensated 3.6%, which penalised growth by 4.4 points.

The implementation of macroeconomic policy was on the whole satisfactory in 2010. Mauritania performed well under the programme of reforms supported by the Extended Credit Facility (ECF). In terms of fiscal policy implementation, the government also succeeded in better mobilising domestic resources, controlling spending and reducing instances and arrears on domestic debt. Budgetary receipts increased by 6.9% while overall expenditure and net loans declined by 2.7% between 2009 and 2010. As a result, the budgetary execution in 2010 resulted in an improvement in the overall deficit to 3.7% of nominal GDP, after having reached 5.1% in 2009. The deficit on the current account also improved by almost 4% of GDP, falling from 12.6% to 8.8% of GDP. This improvement was due to the value increase in exports by more than 11% and by the fall in the value of imports by more than 8%.

The Mauritanian ougiya (MRO) experienced a sharp depreciation since the start of 2010, of around 9% vis-à-vis the dollar (USD), so much so that the Central Bank limited its operations. It decided on a three-point drop in the intervention rate, from 12 to 9% in order to promote financing by credit, aimed principally at the private sector. In 2010 consumer prices came under inflationary pressure, because of the rise in international oil prices and certain food products (notably fruit and vegetables, following flooding in Morocco). This shock considerably disrupted market supply for several months. Inflation rose sharply over 2009 (when it was 2.2%) to reach 6.1% according to Central Bank estimates. If the prices of food goods continue on an upward trajectory, with the gradual lifting of subsidies on food staples, inflationary pressures risk continuing during 2011 and 2012, to reach rates of 5.7% and 5.4% respectively.

The authorities have also committed themselves to improving the management of public finances in order to carry out their development programme. The principal reforms aim to control spending and increase public income; decentralise the functions of payment scheduling and financial monitoring with a view to improving management capacities; and computerise the public expenditure and state accounting chains to improve absorption capacity. These reforms consolidate other reforms currently being implemented including: *i)* drawing up a budget based on multi-annual national policies; *ii)* decentralising accounting with the creation of regional general treasury paymasters; *iii)* integrating the information systems of the ministry of finance; *iv)* managing the Treasury (diversifying the Treasury's financing instruments, introducing a single Treasury account and implementing a Treasury plan).

Table 1: Macroeconomic indicators

	2009	2010	2011	2012
Real GDP growth	-1.2	5	5.3	5.5
CPI inflation	2.2	6.1	5.7	5.4
Budget balance % GDP	-5.1	-3.7	-3	-2.9
Current account % GDP	-12.6	-8.8	-8.1	-9.1

Source: National authorities' data; estimates and predictions based on authors' calculations.

Figures for 2010 are estimates; for 2011 and later are projections.

StatLink http://dx.doi.org/10.1787/888932406688

Figure 1: Real GDP growth (N)

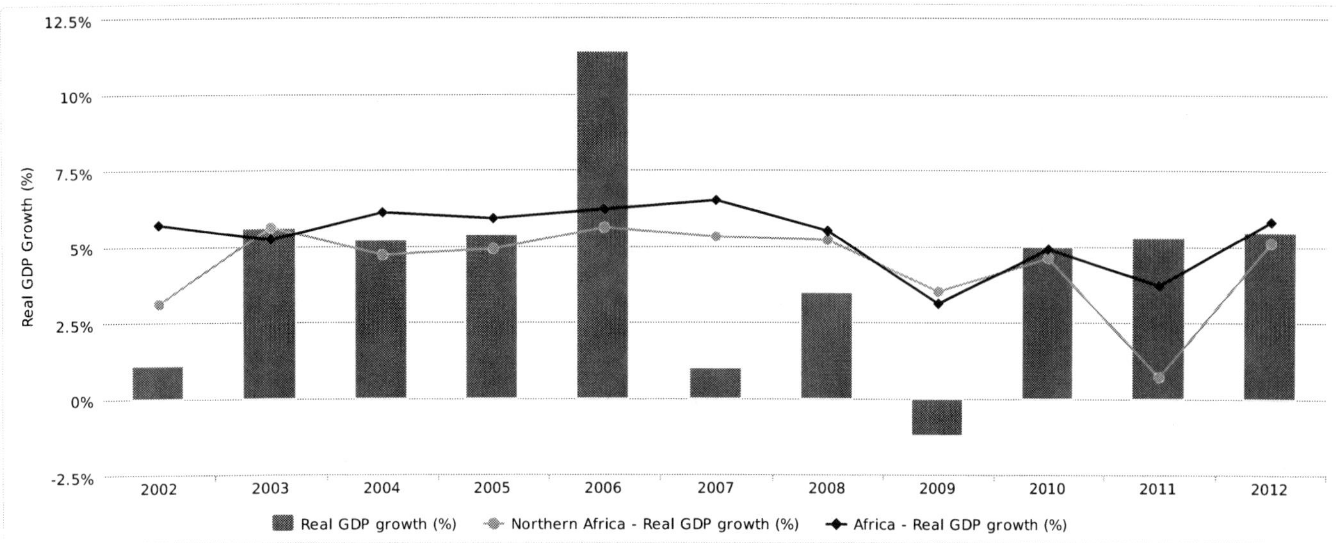

Source: IMF and local authorities' data; estimates and projections based on authors' calculations.

Figures for 2010 are estimates; for 2011 and later are projections.

StatLink http://dx.doi.org/10.1787/888932404332

Mauritius

Despite challenges at home and abroad, Mauritius' gross domestic product (GDP) put on 4.1% in 2010, though its aim to reach 4% in 2011 will depend on the recovery in its main European trade partners.

Mauritius has improved competiveness and financial and political stability, but it must overcome persistent fiscal and current account deficits, low diversification of export markets, high import-dependence, relatively poor infrastructure and rising inequality.

Leading new powers China and India are quickly gaining ground on the traditional traders in providing Mauritius' imports and investment. Malaysia, United Arab Emirates and Singapore are also increasingly important.

Mauritius is striving to diversify its "four-pillar" economy -- sugar, textiles, tourism and financial services -- to make it more resilient to shocks, enhance productivity and competiveness, and support growth and job creation. The 2010 budget focused on job creation, social development and the environment. It maintained previous support measures taken by the government. For 2011, the three main thrusts of the budget are rebalancing growth, boosting productivity and consolidating social justice.

Real gross domestic product (GDP) grew by 4.1% in 2010, up from 3.1% in 2009 but lower than the 5.5% in 2008. Despite challenges at home and abroad, the government has maintained a growth path. In 2011, GDP growth is projected to remain around 4%. However, this will depend on the recovery in the main European trading partners, but could be faster if Mauritius reduces its dependence on sending exports to slow-growing traditional markets and charting a new economic model more resilient to future shocks. Projections for 2012 put economic growth at 4.1%. The overall 2010 budget deficit was estimated at 4.7% of GDP against 6.6% in 2009. It is projected to fall back to 4.4% in 2011 and 4.3% in 2012. The relatively high fiscal deficits are caused by rapidly increasing government expenditure (including capital repayments) compared to revenues.

In 2010, the key Repurchase Agreement (Repo) rate was reduced from 5.75% to 4.75% and the headline inflation rate stood at 2.9% compared to 2.5% in 2009. Inflation is expected to rise to 3.0% in 2011 and 3.9% in 2012. The current account deficit stood at 7.9% of GDP and is projected to rise to 9.2% in 2011 and 9% in 2012. The higher deficits are due to an expected higher trade deficit as imports outstrip exports. Amid volatility in the foreign exchange market, the Mauritius rupee (MUR) ended 2010 appreciating against major currencies. Against the US dollar (USD), it gained from an average of MUR 31.94 in 2009 to MUR 30.89.

In 2010, tourist arrivals were estimated at about 934 000 compared to 871 000 the previous year and 2010 tourism earnings were estimated at about MUR 39.5 billion, up from MUR 35.7 billion in 2009. Gross foreign direct investment (FDI) stood at MUR 10.6 billion at the end of September 2010 against MUR 8.8 billion for the same period in 2009, a 20% gain. The investment went mainly to health and social work activities, real estate, finance and insurance.

Apart from infrastructure development, Mauritius is giving priority to the small and medium enterprise (SME) sector, which has been the main source of employment creation during the financial and economic crises. The government is also increasing support to export-oriented industries, especially textiles and clothing, which have been under severe stress in the crisis.

Mauritian banks are healthy, profitable, well-capitalized and resilient with an overall capital adequacy ratio well up with international standards.

The unemployment rate rose from 7.3% in 2009 to 7.5% in 2010.

Estimates indicate that primary sector activities, mainly related to agriculture, grew by 2.5% in 2010, down from 8.7% in 2009. Sugarcane grew by only 0.6% while "other agriculture" expanded 3.7% in 2010. As part of efforts to make the economy more resilient, an agricultural production and marketing information system is being set up for planters and breeders to optimize revenue. Sugar co-operatives are being helped to get the European Union's Fair Trade accreditation. This will enable them to obtain a premium of USD 60 per tonne of sugar. The government has provided liberal tax regimes for agriculture in the 2011 budget. In addition, the Leasing for Equipment Modernization Scheme is being extended to December 2012 to cover heavy duty agricultural equipment.

Future overall growth will rely in some part on Mauritius tackling its fiscal and current account deficits, high dependency on traditional export partners, high import-dependence, and relatively poor infrastructure. Poverty and inequality are also edging up. Traffic congestion and the high number of road accidents are also a problem.

Table 1: Macroeconomic indicators

	2009	2010	2011	2012
Real GDP growth	3.1	4.1	4	4.1
CPI inflation	2.5	2.9	3	3.9
Budget balance % GDP	-6.6	-4.7	-4.4	-4.3
Current account % GDP	-7.4	-7.9	-9.2	-9

Source: National authorities' data; estimates and predictions based on authors' calculations.

Figures for 2010 are estimates; for 2011 and later are projections.

StatLink http://dx.doi.org/10.1787/888932406707

Figure 1: Real GDP growth (S)

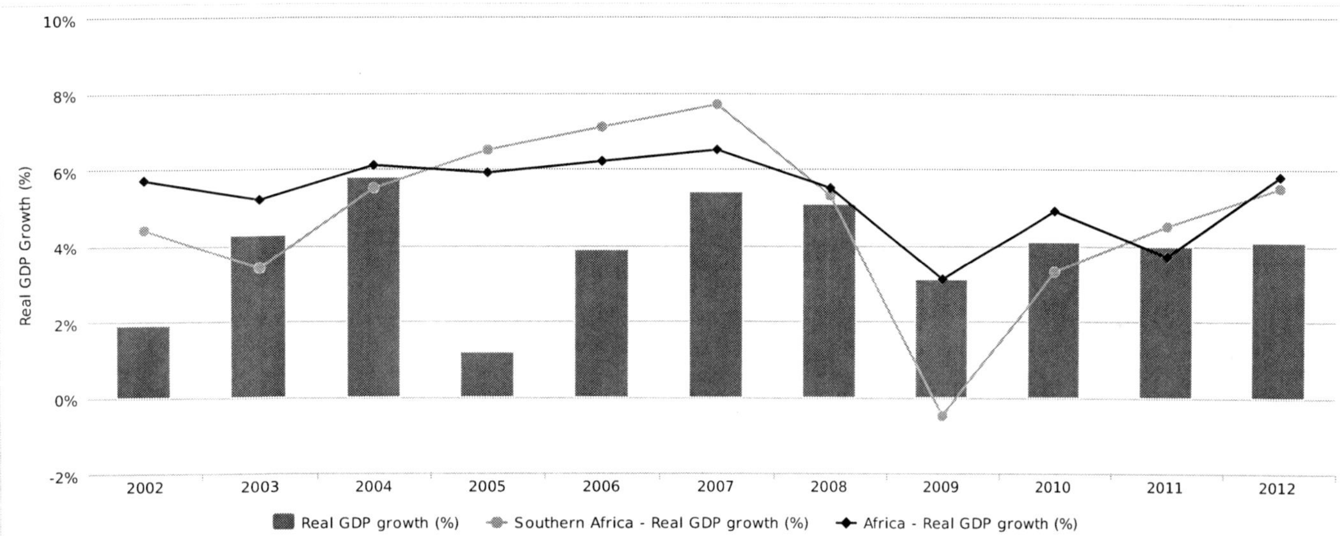

Source: IMF and local authorities' data; estimates and projections based on authors' calculations.

Figures for 2010 are estimates; for 2011 and later are projections.

StatLink http://dx.doi.org/10.1787/888932404351

Morocco

Morocco's deepening involvement with the region and the wider world meant that it was inevitable that it would suffer from the international crisis of 2008.

Nevertheless the continuation of the macroeconomic and structural reforms instituted over the past ten years, combined with a pick-up in non-agricultural activities and in demand from Morocco's partner countries, offer favourable prospects for growth and the economy should record growth of 4.6% in 2011.

Morocco is well aware of its dependence on Europe and has encouraged partnership agreements with several emergent economies with a view to widening the range of its partners. The most important of these are Arab countries (Saudi Arabia and the United Arab Emirates, in particular), Asian states (China and South Korea), Latin American countries (Brazil and Mexico) and Turkey.

The involvement of the Moroccan economy in its regional and global environment has found expression in the signature of several free-trade agreements with its main trading partners. But it also exposed the country to the fall-out of the international crisis which hit world markets in 2008. The basics of the national economy remained stable in spite of the crisis and the country displayed a degree of resilience in the face of external shock, with a growth in gross domestic product (GDP) of 4.9% in 2009 and 3.3% in 2010. Nevertheless, the crisis has highlighted structural weaknesses, in particular in certain export-oriented sectors such as textiles and clothing.

The problems that the government has to confront were summarised by King Mohammed VI in July 2010. In a speech from the throne he identified priorities including:

"To take up the challenges of opening-up and competitiveness by undertaking the necessary reforms to restructure the sectors whose weaknesses have been exposed by the global crisis and turn the first fruits of the pick-up in the world economy to our account."

He also said that preserving macroeconomic balances was an absolute necessity, like the rationalisation of public spending and the updating of the legal and regulatory framework to make the country more attractive to enterprise and business.

He added that there was a further need to pay attention to a judicious use of the credibility enjoyed by the national banking and financial sector and the confidence in Morocco as a centre of attraction to international capital and investment.

In this context the continuation of the macroeconomic and structural reforms put in place over the past decade, combined with the revival of non-agricultural activities and demand from Morocco's partners, offer favourable prospects for growth and the economy should expand by 4.6% in 2011 and 5.0% in 2012.

Table 1: Macroeconomic indicators

	2009	2010	2011	2012
Real GDP growth	4.9	3.3	4.6	5
CPI inflation	1	0.9	2.1	2.7
Budget balance % GDP	-2.2	-4.1	-3.5	-3.4
Current account % GDP	-5.1	-4.2	-4.5	-5.2

Source: National authorities' data; estimates and predictions based on authors' calculations.

Figures for 2010 are estimates; for 2011 and later are projections.

StatLink http://dx.doi.org/10.1787/888932406726

Figure 1: Real GDP growth (N)

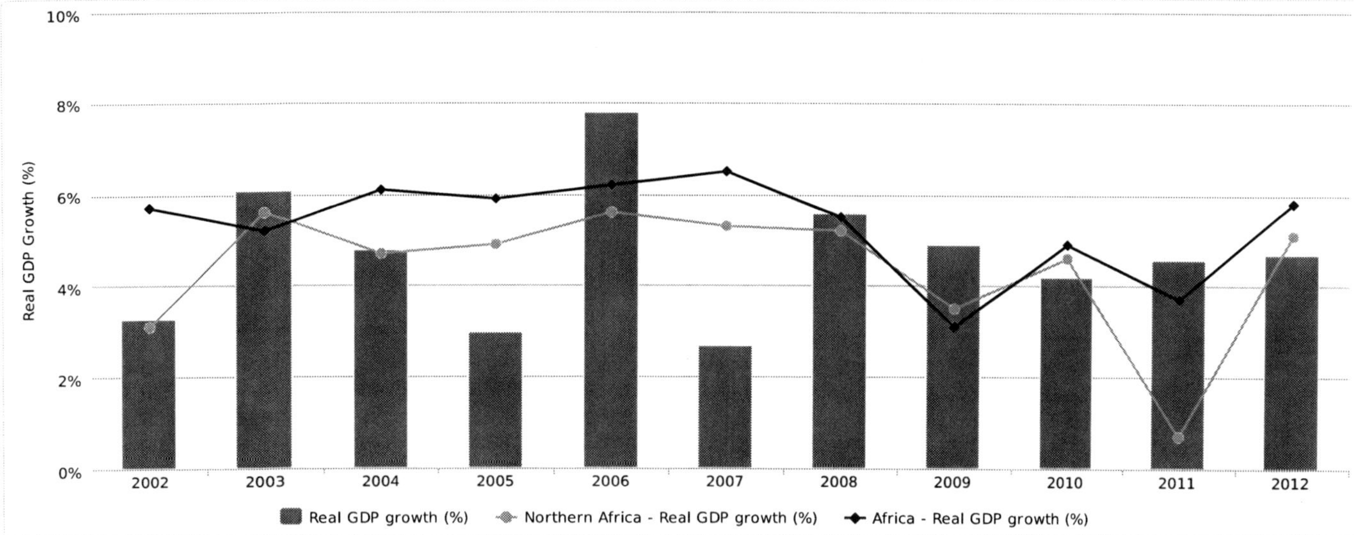

Source: IMF and local authorities' data; estimates and projections based on authors' calculations.

Figures for 2010 are estimates; for 2011 and later are projections.

StatLink http://dx.doi.org/10.1787/888932404370

Mozambique

Although Mozambique's growth remains high, the government, donors and civil society are questioning the development model based on mega-projects.

The difficulty of sustainably lowering consumption poverty rates combined with high international oil and food prices could lead to further political unrest.

Mozambique aims to lower its dependence on Western donors by cautiously engaging with emerging partners through foreign direct investment (FDI).

Mozambique's economy continued to perform well in 2010, growing by an estimated 8.1%. Growth in 2009 had been achieved despite a drop in aluminium prices, offset by massive inflows of foreign direct investment (FDI) in coal projects, whereas in 2010 the economy benefited from both FDI and recovering aluminium prices. In addition, coal extracted from the "mega-projects" in Tete province will start adding to exports in 2011. Exports are therefore expected to increase, although the current account balance will remain structurally negative due to the country's dependence on imports of food, oil and manufactured products. Mozambique is expected to maintain high growth rates in the medium term, driven by mega-projects.

The inflation rate hit double digits in 2010, as a result of the scrapping of fuel subsidies in March-August 2010, the rise in international oil and food prices, the depreciation of the currency against the US dollar (USD) and the South African rand (ZAR), a poor agricultural year and loose monetary policies. Inflation should decline to single digits in 2011, contained by urban transport and wheat flour subsidies, a tighter monetary policy and reinforcement of the domestic food production strategy. The main risk in the growth forecast is that the recovery of international oil and food prices and poor weather will result in failure to control inflation.

However impressive the growth rate, riots in September 2010 and new data on poverty highlighted the weak linkages between macroeconomic performance and the bulk of the population. Social unrest forced the government, donors and international institutions to reconsider Mozambique's growth model. This model has been based on FDI mega-projects in the extractive industries, which are largely exempt from taxation, with human development supported by donor contributions. The government launched the 2010-14 Poverty Reduction Strategy Paper (PARPA) III, which apart from human development focuses on agricultural output and productivity and on the creation of jobs in small and medium-sized enterprises (SMEs).

The government's ambitious public works programme over the next few years is expected to result in a substantial widening of the deficit. Capital expenditure should rise by over 1.5 percentage points of GDP between 2008 and 2012. Public investment funded by non-concessional loans will focus on infrastructure based on public-private partnerships (PPPs) along the development corridors. Such projects will absorb all fiscal space over the 2011-13 period, favouring in a first stage large foreign investments linking extractive areas with the coast. Agriculture and SME jobs are expected to benefit through spill-over effects along the development corridors. Donors continue to support human development, although their budget contribution, which accounted for almost 50% of revenues in 2010, will start being phased out.

Mozambique's new growth model remains based on extractive industries. Two Industrial Free Zones (IFZs) will be created in Nacala in 2011, followed by five more IFZs and one Special Economic Zone (SEZ) before 2014. The extent to which this model will create spill-over effects that benefit the population is yet to be proven, after the government's failure to promote domestic manufacturing and services around existing mega-projects. The Moatize-Nacala corridor has nevertheless the potential to have a large impact on the economy. Nampula and Zambezia provinces have considerable agricultural potential and large populations, and exchanges with landlocked Malawi, Zambia and Zimbabwe could be exploited.

Mozambique benefits from the diversification of its development partners, notably China, Brazil and India. These emerging partners complement traditional donors' strong focus on social sectors with an interest in infrastructure and agriculture. During the global economic crisis, their rising demand for natural resources helped to sustain Mozambique's economy. Emerging partners also finance various research projects seeking to boost agricultural productivity. To date, however, large investments in infrastructure have mostly been geared towards enhancing the productivity of extractive industries, rather than benefiting the local economy. A more structured engagement with emerging and traditional partners alike is required to embed future projects in the national development plan.

Poverty remains widespread in Mozambique, notwithstanding sustained GDP growth over the past decade. The poverty rate declined from 69.4% of the population in 1997 to 55% in 2010, but poverty is now stagnating and regional disparities remain acute. Growing inequality could lead to further social tension if food prices remain high and the government out of touch with ordinary Mozambicans.

Development indicators have improved in recent years, but most of the Millennium Development Goals (MDGs) will not be attained unless the government and donors reinforce their commitment over the next five years. Basic challenges, such as improving the quality of education and health services and the fight against HIV/AIDS, remain daunting.

Table 1: Macroeconomic indicators

	2009	2010	2011	2012
Real GDP growth	6.4	8.1	7.7	7.9
CPI inflation	3.5	12.7	9.2	7.3
Budget balance % GDP	-5.1	-5.4	-6	-5.4
Current account % GDP	-10.9	-11.2	-10.3	-11

Source: National authorities' data; estimates and predictions based on authors' calculations.

Figures for 2010 are estimates; for 2011 and later are projections.

StatLink http://dx.doi.org/10.1787/888932406745

Figure 1: Real GDP growth (S)

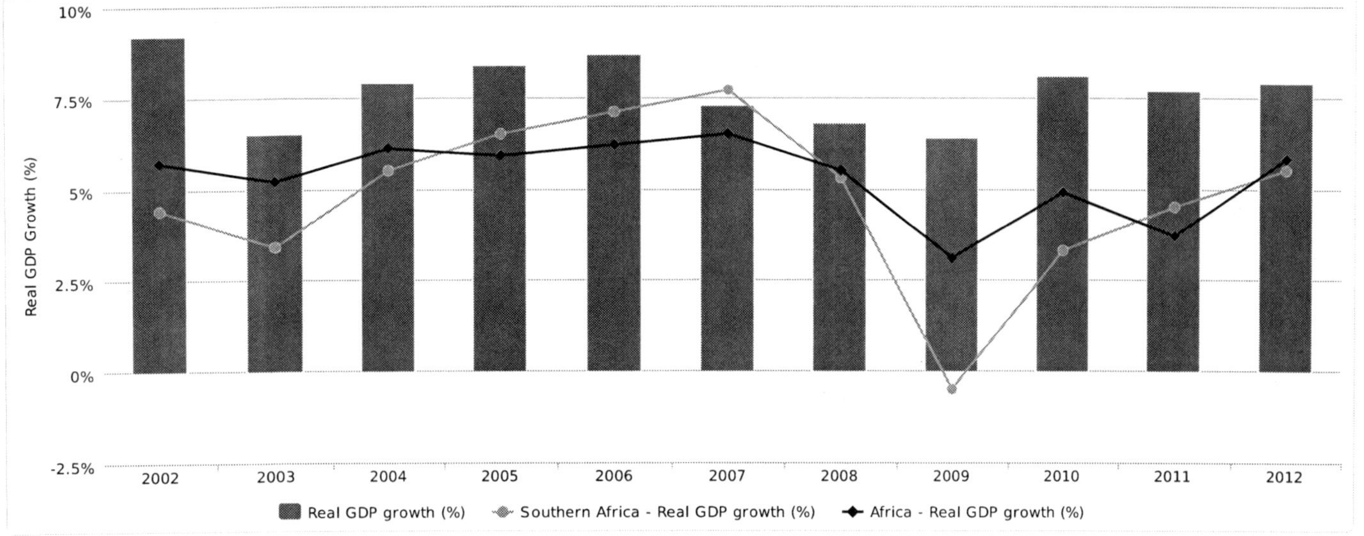

Source: IMF and local authorities' data; estimates and projections based on authors' calculations.

Figures for 2010 are estimates; for 2011 and later are projections.

StatLink http://dx.doi.org/10.1787/888932404389

Namibia

After contracting by 0.7% in 2009, following the global economic downturn, the economy grew by 4.2% in 2010 due to rapid recovery in mining activities. In the medium term, the main policy challenge will be to ensure balance between fostering growth, maintaining fiscal sustainability and a stable currency peg with the South African rand.

The Namibian economic and social environment is clouded by massive structural challenges, notably, very high unemployment, heavy reliance on a few mineral products and deficiencies in energy and water infrastructure, which limit growth potential.

Emerging partners, especially China, are becoming increasingly important participants in the Namibian economy. The challenge is to engage the new partners purposefully to reap the full benefits of buoyant trade ties and ensure that development assistance received is integrated into the national development plan and form part of the long-term national and regional development agenda.

The Namibian economy grew by 4.2% in 2010, following a 0.7% contraction in 2009. Growth was due primarily to a rapid recovery in diamond and uranium mining activities, but also to credit extension. The sustained improvement in global demand for mineral products is expected to maintain gross domestic product (GDP) growth in 2011 with a slight rise to 4.8% in 2011, and then a minor drop to 4.6% in 2012.

Outputs in mining recovered as global demand improved, while agricultural outputs recovered due to good weather conditions. Manufacturing has not only remained resilient amid the global downturn but also expanded in 2010. However, construction contracted in 2010 driven mainly by the decline in residential building construction, which was caused by the tightening of credit and a high level of household indebtedness.

Namibia implemented strong and co-ordinated counter-cyclical fiscal and monetary policies to shield the economy from the effects of the global economic downturn. Fiscal stimulus measures together with the sharp decline in Southern African Customs Union (SACU) receipts may lead to a fiscal deficit of 2.3% of GDP in 2010/11. Namibia is one of the five member states of the SACU. Due to prudent fiscal management during the years immediately prior to the 2009 recession (2005-08), levels of public indebtedness have remained moderate. In 2009/10, total debt stood at 15.1% of GDP, of which 10.9% constituted domestic borrowings, while 4.2% represented foreign borrowing. The Bank of Namibia responded to the crisis by cutting the repo rate by 450 basis points between December 2008 and December 2010, resulting in the rate of 6%. The slowdown in domestic demand, low imported inflation, primarily from South Africa, and a strong currency have led to a decline in inflation from 8.7% in 2009 to 4.5% in 2010. Inflation is expected to be around 6.1% and 5.5% in 2011 and 2012, respectively.

In the medium term, the main policy challenge will continue to be the need to ensure balance between fostering growth, maintaining fiscal sustainability and a stable currency peg with the South African rand.

The Namibian economic and social environment is overshadowed by massive structural challenges, notably, very high unemployment, heavy reliance on a few mineral products and deficiencies in water and energy infrastructure, which limit growth potential. While public service delivery has improved, more must be done to address both quality and coverage of basic services, particularity in rural areas. Human resource development remains one of the most important long-term investments to ensure sustainable economic growth that will benefit the majority of the population.

The ruling party, Swapo, must re-invigorate efforts towards alleviating poverty and inequality – against the backdrop of extremely high unemployment levels – to ensure future social and political stability in the country. Further, the government needs to ensure that the political climate does not deteriorate in election years.

China, India and Russia remain the three most important emerging economic partners of Namibia. Emerging economic partnerships can provide better terms of bilateral co-operation compared to traditional partnerships, as well as benefit the local economy through job creation, economic diversification and transfer of technology, even if at a limited level. The main challenge is to negotiate advantageous terms so that the country fully benefits from the expanding trade, and that assistance received is integrated into the long-term national and regional development agenda.

Table 1: Macroeconomic indicators

	2009	2010	2011	2012
Real GDP growth	-0.7	4.2	4.8	4.6
CPI inflation	8.7	4.5	6.1	5.5
Budget balance % GDP	2.1	-3	-2.3	-1.1
Current account % GDP	1.5	-2.9	-3.5	-3

Source: National authorities' data; estimates and predictions based on authors' calculations.

Figures for budget balance refer to fiscal year April (n)/ March (n+1).

Figures for 2010 are estimates; for 2011 and later are projections.

StatLink http://dx.doi.org/10.1787/888932406764

Figure 1: Real GDP growth (S)

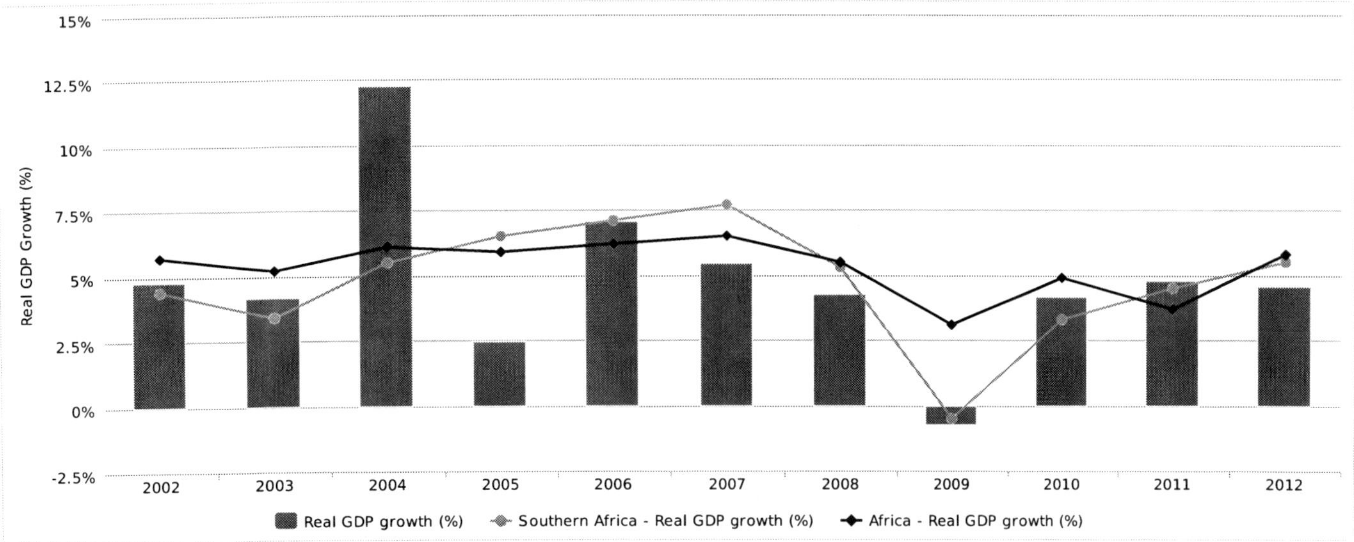

Source: IMF and local authorities' data; estimates and projections based on authors' calculations.

Figures for 2010 are estimates; for 2011 and later are projections.

StatLink http://dx.doi.org/10.1787/888932404408

Niger

Economic growth remains dependent on a good harvest, which means that there is great uncertainty about short-term trends and a lack of visibility in the medium term.

The development and poverty reduction strategy is being speeded up with the aim of reducing dependence on climatic factors and creating conditions for sustainable development based on private sector growth.

Niger has very dynamic bilateral cooperation arrangements, notably with China, which can bring clear dividends in the mining and oil sectors provided that Niger strengthens its negotiating capacities

Real gross domestic product (GDP) growth in 2010 was estimated at 5.5%, essentially driven by the agricultural sector which achieved good results throughout the country. This situation contrasts with that of 2009 when, as a result of low rainfall, GDP dropped -1.2% after growth of 9.5% in 2008, which was an exceptional year. Growth should return to 4.9% in 2011 and then recover to 11.5% in 2012 as production starts at the Imouraren uranium mine, the biggest in Africa.

Niger's trade balance remains in deficit. The poor 2009 harvest only served to aggravate the situation. To deal with the acute food crisis which resulted, Niger had to import 60% of its food needs, particularly rice, the principal food staple.

The general level of prices, as measured by the harmonised index of consumer prices which uses 2008 as its 100% base year, came out at 98.6% in April 2010, compared to 100.1% in January and February and 98.2% in March. On a month to month basis, prices rose 0.4% in March 2010 and this trend was maintained in April when it is estimated that there was a 0.3% increase following a 0.9% increase in the prices of food and non-alcoholic drinks. Overall, the inflation rate in 2010 was 3.4%, quite close to the 3% convergence level set by the West African Economic and Monetary Union (WAEMU). Inflation, therefore, has been kept under control in Niger.

At the current level of mobilisation of fiscal revenue, the fiscal pressure level in 2010 is estimated at 14.1% of GDP compared to 13.6% in 2009. Grants represented 7.2% of GDP up to the end of September, compared to 4.5% in 2009 and 8.6% in 2008. The downward trend in grant revenue began in 2009 when certain development partners suspended their cooperation after the president announced that he intended to prolong his mandate beyond its constitutional term.

The monetary position was affected by policy softening by the Central Bank of West African States (BCEAO) on 16 June 2009 when it reduced base rates by 0.5%. The discount rate was reduced from 6.75% to 6.25% and repurchase rates from 4.75% to 4.25%. These changes stimulated lending to the economy in 2009 and 2010 and should have the same effect in 2011, mainly as a result of the recovery expected in the mining and oil sectors.

The business environment in Niger is not generally favourable to private sector development. There is no shortage of obstacles, including corruption, uncertainty about regulations and their application, institutional weaknesses and difficulty of access to credit and land ownership. According to the 2011 edition of the World Bank report *Doing Business*, Niger is in 173rd position among 183 countries. The prospects of the private sector in Niger are, nevertheless, fairly good, taking into account the measures envisaged under the Accelerated Development and Poverty Reduction Strategy (ADPRS). It provides for concerted action based on the four following principles: *i)* stronger support for the private sector; *ii)* improvement of the micro-economic business environment; *iii)* improvement of financing of the economy; and *iv)* better integration in regional and global trade.

Table 1: Macroeconomic indicators

	2009	2010	2011	2012
Real GDP growth	-1.2	5.5	4.9	11.5
CPI inflation	4.9	3.4	3.1	3.3
Budget balance % GDP	-6.6	-3.2	-3.6	-1.8
Current account % GDP	-23.4	-18.1	-21	-17.6

Source: National authorities' data; estimates and predictions based on authors' calculations.

Figures for 2010 are estimates; for 2011 and later are projections.

StatLink http://dx.doi.org/10.1787/888932406783

Figure 1: Real GDP growth (W)

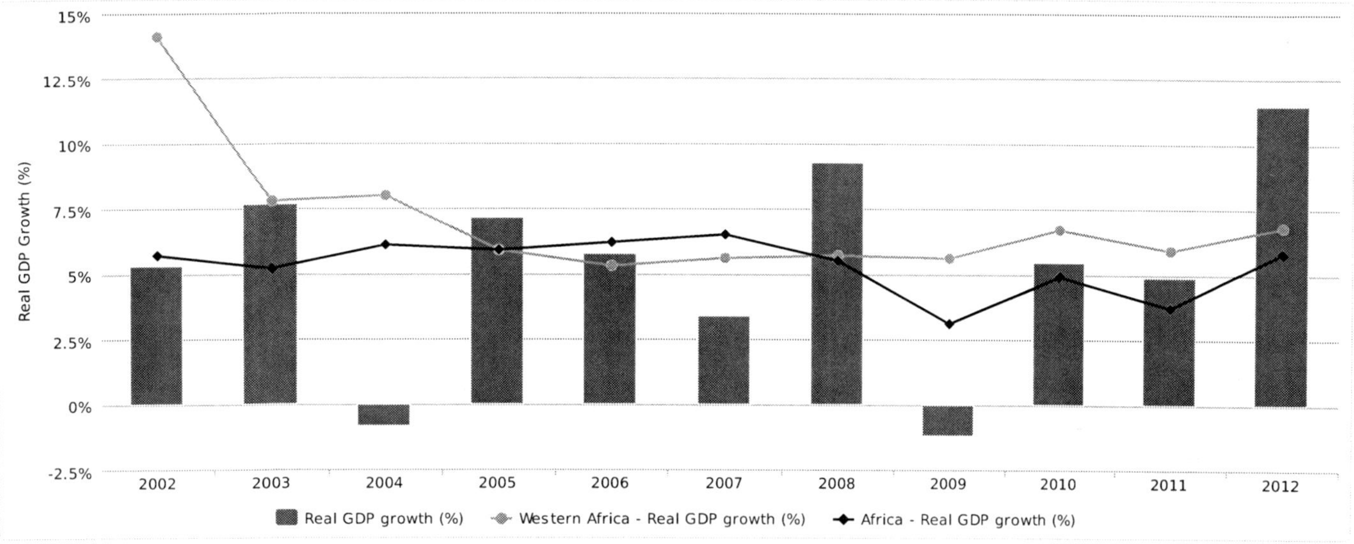

Source: IMF and local authorities' data; estimates and projections based on authors' calculations.

Figures for 2010 are estimates; for 2011 and later are projections.

StatLink http://dx.doi.org/10.1787/888932404427

Nigeria

The high price of crude oil and prudence in economic management are delivering economic progress, with real gross domestic product (GDP) growth expected to be strong at 6.9% in 2011.

A strong adherence to reforms and reduction in ethnic and sectarian violence are needed to enhance private-sector participation in the economy.

Economic diversification, moving away from excessive dependence on oil, will increase opportunities for greater co-operation with emerging partners.

Nigeria is making progress with economic reforms that are delivering strong economic fundamentals. The government has maintained prudent macroeconomic policies, strengthened financial institutions and, albeit slowly and unevenly, is undertaking reforms to transform the economy structurally. The reform effort, aided by revenue from high oil prices, has led to significantly improved macroeconomic outcomes, including weaker inflation and strong GDP growth. Real GDP growth rose from 7.0% in 2009 to an estimated 8.1% in 2010. The robust growth in 2010, in the aftermath of the global financial and economic crisis, underscored the resilience of the Nigerian economy and to some extent, the prudence of its economic policies. Medium-term prospects are also bright, with real GDP growth projected to remain strong and stable at 6.9% in 2011 and 6.7% in 2012.

Notwithstanding these positive developments, the Nigerian economy remains confronted with many serious challenges. Structural imbalance and lack of diversification – with the economy excessively dependent on oil – is preventing the domestic economy from flourishing. High youth unemployment, poor infrastructure facilities and widespread insecurity are the key challenges the government will have to take on.

Deepening the reform process is clearly necessary. Medium- to long-term prospects hinge on Nigeria's addressing key reforms successfully in order to advance infrastructure development and broaden the economic base through enhanced private-sector participation. In addition, containing political, civil and ethnic unrest, especially in the Niger Delta region, remains a challenge for the political stability that is needed to consolidate the achievements of the past few years.

Table 1: Macroeconomic indicators

	2009	2010	2011	2012
Real GDP growth	7	8.1	6.9	6.7
CPI inflation	12.5	13.7	11.1	9
Budget balance % GDP	-10.4	-6.8	-0.7	0.3
Current account % GDP	13.1	13.3	17.6	16.6

Source: National authorities' data; estimates and predictions based on authors' calculations.

Figures for 2010 are estimates; for 2011 and later are projections.

StatLink http://dx.doi.org/10.1787/888932406802

Figure 1: Real GDP growth (W)

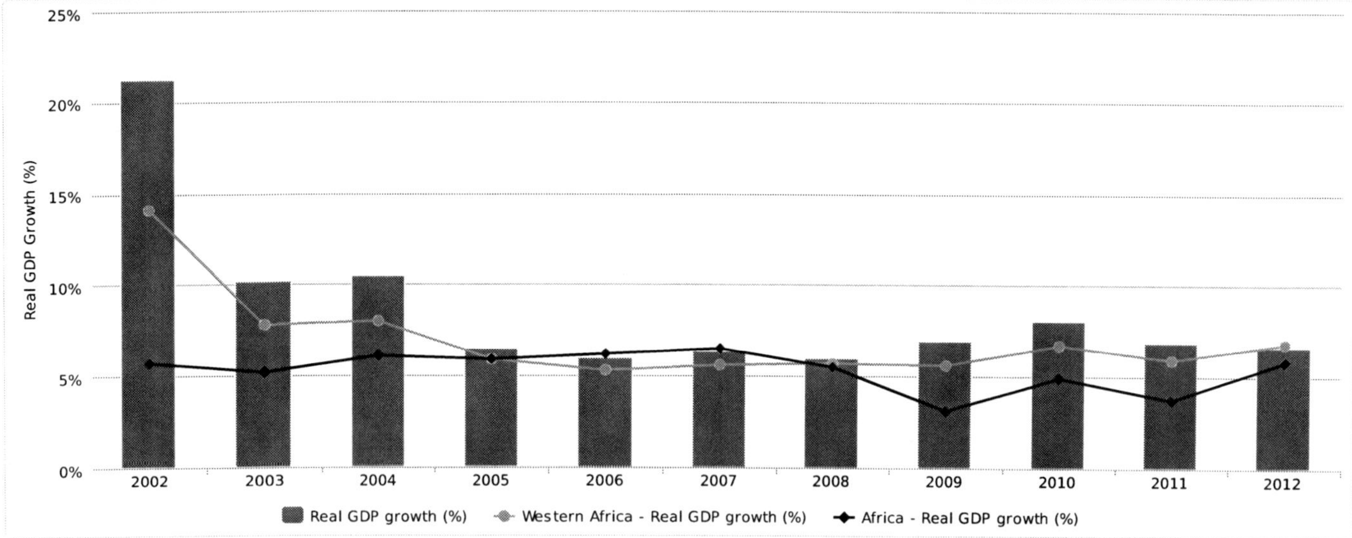

Source: IMF and local authorities' data; estimates and projections based on authors' calculations.

Figures for 2010 are estimates; for 2011 and later are projections.

StatLink http://dx.doi.org/10.1787/888932404446

Rwanda

Rwanda's economy grew 7.4% in 2010, up from 4.1% in 2009, as it recovered from the global economic crisis and domestic liquidity constraints faced by banks. The outlook for the coming three years is one of robust growth.

Rwanda is on the path to becoming a knowledge-based, service economy in the region by investing in ICT capability, e-government, power generation, and air and land transport.

Rwanda's South-South partnerships have made notable progress in the last few years, particularly with China, and to a certain extent with India, in the areas of trade, investment and technical co-operation.

In 2010, the economy of Rwanda recovered from the sharp downturn it experienced in the previous year by growing at 7.4%. The outlook for 2011 and 2012 remains robust. The rebound is driven mainly by increased exports, expansion in the growth of services and construction sector. Inflation also has declined considerably in 2010 compared with 2009 when food prices increased by more than 20% in the wake of the global food crisis. The macroeconomic balance also improved in 2010 and is expected to remain stable in the mid-term.

Table 1: Macroeconomic indicators

	2009	2010	2011	2012
Real GDP growth	4.1	7.4	6.5	7
CPI inflation	10.3	2.3	5.2	5.5
Budget balance % GDP	-2.2	-0.5	-3.5	-1.4
Current account % GDP	-8.4	-6.7	-9.1	-6.5

Source: National authorities' data; estimates and predictions based on authors' calculations.

Figures for 2010 are estimates; for 2011 and later are projections.

StatLink http://dx.doi.org/10.1787/888932406821

In the last decade and a half, Rwanda's economy has progressed by improving factor productivity, achieving a considerably higher level of output per worker. The mid-term outlook now depends on increased investment in core sectors. Public investment to improve power generation capacity, air transport, e-government and other sectors is expected to help sustain current growth. But the country's continued dependence on a few export commodities represents a serious constraint and the mobilisation of domestic resources to finance investment remains low.

Rwanda has undertaken impressive reforms to create a business-friendly environment for the private sector. It has the status of best reformer in the world and is one of the freer countries in economic terms. The hope is that these achievements will translate into increased economic activity in the private sector and attract investment from around the world.

There is impressive social as well as economic progress. Rwanda is on track to meet most of the Millennium Development Goals (MDGs).

Rwanda has the potential to achieve a much higher rate economic growth. Investment in creating a skilled labor force, removing infrastructure bottlenecks and improving farm productivity could make a huge difference in the years to come. These are some of the priorities of the government's Economic Development and Poverty Reduction Strategy and Vision 2020.

Figure 1: Real GDP growth (E)

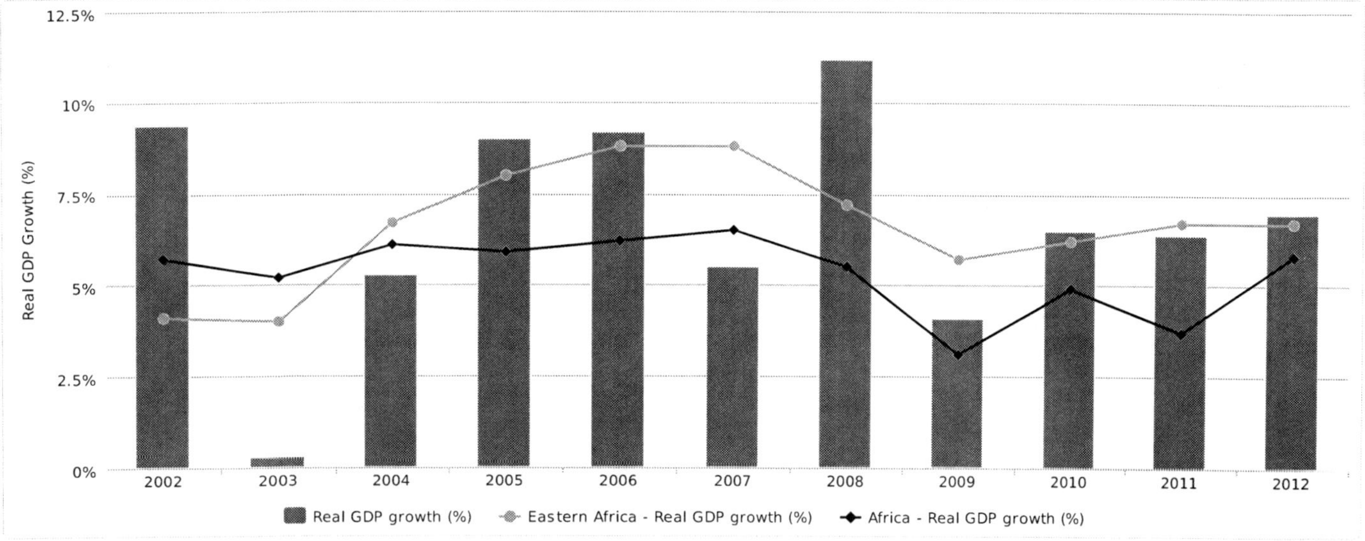

Source: IMF and local authorities' data; estimates and projections based on authors' calculations.

Figures for 2010 are estimates; for 2011 and later are projections.

StatLink http://dx.doi.org/10.1787/888932404465

São Tomé & Príncipe

The economy grew by an estimated 4.5% in 2010. From 2011 onwards, large private investments in oil exploration and the construction of a deepwater seaport should boost growth back to pre-crisis levels of 6% by 2012.

The new Prime Minister is actively diversifying trade and diplomatic ties with emerging partners, particularly in the African sub region, to push the project of turning the archipelago into a regional transport hub and spur the country's development.

Social indicators remain weak despite some progress. Economic growth so far is not broad based and has failed to create employment opportunities for the rural poor and the urban youth.

The gross domestic product (GDP) of the Democratic Republic of São Tomé and Príncipe (STP) slowed down in 2009 but picked up timidly in 2010 to an estimated 4.5%. Growth was sustained by foreign aid and the tertiary sector, including tourism, construction and retail. The economy is forecast to expand by 5.0% in 2011 and 6.0% in 2012, supported by foreign direct investment (FDI) in oil exploration and the construction of a new deepwater seaport. The longer-term outlook, however, remains highly dependent on uncertain oil prospects, with production not expected before 2016.

Macroeconomic policies will remain restrictive. Fiscal policy aims to contain further current primary expenditure through better management of public finances. At the same time, legal and technical measures, combined with higher import duties related to future investment projects, should gradually improve fiscal revenues. Monetary policy is geared towards maintaining the euro currency peg introduced in January 2010. Inflation, still largely determined by imported food and oil prices, slowed to about 11.4% in 2010, down from 16.7% in 2009, thanks to the economic rigour imposed by the peg. This downward trend is expected to continue, provided fiscal policies stay on track and international food prices remain stable. In the meantime, major structural challenges remain: the growing debt burden, vulnerability to external shocks and the lack of economic diversification.

Until and unless oil revenues materialise, the government will remain heavily dependent on external financing. FDI is not expected to return to its pre-crisis levels until after the presidential elections in 2011. In 2010, investments were driven by the public sector, financed by grants and concessional loans. Official development assistance (ODA) remained at the same level as in 2009, although disbursements were held back until after the legislative elections in August. So far, ODA compensated for sluggish FDI throughout 2010, sustaining the slight increase in economic growth. ODA might drop in 2011, however, given the increasing pressures on donors' budgets.

Emerging partners have long played a crucial role in STP's economic and social development. Chinese Taipei has the longest track record, but India and Brazil are intensifying their bilateral cooperation. Nigeria, Angola and increasingly other neighbouring countries are engaging more pro-actively with STP. The new Prime Minister has expressed his interest in diversifying trade and diplomatic ties with emerging partners in order to spur STP's development. In a time of increased competition for scarce resources, STP is seeking to engage with various emerging partners while nurturing the collaboration with traditional partners.

The most pivotal event in 2010 was the local government and parliamentary election in August, resulting in a minority government that may struggle to pass legislation or even remain in charge for long. The new Prime Minister remains committed to transforming STP's economy into a regional hub for transhipment activity. He will promote the diversification of the economy in order to lessen the country's dependence on uncertain oil prospects. Prospects for the economy in the short term will depend on the stability of the new government and the success of presidential elections in June 2011.

Poverty, estimated at about 54% in 2009, remains widespread in rural and periurban areas. The search for employment opportunities is resulting in urban migration, which puts increasing pressure on the capital's infrastructure and feeds the informal sector – estimated at 63% of the economy. Public services such as electricity, sanitation, health and waste management need to be ramped up if STP's social indicators are to maintain their upward trend.

Table 1: Macroeconomic indicators

	2009	2010	2011	2012
Real GDP growth	4	4.5	5	6
CPI inflation	16.7	11.4	7.5	6.7
Budget balance % GDP	17.6	-7.7	3.3	-8.4
Current account % GDP	-26.2	-28.1	-35.8	-34.2

Source: National authorities' data; estimates and predictions based on authors' calculations.

Figures for 2010 are estimates; for 2011 and later are projections.

StatLink http://dx.doi.org/10.1787/888932406859

Figure 1: Real GDP growth (W)

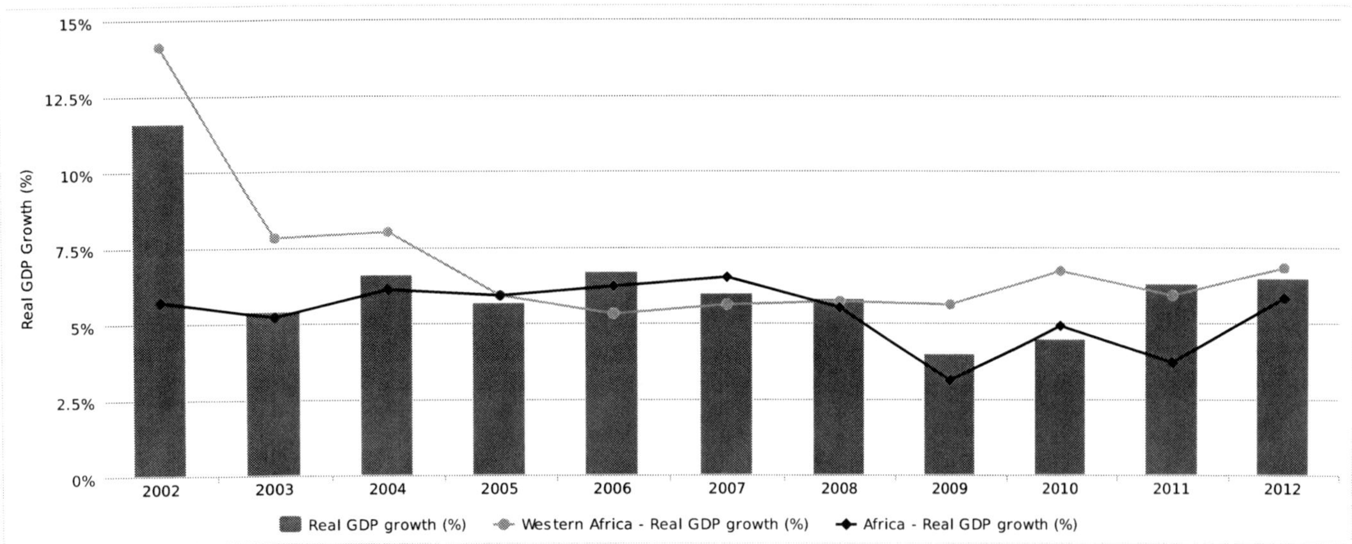

Source: IMF and local authorities' data; estimates and projections based on authors' calculations.

Figures for 2010 are estimates; for 2011 and later are projections.

StatLink http://dx.doi.org/10.1787/888932404503

Senegal

Senegal's economy initiated its recovery in 2010.

Difficulties in the energy sector are one of the main obstacles to this recovery.

A new partnership for the economic development in Senegal has been sealed this year.

After two years marked by the effects of the global financial crisis, the Senegalese economy began to recover in 2010 thanks to the global economic recovery and the measures taken by the authorities to boost national economic activity. Gross domestic product (GDP) was estimated to have grown from 2.2% in 2009 to 4.2% in 2010, and is projected to reach 4.5% in 2011. This will be largely due to the performance of the three sectors of the economy - primary, secondary and tertiary - which respectively accounted for 14.7%, 20.4% and 64.9% (including administration) of GDP in 2010.

Analysis of the basic macroeconomic indicators in 2010 reveals the start of a recovery in the Senegalese economy. The real growth rate thus rose from 2.2% in 2009 to 4.2% in 2010 and 4.5% in 2011 (forecasts). The average annual rate of inflation (-1.0% in 2009) was 1.2% in 2010. In 2011 inflation measured by the GDP deflator is forecast at 3% largely as a result of higher energy prices. The expected change in the investment rate measured by the Gross Fixed Capital Formation (GFCF) is positive: 23.9% of GDP in 2010 and 24.1% in 2011. The tax-burden rate of 18.9% in 2010 also complies with the requirements of the sub-regional convergence criteria (greater than or equal to 17%).

Senegal's external position in 2009 and 2010 resulted in an improved current account deficit (6.7% of GDP in 2009 and 5.9% of GDP in 2010, compared to 14.2% in 2008). The good rate of revenue collection, up by 11% compared to 2009, and control of the increase in public expenditure (7.1%) characterised Senegal's fiscal policy in 2010. The overall budget deficit, including grants, improved 0.4 percentage points, from 4.9% of GDP in 2009 to 4.5% in 2010. It was estimated at 5.8% in 2011.

Since 2000, Senegal has initiated new partnerships with emerging countries, particularly China, India and Iran. The main achievements are to be found in the areas of training, infrastructure and transport.

In 2010 was marked by social movements linked to demands for better access to basic services, sometimes at the initiative of citizens' movements unrelated to opposition political parties. New armed clashes resulted in seven deaths among the armed forces in the Casamance region in December 2010. Specific development programmes are being implemented with the objective of re-establishing peace in the region.

Table 1: Macroeconomic indicators

	2009	2010	2011	2012
Real GDP growth	2.2	4.2	4.5	5
CPI inflation	-1	1.2	3	2.3
Budget balance % GDP	-4.9	-4.5	-5.8	-6.3
Current account % GDP	-6.7	-5.9	-5.9	-10.3

Source: National authorities' data; estimates and predictions based on authors' calculations.

Figures for 2010 are estimates; for 2011 and later are projections.

StatLink http://dx.doi.org/10.1787/888932406840

Figure 1: Real GDP growth (W)

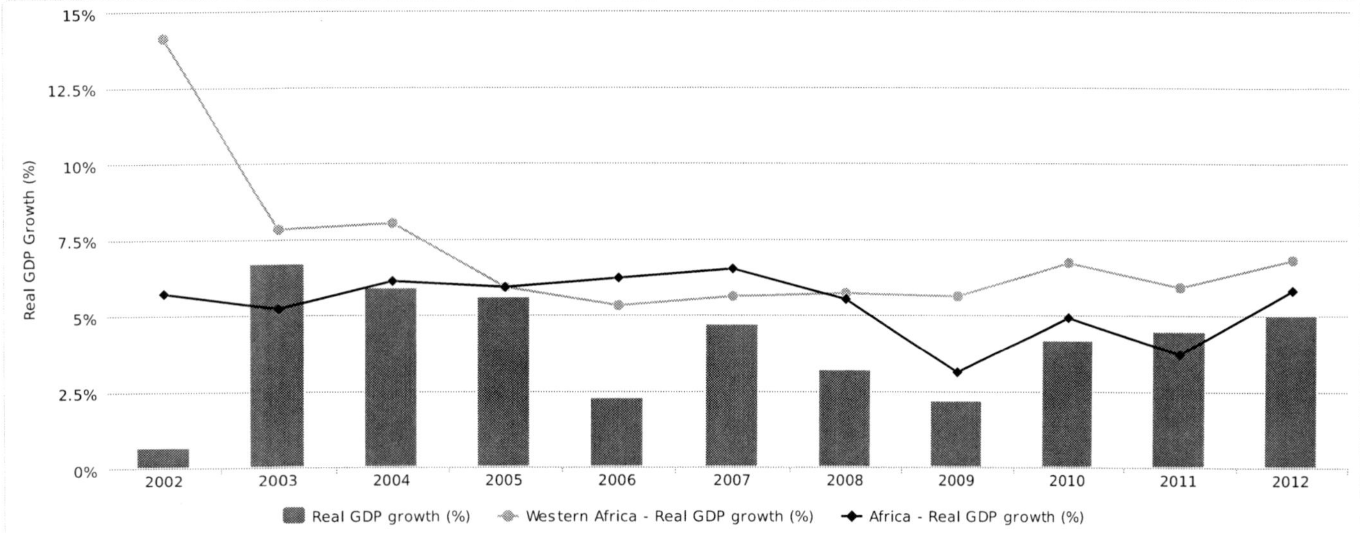

Source: IMF and local authorities' data; estimates and projections based on authors' calculations.

Figures for 2010 are estimates; for 2011 and later are projections.

StatLink http://dx.doi.org/10.1787/888932404484

Seychelles

In 2010, the Seychelles economy recovered strongly because of strong measures to address the 2008 debt crisis. It also weathered the recent global financial and economic crisis relatively well, growing at an estimated rate of 6%.

The government continued with reforms in public financial management, public expenditure and public enterprise during 2010, introducing a medium-term budgeting framework for its fiscal and economic projections over a 3-year period in the 2011 budget.

The most established emerging partners of Seychelles – China, United Arab Emirates (UAE) and India – focus on trade, investment and aid and have intensified their relationships in the past five years.

In 2010, the Seychelles economy recovered after important measures were taken to address the 2008 debt crisis. The country also weathered the recent global financial and economic crisis relatively well. Driven by the tourism industry, which accounts for 25.5% of the gross domestic product (GDP), the economy grew by over 5% from 0.7% in 2009 to an estimated 6% in 2010. There were higher numbers of visitor arrivals with a longer average stay, which increased by 13% and 5%, respectively. This was supported by a rebound in the global economy, a weaker rupee and price discounting by operators. Piracy attacks and threats in the Indian Ocean continue to affect the fishing sector adversely, however. The economy is projected to grow by 4% in 2011 and 4.5% in 2012.

The authorities have eliminated the foreign currency black market and have brought price increases under control, with inflation estimated to have been contained to negative 2.4% in 2010 and projected to reach 4.2% and 2.9% in 2011 and 2012, respectively. The Central Bank of the Seychelles (CBS) foreign exchange reserves are now in excess of two months' worth of imports and are projected to increase to three months of imports by December 2012. Renewed domestic confidence is supporting macroeconomic stabilisation. Since October 2009, the nominal effective exchange rate has stabilised, the depreciation against the US dollar (USD) is offset by the appreciation against the euro (EUR) and the British pound (GBP).

The country now has a sustainable debt position after having re-structured the debt profile. The authorities continue to maintain fiscal discipline. The primary fiscal surplus is estimated at 11.9% of GDP in 2010. The current account deficit, which was 30.3% of GDP in 2009, widened to 33.2% of GDP in 2010 owing to the recovery of domestic demand and rising costs of insurance premiums due to piracy in the Indian Ocean. Foreign direct investment (FDI) resumed, thus financing a larger part of the deficit. The deficit is expected to gradually narrow in 2011 and 2012, as exports of tourism services will benefit from the global economic recovery and additional hotel accommodation.

A number of constraints still affect the business environment despite the measures that the government has recently put in place. The World Bank *2011 Doing Business* report shows that Seychelles slipped to a rank of 95 out of 183 countries in 2010 in the ease of doing business index, compared to a ranking of 92 in 2009.

The Seychelles is an open economy that relies heavily on tourism. As a result, growth prospects in the medium term will largely remain dependent on the global economy's performance, especially in the Euro zone, where 75% of the country's tourists come from as well as on the levels of piracy in the Indian Ocean.

In 2009, the Seychelles received balance of payments and budget support assistance from development partners, namely the International Monetary Fund (IMF), the World Bank, the African Development Bank (AfDB) and the European Union, amounting to EUR 21.9 million to support directly the 2008 economic reform programme. The first part of the reform programme was successfully implemented, which led the IMF to approve an Extended Fund Facility (EFF) in December 2009 to replace the two-year Stand-by Arrangements (SBA). Seychelles made a good start on its second stage of reforms under the EFF despite the global economic crisis and its external debt crisis. By the end of 2010, it had met the quantitative benchmarks under the EFF and its structural targets, and remains on track with key reforms, including an overhaul of the tax system, improving public financial management, modernising monetary operations, strengthening financial sector supervision and restructuring parastatals. It is now on a more sustainable development path.

The most established emerging partners (EPs) of Seychelles are China, United Arab Emirates (UAE), India, Saudi Arabia and Brazil. Others include Malaysia, Indonesia, Singapore and Turkey. Most of these EPs are involved in trade, investment and aid. In the past five years (2006-10), the countries that have most intensified their relationships are China, India and UAE.

The on-going socio-economic reforms have led to a more transparent and less partisan society. However, challenges related to building a more independent judiciary and improving press freedom remain.

Seychelles has one of the highest GDPs per capita in Africa and is one of Africa´s six upper-middle-income countries. It leads the continent in human development according to its ranking of 57 in the 2009 Human Development Index (HDI) of the United Nations Development Programme (UNDP), a level comparable to many countries of the Organisation for Economic Co-operation and Development (OECD). It allocated about 43% of the budget in 2010 or 5% of GDP to the social sectors of health and education, reflecting the government's concerns on poverty and social welfare programmes. Seychelles has already met the target for five of the eight Millenium Development Goals (MDGs); only the sixth through eighth remain.

Table 1: Macroeconomic indicators

	2009	2010	2011	2012
Real GDP growth	0.7	6	4	4.5
CPI inflation	31.7	-2.4	4.2	2.9
Budget balance % GDP	5.1	3.2	0.3	-0.2
Current account % GDP	-30.3	-33.2	-24.8	-22.2

Source: National authorities' data; estimates and predictions based on authors' calculations.

Figures for 2010 are estimates; for 2011 and later are projections.

StatLink http://dx.doi.org/10.1787/888932406878

Figure 1: Real GDP growth (E)

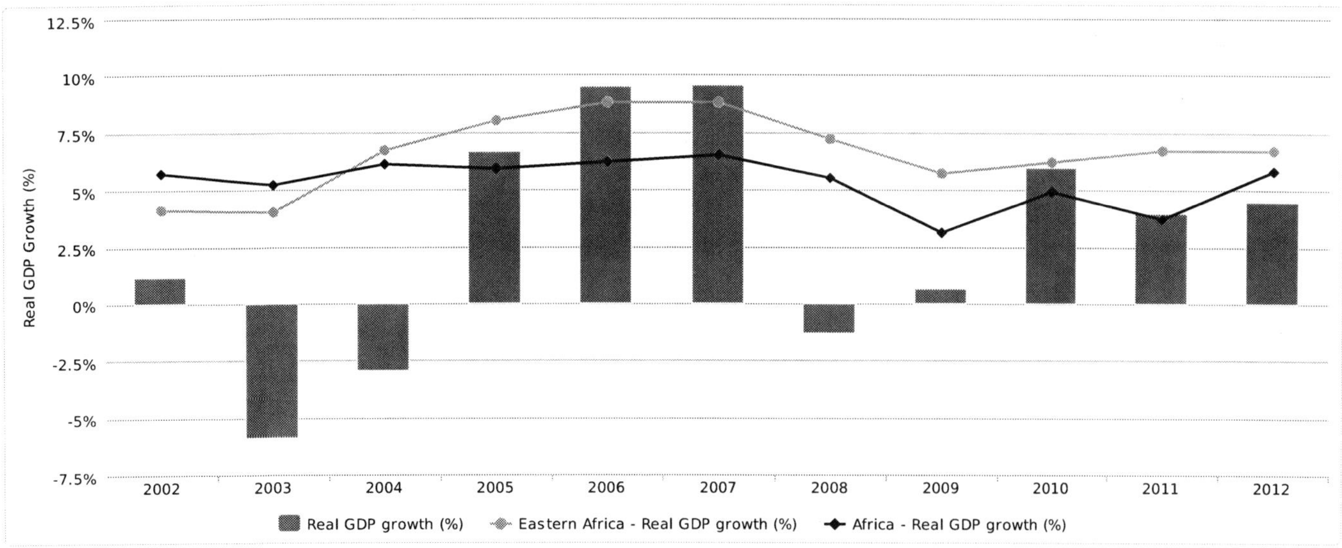

Source: IMF and local authorities' data; estimates and projections based on authors' calculations.

Figures for 2010 are estimates; for 2011 and later are projections.

StatLink http://dx.doi.org/10.1787/888932404522

Sierra Leone

The macroeconomic outlook for Sierra Leone is positive with estimated growth rising to 5.1% in 2011 and 6% in 2012, but the government could do even more to accelerate growth and raise the standard of living.

On the structural reform side, strengthening tax revenue collection, improving the medium term expenditure framework (MTEF), and developing the financial sector are among the key measures that would help mobilise additional resources for development.

New partnerships are becoming more important to Sierra Leone's development agenda. China has been providing support aimed at both growth (e.g. construction of energy projects) and improvement of Sierra Leone's still dismal social indicators (e.g. creation of the China-Sierra Leone Malaria Prevention and Treatment Centre).

Having recorded 4.5% in 2010, growth is projected to rise to 5.1 in 2011 and to gradually recover to 6.0% in 2012. The medium-term outlook for the Sierra Leonean economy is positive, but even more could be done on the structural reform side to help bring the country on a path of high growth with the job creation needed for significant improvements in people's living standards. Growth is being driven by exports of minerals and cash crops due to the global recovery, the expansion of the service sector, increased agricultural productivity, and continued investment in infrastructure. The recent completion of the Bumbuna power station has already started to yield benefits. The government has undertaken key reforms (e.g. in the financial sector, tax reforms) that will bring benefits only later but bode well for the country's future.

Sierra Leone is one of the poorest countries in the world. Its gross domestic product (GDP) per capita was estimated to be only slightly more than 300 US dollars (USD) in 2010. The country faces major development challenges as evidenced by its very low rank on the Human Development Index (HDI) (third from the bottom rank after Afghanistan and Niger) and staggering rates of youth unemployment. Even though Sierra Leone weathered the economic crisis well, the 6% growth forecast for 2012 will still be below pre-crisis growth rates. This points to the need for further growth acceleration if the country is to overcome its economic fragility and reduce the income gap with more advanced economies. Macroeconomic policies can help in this regard by *i)* gradually moving towards a rule-based, counter-cyclical framework and *ii)* making achievement of high growth a key policy priority.

Inflation started to decline in 2011 after rising to 18% in September 2010 due to fiscal expansion and the "one-off effect" from the introduction of goods and service tax (GST). On the supply side, expanded domestic food production is expected to offset rising food prices. Supported by appropriate monetary and fiscal policies and a stabilised nominal exchange rate, average inflation is expected to decline to upper single digits in 2011 and ease further by the end of 2012. Additional pressures to raise public sector wages, a weakening of the exchange rate, and higher than expected increases in food and fuel prices constitute the main risks to the inflation outlook.

Table 1: Macroeconomic indicators

	2009	2010	2011	2012
Real GDP growth	3.2	4.5	5.1	6
CPI inflation	9.2	17.8	9.6	8.2
Budget balance % GDP	-3.2	-4.6	-5.9	-5.3
Current account % GDP	-8.7	-9	-9.6	-9.2

Source: National authorities' data; estimates and predictions based on authors' calculations.

Figures for 2010 are estimates; for 2011 and later are projections.

StatLink http://dx.doi.org/10.1787/888932406897

According to the 2011 budget, fiscal space will be created and expenditures reprioritised to raise capital and social spending. These will be financed by a combination of higher tax revenues, the proceeds of privatisation and external grants (such as EUR 52.5 million from the EU to finance roads and agriculture, etc.) as well as by savings from cutting non-essential current outlays. The authorities are expected to further improve tax administration and minimise discretionary tax exemptions in order to meet revenue targets. Due to higher capital spending, the budget deficit is projected to expand from 4.6% of GDP in 2010 to 5.9% of GDP in 2011; in 2012, it is expected to decline to 5.3% of GDP.

Following the successful implementation of the previous economic reform programme, the International Monetary Fund (IMF) in June 2010 approved a new three-year programme for Sierra Leone, supported under the Extended Credit Facility (ECF) arrangement, amounting to USD 45.4 million. This new programme has been designed to support the government's efforts to enhance economic growth by increasing investment in infrastructure and developing an accessible financial sector, while maintaining macroeconomic stability. Care needs to be taken to support the programme as it progresses with the right macroeconomic policies. Specifically, given the country's enormous development needs, future macroeconomic policy will need to steer clear of overly tight stances that would bring about short-term stability at the expense of longer term growth. Flexible macroeconomic policies need to be accompanied by reforms to improve the business environment, training programmes to create job opportunities, especially for young people entering the labour market, and the building of a social safety net for the most vulnerable.

Figure 1: Real GDP growth (W)

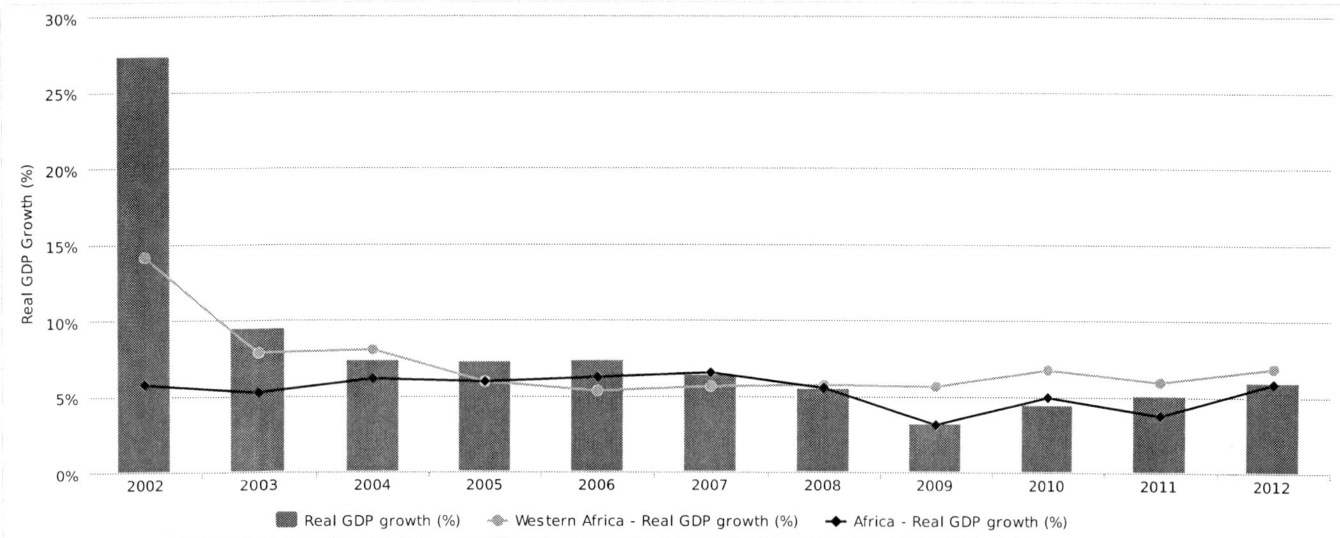

Source: IMF and local authorities' data; estimates and projections based on authors' calculations.

Figures for 2010 are estimates; for 2011 and later are projections.

StatLink http://dx.doi.org/10.1787/888932404541

South Africa

Real gross domestic product (GDP) growth recovered in 2010 to reach 2.8% but unemployment remains painfully high around 25%. Real GDP growth is projected to increase to 3.6% in 2011, and to 4.3% in 2012.

South Africa has achieved the Millennium Development Goal (MDG) of eradicating extreme poverty and hunger but, as highlighted by the New Growth Path framework, progress still needs to be made in health, education and especially job creation.

China is the topmost destination for South Africa's exports and leading source of imports, highlighting the need to engage purposefully with the newly joined BRIC (Brazil-Russia-India-China) group and to prioritise productive capacity.

Real GDP has recovered from -1.7% in 2009 to 2.8% in 2010; this rate of GDP growth remained clearly below potential, estimated around 4% per annum for South Africa. GDP is expected to grow at a rate of 3.6% in 2011 and 4.3% in 2012. GDP growth for 2010 was driven primarily by a steady recovery in consumer spending, partially attributed to the FIFA World Cup. Inflation fell to 3.5% by the end of 2010, averaged 4.3% in 2010, and is expected to reach 5.3% in 2011.

The consolidated government deficit rose to 6.9% of GDP in fiscal year 2009/10, and the central bank's policy rate declined by 6.5 percentage points since the end of 2008. Fiscal policy is now taking a less expansionary turn, with the consolidated government deficit slowing to an estimated 5.4% in fiscal year 2010/11 and projected to decline further to 5.0% in fiscal year 2011/12. Likely increases in the wage bill pose a downward risk to the fiscal balance outlook as do the possible introduction of a new public health insurance system and youth employment subsidy. The repo rate, the price at which the South African Reserve Bank lends cash to the banking system, is expected to remain close to 5.5% throughout 2011 and to start rising moderately only towards the end of the year.

China has become the top destination for South Africa's exports since mid-2009 and is also South Africa's leading source of imports. China is the dominant investment partner among emerging partners with its foreign direct investment (FDI) ranked fifth in terms of value in early 2010, at 33 billion South African rand (ZAR). Many emerging partners use South Africa as a gateway to other African countries. In December 2010, South Africa became an official member of the BRICS (Brazil-Russia-India-China-South Africa) group. The challenge for the government is to show that it has a purposeful plan to engage with BRIC countries, to prioritise its productive capacity, and to maximise its contribution to the national economy. Another challenge is to avoid neglecting traditional partners while nurturing its strategically important emerging partnerships. Indeed, the EU is still South Africa's topmost regional export destination. The year 2011 will also see the launch of the South African Development Agency (SADPA) to inform and direct the country's development assistance.

In the political arena, 2010 was characterised by a clearer elaboration of the Zuma administration's goals, and progress in achieving some of them. The administration has shown strong commitment to fighting crime. Significant progress has been made, for example, in crime prevention. Corruption, however, remains a major challenge, and both unemployment and inequality are on the rise. South Africa has achieved the 1st Millennium Development Goal (MDG) – reducing the proportion of the population living on less than 1 USD a day by half – but the government still needs to tackle issues such as providing adequate public health services, improving the quality of education, and reducing unemployment, especially for the youth. HIV/AIDS remains a critical issue: South Africa has the world's largest population of people living with HIV: 5.6 million. In April 2010, the Zuma administration launched a campaign to test 15 million people for HIV by end-2011; five million people have been tested since the launch began.

Structural challenges such as infrastructure bottlenecks hampered recovery in private investment in 2010. Unemployment remained very high in 2010 even though it declined marginally in the fourth quarter of 2010 to 24% from 25.3% in the previous quarter. The government outlined a number of measures to address these challenges in the New Growth Path framework (November 2010), including more investment in infrastructure, skills enhancement, public service and regional economic ties.

Table 1: Macroeconomic indicators

	2009	2010	2011	2012
Real GDP growth	-1.7	2.8	3.6	4.3
CPI inflation	7.1	4.3	5.3	5.6
Budget balance % GDP	-6.9	-5.4	-5	-4.5
Current account % GDP	-4.1	-2.8	-3.4	-4.3

Source: National authorities' data; estimates and predictions based on authors' calculations.

Figures for budget balance refer to fiscal years; thus 2009 corresponds to FY 2009/10, running from April 2009 to March 2010, for instance.

Figures for 2010 are estimates; for 2011 and later are projections.

StatLink http://dx.doi.org/10.1787/888932406916

Figure 1: Real GDP growth (S)

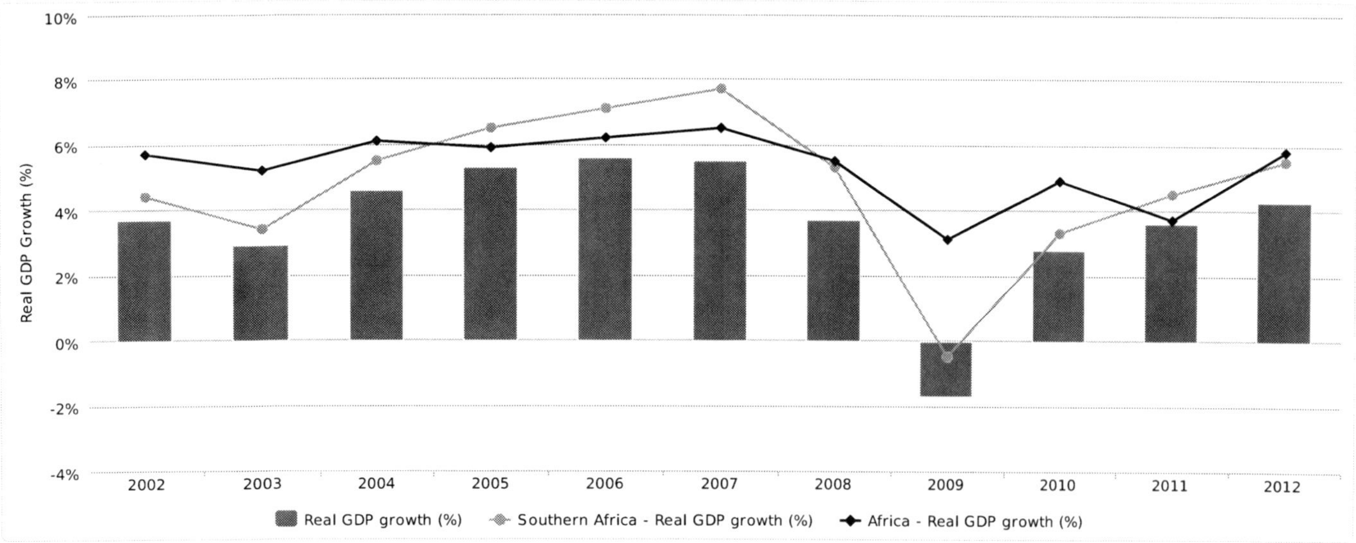

Source: IMF and local authorities' data; estimates and projections based on authors' calculations.

Figures for 2010 are estimates; for 2011 and later are projections.

StatLink http://dx.doi.org/10.1787/888932404560

Sudan

Sudan's economy grew 5% in 2010, up from 4.5% in 2009 on the back of rising oil prices. As the country embarks on a historic political transformation, the challenge will be to ensure macroeconomic sustainability by controlling the fiscal deficit, rebuilding foreign reserves and lowering low inflation.

Sudan faces major economic, social and political hurdles in addition to the major structural economic shifts following the referendum in January 2011 in which the people of South Sudan voted for independence. Separation is due to be completed on 9 July 2011 but there remain significant contentious issues over border demarcation, currency, the division of public assets – especially oil -- and external debt.

Sudan has attracted substantial 'resource-seeking' foreign direct investment (FDI) from emerging country partners, notably China, Malaysia and India. The challenge is to sustain the key oil industry, which is a major resource for both North and South Sudan, and to attract more diversified FDI, especially in joint ventures with the private sector.

Sudan's economy picked up slightly in 2010 to grow 5%, after 4.5% in 2009 but this was one percentage point lower than expected. The economy is projected to grow 5.1% in 2011 and then 5.3% in 2012 largely due to increased oil production and sustained gains in the non-oil sector. The non-oil sector remains buoyant and should underpin economic growth in the medium term through the continued revival of agriculture and increased investment in infrastructure, especially roads and electricity, and manufacturing.

A major feature of 2010 was continued expansionary public sector spending. This was driven firstly by implementation of various regional peace agreements and the financing of April 2010 presidential and parliamentary elections in the North and South. Additionally, the government continued costly subsidies for fuel and electricity. As a result, the budget deficit rose to 2.1% of gross domestic product (GDP) in 2010 from 1.9% in 2009. The Central Bank of Sudan increased money supply partly to provide credit to the government and partly to offset the negative effects of a decline in credit to the private sector in the aftermath of the global financial crisis. The Sudanese Pound (SDG) fell 16% against the US dollar (USD) due to political uncertainties associated with the January 2011 referendum as well as growing concerns over the low level of foreign reserves. Inflation rose to 13.8% from 11%.

The challenge ahead for the authorities is to ensure macroeconomic stability and sustainability of internal and external balances by controlling the fiscal deficit, rebuilding foreign reserves and maintaining low inflation.

As a result of increased public investment in infrastructure, the national road network and electricity generation have improved but many parts of the country, particularly conflict areas in the South and Darfur, suffer from a severe infrastructure deficit -- even by national standards. Poor infrastructure means higher production costs and constrains opportunities for broad-based non-oil growth. At the same time, the authorities face tremendous challenges in providing public services, particularly education and clean water, to these areas, due to financial constraints and insecurity in some cases. Sudan has had limited access to external financing from donors and multilateral financial institutions over the last two decades. It remains among the heavily indebted least developed countries, with no signs of qualifying for debt relief on the horizon. Sudan has increased its ties with emerging country partners and this offers the possibility of resource-backed loans for infrastructure and public services projects as well as private sector development.

Sudan continues to strengthen links with key emerging country partners, especially China, Malaysia and India following the attraction of substantial 'resource-seeking' FDI from these countries since the late 1990s. The oil sector has contributed significantly to economic development. A peaceful conclusion to the North-South separation process is critical for sustaining oil production and for protecting the stock of committed oil-related FDI. This is also an important catalyst for attracting further resource- and market-seeking FDI, and for paving the way to normalising relations with key global players, particularly the United States and the European Union.

The division of the country poses unprecedented challenges. The demarcation of the border presents major risks given the presence of several active conflict zones but the ruling National Congress Party (NCP) in the North and the Sudan People's Liberation Army (SPLA) in the South have agreed to form joint forces to protect oil fields and infrastructure through the secession process. Despite progress in some areas of social development, the challenge of reducing poverty and achieving other Millennium Development Goals (MDGs) remains formidable, with a real per capita income growth rate of about 3% in 2010 and skewed income distribution across regions and social groups.

Table 1: Macroeconomic indicators

	2009	2010	2011	2012
Real GDP growth	4.5	5	5.1	5.3
CPI inflation	11	13.8	14.3	10.7
Budget balance % GDP	-1.9	-2.1	-0.5	-1.5
Current account % GDP	-10.1	-8.3	-6.1	-7.2

Source: National authorities' data; estimates and predictions based on authors' calculations.

Figures for 2010 are estimates; for 2011 and later are projections.

StatLink http://dx.doi.org/10.1787/888932406935

Figure 1: Real GDP growth (E)

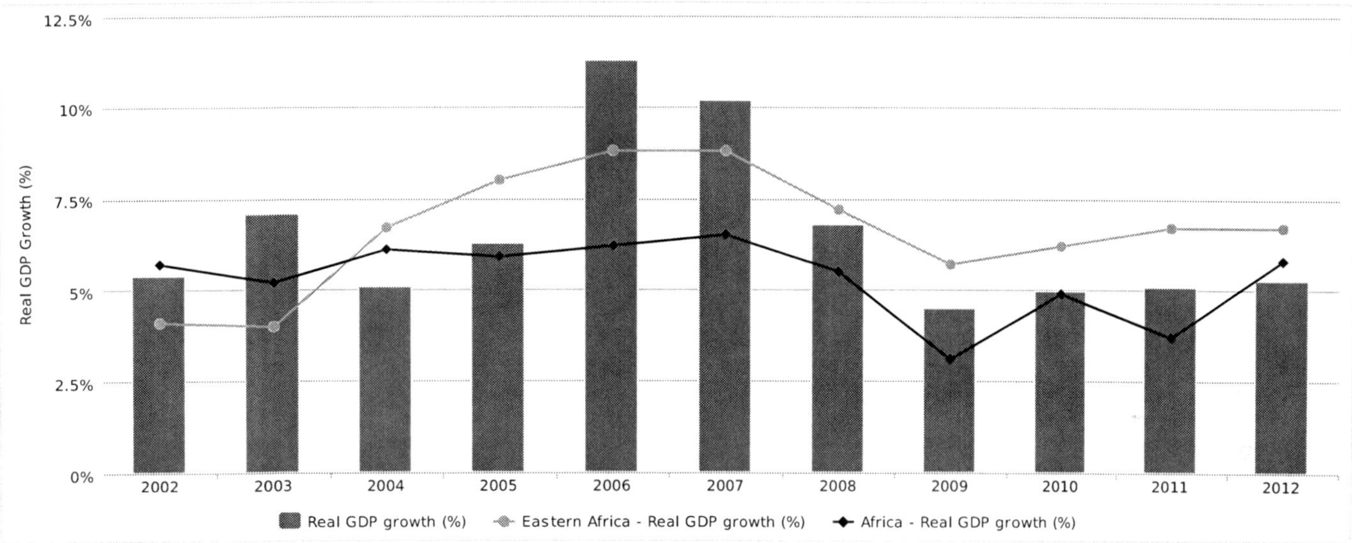

Source: IMF and local authorities' data; estimates and projections based on authors' calculations.

Figures for 2010 are estimates; for 2011 and later are projections.

StatLink http://dx.doi.org/10.1787/888932404579

Swaziland

The Swaziland economy moderately improved, recording an estimated gross domestic product (GDP) growth of 2.1% in 2010. While the constraints that limited the government's countercyclical measures in 2010 continue, the economy is projected to grow at 1.9% in 2011. Growth is premised on an improved global economic environment (providing some stimulus to tourism and manufacturing) and an increase in domestic absorption, in particular, public investment.

In 2010, the economy experienced critical structural challenges related to an unfavourable business environment. Improvement in areas of weakness identified by the 2011 *Doing Business* report coupled with proposed reform measures in the financial services regulatory bill and regulation of the utility sector should promote private investment. High prevalence of HIV, unemployment and poverty are critical social challenges that continue to undermine social and economic progress.

In the context of a small domestic market of 1.2 million people and GDP per capita estimated at USD 2 452, external markets for exports are critical for sustained economic growth in the short to medium term. The country's membership in various trade partnerships points to the right direction.

After averaging 2.9% during 2004-08, economic growth in Swaziland significantly dropped in 2009, mainly due to the impact of the global economic downturn on export-oriented sectors, in particular textiles and wood pulp. Other contributory factors were prolonged drought and low levels of foreign direct investment (FDI). In 2010, the economy moderately recovered with a rebound in global demand mainly for sugar and textiles. However, falling receipts from the Southern African Customs Union (SACU) coupled with lower internal revenues constrained the government's ability to implement counter-cyclical measures. In order to support economic activity in 2010, low interest rates were maintained in line with those of South Africa. However, the main focus of the Central Bank of Swaziland continued to be price stability. Inflation was 4.5% in 2010, down from 7.5% in 2009. This was mainly driven by lower prices for food and transport. Inflation is forecast at 7.7% in 2011, reflecting the lagged impact of increases in tariffs for water and electricity in 2010. The anticipated fuel and food crises are also expected to impact domestic price levels.

The economic outlook for 2011 appears bullish with unchanged international prices for sugar and wood pulp. However, supply for wood pulp is expected to be affected by the closure of the Sappi Company in 2010. The continued appreciation of the South African rand (ZAR) against the US dollar (USD) and other major currencies has reduced profitability in export-oriented sectors including mining, which might lead to a scaling down of operations and postponement of planned investments. In addition, the high cost of doing business and the high rate of HIV/AIDS prevalence will continue to subdue growth in 2011.

In order to deal with the fiscal challenges caused by the drop in Southern Africa Customs Union (SACU) revenues and burgeoning wage salary expenditures, the Government of Swaziland (GoS) has prepared a Fiscal Adjustment Roadmap (FAR) that runs from 2010/11 to 2014/15. This became the basis for negotiations with the International Monetary Fund (IMF) for an IMF Staff Monitored Program (SMP) since late October 2010. Once concluded, the SMP will unlock external donor support for the FAR and lay a solid foundation for sustainable economic growth. The SMP among other things advocates for quick implementation of the Value Added Tax (VAT) and reduction of the budget, particularly wages and salaries (16.4% of GDP in 2010/11) by 5% per annum beginning 2011/12 until 2013/2014. Revitalising the private sector through improving the business environment and using existing and emerging partnerships will be critical to a quick economic turnaround and for putting the economy onto a path of sustainable economic growth.

Table 1: Macroeconomic indicators

	2009	2010	2011	2012
Real GDP growth	1.2	2.1	1.9	2.2
CPI inflation	7.5	4.5	7.7	10
Budget balance % GDP	-0.2	-6.7	-10.8	-13.6
Current account % GDP	-12	-16.6	-14.2	-12.5

Source: National authorities' data; estimates and predictions based on authors' calculations.

Figures for budget balance refer to fiscal year April (n)/ March (n+1).

Figures for 2010 are estimates; for 2011 and later are projections.

StatLink http://dx.doi.org/10.1787/888932406954

Figure 1: Real GDP growth (S)

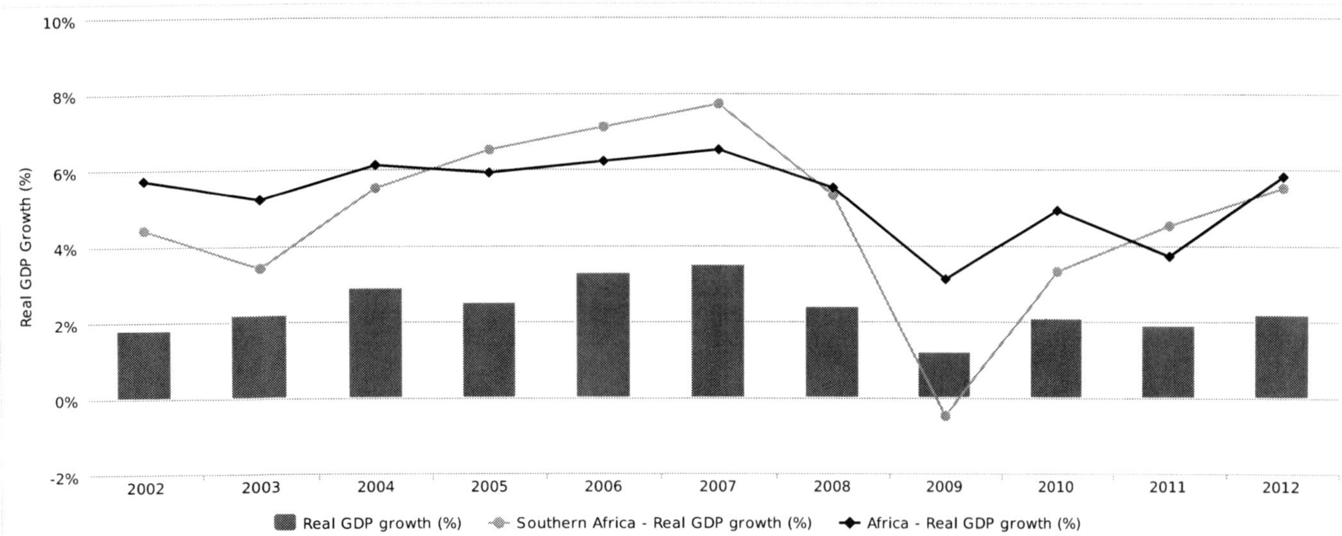

Source: IMF and local authorities' data; estimates and projections based on authors' calculations.

Figures for 2010 are estimates; for 2011 and later are projections.

StatLink http://dx.doi.org/10.1787/888932404598

Tanzania

Tanzania's real gross domestic product (GDP) grew at an estimated 6.8% in 2010, with economic prospects for the medium term looking bright with the exception of a growing fiscal deficit.

The country remains one of the poorest in the world, and will likely fail to meet all the Millennium Development Goals (MDGs).

Emerging economic partners include historic ideological allies, India and China, but also relative newcomers such as the United Arab Emirates, Turkey, Russia and others.

Tanzania registered eight consecutive years of gross domestic product (GDP) growth in excess of 6% until the global economic downturn began to affect growth in 2009. Consequently, the country achieved one of the most impressive rates of growth for a non-oil-producing sub-Saharan African country in the 2000s. Available data suggest that Tanzania's real GDP growth is firmly on the recovery path with growth at an estimated 6.8% in 2010. Economic prospects for the medium term continue to look bright: inflationary pressures are low, gold prices (a major Tanzanian export) are at historic highs and investor sentiment towards East Africa's second largest economy remains upbeat.

Key drivers of growth in the short and medium term include private consumption, exports and gross fixed capital, tourism revenues, foreign investment and aid. The government also intends to direct interventions to ensure that GDP growth is propelled mainly by key sectors, namely agriculture, manufacturing, tourism, mining and infrastructure. Given these factors, which should see the economy continuing its robust expansion in real terms, and in the absence of major adverse effects from the global economy, the forecast is a real GDP growth rate of 6.9% in 2011 and 7.3% in 2012.

The greatest risk to economic growth in the short and medium term is the growing fiscal deficit and the implied potential need to raise bridging funds. In turn, this could translate into an even greater reliance on foreign grants and investment or the government's need to raise such funds from non-concessional borrowing. Any significant disruption to either of these sources of funding would have negative ramifications for macroeconomic stability, and in turn, for economic development.

The government started using a revised methodology to calculate inflation in October 2010. That month, headline inflation declined to 4.2% from 4.5% in September, and followed on from a generally disinflationary trend in place for most of 2010. That trend is expected to bottom out in early 2011 before rising to a forecast 5.1% for the year. Higher energy and food prices, coupled with potential adverse weather conditions bode ill for inflation, especially given that food is the largest single contributor in the consumer price basket. Nonetheless, inflation is expected to be contained at around 6.9% and decline to just above 6% in 2012.

At a more fundamental level, Tanzania remains one of the world's poorest countries despite the huge strides made in recent years to promote economic development. The country still lags behind most of its neighbours in terms of economic development and is unlikely to meet all the Millennium Development Goals (MDGs). With rapid population growth forecast for the next 50 years, it will prove very challenging to stem poverty in the medium to longer term, particularly as government revenues are spread very thinly.

Having won the elections in 2010, the ruling Chama Cha Mapinduzi (CCM) party faces no serious threats in 2011. Confident of his political base, President Kikwete has vowed to continue the economic reforms that have allowed Tanzania to have one of Africa's fastest-growing economies in the 2000s. There are, however, potentially destabilising political factors including Zanzibari separatism and periodic unrest along Tanzania's borders. However, neither is a severe threat for the short term.

Table 1: Macroeconomic indicators

	2009	2010	2011	2012
Real GDP growth	6	6.8	6.9	7.3
CPI inflation	12.1	8.9	6.9	6.2
Budget balance % GDP	-4.8	-5.4	-7.8	-9.2
Current account % GDP	-8.2	-10.3	-10.5	-12

Source: IMF and local authorities' data; estimates and projections ased on author's calculations.

Figures for budget balance refer to fiscal year July (n-1)/ June (n).

Figures for 2010 are estimates; for 2011 and later are projections.

StatLink http://dx.doi.org/10.1787/888932406973

Figure 1: Real GDP growth (E)

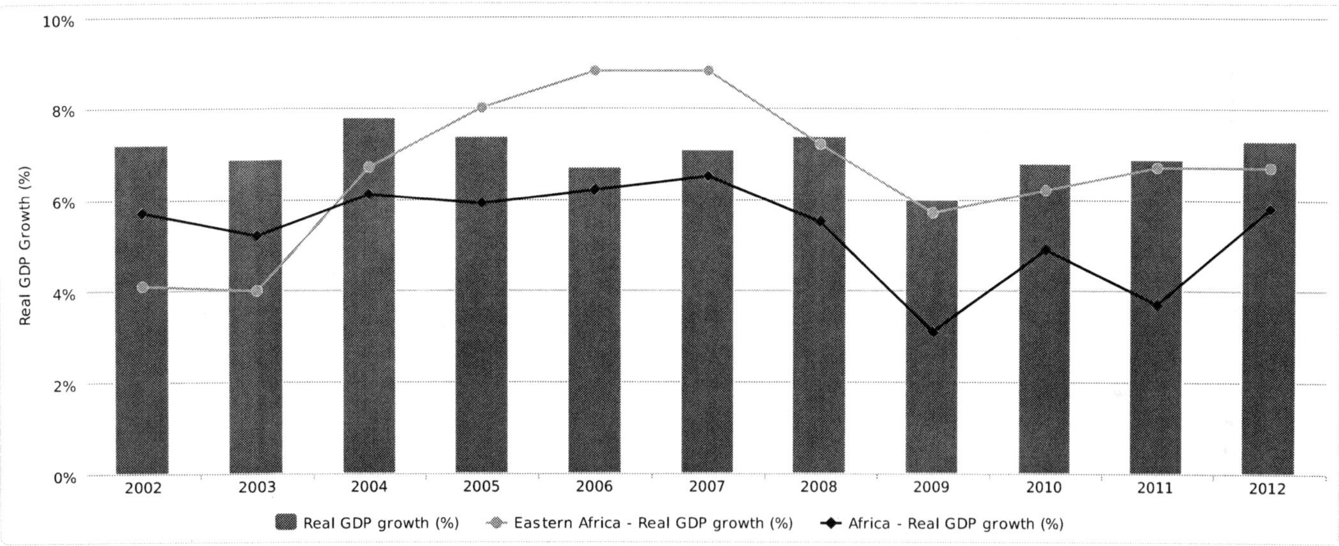

Source: IMF and local authorities' data; estimates and projections based on authors' calculations.

Figures for 2010 are estimates; for 2011 and later are projections.

StatLink http://dx.doi.org/10.1787/888932404617

Togo

Despite a difficult international environment, Togo remained on the road to recovery in 2010.

Authorities intend to pursue reforms to consolidate recent progress, accelerate growth to help the population and restore the solidity of public finances.

Togo is counting on support from foreign partners to achieve its development objectives and China is among the leaders in financing development.

Despite a difficult international environment, Togo maintained growth at 3.4%, which though not very strong, allowed the country to achieve the Heavily Indebted Poor Countries (HIPC) Initiative completion point. Growth is projected to continue at a slightly higher rate in 2011 and 2012, at 3.7% and 4%, respectively. The inflation rate has been estimated at 5.3% for 2010 versus 2.9% in 2009, and is projected at 2.4% for 2011.

The primary sector, on which the Togolese economy relies, was negatively affected by bad rainfall in 2010. Nonetheless, thanks to support from the public authorities, its share of contribution to growth amounted to 1.3%. The good performance of the mining industries, with in particular a 14.3% increase in the production of clinker mining, also supported growth in 2010. On the other hand, renovation of the production facilities of the national phosphate company SNPT had no major effects in 2010.

Driven by the Port of Lomé, the tertiary sector reinforced its position as second most important contributor to growth. The authorities decided in 2010 to institute a one-stop window at the port in order to promote its competitiveness. The country's absorption capacity improved, as well as the rate of budget execution for public investments, which rose to 6.7% in 2010 versus 5.6% in 2009.

In 2010, the authorities continued to implement the economic and financial programme with support from the Extended Credit Facility (ECF). Thanks to the satisfactory performance of public finances and to compliance with economic and financial programme criteria, Togo was able to achieve the HIPC Initiative completion point in December 2010. Indebtedness will therefore decline and comply with the community standard of outstanding public debt lower than 70% of GDP. Togo's external debt could be brought down to 12.3% of GDP in current value. Combined with an internal debt at 17.9% of GDP, this would bring total public debt in current value within the limits of 30% of GDP.

Togo, which is a low-revenue country, counts on support from its technical and financial partners to achieve its development goals. Emerging partners such as China and India play an important role in the country's development-financing strategy.

Table 1: Macroeconomic indicators

	2009	2010	2011	2012
Real GDP growth	3.2	3.4	3.7	4
CPI inflation	2.9	5.3	2.4	2.3
Budget balance % GDP	-5.5	-5.8	-5.6	-5.2
Current account % GDP	-6.6	-6.8	-5.5	-5

Source: National authorities' data; estimates and predictions based on authors' calculations.

Figures for 2010 are estimates; for 2011 and later are projections.

StatLink http://dx.doi.org/10.1787/888932406992

Figure 1: Real GDP growth (W)

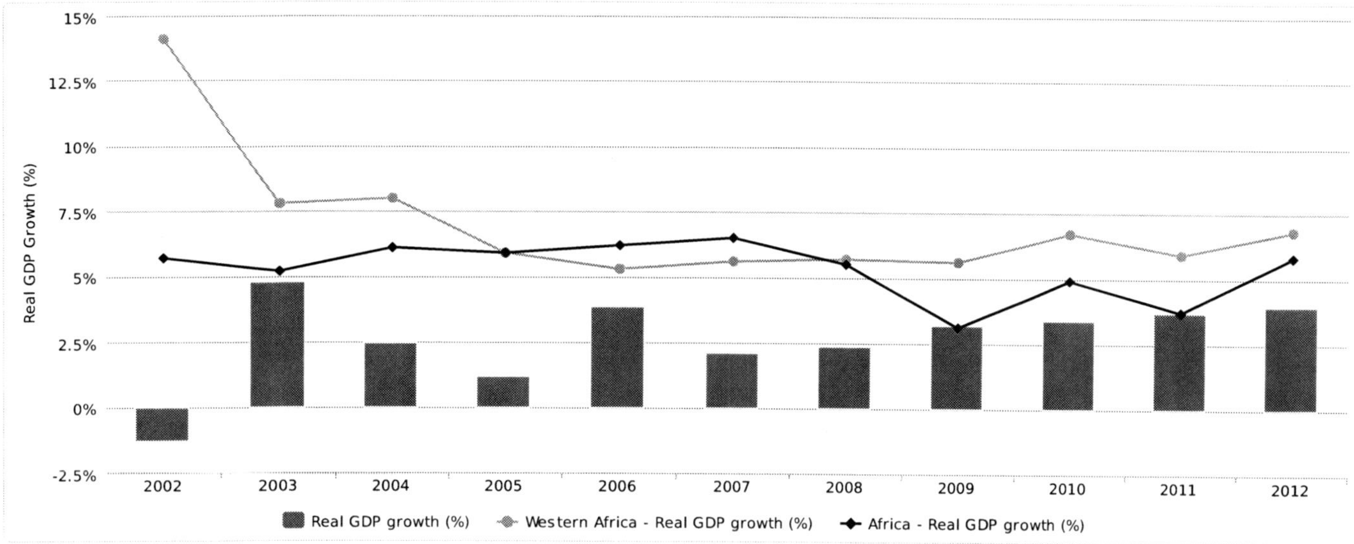

Source: IMF and local authorities' data; estimates and projections based on authors' calculations.

Figures for 2010 are estimates; for 2011 and later are projections.

StatLink http://dx.doi.org/10.1787/888932404636

Tunisia

Economic growth is expected to slow to 1.1% in 2011 (from 3.7% in 2010) because of the country's political revolution.

The root causes of the uprising -- regional economic disparities and high unemployment among school-leavers and college graduates -- will have to be quickly tackled by the new government.

Partners for Tunisia's emerging economy are still few but are investing more and more in the phosphate industry.

When a young man died after setting fire to himself in the town of Sidi Bouzid, 265 kilometers from Tunis, in mid-December, students, young people and others took to the streets to protest against unemployment and the high cost of living. Unrest and clashes with police and troops spread to other parts of Tunisia, including Jendouba, Kasserine, Le Kef and Gafsa, and then to big cities and the capital. President Zine El Abidine Ben Ali and his aides fled into exile in Saudi Arabia on 14 January 2011, ending his 23-year rule. The shock-wave of the revolution was felt in neighbouring countries. It also shook Tunisia's economic, social and political stability and sharply changed prospects for the future.

Budget and current deficits are expected to increase, due to the revolution's effect on tourism and foreign investment. Hopes for recovery are good thanks to sound macroeconomic policy in recent years. Corrective measures were taken early in the 2008/09 world economic crisis but growth should slow sharply to 1.1% in 2011, down from 3.7% in 2010 and 3% in 2009.

The interim government must organise the election of a constituent assembly in July 2011, but also end corruption and bad governance, restore the economy and meet numerous social demands. A return to normality and economic prospects for 2012 depend on how these challenges are met. The government will have to keep subsidies for staple products and energy to avoid unrest. It will also have to create jobs, both in the civil service and through public investment. Higher spending will increase the budget deficit to 5.2% of gross domestic product (GDP) in 2011 and 4.8% in 2012, up from a moderate 2.7% in 2009 and 2.6% in 2010. Inflation (4.4% in 2010) has already exceeded the 3% target for 2011 and should reach 4.7%. The external account will be affected by a drop in tourist revenue and bigger trade deficit. The current deficit is expect to rise substantially to 7.6% of GDP in 2011, from 4.7% in 2010 and 2.8% in 2009.

Tunisia has privileged ties with the European Union (EU) and is close to Arab League and North African countries through several free-trade agreements. Partners among the new economic powers are still few despite the attractive phosphate industry. Oil exploration and increasing mineral output should keep total exports at about a third of GDP. Nearly all the 18 targets under the Millennium Development Goals (MDGs) have been achieved, but more must be done to reach the goal of developing "strategies for decent and productive work for youth." Unemployment of qualified school-leavers and college graduates, as well as sharp economic disparities between the tourist-dominated coastal areas and the interior of the country, set off the uprising. Authorities have long recognised these problems but reforms have not sufficiently boosted competitiveness and employment. The country has made little progress with reforms, moving with a caution often criticised by international financial institutions. This hesitance increased during the world financial crisis. The revolution is therefore a new chance to speed up reform and improve governance, competitiveness and respect for human rights.

Table 1: Macroeconomic indicators

	2009	2010	2011	2012
Real GDP growth	3	3.7	1.1	3.3
CPI inflation	3.5	4.4	4.7	4.6
Budget balance % GDP	-2.7	-2.6	-5.2	-4.8
Current account % GDP	-2.8	-4.7	-7.6	-5.6

Source: National authorities' data; estimates and predictions based on authors' calculations.

Figures for 2010 are estimates; for 2011 and later are projections.

StatLink http://dx.doi.org/10.1787/888932407011

Figure 1: Real GDP growth (N)

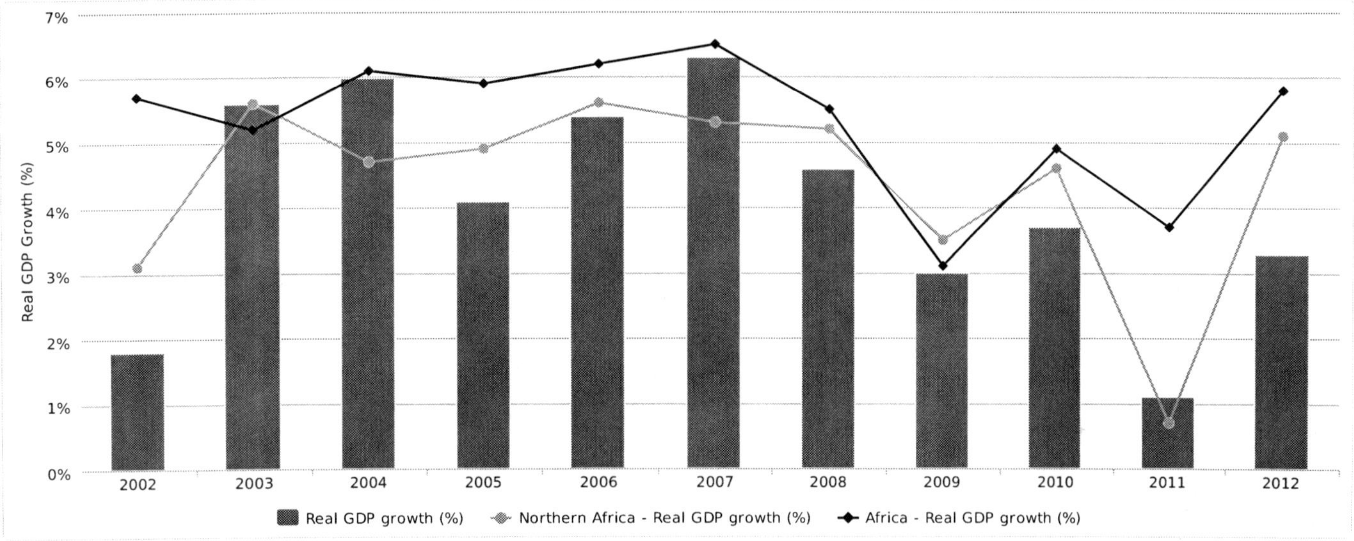

Source: IMF and local authorities' data; estimates and projections based on authors' calculations.

Figures for 2010 are estimates; for 2011 and later are projections.

StatLink http://dx.doi.org/10.1787/888932404655

Uganda

Uganda's economy weathered adverse external and internal shocks to record 5.1% growth in 2010 because of sluggish aggregate demand and external demand for traditional exports. Growth is projected to edge up slightly to 5.6% in 2011 thanks to a rebound in regional demand and the improved global economic outlook.

The overall World Bank *Doing Business* ranking dropped by six places to 112th in 2010 compared with 2009, with limited access to credit, inadequate transport and energy infrastructure, and weak private sector regulatory framework remaining key impediments. Uganda has achieved the Millennium Development Goals (MDGs) target of halving the population living under the poverty line but progress on the health indicators is insufficient to meet the MDG targets.

Major emerging partners in 2009 were the United Arab Emirates (UAE); China; Hong Kong, China; Singapore and India, with the UAE; China and Hong Kong, China accounting for 29% of total foreign direct investment (FDI) in 2009. Emerging partners in Asia and the Middle East accounted for 13% of Uganda's export earnings and 57% of imports.

The Ugandan economy recorded weaker growth of 5.1% in 2010 because of receding aggregate demand, mainly in private consumption, and weak external demand for traditional exports, in particular coffee. In spite of the declines, regional demand for Uganda's exports remained high. Export earnings fell from 2.9 billion US dollars (USD) in the financial year 2008/09 to USD 2.8 billion in 2009/10. Although lower than 2008/09 levels (USD 883 million), remittance receipts in 2009/10 (USD 820 million) surpassed traditional foreign exchange earners coffee and tourism. Earnings from coffee and tourism in 2009/10 were USD 262 million and USD 400 million respectively. Sustained public investment in infrastructure and the global recovery are expected to spur growth in the short to medium term. The near-term prospects for the oil and gas sector remain uncertain because of disputes between the government and oil exploration firms. The real gross domestic product (GDP) growth rate is projected to increase to 5.6% in 2011 and 6.9% in 2012 because of increasing regional demand and the improved global outlook.

Growth in 2010 was primarily driven by the telecommunications, financial services and construction sectors, while the services and agriculture, forestry, fishing and hunting sectors, which account for 54.4% and 24.8% of GDP respectively, showed weaker growth. Growth in telecommunications was bolstered by expansion in mobile telephony while financial sector growth was boosted by the licensing of an additional commercial bank and expansion in the size and outreach of the existing financial institutions. The rebound in fishing and food production was offset by falling growth for the cash crops of coffee and cotton, leading to stagnation in the agriculture sector. In the recent past the declining GDP share of the agriculture sector has been the result of low productivity, limited value addition and lack of commercialisation. On the demand side, growth was driven by private consumption and investment growth, albeit at rates lower than in 2009. Private consumption and private investment projections are for weaker growth in 2011 but recovery in 2012.

Inflation declined markedly from 13.4% in 2009 to 7.3% in 2010 as a consequence of falling food prices resulting from favourable weather conditions and subsequent improved food production. Projections are for further reductions in 2011 and 2012. The monetary policy stance over the medium term remains focused on seeking to restrict inflation at the target of 5%. The fiscal policy stance will remain expansionary in view of the government's sustained public investment in infrastructure, including roads and energy. Tax receipts are expected to recover in tandem with the improving economic prospects and tax administration efficiency gains, although these gains will not be sufficient to cover the shortfall in grants. Thus the overall fiscal deficit (including grants) as a percentage of GDP is expected to increase in 2011.

The external position weakened as a result of a decline in export earnings from the traditional export crops, in particular coffee. International reserves, currently covering slightly under five months of imports, are expected to remain healthy, in part because of the weekly purchase of foreign exchange by the central bank.

The social sector also saw marked improvements with a reduction in the poverty rate from 31% in 2005/06 to 23% in 2009/10 although income inequality worsened. Progress was also recorded in education thanks to the universal primary and secondary education programmes. However, stagnation and reversals were reported for the health-related indicators.

Weak infrastructure, inadequate financial services to the private sector, and weaknesses in public sector management and administration are the major constraints to growth. The recently launched National Development Plan (NDP) is expected to prioritise reforms aimed at addressing these constraints.

Uganda's major Emerging Partners (EPs) in 2009 were China, Hong Kong, India, Singapore and United Arab Emirates (UAE). The UAE, China and Hong Kong accounted for 29% of total foreign direct investment (FDI) in 2009, with 54% of these investments in equity capital. In addition, the bulk of this FDI is concentrated in three sectors: finance, insurance and business services; manufacturing; and wholesale, retail, catering, accommodation and tourism. Emerging partners in Asia and the Middle East[1] accounted for 13% of Uganda's export earnings and 57% of imports.

Table 1: Macroeconomic indicators

	2009	2010	2011	2012
Real GDP growth	5.3	5.1	5.6	6.9
CPI inflation	13.4	7.3	4.1	5.1
Budget balance % GDP	0.1	-1.8	-2.5	-3.9
Current account % GDP	-3.7	-9	-10.3	-10.8

Source: National authorities' data; estimates and predictions based on authors' calculations.

Figures for 2010 are estimates; for 2011 and later are projections.

StatLink http://dx.doi.org/10.1787/888932407030

Figure 1: Real GDP growth (E)

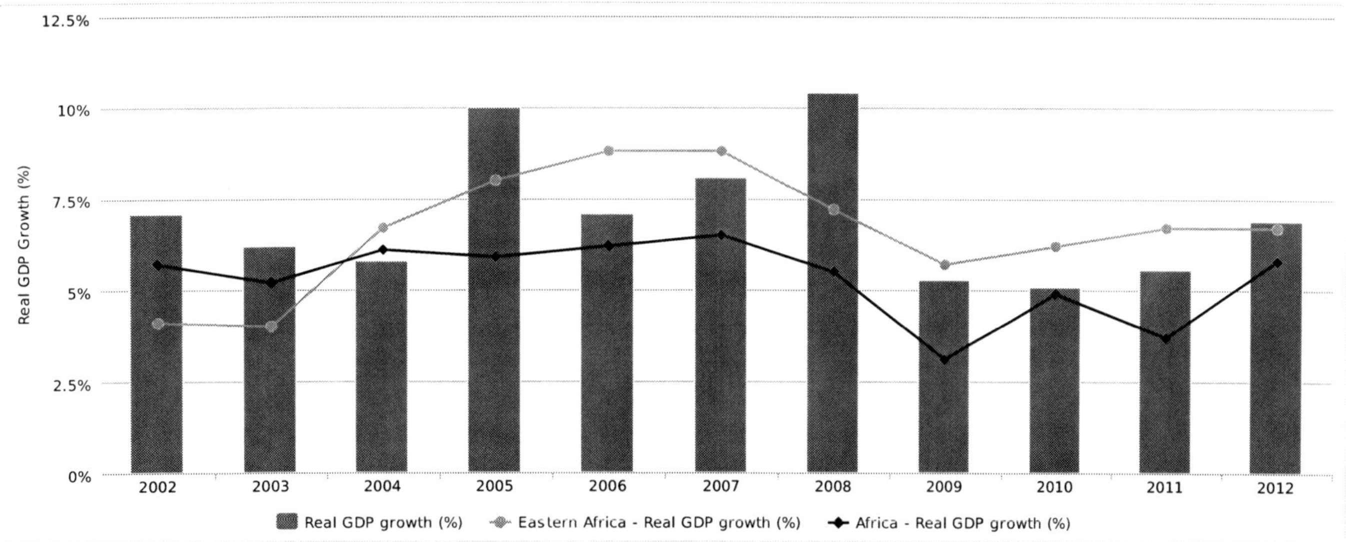

Source: IMF and local authorities' data; estimates and projections based on authors' calculations.

Figures for 2010 are estimates; for 2011 and later are projections.

StatLink http://dx.doi.org/10.1787/888932404674

Zambia

The Zambian economy is recovering from the global financial and economic crisis, with 2010 gross domestic product (GDP) projected at 6.6%, mainly driven by mining, agriculture, tourism, construction and manufacturing.

The government is seeking to lower expenditure, stimulate growth and diversify the economy in a bid to get the economy through the recession and get growth back to pre-crisis levels.

Zambia has intensified co-operation with China, India and Brazil. This has reduced co-operation with traditional partners, which have in turn cut financial support due to the financial crisis.

The projected 6.6% growth in Zambia's GDP in 2010 is up from 6.4% in 2009. Agriculture, tourism, construction, manufacturing and mining are driving growth which is expected to expand by 6.5% and 6.7% in 2011 and 2012 respectively.

Overall, primary industries performed well in 2010 with agriculture growing by 7.6%. In 2011 and 2012 agriculture growth is projected at 3.2% and 4.6%, respectively. The largest contribution to 2010 growth came from maize production. The harvest reached 2.8 million tonnes compared to 1.9 million tonnes in the previous season. Zambia is Africa's biggest copper producer and the mining sector's big recovery was due to improved global copper prices. The sector is estimated to have grown by 7.4% in 2010.

Manufacturing, which historically has contributed about 10% of GDP, grew by 2.5% in 2010. The government has made substantial progress in infrastructure construction and has invested in manufacturing through the establishment of Multi Facility Economic Zones. Tourism, which was hard hit by the financial crisis, is expected to rebound strongly with estimated growth of 25% in 2010. Construction was expected to expand by 10% in 2010 and maintain double-digit growth in the next few years.

Monetary policy focused on sustaining stability by maintaining single digit inflation while ensuring adequate liquidity for the growing economy. Annual inflation declined to an estimated 7.9% at the end of 2010, down from 9.9% in December 2009. Annual food inflation declined sharply from 8.0% in December 2009 to 2.8% in September 2010.

The Zambian government is pursuing aggressive business reforms to encourage increased private investment and reduce business costs. The Private Sector Development Reform Programme is intended to ease private sector development. The barriers include: (i) limited and high cost credit; (ii) excessive bureaucratic trade procedures due to the involvement of multiple government agencies and border clearance systems; (iii) lengthy inspection and certification processes; (iv) poor border information technology; (v) outdated customs techniques; (vi) inadequate skilled personnel; (vi) inadequate infrastructure.

Progress in improving public financial management has led to the publishing of work plans by government agencies, and the introduction of a Treasury Single Account to improve budget execution and cash management.

In the past few years, donor assistance has shifted from developed countries to emerging economies, especially from Asia. Zambia has built new partnerships with China and India. There is, however, growing concern that the motives of these new powers may not be very different from the traditional partners -- all are interested mainly in Zambia's vast mineral and energy resources.

Zambia remains one of the most politically stable countries in the Southern African Development Community (SADC) and Africa as a whole. There has been democracy since 1991 when a two-decade old single party system was ended. The Movement for Multiparty Democracy (MMD) which has been in power since 1991 is likely to face a formidable challenge from a possible merger between the Patriotic Front (PF) and the United Party for National Development (UPND) going into presidential and general elections in 2011. The vote is expected to be peaceful and whatever the outcome, the country is likely to remain stable.

Table 1: Macroeconomic indicators

	2009	2010	2011	2012
Real GDP growth	6.4	6.6	6.5	6.7
CPI inflation	9.9	7.9	7.1	6.2
Budget balance % GDP	-2.1	-3.1	-4.5	-5.9
Current account % GDP	-3.2	-1.5	-1.8	-2.7

Source: National authorities' data; estimates and predictions based on authors' calculations.

Figures for 2010 are estimates; for 2011 and later are projections.

StatLink http://dx.doi.org/10.1787/888932407049

Figure 1: Real GDP growth (S)

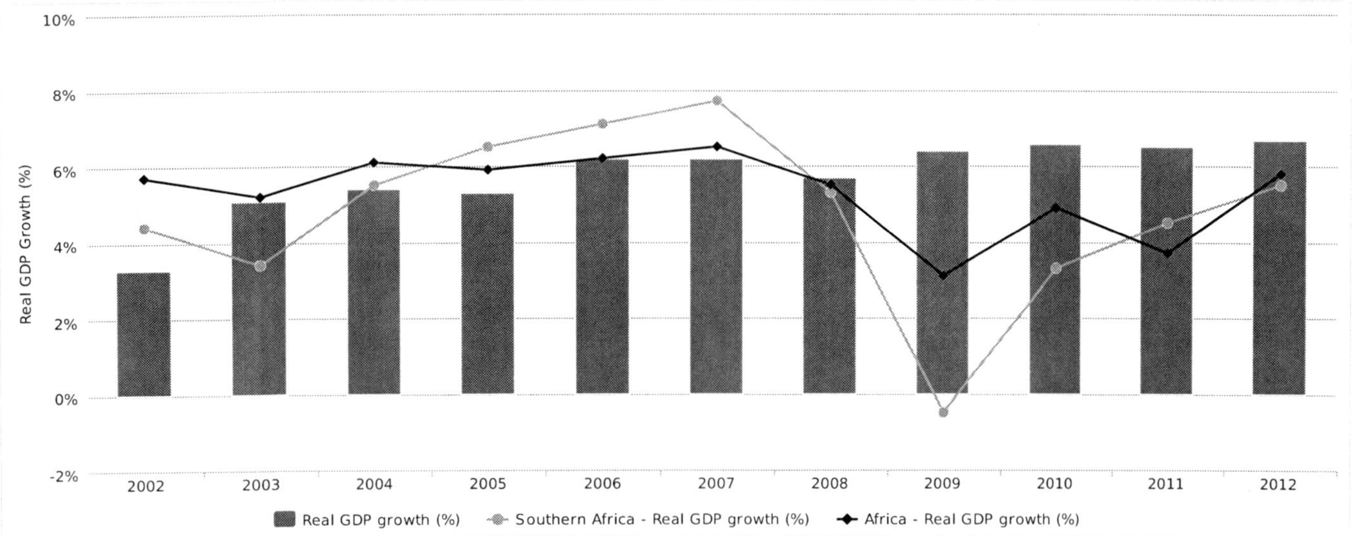

Source: IMF and local authorities' data; estimates and projections based on authors' calculations.

Figures for 2010 are estimates; for 2011 and later are projections.

StatLink http://dx.doi.org/10.1787/888932404693

Zimbabwe

After a decade of economic decline, the introduction of a multi-currency regime and other policies halted hyper-inflation and put the economy on the route to recovery, though the government must act to sustain recent expansion.

The national unity government has to organise elections and businessmen are wary about conserving the economic momentum – driven by higher mining and agriculture – that produced estimated growth of 8.2% in 2010.

South Africa is Zimbabwe's main emerging power trade partner followed by China and India. The parterships have provided foreign direct investment (FDI) in mining and deepened co-operation beyond trade and aid.

The Zimbabwe economy is rebounding after a decade of economic decline during which time real gross domestic product (GDP) fell by more than a third and per capita income fell by 40%, combined with prolonged or chronic inflation and hyperinflation.

The establishment of a Government of National Unity (GNU) in February 2009 and the adoption of macroeconomic stabilisation policies including the multi-currency regime resulted in early signs of economic recovery. GDP growth was estimated at 8.2% in 2010 and 7.8% in 2011, driven by rapid expansion of mining output and exports, and agriculture.

Mining output has risen spectacularly -- 8.5% in 2009 and a record level of 47% in 2010 largely due to increased mining investment. Agricultural output rose 15% in 2009 and 34% in 2010, largely from a doubling of tobacco production. Manufacturing growth, however, slowed down to less than 3% in 2010 compared to 10% in 2009.

Following the adoption of the multi-currency regime, consumer prices fell by 7.7% during 2009, before rising by 2.5% in the first ten months of 2010. Inflation is estimated to have averaged 4.9% in 2010 – year-on-year inflation was 4.2% in November 2010 – and is officially forecast to increase marginally to 5.9% in 2011. However, food inflation remains a problem with food prices up 7.3% in the year to December 2010.

Exports are estimated to have increased by 35% in 2010 to 2.1 billion US dollars (USD) while imports increased by 13.5% to USD 3.6 billion leaving a trade deficit of USD 1.5 billion. The overall balance of payments improved from a deficit of USD 1.77 billion in 2009 to USD 460 million in 2010.

During the years of economic decline the budget deficit was financed by credit creation by the Reserve Bank of Zimbabwe, setting off the hyperinflation of 2007/08, which exacerbated the situation. The multi-currency regime contained inflation, revived financial intermediation and imposed fiscal discipline through implementation of cash budgeting.[1]

The improved political climate and the fiscal and monetary reforms by the GNU brightened economic prospects. The Reserve Bank of Zimbabwe asserts that the banking sector has stabilised and is now "sound," with low inflation, foreign direct investment (FDI) and portfolio investment inflows have shown signs of recovery. Emerging partners are exploring new trading opportunities and untapped potential in mining, tobacco and other agricultural sub-sectors. South Africa remains a dominant trading and investment partner while China is becoming more important.

Social conditions remain tough. The poverty rate has increased from 42% in 1995 to 63% in 2003 and is currently estimated to be over 70%. Zimbabwe has a Gini inequality coefficient estimated at 50.1% in 2003, one of the highest in the world. There is also high unemployment which is estimated at 80%.

Despite the deteriorating poverty indicators, significant progress has been made towards meeting the Millennium Development Goals (MDGs) in recent years, with net primary school employment ratio of 91% in 2009. The adult HIV prevalence rate has fallen from 23.7% in 2001 to 13.7% in 2009. Food security improved with production of the maize staple increasing from 600 000 tonnes in 2008 to 1.1 million tonnes in 2009 and an estimated 1.3 million in 2010. Donors have provided significant off-budget humanitarian and social services funding estimated at 12% of GDP in 2009.

The government's main challenge will be to sustain economic growth and deepen structural transformation and diversification of the economy to ensure realisation of its policy on "shared economy, shared development and shared transformation".

Table 1: Macroeconomic indicators

	2009	2010	2011	2012
Real GDP growth	5.7	8.2	7.8	5.4
CPI inflation	6.5	4.9	5.9	4.7
Budget balance % GDP	-0.1	-1.7	-2.2	-3.4
Current account % GDP	-16.5	-19.9	-17.7	-16.8

Source: National authorities' data; estimates and predictions based on authors' calculations.

Figures for 2010 are estimates; for 2011 and later are projections.

StatLink http://dx.doi.org/10.1787/888932407068

Figure 1: Real GDP growth (S)

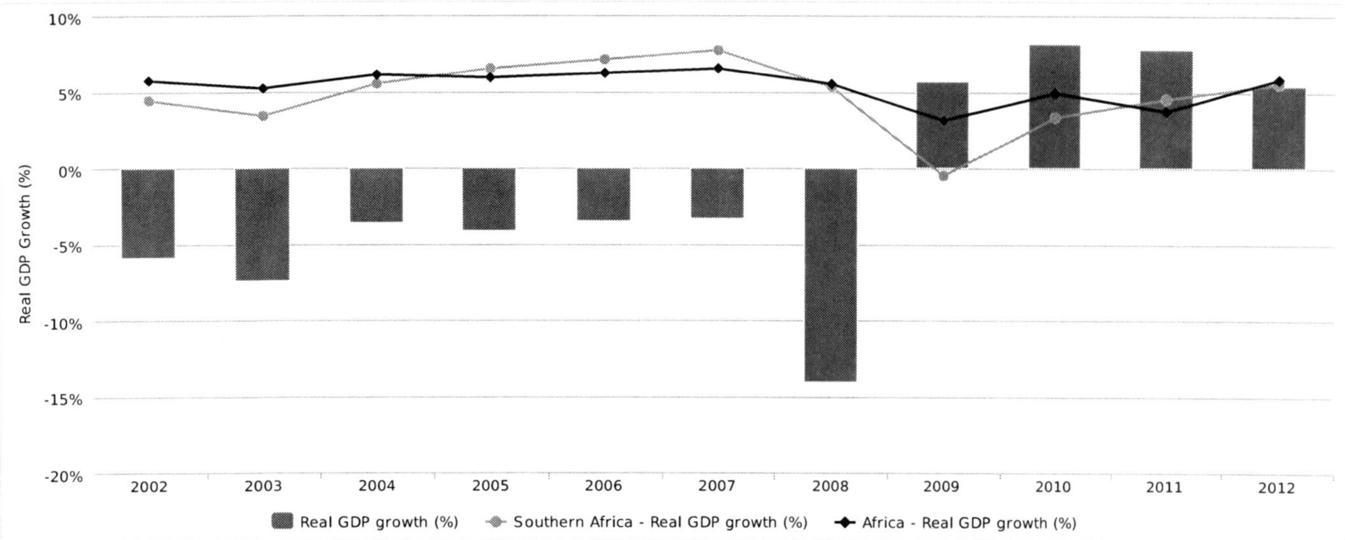

Source: IMF and local authorities' data; estimates and projections based on authors' calculations.

Figures for 2010 are estimates; for 2011 and later are projections.

StatLink http://dx.doi.org/10.1787/888932404712

Part Four

Statistical Annex

List of Tables

Methodology

The aggregate figure for Africa, when reported, does not include countries whose data are unavailable.

When used, the oil exporting countries group refers to Algeria, Angola, Cameroon, Chad, Congo Dem. Rep., Congo Rep., Côte d'Ivoire, Egypt, Equatorial Guinea, Gabon, Libya, Nigeria and Sudan.

Tables 1 to 6.

Where indicated, the figures are reported on a fiscal-year basis. Figures for Egypt, Ethiopia, Kenya, Liberia, Malawi, Mauritius, Tanzania, and Uganda are from July to June in the reference year. For South Africa, Namibia, Swaziland, Lesotho and Botswana, fiscal year 2010 is from April 2009 to March 2010.

Table 7. Exports, 2009

The table is based on exports disaggregated at 6 digit level (following the Harmonised System, rev.2)

Table 8. Diversification and Competitiveness

The diversification indicator measures the extent to which exports are diversified. It is constructed as the inverse of a Herfindahl index, using disaggregated exports at 4 digits (following the Harmonised System, rev.2). A higher index indicates more export diversification. The competitiveness indicator has two aspects: the sectoral effect and the global competitivity effect. In order to compute both competitiveness indicators, we decompose the growth of exports into three components: the growth rate of total international trade over the reference period (2005-2009) (not reported); the contribution to a country's export growth of the dynamics of the sectoral markets where the country sells its products, assuming that its sectoral market shares are constant (a weighted average of the differences between the sectoral export growth rates - measured at the world level - and total international trade growth, the weights being the shares of the corresponding products in the country's total exports); the competitiveness effect, or the balance (export growth minus world growth and sector effect), measuring the contribution of changes in sectoral market shares to a country's export growth.

Table 10. Foreign Direct Investment, 2004-09

The UNCTAD Inward Potential Index is based on 12 economic and structural variables measured by their respective scores on a range of 0-1 (raw data are available on: www.unctad.org/wir). It is the unweighted average of scores of: GDP per capita, the rate of growth of GDP, the share of exports in GDP, telecom infrastructure (the average number of telephone lines per 1 000 inhabitants, and number of mobile phones per 1 000 inhabitants), commercial energy use per capita, share of R&D expenditures in gross national income, share of tertiary students in the population, country risk, exports of natural resources as a percentage of the world total, imports of parts and components of electronics and automobiles as a percentage of the world total, and inward FDI stock as a percentage of the world total (Source: UNCTAD, World Investment Report 2009).

Table 11. Aid Flows, 2004-09

The DAC countries are: Australia, Austria, Belgium, Canada, Denmark, Finland, France, Germany, Greece, Ireland, Italy, Japan, Korea, Luxembourg, Netherlands, New Zealand, Norway, Portugal, Spain, Sweden, Switzerland, United Kingdom, United States and the Commission of the European Communities.

Table 13. Demographic Indicators

Infant mortality rate: under one-year-old child deaths per live birth per year.

Total fertility rate: average number of children per woman.

Mortality under age 5: probability that a newborn infant would die before the age of 5.

Table 14. Poverty and Income Distribution Indicators

National poverty line: absolute poverty line corresponding to the value of consumption necessary to satisfy minimum subsistence needs. International poverty line: absolute poverty line corresponding to a level of income or consumption of 1 USD or 2 USD a day.

Gini index: index measuring the intensity of inequality in income or consumption expenditure distribution. Perfect equality leads to a Gini index of zero and maximum inequality to a Gini index of 100. Share of consumption: share of total consumption for a decile of the population ranked by level of consumption.

Table 15. Access to Services

The Sanitation coverage is the percentage of the population with access to improved sanitation technologies (connection to a public sewer, connection to septic system, pour-flush latrine, simple pit latrine or ventilated improved pit latrine). The water supply coverage is the percentage of the population with access to improved water supply (household connection, public standpipe, borehole, protected dug well and protected spring or rainwater collection).

Table 16. Basic Health Indicators

Life expectancy at birth is the average number of years a newborn infant would live under the hypothesis that, during its life, the conditions of mortality remain the same as observed at its birth.

Life expectancy at birth with AIDS is the estimated average number of years a newborn infant would live under the hypothesis that, during its life, the conditions of mortality remain the same as observed at its birth in particular the characteristics of AIDS epidemic.

Life expectancy at birth without AIDS is the estimated number of years a newborn infant would live under the hypothesis of absence of AIDS during its life. Under nourishment prevalence is the proportion of the population that is suffering insufficient food intake to meet dietary energy requirements continuously.

Food availability is the available nutritious food for human consumption expressed in kilo-calories per person per day (note that the recommended daily caloric intake for an active healthy life is 2 100 calories).

Public share of total health expenditure is calculated by defining public health expenditure as current and capital outlays of government, compulsory social security schemes, extra-budgetary funds dedicated to health services delivery or financing and grants and loans provided by international agencies, other national authorities and commercial banks.

Private share of total health expenditure is calculated by defining private expenditure as private insurance schemes and prepaid medical care plans, services delivered or financed by enterprises, outlays by non-governmental organisations and non-profit institutions serving mainly households, out-of-pocket payments, and other privately funded schemes not elsewhere classified, including investment outlays.

Table 17. Major Diseases

Healthy life expectancy at birth is the average equivalent number of years in full health a newborn infant would live under the hypothesis that, during its life, the conditions of mortality and ill-health remain the same as observed at its birth.

People living with HIV/AIDS is estimated whether or not they have developed symptoms of AIDS. HIV/AIDS adult prevalence is the estimate of the adult population (15-49) living with HIV/AIDS. Malaria notified cases are cases of malaria reported from the different local case detection and reporting systems. These figures should be considered with caution because of the diversity of sources and probable underestimation. The Measles incidence is the number of new cases of measles reported during the reference year.

MCV: Measles Containing Vaccine.

DTP3: Third dose of Diphtheria and Tetanus toxoids and Pertussis vaccine.

Table 19. School Enrolment

Gross enrolment ratio: population enrolled in a specific level of education, regardless of age, expressed as a percentage of the official school-age pupils enrolled in that level. Net enrolment ratio: official school-age population enrolled in a specific level of education expressed as a percentage of the total population enrolled in that level.

Table 20. Employment and Remittances

Participation rate: measure of the proportion of a country's working-age population that engages actively in the labour market, either by working or looking for work. It provides an indication of the relative size of the supply of labour available to engage in the production of goods and services.

Total unemployment: proportion of the labour force that does not have a job and is actively looking for work.

Inactivity rate: percentage of the population that is neither working nor seeking work (that is, not in the labour force).

Table 21. Corruption Perception Index

The Corruption Perception Index (CPI) is a composite indicator based on surveys of business people and assessments of country analysts. A background paper presenting the methodology and validity of the CPI is available on the Transparency International website: http://www.transparency.org/policy_research/surveys_indices/cpi/2009/methodology

Table 22 to 24. Political Indicators

The political indicators presented in tables 22 to 24 and discussed in chapter 5 of this report measure public protests, public violence and political hardening in African countries. The indicators have been assembled on the basis of a detailed monitoring of daily press briefs from Agence France Presse (AFP), with the aim to take into account the daily events and decisions that make up the reality of political life and government attitudes in African countries. The methodology was first proposed by Dessus, Lafay and Morrisson[1]. All three indicators are composites combining 4-value variables (with a scale of 0 to 3: 0: non-occurrence, 1: occurrence but weak intensity, 2: medium intensity and 3: strong intensity) and/or binary variables with values 0 and 1, with 0 being the non-occurrence of the event and 1 its occurrence. The detailed contents of each indicator are listed below.

These indices have been assembled since 1996 for 25 African countries[2] and since 2006 for 51 countries. AFP's daily press briefs have been the source for the indicators since 2008. Before that, the weekly newspaper *Marchés Tropicaux et Méditerranéens* (MTM) served as the source for the indicators. This change in the source introduced a break in the series. Comparing both sources for all 52 countries in two consecutive years (2006 and 2007), we found that the number of reported relevant events was higher in AFP, which reports daily, than in the weekly MTM, requiring a slight upward adjustment of past data to ensure comparability. We estimated correction coefficients for each country in the series (the average coefficients were 1.10 for public protests, 1.04 for public violence and 1.46 for political hardening). The indicators presented in the tables have been adjusted accordingly for the years 1996-2005.

In previous AEO reports the public protest and public violence indicators were combined in a civil tensions indicator. This series has been split up into its components in this report to allow for a separate analysis of these two time series. The civil tensions indicator for 2010 can be found on the AEO website www.africaneconomicoutlook.org, where the indicator measuring political softening from previous years is also being continued.

1 Dessus, S., D. Lafay et C. Morrisson (1994), "A Politico-economic Model for Stabilisation in Africa", *Journal of African Economies*.

2 The following countries are included in this sample: Algeria, Botswana, Burkina Faso, Cameroon, Chad, Côte d'Ivoire, Egypt, Equatorial Guinea, Ethiopia, Gabon, Ghana, Kenya, Mali, Mauritius, Morocco, Mozambique, Namibia, Nigeria, Senegal, South Africa, Tanzania, Tunisia, Uganda, Zambia and Zimbabwe.

Table 22: Public Protest

- **Strikes**

0 = non-occurrence,

1 = 1 strike or number of strikers lower than 1 000 (included),

2 = 2 strikes or number of strikers between 1 000 and 5 000 (included),

3 = 3 strikes or number of strikers strictly higher than 5 000.

- **Demonstrations**

0 = non-occurrence,

1 = 1 demonstration or number of protesters lower than 5 000 (not included),

2 = 2 demonstrations or number of protesters between 5 000 and 10 000 (not included),

3 = 3 demonstrations or number of protesters higher than 10 000.

Table 23: Public Violence

- **Unrest and violence (number of dead and injured)**

Dead

0 = none,

1 = between 1 and 10 (not included),

2 = between 10 and 100 (not included),

3 = higher than 100.

Injured

0 = none,

1 = between 1 and 50 (not included) or if the number of dead is between 1 and 10,

2 = between 50 and 500 (not included) or if the number of dead is between 10 and 100,

3 = higher than 500 or if the number of dead exceeds 100.

- **Coup d'état and attempted coup d'état**

Table 24: Political Hardening

- **State of emergency (0 or 1)**

- **Arrests, incarcerations**

0 = non-occurrence,

1 = between 1 and 10 (not included),

2 = between 10 and 100 (not included),

3 = higher than 100.

- **Additional resources for the police, propaganda or censorship**

- **Toughening of the political environment (expulsions, dismissals, curfew, dissolution of political parties...)**

- **Violence perpetuated by the police (number of dead and injured)**

Dead

0 = none,

1 = between 1 and 10 (not included),

2 = between 10 and 100 (not included),

3 = higher or equal to 100.

Injured

0 = none,

1 = between 1 and 50 (not included),

2 = between 50 and 500 (not included),

3 = higher or equal to 500.

- **Extra juridical prosecutions and executions**

- **Bans on strikes and demonstrations**

- **Bans on press or public debates**

- **Closing of schools**

- **Counter-demonstrations orchestrated by the government**

Table 1: **Basic Indicators, 2010**

	Population (thousands)	Land area (thousands of km^2)	Population density (pop / km^2)	GDP based on PPP valuation (USD million)	GDP per Capita (PPP valuation, USD)	Annual real GDP growth (average over 2002-10)
Algeria	35 423	2 382	15	234 572	6 622	3.9
Angola	18 993	1 247	15	115 805	6 097	12.3
Benin	9 212	115	80	13 833	1 502	3.6
Botswana	1 978	582	3	30 407	15 376	4.3
Burkina Faso	16 287	274	59	20 986	1 289	5.5
Burundi	8 519	28	306	3 176	373	3.3
Cameroon	19 958	476	42	45 971	2 303	3.2
Cape Verde	513	4	127	2 147	4 188	6.1
Central Afr. Rep.	4 506	623	7	3 341	741	1.7
Chad	11 506	1 284	9	17 469	1 518	8.4
Comoros	691	2	309	845	1 223	1.8
Congo	3 759	342	11	15 722	4 183	5.0
Congo Dem. Rep.	67 827	2 345	29	28 080	414	5.6
Côte d'Ivoire	21 571	322	67	36 652	1 699	1.2
Djibouti	879	23	38	2 131	2 424	4.1
Egypt*	84 474	1 001	84	501 752	5 940	5.1
Equatorial Guinea	693	28	25	18 355	26 472	12.9
Eritrea	5 224	118	44	3 432	657	0.0
Ethiopia*	84 976	1 104	77	91 304	1 074	8.6
Gabon	1 501	268	6	22 319	14 866	2.2
Gambia	1 751	11	155	3 525	2 013	5.2
Ghana	24 333	239	102	37 135	1 526	5.9
Guinea	10 324	246	42	11 672	1 131	2.5
Guinea-Bissau	1 647	36	46	17 693	10 740	1.5
Kenya	40 863	593	69	71 304	1 745	4.1
Lesotho	2 084	30	69	2 972	1 426	3.1
Liberia	4 102	111	37	2 266	552	1.7
Libya	6 546	1 760	4	93 233	14 244	5.2

Table 1: **Basic Indicators, 2010** (cont.)

	Population (thousands)	Land area (thousands of km²)	Population density (pop / km²)	GDP based on PPP valuation (USD million)	GDP per Capita (PPP valuation, USD)	Annual real GDP growth (average over 2002-10)
Madagascar	20 146	587	34	18 454	916	2.4
Malawi	15 692	118	132	13 650	870	5.7
Mali	13 323	1 240	11	15 243	1 144	4.9
Mauritania	3 366	1 026	3	8 250	2 451	4.1
Mauritius	1 297	2	636	18 513	14 278	3.9
Morocco	32 381	711	46	156 306	4 827	4.6
Mozambique	23 406	802	29	26 386	1 127	7.7
Namibia	2 212	824	3	14 949	6 758	4.9
Niger	15 891	1 267	13	10 979	691	4.7
Nigeria	158 259	924	171	384 084	2 427	9.1
Rwanda	10 277	26	390	9 478	922	6.8
São Tomé & Príncipe	165	1	172	327	1 978	6.3
Senegal	12 861	197	65	22 009	1 711	3.9
Seychelles	85	0.455	186	2 303	27 222	2.6
Sierra Leone	5 836	72	81	5 128	879	8.7
Somalia	9 359	638	15	...	...	...
South Africa	50 492	1 221	41	521 779	10 334	3.6
Sudan	43 192	2 506	17	92 741	2 147	6.9
Swaziland	1 202	17	69	6 389	5 315	2.4
Tanzania	45 040	945	48	63 549	1 411	7.0
Togo	6 780	57	119	6 289	928	2.5
Tunisia	10 374	164	63	100 606	9 698	4.5
Uganda	33 796	241	140	48 068	1 422	7.2
Zambia	13 257	753	18	22 571	1 703	5.6
Zimbabwe	12 644	391	32	3 238	256	-3.1
Africa	1031 472	30 323	34	3 049 131	2 956	5.5

Note: * Fiscal year July (n-1)/June (n)

Sources: United Nations, Department of Economic and Social Affairs, Population Division, *World Population Prospects, The 2008 Revision.*
AfDB Statistics Department, Various domestic authorities and IMF *World Economic Outlook* (march 2011) and author's estimates and projections.

StatLink http://dx.doi.org/10.1787/888932419399

Table 2: **Real GDP Growth Rates, 2002-12**

	2002	2003	2004	2005	2006	2007	2008	2009	2010 (e)	2011 (p)	2012 (p)
Algeria	4.7	6.9	5.2	5.1	2.0	3.0	2.4	2.4	3.5	3.9	3.6
Angola	14.5	3.3	11.2	20.6	18.6	22.6	13.8	2.4	3.4	7.5	11.1
Benin	4.4	3.9	3.1	2.9	3.8	4.6	5.0	2.7	2.1	2.5	3.7
Botswana	8.8	6.3	6.0	1.6	5.1	4.8	3.1	-3.7	6.4	6.9	7.0
Burkina Faso	4.7	8.0	4.6	8.7	5.5	3.6	5.2	3.2	5.7	6.5	6.2
Burundi	4.5	-1.2	4.8	0.9	5.2	3.5	4.5	3.4	3.9	4.5	5.2
Cameroon	4.0	4.0	3.7	2.3	3.2	3.3	2.9	2.0	3.0	3.8	5.3
Cape Verde	5.3	4.7	4.3	6.5	10.8	8.6	6.2	3.6	5.3	5.6	6.1
Central Afr. Rep.	0.4	-4.7	2.8	2.0	3.8	3.7	2.0	1.7	3.4	4.3	4.5
Chad	8.6	13.2	34.3	7.5	1.4	4.0	-0.6	1.7	5.9	5.7	6.9
Comoros	2.3	2.1	1.9	2.8	2.6	0.8	0.6	1.1	2.1	2.5	3.2
Congo	4.6	0.8	3.7	7.6	6.2	-1.6	6.4	6.8	10.2	8.4	3.1
Congo Dem. Rep.	3.5	5.8	6.6	7.9	5.6	6.3	6.2	2.8	6.1	6.7	6.4
Côte d'Ivoire	-1.6	-1.7	1.6	1.8	0.7	1.6	2.3	3.7	2.0	-7.3	5.9
Djibouti	2.6	3.2	3.0	3.2	4.8	5.1	5.8	5.0	4.4	4.6	5.1
Egypt*	3.2	3.2	4.1	4.5	6.8	7.1	7.2	4.7	5.1	1.6	4.0
Equatorial Guinea	20.4	14.4	32.7	8.8	1.3	21.4	10.7	5.3	1.2	5.0	7.5
Eritrea	3.0	-2.7	1.5	2.6	-1.0	1.4	-9.8	3.9	2.2	7.9	6.1
Ethiopia*	1.6	-2.1	11.7	12.6	11.5	11.8	11.2	9.9	8.8	10.0	8.6
Gabon	-0.3	2.5	1.4	3.0	1.2	5.6	2.3	-1.4	5.5	4.2	4.9
Gambia	-3.2	6.9	7.0	5.1	6.5	6.0	6.3	6.7	5.4	5.6	5.6
Ghana	4.5	5.2	5.6	5.9	6.4	6.5	8.4	4.7	5.9	12.0	11.0
Guinea	5.2	1.2	2.3	3.0	2.5	1.8	4.9	-0.3	1.6	4.6	5.5
Guinea-Bissau	-4.2	-0.6	2.2	3.5	0.6	2.7	3.2	3.0	3.6	4.5	4.8
Kenya	0.5	2.9	5.1	5.9	6.3	7.1	1.7	2.6	5.0	5.3	5.5
Lesotho	0.4	4.8	2.2	1.4	6.6	2.3	4.4	1.9	3.8	2.9	3.3
Liberia	3.7	-31.3	2.6	5.3	7.8	9.4	7.1	4.6	6.1	7.3	8.9
Libya	-1.3	13.0	4.4	9.9	5.9	6.0	2.8	-1.6	7.4	-19.0	16.0

Table 2: Real GDP Growth Rates, 2002-12 (cont.)

	2002	2003	2004	2005	2006	2007	2008	2009	2010 (e)	2011 (p)	2012 (p)
Madagascar	-12.7	9.8	5.3	4.6	5.0	6.2	7.1	-3.7	0.3	0.6	2.0
Malawi	1.7	5.7	5.4	2.6	7.7	5.5	8.6	7.6	6.7	6.4	6.0
Mali	4.3	7.6	2.3	6.1	5.3	4.3	5.0	4.5	4.5	5.4	5.3
Mauritania	1.1	5.6	5.2	5.4	11.4	1.0	3.5	-1.2	5.0	5.3	5.5
Mauritius	1.9	4.3	5.8	1.2	3.9	5.4	5.1	3.1	4.1	4.0	4.1
Morocco	3.3	6.1	4.8	3.0	7.8	2.7	5.6	4.9	3.3	4.6	5.0
Mozambique	9.2	6.5	7.9	8.4	8.7	7.3	6.8	6.4	8.1	7.7	7.9
Namibia	4.8	4.2	12.3	2.5	7.1	5.5	4.3	-0.7	4.2	4.8	4.6
Niger	5.3	7.7	-0.8	7.2	5.8	3.4	9.3	-1.2	5.5	4.9	11.5
Nigeria	21.3	10.2	10.5	6.5	6.0	6.4	6.0	7.0	8.1	6.9	6.7
Rwanda	9.4	0.3	5.3	9.0	9.2	5.5	11.2	4.1	7.4	6.5	7.0
São Tomé & Príncipe	11.6	5.4	6.6	5.7	6.7	6.0	5.8	4.0	4.5	5.0	6.0
Senegal	0.7	6.7	5.9	5.6	2.3	4.7	3.2	2.2	4.2	4.5	5.0
Seychelles	1.2	-5.9	-2.9	6.7	9.5	9.6	-1.3	0.7	6.0	4.0	4.5
Sierra Leone	27.4	9.5	7.4	7.3	7.4	6.4	5.5	3.2	4.5	5.1	6.0
Somalia	...	...	...	...	...	...	...	...	...	...	...
South Africa	3.7	2.9	4.6	5.3	5.6	5.5	3.7	-1.7	2.8	3.6	4.3
Sudan	5.4	7.1	5.1	6.3	11.3	10.2	6.8	4.5	5.0	5.1	5.3
Swaziland	1.8	2.2	2.9	2.5	3.3	3.5	2.4	1.2	2.1	1.9	2.2
Tanzania	7.2	6.9	7.8	7.4	6.7	7.1	7.4	6.0	6.8	6.9	7.3
Togo	-1.3	4.8	2.5	1.2	3.9	2.1	2.4	3.2	3.4	3.7	4.0
Tunisia	1.8	5.6	6.0	4.1	5.4	6.3	4.6	3.0	3.7	1.1	3.3
Uganda	7.1	6.2	5.8	10.0	7.1	8.1	10.4	5.3	5.1	5.6	6.9
Zambia	3.3	5.1	5.4	5.3	6.2	6.2	5.7	6.4	6.6	6.5	6.7
Zimbabwe	-5.9	-7.4	-3.6	-4.1	-3.5	-3.3	-14.0	5.7	8.2	7.8	5.4
Africa	5.7	5.3	6.1	5.9	6.2	6.5	5.5	3.1	4.9	3.7	5.8

Note: * Fiscal year July (n-1)/June (n)

Sources: AfDB Statistics Department. Various domestic authorities; IMF *World Economic Outlook* (march 2011) and author's estimates and projections.

StatLink http://dx.doi.org/10.1787/888932419418

Table 3: **Demand Composition and Growth Rate, 2009-12**

	2009						2010 (e)				2011 (p)				2012 (p)			
	Final consumption		Gross capital formation		External sector		Total final consump-tion	Gross capi-tal formation - Total	Exports	Imports	Total final consump-tion	Gross capital formation - Total	Exports	Imports	Total Final Consump-tion	Gross capi-tal formation - Total	Exports	Imports
	Private	Public	Private	Public	Exports	Imports												
	% of GDP						Real Percentage Growth				Real Percentage Growth				Real Percentage Growth			
Algeria	37.4	16.4	22.3	24.5	35.2	35.8	5.3	5.3	-2.0	5.1	5.5	5.7	-0.5	6.1	3.9	5.0	1.9	4.9
Angola	52.0	24.9	2.4	12.4	54.5	46.2	5.8	-23.5	-1.0	-2.7	7.3	13.1	3.4	4.9	2.0	6.6	7.6	0.2
Benin	76.1	12.0	11.1	10.1	15.8	25.1	2.2	1.7	3.6	3.2	2.6	3.4	3.8	4.3	3.2	3.7	6.3	4.1
Botswana	57.3	24.2	9.1	14.9	37.7	43.2	2.1	5.8	12.3	4.2	1.8	16.9	8.5	6.0	2.6	13.9	8.6	6.0
Burkina Faso	70.9	18.7	15.7	5.4	13.1	23.9	4.1	9.2	6.9	4.1	4.3	10.7	14.4	7.4	4.7	10.0	10.1	6.9
Burundi	83.6	25.3	4.8	20.2	10.0	43.9	4.7	9.6	-0.6	8.5	-1.0	17.3	10.9	3.0	6.1	7.2	0.0	7.5
Cameroon	75.2	11.3	16.3	2.2	22.6	27.6	3.4	7.4	-4.1	1.7	3.9	6.3	0.6	3.8	3.8	8.1	8.2	5.0
Cape Verde	70.1	13.8	30.5	14.3	37.2	65.7	4.1	15.2	2.6	8.6	7.0	-2.4	9.6	4.0	5.6	0.3	8.6	3.3
Central Afr. Rep.	92.3	8.4	7.1	4.2	10.2	22.2	2.9	5.7	5.8	3.3	3.9	3.8	5.7	2.9	3.5	9.0	8.5	4.9
Chad	45.7	28.0	13.4	5.2	48.4	40.8	3.9	11.0	7.1	6.0	9.9	4.7	5.8	12.6	8.4	1.6	8.1	8.0
Comores	92.2	13.5	7.0	5.9	12.7	31.3	-1.8	27.3	3.1	0.5	2.9	6.5	4.8	5.8	3.3	6.9	6.1	5.9
Congo	31.2	10.2	32.3	11.1	76.5	61.3	6.7	4.9	7.7	0.7	5.6	7.2	6.3	3.1	6.0	6.5	-1.5	4.6
Congo DRC	84.2	12.1	14.8	4.6	45.2	60.9	7.2	34.5	9.4	18.6	7.9	14.4	4.5	10.6	3.8	2.7	6.4	1.1
Côte d'Ivoire	74.1	8.5	6.5	2.9	49.0	41.0	1.8	-0.1	2.3	1.6	-11.5	-18.3	-5.0	-14.4	6.4	16.7	5.2	8.1
Djibouti	62.8	19.3	24.1	15.4	52.2	73.7	2.9	5.3	2.8	2.1	3.3	25.7	0.0	11.5	6.7	9.4	0.9	6.7
Egypt*	76.0	11.3	9.6	9.7	24.9	31.5	6.3	-1.2	-0.3	-0.6	1.8	-2.6	-1.8	-3.1	3.8	8.8	4.1	6.7
Equatorial Guinea	7.8	4.7	17.6	51.9	89.4	71.4	7.5	-2.7	0.3	-0.6	7.7	4.5	2.2	2.7	4.1	2.3	3.9	1.7
Ethiopia*	87.5	8.2	4.9	17.5	10.5	28.6	7.8	11.5	1.3	5.7	1.9	13.3	14.8	-3.4	8.3	8.6	1.0	5.0
Gabon	39.7	15.4	18.0	6.9	56.4	36.4	4.0	2.4	4.5	-0.2	4.1	11.0	3.7	8.2	3.9	2.5	5.3	2.1
Gambia	87.4	9.3	10.8	7.5	23.7	38.6	10.3	2.1	-8.7	8.0	7.3	0.5	1.2	5.6	6.5	0.5	1.8	3.9
Ghana	76.3	19.6	20.4	9.5	50.9	76.7	1.8	17.9	13.7	10.1	6.4	15.3	15.1	9.0	6.4	9.9	11.8	6.1
Guinea	85.6	9.0	11.8	5.5	25.6	37.6	-6.5	20.9	3.1	-0.6	3.9	7.7	13.2	11.8	-0.1	10.3	9.5	1.3
Guinea-Bissau	92.2	13.5	4.4	3.6	15.3	29.0	-0.1	4.0	13.2	0.8	3.8	7.9	4.2	3.5	3.8	8.4	5.5	3.8
Kenya	75.5	16.3	15.7	5.2	25.3	37.9	5.2	3.4	5.9	5.2	3.4	4.1	8.0	3.0	5.1	4.9	6.0	4.8
Lesotho	93.5	39.3	14.4	13.0	56.8	117.1	5.3	8.7	2.3	5.6	2.5	3.8	3.0	2.9	2.3	2.5	3.2	2.1
Liberia	143.0	26.8	56.3	10.6	55.8	192.5	-5.8	14.7	4.5	1.7	-0.6	11.8	4.7	4.1	0.8	13.0	4.4	5.2
Libya	29.5	17.5	9.5	25.4	64.0	45.8	5.7	12.6	8.4	10.7	-3.8	-18.5	-31.3	-12.6	6.9	20.0	26.9	15.5

Table 3: Demand Composition and Growth Rate, 2009-12 (cont.)

	2009						2010 (e)				2011 (p)				2012 (p)			
	Final consumption		Gross capital formation		External sector		Total final consump-tion	Gross capi-tal formation - Total	Exports	Imports	Total final consump-tion	Gross capital formation - Total	Exports	Imports	Total Final Consump-tion	Gross capi-tal formation - Total	Exports	Imports
	Private	Public	Private	Public	Exports	Imports												
	% of GDP						Real Percentage Growth				Real Percentage Growth				Real Percentage Growth			
Madagascar	82.0	11.9	28.0	4.1	24.7	50.7	-2.9	-8.4	5.7	-8.1	-1.2	0.0	2.9	-1.8	1.5	0.3	3.8	1.2
Malawi	88.8	10.2	12.2	14.1	23.4	48.7	4.9	16.6	9.1	8.4	4.0	13.9	10.2	6.5	5.3	6.1	10.3	5.9
Mali	70.7	17.3	13.0	7.0	26.6	34.6	3.8	6.4	4.4	3.7	5.1	2.7	18.0	11.4	6.0	5.0	3.7	5.6
Mauritania	73.9	20.5	18.8	5.3	50.2	68.8	4.5	9.3	0.1	4.3	5.1	5.8	-0.1	3.6	4.7	6.9	3.2	4.4
Mauritius	73.7	9.3	19.7	6.6	48.8	58.1	5.1	-0.7	3.9	3.2	5.2	6.5	3.2	6.1	4.1	6.8	3.5	4.7
Morocco	57.0	18.0	30.7	5.3	28.6	39.5	3.6	6.4	1.8	5.5	5.4	6.7	2.4	6.4	5.1	7.6	3.1	6.1
Mozambique	80.0	14.0	5.5	9.3	26.0	34.8	4.8	18.1	4.8	1.5	4.3	13.6	10.1	4.4	7.4	14.7	5.6	8.0
Namibia	57.2	24.4	20.8	6.4	44.4	53.3	4.3	22.3	5.0	11.9	1.6	3.1	5.8	1.7	2.1	6.0	5.3	3.3
Niger	74.3	16.3	21.5	7.8	19.5	39.4	8.7	5.7	-5.3	6.9	1.7	12.6	8.8	5.9	9.3	17.7	13.6	13.2
Nigeria	42.1	21.0	19.9	8.1	36.9	27.9	6.5	4.5	2.7	-1.5	5.6	6.8	3.3	1.7	6.4	6.2	3.7	3.6
Rwanda	81.3	14.5	14.4	7.1	11.6	29.0	8.8	8.9	3.7	10.9	7.5	6.0	3.8	7.8	8.2	6.0	3.6	8.5
São Tomé & Príncipe	81.8	16.7	19.0	29.6	10.9	58.0	-0.2	13.3	3.9	5.0	2.9	9.4	5.7	6.3	4.4	7.7	7.9	5.8
Senegal	78.6	14.2	20.4	6.7	23.2	43.1	2.2	9.2	4.6	3.5	2.4	11.1	3.7	4.2	2.6	12.2	3.3	4.6
Seychelles	85.0	13.3	23.6	5.7	103.4	131.0	5.8	21.4	2.4	6.9	1.5	14.1	4.5	4.5	1.6	11.2	4.8	3.9
Sierra Leone	98.4	1.4	10.1	3.6	17.5	30.9	6.2	10.9	0.4	10.4	6.3	8.6	1.2	8.3	7.0	9.0	2.9	8.8
South Africa	60.2	21.1	11.0	8.6	27.4	28.3	2.6	4.0	4.3	8.9	3.1	5.4	3.3	3.3	4.1	7.7	3.5	5.4
Sudan	66.2	15.9	17.2	5.8	16.0	21.1	6.9	7.3	-4.4	8.2	3.7	10.0	9.4	7.6	5.1	9.5	-0.9	6.1
Swaziland	88.2	13.7	4.9	5.4	55.5	67.7	2.4	15.0	2.8	4.7	-1.3	15.0	2.7	1.2	-2.0	7.4	1.7	-1.4
Tanzania	65.5	17.5	21.0	7.9	23.2	35.2	6.1	6.3	11.6	7.8	5.0	9.2	10.5	6.5	6.5	9.2	9.7	8.7
Togo	82.6	14.2	12.5	6.2	35.5	51.0	2.3	11.0	3.1	3.8	2.4	9.7	4.2	4.1	2.8	8.3	4.2	3.8
Tunisia	61.9	16.2	19.9	4.9	45.0	48.0	4.5	12.0	2.6	8.9	5.2	-8.0	-3.6	-0.6	2.8	4.0	4.8	3.9
Uganda	78.0	8.6	16.4	4.7	23.7	31.3	5.3	9.7	3.7	7.7	5.3	10.4	3.1	6.1	5.8	13.8	5.6	8.2
Zambia	57.0	19.4	17.6	3.5	34.6	32.0	8.2	14.7	6.8	13.7	7.1	4.6	5.6	5.7	7.9	6.5	6.0	7.8
Zimbabwe	98.6	14.3	12.0	4.5	35.7	65.1	5.2	20.9	11.2	8.2	2.6	28.4	11.2	7.4	0.0	24.5	7.2	5.2

Note: * Fiscal year July (n-1)/June (n)

Sources: AfDB Statistics Department. Various domestic authorities and IMF *World Economic Outlook* (march 2011) and author's estimates and projections.

StatLink http://dx.doi.org/10.1787/888932419437

Table 4: **Public Finances, 2009-12 (percentage of GDP)**

	2009			2010 (e)			2011 (p)			2012 (p)		
	Total revenue and grants	Total expenditure and net lending	Overall balance	Total revenue and grants	Total expenditure and net lending	Overall balance	Total revenue and grants	Total expenditure and net lending	Overall balance	Total revenue and grants	Total expenditure and net lending	Overall balance
Algeria	36.7	43.6	-6.9	37.3	41.7	-4.4	36.9	42.2	-5.3	36.4	42.1	-5.7
Angola	30.9	39.5	-8.6	39.1	31.8	7.3	38.0	31.3	6.7	38.0	29.9	8.1
Benin	21.7	25.9	-4.2	21.3	23.9	-2.6	21.6	24.1	-2.5	21.6	23.2	-1.6
Botswana**	34.0	39.3	-5.2	35.2	46.3	-11.1	34.9	41.8	-6.9	34.4	40.4	-6.0
Burkina Faso	19.6	23.1	-3.5	20.5	24.9	-4.5	19.1	23.5	-4.4	19.1	24.2	-5.1
Burundi	31.0	33.0	-2.0	30.5	33.7	-3.2	29.1	33.7	-4.5	30.8	34.7	-3.9
Cameroon	17.1	17.5	-0.4	17.4	18.3	-0.9	17.4	18.7	-1.3	17.4	17.8	-0.4
Cape Verde	29.3	35.7	-6.3	30.5	44.2	-13.7	28.8	40.0	-11.3	27.9	36.9	-8.9
Central Afr. Rep.	16.1	15.4	0.7	15.7	15.9	-0.3	15.5	15.9	-0.3	15.4	16.0	-0.5
Chad	19.4	29.3	-9.8	20.0	32.5	-12.5	20.5	29.6	-9.1	20.5	29.0	-8.5
Comoros	22.7	22.1	0.6	26.8	22.7	4.1	20.2	23.3	-3.1	20.1	23.7	-3.6
Congo	32.5	27.1	5.4	35.5	21.7	13.9	36.9	20.4	16.5	37.7	22.1	15.6
Congo Dem. Rep.	24.1	28.2	-4.1	29.3	29.9	-0.5	26.0	34.2	-8.3	26.4	33.0	-6.6
Côte d'Ivoire	19.5	21.1	-1.6	19.3	21.7	-2.5	19.3	21.2	-1.9	19.5	22.9	-3.4
Djibouti	38.7	43.8	-5.1	38.8	41.5	-2.7	39.1	41.6	-2.5	37.7	39.1	-1.3
Egypt *	27.1	33.7	-6.6	22.2	30.3	-8.1	22.1	31.9	-9.8	22.4	31.7	-9.4
Equatorial Guinea	49.5	59.1	-9.6	46.3	48.9	-2.6	45.5	48.3	-2.8	44.9	47.6	-2.7
Eritrea	..	..	..	..	..	..	...	...	...	...	...	...
Ethiopia*	16.3	17.2	-0.9	15.8	18.1	-2.3	15.9	19.4	-3.5	15.6	19.7	-4.1
Gabon	25.0	24.8	0.2	24.8	21.1	3.7	24.8	20.4	4.4	24.6	20.0	4.6
Gambia	19.0	22.0	-3.0	18.5	21.2	-2.7	18.2	20.6	-2.4	17.8	19.3	-1.5
Ghana	34.0	41.5	-7.6	31.9	39.8	-7.9	29.7	37.5	-7.7	29.3	34.4	-5.0
Guinea	16.7	25.1	-8.4	16.7	28.7	-12.0	15.3	26.1	-10.8	13.9	23.2	-9.3
Guinea-Bissau	24.7	21.8	2.8	20.9	21.1	-0.2	18.8	20.8	-2.0	19.8	20.9	-1.2
Kenya*	23.3	28.7	-5.4	24.9	30.8	-5.8	24.5	31.3	-6.8	23.7	30.7	-7.1
Lesotho**	66.2	71.1	-4.9	44.1	53.9	-9.8	40.5	51.8	-11.3	45.5	48.9	-3.4
Liberia*	27.4	29.0	-1.6	31.7	30.4	1.3	30.6	32.5	-1.9	30.1	32.3	-2.2
Libya	60.2	53.1	7.1	68.3	47.4	20.9	50.5	57.5	-7.1	59.9	53.1	6.8

Table 4: **Public Finances, 2009-12 (percentage of GDP)** (cont.)

	2009			2010 (e)			2011 (p)			2012 (p)		
	Total revenue and grants	Total expenditure and net lending	Overall balance	Total revenue and grants	Total expenditure and net lending	Overall balance	Total revenue and grants	Total expenditure and net lending	Overall balance	Total revenue and grants	Total expenditure and net lending	Overall balance
Madagascar	12.1	14.6	-2.5	11.4	13.0	-1.6	11.3	12.6	-1.3	11.0	12.2	-1.2
Malawi*	31.9	35.5	-3.6	33.9	35.0	-1.1	31.5	37.9	-6.3	29.9	37.3	-7.4
Mali	21.7	25.9	-4.2	22.1	26.2	-4.1	22.4	26.5	-4.1	22.5	26.4	-3.9
Mauritania	25.5	30.6	-5.1	23.3	27.0	-3.7	23.9	26.9	-3.0	24.5	27.4	-2.9
Mauritius*	18.8	25.4	-6.6	19.8	24.5	-4.7	20.5	24.9	-4.4	20.6	24.9	-4.3
Morocco	25.9	28.0	-2.2	26.4	30.5	-4.1	26.5	30.0	-3.5	26.1	29.5	-3.4
Mozambique	27.0	32.0	-5.1	26.6	32.0	-5.4	26.8	32.7	-6.0	26.5	31.9	-5.4
Namibia**	32.1	30.0	2.1	31.0	34.0	-3.0	28.4	30.7	-2.3	27.8	28.9	-1.1
Niger	18.9	25.5	-6.6	22.1	25.3	-3.2	23.6	27.2	-3.6	25.8	27.6	-1.8
Nigeria	19.9	30.4	-10.4	23.6	30.4	-6.8	27.1	27.8	-0.7	26.1	25.8	0.3
Rwanda	24.6	26.8	-2.2	25.0	25.5	-0.5	24.0	27.6	-3.5	23.9	25.4	-1.4
São Tomé & Príncipe	58.8	41.2	17.6	36.9	44.5	-7.7	47.2	43.9	3.3	33.6	42.1	-8.4
Senegal	21.7	26.8	-4.9	21.4	27.6	-4.5	21.2	28.0	-5.8	21.4	27.7	-6.3
Seychelles	38.8	33.8	5.1	37.0	33.7	3.2	37.6	37.3	0.3	36.7	36.9	-0.2
Sierra Leone	19.7	22.9	-3.2	18.9	23.5	-4.6	17.8	23.7	-5.9	18.1	23.4	-5.3
Somalia	..	..	..	..	..	..	...	...	...	...	...	...
South Africa**	23.7	30.6	-6.9	25.0	30.4	-5.4	24.2	29.2	-5.0	24.3	28.7	-4.5
Sudan	16.7	18.6	-1.9	16.6	18.7	-2.1	16.9	17.4	-0.5	15.7	17.2	-1.5
Swaziland**	37.9	38.1	-0.2	34.2	40.9	-6.7	31.1	41.9	-10.8	30.0	43.7	-13.6
Tanzania*	20.9	25.7	-4.8	26.0	31.4	-5.4	22.9	30.7	-7.8	21.1	30.2	-9.2
Togo	16.4	21.9	-5.5	16.7	22.5	-5.8	16.8	22.4	-5.6	16.7	21.8	-5.2
Tunisia	23.1	25.8	-2.7	23.1	25.7	-2.6	23.3	28.5	-5.2	23.1	27.9	-4.8
Uganda*	15.4	15.3	0.1	14.9	16.7	-1.8	13.9	16.4	-2.5	13.4	17.3	-3.9
Zambia	20.3	22.4	-2.1	16.4	19.5	-3.1	14.4	18.9	-4.5	13.6	19.5	-5.9
Zimbabwe	17.3	17.4	-0.1	18.1	19.9	-1.7	18.8	21.0	-2.2	18.2	21.6	-3.4
Africa	26.5	31.7	-5.2	27.5	30.8	-3.3	26.6	30.6	-3.9	26.8	29.9	-3.2

Note: * Fiscal year July (n-1)/June (n) ; ** Fiscal year April (n)/March (n+1)

Sources: AfDB Statistics Department, Various domestic authorities and IMF World Economic Outlook (march 2011) and author's estimates and projections.

StatLink http://dx.doi.org/10.1787/888932419456

Table 5: Monetary Indicators

	Inflation (%)				Exchange rate (LCU / USD)			Broad Money (LCU billion) 2010			Reserves, excluding gold, (USD million) 2010	
	2009	2010 (e)	2011 (p)	2012 (p)	2008	2009	2010	Level	% of GDP	Growth 2009-10	Stock at year-end	Eq. Months of imports
Algeria	5.7	4.1	4.5	4.1	64.6	72.6	74.4	7 323.2	65.6	2.1	162 614.0	48.2
Angola	13.7	14.7	11.7	12.1	75.0	79.3	91.9	2 411.0	30.5	4.7	19 667.3	11.5
Benin	2.2	2.1	2.2	2.9	447.8	472.2	495.3	1 204.2	37.0	1.3	1 020.7	8.2
Botswana	8.2	7.0	6.1	5.3	6.8	7.2	6.8	42.9	43.2	10.7	8 125.7	21.2
Burkina Faso	2.6	0.9	2.5	2.6	447.8	472.2	495.3	1 219.4	27.1	16.3	1 018.7	6.9
Burundi	10.7	7.1	8.3	6.9	1 185.7	1 230.2	1 230.9	713.8	41.4	10.0	330.7	11.2
Cameroon	3.0	1.4	2.9	3.0	447.8	472.2	495.3	2 491.7	21.6	7.2	3 516.4	9.3
Cape Verde	1.2	2.1	3.0	2.1	75.3	79.4	83.3	109.2	70.6	3.7	365.1	5.8
Central Afr. Rep.	3.5	1.8	2.5	1.8	447.8	472.2	495.3	170.7	17.7	9.2	168.6	6.5
Chad	10.1	0.6	3.1	3.2	447.8	472.2	495.3	599.7	15.2	26.0	712.3	2.9
Comoros	4.8	2.9	3.0	2.8	335.9	354.1	371.5	66.4	31.3	15.4	138.4	8.8
Congo	3.8	4.8	5.2	3.3	447.8	472.2	495.3	1 227.3	22.7	19.3	4 288.2	15.9
Congo Dem. Rep.	46.2	23.2	10.2	9.8	559.3	809.8	905.9	1 832.0	12.2	22.0	1 840.9	3.0
Côte d'Ivoire	4.7	2.7	6.3	3.3	447.8	472.2	495.3	3 983.9	35.5	13.4	3 542.5	6.2
Djibouti	1.7	4.2	4.0	3.0	177.7	177.7	177.7	182.7	89.1	9.3	254.5	6.1
Egypt	16.2	11.7	13.4	12.2	5.4	5.5	....	963.3	79.8	11.1	33 153.6	8.1
Equatorial Guinea	7.2	4.7	6.3	5.6	447.8	472.2	495.3	1 019.0	18.6	46.5	2 286.8	7.7
Eritrea	33.0	12.7	13.3	12.3	15.4	15.4	15.4	37.8	...	9.0	88.1	2.8
Ethiopia	36.0	11.2	17.6	14.3	9.6	11.8	13.4	...	...	...	1 780.9	2.6
Gabon	1.9	3.2	2.7	2.7	447.8	472.2	495.3	1 221.9	19.1	4.9	1 952.2	9.7
Gambia	4.6	5.8	5.9	6.3	22.2	26.6	28.1	12.3	41.4	4.8	207.4	7.9
Ghana	19.3	8.0	8.5	6.9	1.1	1.4	1.4	13.7	0.0	29.0	...	...
Guinea	4.7	15.8	13.5	8.2	5 500.0	....	....	...	...	...	...	...
Guinea-Bissau	-1.6	2.6	2.7	2.6	447.8	472.2	495.3	121.9	2.9	27.9	147.8	11.2
Kenya	10.5	4.1	9.8	7.6	69.2	77.4	79.2	1 249.2	45.4	19.6	4 326.2	4.8
Lesotho	7.3	7.3	7.8	6.8	8.3	8.5	7.3	6.6	51.8	14.5	...	...
Liberia	7.6	7.7	4.4	4.8	63.2	68.3	71.9	29.0	2239.9	16.1	418.7	7.2
Libya	2.4	4.7	12.1	5.1	1.2	1.3	1.2	43.6	46.1	-4.0	101 882.0	52.3

Table 5: **Monetary Indicators** (cont.)

	Inflation (%)				Exchange rate (LCU / USD)			Broad Money (LCU billion) 2009			Reserves, excluding gold, (USD million) 2009	
	2009	2010 (e)	2011 (p)	2012 (p)	2007	2008	2009	Level	% of GDP	Growth 2008/-9	Stock at year-end	Eq. Months of imports
Madagascar	8.5	9.6	10.1	9.8	1 708.4	1 956.2	2 090.0	4 277.0	25.0	9.6	1 133.7	6.0
Malawi	8.4	7.7	7.6	6.2	140.5	141.2	150.8	180.0	22.3	3.4	245.1	1.8
Mali	2.2	1.4	4.1	2.5	447.8	472.2	495.3	1 204.4	28.9	5.2	1 295.2	6.1
Mauritania	2.2	6.1	5.7	5.4	238.2	262.4	286.6	292.7	24.6	5.3	210.8	1.5
Mauritius	2.5	2.9	3.0	3.9	28.5	32.0	30.8	300.6	95.0	1.4	2 441.8	8.1
Morocco	1.0	0.9	2.1	2.7	7.8	8.1	8.4	903.9	112.1	4.8	22 588.4	8.2
Mozambique	3.5	12.7	9.2	7.3	24.3	27.5	35.6	128.8	0.0	20.3	1 924.8	6.4
Namibia	8.7	4.5	6.1	5.5	8.3	8.5	7.3	34.3	37.6	10.7	1 856.5	4.5
Niger	4.9	3.4	3.1	3.3	447.8	472.2	495.3	545.7	19.5	15.5	650.2	4.2
Nigeria	12.5	13.7	11.1	9.0	118.5	148.9	150.3	10 844.3	35.3	6.2	34 919.3	13.4
Rwanda	10.3	2.3	5.2	5.5	546.8	568.3	583.1	...	...	...	812.8	8.4
São Tomé & Príncipe	16.7	11.4	7.5	6.7	14 695.2	16 208.5	18 498.6	1 315.7	33.7	16.1	...	...
Senegal	-1.0	1.2	2.0	2.3	447.8	472.2	495.3	2 469.0	42.2	10.5	1 945.0	5.3
Seychelles	31.7	-2.4	4.2	2.9	9.5	13.6	12.1	7.3	60.0	13.7	235.6	3.4
Sierra Leone	9.2	17.8	9.6	8.2	2 981.5	3 385.7	3 874.5	2 236.5	28.0	32.7	389.3	8.7
Somalia	...	...	...	...	....	....	....	...	...	...	...	...
South Africa	7.1	4.3	5.3	5.6	8.3	8.5	7.3	2 083.0	78.2	6.9	38 175.0	6.1
Sudan	11.0	13.8	14.3	10.7	2.1	2.3	2.2	32.7	22.8	15.6	1 263.2	1.7
Swaziland	7.5	4.5	7.7	10.0	8.3	8.5	7.3	8.3	29.1	7.9	756.3	5.4
Tanzania	12.1	8.9	6.9	6.2	1 196.3	1 320.3	1 409.3	11 012.6	33.9	25.4	3 904.7	7.1
Togo	2.9	5.3	2.4	2.3	447.8	472.2	495.3	690.6	41.5	12.0	693.6	7.8
Tunisia	3.5	4.4	4.7	4.6	1.2	1.4	1.4	40.4	61.8	11.4	9 459.3	5.9
Uganda	13.4	7.3	4.1	5.1	1 720.4	2 030.5	2 177.6	9 354.7	23.9	37.6	2 960.4	8.6
Zambia	9.9	7.9	7.1	6.2	3 745.7	5 046.1	4 797.1	17 597.2	20.3	27.5	2 093.8	5.4
Zimbabwe	6.5	5	5.9	4.7	...	....	....	...	...	...	...	...
Africa	10.0	7.7	8.4	7.4	...	...	...	...	...	...	483 802.4	13.6

Sources: AfDB Statistics Department, Various domestic authorities; IMF *World Economic Outlook* (march 2011) & *International Financial Statistics* and authors' estimates and forecasts.

StatLink http://dx.doi.org/10.1787/888932419475

Table 6: Balance of payments Indicators

	Trade balance (USD million)				Current account balance (USD million)				Current account balance (as % of GDP)			
	2009	2010(e)	2011(p)	2012(p)	2009	2010(e)	2011(p)	2012(p)	2009	2010(e)	2011(p)	2012(p)
Algeria	7 775	10 217	9 250	8 244	417	8 294	8 318	8 304	0.3	5.5	5.0	4.7
Angola	18 168	28 684	34 928	40 369	-7 571	881	-3 936	3 884	-10.0	1.0	-3.8	3.5
Benin	- 797	- 741	- 858	- 872	- 492	- 471	- 588	- 577	-7.7	-7.1	-8.2	-7.6
Botswana	- 681	- 270	- 51	129	- 666	212	307	473	-5.7	1.5	1.9	2.7
Burkina Faso	- 483	- 255	- 163	- 103	- 385	- 248	- 136	- 46	-4.6	-2.7	-1.3	-0.4
Burundi	- 194	- 263	- 252	- 316	- 193	- 127	- 125	- 204	-15.5	-9.4	-7.9	-11.7
Cameroon	- 251	- 642	-1 176	- 938	- 782	- 855	- 920	- 669	-3.3	-3.6	-3.8	-2.6
Cape Verde	- 630	- 819	- 906	- 945	- 156	- 344	- 324	- 296	-9.9	-18.4	-15.5	-13.2
Central Afr. Rep.	- 147	- 162	- 183	- 185	- 182	- 194	- 252	- 276	-9.2	-9.9	-12.3	-12.7
Chad	368	984	1 161	1 302	-1 207	- 900	- 869	- 933	-16.9	-11.3	-9.5	-9.4
Comoros	- 144	- 157	- 172	- 181	- 43	- 58	- 75	- 83	-7.6	-10.2	-11.7	-12.2
Congo	3 179	4 815	5 672	4 694	-1 809	- 284	44	-1 078	-20.8	-2.6	0.3	-8.4
Congo Dem. Rep.	- 583	- 728	-1 175	- 513	-1 133	-2 591	-2 974	-2 623	-10.1	-15.7	-16.7	-14.3
Côte d'Ivoire	4 192	4 469	5 037	5 073	1 674	1 345	1 178	1 034	7.2	5.9	5.2	4.2
Djibouti	- 507	- 592	- 706	- 768	- 175	- 105	- 180	- 186	-17.5	-9.1	-14.3	-13.6
Egypt *	-25 173	-25 120	-22 576	-25 848	-4 424	-4 318	-7 395	-7 894	-2.3	-2.0	-3.2	-2.9
Equatorial Guinea	3 671	4 984	5 630	6 071	- 744	309	371	524	-7.6	2.7	2.9	3.8
Eritrea	- 316	- 328	- 103	- 142	- 93	- 29	84	- 20	-5.0	-1.4	3.2	-0.7
Ethiopia*	-6 279	-7 580	-7 102	-8 405	-1 621	-2 209	-1 890	-3 623	-5.0	-6.6	-6.4	-11.9
Gabon	4 183	6 025	7 159	7 724	1 485	1 862	2 460	2 675	13.6	14.3	16.4	16.6
Gambia	- 203	- 236	- 264	- 268	- 97	- 128	- 141	- 142	-10.1	-12.2	-11.9	-11.0
Ghana	-2 177	-1 637	- 676	- 170	-1 168	-1 345	-1 383	- 587	-8.1	-7.6	-6.4	-2.5
Guinea	- 10	149	193	310	- 403	- 376	- 304	- 208	-9.2	-8.3	-5.6	-3.6
Guinea-Bissau	- 796	- 687	- 781	- 823	- 346	- 472	- 577	- 603	-4.1	-5.6	-6.2	-6.1
Kenya	-5 729	-7 250	-7 909	-8 356	-1 558	-2 695	-3 127	-3 599	-5.3	-7.8	-8.5	-9.1
Lesotho	- 918	- 930	- 984	-1 009	- 3	- 288	- 297	- 119	-0.2	-14.9	-14.5	-5.4
Liberia	- 410	- 651	- 695	- 714	- 292	- 530	- 527	- 606	-33.2	-40.9	-38.1	-40.6
Libya	15 163	24 615	10 772	19 697	10 969	21 264	8 241	17 276	18.5	28.4	13.7	22.7

Table 6: **Balance of payments Indicators** (cont.)

	Trade balance (USD million)				Current account balance (USD million)				Current account balance (as % of GDP)			
	2009	2010(e)	2011(p)	2012(p)	2009	2010(e)	2011(p)	2012(p)	2009	2010(e)	2011(p)	2012(p)
Madagascar	-1 677	-1 416	-1 443	-1 503	-1 818	-1 382	-1 350	-1 386	-20.9	-17.0	-15.9	-15.3
Malawi	- 805	- 843	- 961	-1 001	- 101	61	- 92	- 214	-2.1	1.1	-1.6	-3.3
Mali	- 271	- 115	- 790	- 972	- 670	- 739	- 887	-1 057	-7.5	-8.8	-9.6	-10.9
Mauritania	- 83	540	388	186	- 382	- 394	- 387	- 451	-12.6	-8.8	-8.1	-9.1
Mauritius	-1 540	-1 809	-2 177	-2 351	- 652	- 816	-1 043	-1 085	-7.4	-7.9	-9.2	-9.0
Morocco	-16 535	-20 577	-24 565	-26 918	-4 685	-3 993	-4 717	-5 734	-5.1	-4.2	-4.5	-5.2
Mozambique	-1 275	- 937	- 835	- 975	-1 063	-1 246	-1 267	-1 524	-10.9	-11.2	-10.3	-11.0
Namibia	- 768	-1 109	- 801	- 724	141	- 365	- 472	- 430	1.5	-2.9	-3.5	-3.0
Niger	- 619	- 874	- 936	- 925	-1 234	-1 033	-1 278	-1 249	-23.4	-18.1	-21.0	-17.6
Nigeria	29 500	47 420	57 845	60 710	22 100	28 220	42 945	44 692	13.1	13.3	17.6	16.6
Rwanda	- 832	- 841	-1 017	-1 158	- 444	- 301	- 454	- 359	-8.4	-6.7	-9.1	-6.5
São Tomé & Príncipe	- 70	- 87	- 100	- 107	- 49	- 60	- 87	- 92	-26.2	-28.1	-35.8	-34.2
Senegal	-2 462	-2 435	-2 737	-2 923	- 978	-1 108	-1 314	-1 500	-6.7	-5.9	-5.9	-10.3
Seychelles	- 321	- 336	- 349	- 342	- 288	- 342	- 278	- 268	-30.3	-33.2	-24.8	-22.2
Sierra Leone	- 187	- 258	- 330	- 363	- 175	- 234	- 282	- 310	-8.7	-9.0	-9.6	-9.2
Somalia	...	...	...	...	...	...	...	...	...	...	...	...
South Africa	268	2 797	3 017	242	-11 455	-10 167	-12 360	-16 699	-4.1	-2.8	-3.4	-4.3
Sudan	1 095	2 131	3 577	3 010	-5 254	-5 354	-4 794	-6 496	-10.1	-8.3	-6.1	-7.2
Swaziland	- 131	- 158	- 208	- 196	- 380	- 648	- 617	- 552	-12.0	-16.6	-14.2	-12.5
Tanzania	-2 679	-3 035	-3 455	-4 002	-1 746	-2 370	-2 600	-3 230	-8.2	-10.3	-10.5	-12.0
Togo	- 400	- 445	- 469	- 459	- 209	- 231	- 205	- 197	-6.6	-6.8	-5.5	-5.0
Tunisia	-3 699	-4 977	-5 877	-5 874	-1 234	-2 136	-3 593	-2 807	-2.8	-4.7	-7.6	-5.6
Uganda	-1 250	-1 718	-2 148	-2 459	- 628	-1 707	-2 110	-2 458	-3.7	-9.0	-10.3	-10.8
Zambia	906	2 472	3 491	3 264	- 403	- 266	- 374	- 619	-3.2	-1.5	-1.8	-2.7
Zimbabwe	-1 622	-1 654	-1 778	-1 855	- 928	-1 268	-1 327	-1 397	-16.5	-19.9	-17.7	-16.8
Africa	4 816	47 631	50 412	55 360	-23 532	7 721	-3 956	4 375	-1.6	0.4	-0.2	0.2

Note: * Fiscal year July (n-1)/June (n)

Sources: AfDB Statistics Department, IMF WEO, March 2011 and authors' estimates and forecasts.

StatLink http://dx.doi.org/10.1787/888932419494

Table 7: Exports, 2009

	Three main exports*, with their share in total exports**			Nº of products accounting for more than 75 per cent of exports
	Product I	Product II	Product III	
Algeria	Petroleum oils and oils obtained from bituminous minerals, crude (46.8%)	Natural gas, in gaseous state (21.0%)	Natural gas, liquefied (10.8%)	3
Angola	Petroleum oils and oils obtained from bituminous minerals, crude (96.3%)			1
Benin	Cashew nuts :-- In shell (29.5%)	Cotton, not carded or combed (28.7%)	Copper waste and scrap (6.0%)	6
Botswana	Diamonds non-industrial unworked or simply sawn, cleaved or bruted (27.9%)	Nickel mattes (19.9%)	Diamonds non-industrial nes excluding mounted or set diamonds (8.6%)	16
Burkina Faso	Cotton, not carded or combed (52.1%)	Gold in oth semi-manufactd form n-monetary(inc gold platd w platinum) (19.6%)	Sesamum seeds (9.1%)	3
Burundi	Coffee, not roasted, not decaffeinated (76.1%)	Black tea (fermented) and other partly fermented tea (9.3%)		1
Cameroon	Petroleum oils and oils obtained from bituminous minerals, crude (39.6%)	Cocoa beans, whole or broken, raw or roasted (18.7%)	Bananas, including plantains, fresh (8.4%)	5
Cape Verde	Yellowfin tunas (Thunnus albacares) (16.4%)	Fish, whole or in pieces (13.5%)	Mens/boys trousers and shorts, of cotton, not knitted (10.4%)	9
Central Afr. Rep.	Logs, tropical hardwoods nes (25.8%)	Diamonds unsorted whether or not worked (25.4%)	Logs, tropical wood specified in Subhe (16.7%)	4
Chad	Petroleum oils and oils obtained from bituminous minerals, crude (90.9%)	Petroleum oils & oils obtained from bituminous minerals (other than crude) & preparations (5.6%)		1
Comoros	Cloves (whole fruit, cloves and stems) (32.1%)	Vessels and other floating structures for breaking up (26.8%)	Essential oils, nes (18.6%)	3
Congo	Petroleum oils and oils obtained from bituminous minerals, crude (87.8%)			1
Congo Dem. Rep.	Cobalt ores and concentrates (20.7%)	Petroleum oils and oils obtained from bituminous minerals, crude (16.6%)	Copper ores and concentrates (14.1%)	6
Côte d'Ivoire	Cocoa beans, whole or broken, raw or roasted (36.3%)	Petroleum oils and oils obtained from bituminous minerals, crude (14.6%)	Cocoa paste, not defatted (8.0%)	7
Djibouti	Bovine, live except pure-bred breeding (27.4%)	Sheep (17.8%)	Goats (13.2%)	5
Egypt	Natural gas, liquefied (15.8%)	Petroleum oils and oils obtained from bituminous minerals, crude (15.3%)	Light oils and preparations (5.3%)	65
Equatorial Guinea	Petroleum oils and oils obtained from bituminous minerals, crude (72.7%)	Natural gas, liquefied (22.2%)		2

Table 7: **Exports, 2009** (cont.)

	Three main exports*, with their share in total exports**			N° of products accounting for more than 75 per cent of exports
	Product I	Product II	Product III	
Eritrea	Prefabricated buildings (19.3%)	Sheep (14.2%)	Mens/boys's shirts; of cotton (6.9%)	19
Ethiopia	Coffee, not roasted, not decaffeinated (31.0%)	Sesamum seeds (24.9%)	Cut flowers fresh (10.9%)	7
Gabon	Petroleum oils and oils obtained from bituminous minerals, crude (69.9%)	Manganese ores and concentrates (9.8%)	Logs, tropical hardwoods nes (7.0%)	2
Gambia	Cashew nuts :-- In shell (44.5%)	Crude oil (14.3%)	Titanium ores and concentrates (12.3%)	4
Ghana	Cocoa beans, whole or broken, raw or roasted (49.7%)	Manganese ores and concentrates, in (8.5%)	Cocoa butter, fat and oil (5.6%)	7
Guinea	Aluminium ores and concentrates (62.9%)	Aluminium oxide, nes (11.2%)	Coffee, not roasted, not decaffeinated (4.0%)	3
Guinea-Bissau	Cashew nuts :-- In shell (92.2%)			1
Kenya	Black tea (fermented) and other partly fermented tea (14.3%)	Cut flowers fresh (13.8%)	Coffee, not roasted, not decaffeinated (5.9%)	54
Lesotho	Diamonds non-industrial unworked or simply sawn, cleaved or bruted(33.3%)	Mens/boys trousers and shorts, of cotton, not knitted (13.8%)	Pullovers, cardigans and similar articles of cotton, knitted (11.0%)	6
Liberia	Cargo vessels nes & other vessels for the transport of both persons & goods (42.1%)	Tankers (19.3%)	Petroleum oils and oils obtained from bituminous minerals, crude (13.3%)	4
Libya	Petroleum oils and oils obtained from bituminous minerals, crude (79.3%)	Natural gas, in gaseous state (9.1%)	Petroleum oils & oils obtained from bituminous minerals (other than crude) & preparations (4.8%)	1
Madagascar	Shrimps and prawns (9.3%)	Women's/girls', trousers, bib & brace overalls, breeches & shorts, of cotton (6.7%)	Vanilla (5.6%)	31
Malawi	Tobacco, partly or wholly stemmed/stripped (63.0%)	Dried leguminous vegetables, n.e.s., shelled, whether/ not skinned/split (8.8%)	Black tea (fermented) and partly fermented tea (6.3%)	3
Mali	Cotton, not carded or combed (39.3%)	Mineral or chemical fertilisers containing the three fertilising elements nitrogen, phosphorus and potassium(12.5%)	Sesamum seeds (8.1%)	8
Mauritania	Iron ores & concentrates, non-agglomerated (45.4%)	Octopus, other than live/fresh/chilled (14.4%)	Petroleum oils and oils obtained from bituminous minerals, crude (13.2%)	4
Mauritius	T-shirts, singlets and other vests, of cotton, knitted (13.4%)	Raw sugar, cane (12.2%)	Tunas, skipjack and bonito (11.2%)	36
Morocco	Phosphoric acid and polyphosphoric acids (6.6%)	Ignition wiring sets and other wiring sets of a kind used in vehicles, aircraft or ships (4.8%)		76

Table 7: Exports, 2009 (cont.)

	Three main exports*, with their share in total exports**			N° of products accounting for more than 75 per cent of exports
	Product I	Product II	Product III	
Mozambique	Aluminium unwrought, not alloyed (38.1%)	Electrical energy (10.5%)	Light oils and preparations (9.0%)	8
Namibia	Natural uranium and its compounds; (16.4%)	Unwrought zinc, containing by weight 99.99 % or more of zinc (14.5%)	Uranium ores and concentrates (13.3%)	7
Niger	Natural uranium and its compounds; (70.5%)	Light oils and preparations (23.8%)		2
Nigeria	Petroleum oils and oils obtained from bituminous minerals, crude (86.3%)	Natural gas, liquefied (7.5%)		1
Rwanda	Coffee, not roasted, not decaffeinated (29.0%)	Niobium, tantalum and vanadium ores and concentrates (20.6%)	Tin ores and concentrates (11.2%)	5
São Tomé & Príncipe	Cocoa beans, whole or broken, raw or roasted (47.1%)	Wrist-watches other than automatic winding (12.3%)	Aeroplanes and other aircraft, of an unladen weight exceeding 2,000 kg but not exceeding 15,000 kg (9.7%)	4
Senegal	Phosphoric acid and polyphosphoric acids (25.5%)	Fish, n.e.s., fresh/chilled (6.8%)	Fish, n.e.s., frozen (6.0%)	19
Seychelles	Tunas, skipjack and bonito (Sarda s (59.2%)	Bigeye tunas (Thunnus obesus) (7.3%)	Skipjack or stripbellied bonito (5.4%)	4
Sierra Leone	Diamonds non-industrial unworked or simply sawn, cleaved or bruted (21.5%)	Titanium ores and concentrates (11.8%)	Cocoa beans, whole or broken, raw or roasted (8.5%)	22
Somalia	Goats (28.3%)	Sheep (24.3%)	Live bovine animals (21.6%)	4
South Africa	Platinum unwrought or in powder form (9.3%)	Gold in unwrought forms non-monetary (6.4%)	Iron ores & concentrates,non-agglomerated (5.6%)	103
Sudan	Petroleum oils and oils obtained from bituminous minerals, crude (91.3%)			1
Swaziland	Raw sugar, cane (15.7%)	Mixtures of odoriferous substances for the food or drink industries (13.4%)	Food preparations nes (10.6%)	25
Tanzania	Coffee, not roasted, not decaffeinated (9.6%)	Tobacco, partly or wholly stemmed/stripped (9.2%)	Other Precious metal ores and concentrates, other than silver (8.3%)	31
Togo	Cocoa beans, whole or broken, raw or roasted (47.1%)	Ground (8.3%)	Gold in unwrought forms non-monetary (7.7%)	5
Tunisia	Petroleum oils and oils obtained from bituminous minerals, crude (9.4%)	Ignition wiring sets and other wiring sets of a kind used in vehicles, aircraft or ships (6.1%)	Mens/boys trousers and shorts, of cotton, not knitted (5.5%)	94
Uganda	Coffee, not roasted, not decaffeinated (35.4%)	Fish fillets and other fish meat, minced or not, fresh or chilled (8.8%)	Tobacco, partly or wholly stemmed/stripped (7.5%)	15

Table 7: **Exports, 2009** (cont.)

	Three main exports*, with their share in total exports**			N° of products accounting for more than 75 per cent of exports
	Product I	Product II	Product III	
Zambia	Copper cathodes and sections of cathodes unwrought (56,4%)	Copper ores and concentrates (8,2%)	Cobalt,unwrought,matte&oth intermediate products,waste,scrap&powders (6,0%)	4
Zimbabwe	Ferro-chromium containing by weight more than 4% of carbon (13,4%)	Tobacco, unmanufactured, partly or wholly stemmed or stripped (12,3%)	Nickel mattes (11,0%)	14
Africa**	Petroleum oils and oils obtained from bituminous minerals, crude (51,6%) [19,0%]	Natural gas, liquefied (4,2%) [24,2%]	Petroleum oils&oils obtained from bituminous minerals,o/than crude etc (3,9%) [3,3%]	25

Notes: * Products are reported when accounting for more than 4 per cent of total exports.
** Figures in [ ] represent the share of Africa in the World export for each product.

Sources: AfDB Statistics Department; COMTRADE Database (Harmonized system, Rev.2) - UN Statistics Division.

StatLink http://dx.doi.org/10.1787/888932419513

Table 8: Diversification and Competitiveness

	Diversification index					Annual export growth (%)	Competitiveness Indicator 2005-09 (%)	
	2005	2006	2007	2008	2009	2005-2009	Sectoral effect	Global competitiveness effect
Algeria	2.4	2.3	2.4	2.5	3.5	3.9	1.9	-1.5
Angola	1.1	1.1	1.1	1.1	1.1	19.3	-0.2	16.0
Benin	5.5	7.4	7.9	7.9	5.5	-11.7	-1.3	-13.9
Botswana	1.4	1.8	2.7	4.0	7.7	-12.4	-15.8	-6.4
Burkina Faso	1.6	1.8	1.9	2.8	3.1	1.0	-8.2	5.7
Burundi	1.4	4.0	3.0	3.6	1.7	-1.4	6.5	-11.5
Cameroon	4.1	3.0	3.4	3.3	4.8	0.7	-0.1	-2.7
Cape Verde	8.9	10.9	14.4	5.8	11.5	14.3	-0.7	11.5
Central Afr. Rep.	4.3	4.2	4.3	5.9	5.3	-1.7	-3.2	-2.1
Chad	1.7	1.2	1.1	1.1	1.2	1.4	0.9	-3.0
Comoros	4.9	6.3	5.2	6.8	4.5	0.3	-0.2	-3.0
Congo	1.4	1.3	1.5	1.4	1.3	4.2	0.0	0.6
Congo Dem. Rep.	4.6	6.2	7.5	7.0	7.9	21.1	-2.8	20.3
Côte d'Ivoire	7.4	7.8	7.7	8.4	5.9	7.5	7.1	-3.1
Djibouti	40.1	21.9	6.0	8.9	6.6	17.3	1.4	12.3
Egypt	26.1	15.6	19.4	15.9	17.5	13.4	1.2	8.6
Equatorial Guinea	1.2	1.2	1.3	1.6	1.7	8.2	-0.9	5.6
Eritrea	9.2	22.3	2.1	15.2	13.7	3.1	-2.5	2.0
Ethiopia	4.1	4.5	6.0	6.4	5.7	15.3	7.4	4.3
Gabon	1.6	1.8	1.8	2.1	2.0	-0.8	-0.1	-4.3
Gambia	5.4	5.3	8.2	3.9	4.2	23.0	0.4	19.1
Ghana	5.0	4.7	4.3	4.7	3.8	10.9	8.2	-0.8
Guinea	4.0	4.8	3.7	3.5	2.4	-1.2	1.6	-6.4
Guinea-Bissau	1.2	1.5	1.3	1.2	1.2	-2.5	-2.6	-3.4
Kenya	21.2	21.3	23.4	22.7	20.2	6.5	1.9	1.1
Lesotho	7.2	7.9	6.4	4.8	6.3	-1.7	-3.0	-4.3
Liberia	3.4	4.8	3.4	7.0	4.1	-1.6	11.4	-16.5
Libya	1.3	1.3	1.4	1.3	1.6	6.0	-0.3	2.8

Table 8: **Diversification and Competitiveness** (cont.)

	Diversification index					Annual export growth (%)	Competitiveness Indicator 2005-09 (%)	
	2005	2006	2007	2008	2009	2005-2009	Sectoral effect	Global competitiveness effect
Madagascar	21.3	22.9	26.1	29.0	31.5	3.0	-0.8	0.3
Malawi	2.9	3.0	3.8	3.7	2.4	12.4	9.2	-0.4
Mali	1.6	3.0	1.9	2.0	5.4	-10.6	-8.9	-5.2
Mauritania	4.0	4.4	4.0	3.9	3.8	20.5	12.4	4.5
Mauritius	12.0	12.6	13.6	15.1	18.5	1.6	0.9	-2.9
Morocco	66.7	73.2	68.9	36.0	59.6	3.7	2.4	-2.2
Mozambique	3.0	2.6	3.5	6.4	5.8	4.1	-3.4	4.0
Namibia	5.7	5.1	8.9	11.3	10.3	4.6	-2.4	4.0
Niger	2.6	2.7	1.4	5.6	1.8	17.7	7.6	6.6
Nigeria	1.3	1.3	1.3	1.4	1.3	3.9	0.8	-0.4
Rwanda	3.5	3.4	5.1	4.7	6.1	26.1	1.7	21.0
São Tomé & Príncipe	3.8	5.4	5.1	2.4	3.9	15.2	11.5	0.2
Senegal	11.5	24.7	25.8	10.2	11.7	-4.3	2.0	-9.8
Seychelles	4.7	3.3	3.9	3.2	2.8	-4.6	6.1	-14.2
Sierra Leone	2.8	5.3	7.5	8.8	12.6	7.3	-5.9	9.7
Somalia	8.6	9.5	13.4	11.9	5.1	8.2	-0.2	5.0
South Africa	43.3	42.5	41.6	38.7	39.4	5.6	2.7	-0.5
Sudan	1.4	1.3	1.2	1.2	1.2	7.3	0.2	3.6
Swaziland	17.5	19.8	22.4	21.1	15.9	-0.6	1.8	-5.9
Tanzania	20.0	31.0	31.0	36.3	26.5	6.0	6.1	-3.6
Togo	15.7	15.4	8.4	4.8	4.0	0.6	1.6	-4.5
Tunisia	43.8	45.2	36.4	35.2	45.2	8.8	-0.4	5.7
Uganda	7.8	8.5	11.1	7.7	6.9	14.5	4.4	6.5
Zambia	3.4	2.2	2.5	2.4	3.5	6.8	5.7	-2.4
Zimbabwe	14.9	15.3	10.5	13.2	11.9	-10.7	2.7	-16.9
Africa	4.6	3.9	4.2	3.7	4.9	6.1	1.4	1.2

Sources: AfDB Statistics Department ; COMTRADE Database (Harmonized system, Rev.2) - UN Statistics Division and authors' calculations.

StatLink http://dx.doi.org/10.1787/888932419532

Table 9: **International Prices of Exports, 2003-10**

	Unit	2003	2004	2005	2006	2007	2008	2009	2010
Aluminum	**(USD/mt)**	**1 431.29**	**1 715.54**	**1 898.31**	**2 569.90**	**2 638.18**	**2 572.79**	**1 664.83**	**2 173.12**
Banana (US)	**(USD/mt)**	**374.79**	**524.58**	**602.84**	**677.24**	**675.81**	**844.21**	**847.14**	**868.32**
Coal (Australia)	**(USD/mt)**	...	...	...	**49.09**	**65.73**	**127.10**	**71.84**	**98.97**
Cocoa	**(cents/kg)**	**175.09**	**154.98**	**153.81**	**159.19**	**195.23**	**257.71**	**288.88**	**313.30**
Coffee (Arabica)	**(cents/kg)**	**141.54**	**177.40**	**253.22**	**252.21**	**272.37**	**308.16**	**317.11**	**432.01**
Coffee (Robusta)	**(cents/kg)**	**81.45**	**79.30**	**111.45**	**148.93**	**190.92**	**232.09**	**164.42**	**173.59**
Copper	**(USD/mt)**	**1 779.14**	**2 865.88**	**3 678.88**	**6 722.13**	**7 118.23**	**6 955.88**	**5 149.74**	**7 534.78**
Cotton	**(c/kg)**	**139.91**	**136.57**	**121.70**	**126.66**	**139.52**	**157.39**	**138.20**	**228.34**
Fish Meal	**(USD/mt)**	**610.71**	**648.58**	**730.96**	**1 166.33**	**1 177.25**	**1 133.08**	**1 230.25**	**1 687.42**
Gold	**(USD/toz)**	**363.51**	**409.21**	**444.84**	**604.34**	**696.72**	**871.71**	**972.97**	**1 224.66**
Groundnut oil	**(USD/mt)**	**1 243.17**	**1 161.00**	**1 060.44**	**970.23**	**1 352.08**	**2 131.12**	**1 183.67**	**1 403.96**
Iron ore	**(c/dmtu)**	**31.95**	**37.90**	**65.00**	**77.35**	**84.70**	**140.60**	**100.95**	...
Lead	**(c/kg)**	**51.50**	**88.65**	**97.64**	**128.97**	**258.00**	**209.07**	**171.93**	**214.84**
Logs Cameroon	**(USD/CM)**	...	...	...	**318.48**	**381.32**	**526.89**	**421.47**	**428.56**
Maize	**(USD/mt)**	**105.37**	**111.80**	**98.67**	**121.85**	**163.66**	**223.12**	**165.51**	**185.91**
Oil (crude)	**(USD/bbl)**	**28.85**	**38.30**	**54.43**	**65.39**	**72.70**	**97.64**	**61.86**	**79.64**
Palm oil	**(USD/mt)**	**443.25**	**471.33**	**422.08**	**478.35**	**780.25**	**948.54**	**682.83**	**900.83**
Phosphate (rock)	**(USD/mt)**	**38.00**	**40.98**	**42.00**	**44.21**	**70.93**	**345.59**	**121.66**	**123.02**
Rubber (US)	**(cents/kg)**	...	...	...	**231.28**	**248.03**	**284.08**	**214.64**	**386.62**

Table 9: **International Prices of Exports, 2003-10** (cont.)

	Unit	2003	2004	2005	2006	2007	2008	2009	2010
Sugar (EU)	**(cents/kg)**	**59.72**	**66.97**	**66.54**	**64.56**	**68.09**	**69.69**	**52.44**	**44.18**
Sugar (World)	**(c/kg)**	**15.63**	**15.80**	**21.79**	**32.59**	**22.22**	**28.21**	**40.00**	**46.93**
Sugar (US)	**(cents/kg)**	**47.37**	**45.47**	**46.93**	**48.76**	**45.77**	**46.86**	**54.88**	**79.25**
Tea (Avg. 3 auctions)	**(c/kg)**	**151.66**	**168.56**	**164.71**	**187.21**	**203.61**	**242.05**	**272.40**	**288.49**
Tea (Mombasa)	**(c/kg)**	**154.36**	**155.42**	**147.75**	**195.23**	**166.49**	**221.76**	**251.96**	**256.00**
Tobacco	**(USD/mt)**	**2 646.25**	**2 740.50**	**2 789.83**	**2 969.33**	**3 315.06**	**3 569.72**	**4 236.55**	...

Sources: World Bank, *Global Commodity Price Prospects*, March 2011.

StatLink http://dx.doi.org/10.1787/888932419551

Table 10: **Foreign Direct Investment, 2004-09 (USD million)**

	FDI inflows						FDI outflows						FDI inflows/GFCF (%)			Inward FDI* Potential Index
	2004	2005	2006	2007	2008	2009	2004	2005	2006	2007	2008	2009	2007	2008	2009	2008
Algeria	882	1081	1795	1662	2646	2847	258	57	35	295	318	309	4.7	5.6	5.9	70
Angola	5606	6794	9064	9796	16581	13101	35	221	194	912	2570	8	118.1	123.2	109.0	64
Benin	65	53	55	261	174	93	-1	0	-2	-6	-3	-4	23.8	12.9	5.7	138
Botswana	391	279	486	495	521	234	-39	56	50	51	-91	3	16.7	16.7	7.2	88
Burkina Faso	14	34	34	344	137	171	-9	0	1	0	0	1	24.3	8.2	11.8	129
Burundi	0	1	0	1	14	10	...	...	...	0	...	...	0.5	9.3	5.7	...
Cameroon	319	225	309	284	270	337	2	-9	-1	-2	2	-9	8.2	6.1	8.6	105
Cape Verde	68	82	131	190	212	120	...	...	...	0	-3	0	27.5	28.7	15.7	...
Central Afr. Rep.	29	32	35	57	117	42	...	...	...	...	...	...	37.8	57.5	21.2	...
Chad	467	-99	-279	-69	234	462	...	...	...	...	...	...	-6.2	18.5	35.1	...
Comoros	1	1	1	8	8	9	...	...	...	...	...	...	15.6	10.5	13.5	...
Congo	513	1475	1925	2275	2483	2083	5	...	...	...	...	...	57.2	65.9	60.7	92
Congo Dem. Rep.	409	...	256	1808	1727	951	8	13	18	18	54	30	92.8	61.4	40.0	130
Côte d'Ivoire	283	312	319	427	482	409	-26	52	-27	0	8	-7	22.6	18.5	16.3	126
Djibouti	39	59	164	195	234	100	...	...	...	...	...	...	54.6	51.1	26.3	...
Egypt	2157	5376	10043	11578	9495	6712	159	92	148	665	1920	571	42.2	31.2	22.3	93
Equatorial Guinea	341	769	470	1243	-794	1636	...	...	...	...	...	...	37.3	-19.8	29.0	...
Eritrea	-8	-1	0	0	0	0	...	...	...	...	...	...	-0.1	-0.1	0.0	...
Ethiopia	545	265	545	222	109	94	...	...	...	...	...	...	4.7	2.0	1.3	134
Gabon	320	242	268	269	209	33	-25	65	106	59	96	87	10.1	6.4	1.2	94
Gambia	49	45	71	76	70	47	...	...	...	...	...	...	132.4	59.5	41.5	111
Ghana	139	145	636	855	1220	1685	-1	...	...	...	9	7	16.7	20.5	36.0	106
Guinea	98	105	125	386	382	141	-1	-5	...	...	126	...	83.5	54.2	27.1	136
Guinea-Bissau	9	8	17	19	6	14	-8	1	0	0	0	0	34.7	9.5	15.3	...
Kenya	46	21	51	729	96	141	4	10	24	36	44	46	13.9	1.9	3.0	125
Lesotho	53	57	89	97	56	48	0	...	...	...	...	...	23.7	12.1	9.4	...
Liberia	75	83	108	132	200	378	304	437	346	363	382	364	100.8	128.1	239.3	...
Libya	357	1038	2013	4689	4111	2674	-286	128	-534	3933	5888	1165	76.0	46.7	37.2	36

Table 10: Foreign Direct Investment, 2004-09 (USD million) (cont.)

	FDI inflows						FDI outflows						FDI inflows/GFCF (%)			Inward FDI* Potential Index
	2004	2005	2006	2007	2008	2009	2004	2005	2006	2007	2008	2009	2007	2008	2009	2008
Madagascar	95	86	294	777	1180	543	...	...	...	...	...	...	38.3	37.2	26.1	135
Malawi	108	52	72	92	170	60	2	1	1	1	1	1	35.0	56.2	15.4	132
Mali	100	225	82	65	180	109	1	-1	1	7	3	4	4.7	11.4	7.2	123
Mauritania	392	814	106	138	338	-38	4	2	5	4	4	...	22.0	49.8	-5.1	...
Mauritius	11	42	105	339	383	257	32	48	10	58	52	38	17.9	16.7	11.7	...
Morocco	895	1653	2450	2803	2487	1331	31	75	445	621	485	470	11.9	9.0	4.5	96
Mozambique	245	108	154	427	592	881	0	0	0	0	0	3	30.7	28.5	32.1	115
Namibia	226	348	387	733	720	516	-22	-13	-12	3	5	-3	35.3	34.9	25.1	89
Niger	20	30	51	129	566	739	7	-4	-1	8	24	10	13.1	42.7	44.7	131
Nigeria	2127	4978	13956	6087	6814	5851	261	15	16	468	972	141	40.0	34.8	30.9	86
Rwanda	11	14	31	82	103	119	...	...	14	13	14	14	13.4	10.2	11.6	139
São Tomé & Príncipe	4	16	38	35	33	36	...	15	3	3	7	4	38.0	28.0	28.3	...
Senegal	64	52	210	273	272	208	13	-8	10	25	9	15	9.0	6.7	6.2	127
Seychelles	38	86	146	239	252	243	8	33	8	26	30	6	71.6	75.7	83.2	...
Sierra Leone	61	83	59	97	53	33	...	-8	...	...	...	...	73.9	15.7	12.0	114
Somalia	-5	24	96	141	87	108	...	...	...	...	...	...	25.9	16.1	21.2	...
South Africa	798	6647	-527	5695	9006	5696	1350	930	6063	2966	-3134	1584	9.9	14.5	8.9	72
Sudan	1511	2305	3541	2436	2601	3034	...	...	7	11	98	45	21.4	21.2	27.6	119
Swaziland	71	-46	121	37	106	66	-1	21	1	-23	8	-7	10.0	26.9	15.8	...
Tanzania	331	494	597	647	679	645	...	...	...	...	...	...	12.9	10.3	9.8	118
Togo	59	77	77	49	24	50	-13	-15	-14	-1	-16	-10	11.0	6.7	11.5	133
Tunisia	639	783	3308	1616	2758	1688	4	13	33	20	42	77	19.0	27.0	15.6	68
Uganda	295	380	644	733	787	799	...	...	...	...	...	...	23.8	23.9	21.1	128
Zambia	364	357	616	1324	939	959	...	...	...	86	...	...	43.2	25.9	26.3	122
Zimbabwe	9	103	40	69	52	60	0	1	0	3	8	0	6.6	9.5	9.9	141
Africa	21736	38192	55382	63091	72179	58565	2056	2222	6951	10622	9934	4962	23.9	22.9	18.7	...

Note: * The potential Index is based on 12 economic and policy variables. See note on methodology for further details.

Sources: UNCTAD, FDI Online Database (March 2011) and World investment Report 2010.

StatLink http://dx.doi.org/10.1787/888932419570

Table 11: Aid Flows*, 2004-09 (USD million)

	ODA net total, All donors						ODA net total, DAC countries						ODA net total, Multilateral					
	2004	2005	2006	2007	2008	2009	2004	2005	2006	2007	2008	2009	2004	2005	2006	2007	2008	2009
Algeria	315	346	209	390	319	319	235	267	206	292	245	200	80	69	- 3	93	101	107
Angola	1 144	415	164	248	369	239	1 016	248	- 45	103	210	131	131	167	117	144	151	98
Benin	394	347	378	474	641	683	210	208	229	238	305	326	184	140	150	233	332	354
Botswana	50	48	69	108	720	280	32	30	36	64	683	223	20	20	34	45	39	57
Burkina Faso	642	693	874	951	1 001	1 084	331	339	386	412	475	453	306	347	478	524	519	629
Burundi	364	364	431	475	509	549	186	180	223	202	255	261	178	183	208	273	253	288
Cameroon	791	413	1 704	1 926	549	649	573	332	1 506	1 697	298	268	218	79	193	220	240	381
Cape Verde	143	162	138	165	222	196	91	104	99	114	163	162	51	56	38	50	59	34
Central Afr. Rep.	110	89	134	177	256	237	55	61	65	118	129	99	55	28	68	59	128	138
Chad	337	380	288	358	419	561	163	162	153	227	277	356	171	214	132	130	141	206
Comoros	26	23	31	44	37	51	14	15	20	20	21	28	12	8	10	25	15	22
Congo	115	1 425	258	119	485	283	48	1 344	169	49	383	226	68	81	88	70	102	56
Congo Dem. Rep.	1 919	1 881	2 197	1 356	1 769	2 354	1 165	990	1 501	789	986	1 099	754	894	697	567	778	1 252
Côte d'Ivoire	161	91	247	171	623	2 366	197	129	200	112	200	1 723	- 37	- 38	48	59	421	641
Djibouti	64	74	115	112	121	162	40	54	90	76	66	98	27	21	24	37	45	54
Egypt	1 506	994	873	1 107	1 344	925	1 178	667	542	793	967	580	311	240	287	238	270	223
Equatorial Guinea	29	38	26	31	32	32	23	30	19	26	19	25	6	9	7	6	13	7
Eritrea	265	349	126	158	144	145	177	226	63	47	53	43	92	127	64	109	84	87
Ethiopia	1 828	1 927	1 980	2 578	3 328	3 820	1 027	1 187	1 026	1 245	1 843	1 817	766	714	931	1 302	1 453	1 984
Gabon	40	60	29	51	62	78	24	30	32	34	38	53	16	31	- 3	16	24	25
Gambia	55	60	73	73	94	128	12	15	25	33	28	22	43	45	43	37	62	105
Ghana	1 417	1 149	1 213	1 164	1 305	1 583	929	615	595	710	726	820	484	529	618	453	576	756
Guinea	278	198	170	228	328	215	178	126	103	124	210	171	100	61	64	96	117	48
Guinea-Bissau	76	66	87	122	132	146	29	27	39	44	53	51	48	39	48	78	78	94
Kenya	658	752	943	1 323	1 363	1 778	470	521	776	827	953	1 224	188	230	167	496	408	549
Lesotho	98	67	71	129	144	123	35	40	38	62	66	71	64	29	33	67	78	48
Liberia	213	222	260	701	1 249	505	163	144	187	229	819	341	50	78	73	471	403	163
Libya**	...	24	38	19	60	39	...	17	33	16	52	32	...	3	3	3	6	6

Table 11: **Aid Flows*, 2004-09 (USD million)** (cont.)

	ODA net total, All donors						ODA net total, DAC countries						ODA net total, Multilateral					
	2004	2005	2006	2007	2008	2009	2004	2005	2006	2007	2008	2009	2004	2005	2006	2007	2008	2009
Madagascar	1 263	913	757	894	843	445	685	498	261	387	274	242	579	416	492	502	565	202
Malawi	506	573	698	744	924	772	308	325	398	401	432	435	196	247	288	332	482	333
Mali	588	704	831	1 020	964	985	328	371	398	558	531	575	261	326	424	458	433	409
Mauritania	194	187	208	346	320	287	84	105	94	133	139	122	110	81	113	212	156	144
Mauritius	33	34	19	69	110	156	15	22	9	44	16	64	21	10	13	28	95	94
Morocco	705	691	1 044	1 073	1 063	912	396	288	569	631	614	705	241	313	361	327	370	305
Mozambique	1 243	1 297	1 606	1 778	1 996	2 013	731	760	938	1 073	1 341	1 288	508	535	664	682	652	724
Namibia	173	125	152	217	210	326	124	88	106	144	150	247	33	33	44	73	58	78
Niger	547	520	526	542	607	470	306	254	235	233	269	255	241	265	291	307	336	213
Nigeria	577	6 409	11 428	1 956	1 290	1 659	314	5 931	10 820	1 385	637	688	263	477	607	570	651	969
Rwanda	490	577	589	722	933	934	217	281	321	375	452	520	273	296	267	347	480	412
São Tomé & Príncipe	34	32	23	36	47	31	22	18	18	31	26	20	12	14	5	5	21	11
Senegal	1 070	698	838	872	1 064	1 018	756	444	510	453	554	514	316	254	318	390	472	499
Seychelles	10	15	14	9	13	23	6	8	7	1	5	12	3	7	7	8	7	11
Sierra Leone	376	340	347	545	367	437	163	129	180	381	175	196	213	211	167	164	193	241
Somalia	199	237	391	384	758	662	140	145	263	257	566	500	58	92	124	124	185	152
South Africa	629	690	715	807	1 125	1 075	459	466	561	594	882	861	169	224	154	213	242	211
Sudan	992	1 823	2 044	2 112	2 384	2 289	849	1 455	1 518	1 665	1 821	1 911	119	319	440	334	459	317
Swaziland	25	47	35	51	70	58	7	21	12	12	18	19	17	26	23	39	53	40
Tanzania	1 768	1 499	1 839	2 820	2 331	2 934	1 030	861	996	1 839	1 373	1 409	737	629	846	982	960	1 527
Togo	64	82	79	121	330	499	52	59	55	65	176	362	12	23	24	58	154	136
Tunisia	352	362	431	321	332	474	232	268	286	194	251	350	120	101	154	137	90	130
Uganda	1 216	1 192	1 554	1 737	1 641	1 786	684	691	938	1 003	1 006	1 013	530	499	613	731	632	769
Zambia	1 130	1 172	1 449	1 008	1 116	1 269	746	823	1 115	714	704	701	382	347	331	295	412	566
Zimbabwe	187	373	278	479	612	737	167	187	200	372	532	620	20	186	78	106	80	116
Africa Unspecified	2 221	2 228	2 577	3 432	4 313	5 252	1 710	1 799	2 051	2 508	3 317	3 052	511	406	484	854	971	2 139
Africa Total	**29 631**	**35 480**	**43 597**	**38 854**	**43 385**	**47 030**	**19 128**	**24 404**	**31 177**	**24 154**	**26 782**	**27 579**	**10 333**	**10 742**	**11 948**	**14 179**	**16 103**	**19 159**

Note: ODA : Official Development Assistance.
DAC : Development Assistance Committee of OECD.
* Net disbursements.
** Libya has belonged to the recipient countries of Official Aid (OA) from 2000 to 2004 and has been re-included in the new list of ODA recipients in 2005.

Source: OECD Development Assistance Committee 2011.

StatLink http://dx.doi.org/10.1787/888932419589

Table 12: External Debt Indicators

Country	Debt outstanding, at year end: Total (Million USD)	Of Which: Multilateral (as % of total)	Of Which: Bilateral (as % of total)	Of Which: Private (as % of total)	Total debt outstanding (as % of GDP)				Debt Service (as % of Exports of goods and services)			
	2009	2009	2009	2009	2009	2010 (e)	2011 (p)	2012 (p)	2009	2010 (e)	2011 (p)	2012 (p)
Algeria	5 268	0.2	99.8	0.0	3.8	3.1	2.3	1.7	1.1	2.6	2.8	2.8
Angola	17 902	2.6	97.4	0.0	23.7	22.2	17.8	17.3	12.5	10.0	10.6	7.5
Benin	1 141	74.7	25.3	0.0	17.9	20.8	20.5	20.7	4.5	6.3	7.3	7.1
Botswana	2 381	56.5	0.0	43.5	20.5	18.5	21.2	25.4	10.2	9.2	12.8	15.5
Burkina Faso	1 931	76.4	23.6	0.0	23.1	27.0	24.1	25.5	4.8	4.9	4.6	4.7
Burundi	364	62.1	37.9	0.0	29.3	31.1	30.2	29.2	1.9	2.6	5.4	8.9
Cameroon	1 096	23.2	76.8	0.0	4.7	5.9	7.9	9.2	9.5	7.1	6.7	5.7
Cape Verde	1 029	75.3	1.4	23.3	65.3	65.0	65.7	67.6	18.8	21.7	19.9	18.0
Central Afr.Rep.	264	15.1	84.9	0.0	13.3	15.2	15.4	14.9	25.7	39.3	34.4	30.8
Chad	1 701	84.9	10.5	4.6	23.8	26.5	25.7	23.7	2.8	3.0	2.9	3.2
Comoros	289	76.8	23.2	0.0	51.9	39.5	34.9	31.6	10.6	7.4	5.0	6.7
Congo	13 705	34.4	65.6	0.0	122.3	26.6	46.5	62.2	21.2	2.3	1.0	1.1
Congo Dem. Rep.	5 049	9.2	90.8	0.0	58.0	16.5	13.6	13.0	2.1	9.4	0.7	0.8
Côte d'Ivoire	17 786	20.3	50.5	29.2	77.0	75.0	75.0	70.3	10.6	10.9	10.8	14.2
Djibouti	626	53.6	46.4	0.0	62.5	58.1	54.9	52.3	7.2	7.5	8.0	8.0
Egypt	31 531	25.3	71.4	3.3	16.7	14.1	13.6	11.9	12.0	9.7	9.1	8.3
Equatorial Guinea	620	NM	100.0	0.0	6.3	9.7	12.9	15.5	0.2	0.3	0.6	2.7
Eritrea	895	64.5	35.5	0.0	48.2	43.5	35.8	30.5	35.9	34.1	10.4	10.1
Ethiopia	4 552	46.0	41.5	12.5	14.1	15.5	25.1	28.5	2.4	3.8	5.5	6.8
Gabon	2 035	18.8	83.4	-2.2	18.7	14.9	15.3	15.2	7.4	6.7	5.2	4.8
Gambia	330	60.3	39.7	0.0	34.2	32.5	30.7	29.5	30.9	31.2	31.4	30.8
Ghana	7 269	39.0	29.9	31.1	50.5	48.0	43.0	43.4	4.5	3.8	3.2	2.6
Guinea	3 015	62.4	37.6	0.0	68.8	67.4	58.6	22.6	8.3	12.2	7.8	150.6
Guinea-Bissau	1 064	45.6	54.4	0.0	12.7	1.9	1.9	1.9	6.4	458.0	2.7	2.8
Kenya	7 831	48.2	48.9	2.9	26.6	25.0	26.1	27.1	5.0	5.4	4.9	6.3
Lesotho	748	86.1	13.9	0.0	44.5	46.5	55.9	62.6	4.3	4.3	4.4	4.6
Liberia	1 660	9.3	91.7	-1.1	188.9	11.6	10.8	11.4	335.7	126.0	2.0	3.3
Libya	5 574	NM	0.0	100.0	9.4	7.5	9.3	7.3	0.0	0.0	0.0	0.0

Table 12: External Debt Indicators (cont.)

Country	Debt outstanding, at year end: Total (Million USD)	Of Which: Multilateral (as % of total)	Bilateral (as % of total)	Private (as % of total)	Total debt outstanding (as % of GDP)				Debt Service (as % of Exports of goods and services)			
	2009	2009	2009	2009	2009	2010 (e)	2011 (p)	2012 (p)	2009	2010 (e)	2011 (p)	2012 (p)
Madagascar	2 346	65.4	34.6	0.0	26.9	29.3	31.5	33.6	6.7	7.1	4.4	7.9
Malawi	900	49.4	50.6	0.0	19.1	18.8	19.2	19.6	1.2	0.9	1.9	2.0
Mali	3 260	56.4	9.3	34.3	36.4	43.1	43.4	45.5	3.3	2.5	2.6	2.2
Mauritania	3 123	54.9	35.3	9.9	103.2	54.0	57.6	63.4	3.7	5.5	5.5	6.5
Mauritius	1 337	49.9	7.2	42.9	15.1	12.8	15.7	17.7	4.5	4.2	4.2	3.6
Morocco	21 163	42.2	49.3	8.5	23.2	23.3	23.0	23.3	7.5	7.2	7.1	6.8
Mozambique	5 073	47.9	0.8	51.4	51.8	48.9	53.8	55.8	20.0	17.1	11.3	12.8
Namibia	2 262	NM	20.7	79.3	24.6	19.3	19.2	18.5	14.8	10.9	9.7	9.2
Niger	832	69.1	30.9	0.0	15.8	17.2	18.9	18.8	2.0	1.7	2.6	2.3
Nigeria	4 438	43.2	56.8	0.0	2.6	2.4	2.3	2.3	1.0	0.7	0.6	0.5
Rwanda	749	84.5	15.5	0.0	14.2	20.2	23.3	22.7	1.8	3.0	6.3	7.0
São Tomé & Príncipe	124	23.3	76.7	0.0	66.7	67.8	68.4	66.1	7.9	22.4	15.4	13.8
Senegal	3 775	51.7	33.3	15.0	29.5	30.3	29.3	29.0	5.5	5.4	6.9	6.7
Seychelles	729	3.1	96.9	0.0	76.7	47.7	46.1	45.6	14.1	8.3	5.8	4.5
Sierra Leone	683	69.4	30.6	0.0	34.1	29.3	19.7	19.9	4.7	4.0	4.4	3.5
Somalia	2 973	27.1	0.0	72.9	...	...	...	...	...	...	...	...
South Africa	79 031	0.5	26.6	72.9	28.0	24.8	27.1	29.1	46.6	39.4	32.1	40.7
Sudan	35 687	15.7	84.3	0.0	68.9	58.4	51.1	47.3	3.7	5.9	7.1	6.7
Swaziland	531	61.0	24.2	14.8	16.8	14.6	14.4	15.5	2.5	2.8	3.6	4.7
Tanzania	7 137	48.8	36.9	14.3	33.4	30.9	30.3	29.8	5.0	3.6	4.4	5.9
Togo	1 740	51.0	49.0	0.0	55.0	12.6	14.0	14.1	5.9	6.1	2.3	2.6
Tunisia	21 444	30.0	41.2	28.8	49.3	44.3	43.4	41.0	55.3	58.4	54.7	52.4
Uganda	2 420	81.0	19.0	0.0	14.4	15.0	15.6	14.4	1.8	2.8	3.0	3.0
Zambia	1 578	28.9	71.1	0.0	12.3	9.7	10.3	12.6	1.9	1.3	1.4	1.5
Zimbabwe	6 853	0.0	0.0	100.0	121.8	116.7	109.1	107.0	26.5	23.5	20.1	19.0
Africa	347 844	23.2	48.4	28.4	23.6	20.3	20.5	20.4	14.6	12.1	10.3	11.4

Sources: AfDB Statistics Department; IMF, World Economic Outlook Database, March 2011; GDF Online Database, Worldbank and author's estimates and projections.

StatLink http://dx.doi.org/10.1787/888932419608

Table 13: Demographic Indicators

	Total population (thousands)	Urban population (% of total)	Sex ratio (males per 100 females)	Population growth rate (%)		Infant mortality rate (per 1000)	Total fertility rate (per woman)	Mortality under age 5 (per 1000)	Distribution by age (%)		
									0-14	15-64	65+
	2010	2010	2010	2000-05	2005-10	2010	2010	2010	2010		
Algeria	35 423	66.5	101.9	1.5	1.6	28.2	2.3	30	27.0	68.4	5.4
Angola	18 993	58.5	97.2	3.3	2.9	110.9	5.5	193	44.7	52.9	2.7
Benin	9 212	42.0	102.0	3.6	3.4	80.8	5.3	113	42.9	53.8	3.6
Botswana	1 978	61.1	100.1	1.4	1.5	32.2	2.8	44	32.9	63.2	4.3
Burkina Faso	16 287	20.4	99.9	3.5	3.7	77.8	5.8	150	46.4	51.6	2.1
Burundi	8 519	11.0	96.3	2.8	3.1	94.6	4.3	159	37.9	59.3	3.2
Cameroon	19 958	58.4	100.0	2.5	2.4	83.7	4.5	138	40.8	55.7	4.0
Cape Verde	513	61.1	91.7	1.8	1.5	23.4	2.6	28	35.5	60.4	4.8
Central Afr. Rep.	4 506	38.9	96.6	1.9	2.0	101.4	4.6	172	40.3	55.8	4.4
Chad	11 506	27.6	98.9	3.8	3.0	127.0	6.0	205	45.6	51.6	3.1
Comoros	691	28.2	100.7	2.3	2.4	44.1	3.8	56	38.1	58.8	3.5
Congo	3 759	62.1	99.7	2.5	2.0	79.1	4.2	128	40.2	56.0	4.3
Congo Dem. Rep.	67 827	35.2	98.3	3.2	3.0	113.9	5.8	194	46.4	51.0	2.9
Côte d'Ivoire	21 571	50.1	103.6	2.3	2.4	83.3	4.4	117	40.4	55.7	4.3
Djibouti	879	88.1	99.9	2.1	1.8	80.1	3.7	117	35.6	61.1	3.6
Egypt	84 474	42.8	101.1	2.0	1.9	32.5	2.8	38	32.1	63.2	5.2
Equatorial Guinea	693	39.7	98.4	3.0	2.8	95.4	5.2	161	40.7	56.4	3.3
Eritrea	5 224	21.6	96.9	4.5	3.4	51.0	4.4	70	41.5	56.0	2.8
Ethiopia	84 976	17.6	99.0	2.8	2.8	74.9	5.1	123	43.2	53.6	3.6
Gabon	1 501	86.0	99.9	2.2	1.9	47.2	3.2	73	35.6	60.1	5.1
Gambia	1 751	58.1	98.4	3.4	2.9	74.0	4.9	112	42.1	55.1	3.0
Ghana	24 333	51.5	102.8	2.4	2.2	70.9	4.2	114	38.1	58.2	4.1
Guinea	10 324	35.4	102.0	2.0	2.4	93.0	5.2	136	42.6	54.1	3.6
Guinea-Bissau	1 647	30.0	98.2	2.6	2.4	109.4	5.6	188	42.6	53.9	3.9
Kenya	40 863	22.2	100.0	2.8	2.8	60.4	4.8	97	42.8	54.5	3.0
Lesotho	2 084	26.9	89.6	1.1	0.9	65.0	3.2	96	38.5	56.7	5.4
Liberia	4 102	61.5	98.8	3.6	4.6	91.3	4.9	132	42.5	54.4	3.4
Libya	6 546	77.9	106.8	2.2	2.1	16.9	2.6	18	30.1	65.6	5.0

Table 13: **Demographic Indicators** (cont.)

	Total population (thousands)	Urban population (% of total)	Sex ratio (males per 100 females)	Population growth rate (%)		Infant mortality rate (per 1000)	Total fertility rate (per woman)	Mortality under age 5 (per 1000)	Distribution by age (%) 0-14	15-64	65+
	2010	2010	2010	2000-05	2005-10	2010	2010	2010	2010		
Madagascar	20 146	30.2	99.2	3.1	2.9	61.0	4.5	93	42.5	54.5	3.5
Malawi	15 692	19.8	98.9	3.1	3.0	78.4	5.4	111	45.9	51.0	3.5
Mali	13 323	33.3	97.6	2.5	2.5	102.9	5.3	182	44.1	53.6	2.4
Mauritania	3 366	41.4	102.9	2.9	2.5	71.0	4.3	116	39.2	58.1	2.8
Mauritius*	1 297	42.6	98.1	1.0	0.7	14.0	1.8	17	22.2	70.3	8.8
Morocco	32 381	56.7	96.4	1.2	1.2	27.7	2.3	32	28.0	66.6	6.2
Mozambique	23 406	38.4	94.9	2.8	2.5	83.3	4.9	140	43.9	52.8	3.7
Namibia	2 212	38.0	97.4	2.0	2.0	30.4	3.2	43	36.4	59.9	4.2
Niger	15 891	16.7	100.4	3.8	4.3	83.7	7.0	162	50.1	47.9	2.1
Nigeria	158 259	49.8	100.5	2.6	2.5	106.6	5.1	181	42.4	54.5	3.5
Rwanda	10 277	18.9	94.0	2.6	2.9	95.9	5.3	148	42.4	55.2	2.8
São Tomé & Príncipe	165	62.2	98.1	1.8	1.7	70.1	3.6	91	40.3	55.8	4.5
Senegal	12 861	42.9	98.3	2.8	2.8	57.0	4.8	115	43.3	54.3	2.5
Seychelles	85	...	...	0.4	0.5	...	...		...	...	...
Sierra Leone	5 836	38.4	95.1	4.2	2.9	101.5	5.1	143	43.5	54.7	1.9
Somalia	9 359	37.4	98.4	2.6	2.4	105.9	6.3	173	44.9	52.4	3.0
South Africa	50 492	61.7	97.3	1.4	1.0	42.8	2.5	61	30.3	65.1	5.2
Sudan	43 192	45.2	101.4	2.2	2.3	65.7	4.0	105	38.7	57.7	4.1
Swaziland	1 202	25.5	95.9	0.8	1.4	58.9	3.4	88	38.8	57.8	3.8
Tanzania	45 040	26.4	99.5	2.9	3.1	59.8	5.5	97	44.7	52.1	3.5
Togo	6 780	43.4	98.1	2.8	2.6	68.3	4.1	92	39.5	56.9	4.0
Tunisia	10 374	67.3	101.1	0.9	1.0	18.5	1.8	21	22.8	70.4	7.9
Uganda	33 796	13.3	100.4	3.5	3.6	70.3	6.2	115	48.7	48.7	2.9
Zambia	13 257	35.7	99.6	2.4	2.6	86.5	5.6	146	46.2	50.8	3.4
Zimbabwe	12 644	38.3	93.7	0.0	0.3	51.4	3.3	83	39.5	56.4	4.8
Africa	1 031 472	40.0	99.5	2.5	2.4	78.6	4.4	127.2	40.3	56.3	3.8

Note: * Including Agalega, Rodrigues and Saint Brandon.

Source: AfDB Statistics Department ; United Nations, Department of Economic and Social Affairs, Population Division, *World Population Prospects*, The 2008 Revision.

StatLink http://dx.doi.org/10.1787/888932419627

Table 14: Poverty and Income Distribution Indicators

	National poverty line*				International poverty line			Gini coefficient**		Share of consumption (%)	
		Population below the poverty line (%)			Population below the poverty line (%)						
	Survey year	Rural	Urban	National	Survey year	Below 1 USD	Below 2 USD	Survey year	Index	Lowest 10%	Highest 10%
Algeria	2000	...	...	15.0	2000	0.9	...	2000	35.3	2.8	26.9
Angola	2001	94.3	57.0	68.0	2000	54.3	...	2000	58.6	0.6	44.7
Benin	1999	33.0	23.3	29.0	2003	47.3	73.7	2003	38.6	2.9	31.0
Botswana	2003	...	...	30.3	1994	31.2	...	2003	61.0	1.3	51.2
Burkina Faso	2003	52.3	19.9	46.4	2003	56.5	81.0	2003	39.6	3.0	32.4
Burundi	2006	37.0	...	36.2	2006	81.3	87.6	2006	33.3	4.1	28.0
Cameroon	2001	49.9	22.1	40.2	2001	32.8	50.6	2001	44.6	2.4	35.5
Cape Verde	2002	55.1	25.0	36.7	2001	20.6	...	2001	50.5	1.9	40.6
Central Afr. Rep.	2003	...	...	50.2	2003	62.4	...	2003	43.6	2.1	33.0
Chad	1996	67.0	63.0	64.0	2003	61.9	...	2003	39.8	2.6	30.8
Comoros	...	...	...	...	2004	46.1	...	2004	64.3	0.9	55.2
Congo	2005	57.7	55.4	50.1	2005	54.1	...	2005	47.3	2.1	37.1
Congo Dem. Rep.	2005	...	...	71.3	2006	59.2	...	2006	44.4	2.3	34.7
Côte d'Ivoire	2002	49.0	24.0	38.4	2002	23.3	48.8	2002	48.4	2.0	39.6
Djibouti	2002	...	...	42.1	2002	18.8	...	2002	40.0	2.4	30.9
Egypt	1999-00	...	...	16.7	2005	2.0	43.9	2005	32.1	3.9	27.6
Equatorial Guinea	2003	...	...	38.1	...	...	...	...	...	...	...
Eritrea	1993-94	...	...	53.0	...	...	...	...	...	...	...
Ethiopia	1999-00	45.0	37.0	44.2	2005	39.0	77.8	2005	29.8	4.1	25.6
Gabon	2005	45.0	30.0	33.0	2005	4.8	...	2005	41.5	2.5	32.7
Gambia	2003	63.0	...	61.3	2003	34.3	82.9	2003	47.3	2.0	36.9
Ghana	2006	39.2	10.8	28.5	2006	30.0	78.5	2006	42.8	2.0	32.8
Guinea	1994	...	...	40.0	2003	70.1	50.2	2003	43.3	2.4	34.4
Guinea-Bissau	2002	...	...	65.7	2002	48.8	96.7	2002	35.5	2.9	28.0
Kenya	2005-06	49.1	33.7	45.9	2005	19.7	58.3	2005	47.7	1.8	37.8
Lesotho	2002-03	...	...	56.6	2003	43.4	56.1	2003	52.5	1.0	39.4
Liberia	2002	...	...	76.2	2007	83.7	...	2007	52.6	2.4	30.1
Libya	2000-05	...	...	14.0	...	...	...	...	...	...	

Table 14: Poverty and Income Distribution Indicators (cont.)

	National poverty line* Population below the poverty line (%)				International poverty line Population below the poverty line (%)			Gini coefficient**		Share of consumption (%)	
	Survey year	Rural	Urban	National	Survey year	Below 1 USD	Below 2 USD	Survey year	Index	Lowest 10%	Highest 10%
Madagascar	2005	73.5	52.0	68.7	2005	67.8	85.1	2005	47.2	2.6	41.5
Malawi	2006	47.0	25.0	45.0	2004	73.9	76.1	2004	39.0	3.0	31.9
Mali	2005	...	...	47.5	2006	51.4	90.6	2006	39.0	2.7	30.5
Mauritania	2000	61.2	25.4	46.3	2000	21.2	63.1	2000	39.0	2.5	29.6
Mauritiusa	...	...	...	...	...	...	...	2006	38.9	...	...
Morocco	1999	27.2	12.0	19.0	2007	2.5	14.3	2007	40.9	2.7	33.2
Mozambique	2002-03	55.3	51.5	54.1	2003	74.7	78.4	2003	47.1	2.1	39.2
Namibia	...	...	...	...	2004	32.8	55.8	2004	60.0	0.6	65.0
Niger	1993	66.0	52.0	63.0	2005	65.9	85.3	2005	43.9	2.3	35.7
Nigeria	1996	...	...	65.6	2004	64.4	90.8	2004	42.9	2.0	32.4
Rwanda	2005-06	62.5	41.5	56.9	2006	57.0	83.7	2006	46.7	2.1	37.8
São Tomé & Príncipe	2001	...	...	53.8	...	...	...	...	...	...	...
Senegal	2001	...	...	53.9	2005	33.5	63.0	2005	39.2	2.5	30.1
Seychelles	...	...	...	...	...	...	...	...	...	...	...
Sierra Leone	2004	79.0	56.4	70.2	2003	53.4	74.5	2003	42.5	2.6	33.6
Somalia	...	...	...	...	...	...	...	...	...	...	...
South Africa	2000	...	...	45.0	2000	26.2	34.1	2000	57.8	1.3	44.9
Sudan	...	...	...	...	...	...	...	...	...	...	...
Swaziland	2001	75.0	...	69.2	2001	62.9	22.5	2001	50.7	1.8	40.8
Tanzania	2000-01	38.7	29.5	35.7	2000	88.5	89.9	2000	34.6	3.1	27.0
Togo	1995	...	...	72.2	2006	38.7	...	2006	34.4	3.3	27.1
Tunisia	2005	...	...	3.8	2000	2.6	6.6	2000	40.8	2.4	31.6
Uganda	2003	41.7	12.2	37.7	2005	51.5	...	2005	42.6	2.6	34.1
Zambia	2003	74.0	52.0	68.0	2004	64.3	94.1	2004	50.7	1.3	38.9
Zimbabwe	1995-96	48.0	7.9	34.9	2004	61.9	...	2004	50.1	1.8	40.3

Notes: * The national poverty line is defined as two-thirds of the average consumption.
** The Gini coefficient is defined on income distribution.

Sources: Domestic authorities and World Bank (Povcal 2009), World Development Indicators, online Database, Country DHS,

StatLink http://dx.doi.org/10.1787/888932419646

Table 15: Access to Services

	Telecommunications						Access to electricity		Water supply coverage			Sanitation coverage		
	Main telephone line per 100 inhabitants		Mobile line per 100 inhabitants		Internet users per 100 inhabitants		Electricity consumption (KWh - millions)		Total	Urban	Rural	Total	Urban	Rural
	2002	2009	2002	2009	2002	2009	2002	2007	2008			2008		
Algeria	6.21	7.38	1.43	93.79	1.59	13.47	25 542	34 455	83	85	79	95	98	88
Angola	0.53	1.64	0.92	43.84	0.27	3.28	1 671	2 969	50	60	38	57	86	18
Benin	0.88	1.42	3.08	56.33	0.70	2.24	596	720	75	84	69	12	24	4
Botswana	8.36	7.05	18.75	96.12	3.39	6.15	2 139	2 781	95	99	90	60	74	39
Burkina Faso	0.50	0.97	0.89	24.27	0.20	1.13	465	727	76	95	72	11	33	6
Burundi	0.33	0.38	0.77	10.10	0.12	1.90	155	189	72	83	71	46	49	46
Cameroon	0.67	2.23	4.22	41.00	0.36	3.84	3 300	5 253	74	92	51	47	56	35
Cape Verde	15.44	14.22	9.45	57.48	3.52	29.67	178	261	84	85	82	54	65	38
Central Afr. Rep.	0.23	0.27	0.32	13.57	0.13	0.51	108	160	67	92	51	34	43	28
Chad	0.13	0.52	0.38	20.36	0.17	1.50	84	94	50	67	44	9	23	4
Comoros	1.78	3.18	0.00	18.49	0.55	3.59	31	47	95	91	97	36	50	30
Congo	0.69	0.66	6.98	58.94	0.16	6.66	577	798	71	95	34	30	31	29
Congo Dem. Rep.	0.02	0.06	1.04	14.33	0.09	...	4 767	7 334	46	80	28	23	23	23
Côte d'Ivoire	1.80	1.34	5.68	62.56	0.50	4.59	3 690	4 821	80	93	68	23	36	11
Djibouti	1.33	1.95	1.97	14.90	0.49	3.00	190	280	92	98	52	56	63	10
Egypt	10.69	12.42	6.17	66.69	2.72	24.26	82 228	123 345	99	100	98	94	97	92
Equatorial Guinea	1.57	1.48	5.71	29.57	0.32	2.13	67	95	...	...	...	...	...	...
Eritrea	0.91	0.96	0.00	2.78	0.23	...	245	273	61	74	57	14	52	4
Ethiopia	0.51	1.10	0.07	4.89	0.07	0.54	1 905	3 479	38	98	26	12	29	8
Gabon	2.49	1.80	21.67	93.11	1.94	6.70	1 405	1 778	87	95	41	33	33	30
Gambia	2.76	2.87	7.19	84.04	1.80	7.63	147	223	92	96	86	67	68	65
Ghana	1.34	1.12	1.89	63.38	0.83	5.44	7 790	6 819	82	90	74	13	18	7
Guinea	0.30	0.22	1.04	34.65	0.40	0.94	1 005	958	71	89	61	19	34	11
Guinea-Bissau	0.82	0.30	0.00	34.79	1.02	2.30	60	70	61	83	51	21	49	9
Kenya	0.97	1.67	3.58	48.65	1.21	10.04	5 362	6 721	59	83	52	31	27	32
Lesotho	1.48	1.94	7.12	31.98	1.08	3.72	341	223	85	97	81	29	40	25
Liberia	0.23	0.05	0.16	21.29	0.03	0.51	315	333	68	79	51	17	25	4
Libya	12.93	17.15	1.26	77.94	2.24	5.51	15 266	23 667	...	...	...	97	97	96

Table 15: Access to Services (cont.)

	Telecommunications						Access to electricity		Water supply coverage			Sanitation coverage		
	Main telephone line per 100 inhabitants		Mobile line per 100 inhabitants		Internet users per 100 inhabitants		Electricity consumption (KWh - millions)		Total	Urban	Rural	Total	Urban	Rural
	2002	2009	2002	2009	2002	2009	2002	2007	2008			2008		
Madagascar	0.37	0.95	1.01	32.02	0.34	1.63	760	900	41	71	29	11	15	10
Malawi	0.58	1.15	0.69	15.72	0.22	4.69	1 278	1 620	80	95	77	56	51	57
Mali	0.51	0.65	0.42	34.17	0.23	1.92	409	487	56	81	44	36	45	32
Mauritania	1.15	2.26	8.98	66.32	0.36	2.28	276	688	49	52	47	26	50	9
Mauritius	26.07	29.63	28.50	84.36	10.25	22.51	1 904	2 424	99	100	99	91	93	90
Morocco	3.82	10.99	21.02	79.11	2.37	41.30	17 128	25 358	81	98	60	69	83	52
Mozambique	0.43	0.32	1.32	26.08	0.26	2.68	6 103	12 398	47	77	29	17	38	4
Namibia	6.40	6.54	7.90	56.05	2.63	5.87	2 265	3 699	92	99	88	33	60	17
Niger	0.19	0.43	0.49	17.00	0.13	0.76	412	585	48	96	39	9	34	4
Nigeria	0.54	0.92	1.20	48.16	0.32	28.43	20 928	22 383	58	75	42	32	36	28
Rwanda	0.29	0.33	0.96	24.30	0.29	4.50	214	234	65	77	62	54	50	55
São Tomé & Príncipe	4.39	4.79	1.36	39.32	7.58	16.41	32	43	89	89	88	26	30	19
Senegal	2.15	2.22	5.30	55.06	1.01	14.50	1 974	2 237	69	92	52	51	69	38
Seychelles	25.90	30.95	54.52	131.36	14.30	...	193	251	...	100	...	...	97	...
Sierra Leone	0.53	0.58	1.48	20.36	0.18	0.26	153	58	49	86	26	13	24	6
Somalia	0.45	1.09	1.28	7.02	0.12	1.16	274	326	30	67	9	23	52	6
South Africa	10.49	8.62	29.66	92.67	6.71	8.82	207 031	245 652	91	99	78	77	84	65
Sudan	1.85	0.88	0.52	36.29	0.44	...	2 880	4 523	57	64	52	34	55	18
Swaziland	3.18	3.71	6.18	55.36	1.82	7.60	1 147	1 374	69	92	61	55	61	53
Tanzania	0.45	0.40	1.69	39.94	0.22	1.55	2 933	4 232	54	80	45	24	32	21
Togo	0.92	2.70	2.97	33.05	3.60	5.38	576	708	60	87	41	12	24	3
Tunisia	11.94	12.45	5.97	95.38	5.25	34.07	10 345	13 339	94	99	84	85	96	64
Uganda	0.21	0.71	1.51	28.69	0.38	9.78	1 476	1 879	67	91	64	48	38	49
Zambia	0.80	0.70	1.27	34.07	0.48	6.31	7 177	9 352	60	87	46	49	59	43
Zimbabwe	2.30	3.08	2.71	23.88	3.99	11.36	12 416	11 516	82	99	72	44	56	37
Africa	2.66	3.12	4.30	43.86	1.18	11.07	459 914	595 139	65	86	53	41	55	32

Sources: Telecommunications : International telecommunication Union - ICT Indicators Database, December 2010.
Electricity : United Nations Statistics Division, Energy Statistics Database - online database
Water supply coverage and sanitation coverage: WHO, 2009, Joint Reporting Form and WHO regional offices reports; March 2009
Domestic authorities

StatLink http://dx.doi.org/10.1787/888932419665

Table 16: Basic Health Indicators

	Life expectancy at birth (years)			Prevalence of Undernourished in tot. population	Food availability (Kcal/ person/day)	Total health expenditure				Health personnel (per 100 000)		
								Distribution				
		With AIDS	No-AIDS scenario			as % of GDP	Per capita** (US USD)	Public (%)	Private (%)	Survey	Physi-cians	Nurses
	2010	2005-10		2005-07	2007	2008				year		
Algeria	72.9	72	...	...	3 153	4.5	223.0	83.8	16.2	2007-08	118.9	170
Angola	48.1	47.0	48.0	41	1 973	2.7	126.0	81.7	18.3	2004-05	7.0	115
Benin	62.3	61.0	62.0	12	2 533	4.8	38.0	52.8	47.2	2008-09	6.1	69
Botswana	55.5	55.0	69.0	25	2 264	5.6	392.0	74.3	25.7	2006-07	31.2	268
Burkina Faso	53.7	53.0	54.0	9	2 677	5.6	31.0	54.4	45.6	2008-09	5.8	44
Burundi	51.4	50.0	53.0	62	1 685	13.6	20.0	41.8	58.2	2004-05	2.7	19
Cameroon	51.7	51.0	56.0	21	2 269	5.5	67.0	28.4	71.6	2004-05	17.5	149
Cape Verde	71.9	71.0	...	10	2 572	4.3	149.0	72.5	27.5	2008-09	61.3	143
Central Afr. Rep.	47.7	47.0	51.0	40	1 986	4.4	20.0	39.4	60.6	2004-05	8.1	23
Chad	49.2	49.0	51.0	37	2 056	4.9	37.0	54.1	45.9	2004-05	3.4	22
Comoros	66.2	65.0	...	46	1 884	3.3	27.0	58.7	41.3	2004-05	18.7	80
Congo	53.9	54.0	57.0	15	2 512	1.8	53.0	65.4	34.6	2007-08	11.1	80
Congo Dem. Rep.	48.0	47.0	48.0	69	1 605	5.4	10.0	22.3	77.7	2004-05	9.9	50
Côte d'Ivoire	58.4	57.0	62.0	14	2 528	4.2	47.0	24.2	75.8	2008-09	13.0	34
Djibouti	56.1	55.0	58.0	28	2 291	8.5	88.0	76.1	23.9	2007-08	22.2	78
Egypt	70.5	70.0	...	...	3 195	6.4	124.0	38.3	61.7	2008-09	247.9	338
Equatorial Guinea	51.0	50.0	52.0		...	1.7	472.0	81.8	18.2	2004-05	25.1	37
Eritrea	60.4	59.0	61.0	64	1 605	3.1	10.0	44.4	55.6	2004-05	4.8	55
Ethiopia	56.1	55.0	57.0	41	1 980	3.4	11.0	56.8	43.2	2007-08	2.2	23
Gabon	61.3	60.0	52.0	...	2 755	4.1	411.0	60.5	39.5	2004-05	28.8	467
Gambia	56.6	56.0	...	19	2 385	5.3	25.0	46.0	54.0	2008-09	3.6	45
Ghana	57.1	57.0	58.0	5	2 907	7.8	56.0	49.7	50.3	2009	10.9	105
Guinea	58.9	58.0	59.0	17	2 568	5.5	37.0	11.0	89.0	2004-09	10.0	45
Guinea-Bissau	48.6	48.0	49.0	22	2 306	5.8	17.0	26.1	73.9	2008-09	4.8	50
Kenya	55.6	54.0	61.0	31	2 089	4.5	40.0	37.4	62.6	2002-03	13.3	112
Lesotho	45.9	45.0	63.0	14	2 476	6.4	51.0	56.4	43.6	2003-04	4.5	57
Liberia	59.1	58.0	60.0	33	2 204	11.7	26.0	33.0	67.0	2008-09	1.3	16
Libya	74.5	74.0	...	...	3 143	2.8	416.0	75.9	24.1	2009	173.9	670

Table 16: Basic Health Indicators (cont.)

	Life expectancy at birth (years)			Prevalence of Undernourished in tot. population	Food availability (Kcal/ person/day)	Total health expenditure				Health personnel (per 100 000)		
		With AIDS	No-AIDS scenario			as % of GDP	Per capita** (US USD)	Distribution Public (%)	Private (%)	Survey	Physicians	Nurses
	2010	2005-10		2005-07	2007	2008				year		
Madagascar	61.2	60.0	...	25	2 160	4.5	22.0	69.6	30.4	2004-08	16.5	21
Malawi	54.6	53.0	64.0	28	2 172	9.7	19.0	59.4	40.6	2008-09	1.7	26
Mali	49.2	48.0	49.0	12	2 614	5.5	38.0	47.5	52.5	2008-09	5.6	21
Mauritania	57.3	57.0	...	7	2 841	2.6	26.0	67.3	32.7	2005-09	10.5	59
Mauritius*	72.1	72.0	73.0	5	2 965	4.2	303.0	46.2	53.8	2004-05	104.0	357
Morocco	71.8	71.0	...	...	3 236	5.3	144.0	35.0	65.0	2008-09	57.8	93
Mozambique	48.4	48.0	56.0	38	2 067	5.6	24.0	76.0	24.0	2006-07	2.5	29
Namibia	62.1	61.0	70.0	19	2 383	6.7	269.0	54.4	45.6	2007-08	36.3	275
Niger	52.5	51.0	...	20	2 376	5.0	22.0	56.8	43.2	2008-09	1.9	11
Nigeria	48.4	48.0	50.0	6	2 741	6.8	90.0	24.7	75.3	2008-09	35.8	88
Rwanda	51.1	50.0	52.0	34	2 085	10.4	48.0	47.0	53.0	2005-06	2.4	45
São Tomé & Príncipe	66.1	66.0	...	...	2 684	9.5	104.0	41.3	58.7	2004-05	53.1	171
Senegal	56.2	55.0	...	17	2 348	5.7	63.0	55.8	44.2	2008-09	5.9	36
Seychelles	72.9	...	...	7	2 463	4.1	405.0	67.0	33.0	2004-05	146.4	769
Sierra Leone	48.2	47.0	48.0	35	2 170	4.2	15.0	28.5	71.5	2008-09	1.7	16
Somalia	50.4	50.0	...	...	...	...	...	...	...	2006-07	3.4	11
South Africa	52.0	52.0	65.0	...	2 999	8.3	464.0	40.3	59.7	2004-05	72.4	389
Sudan	58.9	58.0	59.0	22	2 282	3.6	49.0	36.6	63.4	2008-09	25.6	78
Swaziland	47.0	46.0	64.0	18	2 292	5.9	132.0	64.8	35.2	2004-05	15.2	412
Tanzania	56.9	55.0	61.0	34	2 032	5.1	25.0	65.6	34.4	2006-07	0.7	17
Togo	63.3	62.0	66.0	30	2 161	6.4	38.0	24.2	75.8	2008-09	5.3	19
Tunisia	74.3	74.0	...	...	3 326	6.0	231.0	49.6	50.4	2009	117.8	336
Uganda	54.1	52.0	59.0	21	2 211	6.3	33.0	22.6	77.4	2005-06	11.3	131
Zambia	47.3	45.0	55.0	43	1 873	6.0	68.0	61.8	38.2	2006-07	5.3	51
Zimbabwe	47.0	44.0	65.0	30	2 238	12.2	...	41.6	58.4	2004-05	16.7	75
Africa	56.0	54.0	...	28	2 398	5.7	90.1	50.6	49.4	...	...	...

Note: * Including Agalega, Rodrigues and Saint Brandon
** at average exchange rate

Sources: Life expectancy at birth (2010: from UN Revision 2008) : United Nations, Department of Economic and Social Affairs, Population Division, World Population Prospects, Population and HIV/AIDS 2010 , AfDB Statistics Department.
Undernourishment prevalence and food availability: FAO, Food Insecurity Online Database, September 2010
Total health expenditure and public health expenditure: WHO , The World Health Report 2010

StatLink http://dx.doi.org/10.1787/888932419684

Table 17: Major Diseases

	Healthy life expectancy at birth (years)			HIV / AIDS			Malaria* (reported cases) Probable and confirmed		Tuberculosis (reported cases)	Measles Incidence (reported cases)	Vaccination (%)	
	Total	Male	Female	People living with HIV / AIDS (000)	Adult prevalence (%)	AIDS deaths in adults & children (000)					MCV	DTP3
	2007			2009			Survey year		2008	2008	2009	
Algeria	62.0	62.0	63.0	18	0.1	<1	2008	11 964	8 643	217	88	93
Angola	45.0	44.0	47.0	200	2.0	11.0	2009	2221 076	22 562	265	77	73
Benin	50.0	50.0	50.0	60	1.2	2.7	2009	1256 708	2 966	928	72	83
Botswana	49.0	49.0	48.0	320	24.8	5.8	2009	14 878	3 351	0	94	96
Burkina Faso	43.0	42.0	43.0	110	1.2	7.1	2009	4399 837	2 756	395	75	82
Burundi	43.0	42.0	43.0	180	3.3	15.0	2009	1757 387	3 610	173	91	92
Cameroon	45.0	45.0	45.0	610	5.3	37.0	2009	1883 199	14 232	495	74	80
Cape Verde	61.0	59.0	64.0	...	...	...	2009	65	197	0	96	99
Central Afr. Rep.	42.0	43.0	42.0	130	4.7	11.0	2009	175 210	4 232	12	62	54
Chad	40.0	40.0	40.0	210	3.4	11.0	2009	182 415	3 309	63	23	23
Comoros	56.0	55.0	58.0	<0.5	0.1	<0.1	2009	49 679	77	0	79	83
Congo	48.0	48.0	49.0	77	3.4	5.1	2009	92 855	3 371	2	76	91
Congo Dem. Rep.	45.0	44.0	46.0	...	...	...	2009	6749 112	69 477	12 461	76	77
Côte d'Ivoire	47.0	45.0	48.0	450	3.4	36.0	2009	1847 367	15 294	12	67	81
Djibouti	48.0	47.0	50.0	14	2.5	1.0	2009	7 120	1 375	143	73	89
Egypt	60.0	59.0	62.0	11	<0.1	<0.5	2009	94	5 102	668	95	97
Equatorial Guinea	46.0	45.0	46.0	20	5.0	<1	2009	78 983	541	436	51	33
Eritrea	55.0	54.0	56.0	25	0.8	1.7	2009	21 298	839	0	95	99
Ethiopia	50.0	49.0	51.0	...	...	...	2009	3043 203	40 794	3 511	75	79
Gabon	52.0	50.0	53.0	46	5.2	2.4	2009	112 840	1 502	3	55	45
Gambia	51.0	50.0	53.0	18	2.0	<1	2009	479 409	1 300	0	96	98
Ghana	50.0	49.0	50.0	260	1.8	18.0	2009	1 899 544	7 904	82	93	94
Guinea	47.0	46.0	48.0	79	1.3	4.7	2009	812 471	6 561	89	51	57
Guinea-Bissau	42.0	40.0	43.0	22	2.5	1.2	2009	143 011	1 223	12	76	68
Kenya	48.0	47.0	48.0	1 500	6	80.0	2009	8 123 689	36 811	1 282	74	75
Lesotho	40.0	38.0	41.0	290	23.6	14.0	...	...	3 862	0	85	83
Liberia	48.0	47.0	49.0	37	1.5	3.6	2009	871 560	3 038	1	64	64
Libya	64.0	63.0	66.0	...	...	...	...	...	871	8	98	98

Table 17: Major Diseases (cont.)

	Healthy life expectancy at birth (years)			HIV / AIDS			Malaria* (reported cases) Probable and confirmed		Tuberculosis (reported cases)	Measles Incidence (reported cases)	Vaccination (%)	
	Total	Male	Female	People living with HIV / AIDS (000)	Adult prevalence (%)	AIDS deaths in adults & children (000)					MCV	DTP3
	2007			2009			Survey year		2008	2008	2009	
Madagascar	52.0	51.0	53.0	24	0.2	1.7	2009	215 110	15 391	3	64	78
Malawi	44.0	43.0	44.0	920	11.0	51.0	2009	5455 423	7 627	20	92	93
Mali	42.0	41.0	43.0	76	1.0	4.4	2009	1633 423	4 734	98	71	74
Mauritania	51.0	49.0	52.0	14	0.7	<1	2009	167 705	1 605	4	59	64
Mauritius	63.0	61.0	65.0	9	1.0	<0.5	...	...	85	12	99	99
Morocco	62.0	61.0	63.0	26	0.1	1.2	2009	145	11 825	1 455	98	99
Mozambique	42.0	42.0	42.0	1 400	11.5	74.0	2009	4310 086	18 824	4	77	76
Namibia	52.0	52.0	53.0	180	13.1	6.7	2009	81 812	4 828	0	76	83
Niger	44.0	44.0	45.0	61	0.8	4.3	2009	309 675	5 853	1 317	73	70
Nigeria	42.0	42.0	42.0	3 300	3.6	220.0	2009	4295 686	46 026	9 960	41	42
Rwanda	43.0	43.0	44.0	170	2.9	4.1	2009	1 247 583	4 173	6	92	97
São Tomé & Príncipe	53.0	52.0	54.0	...	...	...	2009	3 893	52	0	90	98
Senegal	51.0	50.0	52.0	59	0.9	2.6	2009	222 232	7 584	4	79	86
Seychelles	63.0	60.0	65.0	...	...	...	...	...	4	0	97	99
Sierra Leone	35.0	34.0	37.0	49	1.6	2.8	2009	646 808	5 826	44	71	75
Somalia	45.0	44.0	46.0	34	0.7	1.6	2009	56 153	6 520	1 081	24	31
South Africa	48.0	47.0	48.0	5 600	17.8	310.0	2009	6 072	138 803	39	62	69
Sudan	50.0	50.0	50.0	260	1.1	12.0	2009	2 686 822	10 800	129	82	84
Swaziland	42.0	42.0	42.0	180	25.9	7.0	2009	6 639	3 105	1	95	95
Tanzania	45.0	45.0	45.0	1 400	5.6	86.0	2009	0 040	24 171	3 413	91	85
Togo	51.0	49.0	52.0	120	3.2	7.7	2009	618 842	2 234	187	84	89
Tunisia	66.0	65.0	67.0	2	<0.1	<0.1	...	...	1 005	2	98	99
Uganda	42.0	41.0	44.0	1 200	6.5	64.0	2009	9775 318	22 766	1 319	68	64
Zambia	40.0	39.0	40.0	980	13.5	45.0	2009	2 976 395	13 211	140	85	81
Zimbabwe	39.0	40.0	38.0	1 200	14.3	83.0	2009	736 897	9 830	0	76	73
Africa	47.1	46.5	47.7	21 951	4.9	1 257.4	2009	71687 733	632 682	40 496	71	73

Notes: DTP: Diphtheria, tetanus toxoids and pertussis antigen. MCV: Measles Contaning Vaccine.

Sources: UNAIDS and WHO, Global report: UNAIDS report on the global AIDS epidemic 2010. UNAIDS, 2010.;
Malaria reported cases: WHO, Roll Back Malaria (RBM) 2010 online Database; World Malaria Report 2010;
Tuberculosis reported cases: WHO, 2010, Global Tuberculosis Database; Vaccination coverage and Measles incidence: WHO, March 2010
* : New series which now includes both probable and confirmed cases of malaria.

StatLink http://dx.doi.org/10.1787/888932419703

Table 18: **Basic Education Indicators**

	Estimated adult illiteracy rate, 2005-08 (%) (people over 15)			Estimated youth illiteracy rate, 2005-08 (%) (people between 15 and 24)			Public expenditure on education 1999-2008
	Total	Male	Female	Total	Male	Female	(% of GDP)
Algeria	72.6	81.3	63.9	91.8	94.4	89.1	4.3
Angola	69.6	82.8	57.0	72.9	80.8	65.2	2.6
Benin	40.8	53.5	28.1	53.3	64.1	42.1	3.5
Botswana	83.3	83.1	83.5	95.1	93.8	96.3	7.9
Burkina Faso	28.7	36.7	21.6	39.3	46.7	33.1	4.6
Burundi	65.9	72.3	59.9	75.9	76.5	75.3	8.3
Cameroon	75.9	84.0	67.8	85.8	88.2	83.5	3.7
Cape Verde	84.1	89.6	79.3	98.0	97.2	98.9	5.9
Central Afr. Rep.	54.6	68.8	41.1	64.2	72.1	56.4	1.3
Chad	32.7	43.8	21.9	45.4	53.5	37.2	3.2
Comoros	73.6	79.3	67.8	84.9	85.7	84.1	7.6
Congo	...	...	...	80.5	86.8	78.0	1.8
Congo Dem. Rep.	66.6	77.5	56.1	65.3	68.8	61.8	...
Côte d'Ivoire	54.6	64.2	44.3	66.1	72.0	60.1	4.6
Djibouti	...	...	...	...	...	...	8.4
Egypt	66.4	74.6	57.8	84.9	87.9	81.8	3.8
Equatorial Guinea	93.0	96.9	89.1	97.8	97.6	98.1	0.6
Eritrea	65.3	77.0	54.5	87.8	91.1	84.4	2.0
Ethiopia	35.9	50.0	22.8	49.9	62.2	38.5	5.5
Gabon	87.0	90.9	83.2	97.4	98.4	96.4	3.8
Gambia	45.3	56.7	34.3	64.1	70.1	58.1	2.0
Ghana	65.8	72.3	59.3	79.3	80.6	77.9	5.4
Guinea	38.0	49.6	26.4	58.7	66.5	50.6	2.4
Guinea-Bissau	51.0	66.1	36.5	69.6	77.6	61.6	5.2
Kenya	86.5	90.3	82.8	92.3	91.8	92.9	6.7
Lesotho	89.5	82.6	95.1	91.9	85.6	98.0	12.4
Liberia	58.1	63.3	53.0	74.8	70.1	79.5	2.8
Libya	88.4	94.9	81.3	99.8	99.9	99.7	2.7

Table 18: **Basic Education Indicators** (cont.)

	Estimated adult illiteracy rate, 2005-08 (%) (people over 15)			Estimated youth illiteracy rate, 2005-08 (%) (people between 15 and 24)			Public expenditure on education 1999-2008
	Total	Male	Female	Total	Male	Female	(% of GDP)
Madagascar	70.7	76.5	65.3	70.2	72.7	68.2	3.0
Malawi	72.8	80.2	65.8	85.7	86.5	85.0	4.2
Mali	26.2	34.9	18.2	38.8	47.4	30.8	4.4
Mauritania	56.8	64.1	49.5	67.0	70.5	63.4	2.9
Mauritius	87.5	90.4	84.8	96.4	95.4	97.4	3.2
Morocco	56.4	69.4	44.1	76.6	84.8	68.4	5.6
Mozambique	54.0	69.5	40.1	69.9	77.7	62.1	5.0
Namibia	88.2	88.7	87.7	92.9	91.1	94.8	6.4
Niger	28.7	42.9	15.1	36.5	52.4	23.2	4.5
Nigeria	60.1	71.5	48.8	71.5	78.3	64.6	...
Rwanda	70.3	74.8	66.1	77.1	77.1	77.1	4.9
São Tomé & Príncipe	88.3	93.5	83.3	95.2	94.7	95.6	...
Senegal	41.9	52.3	33.0	50.9	58.1	44.5	5.8
Seychelles	91.8	91.4	92.3	99.1	98.8	99.4	5.0
Sierra Leone	39.8	51.7	28.9	55.7	66.0	45.9	4.3
Somalia	...	...	...	...	...	...	...
South Africa	89.0	89.9	88.1	96.8	96.1	97.5	5.4
Sudan	69.3	79.0	59.6	85.2	88.6	81.7	...
Swaziland	86.5	87.4	85.6	93.2	91.8	94.7	7.8
Tanzania	72.6	79.0	66.3	77.5	78.7	76.3	6.8
Togo	64.9	76.6	53.7	83.5	87.0	80.0	4.6
Tunisia	77.6	86.4	71.0	96.8	98.1	95.8	7.1
Uganda	74.6	82.4	66.8	87.3	89.1	85.5	3.2
Zambia	70.7	80.6	61.0	74.8	82.1	67.5	1.3
Zimbabwe	91.4	94.4	88.8	98.9	98.3	99.4	5.2
Africa	64.8	74.0	55.9	67.3	74.0	60.4	4.6

Sources: AfDB Statistics Department ; UNESCO Institute for Statistics (UIS) Database ; Domestic Authorities.

StatLink http://dx.doi.org/10.1787/888932419722

Table 19: School Enrolment

	Primary School, 2006-10							Secondary School, 2006-10				Enrolment ratio in technical and vocational programmes		
	Gross enrolment ratio			Net enrolment ratio			Pupil / teacher	Gross enrolment ratio			Pupil / teacher	2006-08*		
	Total	Male	Female	Total	Male	Female	ratio	Total	Male	Female	ratio	Total secondary	Lower secondary	Upper secondary
Algeria	107.7	111.0	104.2	93.8	94.8	92.9	23.0	83.2	80.3	86.3	20.8	...	...	...
Angola	127.7	141.1	114.4	51.4	55.2	47.6	41.8	15.2	18.9	15.7	19.0	...	...	...
Benin	121.9	129.2	114.2	94.7	98.9	86.5	44.9	36.3	46.1	26.1	23.9	...	...	...
Botswana	109.4	110.9	107.9	86.9	86.1	87.8	25.2	81.5	79.4	83.7	13.9	6.1	...	19.1
Burkina Faso	79.2	82.9	75.4	63.3	67.1	59.4	47.8	21.4	24.3	18.5	30.3	6.0	1.9	23.8
Burundi	146.6	149.1	144.2	98.9	98.2	99.6	51.4	21.2	24.6	17.8	26.5	5.2	1.8	19.0
Cameroon	113.8	122.0	105.5	91.6	97.5	85.6	46.3	41.5	45.2	37.7	16.2	19.1	19.7	17.7
Cape Verde	98.1	101.8	94.4	82.6	83.6	81.5	23.9	81.5	74.7	88.2	18.2	...	...	...
Central Afr. Rep.	88.6	103.8	73.6	66.7	76.9	56.6	94.6	13.6	17.5	9.8	80.1	...	...	...
Chad	89.7	105.2	74.2	61.0	71.8	50.0	60.9	24.1	34.1	14.0	32.3	1.1	0.1	4.2
Comoros	119.4	124.6	114.1	87.3	90.7	83.8	30.2	45.8	52.1	39.3	13.8	...	...	...
Congo	119.5	123.5	115.5	58.9	61.8	56.0	64.4	43.1	46.3	40.0	29.9	...	...	...
Congo Dem. Rep.	90.3	97.5	83.0	32.4	33.3	31.5	37.3	36.7	47.0	26.2	16.0	19.2	1.9	34.1
Côte d'Ivoire	73.6	81.2	66.0	57.2	62.5	52.0	42.1	26.3	33.8	18.7	29.4	...	...	...
Djibouti	54.5	57.6	51.3	44.4	46.8	42.1	34.1	30.5	35.1	25.8	28.5	5.4	1.4	15.9
Egypt	99.7	102.1	97.1	93.6	95.5	91.7	27.1	79.3	81.7	76.9	17.1	...	...	...
Equatorial Guinea	81.9	83.6	80.1	53.5	54.0	53.0	24.2	26.2	33.3	19.0	23.2	...	...	...
Eritrea	48.3	52.8	43.8	35.7	38.1	33.2	38.5	31.8	37.1	26.4	42.7	0.7	...	1.9
Ethiopia	102.5	107.1	97.8	82.7	85.2	80.1	57.9	34.4	38.8	30.0	47.9	6.2	...	54.2
Gabon	134.3	134.7	133.9	80.3	80.5	80.0	36.0	53.1	51.9	44.7	28.1	...	...	...
Gambia	84.7	83.8	85.5	67.2	66.1	68.2	34.4	50.3	51.2	49.5	24.1	...	...	...
Ghana	105.2	105.7	104.6	75.9	75.5	76.2	33.1	57.2	60.5	53.6	18.3	4.0	...	13.5
Guinea	89.8	96.7	82.8	72.9	77.9	67.8	43.7	37.0	46.3	27.4	31.9	2.1	0.2	6.9
Guinea-Bissau	119.7	96.0	64.8	52.1	60.7	43.5	62.2	35.9	25.6	14.1	37.3	1.8	...	...
Kenya	112.7	113.9	111.4	82.6	82.2	83.0	46.8	59.5	62.4	56.5	29.7	1.0	...	2.1
Lesotho	104.4	104.6	104.2	73.1	71.2	75.0	33.8	45.0	37.8	52.3	16.9	1.6	3.8	3.3
Liberia	90.6	95.6	85.6	75.2	84.7	65.6	24.3	36.9	43.1	30.6	26.4	...	...	...
Libya	110.3	113.0	107.5	98.3	100.0	96.5	16.9	93.5	86.3	101.0	11.1	...	...	...

Table 19: School Enrolment (cont.)

	Primary School, 2006-10							Secondary School, 2006-10				Enrolment ratio in technical and vocational programmes		
	Gross enrolment ratio			Net enrolment ratio			Pupil / teacher	Gross enrolment ratio			Pupil / teacher	2006-08*		
	Total	Male	Female	Total	Male	Female	ratio	Total	Male	Female	ratio	Total second-ary	Lower second-ary	Upper second-ary
Madagascar	151.7	154.0	149.5	98.5	98.1	98.9	47.2	30.1	30.9	29.2	26.7	3.5	0.9	14.5
Malawi	120.2	118.5	121.8	90.6	87.9	93.4	92.8	29.4	31.8	27.0	27.8	...	...	...
Mali	91.3	99.8	82.7	72.0	78.0	65.0	51.4	34.8	42.4	27.1	23.5	12.3	...	39.6
Mauritania	102.3	99.4	105.3	79.7	77.4	82.1	42.5	24.5	25.9	22.9	26.6	3.2	1.6	5.4
Mauritius	99.4	99.7	99.1	93.1	92.8	93.5	21.7	87.6	87.0	88.2	16.4	...	13.6	...
Morocco	106.9	112.2	101.5	89.5	91.5	87.3	26.5	55.8	60.1	51.4	18.7	5.6	2.1	5.2
Mozambique	114.2	121.5	106.9	79.9	82.4	77.3	64.1	20.6	23.5	17.6	32.8	5.8	5.5	7.4
Namibia	112.4	113.0	111.7	89.0	86.9	91.1	29.4	65.8	60.7	70.9	24.5	...	...	...
Niger	57.8	64.7	50.6	49.5	55.4	43.2	40.7	11.0	13.7	8.2	27.9	1.0	0.7	3.5
Nigeria	93.1	99.2	86.8	61.4	64.4	58.3	46.3	30.5	34.3	26.5	28.4	4.3	4.1	4.5
Rwanda	150.9	149.8	152.0	95.9	94.7	97.0	67.7	21.9	23.1	20.8	26.9	16.2	...	44.8
São Tomé & Príncipe	130.2	131.4	129.0	97.1	97.8	96.5	30.8	46.3	44.7	47.9	21.7	1.6	...	10.9
Senegal	83.5	82.5	84.5	72.9	72.1	73.8	36.4	30.6	33.9	27.3	26.4	5.9	6.1	4.9
Seychelles	125.3	126.1	124.6	98.4	98.9	100.0	12.5	111.8	105.3	119.1	13.3	...	...	...
Sierra Leone	157.7	167.8	148.0	65.2	54.9	62.7	43.7	34.6	41.8	27.7	23.9	4.9	1.2	16.0
Somalia	20.7	26.0	15.4	9.8	12.7	6.9	30.8	...	...	...	...	...	...	...
South Africa	104.5	106.5	102.6	87.5	87.4	87.6	31.0	95.1	92.9	97.2	29.0	...	...	...
Sudan	74.0	77.8	70.0	41.2	44.9	37.0	38.4	38.0	40.3	35.5	22.2	1.9	...	4.5
Swaziland	107.9	111.9	103.8	82.8	81.9	83.7	32.4	53.3	56.0	50.5	19.1	...	...	...
Tanzania	110.2	111.0	109.3	99.3	99.6	99.1	52.2	...	...	...	...	...	...	...
Togo	105.0	112.6	97.4	83.5	88.9	78.1	39.1	41.3	54.1	28.5	35.5	7.8	1.4	25.0
Tunisia	107.6	109.0	106.1	97.7	97.3	98.2	18.2	90.2	83.1	91.1	15.9	9.5	1.0	8.5
Uganda	117.2	116.7	117.7	95.5	94.0	96.9	57.0	22.9	25.1	20.8	18.6	5.0	1.8	20.9
Zambia	119.1	120.4	117.9	95.2	94.6	95.8	60.5	51.8	56.4	47.2	25.2	7.9	...	19.6
Zimbabwe	103.6	104.1	103.1	89.9	89.3	90.5	38.2	41.0	42.6	39.4	...	...	...	...
Africa	100.9	105.0	96.3	75.1	77.2	73.0	40.5	40.7	48.2	40.8	22.0	...	...	...

Sources: AfDB Statistics Department ; UNESCO Institute for Statistics (UIS) Database, March 2011; Various Domestic Authorities.

StatLink http://dx.doi.org/10.1787/888932419741

Table 20: Employment and Remittances*

	Year	Unemployment rate			Participation rate (>15)	Inactivity rate (15-64)			Worker remittances (USD million)				
					2009	2009			2005	2006	2007	2008	2009
		Total	Male	Female	Total	Total	Male	Female					
Algeria	2008	11.30	11.00	10.10	58.5	38.9	17.2	61.2	2 060	1 610	2 120	2 202	2 059
Angola	2006	25.20	...	...	81.3	17.4	10.9	23.6	..	..	..	82	..
Benin	2002	0.70	0.90	0.40	72.7	26.5	21.8	31.2	173	224	282	271	243
Botswana	2006	17.60	15.30	19.90	76.6	21.2	17.9	24.5	127	117	105	114	111
Burkina Faso	1998	2.4	2.3	2.6	84.4	14.3	8.6	19.8	50	50	50	50	49
Burundi	1990	0.47	0.71	0.25	89.3	10.1	11.9	8.4	0	0	0	4	3
Cameroon	2007	2.90	2.50	3.30	67.0	31.7	18.0	45.5	77	130	167	162	148
Cape Verde	2008	17.80	15.00	28.00	66.4	30.8	17.2	43.0	137	137	139	155	145
Central Afr. Rep.	...	...	...	...	79.0	20.7	12.9	28.3	..	..	..	..	..
Chad	1993	0.69	1.1	0.3	70.4	29.4	22.2	36.5	..	..	..	..	..
Comoros	1991	19.95	21.27	16.93	79.6	19.4	14.1	24.7	12	12	12	12	11
Congo	...	...	...	...	72.7	26.9	16.5	37.2	11	13	15	15	14
Congo Dem. Rep.	...	...	...	...	70.8	27.9	13.0	42.3	..	..	..	..	..
Côte d'Ivoire	1998	4.1	...	...	66.9	32.5	17.4	48.5	163	167	185	199	185
Djibouti	2002	59.50	54.60	68.60	70.1	28.2	20.0	36.4	26	28	29	30	28
Egypt	2009	9.40	5.20	22.90	48.8	48.4	20.9	76.1	5 017	5 330	7 656	8 694	7 150
Equatorial Guinea	1983	24.19	27.37	18.53	65.5	33.1	6.2	59.3	..	..	..	..	..
Eritrea	...	...	...	...	72.6	26.0	15.4	36.1	..	..	..	..	..
Ethiopia	2006	17.00	11.70	22.60	85.4	13.0	9.1	16.9	174	172	358	387	353
Gabon	1993	17.80	19.10	16.10	75.5	22.5	17.2	27.9	11	11	11	11	10
Gambia	...	...	...	...	77.8	22.0	14.9	28.9	57	64	63	67	60
Ghana	2000	10.40	10.10	10.70	74.6	24.4	24.2	24.7	99	105	117	126	114
Guinea	1994	3.09	4.6	1.7	84.2	13.7	10.1	17.4	78	114	151	72	68
Guinea-Bissau	...	...	...	...	71.5	26.7	14.4	38.7	28	28	29	30	28
Kenya	1999	9.8	...	...	82.2	16.5	11.2	21.8	805	1 128	1 588	1 692	1 686
Lesotho	1999	27.26	21.47	33.09	74.0	24.8	21.5	27.6	327	361	451	439	450
Liberia	2007	5.55	6.83	4.18	71.1	27.1	23.2	30.9	32	79	62	58	54
Libya	2007	13.50	...	...	52.8	45.0	18.4	73.9	15	16	16	16	14

Table 20: Employment and Remittances* (cont.)

	Year	Unemployment rate			Participation rate (>15)	Inactivity rate (15-64)			Worker remittances (USD million)				
					2009	2009			2005	2006	2007	2008	2009
		Total	Male	Female	Total	Total	Male	Female					
Madagascar	2005	2.60	1.70	3.50	86.4	12.3	10.6	14.0	11	11	11	11	10
Malawi	2004	7.80	5.40	10.00	76.8	23.9	22.1	25.6	1	1	1	1	1
Mali	2004	8.8	7.2	10.9	51.9	46.9	31.7	61.3	177	212	344	431	405
Mauritania	2004	33.00	...	...	70.0	28.4	18.0	39.1	2	2	2	2	2
Mauritius	2009	7.30	4.40	12.30	57.5	37.4	20.2	54.6	215	215	215	215	211
Morocco	2009	10.00	9.80	10.50	52.3	44.7	16.3	71.7	4 590	5 451	6 730	6 895	6 271
Mozambique	1997	2.24	3.39	1.32	85.8	13.9	13.4	14.4	57	80	99	116	111
Namibia	2008	37.60	32.50	43.00	57.1	41.4	36.1	46.5	18	17	16	14	14
Niger	2001	1.46	1.72	0.93	62.7	36.7	12.0	60.6	66	78	79	79	75
Nigeria	1986	3.94	3.71	4.39	56.2	42.7	25.3	60.1	3 329	5 435	9 221	9 980	9 585
Rwanda	1996	0.6	0.9	0.4	86.0	12.8	14.0	11.6	21	21	51	68	93
São Tomé & Príncipe	2006	16.65	11.04	24.51	59.8	37.5	21.5	52.9	2	2	2	3	2
Senegal	2006	10.00	7.90	13.60	76.4	22.5	10.3	34.3	789	925	1 192	1 288	1 191
Seychelles	2005	5.45	6.12	4.85					12	13	11	8	12
Sierra Leone	2004	3.40	4.50	2.30	66.4	32.6	32.1	33.2	2	16	42	28	47
Somalia	...	...	...	...	70.3	28.2	13.9	42.1	..	..	..	..	..
South Africa	2009	23.80	22.00	25.90	55.0	41.4	33.4	49.2	658	734	834	823	902
Sudan	...	...	...	...	52.3	46.8	26.0	67.8	1 016	1 179	1 769	3 100	2 993
Swaziland	1997	22.54	19.97	25.97	63.6	34.7	24.2	44.5	95	99	100	100	102
Tanzania	2006	4.30	2.80	5.80	88.4	10.0	8.8	11.2	19	15	14	19	16
Togo	...	...	...	...	74.4	24.4	13.6	35.0	193	232	284	337	307
Tunisia	2008	14.2	...	...	48.0	49.1	26.2	72.2	1 393	1 510	1 716	1 977	1 966
Uganda	2003	3.2	2.5	3.9	84.5	14.2	8.8	19.5	322	411	452	724	694
Zambia	2000	12.90	14.10	11.30	69.2	30.3	20.7	40.0	53	58	59	68	68
Zimbabwe	2004	4.16	4.19	4.14	66.8	32.1	24.6	38.8	..	..	..	..	..
Africa	...	...	...	...	...	...	...	...	22 518	26 613	36 851	41 174	38 063

Sources: Employment: ILO. KILM database, sixth edition.
World Bank staff estimates based on the International Monetary Fund's Balance of Payments Statistics Yearbook 2008.
* See note on methodology for definitions.

StatLink http://dx.doi.org/10.1787/888932419760

Table 21: **Corruption Perception Index (CPI)***

	2004		2005		2006		2007		2008		2009		2010	
	Index	Country Rank / 145	Index	Country Rank / 158	Index	Country Rank / 163	Index	Country Rank / 179	Index	Country Rank / 180	Index	Country Rank / 180	Index	Country Rank / 178
Algeria	2.7	97	2.8	97	3.1	84	3	99	3.2	92	2.8	111	2.9	105
Angola	2	133	2	151	2.2	142	2.2	147	1.9	158	1.9	162	1.9	168
Benin	3.2	77	2.9	88	2.5	121	2.7	118	3.1	96	2.9	106	2.8	110
Botswana	6	31	5.9	32	5.6	37	5.4	38	5.8	36	5.6	37	5.8	33
Burkina Faso	...	...	3.4	70	3.2	79	2.9	105	3.5	80	3.6	79	3.1	98
Burundi	...	...	2.3	130	2.4	130	2.5	131	1.9	158	1.8	168	1.8	170
Cameroon	2.1	129	2.2	137	2.3	138	2.4	138	2.3	141	2.2	146	2.2	146
Cape Verde	...	...	...	...	...	...	4.9	49	5.1	47	5.1	46	5.1	45
Central Afr. Rep.	...	...	...	...	2.4	130	2	162	2	151	2	158	2.1	154
Chad	1.7	142	1.7	158	2	156	1.8	172	1.6	173	1.6	175	1.7	171
Comoros	...	...	...	...	...	...	2.6	123	2.5	134	2.3	143	2.1	154
Congo	2.3	114	2.3	130	2.2	142	2.1	150	1.9	158	1.9	162	2.1	154
Congo Dem. Rep.	2	133	2.1	144	2	156	1.9	168	1.7	171	1.9	162	2.2	146
Côte d'Ivoire	2	133	1.9	152	2.1	151	2.1	150	...	...	2.1	154	2	164
Djibouti	...	...	...	...	...	...	2.9	105	3	102	2.8	111	3.2	91
Egypt	3.2	77	3.4	70	3.3	70	2.9	105	2.6	115	2.8	111	3.1	98
Equatorial Guinea	...	...	1.9	152	2.1	151	1.9	168	1.7	171	1.8	168	1.9	168
Eritrea	2.6	102	2.6	107	2.9	93	2.8	111	2.6	126	2.6	126	2.6	123
Ethiopia	2.3	114	2.2	137	2.4	130	2.4	138	2.6	126	2.7	120	2.7	116
Gabon	3.3	74	2.9	88	3	90	3.3	84	3.1	96	2.9	106	2.8	110
Gambia	2.8	90	2.7	103	2.5	121	2.3	143	1.9	158	2.9	106	3.2	91
Ghana	3.6	64	3.5	65	3.3	70	3.7	69	3.9	67	3.9	69	4.1	62
Guinea	...	...	...	...	1.9	160	1.9	168	1.6	173	1.8	168	2	164
Guinea-Bissau	...	...	...	...	...	...	2.2	147	1.9	158	1.9	162	2.1	154
Kenya	2.1	129	2.1	144	2.2	142	2.1	150	2.1	147	2.2	146	2.1	154
Lesotho	...	...	3.4	70	3.2	79	3.3	84	3.2	92	3.3	89	3.5	78
Liberia	...	...	2.2	137	...	...	2.1	150	2.4	138	3.1	97	3.3	87
Libya	2.5	108	2.5	117	2.7	105	2.5	131	2.6	126	2.5	130	2.2	146

Table 21: Corruption Perception Index (CPI)* (cont.)

	2004		2005		2006		2007		2008		2009		2010	
	Index	Country Rank / 145	Index	Country Rank / 158	Index	Country Rank / 163	Index	Country Rank / 179	Index	Country Rank / 180	Index	Country Rank / 180	Index	Country Rank / 178
Madagascar	3.1	82	2.8	97	3.1	84	3.2	94	3.4	85	3	99	2.6	123
Malawi	2.8	90	2.8	97	2.7	105	2.7	118	2.8	115	3.3	89	3.4	85
Mali	3.2	77	2.9	88	2.8	99	2.7	118	3.1	96	2.8	111	2.7	116
Mauritania	...	...	...	...	3.1	84	2.6	123	2.8	115	2.5	130	2.3	143
Mauritius	4.1	54	4.2	51	5.1	42	4.7	53	5.5	41	5.4	42	5.4	39
Morocco	3.2	77	3.2	78	3.2	79	3.5	72	3.5	80	3.3	89	3.4	85
Mozambique	2.8	90	2.8	97	2.8	99	2.8	111	2.6	126	2.5	130	2.7	116
Namibia	4.1	54	4.3	47	4.1	55	4.5	57	4.5	61	4.5	56	4.4	56
Niger	2.2	122	2.4	126	2.3	138	2.6	123	2.8	115	2.9	106	2.6	123
Nigeria	1.6	144	1.9	152	2.2	142	2.2	147	2.7	121	2.5	130	2.4	134
Rwanda	...	...	3.1	83	2.5	121	2.8	111	3	102	3.3	89	4	66
São Tomé & Príncipe	...	...	...	...	...	...	2.7	118	2.7	121	2.8	111	3	101
Senegal	3	85	3.2	78	3.3	70	3.6	71	3.4	85	3	99	2.9	105
Seychelles	4.4	48	4	55	3.6	63	4.5	57	4.8	55	4.8	54	4.8	49
Sierra Leone	2.3	114	2.4	126	2.2	142	2.1	150	1.9	158	2.2	146	2.4	134
Somalia	...	...	2.1	144	...	...	1.4	179	1	180	1.1	180	1.1	178
South Africa	4.6	44	4.5	46	4.6	51	5.1	43	4.9	54	4.7	55	4.5	54
Sudan	2.2	122	2.1	144	2	156	1.8	172	1.6	173	1.5	176	1.6	172
Swaziland	...	...	2.7	103	2.5	121	3.3	84	3.6	72	3.6	79	3.2	91
Tanzania	2.8	90	2.9	88	2.9	93	3.2	94	3	102	2.6	126	2.7	116
Togo	...	...	...	...	2.4	130	2.3	143	2.7	121	2.8	111	2.4	134
Tunisia	5	39	4.9	43	4.6	51	4.2	61	4.4	62	4.2	65	4.3	59
Uganda	2.6	102	2.5	117	2.7	105	2.8	111	2.6	126	2.5	130	2.5	127
Zambia	2.6	102	2.6	107	2.6	111	2.6	123	2.8	115	3	99	3	101
Zimbabwe	2.3	114	2.6	107	2.4	130	2.1	150	1.8	166	2.2	146	2.4	134

Note: * Index (CPI) Score relates to perceptions of the degree of corruption as seen by business people and country analysts, and ranges between 10 (highly clean) and 0 (highly corrupt).

Source: Transparency International: http://www.transparency.org/.

StatLink http://dx.doi.org/10.1787/888932419779

Table 22: Public Protest

	1996	1997	1998	1999	2000	2001	2002	2003	2004	2005	2006	2007	2008	2009	2010
Algeria	4.0	2.3	6.7	1.4	0.0	9.9	10.0	6.6	1.3	0.7	4.0	1.5	2.5	1.8	9.0
Angola	-	-	-	-	-	-	-	-	1.5	0.0	1.0	0.0	0.0	0.3	0.0
Benin	-	-	-	-	-	-	-	-	1.5	0.0	0.5	0.0	0.0	0.0	0.0
Botswana	0.0	0.0	0.0	0.0	0.0	0.0	0.0	0.0	0.0	0.0	0.0	0.0	0.0	0.0	0.3
Burkina Faso	0.0	1.5	0.8	3.2	9.4	0.5	1.1	0.0	1.6	0.9	3.8	0.5	2.5	4.3	0.8
Burundi	-	-	-	-	-	-	-	-	-	-	2.3	11.8	0.0	4.8	3.8
Cameroon	8.2	4.4	0.3	2.2	0.3	0.0	1.5	2.0	1.0	2.7	4.5	2.8	1.0	4.0	6.8
Cape Verde	-	-	-	-	-	-	-	-	-	-	0.0	0.0	0.0	0.0	0.5
Central Afr. Rep.	-	-	-	-	-	-	-	-	-	-	12.8	3.5	1.8	1.8	3.3
Chad	0.3	3.0	0.7	0.5	0.0	2.2	0.0	1.5	0.0	1.6	1.3	5.3	1.0	2.5	0.5
Comoros	-	-	-	-	-	-	-	-	-	-	0.5	1.0	1.8	1.8	0.0
Congo	-	-	-	-	-	-	-	-	1.5	0.0	0.3	0.0	0.0	0.8	0.0
Congo Dem. Rep.	-	-	-	-	-	-	-	-	2.0	2.8	7.3	4.8	1.8	6.0	1.8
Côte d'Ivoire	1.0	8.2	6.7	10.0	6.7	0.0	2.9	0.8	2.4	1.1	12.8	6.8	4.9	7.2	3.0
Djibouti	-	-	-	-	-	-	-	-	-	-	0.0	0.8	0.0	0.0	0.0
Egypt	0.0	4.2	0.0	0.0	1.6	3.2	2.6	1.3	3.1	2.3	4.1	5.8	4.6	3.0	3.5
Equatorial Guinea	0.0	0.0	0.0	0.0	0.0	0.0	0.0	0.0	0.0	0.0	0.0	0.0	0.0	0.0	1.0
Ethiopia	1.3	1.2	0.8	0.0	0.0	1.3	0.3	0.0	0.0	2.3	0.6	0.3	0.0	0.3	0.0
Gabon	8.0	0.0	2.1	1.3	0.0	0.0	1.3	0.0	0.5	5.0	6.1	1.5	0.9	4.5	7.5
Gambia	-	-	-	-	-	-	-	-	-	-	0.0	0.0	0.0	0.0	0.0
Ghana	0.5	0.0	0.3	2.0	0.0	0.0	0.0	0.5	0.0	0.0	0.0	0.0	0.5	0.0	0.0
Guinea	-	-	-	-	-	-	-	-	-	-	3.8	11.8	0.8	3.5	3.0
Guinea-Bissau	-	-	-	-	-	-	-	-	-	-	4.0	1.8	0.5	0.0	0.8
Kenya	2.3	4.4	8.1	0.0	0.0	0.5	0.0	0.9	2.4	2.2	2.5	1.0	5.1	1.4	0.5
Lesotho	-	-	-	-	-	-	-	-	-	-	0.0	0.8	0.0	0.0	0.0
Liberia	-	-	-	-	-	-	-	-	-	-	3.3	0.3	0.0	0.3	0.0
Libya	-	-	-	-	-	-	-	-	-	-	0.3	0.0	0.0	0.0	0.0

Table 22: **Public Protest** (cont.)

	1996	1997	1998	1999	2000	2001	2002	2003	2004	2005	2006	2007	2008	2009	2010
Madagascar	-	-	-	-	-	-	-	-	1.0	3.3	0.8	1.0	0.0	8.3	0.8
Malawi	-	-	-	-	-	-	-	-	-	0.8	0.3	0.8	0.0	0.0	0.5
Mali	1.4	3.9	1.2	0.9	0.0	0.0	0.0	0.7	0.5	0.4	0.5	2.1	0.0	1.4	0.8
Mauritania	-	-	-	-	-	-	-	-	-	-	1.8	0.5	5.3	2.3	0.3
Mauritius	0.0	0.0	0.0	0.8	0.0	0.0	0.0	0.0	0.0	0.0	0.0	0.3	0.0	0.0	0.0
Morocco	5.9	1.6	1.4	0.7	0.7	0.0	0.0	0.0	1.2	0.5	2.0	3.9	2.7	2.2	1.0
Mozambique	1.3	0.0	0.0	1.5	0.5	0.0	0.0	0.8	0.0	0.0	0.0	0.0	0.5	0.8	0.5
Namibia	3.0	0.0	0.0	0.0	0.0	0.0	0.0	0.0	0.0	0.0	0.0	0.0	0.0	0.0	0.3
Niger	-	-	-	-	-	-	-	-	1.3	1.5	6.0	1.8	1.0	7.3	0.0
Nigeria	3.7	2.3	2.8	6.3	4.1	5.3	1.0	0.8	2.9	0.5	3.2	2.3	2.8	3.6	3.8
Rwanda	-	-	-	-	-	-	-	-	0.0	0.0	0.0	0.0	0.8	0.0	0.0
São Tomé & Príncipe	-	-	-	-	-	-	-	-	-	-	0.8	2.3	0.0	0.5	0.0
Senegal	1.2	5.0	1.9	1.1	0.0	1.4	0.0	0.0	1.3	2.2	5.4	4.5	2.5	2.9	2.5
Seychelles	-	-	-	-	-	-	-	-	-	-	0.3	0.0	0.0	0.0	0.0
Sierra Leone	-	-	-	-	-	-	-	-	-	-	0.5	1.3	0.3	0.0	0.3
South Africa	6.3	10.3	2.0	5.6	1.9	1.5	1.0	0.6	3.0	1.0	3.6	7.5	2.3	8.8	6.3
Sudan	-	-	-	-	-	-	-	-	-	-	2.0	0.5	1.0	1.3	1.3
Swaziland	-	-	-	-	-	-	-	-	-	-	0.0	1.8	0.0	0.0	0.0
Tanzania	0.8	0.0	0.8	0.0	0.0	1.0	0.0	0.3	0.3	0.3	0.0	0.0	0.3	0.0	0.3
Togo	-	-	-	-	-	-	-	-	-	-	0.0	0.3	0.0	0.5	1.8
Tunisia	0.0	0.0	0.3	0.7	0.7	0.0	0.0	2.8	0.0	1.3	5.6	1.9	1.7	3.4	0.8
Uganda	0.8	0.0	0.0	0.0	0.0	0.0	0.0	0.0	1.0	1.0	0.3	1.3	0.0	0.5	0.0
Zambia	2.5	1.5	2.1	1.5	0.5	5.0	0.5	3.4	1.8	0.9	6.6	2.4	1.5	1.6	0.3
Zimbabwe	7.3	3.7	4.8	4.6	1.3	1.4	1.0	5.9	0.3	1.0	2.0	6.9	2.7	4.4	3.5

Sources: Authors' calculations based on Marchés Tropicaux et Méditerranéens, between 1996 and 2007, and Agence Fance Presse for 2008 and 2009. The change in the source might affect the comparability of 2008 indicator to its historical values. For more details, see note on methodology .

StatLink http://dx.doi.org/10.1787/888932419798

Table 23: Public Violence

	1996	1997	1998	1999	2000	2001	2002	2003	2004	2005	2006	2007	2008	2009	2010
Algeria	35.2	31.3	37.6	43.0	37.8	35.0	15.4	5.5	19.2	10.7	12.8	14.8	10.8	11.0	5.8
Angola	-	-	-	-	-	-	-	-	13.5	0.8	0.3	0.0	0.3	0.5	1.3
Benin	-	-	-	-	-	-	-	-	0.3	0.0	0.3	0.0	0.0	0.8	0.0
Botswana	0.0	0.0	0.0	0.0	0.0	0.0	0.0	0.0	0.0	0.0	0.0	0.0	0.0	0.0	0.0
Burkina Faso	0.0	0.0	0.0	0.3	0.0	0.5	0.5	0.0	0.5	0.0	0.0	0.0	0.3	0.0	0.0
Burundi	-	-	-	-	-	-	-	-	-	-	6.3	2.8	2.3	4.3	3.0
Cameroon	4.8	14.2	0.3	0.0	0.7	0.4	0.0	0.0	0.3	0.9	1.8	1.3	1.3	3.3	0.0
Cape Verde	-	-	-	-	-	-	-	-	-	-	0.0	0.0	0.0	0.0	0.0
Central Afr. Rep.	-	-	-	-	-	-	-	-	-	-	6.0	2.8	2.5	7.3	9.0
Chad	2.4	2.4	1.3	6.4	7.7	4.7	3.0	4.5	1.0	3.2	13.8	8.3	3.4	3.0	1.3
Comoros	-	-	-	-	-	-	-	-	-	-	0.0	1.5	0.8	0.0	0.0
Congo	-	-	-	-	-	-	-	-	0.0	0.5	0.0	0.5	0.0	1.0	0.0
Congo Dem. Rep.	-	-	-	-	-	-	-	-	4.5	4.5	12.0	17.3	10.3	18.8	11.5
Côte d'Ivoire	4.5	0.0	0.0	1.7	6.2	1.2	3.1	4.7	6.0	5.7	7.0	1.3	1.0	1.0	2.5
Djibouti	-	-	-	-	-	-	-	-	-	-	0.0	0.0	0.8	0.5	0.0
Egypt	6.5	10.8	0.0	0.5	2.0	1.0	0.0	1.2	1.3	2.3	3.5	2.0	4.3	4.1	1.3
Equatorial Guinea	0.5	0.0	0.5	0.0	0.0	0.0	0.0	0.3	0.3	0.0	0.0	0.0	0.0	0.8	0.0
Ethiopia	13.3	4.1	0.0	7.2	2.0	1.5	12.4	4.7	8.1	3.6	7.4	7.9	4.2	5.0	2.0
Gabon	0.5	0.3	0.0	0.0	0.0	0.0	0.0	0.0	0.0	0.3	0.0	0.0	0.0	0.8	0.0
Gambia	-	-	-	-	-	-	-	-	-	-	0.0	0.0	0.0	0.0	0.0
Ghana	1.1	0.0	0.0	0.5	0.5	1.0	1.0	0.0	0.5	0.0	0.0	0.5	0.5	0.0	0.0
Guinea	-	-	-	-	-	-	-	-	-	-	0.0	0.5	1.3	0.3	2.0
Guinea-Bissau	-	-	-	-	-	-	-	-	-	-	1.5	0.3	0.0	0.3	0.0
Kenya	3.0	5.3	6.5	0.0	0.0	2.8	0.5	1.5	0.5	2.3	8.3	6.3	8.3	4.8	0.8
Lesotho	-	-	-	-	-	-	-	-	-	-	0.3	0.3	0.0	0.0	0.0
Liberia	-	-	-	-	-	-	-	-	-	-	2.5	0.3	0.8	0.8	0.5
Libya	-	-	-	-	-	-	-	-	-	-	0.0	0.0	0.3	0.0	0.0

Table 23: **Public Violence** (cont.)															
	1996	1997	1998	1999	2000	2001	2002	2003	2004	2005	2006	2007	2008	2009	2010
Madagascar	-	-	-	-	-	-	-	-	1.3	1.3	0.8	0.0	0.0	2.8	0.5
Malawi	-	-	-	-	-	-	-	-	-	1.3	0.3	0.0	0.0	0.0	0.0
Mali	0.6	2.3	0.0	2.0	0.0	0.0	0.0	0.0	0.0	0.6	1.0	2.3	4.2	2.6	1.0
Mauritania	-	-	-	-	-	-	-	-	-	-	0.0	1.3	1.5	1.3	0.8
Mauritius	0.0	0.0	0.0	1.0	0.0	0.0	0.0	0.0	0.5	0.3	0.0	0.0	0.0	0.0	0.0
Morocco	1.5	0.0	0.0	0.0	0.0	0.0	0.0	0.0	0.5	0.3	0.0	1.3	1.0	0.0	0.0
Mozambique	9.5	0.0	0.0	0.3	1.5	0.0	0.0	0.8	1.0	0.3	0.0	0.0	0.8	0.3	0.8
Namibia	0.0	0.0	0.0	2.0	1.0	0.0	0.0	0.0	0.0	0.0	0.0	0.0	0.0	0.3	0.0
Niger	-	-	-	-	-	-	-	-	1.0	0.3	0.3	7.3	5.5	2.8	0.3
Nigeria	12.8	16.6	5.7	16.0	12.4	12.7	6.4	6.0	11.3	0.8	16.4	22.5	12.9	13.8	12.5
Rwanda	-	-	-	-	-	-	-	-	0.0	0.0	0.0	0.3	0.5	0.8	1.0
São Tomé & Príncipe	-	-	-	-	-	-	-	-	-	-	0.0	0.0	0.0	0.0	0.0
Senegal	0.0	4.2	0.6	1.4	1.6	1.4	2.2	1.9	2.1	0.3	1.9	1.9	0.3	4.1	4.8
Seychelles	-	-	-	-	-	-	-	-	-	-	0.0	0.0	0.0	0.3	0.0
Sierra Leone	-	-	-	-	-	-	-	-	-	-	0.0	0.5	0.0	1.5	0.0
South Africa	20.0	7.0	4.5	8.3	4.5	0.0	0.5	0.3	2.0	0.3	0.5	0.0	4.3	4.3	0.5
Sudan	-	-	-	-	-	-	-	-	-	-	8.8	9.5	9.5	24.0	18.3
Swaziland	-	-	-	-	-	-	-	-	-	-	0.5	0.0	0.0	0.5	0.0
Tanzania	1.0	0.5	0.0	0.0	0.0	1.0	0.0	0.0	0.0	1.3	0.0	0.0	0.0	0.0	0.0
Togo	-	-	-	-	-	-	-	-	-	-	0.0	0.0	0.0	0.8	0.0
Tunisia	0.0	0.0	0.0	0.5	0.0	0.0	0.8	0.0	0.0	0.3	0.0	0.0	0.3	0.3	0.0
Uganda	21.0	4.0	2.8	2.5	0.0	6.3	3.8	4.5	10.3	1.8	3.8	2.5	1.8	3.5	0.0
Zambia	0.8	0.8	0.5	0.5	0.0	2.8	0.0	0.8	0.0	0.3	0.5	0.0	0.3	0.0	0.0
Zimbabwe	0.0	1.5	1.0	0.0	3.8	3.0	3.8	0.3	0.8	0.8	0.0	0.0	8.0	0.8	0.8

Sources: Authors' calculations based on Marchés Tropicaux et Méditerranéens, between 1996 and 2007, and Agence Fance Presse for 2008 and 2009. The change in the source might affect the comparability of 2008 indicator to its historical values. For more details, see note on methodology .

StatLink http://dx.doi.org/10.1787/888932419817

Table 24: Political Hardening

	1996	1997	1998	1999	2000	2001	2002	2003	2004	2005	2006	2007	2008	2009	2010
Algeria	8.2	7.0	6.5	6.1	5.6	7.4	9.0	6.5	7.5	5.5	4.6	6.1	6.8	5.1	1.8
Angola	-	-	-	-	-	-	-	-	1.4	0.1	0.5	0.2	0.8	0.4	0.7
Benin	-	-	-	-	-	-	-	-	0.1	0.1	0.3	0.1	0.5	0.1	0.2
Botswana	0.1	0.1	0.0	0.2	0.0	0.0	0.0	0.0	0.3	0.1	0.0	0.0	0.0	0.0	0.0
Burkina Faso	0.2	0.5	0.2	1.2	0.4	0.3	0.7	0.6	0.7	0.2	0.2	0.1	0.8	0.3	0.1
Burundi	-	-	-	-	-	-	-	-	-	-	3.6	1.4	1.2	1.8	2.5
Cameroon	2.7	2.3	1.3	1.3	1.1	1.7	1.1	1.4	1.5	0.9	1.9	1.2	1.6	1.5	1.8
Cape Verde	-	-	-	-	-	-	-	-	-	-	0.0	0.3	0.2	0.0	0.0
Central Afr. Rep.	-	-	-	-	-	-	-	-	-	-	4.2	0.8	0.5	1.7	1.9
Chad	0.7	0.3	0.3	0.0	0.3	0.6	0.4	1.6	0.2	1.7	4.3	2.2	5.7	1.2	0.8
Comoros	-	-	-	-	-	-	-	-	-	-	0.4	0.9	0.6	0.4	0.0
Congo	-	-	-	-	-	-	-	-	0.3	0.3	0.5	0.4	0.2	0.9	0.3
Congo, Dem. Rep.	-	-	-	-	-	-	-	-	6.9	8.1	10.5	8.9	4.0	4.7	5.0
Côte d'Ivoire	1.0	0.9	0.5	2.8	2.3	0.7	1.1	2.1	2.7	2.1	3.3	1.2	1.5	0.6	4.0
Djibuti	-	-	-	-	-	-	-	-	-	-	0.2	0.1	0.6	0.0	0.1
Egypt	5.9	5.3	4.9	4.1	5.4	4.6	6.4	4.8	4.6	6.4	5.7	7.1	7.9	4.7	5.4
Equatorial Guinea	0.0	0.3	1.3	0.0	0.0	0.2	1.5	0.2	2.1	0.0	0.5	0.3	0.5	0.8	0.5
Ethiopia	4.0	3.2	2.8	2.2	2.4	3.1	4.2	2.5	2.5	5.2	3.4	3.4	1.9	2.0	1.4
Gabon	0.4	1.4	0.3	0.7	0.2	0.1	0.3	0.5	1.0	2.1	0.7	0.5	0.2	1.3	0.9
Gambia	-	-	-	-	-	-	-	-	-	-	1.4	0.3	0.9	2.1	0.2
Ghana	0.6	0.2	0.6	0.6	0.0	0.2	0.3	0.0	0.1	0.0	0.0	0.0	0.1	0.0	0.2
Guinea	-	-	-	-	-	-	-	-	-	-	1.7	3.0	2.8	5.4	1.6
Guinea-Bissau	-	-	-	-	-	-	-	-	-	-	1.2	0.8	0.6	2.0	0.1
Kenya	1.0	2.7	0.9	0.0	0.0	0.2	0.3	0.5	0.6	0.7	1.8	2.6	7.4	0.4	0.0
Lesotho	-	-	-	-	-	-	-	-	-	-	0.1	0.3	0.0	0.0	0.0
Liberia	-	-	-	-	-	-	-	-	-	-	0.8	0.3	0.5	0.2	0.0
Libya	-	-	-	-	-	-	-	-	-	-	0.6	0.5	0.5	0.4	0.1

Table 24: **Political Hardening** (cont.)

	1996	1997	1998	1999	2000	2001	2002	2003	2004	2005	2006	2007	2008	2009	2010
Madagascar	-	-	-	-	-	-	-	-	0.8	0.3	1.1	0.9	0.0	2.7	0.7
Malawi	-	-	-	-	-	-	-	-	-	0.8	0.3	0.3	0.3	0.6	0.5
Mali	0.1	1.3	0.0	0.1	0.3	0.3	0.1	0.3	0.1	0.0	0.4	0.5	1.9	1.2	0.1
Mauritania	-	-	-	-	-	-	-	-	-	-	1.3	1.1	9.0	1.3	0.6
Mauritius	0.1	0.0	0.0	0.1	0.0	0.0	0.0	0.6	0.1	0.2	0.0	0.0	0.0	0.0	0.0
Morocco	4.7	4.4	3.9	3.8	4.3	4.2	4.1	4.4	4.9	4.0	4.3	4.4	4.6	2.0	2.2
Mozambique	0.1	0.2	0.6	0.3	0.9	0.3	0.0	0.1	0.4	0.0	0.0	0.0	0.4	0.5	0.9
Namibia	0.0	0.1	0.0	0.3	0.4	0.1	0.1	0.2	0.1	0.0	0.0	0.0	0.0	0.1	0.0
Niger	-	-	-	-	-	-	-	-	0.4	0.8	1.3	1.4	2.2	3.9	0.7
Nigeria	5.7	4.2	3.4	3.1	3.1	2.7	2.6	2.9	5.0	2.7	4.6	3.7	4.3	2.9	0.6
Rwanda	-	-	-	-	-	-	-	-	1.1	0.1	0.1	0.1	0.2	0.2	0.6
São Tomé & Príncipe	-	-	-	-	-	-	-	-	-	-	0.1	0.3	0.1	0.7	0.0
Senegal	1.7	2.0	1.9	1.3	1.2	1.7	1.5	1.6	1.5	1.9	1.5	2.6	1.8	1.2	1.4
Seychelles	-	-	-	-	-	-	-	-	-	-	0.4	0.0	0.0	0.4	0.0
Sierra Leone	-	-	-	-	-	-	-	-	-	-	0.4	0.6	0.2	1.0	0.2
South Africa	4.6	3.6	1.5	1.1	0.5	0.3	0.5	0.4	1.0	1.1	0.5	1.2	1.5	1.6	0.4
Sudan	-	-	-	-	-	-	-	-	-	-	3.5	3.6	7.6	5.0	6.2
Swaziland	-	-	-	-	-	-	-	-	-	-	0.3	0.3	0.9	0.2	0.0
Tanzania	0.3	0.1	0.1	0.0	0.1	0.1	0.0	0.1	0.0	0.4	0.0	0.0	0.0	0.3	0.2
Togo	-	-	-	-	-	-	-	-	-	-	0.0	0.0	0.0	0.7	0.8
Tunisia	2.4	1.8	1.8	2.0	1.8	2.2	2.1	1.8	3.0	2.1	1.3	1.9	3.4	2.1	1.1
Uganda	1.2	0.4	0.6	0.7	0.4	1.9	0.8	1.4	3.5	1.1	3.3	2.0	0.9	3.0	0.9
Zambia	1.9	2.7	1.6	1.3	0.9	1.8	1.9	1.0	1.2	0.9	1.7	0.5	0.2	0.5	0.6
Zimbabwe	1.0	0.9	1.9	1.3	1.2	3.1	4.4	3.9	4.1	3.3	2.2	3.0	9.9	3.3	0.7

Sources: Authors' calculations based on Marchés Tropicaux et Méditerranéens, between 1996 and 2007, and Agence Fance Presse for 2008 and 2009. The change in the source might affect the comparability of 2008 indicator to its historical values. For more details, see note on methodology .

StatLink http://dx.doi.org/10.1787/888932419836

THE AFRICAN DEVELOPMENT BANK GROUP

The African Development Bank Group is a regional multilateral development finance institution the members of which are all of the 53 countries in Africa and 24 countries from Asia, Europe, North and South America.

The purpose of the Bank is to further the economic development and social progress of African countries, individually and collectively. To this end, the Bank promotes the investment of public and private capital for development, primarily by providing loans and grants for projects and programmes that contribute to poverty reduction and broad-based sustainable development in Africa.

The non-concessional operations of the Bank are financed from its ordinary capital resources. In addition, the Bank's soft window affiliates – the African Development Fund and the Nigeria Trust Fund – provide concessional financing to low-income countries that are not able to sustain loans on market terms.

By the end of 2010, the African Development Bank Group cumulatively approved 3 526 loans and grants for commitments of close to UA 55.93 billion (USD 79.23 billion). The commitments were made to 53 regional member countries and institutions to support development projects and programmes in agriculture, transport, public utilities, industry, education and health services. Since the mid-1980s, a significant share of commitments has also gone to promoting economic reform and adjustment programmes that help to accelerate socio-economic development. About 58.8% of the total Bank Group commitments were financed on non-concessional terms, while the balance benefited from concessional financing.

For more information on the African Development Bank, please see www.afdb.org

UNITED NATIONS DEVELOPMENT PROGRAMME

The UNDP is the United Nations' global development network, an organisation advocating for change and connecting countries to knowledge, experience and resources to help people build a better life. The UNDP is present in 166 countries, of which 45 are in Africa, working with them on their own solutions to global and national development challenges. As these countries develop local capacity, they draw on the people of UNDP and its wide range of partners.

The UNDP's network links and co-ordinates global and national efforts to reach the Millennium Development Goals. In all its activities, it encourages the protection of human rights and the empowerment of women. The annual *Human Development Report*, commissioned by the UNDP, focuses the global debate on key development issues, providing new measurement tools, innovative analysis and often controversial policy proposals.

For more information on the United Nations Development Programme, please see www.undp.org/

ORGANISATION FOR ECONOMIC CO-OPERATION AND DEVELOPMENT

The OECD is a unique forum where governments work together to address the economic, social and environmental challenges of globalisation. The OECD is also at the forefront of efforts to understand and to help governments respond to new developments and concerns, such as corporate governance, the information economy and the challenges of an ageing population. The Organisation provides a setting where governments can compare policy experiences, seek answers to common problems, identify good practice and work to co-ordinate domestic and international policies.

The OECD member countries are: Australia, Austria, Belgium, Canada, Chile, the Czech Republic, Denmark, Estonia, Finland, France, Germany, Greece, Hungary, Iceland, Ireland, Israel, Italy, Japan, Korea, Luxembourg, Mexico, the Netherlands, New Zealand, Norway, Poland, Portugal, the Slovak Republic, Slovenia, Spain, Sweden, Switzerland, Turkey, the United Kingdom and the United States. The European Union takes part in the work of the OECD.

OECD Publishing disseminates widely the results of the Organisation's statistics gathering and research on economic, social and environmental issues, as well as the conventions, guidelines and standards agreed by its members.

The OECD Development Centre was established in 1962 as an independent platform for knowledge-sharing and policy dialogue between OECD member countries and developing economies, allowing these countries to interact on an equal footing. As of March 2011, 16 non-OECD countries are full members of the Centre's Governing Board. The Centre draws attention to emerging systemic issues likely to have an impact on global development and more specific development challenges faced by today's emerging and developing countries. It uses evidence-based analysis and strategic partnerships to help countries formulate innovative policy solutions to the global challenges of development.

For more information on the Centre and its members, please see www.oecd.org/dev

ECONOMIC COMMISSION FOR AFRICA

The Economic Commission for Africa (ECA) was established by the Economic and Social Council (ECOSOC) of the United Nations (UN) in 1958 as one of the UN's five regional commissions. ECA's mandate is to promote the economic and social development of its member states, foster intraregional integration, and promote international co-operation for Africa's development.

ECA's dual role as a regional arm of the UN, and a part of the regional institutional landscape in Africa, positions it well to make unique contributions to member states' efforts to address their development challenges.

In terms of strategy, ECA focuses on achieving results in the areas of regional integration in support of the African Union vision and priorities and meeting Africa's special needs and emerging global challenges. In that regard, the Commission places special attention on policy relevant analytical work and has positioned itself to be at the cutting edge of economic and social development thinking in support to member states, sub-regional and regional organisations. Drawing on its analytical work, ECA serves as a policy advocate on critical development issues, and plays a leading role in consensus building on the continent.

For more information on the Economic Commission for Africa, please see www.uneca.org

OECD PUBLISHING, 2, rue André Pascal, 75775 PARIS CEDEX
(412011031 P) ISBN 978-92-64-11175-2 - No. 58117 2011

CPSIA information can be obtained at www.ICGtesting.com
Printed in the USA
241981LV00001B/17/P

9 789264 111752